T0178505

Lecture Notes in Computer Science 14262

The series Lecture Notes in Computer Science (LNCS), including its subseries Lecture Notes in Artificial Intelligence (LNAI) and Lecture Notes in Bioinformatics (LNBI), has established itself as a medium for the publication of new developments in computer science and information technology research, teaching, and education.

LNCS enjoys close cooperation with the computer science R & D community, the series counts many renowned academics among its volume editors and paper authors, and collaborates with prestigious societies. Its mission is to serve this international community by providing an invaluable service, mainly focused on the publication of conference and workshop proceedings and postproceedings. LNCS commenced publication in 1973.

Lazaros Iliadis · Antonios Papaleonidas ·
Plamen Angelov · Chrisina Jayne
Editors

Artificial Neural Networks and Machine Learning – ICANN 2023

32nd International Conference on Artificial Neural Networks
Heraklion, Crete, Greece, September 26–29, 2023
Proceedings, Part IX

 Springer

Editors
Lazaros Iliadis
Democritus University of Thrace
Xanthi, Greece

Antonios Papaleonidas
Democritus University of Thrace
Xanthi, Greece

Plamen Angelov
Lancaster University
Lancaster, UK

Chrisina Jayne
Teesside University
Middlesbrough, UK

ISSN 0302-9743 ISSN 1611-3349 (electronic)
Lecture Notes in Computer Science
ISBN 978-3-031-44200-1 ISBN 978-3-031-44201-8 (eBook)
https://doi.org/10.1007/978-3-031-44201-8

This Springer imprint is published by the registered company Springer Nature Switzerland AG
The registered company address is: Gewerbestrasse 11, 6330 Cham, Switzerland

Paper in this product is recyclable.

Preface

The European Neural Network Society (ENNS) is an association of scientists, engineers and students, conducting research on the modelling of behavioral and brain processes, and on the development of neural algorithms. The core of these efforts is the application of neural modelling to several diverse domains. According to its mission statement ENNS is the European non-profit federation of professionals that aims at achieving a worldwide professional and socially responsible development and application of artificial neural technologies.

The flagship event of ENNS is ICANN (the International Conference on Artificial Neural Networks) at which contributed research papers are presented after passing through a rigorous review process. ICANN is a dual-track conference, featuring tracks in brain-inspired computing on the one hand, and machine learning on the other, with strong crossdisciplinary interactions and applications.

The response of the international scientific community to the ICANN 2023 call for papers was more than satisfactory. In total, 947 research papers on the aforementioned research areas were submitted and 426 (45%) of them were finally accepted as full papers after a peer review process. Additionally, 19 extended abstracts were submitted and 9 of them were selected to be included in the front matter of ICANN 2023 proceedings. Due to their high academic and scientific importance, 22 short papers were also accepted.

All papers were peer reviewed by at least two independent academic referees. Where needed, a third or a fourth referee was consulted to resolve any potential conflicts. Three workshops focusing on specific research areas, namely Advances in Spiking Neural Networks (ASNN), Neurorobotics (NRR), and the challenge of Errors, Stability, Robustness, and Accuracy in Deep Neural Networks (ESRA in DNN), were organized.

The 10-volume set of LNCS 14254, 14255, 14256, 14257, 14258, 14259, 14260, 14261, 14262 and 14263 constitutes the proceedings of the 32nd International Conference on Artificial Neural Networks, ICANN 2023, held in Heraklion city, Crete, Greece, on September 26–29, 2023.

The accepted papers are related to the following topics:

Machine Learning: Deep Learning; Neural Network Theory; Neural Network Models; Graphical Models; Bayesian Networks; Kernel Methods; Generative Models; Information Theoretic Learning; Reinforcement Learning; Relational Learning; Dynamical Models; Recurrent Networks; and Ethics of AI.

Brain-Inspired Computing: Cognitive Models; Computational Neuroscience; Self-Organization; Neural Control and Planning; Hybrid Neural-Symbolic Architectures; Neural Dynamics; Cognitive Neuroscience; Brain Informatics; Perception and Action; and Spiking Neural Networks.

Neural applications in Bioinformatics; Biomedicine; Intelligent Robotics; Neuro-robotics; Language Processing; Speech Processing; Image Processing; Sensor Fusion; Pattern Recognition; Data Mining; Neural Agents; Brain-Computer Interaction; Neuromorphic Computing and Edge AI; and Evolutionary Neural Networks.

September 2023

Lazaros Iliadis
Antonios Papaleonidas
Plamen Angelov
Chrisina Jayne

Organization

General Chairs

Iliadis Lazaros   Democritus University of Thrace, Greece
Plamen Angelov   Lancaster University, UK

Program Chairs

Antonios Papaleonidas   Democritus University of Thrace, Greece
Elias Pimenidis   UWE Bristol, UK
Chrisina Jayne   Teesside University, UK

Honorary Chairs

Stefan Wermter   University of Hamburg, Germany
Vera Kurkova   Czech Academy of Sciences, Czech Republic
Nikola Kasabov   Auckland University of Technology, New Zealand

Organizing Chairs

Antonios Papaleonidas   Democritus University of Thrace, Greece
Anastasios Panagiotis Psathas   Democritus University of Thrace, Greece
George Magoulas   University of London, Birkbeck College, UK
Haralambos Mouratidis   University of Essex, UK

Award Chairs

Stefan Wermter   University of Hamburg, Germany
Chukiong Loo   University of Malaysia, Malaysia

Communication Chairs

Sebastian Otte	University of Tübingen, Germany
Anastasios Panagiotis Psathas	Democritus University of Thrace, Greece

Steering Committee

Stefan Wermter	University of Hamburg, Germany
Angelo Cangelosi	University of Manchester, UK
Igor Farkaš	Comenius University in Bratislava, Slovakia
Chrisina Jayne	Teesside University, UK
Matthias Kerzel	University of Hamburg, Germany
Alessandra Lintas	University of Lausanne, Switzerland
Kristína Malinovská (Rebrová)	Comenius University in Bratislava, Slovakia
Alessio Micheli	University of Pisa, Italy
Jaakko Peltonen	Tampere University, Finland
Brigitte Quenet	ESPCI Paris, France
Ausra Saudargiene	Lithuanian University of Health Sciences, Lithuania
Roseli Wedemann	Rio de Janeiro State University, Brazil

Local Organizing/Hybrid Facilitation Committee

Aggeliki Tsouka	Democritus University of Thrace, Greece
Anastasios Panagiotis Psathas	Democritus University of Thrace, Greece
Anna Karagianni	Democritus University of Thrace, Greece
Christina Gkizioti	Democritus University of Thrace, Greece
Ioanna-Maria Erentzi	Democritus University of Thrace, Greece
Ioannis Skopelitis	Democritus University of Thrace, Greece
Lambros Kazelis	Democritus University of Thrace, Greece
Leandros Tsatsaronis	Democritus University of Thrace, Greece
Nikiforos Mpotzoris	Democritus University of Thrace, Greece
Nikos Zervis	Democritus University of Thrace, Greece
Panagiotis Restos	Democritus University of Thrace, Greece
Tassos Giannakopoulos	Democritus University of Thrace, Greece

Program Committee

Abraham Yosipof	CLB, Israel
Adane Tarekegn	NTNU, Norway
Aditya Gilra	Centrum Wiskunde & Informatica, Netherlands
Adrien Durand-Petiteville	Federal University of Pernambuco, Brazil
Adrien Fois	LORIA, France
Alaa Marouf	Hosei University, Japan
Alessandra Sciutti	Istituto Italiano di Tecnologia, Italy
Alessandro Sperduti	University of Padua, Italy
Alessio Micheli	University of Pisa, Italy
Alex Shenfield	Sheffield Hallam University, UK
Alexander Kovalenko	Czech Technical University in Prague, Czech Republic
Alexander Krawczyk	Fulda University of Applied Sciences, Germany
Ali Minai	University of Cincinnati, USA
Aluizio Araujo	Universidade Federal de Pernambuco, Brazil
Amarda Shehu	George Mason University, USA
Amit Kumar Kundu	University of Maryland, USA
Anand Rangarajan	University of Florida, USA
Anastasios Panagiotis Psathas	Democritus University of Thrace, Greece
Andre de Carvalho	Universidade de São Paulo, Brazil
Andrej Lucny	Comenius University, Slovakia
Angel Villar-Corrales	University of Bonn, Germany
Angelo Cangelosi	University of Manchester, UK
Anna Jenul	Norwegian University of Life Sciences, Norway
Antonios Papaleonidas	Democritus University of Thrace, Greece
Arnaud Lewandowski	LISIC, ULCO, France
Arul Selvam Periyasamy	Universität Bonn, Germany
Asma Mekki	University of Sfax, Tunisia
Banafsheh Rekabdar	Portland State University, USA
Barbara Hammer	Universität Bielefeld, Germany
Baris Serhan	University of Manchester, UK
Benedikt Bagus	University of Applied Sciences Fulda, Germany
Benjamin Paaßen	Bielefeld University, Germany
Bernhard Pfahringer	University of Waikato, New Zealand
Bharath Sudharsan	NUI Galway, Ireland
Binyi Wu	Dresden University of Technology, Germany
Binyu Zhao	Harbin Institute of Technology, China
Björn Plüster	University of Hamburg, Germany
Bo Mei	Texas Christian University, USA

Brian Moser	Deutsches Forschungszentrum für künstliche Intelligenz, Germany
Carlo Mazzola	Istituto Italiano di Tecnologia, Italy
Carlos Moreno-Garcia	Robert Gordon University, UK
Chandresh Pravin	Reading University, UK
Chao Ma	Wuhan University, China
Chathura Wanigasekara	German Aerospace Centre, Germany
Cheng Shang	Shanghai Jiaotong University, China
Chengqiang Huang	Huawei Technologies, China
Chenhan Zhang	University of Technology, Sydney, Australia
Chenyang Lyu	Dublin City University, Ireland
Chihuang Liu	Meta, USA
Chrisina Jayne	Teesside University, UK
Christian Balkenius	Lund University, Sweden
Chrysoula Kosma	Ecole Polytechnique, Greece
Claudio Bellei	Elliptic, UK
Claudio Gallicchio	University of Pisa, Italy
Claudio Giorgio Giancaterino	Intesa SanPaolo Vita, Italy
Constantine Dovrolis	Cyprus Institute, USA
Coşku Horuz	University of Tübingen, Germany
Cunjian Chen	Monash, Australia
Cunyi Yin	Fuzhou University, Singapore
Damien Lolive	Université Rennes, CNRS, IRISA, France
Daniel Stamate	Goldsmiths, University of London, UK
Daniel Vašata	Czech Technical University in Prague, Czech Republic
Dario Pasquali	Istituto Italiano di Tecnologia, Italy
David Dembinsky	German Research Center for Artificial Intelligence, Germany
David Rotermund	University of Bremen, Germany
Davide Liberato Manna	University of Strathclyde, UK
Dehao Yuan	University of Maryland, USA
Denise Gorse	University College London, UK
Dennis Wong	Macao Polytechnic University, China
Des Higham	University of Edinburgh, UK
Devesh Jawla	TU Dublin, Ireland
Dimitrios Michail	Harokopio University of Athens, Greece
Dino Ienco	INRAE, France
Diptangshu Pandit	Teesside University, UK
Diyuan Lu	Helmholtz Center Munich, Germany
Domenico Tortorella	University of Pisa, Italy
Dominik Geissler	American Family Insurance, USA

DongNyeong Heo	Handong Global University, South Korea
Dongyang Zhang	University of Electronic Science and Technology of China, China
Doreen Jirak	Istituto Italiano di Tecnologia, Italy
Douglas McLelland	BrainChip, France
Douglas Nyabuga	Mount Kenya University, Rwanda
Dulani Meedeniya	University of Moratuwa, Sri Lanka
Dumitru-Clementin Cercel	University Politehnica of Bucharest, Romania
Dylan Muir	SynSense, Switzerland
Efe Bozkir	Uni Tübingen, Germany
Eleftherios Kouloumpris	Aristotle University of Thessaloniki, Greece
Elias Pimenidis	University of the West of England, UK
Eliska Kloberdanz	Iowa State University, USA
Emre Neftci	Foschungszentrum Juelich, Germany
Enzo Tartaglione	Telecom Paris, France
Erwin Lopez	University of Manchester, UK
Evgeny Mirkes	University of Leicester, UK
F. Boray Tek	Istanbul Technical University, Turkey
Federico Corradi	Eindhoven University of Technology, Netherlands
Federico Errica	NEC Labs Europe, Germany
Federico Manzi	Università Cattolica del Sacro Cuore, Italy
Federico Vozzi	CNR, Italy
Fedor Scholz	University of Tuebingen, Germany
Feifei Dai	Chinese Academy of Sciences, China
Feifei Xu	Shanghai University of Electric Power, China
Feixiang Zhou	University of Leicester, UK
Felipe Moreno	FGV, Peru
Feng Wei	York University, Canada
Fengying Li	Guilin University of Electronic Technology, China
Flora Ferreira	University of Minho, Portugal
Florian Mirus	Intel Labs, Germany
Francesco Semeraro	University of Manchester, UK
Franco Scarselli	University of Siena, Italy
François Blayo	IPSEITE, Switzerland
Frank Röder	Hamburg University of Technology, Germany
Frederic Alexandre	Inria, France
Fuchang Han	Central South University, China
Fuli Wang	University of Essex, UK
Gabriela Sejnova	Czech Technical University in Prague, Czech Republic
Gaetano Di Caterina	University of Strathclyde, UK
George Bebis	University of Nevada, USA

Gerrit Ecke	Mercedes-Benz, Germany
Giannis Nikolentzos	Ecole Polytechnique, France
Gilles Marcou	University of Strasbourg, France
Giorgio Gnecco	IMT School for Advanced Studies, Italy
Glauco Amigo	Baylor University, USA
Greg Lee	Acadia University, Canada
Grégory Bourguin	LISIC/ULCO, France
Guillermo Martín-Sánchez	Champalimaud Foundation, Portugal
Gulustan Dogan	UNCW, USA
Habib Khan	Islamia College University Peshawar, Pakistan
Haizhou Du	Shanghai University of Electric Power, China
Hanli Wang	Tongji University, China
Hanno Gottschalk	TU Berlin, Germany
Hao Tong	University of Birmingham, UK
Haobo Jiang	NJUST, China
Haopeng Chen	Shanghai Jiao Tong University, China
Hazrat Ali	Hamad Bin Khalifa University, Qatar
Hina Afridi	NTNU, Gjøvik, Norway
Hiroaki Aizawa	Hiroshima University, Japan
Hiromichi Suetani	Oita University, Japan
Hiroshi Kawaguchi	Kobe University, Japan
Hiroyasu Ando	Tohoku University, Japan
Hiroyoshi Ito	University of Tsukuba, Japan
Honggang Zhang	University of Massachusetts, Boston, USA
Hongqing Yu	Open University, UK
Hongye Cao	Northwestern Polytechnical University, China
Hugo Carneiro	University of Hamburg, Germany
Hugo Eduardo Camacho Cruz	Universidad Autónoma de Tamaulipas, Mexico
Huifang Ma	Northwest Normal University, China
Hyeyoung Park	Kyungpook National University, South Korea
Ian Nabney	University of Bristol, UK
Igor Farkas	Comenius University Bratislava, Slovakia
Ikuko Nishikawa	Ritsumeikan University, Japan
Ioannis Pierros	Aristotle University of Thessaloniki, Greece
Iraklis Varlamis	Harokopio University of Athens, Greece
Ivan Tyukin	King's College London, UK
Iveta Bečková	Comenius University in Bratislava, Slovakia
Jae Hee Lee	University of Hamburg, Germany
James Yu	Southern University of Science and Technology, China
Jan Faigl	Czech Technical University in Prague, Czech Republic

Koichiro Yamauchi	Chubu University, Japan
Koloud Alkhamaiseh	Western Michigan University, USA
Konstantinos Demertzis	Democritus University of Thrace, Greece
Kostadin Cvejoski	Fraunhofer IAIS, Germany
Kristína Malinovská	Comenius University in Bratislava, Slovakia
Kun Zhang	Inria and École Polytechnique, France
Laurent Mertens	KU Leuven, Belgium
Laurent Perrinet	AMU CNRS, France
Lazaros Iliadis	Democritus University of Thrace, Greece
Leandro dos Santos Coelho	Pontifical Catholic University of Parana, Brazil
Leiping Jie	Hong Kong Baptist University, China
Lenka Tětková	Technical University of Denmark, Denmark
Lia Morra	Politecnico di Torino, Italy
Liang Ge	Chongqing University, China
Liang Zhao	Dalian University of Technology, China
Limengzi Yuan	Shihezi University, China
Ling Guo	Northwest University, China
Linlin Shen	Shenzhen University, China
Lixin Zou	Wuhan University, China
Lorenzo Vorabbi	University of Bologna, Italy
Lu Wang	Macao Polytechnic University, China
Luca Pasa	University of Padova, Italy
Ľudovít Malinovský	Independent Researcher, Slovakia
Luis Alexandre	Universidade da Beira Interior, Portugal
Luis Lago	Universidad Autonoma de Madrid, Spain
Lukáš Gajdošech Gajdošech	Comenius University Bratislava, Slovakia
Lyra Puspa	Vanaya NeuroLab, Indonesia
Madalina Erascu	West University of Timisoara, Romania
Magda Friedjungová	Czech Technical University in Prague, Czech Republic
Manuel Traub	University of Tübingen, Germany
Marcello Trovati	Edge Hill University, UK
Marcin Pietron	AGH-UST, Poland
Marco Bertolini	Pfizer, Germany
Marco Podda	University of Pisa, Italy
Markus Bayer	Technical University of Darmstadt, Germany
Markus Eisenbach	Ilmenau University of Technology, Germany
Martin Ferianc	University College London, Slovakia
Martin Holena	Czech Technical University, Czech Republic
Masanari Kimura	ZOZO Research, Japan
Masato Uchida	Waseda University, Japan
Masoud Daneshtalab	Mälardalen University, Sweden

Mats Leon Richter	University of Montreal, Germany
Matthew Evanusa	University of Maryland, USA
Matthias Karlbauer	University of Tübingen, Germany
Matthias Kerzel	University of Hamburg, Germany
Matthias Möller	Örebro University, Sweden
Matthias Müller-Brockhausen	Leiden University, Netherlands
Matus Tomko	Comenius University in Bratislava, Slovakia
Mayukh Maitra	Walmart, India
Md. Delwar Hossain	Nara Institute of Science and Technology, Japan
Mehmet Aydin	University of the West of England, UK
Michail Chatzianastasis	École Polytechnique, Greece
Michail-Antisthenis Tsompanas	University of the West of England, UK
Michel Salomon	Université de Franche-Comté, France
Miguel Matey-Sanz	Universitat Jaume I, Spain
Mikołaj Morzy	Poznan University of Technology, Poland
Minal Suresh Patil	Umea universitet, Sweden
Minh Tri Lê	Inria, France
Mircea Nicolescu	University of Nevada, Reno, USA
Mohamed Elleuch	ENSI, Tunisia
Mohammed Elmahdi Khennour	Kasdi Merbah University Ouargla, Algeria
Mohib Ullah	NTNU, Norway
Monika Schak	Fulda University of Applied Sciences, Germany
Moritz Wolter	University of Bonn, Germany
Mostafa Kotb	Hamburg University, Germany
Muhammad Burhan Hafez	University of Hamburg, Germany
Nabeel Khalid	German Research Centre for Artificial Intelligence, Germany
Nabil El Malki	IRIT, France
Narendhar Gugulothu	TCS Research, India
Naresh Balaji Ravichandran	KTH Stockholm, Sweden
Natalie Kiesler	DIPF Leibniz Institute for Research and Information in Education, Germany
Nathan Duran	UWE, UK
Nermeen Abou Baker	Ruhr West University of Applied Sciences, Germany
Nick Jhones	Dundee University, UK
Nicolangelo Iannella	University of Oslo, Norway
Nicolas Couellan	ENAC, France
Nicolas Rougier	University of Bordeaux, France
Nikolaos Ioannis Bountos	National Observatory of Athens, Greece
Nikolaos Polatidis	University of Brighton, UK
Norimichi Ukita	TTI-J, Japan

Oleg Bakhteev   EPFL, Switzerland
Olga Grebenkova   Moscow Institute of Physics and Technology,
                                         Russia
Oliver Sutton   King's College London, UK
Olivier Teste   Université de Toulouse, France
Or Elroy   CLB, Israel
Oscar Fontenla-Romero   University of A Coruña, Spain
Ozan Özdenizci   Graz University of Technology, Austria
Pablo Lanillos   Spanish National Research Council, Spain
Pascal Rost   Universität Hamburg, Germany
Paul Kainen   Georgetown, USA
Paulo Cortez   University of Minho, Portugal
Pavel Petrovic   Comenius University, Slovakia
Peipei Liu   School of Cyber Security, University of Chinese
                                         Academy of Sciences, China
Peng Qiao   NUDT, China
Peter Andras   Edinburgh Napier University, UK
Peter Steiner   Technische Universität Dresden, Germany
Peter Sutor   University of Maryland, USA
Petia Georgieva   University of Aveiro/IEETA, Portugal
Petia Koprinkova-Hristova   Bulgarian Academy of Sciences, Bulgaria
Petra Vidnerová   Czech Academy of Sciences, Czech Republic
Philipp Allgeuer   University of Hamburg, Germany
Pragathi Priyadharsini   Indian Institute of Technology Kanpur, India
  Balasubramani
Qian Wang   Durham University, UK
Qinghua Zhou   King's College London, UK
Qingquan Zhang   Southern University of Science and Technology,
                                         China
Quentin Jodelet   Tokyo Institute of Technology, Japan
Radoslav Škoviera   Czech Technical University in Prague,
                                         Czech Republic
Raoul Heese   Fraunhofer ITWM, Germany
Ricardo Marcacini   University of São Paulo, Brazil
Riccardo Renzulli   University of Turin, Italy
Richard Duro   Universidade da Coruña, Spain
Robert Legenstein   Graz University of Technology, Austria
Rodrigo Clemente Thom de Souza   Federal University of Parana, Brazil
Rohit Dwivedula   Independent Researcher, India
Romain Ferrand   IGI TU Graz, Austria
Roman Mouček   University of West Bohemia, Czech Republic
Roseli Wedemann   Universidade do Estado do Rio de Janeiro, Brazil

Rufin VanRullen	CNRS, France
Ruijun Feng	China Telecom Beijing Research Institute, China
Ruxandra Stoean	University of Craiova, Romania
Sanchit Hira	JHU, USA
Sander Bohte	CWI, Netherlands
Sandrine Mouysset	University of Toulouse/IRIT, France
Sanka Rasnayaka	National University of Singapore, Singapore
Sašo Karakatič	University of Maribor, Slovenia
Sebastian Nowak	University Bonn, Germany
Seiya Satoh	Tokyo Denki University, Japan
Senwei Liang	LBNL, USA
Shaolin Zhu	Tianjin University, China
Shayan Gharib	University of Helsinki, Finland
Sherif Eissa	Eindhoven University of Technology, Afghanistan
Shiyong Lan	Independent Researcher, China
Shoumeng Qiu	Fudan, China
Shu Eguchi	Aomori University, Japan
Shubai Chen	Southwest University, China
Shweta Singh	International Institute of Information Technology, Hyderabad, India
Simon Hakenes	Ruhr University Bochum, Germany
Simona Doboli	Hofstra University, USA
Song Guo	Xi'an University of Architecture and Technology, China
Stanislav Frolov	Deutsches Forschungszentrum für künstliche Intelligenz (DFKI), Germany
Štefan Pócoš	Comenius University in Bratislava, Slovakia
Steven (Zvi) Lapp	Bar Ilan University, Israel
Sujala Shetty	BITS Pilani Dubai Campus, United Arab Emirates
Sumio Watanabe	Tokyo Institute of Technology, Japan
Surabhi Sinha	Adobe, USA
Takafumi Amaba	Fukuoka University, Japan
Takaharu Yaguchi	Kobe University, Japan
Takeshi Abe	Yamaguchi University, Japan
Takuya Kitamura	National Institute of Technology, Toyama College, Japan
Tatiana Tyukina	University of Leicester, UK
Teng-Sheng Moh	San Jose State University, USA
Tetsuya Hoya	Independent Researcher, Japan
Thierry Viéville	Domicile, France
Thomas Nowotny	University of Sussex, UK
Tianlin Zhang	University of Manchester, UK

Tianyi Wang	University of Hong Kong, China
Tieke He	Nanjing University, China
Tiyu Fang	Shandong University, China
Tobias Uelwer	Technical University Dortmund, Germany
Tomasz Kapuscinski	Rzeszow University of Technology, Poland
Tomasz Szandala	Wroclaw University of Technology, Poland
Toshiharu Sugawara	Waseda University, Japan
Trond Arild Tjostheim	Lund University, Sweden
Umer Mushtaq	Université Paris-Panthéon-Assas, France
Uwe Handmann	Ruhr West University, Germany
V. Ramasubramanian	International Institute of Information Technology, Bangalore, India
Valeri Mladenov	Technical University of Sofia, Bulgaria
Valerie Vaquet	Bielefeld University, Germany
Vandana Ladwani	International Institute of Information Technology, Bangalore, India
Vangelis Metsis	Texas State University, USA
Vera Kurkova	Czech Academy of Sciences, Czech Republic
Verner Ferreira	Universidade do Estado da Bahia, Brazil
Viktor Kocur	Comenius University, Slovakia
Ville Tanskanen	University of Helsinki, Finland
Viviana Cocco Mariani	PUCPR, Brazil
Vladimír Boža	Comenius University, Slovakia
Vojtech Mrazek	Brno University of Technology, Czech Republic
Weifeng Liu	China University of Petroleum (East China), China
Wenxin Yu	Southwest University of Science and Technology, China
Wenxuan Liu	Wuhan University of Technology, China
Wu Ancheng	Pingan, China
Wuliang Huang	ICT, China
Xi Cheng	NUPT, Hong Kong, China
Xia Feng	Civil Aviation University of China, China
Xian Zhong	Wuhan University of Technology, China
Xiang Zhang	National University of Defense Technology, China
Xiaochen Yuan	Macao Polytechnic University, China
Xiaodong Gu	Fudan University, China
Xiaoqing Liu	Kyushu University, Japan
Xiaowei Zhou	Macquarie University, Australia
Xiaozhuang Song	Chinese University of Hong Kong, Shenzhen, China

Xingpeng Zhang	Southwest Petroleum University, China
Xuemei Jia	Wuhan University, China
Xuewen Wang	China University of Geosciences, China
Yahong Lian	Nankai University, China
Yan Zheng	China University of Political Science and Law, China
Yang Liu	Fudan University, China
Yang Shao	Hitachi, Japan
Yangguang Cui	East China Normal University, China
Yansong Chua	China Nanhu Academy of Electronics and Information Technology, Singapore
Yapeng Gao	Taiyuan University of Technology, China
Yasufumi Sakai	Fujitsu, Japan
Ye Wang	National University of Defense Technology, China
Yeh-Ching Chung	Chinese University of Hong Kong, Shenzhen, China
Yihao Luo	Yichang Testing Technique R&D Institute, China
Yikemaiti Sataer	Southeast University, China
Yipeng Yu	Tencent, China
Yongchao Ye	Southern University of Science and Technology, China
Yoshihiko Horio	Tohoku University, Japan
Youcef Djenouri	NORCE, Norway
Yuan Li	Military Academy of Sciences, China
Yuan Panli	Shihezi University, China
Yuan Yao	Tsinghua University, China
Yuanlun Xie	University of Electronic Science and Technology of China, China
Yuanshao Zhu	Southern University of Science and Technology, China
Yucan Zhou	Institute of Information Engineering, Chinese Academy of Sciences, China
Yuchen Zheng	Shihezi University, China
Yuchun Fang	Shanghai University, China
Yue Zhao	Minzu University of China, China
Yuesong Nan	National University of Singapore, Singapore
Zaneta Swiderska-Chadaj	Warsaw University of Technology, Poland
Zdenek Straka	Czech Technical University in Prague, Czech Republic
Zhao Yang	Leiden University, Netherlands
Zhaoyun Ding	NUDT, China
Zhengwei Yang	Wuhan University, China

Invited Talks

Developmental Robotics for Language Learning, Trust and Theory of Mind

Angelo Cangelosi

University of Manchester and Alan Turing Institute, UK

Growing theoretical and experimental research on action and language processing and on number learning and gestures clearly demonstrates the role of embodiment in cognition and language processing. In psychology and neuroscience, this evidence constitutes the basis of embodied cognition, also known as grounded cognition (Pezzulo et al. 2012). In robotics and AI, these studies have important implications for the design of linguistic capabilities in cognitive agents and robots for human-robot collaboration, and have led to the new interdisciplinary approach of Developmental Robotics, as part of the wider Cognitive Robotics field (Cangelosi and Schlesinger 2015; Cangelosi and Asada 2022). During the talk we presented examples of developmental robotics models and experimental results from iCub experiments on the embodiment biases in early word acquisition and grammar learning (Morse et al. 2015; Morse and Cangelosi 2017) and experiments on pointing gestures and finger counting for number learning (De La Cruz et al. 2014). We then presented a novel developmental robotics model, and experiments, on Theory of Mind and its use for autonomous trust behavior in robots (Vinanzi et al. 2019, 2021). The implications for the use of such embodied approaches for embodied cognition in AI and cognitive sciences, and for robot companion applications, was also discussed.

Challenges of Incremental Learning

Barbara Hammer

CITEC Centre of Excellence, Bielefeld University, Germany

Smart products and AI components are increasingly available in industrial applications and everyday life. This offers great opportunities for cognitive automation and intelligent human-machine cooperation; yet it also poses significant challenges since a fundamental assumption of classical machine learning, an underlying stationary data distribution, might be easily violated. Unexpected events or outliers, sensor drift, or individual user behavior might cause changes of an underlying data distribution, typically referred to as concept drift or covariate shift. Concept drift requires a continuous adaptation of the underlying model and efficient incremental learning strategies. Within the presentation, I looked at recent developments in the context of incremental learning schemes for streaming data, putting a particular focus on the challenge of learning with drift and detecting and disentangling drift in possibly unsupervised setups and for unknown type and strength of drift. More precisely, I dealt with the following aspects: learning schemes for incremental model adaptation from streaming data in the presence of concept drift; various mathematical formalizations of concept drift and detection/quantification of drift based thereon; and decomposition and explanation of drift. I presented a couple of experimental results using benchmarks from the literature, and I offered a glimpse into mathematical guarantees which can be provided for some of the algorithms.

Reliable AI: From Mathematical Foundations to Quantum Computing

Gitta Kutyniok[1,2]

[1]Bavarian AI Chair for Mathematical Foundations of Artificial Intelligence, LMU Munich, Germany
[2]Adjunct Professor for Machine Learning, University of Tromsø, Norway

Artificial intelligence is currently leading to one breakthrough after the other, both in public life with, for instance, autonomous driving and speech recognition, and in the sciences in areas such as medical diagnostics or molecular dynamics. However, one current major drawback is the lack of reliability of such methodologies.

In this lecture we took a mathematical viewpoint towards this problem, showing the power of such approaches to reliability. We first provided an introduction into this vibrant research area, focussing specifically on deep neural networks. We then surveyed recent advances, in particular concerning generalization guarantees and explainability methods. Finally, we discussed fundamental limitations of deep neural networks and related approaches in terms of computability, which seriously affects their reliability, and we revealed a connection with quantum computing.

Intelligent Pervasive Applications for Holistic Health Management

Ilias Maglogiannis

University of Piraeus, Greece

The advancements in telemonitoring platforms, biosensors, and medical devices have paved the way for pervasive health management, allowing patients to be monitored remotely in real-time. The visual domain has become increasingly important for patient monitoring, with activity recognition and fall detection being key components. Computer vision techniques, such as deep learning, have been used to develop robust activity recognition and fall detection algorithms. These algorithms can analyze video streams from cameras, detecting and classifying various activities, and detecting falls in real time. Furthermore, wearable devices, such as smartwatches and fitness trackers, can also monitor a patient's daily activities, providing insights into their overall health and wellness, allowing for a comprehensive analysis of a patient's health. In this talk we discussed the state of the art in pervasive health management and biomedical data analytics and we presented the work done in the Computational Biomedicine Laboratory of the University of Piraeus in this domain. The talk also included Future Trends and Challenges.

Contents – Part IX

MEA-TransUNet: A Multiple External Attention Network for Multi-Organ Segmentation

Xianpeng Cao[1], Junfeng Yao[1,2,3(✉)], Qingqi Hong[1], and Rongzhou Zhou[1]

[1] Center for Digital Media Computing, School of Film, Xiamen University, Xiamen, China
yao0010@xmu.edu.cn
[2] School of Informatics, Xiamen University, Xiamen, China
[3] Key Laboratory of Digital Protection and Intelligent Processing of Intangible Cultural Heritage of Fujian and Taiwan Ministry of Culture and Tourism, Xiamen, China

Abstract. Recently, pioneering work has improved segmentation performance by combining the self-attention (SA) mechanism with UNet. However, since SA can only model its own features in a single sample, it ignores the potential relevance of the whole dataset. Additionally, medical image datasets are typically small, making it crucial to obtain as many features as possible within a limited dataset. To address these problems, we propose the Multiple External Attention (MEA) module, which characterizes the overall dataset by mining correlations between different samples based on external concerns. Furthermore, our method applies the Squeeze-and-Excitation (SE) module for the first time to low-level feature extraction of medical images. By using MEA and SE, we construct MEA-TransUNet for accurate segmentation of medical images. We test our method on two datasets and the experimental results demonstrate its superior performance compared to other existing methods. Code and pre-trained models are coming soon.

Keywords: Medical image segmentation · Deep learning · Self-attention · Vision Transformer

1 Introduction

Medical image segmentation aims to identify specific regions of a medical image that have significant diagnostic or clinical importance [1–3]. It is an essential prerequisite for estimating lesion regions, selecting treatment methods, and administering radiation, as the accuracy of segmentation directly impacts treatment outcomes. UNet [4], an encoder-decoder network with skip connections, has gained widespread attention for its excellent image segmentation performance. However, due to the inherent limitations of convolutional operations, both UNet and its variants face the challenge of inadequate long-range correlation modeling capability. Recently, some researchers have attempted to address this issue by combining the Transformer encoder with UNet, as demonstrated in models such as TransUNet [5], Swin-UNet [6], UCTransNet [7], etc.

© The Author(s), under exclusive license to Springer Nature Switzerland AG 2023
L. Iliadis et al. (Eds.): ICANN 2023, LNCS 14262, pp. 1–12, 2023.
https://doi.org/10.1007/978-3-031-44201-8_1

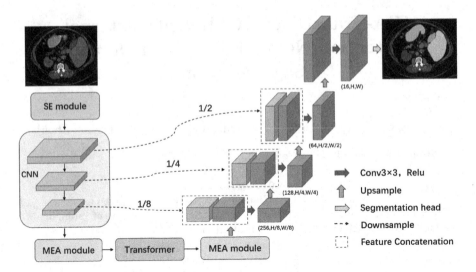

Fig. 1. A schematic view of the proposed MEA-TransUNet. We use the SE module to capture the low-level semantic features and the MEA module to mine the whole dataset for potential relationships.

Although previous research works have yielded better results, they still suffer from these problems as follows: Firstly, medical image segmentation is a layout-specific task, where the shape and location of the same organs are often similar between different samples, but the shape and position of different organs vary widely within the same samples. This results in a small variance between samples and a large variance within samples. However, most recent research has focused on self-attention (SA) modules, which lack the ability to model feature relationships between samples. Secondly, both channel and spatial features can provide richer and more complete information, which is important for segmentation results, but SA overlooks their importance. Finally, due to the limited size of medical image datasets, the utilization of low-level feature information is particularly important. However, SA has paid less attention to low-level feature information.

To address these issues, We propose the proposed Multiple External Attention (MEA) module to acquire external spatial and channel features by two external memory units of learnable parameters, which are learned using the small variance between medical image samples. The MEA module can learn the most discriminative features of the entire dataset, to capture the most informative parts, and to exclude interfering information from other samples. Thus, it is the network that can better characterize the whole dataset and enhance features association between samples. What's more, this allows consistent processing of features in medical images that belong to the same class but are distributed in different samples. Meanwhile, we apply the squeeze-and-excitation (SE) module [8] to low-level feature extraction of medical images for the first time to solve the problem of small medical image datasets that create difficulties for network learning.

Our contributions can be summarized in three folds:

- We propose a novel module named MEA module to obtain external spatial and channel feature information, characterize the samples of the whole dataset, and fuse the information of different samples to generate the corresponding channel and spatial level attention maps.
- Our innovative application of SE module to low-layer feature extraction for medical image segmentation tasks.
- We construct MEA-TransUNet for medical image segmentation and demonstrate its efficacy and generalization on two different datasets.

2 Related Works

2.1 UNet

Full Convolutional Neural Network [9] (FCN) is the pioneer of image segmentation, which extracts feature information by convolution, which makes pixel-level image segmentation significantly better. Based on FCN, Ronneberger et al. [4] proposed the encoder-decoder model UNet and applied it to the field of medical image segmentation, outperformed the state-of-the-art results of numerous medical semantic segmentation tasks [10–12]. The network structure of UNet provides skip-connection to connect same-resolution feature maps and fusion of same-resolution features for encoding and decoding on different scales. In recent years, most of the work on medical image segmentation has been improved based on UNet. UNet++ [13] replaces the cropping and concatenating procedure in the skip-connection section of UNet with a dense convolution operation in order to gain better feature information. ScSE-UNet [14] obtains better network learning results by adding SE module [8] to the sampling to emphasize to reinforce the features that need to be focused on learning. What's more, UNet3+ [15] and Attention U-Net [16] allow decoders to fuse a richer level of semantic information by increasing the number of skip connections or aggregating feature maps in skip connections.

2.2 Vision Transformer

Compared with CNN, Transformer [17], a model structure based on the SA mechanism, has a stronger learning ability, which can model the dependencies between all positions of an image and can improve the segmentation performance of neural networks. Jieneng Chen et al. incorporated the Visual Transformer into UNet and proposed TransUNet [5]. TransUNet utilizes detailed high-resolution spatial information from CNN features and global context encoded by Transformer to learn. The CNN is first used for feature extraction, and then the tokenized image blocks from the extracted feature mapping are encoded into the input sequence used to extract the global context. The encoded features are then upsampled and combined with the previous high-resolution CNN features. Both the limitations of convolution are addressed to some extent and feature loss is prevented. By combining the SA mechanism with spatial attention and channel attention [18], Bo Dong et al. proposed Polyp-PVT [19] with powerful feature expression, which achieved excellent results on polyp segmentation.

The above network design aims to compensate for the lack of UNet's ability to model remote correlations of samples but ignores SA's lack of ability to model external spatial and channel characteristics between samples. Recently, jiacheng ruan et al. proposed MALUNet [20] to optimize the segmentation results by using two external memory units to characterize the dataset. In this paper, based on previous studies, we propose MEA-TransUNet that can accurately locate organ boundaries even in extreme scenarios.

3   Approach

3.1   Overall Structure Design

Figure 1 shows the schematic diagram of MEA-TransUNet. The network is based on the encoder-decoder architecture of TransUNet [5]. As shown in the figure, MEA module improves the feature connections between samples by combining external spatial and channel attention, as a way to compensate for the inability of the SA mechanism of the Transformer layer in TransUNet to learn the feature relationships between samples. Meanwhile, due to the small size of medical image datasets, it is important to obtain as many features as possible in a limited dataset. Low-level features usually contain rich detail information. SE module adaptively enhances the boundary features by explicitly modeling the low-level features of organ boundaries and finding the interdependencies between features.

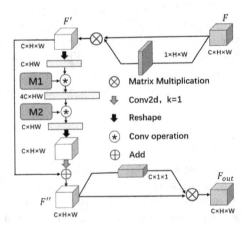

Fig. 2. Overview of the proposed Multiple External Attention module. The MEA module learns the most discriminative features of the entire dataset, capturing the most informative parts while modeling the feature map of the entire dataset.

3.2   Multiple External Attention

Medical image segmentation is an intensive prediction task and the variance between samples is small [20], so acquiring both external spatial and channel features between samples is the key to improving image segmentation performance. The external spatial features learn 'where', that is, where is the most informative part in the input image, which helps to understand the overall structure of the organ and makes it possible to locate the organ position more accurately. The external channel features are learned as 'what', that is, what is meaningful for the input image, which helps to obtain the edge information of the organ and make its segmentation results more continuous and complete. MEA-TransUNet uses MEA module to get external attention. Figure 2 shows the schematic diagram of MEA module.

The MEA module describes the feature interactions between samples using two external memory units $M_1 \in \mathcal{R}^{S \times d}$ and $M_2 \in \mathcal{R}^{S \times d}$ whose weight parameter values are shared. They are learnable parameter matrixs as the memory of the full training dataset. The purpose of the external memory units are to learn the most discriminative features of the entire dataset, to capture the most informative parts, and to exclude interfering information from other samples. Units discover the macroscopic relationships between all samples of the dataset and can model the spatial and channel feature relationships between all samples, This allows consistent processing of features in medical images that belong to the same class but are distributed in different samples.

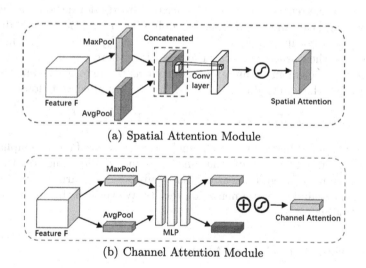

(a) Spatial Attention Module

(b) Channel Attention Module

Fig. 3. Diagram of Spatial and Channel Attention Module

Given a feature map $F \in \mathcal{R}^{C \times H \times W}$ as input, we compress and aggregate the channel information of the input features to efficiently compute the spatial feature map. As shown in Fig. 3(a), after compression and aggregation, two feature maps are obtained: $F^s_{avg} \in \mathbb{R}^{1 \times H \times W}$ and $F^s_{max} \in \mathbb{R}^{1 \times H \times W}$. Then they are concatenated and convolved to obtain our desired spatial attention map $Att_s \in \mathbb{R}^{1 \times H \times W}$. In brief, the spatial attention is computed as follows:

$$Att_s = \sigma \left(f^{7 \times 7}([\text{AvgPool}(F); \text{MaxPool}(F)]) \right) \tag{1}$$

where σ denotes the sigmoid function and $f^{7 \times 7}$ indicates a convolution operation with a convolution kernel of 7×7.

After matrix multiplication, convolution and shaped, we get F' which contains spatial attention of each sample. F' obtains $Att_M \in \mathbb{R}^{C \times HW}$ after the reshape operation so that it can be better learned by external memory units. M_1 establishes connections between samples by learning the spatial features of each sample, while expanding Att_M. This has the advantage of mapping the input to a higher dimensional space for fuller learning, allowing external memory units M_1 and M_2 to model the overall feature information of the dataset more comprehensively. The external memory unit M_2 is then used to perform dimensional recovery and shaping operations to obtain Att'_M. Inspired by ResNet [21], residual information is added to the shaped external spatial feature information and obtain F'' for subsequent computation of external channel features. In short, the external memory units process the feature map Att_M in this way:

$$Att'_M = Att_M M_1^T M_2 \tag{2}$$

As shown in Fig. 3(b), the channel features are complementary to the spatial features, so we aggregate the external spatial feature information through the average pooling layer and the maximum pooling layer to generate two different spatial context descriptors, $F'^c_{avg} \in \mathbb{R}^{C \times 1 \times 1}$ and $F'^c_{max} \in \mathbb{R}^{C \times 1 \times 1}$. These two descriptors are then processed using the multi-layer perceptron (MLP) network and the result of element summation is output as the external channel feature vector. In brief, the external channel Attention is computed as follows:

$$Att_c = \sigma(\text{MLP}(\text{AvgPool}(F'')) + \text{MLP}(\text{MaxPool}(F''))) \tag{3}$$

The reason of spatial first and then channel: learning where first, by emphasizing the range of required feature information, can reduce the learning cost when the subsequent channel attention learns what, improve the learning effect of the network, and obtain better segmentation results. We verified this in the ablation experiment of Sect. 4.4.

3.3   Squeeze-and-Excitation Module

SE module [8] can recalibrate the weights of feature channels, adaptively enhance organ boundary features, and suppress irrelevant features. The module fuses the edge information of organs by performing a one-dimensional convolution operation on the low-level feature information and assigns importance and larger weights to the organ edge features. Therefore, we innovatively apply the SE module to medical image segmentation tasks. Figure 4 shows the schematic diagram of SE module.

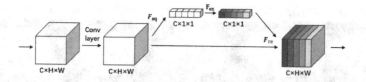

Fig. 4. Diagram of Squeeze-and-excitation module

First, after convolution layer into the Squeeze stage. In the Squeeze phase, each two-dimensional feature channel is transformed into a real number by averaging pooling operations. Each real number possesses a global perceptual field that enables the lower layer convolution to acquire global information. Then, in the Excitation phase, by using an idea based on the gate mechanism in RNN [22] to generate weights for each feature channel. Finally, in the Reweight stage, to complete the recalibration of the original features on the channel dimension, the effect of assigning feature weights is done by multiplying the feature channels with the relevant channel weights.

4   Experiments

4.1   Datasets and Metrics

Synapse: Synapse is a public multi-organ segmentation dataset. There are 30 contrast-enhanced abdominal clinical CT cases in this dataset. Following the settings in [5], 18 cases are used for training and 12 for testing. The annotation of each image includes 8 abdominal organs. We use Dice Similarity Coefficient (DSC) and 95% Hausdorff Distance (HD95) to evaluate our method on this dataset.
ACDC: ACDC is a public cardiac MRI dataset consisting of 100 exams. For each exam, there are two different modalities, and the corresponding label includes left ventricle (LV), right ventricle (RV) and myocardium (Myo). Same to the settings of TranUNet, the dataset is split into 80 for training and 20 for testing.

4.2   Implementation Details

All the experiments are conducted on a Nvidia GTX 3060 GPU. The input image size is set to 224×224 for all the methods. Data augmentation includes random flip and random rotation. All the models are optimized by SGD optimizer with learning rate 0.005, momentum 0.9, weight decay 1e−4 and batch size 16.

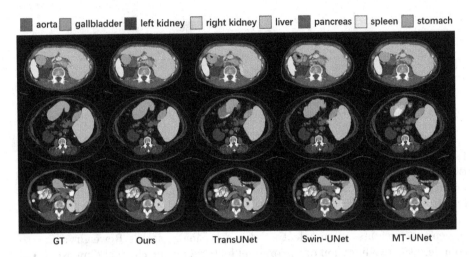

Fig. 5. Qualitative results of different models on the Synapse dataset. Left to right show Ground Truth, our MEA-TransUNet, TransUNet, Swin-UNet and MT-UNet.

4.3   Experimental Results

Segmentation Resluts of Synapse: We compare our MEA-TransUNet network with four state-of-the-art CNN-based approaches and four transformer-based methods. The qualitative segmentation results of different models on the Synapse dataset are given in the Fig. 5, and as shown in the figure, we show an overwhelming advantage in the segmentation of stomach and pancreas. The quantitative segmentation results of the experiments are listed in Table 1 with the best results in bold. All results of our method are averaged over five runs. Our MEA-TransUNet achieves the best performance in terms of DSC (80.04%) and the third-best HD (29.03%). This shows that our MEA-TransUNet is able to learn the most discriminative features in the entire dataset, discover macro-

Table 1. Experimental results of the Synapse Dataset. DSC of each single class is also presented. All results of our method are averaged over five runs.

Methods	DSC ↑	HD ↓	Aorta	Gallbladder	Kidney (L)	Kidney (R)	Liver	Pancreas	Spleen	Stomach
V-Net [23]	68.81	–	75.34	51.87	77.10	**80.75**	87.84	40.05	80.56	56.98
DARR [24]	69.77	–	74.74	53.77	72.31	73.24	94.08	54.18	89.90	45.96
UNet [4]	76.85	39.70	**89.07**	**69.72**	77.77	68.60	93.43	53.98	86.67	75.58
R50 U-Net [5]	74.68	36.87	84.18	62.84	79.19	71.29	93.35	48.23	84.41	73.92
R50 ViT [5]	71.29	32.87	73.73	55.13	75.80	72.20	91.51	45.99	81.99	73.95
Swin-UNet [6]	79.13	**21.55**	85.47	66.53	**83.28**	79.61	94.29	56.58	90.66	76.60
MT-UNet [25]	78.59	26.59	87.92	64.99	81.47	77.29	93.06	59.46	87.75	76.81
TransUNet [5]	77.48	31.69	87.23	63.13	81.87	77.02	94.08	55.86	85.08	75.62
Ours	**80.04**	29.03	86.33	63.70	80.79	80.13	**94.43**	**62.45**	**90.71**	**81.81**

scopic relationships among all samples in the dataset, and model the feature relationships among all samples to obtain excellent segmentation results.

Segmentation Resluts of ACDC: We evaluate MEA-TransUNet network on ACDC dataset to demonstrate the generalization of our model and compare the result with other SOTA methods. Table 2 records Dice Similarity Coefficient (DSC), left ventricle (LV), right ventricle (RV) and myocardium (Myo). Our method achieves the best performance in terms of DSC (90.33%), Myo (87.32%) and LV (95.85%). This shows that our MEA-TransUNet is able to model inter-sample features makes the overall segmentation outperform other visual Transformer methods.

Table 2. Experimental results of the ACDC Dataset. All results of our method are averaged over five runs.

Methods	DSC ↑	RV	Myo	LV
R50 U-Net [5]	87.55	87.10	80.63	94.92
R50 Att-UNet [5]	86.75	87.58	79.20	93.47
R50 ViT [5]	87.57	86.07	81.88	94.75
TransUNet [5]	89.71	**88.86**	84.53	95.73
Swin-UNet [6]	90.00	88.55	85.62	95.83
Ours	**90.33**	87.82	**87.32**	**95.85**

4.4 Ablation Study

On the Impact of MEA and SE Module: To verify the necessity of the MEA and SE modules in our MEA-TransUNet network, we performed several sets of experiments. Also we control whether to use external memory units to verify the importance of external attention mechanisms in feature learning. At first, we tried removing SE module or MEA module to verify their effectiveness. At the same time, We try to remove the external memory units from the MEA module to verify their important role in the network. Then we compared our model with original TransUNet, which serves as the BasicUNet. The experimental results are listed in Table 3. We observed that the DSC scores of MEA modules with external memory units were all higher than those without, which demonstrates that external memory units play an important role in mining potential relationships across the dataset.

On the Impact of the Sequence of Spatial and Channal: As mentioned above, the cooperation of the MEA and SE modules provides better performance for the model than the baseline. In this section we perform ablation experiments on the order of calculation of spatial and channel in the MEA module. The experimental results are listed in Table 4. We observe that the DSC score of spatial first and then channal is always better than the other order, which is

Table 3. Ablation study on Synapse Dataset. M for external memory units in MEA module. The bolded one is the method mentioned in the paper. All results of our method are averaged over five runs.

Methods	M	DSC ↑
BasicUNet (BU)	✗	77.48
BU+SE	✗	78.16
BU+MEA	✗	78.59
BU+MEA	✓	79.56
BU+SE+MEA	✗	79.37
BU+SE+MEA	✓	**80.04**

because learning spatial first can emphasize the range of required feature information, thus reducing the learning cost when subsequent channels pay attention to what to learn, improving the learning effect of the network and obtaining better segmentation results.

Table 4. Ablation study on Synapse Dataset. The bolded one is the method mentioned in the paper. All results of our method are averaged over five runs.

Methods	DSC ↑
BU+MEA (channel first)	79.12
BU+MEA (spatial first)	79.56
BU+SE+MEA (channel first)	79.48
BU+SE+MEA (spatial first)	**80.04**

5   Conclusions

In this paper, we propose an effective medical image segmentation method, MEA-TransUNet. The model has the ability to model inter-sample features to better characterize the entire dataset, enhance inter-sample feature associations, and obtain excellent segmentation results. In experiments the method outperforms other state-of-the-art Visual Transformer methods. We evaluated our approach and performed an ablation study in to demonstrate the effectiveness of our novel design. We also compare MEA-TransUNet with previous work in Sect. 4.3. The proposed method achieved 90.33% DSC on the ACDC dataset and the most advanced performance (80.04% DSC) on the Synapse dataset. The visualization also shows a qualitative comparison to show the superiority of our method.

Acknowledgments. The paper is supported by the Natural Science Foundation of China (No. 62072388), Collaborative Project fund of Fuzhou-Xiamen-Quanzhou Innovation Zone (No. 3502ZCQXT202001), the industry guidance project foundation of science technology bureau of Fujian province in 2020 (No. 2020H0047), and Fujian Sunshine Charity Foundation.

References

1. Azad, R., et al.: Medical image segmentation review: the success of U-Net. arXiv preprint arXiv:2211.14830 (2022)
2. Gupta, A., et al.: SEGPC-2021: a challenge & dataset on segmentation of multiple myeloma plasma cells from microscopic images. Med. Image Anal. **83**, 102677 (2023)
3. Kazerouni, A., et al.: Diffusion models for medical image analysis: a comprehensive survey. arXiv preprint arXiv:2211.07804 (2022)
4. Ronneberger, O., Fischer, P., Brox, T.: U-Net: convolutional networks for biomedical image segmentation. In: Navab, N., Hornegger, J., Wells, W.M., Frangi, A.F. (eds.) MICCAI 2015. LNCS, vol. 9351, pp. 234–241. Springer, Cham (2015). https://doi.org/10.1007/978-3-319-24574-4_28
5. Chen, J., et al.: TransUNet: transformers make strong encoders for medical image segmentation. arXiv preprint arXiv:2102.04306 (2021)
6. Cao, H., et al.: Swin-UNet: UNet-like pure transformer for medical image segmentation. arXiv preprint arXiv:2105.05537 (2021)
7. Wang, H., Cao, P., Wang, J., Zaiane, O.R.: UCTransNet: rethinking the skip connections in U-Net from a channel-wise perspective with transformer. In: Proceedings of the AAAI Conference on Artificial Intelligence, vol. 36, pp. 2441–2449 (2022)
8. Hu, J., Shen, L., Sun, G.: Squeeze-and-excitation networks. In: Proceedings of the IEEE Conference on Computer Vision and Pattern Recognition, pp. 7132–7141 (2018)
9. Long, J., Shelhamer, E., Darrell, T.: Fully convolutional networks for semantic segmentation. In: Proceedings of the IEEE Conference on Computer Vision And Pattern Recognition, pp. 3431–3440 (2015)
10. Bakas, S., et al.: Identifying the best machine learning algorithms for brain tumor segmentation, progression assessment, and overall survival prediction in the brats challenge. arXiv preprint arXiv:1811.02629 (2018)
11. Heller, N., et al.: The kits19 challenge data: 300 kidney tumor cases with clinical context, CT semantic segmentations, and surgical outcomes. arXiv preprint arXiv:1904.00445 (2019)
12. Simpson, A.L., et al.: A large annotated medical image dataset for the development and evaluation of segmentation algorithms. arXiv preprint arXiv:1902.09063 (2019)
13. Zhou, Z., Rahman Siddiquee, M.M., Tajbakhsh, N., Liang, J.: UNet++: a nested U-Net architecture for medical image segmentation. In: Stoyanov, D., et al. (eds.) DLMIA/ML-CDS -2018. LNCS, vol. 11045, pp. 3–11. Springer, Cham (2018). https://doi.org/10.1007/978-3-030-00889-5_1
14. Roy, A.G., Navab, N., Wachinger, C.: Concurrent spatial and channel 'squeeze & excitation' in fully convolutional networks. In: Frangi, A.F., Schnabel, J.A., Davatzikos, C., Alberola-López, C., Fichtinger, G. (eds.) MICCAI 2018. LNCS, vol. 11070, pp. 421–429. Springer, Cham (2018). https://doi.org/10.1007/978-3-030-00928-1_48

15. Huang, H., et al.: UNet 3+: a full-scale connected UNet for medical image segmentation. In: ICASSP 2020–2020 IEEE International Conference on Acoustics, Speech and Signal Processing (ICASSP), pp. 1055–1059. IEEE (2020)
16. Oktay, O., et al.: Attention U-Net: learning where to look for the pancreas. arXiv preprint arXiv:1804.03999 (2018)
17. Vaswani, A., et al.: Attention is all you need. In: Advances in Neural Information Processing Systems, vol. 30 (2017)
18. Woo, S., Park, J., Lee, J.-Y., Kweon, I.S.: CBAM: convolutional block attention module. In: Ferrari, V., Hebert, M., Sminchisescu, C., Weiss, Y. (eds.) ECCV 2018. LNCS, vol. 11211, pp. 3–19. Springer, Cham (2018). https://doi.org/10.1007/978-3-030-01234-2_1
19. Dong, B., Wang, W., Fan, D.P., Li, J., Fu, H., Shao, L.: Polyp-PVT: polyp segmentation with pyramid vision transformers. arXiv preprint arXiv:2108.06932 (2021)
20. Ruan, J., Xiang, S., Xie, M., Liu, T., Fu, Y.: MALUNet: a multi-attention and light-weight unet for skin lesion segmentation. arXiv preprint arXiv:2211.01784 (2022)
21. He, K., Zhang, X., Ren, S., Sun, J.: Deep residual learning for image recognition. In: Proceedings of the IEEE Conference on Computer Vision and Pattern Recognition, pp. 770–778 (2016)
22. Medsker, L.R., Jain, L.: Recurrent neural networks. Des. Appl. 5, 64–67 (2001)
23. Milletari, F., Navab, N., Ahmadi, S.A.: V-Net: fully convolutional neural networks for volumetric medical image segmentation. In: 2016 Fourth International Conference on 3D Vision (3DV), pp. 565–571. IEEE (2016)
24. Fu, S., et al.: Domain adaptive relational reasoning for 3D multi-organ segmentation. In: Martel, A.L., et al. (eds.) MICCAI 2020. LNCS, vol. 12261, pp. 656–666. Springer, Cham (2020). https://doi.org/10.1007/978-3-030-59710-8_64
25. Wang, H., et al.: Mixed transformer U-Net for medical image segmentation. In: ICASSP 2022–2022 IEEE International Conference on Acoustics, Speech and Signal Processing (ICASSP), pp. 2390–2394. IEEE (2022)

Membership-Grade Based Prototype Rectification for Fine-Grained Few-Shot Classification

Sa Ning[ID], Rundong Qi[ID], and Yong Jiang[(✉)]

Southwest University of Science and Technology, Mianyang, China
jiang_yong@swust.edu.cn

Abstract. Few-shot fine-grained classification aims to recognize novel fine-grained categories with the help of a few examples. Under the impact of the low inter-class and high intra-class differences properties of fine-grained datasets, the prototype-based approach, which originally performed well in general FS classification, could not achieve the expected results. In this paper, we propose a transductive method consisting of a feature mapping module and a prototype rectification module. Specifically, the feature mapping module removes redundant attributes from the feature space to enhance the inter-class difference. The prototype rectification module assigns a pseudo-label for each query sample according to the membership-grade between the query samples and the prototypes and uses them to update the prototypes. Experiments on multiple popular fine-grained benchmark datasets and few-shot general classification datasets demonstrate the effectiveness of our approach.

Keywords: Few-shot classification · Prototype rectification · Fine-grained classification

1 Introduction

Few-Shot Learning (FSL) [5,7,18] has recently gained widespread attention thanks to its imitation of the human ability to learn new things. FSL aims to improve the generalization ability of a model, allowing it to generalize efficiently to new classes when only few labeled examples are available. Fine-Grained Few-Shot Learning (FG-FSL) has been studied recently. In FG-FSL, the classes of all images are subclasses within a superclass (e.g., birds, cars). It is non-trivial to employ general FSL methods to finish FG-FSL challenges directly.

In fact, many methods that perform well in general FSL challenges fail to achieve the expected performance in FG-FSL. FG-FSL has the properties of low inter-class difference and high intra-class difference. Meta-Baseline [2] pre-trains a feature encoder on a base dataset and then recognizes novel classes using average-based prototypes. However, this method suffers from a prototype bias problem. Three reasons cause this problem: i) the scarce labeled data cannot provide a reliable estimate for prototypes, resulting in bias between the calculated

---

S. Ning and R. Qi—Contributed equally to this work.

L. Iliadis et al. (Eds.): ICANN 2023, LNCS 14262, pp. 13–24, 2023.
https://doi.org/10.1007/978-3-031-44201-8_2

and the real prototype; ii) the property of low inter-class differences leading to difficulty in having an expected nearest prototype for query samples located at category boundary; iii) the property of high intra-class differences further exacerbates the bias of the prototype. Simply transferring and generalizing the visual representations learned by a model on the base dataset to the novel dataset, as the general FSL approaches do, has fundamental difficulties in FG-FSL.

In recent years, many metric-based FG-FSL methods have been proposed. Among them, FicNet [28] proposed a difference diminishing method that uses a multi-frequency neighborhood and a double-cross modulation to capture the structural representations on both the spatial domain and frequency domain for intra-class differences influencing and modulates the representations according to the inter-class relationship and the global context information for inter-class differences identifying, respectively. BSNet [13] proposed a bi-similarity module to measure the similarity using two distinct similarity measures. Despite their success, they all attempted to solve the problem in FG-FSL from the perspective of fine-grained classification, ignoring the impact of scarce labeled examples and without fully exploiting the potential of the query samples.

In this paper, we propose a transductive method. Specifically, our method consists of a feature mapping module and a prototype rectification module. The feature mapping module is based on principal component analysis, which removes unrepresentative attributes in the feature space to amplify the differences between categories. The prototype rectification module assigns a pseudo-label for each query sample according to the membership-grade between the query samples and the prototypes and then rectifies prototypes in a clustering way. Our main contributions can be summarized as follows:

- We propose a novel fine-grained few-shot classification method and show the significant performance gains obtained using our method.
- We propose a membership-grade-based method, and stronger gains in performance can be obtained.
- We conduct a series of experiments on three popular fine-grained datasets and two few-shot general classification datasets to demonstrate the superiority of our method.

2   Related Works

2.1   Few-Shot Learning

Few-shot learning aims to classify unseen samples with few labeled examples. Existing few-shot learning methods can be roughly divided into two mainstreams: optimization-based and metric-based approaches. The optimization-based method follows meta-learning. The key idea is learning to learn a good initialization of the model, as introduced in MAML [4]. MetaOptNet [11] employs convex base learners and provides a differentiation process for end-to-end learning. The goal of the metric-based [18, 19, 23] approach focuses on learning a task-agnostic metric space and then predicting novel classes by a nearest-neighbor classifier. In this work, we are interested in metric-based approaches due to their validity and malleability.

The metric-based approach mainly consists of a feature extractor and a metric function. The feature extractor extracts image features. The metric function is used to assign labels for the query samples. ProtoNet [18] takes the mean of the features as the prototype and uses the prototype to calculate the distance from the query sample to the category. Meta-Baseline [2] explore the usage of pre-trained models that can help the model better utilize the pre-trained representations with potentially stronger class transferability. CSPN [14] points out that the intra-class bias and the cross-class bias are two key factors affecting the classification performance of the ProtoNet and proposes a method to reduce these biases using label propagation.

2.2 Fine-Grained Classification

Fine-grained classification aims to identify multiple subordinate categories belonging to the same super-category, thus attracting significant interest from the researchers. Fine-grained classification is more challenging than general object classification because local feature variations or subtle feature differences usually distinguish fine-grained objects. Early work relied mainly on part annotations or manually crafted bounding boxes to locate distinctive specific parts, exacerbating the cost of prior information or additional annotations. Thanks to significant advances in robust deep neural networks and large-scale annotated datasets, some deep learning-based methods attempt to learn discriminative features or locate discriminative parts in a weakly supervised manner where only image-level class labels are available.

These methods can be roughly divided into two categories: feature encoding-based and part localization-based methods. For example, Guo et al. [6] introduced a lightweight attention module to locate key regions and learn fine-grained feature representations. In addition, MMAL [27] and AP-CNN [3] propose first finding more vital classification regions and then re-inputting them into the network by cropping and adjusting the original image or feature map size, further enhancing the discriminative ability of object representations. Despite their success, these methods still rely on large-scale datasets. They could be more practical in real-world scenarios due to the difficulty of obtaining large-scale annotated datasets in some cases.

2.3 Few-Shot Fine-Grained Classification

Recently, with the development of few-shot research, some studies have begun to explore few-shot fine-grained classification tasks. That is to say, only a few labeled samples are used to distinguish images in novel classes. Wei et al. [25] use bilinear pooling to extract image encoding features and then use multiple sub-classifiers to classify the extracted image features. MattML [29] adopts a multi-level attention mechanism to initialize the classifier, which helps the network to capture the focused parts of different regions in the image. In contrast to these methods of learning useful categorical information from global features, CPSN [22] introduces two coupled branches to compute the similarity scores between patch-level input pairs to capture subtle and local differences. TOAN [8] proposes a target-oriented matching mechanism to learn explicit feature transformations to reduce the intra-class variance. AGFP [20] proposed an attention-guided refinement strategy to enhance the dominative object and conducted a two-stage meta-learning framework to capture attention-guided pyramidal features.

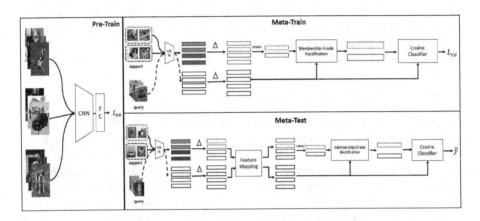

Fig. 1. Method overview. $\triangle$ represents the channel transformation operation.

3 Method

3.1 Problem Formulation

Two datasets are given in the standard few-shot setting: the base dataset C_{base} and the novel dataset C_{novel}. The goal of few-shot learning is to adapt the experience learned in the C_{base} to few-shot tasks derived from C_{novel}. Note that $C_{base} \cap C_{novel} = \emptyset$. Each few-shot task T contains a support set and a query set. Both the support set and the query set contain the same N classes. Each class in the support and query sets contains K labeled examples and Q unlabeled samples, respectively. An "N-way K-shot" task aims to classify $N \times Q$ samples using $N \times K$ examples.

3.2 The Proposed Framework

Our approach is based on the metric learning framework, using the nearest neighbor matching strategy to predict the class for which the query sample belongs. As shown in Fig. 1, the framework consists of three phases: pre-training, meta-learning and meta-test. Next, we detail them respectively.

Pre-training Phase. In the pre-training phase, following [2], pre-train a convolutional neural network W on C_{base} using the standard cross-entropy loss. Then the last fully connected (FC) layer of the neural network W is removed to obtain the feature extractor E.

Meta-Training Phase. In the meta-learning phase, we sample N-way K-shot tasks from C_{base} and optimize the model with these tasks. Specifically, we first use the feature extractor E to obtain the feature vectors X_s and X_q from the support and query sets, respectively. Then we apply the following transformations for each channel of all feature vectors in the X_s and X_q:

$$\phi_\gamma(X_i) = \left\{ \frac{1}{\ln^\gamma\left(\frac{1}{X_i}+1\right)}, \right. \tag{1}$$

where γ is as a learnable parameters and $\gamma > 0$. X_i represents the i-th channel of feature X. $\hat{X}_s$ and $\hat{X}_q$ represent transformed feature vectors of the support set and query set, respectively. Then, we compute the prototype v_i of each class:

$$v_i = \frac{1}{K} \times \sum_{x_s \in \hat{X}_s^i} x_s, \tag{2}$$

where $\hat{X}_s^i$ represents the feature vectors of class i in $\hat{X}_s$. Next, we introduce a membership-grade rectification module to rectify prototype v_i, and we will detail the module in Sect. 3.4. Finally, we classify the query samples based on the cosine similarity between the query sample x_q and the rectified prototype v_i':

$$S(x_q, v_i') = \frac{\exp\left(cosine\left(x_q, v_i'\right)\right)}{\sum_{v_j' \in V} \exp\left(cosine\left(x_q, v_j'\right)\right)}, \tag{3}$$

where $V = [v_1', v_2', ..., v_N']$ and $cosine(\cdot, \cdot)$ represents denotes the cosine similarity.

Meta-Test. The workflow of the meta-test phase is similar to the meta-training. The only difference is that we introduce a feature mapping module after the channel transformation using Eq. 1. We will detail the feature mapping module in Sect. 3.3.

3.3   Feature Mapping Module

Let $X_p = V \cup \hat{X}_q$, and we calculate the covariance matrix M:

$$M = X_p X_p^T. \tag{4}$$

After that, we calculate the eigenvalues and eigenvectors of M and choose the eigenvectors corresponding to the top β biggest eigenvalues from them as the projection matrix $W = [w_1, w_2, ..., w_\beta]$, where the w_i represents the standard orthogonal basis vector (attribute). Then we get the mapped feature matrix X^*:

$$X^* = W^T X_p, \tag{5}$$

where the dimension of the subspace is β.

Algorithm 1. Membership-Grade Prototype Rectification Algorithm

---

Input: scale-parameter α, prototypes V, query samples' features X_q

Output: Rectified prototypes V'

1: Initialize $o = 1$
2: **repeat**
3:   Calculate the membership-grade U using Eq.6;
4:   Find the max u_{ko} for query sample x_q^o;
5:   Assign the label of v_k to x_q^o as a pseudo-label;
6: **until** $o = |X_q|$
7: Initialize $l = 1$
8: **repeat**
9:   Calculate v_l' using Eq.7;
10: **until** $l = N$
11: $V' = \left\{ v_1', ..., v_N' \right\}$

3.4   Membership-Grade Rectification Module

Firstly, we calculate the membership-grade u_{ij} between the query feature x_q^j and the prototype v_i as the basis for query samples:

$$u_{ij} = \frac{1}{\sum_{k=1}^{N} \left(\frac{d_{ij}}{d_{kj}} \right)^{2/(\alpha-1)}}, \tag{6}$$

where d_{ij} denotes the cosine similarity of the $i-th$ prototype to the $j-th$ query sample, $u_{ij} \in U$. α is a learnable parameter. We assign a pseudo-label for each query sample according to the membership-grade and we get a pseudo-support set $\hat{X}_{ps}$.

Secondly, we compute the rectified prototype v_i':

$$v_i' = \frac{1}{K} \times \sum_{x_s \in (\hat{X}_s^i \cup \hat{X}_{ps}^i)} x_s, \tag{7}$$

where $\hat{X}_s^i$ and $\hat{X}_{ps}^i$ represent the support features and pseudo-support features of the i-th class, respectively. The detailed process is summarized in Algorithm 1.

4   Experiments

4.1   Experimental Setup

Datasets. We conducted experiments on three popular fine-grained datasets (CUB-200-2011, Stanford-Cars, Stanford-Dogs) and two few-shot general classification benchmarks (miniImageNet, tieredImageNet). The input images of all datasets are resized to 84×84.

- CUB-200-2011 [24] is a bird dataset. It contains 11788 image data in 200 categories. We use the raw images without human-annotated bounding box as our input and follow [26] to divide the dataset.
- Stanford Dogs [9] contains images of 120 dog species. There are 20580 images in this dataset. We followed [12] to divide the dataset into 70 training sets, 20 evaluation sets, and 30 test sets.
- Stanford Cars [10] contains a total of 16,185 images from 196 cars. Following [12], we divide the dataset into 130 training sets, 17 evaluation sets, and 49 test sets.
- The miniImageNet [23] dataset contains 100 classes and each class contains 600 images. Following [1], we randomly split it into 64, 16 and 20 classes as training, validation, and testing set, respectively.
- The tieredImageNet [17] dataset contains 608 classes and each class contains 1200 images, Following [1], we split it into 351, 97, 160 classes as training, validation, testing set respectively.

Implementation Details. We take a 12-layer ResNet as the backbone network of our method. In the pre-training phase, we train 200 epochs on the Cbase and use an SGD optimizer with a momentum of 0.9. We set the batch size as 128 and the learning rate as 0.001. Moreover, the weight decay is 0.0005, and standard data augmentation methods like random resized crops are also applied. In the meta-learning phase, we train with 100 epochs and choose SGD with a momentum of 0.9 as the optimizer. In particular, the learning rate is 0.001, which will decay at epochs 30 and 50, and the decay factor is 0.1. The learnable parameter γ and α is initialized as 2.5 and 1.5, respectively. The parameter β is fixed to 10.

Evaluation Protocol. To evaluate the performance of our proposed method, we take 10,000 N-way K-shot classification tasks from C_{novel}. We focus on the standard 5-way 1-shot and 5-way 5-shot task settings for each task. The average accuracy of these few-shot tasks is reported with a 95% confidence interval.

Table 1. The accuracy (%) of 5-way 1-shot and 5-shot tasks on three popular fine-grained datasets. The best results are reported in **bold font**.

Methods	CUB-200-2011		Stanford Dogs		Stanford Cars	
	1-shot	5-shot	1-shot	5-shot	1-shot	5-shot
OLSA [26]	77.77 ± 0.44	89.87 ± 0.24	64.15 ± 0.49	78.28 ± 0.32	77.03 ± 0.46	88.85 ± 0.46
CAN [7]	76.98 ± 0.48	87.77 ± 0.30	64.73 ± 0.52	77.93 ± 0.35	86.90 ± 0.42	93.93 ± 0.22
BSNet [13]	73.48 ± 0.92	83.84 ± 0.59	61.95 ± 0.97	79.62 ± 0.63	71.07 ± 1.03	88.38 ± 0.62
FicNet [28]	75.27 ± 0.61	88.48 ± 0.37	64.74 ± 0.69	79.23 ± 0.46	77.31 ± 0.58	89.47 ± 0.32
TOAN [8]	66.10 ± 0.86	82.27 ± 0.60	49.77 ± 0.86	69.29 ± 0.70	75.28 ± 0.72	87.45 ± 0.48
AGPF [20]	78.73 ± 0.84	89.77 ± 0.47	**72.34 ± 0.86**	**84.02 ± 0.57**	85.34 ± 0.74	94.79 ± 0.35
Ours	**82.03 ± 0.73**	**90.32 ± 0.86**	70.61 ± 0.50	81.64 ± 0.47	**87.64 ± 0.57**	**95.17 ± 0.64**

4.2 Results

Results on Fine-Grained Datasets. We conduct few-shot fine-grained classification experiments on CUB, Stanford Dog and Stanford Car, with standard 5-way 1-shot and 5-way 5-shot tasks. Table 1 shows the performance evaluations of our proposed method based on the ResNet-12 backbone. On the CUB-200-2011 dataset, our proposed method can achieve the best performance both in terms of 5-way 1-shot and 5-way 5-shot setting. Specifically, we observe that the our method outperforms AGPF by 3.3% for 5-way 5-shot tasks and OLSA by 0.45% for 5-way 5-shot tasks. On the Stanford Dogs dataset, Compared to the AGPF method, our method is lower than theirs by 1.73% and 2.38% for the 1-shot and 5-shot settings, respectively. But compared to other competitors, our method is competitive. On the Stanford Cars dataset, our method also achieves the best performance and Achieved 87.64% and 95.17% performance on 1-shot and 5-shot settings, respectively. Outperforms CAN by 0.74% for 5-way 5-shot tasks and OLSA by 0.38% for 5-way 5-shot tasks. It is noted that the performance improvement of our method on the 1-shot setting is lower than that on the 5-shot setting. We attribute this phenomenon to the increase in the number of samples used to calculate the prototypes in the 5-shot setup, where the calculated prototypes are more expected, resulting in the reduced role of the membership-grade rectification module.

Table 2. The accuracy (%) of 5-way 1-shot and 5-shot tasks on three popular few-shot benchmarks. The best results are reported in **bold font**.

Methods	backbone	miniImageNet		tieredImageNet	
		1-shot	5-shot	1-shot	5-shot
Meta-Baseline [2]	ResNet-12	63.17 ± 0.23	79.26 ± 0.17	68.62 ± 0.27	83.29 ± 0.18
BD-CSPN [14]	ResNet-12	70.31 ± 0.93	81.89 ± 0.60	78.74 ± 0.95	**86.92 ± 0.63**
MCGN [21]	Conv4	67.32 ± 0.43	82.03 ± 0.54	71.21 ± 0.85	85.98 ± 0.98
LaplacianShot [30]	ResNet-18	72.11 ± 0.19	82.31 ± 0.20	78.98 ± 0.21	86.39 ± 0.16
BaseTransformers [16]	ResNet-18	70.88 ± 0.17	82.37 ± 0.19	72.46 ± 0.20	84.96 ± 0.52
UniSiam [15]	ResNet-12	64.10 ± 0.36	82.26 ± 0.25	67.01±0.39	84.47 ± 0.28
Ours	ResNet-12	**72.29 ± 0.87**	**82.43 ± 0.84**	**79.13 ± 0.87**	85.97 ± 0.94

Results on General Few-Shot Datasets. We conducted general few-shot classification experiments on the miniImageNet and tieredImageNet dataset to further evaluate the generalizability of our method. Table 2 shows the performance evaluations of our proposed method based on the ResNet-12 backbone. On the miniImageNet dataset, our proposed method achieves the best performance than all existing methods by a large margin in terms of 5-way 1-shot setting. Compared with the LaplacianShot method, our proposed method achieves 0.18% and 0.12% performance improvement under 1-shot and 5-shot settings, respectively. On the tieredImageNet dataset, our method can achieve competitive or the best performance than other few-shot classification methods.

Table 3. Effect of sub-modules. MGR: membership-grade rectification module. FMM: Feature Mapping Module.

Methods	CUB-200-2011	
	5-way 1-shot	5-way 5-shot
baseline	67.02 ± 0.51	83.58 ± 0.48
baseline + MGR	80.23 ± 0.63	89.35 ± 0.72
baseline + FMM	70.64 ± 0.47	85.03 ± 0.59
baseline + MGR + FMM	$\mathbf{82.17 \pm 0.72}$	$\mathbf{90.32 \pm 0.68}$

4.3   Ablation Studies

Effect of Sub-modules. Table 3 reports the contribution of the sub-modules. The first row shows the classification performance of the baseline model. The second row shows the performance of the prototype rectification using only the membership-grade rectification module. The third row shows the model's performance using only the feature mapping module. We can find that using both the membership-grade rectification module and the feature mapping module alone improves the model's classification accuracy, which indicates that both modules can improve the classification ability of the model. When we use both modules together, the improvement in classification accuracy is smaller than that of using the two modules separately on the baseline.

Table 4. Effect of using different distance calculation methods on membership-grade rectification module. MGR: membership-grade rectification module.

Methods	CUB-200-2011	
	5-way 1-shot	5-way 5-shot
MGR (Mutual Information)	81.74	89.53
MGR (Euclid)	80.64	88.41
MGR (Cosine)	**82.17**	**90.32**

Effect of Membership-Grade Calculation Function. We used Euclidean distance and mutual information as distance measurement functions to demonstrate the effect of using other distance measures on membership-grade. The experimental results are shown in Table 4. We can see that using cosine similarity as the similarity measurement function achieves the best results, the Euclidean distance method achieves the second best results, and the method using mutual information has the worst accuracy.

5   Conclusion

In this paper, we propose a transductive method for fine-grained few-shot classification. The core idea of this method is to use the membership-grade between query samples and prototypes as the basis for assigning pseudo-labels to query samples. Then we use these query samples to rectification the prototype. To further reduce the impact of low inter-class differences on fine-grained images, we introduce a feature mapping module based on principal component analysis to improve the performance of the model. We have conducted extensive experiments to demonstrate the effectiveness of our method.

Acknowledgment. This study is supported by the Sichuan Science and Technology Program (NO. 2021YFG0031).

References

1. Chen, W.Y., Liu, Y.C., Kira, Z., Wang, Y.C.F., Huang, J.B.: A closer look at few-shot classification. arXiv preprint arXiv:1904.04232 (2019)
2. Chen, Y., Wang, X., Liu, Z., Xu, H., Darrell, T., et al.: A new meta-baseline for few-shot learning. arXiv preprint arXiv:2003.04390 2(3), 5 (2020)
3. Ding, Y., et al.: AP-CNN: weakly supervised attention pyramid convolutional neural network for fine-grained visual classification. IEEE Trans. Image Process. **30**, 2826–2836 (2021)
4. Finn, C., Abbeel, P., Levine, S.: Model-agnostic meta-learning for fast adaptation of deep networks. In: International Conference on Machine Learning, pp. 1126–1135. PMLR (2017)
5. Fu, Y., Fu, Y., Jiang, Y.G.: Meta-FDMixup: cross-domain few-shot learning guided by labeled target data. In: Proceedings of the 29th ACM International Conference on Multimedia, pp. 5326–5334 (2021)
6. Guo, J., Qi, G., Xie, S., Li, X.: Two-branch attention learning for fine-grained class incremental learning. Electronics **10**(23), 2987 (2021)
7. Hou, R., Chang, H., Ma, B., Shan, S., Chen, X.: Cross attention network for few-shot classification. In: Advances in Neural Information Processing Systems, vol. 32 (2019)
8. Huang, H., Zhang, J., Yu, L., Zhang, J., Wu, Q., Xu, C.: TOAN: target-oriented alignment network for fine-grained image categorization with few labeled samples. IEEE Trans. Circuits Syst. Video Technol. **32**(2), 853–866 (2021)
9. Khosla, A., Jayadevaprakash, N., Yao, B., Li, F.F.: Novel dataset for fine-grained image categorization: Stanford dogs. In: Proceedings of the CVPR Workshop on Fine-Grained Visual Categorization (FGVC), vol. 2. Citeseer (2011)
10. Krause, J., Stark, M., Deng, J., Fei-Fei, L.: 3D representations for fine-grained categorization. In: Proceedings of the IEEE International Conference on Computer Vision Workshops, pp. 554–561 (2013)

11. Lee, K., Maji, S., Ravichandran, A., Soatto, S.: Meta-learning with differentiable convex optimization. In: Proceedings of the IEEE/CVF Conference on Computer Vision and Pattern Recognition, pp. 10657–10665 (2019)
12. Li, W., Wang, L., Xu, J., Huo, J., Gao, Y., Luo, J.: Revisiting local descriptor based image-to-class measure for few-shot learning. In: Proceedings of the IEEE/CVF Conference on Computer Vision and Pattern Recognition, pp. 7260–7268 (2019)
13. Li, X., Wu, J., Sun, Z., Ma, Z., Cao, J., Xue, J.H.: BSNet: bi-similarity network for few-shot fine-grained image classification. IEEE Trans. Image Process. **30**, 1318–1331 (2020)
14. Liu, J., Song, L., Qin, Y.: Prototype rectification for few-shot learning. In: Vedaldi, A., Bischof, H., Brox, T., Frahm, J.-M. (eds.) ECCV 2020, Part I. LNCS, vol. 12346, pp. 741–756. Springer, Cham (2020). https://doi.org/10.1007/978-3-030-58452-8_43
15. Lu, Y., Wen, L., Liu, J., Liu, Y., Tian, X.: Self-supervision can be a good few-shot learner. In: Avidan, S., Brostow, G., Cissé, M., Farinella, G.M., Hassner, T. (eds.) ECCV 2022, Part XIX. LNCS, vol. 13679, pp. 740–758. Springer, Cham (2022). https://doi.org/10.1007/978-3-031-19800-7_43 Computer Vision-ECCV 2022: 17th European Conference, Tel Aviv, Israel, October 23–27, 2022, Proceedings
16. Maniparambil, M., McGuinness, K., O'Connor, N.: BaseTransformers: attention over base data-points for one shot learning. arXiv preprint arXiv:2210.02476 (2022)
17. Ren, M., et al.: Meta-learning for semi-supervised few-shot classification. arXiv preprint arXiv:1803.00676 (2018)
18. Snell, J., Swersky, K., Zemel, R.: Prototypical networks for few-shot learning. In: Advances in Neural Information Processing Systems, vol. 30 (2017)
19. Sung, F., Yang, Y., Zhang, L., Xiang, T., Torr, P.H., Hospedales, T.M.: Learning to compare: Relation network for few-shot learning. In: Proceedings of the IEEE Conference on Computer Vision and Pattern Recognition, pp. 1199–1208 (2018)
20. Tang, H., Yuan, C., Li, Z., Tang, J.: Learning attention-guided pyramidal features for few-shot fine-grained recognition. Pattern Recogn. **130**, 108792 (2022)
21. Tang, S., Chen, D., Bai, L., Liu, K., Ge, Y., Ouyang, W.: Mutual CRF-GNN for few-shot learning. In: Proceedings of the IEEE/CVF Conference on Computer Vision and Pattern Recognition, pp. 2329–2339 (2021)
22. Tian, S., Tang, H., Dai, L.: Coupled patch similarity network for one-shot fine-grained image recognition. In: 2021 IEEE International Conference on Image Processing (ICIP), pp. 2478–2482. IEEE (2021)
23. Vinyals, O., Blundell, C., Lillicrap, T., Wierstra, D., et al.: Matching networks for one shot learning. In: Advances in Neural Information Processing Systems, vol. 29 (2016)
24. Wah, C., Branson, S., Welinder, P., Perona, P., Belongie, S.: The caltech-UCSD birds-200-2011 dataset (2011)
25. Wei, X.S., Wang, P., Liu, L., Shen, C., Wu, J.: Piecewise classifier mappings: Learning fine-grained learners for novel categories with few examples. IEEE Trans. Image Process. **28**(12), 6116–6125 (2019)
26. Wu, Y., et al.: Object-aware long-short-range spatial alignment for few-shot fine-grained image classification. arXiv preprint arXiv:2108.13098 (2021)
27. Zhang, F., Li, M., Zhai, G., Liu, Y.: Multi-branch and multi-scale attention learning for fine-grained visual categorization. In: Lokoč, J., Skopal, T., Schoeffmann, K., Mezaris, V., Li, X., Vrochidis, S., Patras, I. (eds.) MMM 2021, Part I. LNCS, vol. 12572, pp. 136–147. Springer, Cham (2021). https://doi.org/10.1007/978-3-030-67832-6_12

28. Zhu, H., Gao, Z., Wang, J., Zhou, Y., Li, C.: Few-shot fine-grained image clas-
    sification via multi-frequency neighborhood and double-cross modulation. arXiv
    preprint arXiv:2207.08547 (2022)
29. Zhu, Y., Liu, C., Jiang, S.: Multi-attention meta learning for few-shot fine-grained
    image recognition. In: IJCAI, pp. 1090–1096 (2020)
30. Ziko, I., Dolz, J., Granger, E., Ayed, I.B.: Laplacian regularized few-shot learning.
    In: International Conference on Machine Learning, pp. 11660–11670. PMLR (2020)

Multi-grained Aspect Fusion for Review Response Generation

Yun Yuan[1], Chen Gong[1], Dexin Kong[1], Nan Yu[1], and Guohong Fu[1,2(✉)]

[1] School of Computer Science and Technology, Soochow University, Suzhou, China
{yyuanwind,kdx,nyu}@stu.suda.edu.cn,
{gongchen18,ghfu}@suda.edu.cn
[2] Institute of Artificial Intelligence, Soochow University, Suzhou, China

Abstract. Review response generation (RRG) aims to automatically generate responses to customer reviews. Responding to reviews in a right manner is important to online customer experience. However, most previous research on RRG focused on exploring coarse review information and ignored fine-grain aspects within reviews, especially those with negative sentiment. As a result, the generated responses are usually not targeted to users' real concerns in their reviews. To this end, we proposed a multi-grained aspect fusion model (MGAF) model to improve the targeting of generated responses. In particular, we first enhance the targeting ability by performing sentence-level aspect selection and response script learning. Then we integrate aspect-level keywords with sentiment information to further improve the diversity of generated responses. Experimental results on both Chinese and English datasets show that our proposed model outperforms the state-of-the-art models available, demonstrating the importance of fusing multi-grained aspect information for targeted response generation.

Keywords: response generation · aspect targeting · script learning

1 Introduction

Review Response Generation (RRG) aims to generate high-quality, targeted responses to customer reviews. In general, reviews play a critical role in customers' purchase decision-making [19]. Effectively responding to these reviews may transform dissatisfied customers into loyal ones and increase sales [16,17,23].

Over the past few years, RRG has been studied in different fields or application scenarios, including e-commerce, mobile apps, and hospitality. In the e-commerce, Clothing [28] and Makeup [3] datasets are introduced for study. Recently, to improve the persuasiveness of responses, Chen et al. [3] proposed to use additional sources of knowledge, such as product titles and retrieved review-response pairs. Although they attempted to utilize aspect information through a multi-aspect attentive network, it does not prioritize responding to the key issues mentioned in the review. As shown in Fig. 1, the negative aspect (as the blue text shows) should be explained first as the gold response did.

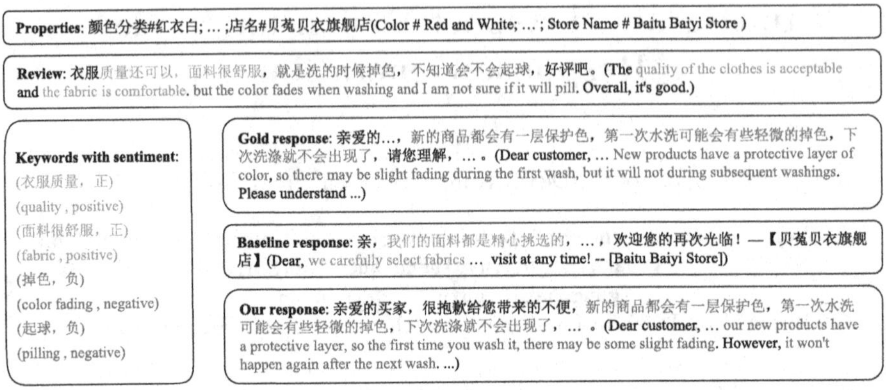

Properties: 颜色分类#红衣白; ... ;店名#贝菟贝衣旗舰店(Color # Red and White; ... ; Store Name # Baitu Baiyi Store)

Review: 衣服质量还可以，面料很舒服，就是洗的时候掉色，不知道会不会起球，好评吧。(The quality of the clothes is acceptable and the fabric is comfortable. but the color fades when washing and I am not sure if it will pill. Overall, it's good.)

Keywords with sentiment:

(衣服质量，正)

(quality , positive)

(面料很舒服，正)

(fabric , positive)

(掉色，负)

(color fading , negative)

(起球，负)

(pilling , negative)

Gold response: 亲爱的...，新的商品都会有一层保护色，第一次水洗可能会有些轻微的掉色，下次洗涤就不会出现了，请您理解，... 。(Dear customer, ... New products have a protective layer of color, so there may be slight fading during the first wash, but it will not during subsequent washings. Please understand ...)

Baseline response: 亲，我们的面料都是精心挑选的，...，欢迎您的再次光临! —【贝菟贝衣旗舰店】(Dear, we carefully select fabrics ... visit at any time! -- [Baitu Baiyi Store])

Our response: 亲爱的买家，很抱歉给您带来的不便，新的商品都会有一层保护色，第一次水洗可能会有些轻微的掉色，下次洗涤就不会出现了，... 。(Dear customer, ... our new products have a protective layer, so the first time you wash it, there may be some slight fading. However, it won't happen again after the next wash. ...)

Fig. 1. One sample of review response generation. The orange text in baseline response is inappropriate, but the blue text represents the targeted response script addressing the issues mentioned in the review. (Color figure online)

In the field of mobile apps, researchers used RNN-based models to incorporate review-specific features to capture users' sentiment and complaint topics. [6,7, 27]. However, these models are not generalizable [8]. Moreover, transformer-based models were shown to be more effective than RNN-based models [2,27]. Therefore, in this paper we adopt a transformer-based BART [10] backbone and add a copy layer to it as our baseline model. In the hospitality domain, researchers proposed large-scale datasets [8] and analyzed the impact of data filtering on performance improvement [9]. However, they did not explore the connection between coarse and fine-grained features.

A major challenge with existing RRG methods is that the responses generated are not targeted to the aspects and opinions that users really care about in their reviews. As illustrated in Fig. 1, the baseline generated response targets the positive aspect of the "fabric" highlighted by the orange text, but it does not address the negative issues of "color fading" and "pilling" highlighted by the blue text. This oversight can adversely affect the user's experience and does not adequately resolve conflicts. Intuitively, high-quality and targeted responses should focus on addressing critical issues from the review, rather than aspects that customers are not concerned about.

In order to alleviate the aforementioned problems, we first complement from a coarse-grained perspective by selecting key points from reviews and choosing scripts[1] used in the responses (as the blue text shows). Then we introduce a fine-grained perspective by using aspect-level keywords and emotions. We fuse multi-grained aspect features to enhance their connection and capture key issues representations of aspects to generate more targeted and persuasive responses. We perform experiments on Chinese clothing and English hospitality datasets. The results demonstrate significant advancements and generalization compared

---

[1] Response script refers to the language skills or templates used by customer service when replying to user reviews.

to previous SOTA methods. Moreover, the targeted F1 score improves significantly, indicating that generated responses are more targeted.

In summary, our contributions can be summarized as follows:

- We propose to explore RRG from two perspectives. At a coarse granularity, we conduct aspect selection and response script learning to enhance targeting ability. At a fine granularity, we incorporate aspect-level keywords with sentiment to further improve diversity.
- We propose a model that adds a script learning auxiliary task to capture coarse features. Moreover, we propose an aspects and sentiments fusion module to incorporate fine-grained features.
- Experimental results demonstrate that our proposed model generates more targeted responses and further improves the fluency and diversity of responses.

2   Related Works

The task of generating review responses has been extensively studied, with a focus on e-commerce, mobile apps, and the hospitality domain. Specifically, in the e-commerce domain, Zhao et al. [28] introduced clothing review response data. They proposed to use gated multi-source attention and a copy mechanism with a dual RNN-encoder architecture to integrate product information. However, using only product information as additional knowledge is insufficient for generating persuasive and informative responses. Thus, Chen et al. [3] introduced the Makeup dataset and proposed to incorporate more sources of prior knowledge, such as product titles and retrieved similar review-response pairs from larger datasets. They added a pointer-generator network to copy factual tokens from reviews under the Transformer-based BART [10] as the backbone network. However, they ignored the aspect-level issues mentioned in reviews and lacked selection, leading to less targeted generated responses.

In the mobile app domain and hospitality domain, Cao et al. [7] proposed the RRGen model, which extends the basic NMT model [5,24] by combining review-specific features (app category, review length, rating, sentiment tendency, keywords). This captures users' emotions and complaint topics, thus improving the performance. However, their approach lacks generality and cannot be effectively applied to other domains [8]. Additionally, Farooq et al. [6] fused seq2seq and machine reading comprehension models with retrieval technology to partially address issues raised in specific app reviews. However, their approach still used RNN-based models, and subsequent studies [2,27] demonstrated that Transformer-based models are more effective than RNN-based models. They proposed the TRRGen model which fuses features such as app category and rating. However, these models lack features contained in the review. In the hospitality domain, Kew et al. [8] proposed large-scale English and German datasets and directly migrated the RRGen model [7] to this domain. They found that adding extra knowledge and keywords had no effect on performance improvement compared to the mobile app domain. Kew et al. [9] analyzed this task from a data filtering perspective and proposed methods for filtering general data. They showed that filtering out meaningless general data can enhance response distinction.

The above studies mainly focus on coarse-grained information, such as review context information and retrieved extra knowledge. Although some models integrated features such as keywords and sentiment orientation, they did not explore the connection between fine-grained information and coarse-grained features. This resulted in models tending to generate meaningless responses that do not effectively address specific issues mentioned in reviews. Therefore, inspired by research on fine-grained sentiment analysis [1,4,13], this paper proposes a model fusing multi-grained features to generate more targeted and persuasive responses.

3   Methods

3.1   Model Overview

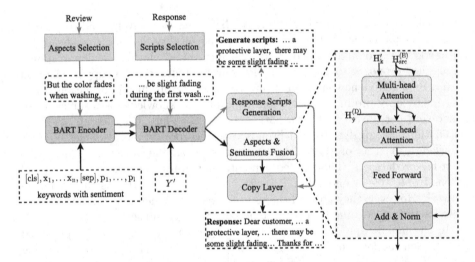

Fig. 2. Framework of our model. The blue arrow indicates the flow of response script learning, while the black arrow represents the flow of response generation with fine-grained keywords and sentiments. (Color figure online)

As shown in Fig. 2, our proposed Multi-Grained Aspect Fusion (MGAF) model for RRG is based on the BART [10], which contains two perspectives. On the one hand, it incorporates a coarse-grained response script learning. On the other hand, it integrates fine-grained aspect-level keywords and sentiments to guide the generation process. Furthermore, to capture replicable tokens mentioned in the review, similar to previous works [3,28], we also incorporate a copy layer to achieve this objective. Most importantly, we hope that the copy layer can copy generated script tokens addressing specific issues mentioned in reviews, thereby further improving the targeting of generated response.

Given a review text with n tokens $X = \{x_1, x_2, ..., x_n\}$, the l pairs of properties associated with the review are denoted as $P = \{p_1, p_2, ..., p_l\}$. The keywords related to aspects and opinions in the review text are denoted as $K = \{k_1, k_2, ..., k_o\}$, and the sentiment of each keyword in K is represented as $S = \{(s_1, b_1), (s_2, b_2), ..., (s_o, b_o)\}$, where o is the number of all keyword tokens. $s_i \in \{0, 1, 2\}$ where 0, 1, and 2 represent negative, positive and neutral sentiment, respectively, and $b_i \in [0, 1]$ represents the probability of the corresponding sentiment s_i. The response with m tokens can be denoted as $Y = \{y_1, y_2, ..., y_m\}$. Therefore, the task can be formalized as $f : (X, P, K, S) \rightarrow Y$.

To substantiate our proposed methodology, similar to the technique adopted in [3], we utilize BART as the backbone. Precisely, we input the review into an embedding layer to obtain the embedded representations $\{x_0, x_1, ..., x_n, x_{n+1}\}$, which are concatenated with the embedded representations of property pairs $\{p_1, p_2, ..., p_{l-1}, p_l\}$:

$$X' = \{x_0, x_1, ..., x_n, x_{n+1}, p_1, p_2, ..., p_{l-1}, p_l\} \tag{1}$$

where x_0, x_{n+1} represent the embedding vectors of the special tokens [CLS] and [SEP], respectively, and $X' \in \mathbb{R}^{(n+l+2) \times D}$, where D is the hidden size of the BART Encoder. The concatenated source embedding X' is fed into the BART Encoder:

$$H_{src}^{(E)} = \text{Encoder}(X') \tag{2}$$

where $H_{src}^{(E)} \in \mathbb{R}^{(n+l+2) \times D}$, and it serves as the representation of the source encoded by BART Encoder. We employ the BART Decoder module to decode the initial representation $H_{\hat{y}}^{(D)}$ of the response:

$$H_{\hat{y}}^{(D)} = \text{Decoder}(H_{src}^{(E)}, Y') \tag{3}$$

During the training phase, teacher forcing is utilized to accelerate convergence, thus the input Y' to the decoder is the true label shifted right by one position. Once we obtain the initial representation of the response, we subsequently refine it using a fine-grained aspect and sentiment fusion module. It is in conjunction with a copy layer that incorporates coarse-grained response scripts to further amplify the targeting of the response.

3.2   Aspect Selection and Response Script Generation

Chen et al. [3] suggested dividing review text into segments based on punctuation, with each segment serving as an aspect for their multi-aspect attentive network. However, this coarse-grained approach might not capture the significance of each aspect within the review, potentially resulting in weak targeted responses and limited response diversity. In our work, we also utilize a coarse-grained approach, but carefully select specific aspects of the review to emphasize. Additionally, we identify key segments from the response to serve as response scripts. By prioritizing these selected aspects, our proposed model demonstrates the capability to generate response sentences that are highly specific and targeted.

Ideally, the selected response scripts should directly address the issues chosen from the review in a targeted manner. However, considering the computational cost and time limitation, we draw from techniques used in the text summarization and utilize the TextRank [15] algorithm combined with BM25 [20] to compute the relevance score for each sentence in the segmented sentences. We first select the salient sentences from review as the chosen aspect sequence, forming a set of tokens $A = \{a_1, a_2, ..., a_{k_1}\}$. Similarly, we select the salient sentences from the segmented response as the corresponding script sequence, forming a set of tokens $R = \{r_1, r_2, ..., r_{k_2}\}$. Note that, we select the important sentences according to a certain proportion that will be detailed in Sect. 4.6. We use the chosen aspect sequence tokens as input and the selected script sequence as the supervised signal to train the response script generation module. As shown in Fig. 2, the response script learning task shares the encoder and decoder with the response generation task, while each task has its own modules to maximize parameter sharing and reduce training costs.

To obtain the aspect selection representation from the aspect sequence tokens A, we feed the embedded representation $A' = \{a_0, a_1, ..., a_{k_1}, a_{k_1+1}\}$ to the BART Encoder:

$$H_a^{(E)} = \text{Encoder}(A') \tag{4}$$

where a_0, a_{k_1+1} represent the embedding vectors of tokens [CLS] and [SEP], respectively. $A' \in \mathbb{R}^{(k_1+2) \times D}$, where D is the hidden size of the BART Encoder. After decoding with BART Decoder and linear layer transformation, the distribution of each token in the response P_r is obtained through the softmax function.

$$H_r^{(D)} = \text{Decoder}(H_a^{(E)}, R') \tag{5}$$

$$P_r = \text{softmax}(W^{(r)} H_r^{(D)} + b^{(r)}) \tag{6}$$

where R' is the embedding representation of the script tokens shifted by one position. $W^{(r)}, b^{(r)}$ are learnable parameters, and softmax is the activation function.

During the training phase, we accelerate the training by using teacher forcing. We use cross entropy as our loss function, which is calculated as follows:

$$L_s = - \sum_{v \in V} \sum_{y_s \in R} Y_{v,t} \cdot \log P_r(y_s) \tag{7}$$

In the inference phase, we first decode the response scripts to obtain their representation and tokens. Then we proceed with generating the final response.

3.3 Aspects and Sentiments Fusion

Different aspects with varying sentiments have a direct impact on the response generation process. Thus, we propose aspects and sentiments fusion module to integrate them into the initial result representation. Specifically, we use the embedding of aspect and opinion keyword tokens $K' = \{k_0, k_1, ..., k_l, k_{l+1}\}$ through the BART Encoder as follows:

$$H_k^{(E)} = \text{Encoder}(K') \tag{8}$$

where k_0 and k_{l+1} represent the embedding vectors of tokens [CLS] and [SEP], respectively, and $H_k^{(D)} \in \mathbb{R}^{(l+2) \times D}$ where D is the dimension of the BART Encoder output.

The sentiment embedding and its corresponding probability are multiplied to obtain the sentiment representation S_k, which can be expressed as follows:

$$S_k = \{b_0 \cdot s_0, b_1 \cdot s_1, b_2 \cdot s_2, \ldots, b_l \cdot s_l, b_{l+1} \cdot s_{l+1}\} \tag{9}$$

where s_0 and s_{l+1} correspond to the embedding vectors for the sentiment of the entire review and are assigned values of $b_0 = 1.0$ and $b_{l+1} = 1.0$, respectively. It should be noted that l represents the length of all keyword tokens and b_i represents the probability of the i-th sentiment label.

Next, we incorporate the sentiment embedding S_k and the fine-grained keyword representation $H_k^{(E)}$ by using multi-head attention modules to produce a response that focuses on relevant fine-grained information. This is achieved through the following:

$$H'_k = S_k + H_k^{(E)} \tag{10}$$

$$H'_k = \text{MultiHead}(Q = H'_k, K = H_{src}^{(E)}, V = H_{src}^{(E)}) \tag{11}$$

$$H_d = \text{MultiHead}(Q = H_{\hat{y}}^{(D)}, K = H'_k, V = H'_k) \tag{12}$$

where $\text{MultiHead}(Q, K, V)$ represents the concatenation of h attention heads. Each $head_i$ is calculated as $head_i = \text{Attention}(QW_i^Q, KW_i^K, VW_i^V)$. The scaled dot-product attention is computed as Vaswani et al. [25] did:

$$\text{Attention}(Q, K, V) = \text{softmax}(\frac{QK^T}{\sqrt{d_k}})V \tag{13}$$

3.4   Copy Layer

To facilitate the direct copying of tokens from the input tokens and previously generated response scripts, we adopt the pointer-generator network [21] as utilized by [3] for copying specific tokens from the multi-source input. This serves as our copy layer for generating the probability $P(y_t)$ of each response token. However, our approach differs in that we copy tokens not only from the review input, but also from the response script tokens generated in Sect. 3.2.

Our model is primarily composed of two types of losses: script learning loss L_s which is calculated by formula (7) in Sect. 3.4. And response generation loss L_r which is computed as follows:

$$L_r = -\sum_{v \in V} \sum_{t}^{T} Y_{v,t} \cdot \log P(y_t) \qquad (14)$$

Finally, the total loss is the weighted summation of them $L = L_r + \beta \cdot L_s$, where β is the weight of loss L_s.

4 Experiments

4.1 Datasets

We carry out experiments on two benchmark datasets specifically designed for RRG tasks. The first dataset, known as the Chinese Taobao[1] Clothing dataset, comprises 100,000 samples and was initially introduced in Zhao et al. [28]. It has since become a popular choice for research in this area. The second dataset [8] is an English hospitality dataset that consists of 400,000 review-response pairs for hotels and restaurants posted on TripAdvisor[2]. Both datasets are divided into 80% for training, 10% for validation, and 10% for testing following the original methodology.

4.2 Evaluation

To evaluate the proposed method, we adopt the evaluation methods employed in prior research [3,8,28] and present the BLEU [18], Rouge-1/2/l [12], and Distinct-1/2 [11] scores. The BLEU and Rouge-1/2/l scores gauge the fluency of the generated results, whereas the Dist-1/2 scores evaluate the diversity of the generated results. All of these scores are higher-the-better metrics.

Furthermore, to evaluate the targeting of the generated responses, we compute the F1 score for the targeted aspect keywords as follows: $F1 = \frac{2*P*R}{P+R}$, where $P = \frac{target\ aspects\ \cap\ predict\ aspects}{predict\ aspects}$ and $R = \frac{target\ aspects\ \cap\ predict\ aspects}{target\ aspects}$, the terms "target aspects" and "predict aspects" denote the aspect and opinion keyword sets found in gold responses and predicted responses, respectively, and "$\cap$" represents the intersection operation.

4.3 Setups

We employ the BART-base [10] model from HuggingFace Transformers [26] as our backbone, and most hyperparameters are the same as the BART-base model. Considering the linguistic differences between Chinese and English, we utilize BART-base-chinese [22] and BART-base [10] to partially initialize the parameters for experiments on clothing and hospitality, respectively. In addition, we set the training batch size to 32 for the Clothing dataset and 24 for the Hospitality dataset. We use the AdamW [14] optimizer with a learning rate of 1e-4

---

[1] https://www.taobao.com/.

[2] https://www.tripadvisor.com/.

Table 1. Results on Clothing dataset.

Model	Rouge-1/2/L	BLEU	Dist-1/2	F1
EPI [28]	36.71/18.07/28.84	15.61	62.30/80.90	–
MsG [3]	41.77/23.28/32.95	21.75	68.00/88.50	–
MsMAAG [3]	43.64/25.67/34.99	24.44	68.80/89.50	–
Baseline	42.85/23.55/33.01	21.86	69.10/93.28	49.18
MGAF (ours)	**44.72/26.19/35.34**	**24.46**	**69.73/93.58**	**51.16**

Table 2. Results on Hospitality dataset.

Model	Rouge-1/2/L	BLEU	Dist-1/2
Seq2Seq [8]	35.62/14.55/28.94	8.17	0.00/0.01
Seq2Seq+A+K [8]	24.24/9.65/20.34	2.92	0.00/0.01
Baseline	36.83/15.07/33.81	9.50	**0.36/1.96**
MGAF (ours)	**37.17/15.20/34.05**	**9.67**	0.34/1.89

to train 30 epochs for the Clothing dataset and 10 epochs for the Hospitality dataset. For response script learning, we choose 25% of the total sentences from the review and responses. We set the loss weight of script learning to 0.25 and 0.1 for the Clothing and Hospitality datasets, respectively. Our model is compared with recent methods, including EPI [28], MsG and MsMAAG [3], and Seq2Seq (+A+K) [8]. The MsMAAG and Seq2Seq are the previous SOTA models. However, due to the unavailability of their source code, we implement our response generation strong baseline by referring to their paper for comparison.

4.4 Main Results

Tables 1 and 2 present the main experimental results on two datasets. The proposed Multi-Grained Aspect Fusion (MGAF) model demonstrates its effectiveness by achieving state-of-the-art performance on all metrics for both Chinese and English datasets. This is attributed to the model's ability to leverage more inherent features of the reviews, including aspect-level keywords and sentiments. In contrast, while MsMAAG attempted to utilize all sentences segmented by punctuations as multi-aspects, it lacks selection and ignores to highlight the issues mentioned in the review. This can also be demonstrated in Sect. 4.6. Our model overcame this challenge through aspect selection and script learning at the sentence level. Specifically, for the Chinese Clothing dataset, the MGAF model achieves a significant improvement over the baseline and the target F1 metric improves approximately 2 points compared to the baseline. These results suggest that our model can better understand information related to the issues raised in the review, thus generating more diverse and targeted responses. For the English Hospitality dataset, our model also generates more fluent and diverse responses compared to previous studies. However, due to the inclusion of more scenarios in the Hospitality dataset (such as hotels and restaurants) and the lack of the accurate aspect and opinion-related keywords, the improvement is not as significant as that on the Clothing dataset. Therefore, further exploration is necessary to better extract aspect-related features from reviews.

4.5 Ablation Results

As stated previously, this study incorporates response script learning to facilitate targeting of our model. Moreover, we integrate aspects, opinion keywords, and sentiments into the model. Thus, we explored the effect of these modules

Table 3. Ablation results. "w/o" means without, "w/" means with. "scripts" represents response script learning, and "senti" means sentiment features.

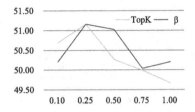

Fig. 3. Influence of TopK and β on target F1.

Model	Rouge-1/2/L	BLEU	Dist-1/2	F1
MGAF	**44.72/26.19/35.34**	**24.46**	69.73/93.58	**51.16**
w/o scripts	44.18 / 25.48 / 34.64	23.88	**69.74/93.69**	50.15
w/o scripts & senti	44.17/25.14/34.29	23.91	67.86/92.67	50.76
w/ punctuation	43.97/25.20/34.39	23.58	69.73/93.65	50.51

and compared them to the approach proposed by [3], which represents aspects using all the sentences segmented by punctuations without aspect selection. The results presented in Table 3 demonstrate that excluding aspect selection and script learning resulted in a decrease in our model's performance by 0.54/0.61/0.7 and 0.58 points on Rouge-1/2/L and BLEU, respectively. This suggests the benefits of script learning in improving the fluency of generated responses. Furthermore, our analysis revealed a decrease of 1.01 points in the target F1 metric, indicating that adopting a coarse-grained perspective improved the targeting of responses, making them more useful in resolving user conflicts. We also notice that removing the script learning has little positive impact on the Dist-1/2 score, this may be because the aspect-level keywords with sentiments are the key factor affecting the Dist-1/2 score. Thus, we further remove the sentiment, only keep the aspect-level keywords but without their sentiments, leading to a significant decrease in the model's response diversity (1.88/1.02 on Dist-1/2). This indicates that the sentiment polarity is more helpful in generating more diverse responses. Finally, we use the multi-aspect representation segmented by punctuation proposed in [3], which resulted in a decline in fluency and relevance, emphasizing the importance of incorporating aspect-level keywords and aspect selection to better represent the issues raised in the review.

4.6   Influence of Hyperparameters

In the ablation experiment, we notice that response script learning has a significant impact on the model. To evaluate the effects of selecting an appropriate number of aspect and scripts sentences, we varied the percentage of selected sentences from reviews as chosen aspects and from responses as scripts to be learned. The TopK line in Fig. 3 demonstrates that an optimal number of selected sentences is necessary for maximizing the effectiveness of this module. Too few or too many selections can negatively affect the model's targeting ability. When TopK equals 1.00, which is no aspect selection, the F1 metric is the lowest. This indicates that selective response to some aspects mentioned in the review, rather than responding to all aspects, are more targeted and persuasive. Additionally, we observe from the β line that the weight of the response script learning task should be appropriately adjusted to prevent a negative impact on the model's convergence speed and performance. Based on our experimentation on the Clothing dataset, we select 25% of the all aspect sentences from the segmented review and scripts from the segmented response and set the weight of the script learning task loss to 0.25.

5   Conclusion

This paper proposes the MGAF model, which combines multi-grained features to improve the targeting of generated responses. The model integrates coarse-grained aspect selection for response script learning and fine-grained aspect-level keywords with sentiment representations. According to the experimental results, the proposed model not only enhances the fluency and diversity of the generated responses compared to previous works, but also generates more targeted and persuasive responses.

In the future, we will explore ways to align aspects and response scripts to obtain more accurate scripts for various issues mentioned in reviews, as well as to improve inference speed.

Acknowledgments. We thank the reviewers for their valuable comments. This work was supported by the National Natural Science Foundation of China (No. 62076173), the High-level Entrepreneurship and Innovation Plan of Jiangsu Province (No. JSS-CRC2021524), and the Project Funded by the Priority Academic Program Development of Jiangsu Higher Education Institutions.

References

1. Alturaief, N., Aljamaan, H., Baslyman, M.: Aware: aspect-based sentiment analysis dataset of apps reviews for requirements elicitation. In: 2021 36th IEEE/ACM International Conference on Automated Software Engineering Workshops (ASEW), pp. 211–218. IEEE (2021)
2. Cao, Y., Fard, F.H.: Pre-trained neural language models for automatic mobile app user feedback answer generation. CoRR abs/2202.02294 (2022). https://arxiv.org/abs/2202.02294
3. Chen, B., Liu, J., Maimaiti, M., Gao, X., Zhang, J.: Generating persuasive responses to customer reviews with multi-source prior knowledge in e-commerce. In: Hasan, M.A., Xiong, L. (eds.) Proceedings of the 31st ACM International Conference on Information & Knowledge Management, Atlanta, GA, USA, 17–21 October 2022, pp. 2994–3002. ACM (2022). https://doi.org/10.1145/3511808.3557122
4. Chen, H., Zhai, Z., Feng, F., Li, R., Wang, X.: Enhanced multi-channel graph convolutional network for aspect sentiment triplet extraction. In: Association for Computational Linguistics (ACL), 22–27 May 2022, pp. 2974–2985 (2022). https://doi.org/10.18653/v1/2022.acl-long.212
5. Cho, K., et al.: Learning phrase representations using RNN encoder-decoder for statistical machine translation. In: Proceedings of the 2014 Conference on Empirical Methods in Natural Language Processing (EMNLP), pp. 1724–1734 (2014)
6. Farooq, U., Siddique, A.B., Jamour, F.T., Zhao, Z., Hristidis, V.: App-aware response synthesis for user reviews. In: 2020 IEEE International Conference on Big Data (IEEE BigData 2020), Atlanta, GA, USA, 10–13 December 2020, pp. 699–708. IEEE (2020). https://doi.org/10.1109/BigData50022.2020.9377983

7. Gao, C., Zhou, W., Xia, X., Lo, D., Xie, Q., Lyu, M.R.: Automating app review response generation based on contextual knowledge. ACM Trans. Softw. Eng. Methodol. **31**(1), 11:1–11:36 (2022). https://doi.org/10.1145/3464969

8. Kew, T., Amsler, M., Ebling, S.: Benchmarking automated review response generation for the hospitality domain. In: Proceedings of Workshop on Natural Language Processing in E-Commerce, pp. 43–52 (2020)

9. Kew, T., Volk, M.: Improving specificity in review response generation with data-driven data filtering. In: Proceedings of The Fifth Workshop on e-Commerce and NLP (ECNLP 5), pp. 121–133 (2022)

10. Lewis, M., Liu, Y., et al.: BART: denoising sequence-to-sequence pre-training for natural language generation, translation, and comprehension. In: Proceedings of the 58th Annual Meeting of the Association for Computational Linguistics, pp. 7871–7880 (2020)

11. Li, J., Galley, M., Brockett, C., Gao, J., Dolan, W.B.: A diversity-promoting objective function for neural conversation models. In: Proceedings of the 2016 Conference of the North American Chapter of the Association for Computational Linguistics: Human Language Technologies, pp. 110–119 (2016)

12. Lin, C.Y.: Rouge: a package for automatic evaluation of summaries. In: Text Summarization Branches Out, pp. 74–81 (2004)

13. Liu, Z., Xia, R., Yu, J.: Comparative opinion quintuple extraction from product reviews. In: Proceedings of the 2021 Conference on Empirical Methods in Natural Language Processing, pp. 3955–3965 (2021)

14. Loshchilov, I., Hutter, F.: Decoupled weight decay regularization. In: International Conference on Learning Representations (2017)

15. Mihalcea, R., Tarau, P.: TextRank: bringing order into text. In: Proceedings of the 2004 Conference on Empirical Methods in Natural Language Processing, pp. 404–411 (2004)

16. Noone, B.M., McGuire, K.A., Rohlfs, K.V.: Social media meets hotel revenue management: opportunities, issues and unanswered questions. J. Revenue Pricing Manag. **10**, 293–305 (2011)

17. Pantelidis, I.S.: Electronic meal experience: a content analysis of online restaurant comments. Cornell Hosp. Q. **51**(4), 483–491 (2010)

18. Papineni, K., Roukos, S., Ward, T., Zhu, W.J.: BLEU: a method for automatic evaluation of machine translation. In: Proceedings of the 40th Annual Meeting of the Association for Computational Linguistics, pp. 311–318 (2002)

19. Park, D.H., Lee, J., Han, I.: The effect of on-line consumer reviews on consumer purchasing intention: the moderating role of involvement. Int. J. Electron. Commer. **11**(4), 125–148 (2007)

20. Robertson, S., Zaragoza, H., et al.: The probabilistic relevance framework: BM25 and beyond. Found. Trends® Inf. Retr. **3**(4), 333–389 (2009)

21. See, A., Liu, P.J., Manning, C.D.: Get to the point: summarization with pointer-generator networks. In: Proceedings of the 55th Annual Meeting of the Association for Computational Linguistics (Volume 1: Long Papers), pp. 1073–1083. Vancouver, Canada, July 2017. https://doi.org/10.18653/v1/P17-1099

22. Shao, Y., et al.: CPT: a pre-trained unbalanced transformer for both Chinese language understanding and generation. arXiv preprint arXiv:2109.05729 (2021)

23. Sparks, B.A., So, K.K.F., Bradley, G.L.: Responding to negative online reviews: the effects of hotel responses on customer inferences of trust and concern. Tour. Manage. **53**, 74–85 (2016)

24. Sutskever, I., Vinyals, O., Le, Q.V.: Sequence to sequence learning with neural networks. In: Proceedings of the 27th International Conference on Neural Information Processing Systems, vol. 2, pp. 3104–3112 (2014)

25. Vaswani, A., et al.: Attention is all you need. In: Advances in Neural Information Processing Systems, vol. 30 (2017)

26. Wolf, T., Debut, L., Sanh, V., Chaumond, et al.: Transformers: state-of-the-art natural language processing. In: Proceedings of the 2020 Conference on Empirical Methods in Natural Language Processing: System Demonstrations, pp. 38–45 (2020)

27. Zhang, W., Gu, W., Gao, C., Lyu, M.R.: A transformer-based approach for improving app review response generation. Softw. Pract. Exp. **53**(2), 438–454 (2023)

28. Zhao, L., Song, K., Sun, C., Zhang, Q., Huang, X., Liu, X.: Review response generation in e-commerce platforms with external product information. In: The World Wide Web Conference, WWW 2019, San Francisco, CA, USA, 13–17 May 2019, pp. 2425–2435. ACM (2019). https://doi.org/10.1145/3308558.3313581

Multiple Object Tracking Based on Variable GIoU-Embedding Matrix and Kalman Filter Compensation

Kelei Sun[1]📷, Qiufen Wen[1]📷, Huaping Zhou[1]([✉])📷, Kaitao Xiong[2]📷,
Jie Zhang[1]📷, Qi Zhao[1]📷, Jingwen Wu[1]📷, and Meiguang Li[1]📷

[1] School of Computer Science and Engineering,
Anhui University of Science and Technology, Huainan 232001, China
13805549155@163.com
[2] State Key Laboratory of Traction Power, Southwest Jiaotong University,
Chengdu 610000, China

Abstract. Despite tracking-by-detection having shown dramatically rapid improvement, most existing approaches are still scrabbling in dense pedestrian tracking. To address this problem, this work presents a new multiple object tracking approach, named VacoTrack. This method combines variable GIoU-Embedding matrix (VGE) and Kalman Filter compensation, which introduces motion compensation operation over trajectory parameters to construct virtual uniform linear trajectories for objects. This method combines GIoU distance and Embedding cosine distance of objects variably as a new association matrix VGE to adjustably calculate similarity matrix in facing different occlusion problem. After association, this method sends all tracked trajectories back to Kalman Filter, including constructed virtual trajectories for re-matched objects, and then operates Kalman Filter compensation to fine tune trajectory parameters. Thus, this approach regards the motion patterns of objects as uniform linear motion patterns to identify them across dense pedestrian, and improve robustness. Our proposed approach achieves 64.43 and 63.14 HOTA on MOT17 and MOT20 benchmarks respectively and outperforms state-of-the-art in most evaluation metrics.

Keywords: Multiple Object Tracking · Variable GIoU-Embedding Matrix · Kalman Filter Compensation · Dense Pedestrian Tracking · Uniform Linear Motion Pattern

Supported by the National Natural Science Foundation of China (Grant no. 61703005) and the Key Research and Development Projects in Anhui Province (Grant no. 202004-b11020029).

1   Introduction

Tracking-by-detection is still a challenging issue for the computer vision applications due to the existence of objects overlapping in dense pedestrian tracking. Recently, several approaches have been presented to against this appearance problem. For example, MO3TR [1] combines spatial and temporal Transformers to predict the locations of all tracked objects in frames. After which, MO3TR can cope with occlusions over consecutive frames. Based on this example, this paper proposes an approach to detect individuals via Deformable-DETR [2] (D-DETR) in video frames, and then utilize the object confidence scores to variably calculate the object GIoU-Embedding cost matrix to help association. And after association, the proposed method performs motion compensation over history and current association results in Kalman Filter to smooth trajectory parameters, after which this method can get better estimation for the following frame.

In association process, the accuracy of similarity cost matrix between trajectories and observations determines the robustness of tracker. The IoU matrix is always utilized as a unique source of object matching [3,4], which is fast but fails in tracking with severe occlusion. To this end, the proposed approach designs a variable similarity matrix in the cascade matching strategy, which extracts object confidence scores to combine GIoU distance and Embedding distance flexibly.

Predicting more accurately for association process, trackers can deal with various appearance problems better. Guo [5] achieves the synergy between the location estimation and the embedding matching, which makes the prediction focus on appearance of targets instead of distractors. Motivated by this, an improved Kalman Filter is implemented in this study to introduce a suitable state vector for better box prediction, and compensates the existing trajectory parameters to model uniform linear motion patterns.

This paper develops a new multiple object tracking (VacoTrack), which contains the object variable GIoU-Embedding matrix and the Kalman Filter compensation. In the current time step, firstly, the proposed method obtains all the detection bounding boxes through D-DETR. Secondly, VacoTrack gets the estimating locations of existing trajectories for this time step, which are predicted by classical Kalman Filter prediction step in the previous time step. Thirdly, according to confidence scores, the presented tracker variably combines the Embedding distance for objects in long-range tracking and the GIoU distance for restricting the Embedding associating range. After association, along existing trajectories, VacoTrack performs Kalman Filter compensation operation over trajectory parameters for purpose of decreasing estimation errors and obtains better estimations in location predicting process. We evaluate the tracker on MOT17 and MOT20 benchmarks, and reach competitive performance. The main contributions of this work can be summarized as follows:

- Fusing location distance matrix and appearance distance matrix as a variable GIoU-Embedding matrix. The tracker presented in this paper utilizes confidence scores of current observations to dynamically adjust the proportion of different distance matrix, which effectively against the occlusion and crossover problems in crowd pedestrian tracking.

- Utilizing motion compensation and feedback receiving to form a Kalman Filter compensation module. The proposed method introduces a suitable state vector for better box prediction and receives the feedback of tracked trajectories to construct Kalman Filter compensation module which will fine tune parameters of Kalman Filter and trajectories.

This paper is organized as follows. Related work is discussed in Sect. 2. The methodology of this approach is presented in Sect. 3. Experimental results are displayed in Sect. 4 followed by the conclusion in Sect. 5.

2   Related Work

Computing the similarity between trajectories and observations is the first step of data association, which determines the upper bound of MOT. Location, motion and appearance are crucial cues for similarity matrix calculation. The IoU distance matrix has been comprehensively used to associate targets in consecutive frames [3], which is fast but inaccurate. In situation of low frame rate or fast camera movement, learning from object motions [6–8] achieves robust results. In short-range association, location and motion similarity are more helpful for matching. And appearance similarity performs better in long-range association. An independent Re-ID model [9,10] is adopted to extract high quality appearance feature to build a more distinguishable association metric for matching. However, they cannot outperform in complicated scenarios such as dense pedestrian tracking. We believe that appearance and location matrix can work together in a more reasonable way that one of them assists another in matching, which is crucially beneficial in dense pedestrian tracking.

Constructed by filter, motion model [3,11] aims at finding out the object motion pattern in the current time step, and then selecting an optimal region to search for each object in the next time step. And it contains rich motion information of objects, which is helpful for associating objects with occlusions and overlapping. Some motion networks [4,6] are designed to extract object motion model. The information of established motion models in MAT [12] are considered as additional cues to promote the prediction process. Conforming to the constant velocity assumption (CVA) [13], traditional Kalman Filter [14] is a popular choice in extracting motion pattern [3,6,15]. However, traditional Kalman Filter is unable to deal with the uncertain noise from observation. In order to solve this problem effectively, many scholars try to improve the tracking performance with different filters [16–18] and variants of the Kalman Filter [19, 20]. Through in-depth analysis of object motion patterns in MOT, it can be seen that more suitable similarity matrix and motion model can help to better associate objects between observation and prediction.

3   Methodology

In this section, the proposed multi-target tracker VacoTrack separates detection and association processes. For detection, this method deploys D-DETR, a Transformer-based detector. For association, VacoTrack designs a variable GIoU-Embedding matrix (VGE) and Kalman Filter compensation operation to enhance association robustness over dense pedestrian tracking.

3.1   Model Architecture

When the appearance of individuals is not clearly identifiable in surveillance videos due to occlusions and overlapping, a more accurate similarity cost matrix and more reasonable motion models of objects play vital roles in their identification. To this end, this text proposes a new multiple object tracking model VacoTrack. At time step t (not the first or the last frame), firstly, the current frame of video is put into the CNN(ResNet-50) and Deformation-DETR(D-DETR) encoder to extract the feature of this frame. Simultaneously, D-DETR outputs all detection bounding boxes on current time step. Secondly, the observation confidence scores (confidence in Fig. 1) are utilizing to variably calculate the GIoU-Embedding cost matrix. By doing this, the trajectory prediction from Kalman Filter in the previous time step could be associated with the current detection boxes by Hungarian algorithm [31] in current frame. Thus, this method constructs virtual uniform linear trajectories for all objects. Then, the association results and the current frame feature are both put into the D-DETR decoder to output the final results, which will be put into Kalman Filter to estimate the positions of reserved trajectories for the following frame. Finally, Kalman Filter receives the feedback from tracking results and performs compensation operation over trajectory parameters. After that, Kalman Filter compensation module can decrease accumulation error in estimation process. The model architecture of VacoTrack is shown as Fig. 1.

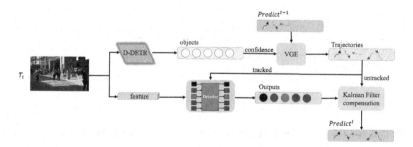

Fig. 1. Model architecture diagram of VacoTrack.

For the first frame of video, VacoTrack initializes all detection bounding boxes detected by D-DETR as new trajectories. And then the method inputs them into the D-DETR decoder along with the frame feature extracted by the CNN(ResNet-50) and D-DETR encoder to obtain the final output. Then, all trajectories are fed into Kalman Filter compensation module for the following frame trajectory predictions.

3.2   Variable GIoU-Embedding Matrix

The tracking performance depends on the precision of similarity matrix in data matching. In dense pedestrian, using IoU distance alone is not enough to retrieve the correct identity. Thus, the approach proposed in this paper proposes the variable GIoU and Embedding matrix (VGE matrix) which combines the Embedding distance for objects in long-range tracking and the GIoU [21] distance for restricting the Embedding associating range. This method extracts weighting factors from current frame observations to adjust the proportions of position distance and appearance distance respectively. Then, the variable GIoU-Embedding matrix can be represented as:

$$\mathbf{VGE} = \mathbf{Conf}_i\mathbf{G} + \mathbf{Conf}_j\mathbf{E} \tag{1}$$

Where two hyper parameters $Conf_i$ and $Conf_j$ represent Weighting factors. G denotes GIoU distance and E denotes Embedding distance. VacoTrack utilizes confidence scores of objects in current frame to flexibly calculate the fusion of GIoU and Embedding distance. Figure 2 shows different association process in dense pedestrian scenario with occlusion.

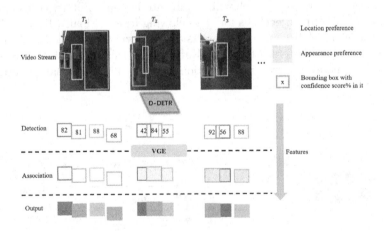

Fig. 2. Different association preference in dense pedestrian scenario with occlusion.

When number of low score objects surpass threshold, this approach gives a low weight to Embedding matrix and a high weight to GIoU matrix. In another word, when the confidence level of target in the current frame is generally low, that is, occlusion proportion between the targets is high, this approach uses appearance distance matrix to assist location distance matrix (location preference in Fig. 2). On the contrary, when number of high score objects surpass threshold, this approach gives a high weight to Embedding matrix and a low weight to GIoU matrix. In another word, when the target confidence is generally high, that is, occlussion proportion between the targets is small, this approach uses location distance matrix to assist appearance distance matrix (appearance preference in Fig. 2). By doing this, VGE matrix could improve the accuracy of tracking method in dense pedestrian tracking.

3.3   Kalman Filter Compensation

Kalman Filter (KF) is an estimator of linear motion. For trajectory prediction in current step, KF only requires the estimated state (x) on the previous time step and the current measurement (the covariance matrix P) for the state estimation. And the prediction process in KF can be described by other parameters such as the state transition model F, the observation model H, the process noise Q and the observation noise R. At time t, the prediction of prior state estimate x and covariance state matrix P are calculated as:

$$\begin{aligned}
\hat{\mathbf{x}}_{t|t-1} &= \mathbf{F}_t \hat{\mathbf{x}}_{t-1|t-1} \\
\mathbf{P}_{t|t-1} &= \mathbf{F}_t \mathbf{P}_{t-1|t-1} \mathbf{F}_t^\top + \mathbf{Q}_t
\end{aligned} \tag{2}$$

In MOT applications, some objects may be untracked on some association process due to occlusion. In response to this problem, the proposed method reuses the estimation of the last tracked time step to the new arrived time step.

In a whole video sequence, both static and dynamic cameras have camera movement due to the change of background and themselves, which lead to shifting of bounding boxes. These camera movements could lead to object tracking failure. Enlightened by the global motion compensation in OpenCV [22], this approach regard camera motion projection as relative movement calculation between two adjacent frames. VacoTrack uses the affine matrix $A_{t|t-1} \in R^{2\times3}$, which is calculated by RANSAC, to transform the predicting boxes from the coordinate system of frame $t-1$ to the coordinates of the next frame t. The affine matrix A is shown as:

$$\mathbf{A}_{t|t-1} = [\mathbf{M}_{2x2} \mid \mathbf{T}_{2x1}] = \begin{bmatrix} a_{11} & a_{12} & a_{13} \\ a_{21} & a_{22} & a_{23} \end{bmatrix} \tag{3}$$

$$\mathbf{M}'_{t|t-1} = \begin{bmatrix} M & 0 & 0 & 0 \\ 0 & M & 0 & 0 \\ 0 & 0 & M & 0 \\ 0 & 0 & 0 & M \end{bmatrix} \tag{4}$$

$$\mathbf{T}'_{t|t-1} = \begin{bmatrix} a_{13} & a_{23} & 0 & 0 & \cdots & 0 \end{bmatrix}^\top \tag{5}$$

Where $M \in R^{2\times2}$ contains the scale and rotation information of affine matrix A. Matrix T contains the translation information. Defining $M'_{t|t-1} \in R^{8\times8}$ and

$T'_{t|t-1} \in R^8$, the prediction of prior state estimate x and covariance state matrix P of update step in Kalman Filter compensation module are corrected as:

$$\hat{x}'_{t|t-1} = M'_{t|t-1}\hat{x}_{t|t-1} + T'_{t|t-1}$$
$$P'_{t|t-1} = M'_{t|t-1}P_{t|t-1}M'^{\top}_{t|t-1} \tag{6}$$

After considering the motion compensation for Kalman Filter, VacoTrack could construct uniform linear trajectories for objects during tracking, including re-matched objects. In loss period, VacoTrack defines the last detection box before being untracked as z_{t_1}, and the detection box that triggered the re-association as z_{t_2}. At time step t, the virtual trajectory can be generated as:

$$\hat{z}_t = z_{t_1} + \frac{t - t_1}{t_2 - t_1}(z_{t_2} - z_{t_1}), t_1 < t < t_2 \tag{7}$$

Thus, motion models can be more effectively established by Kalman Filter compensation. And the update process in the Kalman Filter compensation module is shown as:

$$K_t = P'_{t|t-1}H_t^{\top}\left(H_t P'_{t|t-1}H_t^{\top} + R_t\right)^{-1}$$
$$\hat{x}_{t|t} = F_t\hat{x}'_{t|t-1} + K_t\left(\hat{z}_t - H_t F_t \hat{x}'_{t|t-1}\right) \tag{8}$$
$$P_{t|t} = (I - K_t H_t)P'_{t|t-1}$$

After association process, the associated trajectories are send back to Kalman Filter. Along virtual trajectories, VacoTrack can reversely check the parameters in KF by alternating between the predicting and updating stages. The supervision provided by the observation is introduced to modify the trajectory of the object and decrease the accumulated error of the Kalman Filter. We name this process "Kalman Filter compensation". This method only uses observation data up to the current time step and does not modify past output results of multiple object tracking. By applying this method, this tracker becomes more robust in dense pedestrian tracking. Once a trajectory remains untracked for some frames, this tracker tries to associate the last predicting location of this trajectory with detection box on newly arrived time steps. If this untracked trajectory is still untracked for more than 30 frames, this tracker will terminate this trajectory. By doing this, the estimation error generated by Kalman Filter will no longer accumulate.

4   Experimental Results

In this part, this paper illustrates the experimental setup and provides experimental results to verify the ability of VacoTrack. The presented approach is conducted with PyTorch framework in the python.

4.1   Datasets, Metrics and Experimental Setup

Datasets and Metrics. The presented approach is validated with standard performance criteria on MOT17 and MOT20 benchmarks. MOT17 and MOT20 are dense pedestrian tracking datasets whose motion is almost linear but with mutual occlusion and frequent crossovers. Compared to MOT17, the scenes in MOT20 are more crowded. This paper chooses the common metrics as the standard evaluation protocols to evaluate this approach, including Higher Order Metric for Evaluating Multi-object Tracking (HOTA [25], AssA, DetA), Multiple-Object Tracking Accuracy (MOTA), and Identity F1 Score (IDF1). Compared with MOTA, HOTA keeps a balance between the evaluation within target detection and association.

Experimental Setup. Following the settings in MOTR, VacoTrack resizes the shorter side of the input image to 800 and the maximum size to 1536. This approach is built upon Deformable-DETR and ResNet-50. For MOT17 [23] and MOT20 [24] datasets, we initialize VacoTrack with the official D-DETR weight, which is pretrained on MS COCO dataset. VacoTrack has been trained for 200 epochs both on MOT17 and MOT20 datasets. And we train the proposed approach on two joint datasets, one is combined by MOT17 train set and CrowdHuman val set, and the other is combined by MOT20 train set and CrowdHuman val set. Then, the comparisons between the proposed method and other algorithms have been conducted on MOT17 and MOT20 datasets respectively.

4.2   Experimental Results and Analysis

For the sake of verifying the application performance difference between the proposed approach and the existing trackers on MOT17 and MOT20 benchmarks, the same environment based on Tesla V100 is setup. Table 1 shows the performance of VacoTrack and other trackers on MOT17 and MOT20 respectively.

The experimental results confirm the conclusion that the presented approach constantly outperforms MOTR and the state-of-the-art (SOTA) models on HOTA metric. MOTR[5], a Transformer-based model, only detects new-born targets in detection process and performs TALA module to obtain tracked targets. But these two modules in MOTR inhibit each other and result in the degradation of both detection and association performance. Cutting out TALA module, the proposed method obtains all detection bounding boxes from D-DETR, and then calculates the object variable GIoU-Embedding distance matrix to help association. In addition, Kalman Filter compensation operation is performed over existing trajectory parameters to model uniform linear motion patterns. By doing these, VacoTrack can more accurately predict object locations and hence get better tracking results. In terms of the HOTA metric, the proposed tracker outperforms MOTR by 6.84% on MOT17 test set. It is confirmed that VacoTrack has better application performance than MOTR in multiple object tracking.

Table 1. Comparison results on the MOT17 and MOT20 test set of trackers.

Dataset	Tracker	HOTA	MOTA	IDF1	DetA	AssA
MOT17	JLA [26]	36.03	34.37	46.89	30.33	42.96
	TADAM [5]	48.19	60.44	59.76	48.09	48.56
	LPC [27]	51.09	58.82	66.04	47.56	55.15
	TransCenter [15]	54.59	75.93	65.94	62.59	51.56
	MOTR [28]	57.59	72.91	68.40	59.87	55.77
	GTR [29]	59.01	75.21	71.53	61.49	56.92
	OC-SORT [4]	61.76	75.94	76.12	61.58	62.20
	ByteTrack [3]	62.37	78.69	76.57	63.69	61.39
	BoT SORT [30]	63.76	78.56	78.56	63.52	64.31
	Strong SORT [19]	64.25	79.36	79.45	63.99	**64.79**
	VacoTrack	**64.43**	**79.59**	**79.57**	**64.63**	64.51
MOT20	TADAM [5]	42.68	57.16	52.93	46.83	39.21
	TransTrack [6]	50.74	67.72	58.83	57.06	45.49
	JLA [26]	52.17	51.69	64.10	50.38	54.32
	OC-SORT [4]	60.51	73.10	74.35	60.45	60.76
	ByteTrack [3]	60.95	75.74	75.01	61.99	60.11
	BoT SORT [30]	62.35	76.91	76.10	63.31	61.62
	Strong SORT [19]	62.56	73.84	76.93	61.34	**63.98**
	VacoTrack	**63.14**	**76.96**	**77.01**	**63.37**	63.12

Compared with other SOTA trackers in Table 1, the proposed tracker gets higher HOTA scores, which means VacoTrack holds the better association strategy. Different detectors have an influence on the tracking ability. For example, ByteTrack and OC-SORT use YOLOX to get detection bounding boxes. VacoTrack is also compared with Transformer-based trackers, like GTR, TransCenter, MOTR and TransTrack. Compared with YOLO-based trackers and Transformer-based trackers, Table 1 comprehensively indicates that VGE module and Kalman Filter compensation are effectively enhance the tracking performance in dense pedestrian tracking. The major improvement of HOTA comes from object variable GIoU-Embedding distance matrix and the parameter compensation in improved Kalman Filter for uniform linear motion modeling.

4.3 Ablation Study on MOT17 and MOT20

In order to prove the effectiveness of VGE matrix, we conduct the ablation studies on MOT17 and MOT20 datasets in Fig. 3. Two hyper parameters $Conf_i$ and $Conf_j$ in Eq. (1) represent weighting factors, which are calculated from confidence scores of objects in current frame to flexibly fuse GIoU distance and Embedding distance. The proposed tracker inputs objects with low confidence scores into $array_i$ and objects with high confidence scores into $array_j$ to count object numbers of high or low confidence scores respectively. Thus, this tracker could dynamically adjust the proportions of these two distance matrix for purpose of utilizing different distance matrix combinations to deal with different overlapping situations. This tracker gives a low weight to Embedding matrix and a high weight to GIoU matrix in facing high occlusion. On the contrary, when objects are easily to be detected, this tracker gives a high weight to Embedding matrix and a low weight to GIoU matrix. This paper tests the impact of different proportions of GIoU distance and Embedding distance in dense pedestrian tracking and displays the results in Fig. 3. This tracker fixes one distance matrix and fine tune the other distance matrix. Thus, the tracker sets the weighting factor of fixed distance matrix as 1, and use τ as weighting factor of changing distance matrix. For example, when $\tau = 0.5$, we set $Conf_i = 0.5$, $Conf_j = 1$ = in appearance preference situation and $Conf_i = 1$, $Conf_j = 0.5$ in position preference situation. When $\tau = 1.5$, we set $Conf_i = 1.5$, $Conf_j = 1$ in appearance preference situation and $Conf_i = 1$, $Conf_j = 1.5$ in position preference situation.

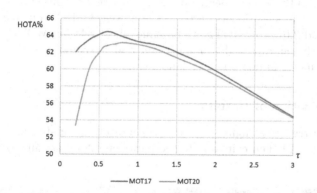

Fig. 3. The ablation study of weighting factor τ in variable GIoU-Embedding matrix on MOT17 and MOT20 test set.

Setting ($Conf_i$ and $Conf_j$), we conduct the ablation studies on MOT17 and MOT20 datasets in Table 2 to measure the impact of two proposed modules in VacoTrack respectively. The results demonstrate the efficiency of each of these two modules. We reconstruct association process in MOTR as baseline. We use classical Kalman Filter to estimate trajectories and update locations. Using GIoU and Hungarian algorithms as baseline to associate the objects between the previous and current time steps. The tracking results of baseline are displayed in the first line in Table 2.

Table 2. The ablation study of components on MOT17 and MOT20 test set.

VGE	KF compensation	MOT17				MOT20			
		HOTA	MOTA	IDF1	IDSW	HOTA	MOTA	IDF1	IDSW
–	–	61.67	75.97	76.16	2199	60.47	73.10	74.25	1496
√	–	62.65	78.83	76.96	2437	60.88	75.69	74.90	1352
–	√	62.86	78.87	77.23	2261	62.12	76.93	75.62	1571
√	√	**64.43**	**79.59**	**79.57**	**1158**	**63.14**	**76.96**	**77.01**	**1321**

With VGE module added, the baseline improves HOTA from 61.67% to 62.65% on MOT17 and from 60.47% to 60.88% on MOT20, which is a HOTA increase of 5.06% to MOTR on MOT17. Further, adding Kalman Filter compensation (KF compensation in Table 2) operation, the baseline improves HOTA from 61.67% to 62.86% on MOT17 and from 60.47% to 62.12% on MOT20, which is a HOTA increase of 5.27% to MOTR on MOT17. It proves that VGE module and Kalman Filter compensation operation can improve the performance in dense pedestrian tracking respectively. And then, we combine VGE module with Kalman Filter compensation as VacoTrack, and we get a HOTA increase of 2.76% on MOT17 and 2.67% on MOT20 to baseline, and 6.84% on MOT17 to MOTR. Combined with the improved Kalman Filter and VGE module, VacoTrack gets better performance in dense pedestrian tracking.

4.4 Visualization of Results

The proposed tracker is managed to more accurately calculate similarity matrix for association and then compensate the parameters of Kalman Filter and tra-

Fig. 4. Qualitative results of VacoTrack on MOT17 test set.

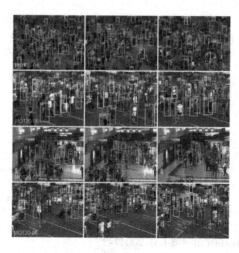

Fig. 5. Qualitative results of VacoTrack on MOT20 test set.

jectories in the dense pedestrian scenarios. In order to demonstrate both the ability of the VGE matrix and Kalman Filter compensation module, this paper shows some qualitative results of each sequence in MOT17 and MOT20 test set in Fig. 4 and Fig. 5. In the case of occlusion, motion blur and large displacement, this tracker can provide crucial cues to recover object relationships. The tracking results of MOT17-06, MOT17-07, MOT17-12 and MOT17-14 show the effectiveness of VacoTrack in irregular camera motion scenarios. MOT20 test results demonstrate that our tracker performs well in scenarios with heavily occlusion and overlapping.

5   Conclusion

This paper has introduced a new MOT model VacoTrack, which is based on object variable GIoU-Embedding distance matrix and Kalman Filter compensation to solve the occlusion and crossover problems in dense pedestrian tracking. The proposed framework achieves better tracking performance via calculating object variable GIoU-Embedding distance matrix for association and performing Kalman Filter compensation over trajectory parameters in current frame. This tracker forms a virtual uniform linear trajectory for a re-matched object from last tracked time step to re-matched time step. Then, the tracker can calculate the locations of this object during loss period and compensate the trajectory parameters in Kalman Filter. After that, VacoTrack can decrease the accumulated error in Kalman Filter estimation process and get better trajectory predictions for the following time step. Our evaluations on the MOT17 and MOT20 datasets illustrate that VacoTrack improves tracking capability considerably.

Besides, VacoTrack is still based on the linear motion assumption and the variant of classical Kalman Filter without a fundamental extension for non-linear object motion. So, there is still room for improvement of non-linear motion-based tracking. In the future, we will conduct researches on this aspect.

Acknowledgments. This work was supported in part by the National Natural Science Foundation of China (Grant no. 61703005) and in part by the Key Research and Development Projects in Anhui Province (Grant no. 202004-b11020029).

References

1. Zhu, T., Hiller, M., Ehsanpour, M., et al.: Looking beyond two frames: end-to-end multi-object tracking using spatial and temporal transformers. IEEE TPAMI, 1–14 (2022)
2. Zhu, X., Su, W., Lu, L., et al.: Deformable DETR: deformable transformers for end-to-end object detection. arXiv preprint arXiv:2010.04159 (2020)
3. Zhang, Y., Sun, P., Jiang, Y., et al.: ByteTrack: multi-object tracking by associating every detection box. In: Avidan, S., Brostow, G., Cissé, M., Farinella, G.M., Hassner, T. (eds.) ECCV. LNCS, vol. 13682, pp. 23–27. Springer, Cham (2022). https://doi.org/10.1007/978-3-031-20047-2_1
4. Cao, J., Weng, X., Khirodkar, R., et al.: Observation-centric sort: Rethinking sort for robust multi-object tracking. arXiv preprint arXiv:2203.14360 (2022)
5. Guo, S., Wang, J., Wang, X., et al.: Online multiple object tracking with cross-task synergy. In: CVPR, pp. 8136–8145 (2021)
6. Sun, P., Cao, J., Jiang, Y., et al.: TransTrack: multiple object tracking with transformer. arXiv preprint arXiv:2012.15460 (2020)
7. Zhou, X., Koltun, V., Krähenbühl, P.: Tracking objects as points. In: Vedaldi, A., Bischof, H., Brox, T., Frahm, J.-M. (eds.) ECCV 2020. LNCS, vol. 12349, pp. 474–490. Springer, Cham (2020). https://doi.org/10.1007/978-3-030-58548-8_28
8. Wu, J., Cao, J., Song, L., et al.: Track to detect and segment: an online multi-object tracker. In: CVPR, pp. 12352–12361 (2021)
9. Lu, Z., Rathod, V., Votel, R., et al.: RetinaTrack: online single stage joint detection and tracking. In: CVPR, pp. 14668–14678 (2020)
10. Pang, J., Qiu, L., Li, X., et al.: Quasi-dense similarity learning for multiple object tracking. In: CVPR, pp. 164–173 (2021)
11. Hornakova, A., Henschel, R., Rosenhahn, B., et al.: Lifted disjoint paths with application in multiple object tracking. In: ICML, pp. 4364–4375 (2020)
12. Han, S., Huang, P., Wang, H., et al.: MAT: motion-aware multi-object tracking. Neurocomputing **476**, 75–86 (2022)
13. Zhang, Y., Sheng, H., Wu, Y., et al.: Long-term tracking with deep tracklet association. IEEE Trans. Image Process. **29**, 6694–6706 (2020)
14. Kalman, R.E.: A new approach to linear filtering and prediction problems, pp. 35–45 (1960)
15. Xu, Y., Ban, Y., Delorme, G., et al.: TransCenter: transformers with dense queries for multiple-object tracking. arXiv e-prints, arXiv: 2103.15145 (2021)
16. Liu, Q., Ren, J., Wang, Y., et al.: EACOFT: an energy-aware correlation filter for visual tracking. Pattern Recogn. **112**, 107766 (2021)
17. Huang, B., Xu, T., Jiang, S., et al.: Robust visual tracking via constrained multi-kernel correlation filters. IEEE Trans. Multimedia **22**(11), 2820–2832 (2020)
18. Bai, S., He, Z., Dong, Y., et al.: Multi-hierarchical independent correlation filters for visual tracking. In: ICME, pp. 1–6 (2020)
19. Du, Y., Zhao, Z., Song, Y., et al.: StrongSORT: make DeepSORT great again. IEEE Trans. Multimedia, 1–14 (2023)

20. Du, Y., Wan, J., Zhao, Y., et al.: GIAOTracker: a comprehensive framework for MCMOT with global information and optimizing strategies in VisDrone 2021. In: ICCV, pp. 2809–2819 (2021)
21. Rezatofighi, H., Tsoi N., Gwak, J Y., et al.: Generalized intersection over union: a metric and a loss for bounding box regression. In: CVPR, pp. 658–666 (2019)
22. Bradski, G.: The openCV library. Dr. Dobb's J. Softw. Tools Prof. Program. **25**(11), 120–123 (2000)
23. Milan, A., Leal-Taixé, L., Reid, I., et al.: MOT16: a benchmark for multi-object tracking. arXiv preprint arXiv:1603.00831 (2016)
24. Dendorfer, P., Rezatofighi, H., Milan, A., et al.: MOT20: a benchmark for multi object tracking in crowded scenes. arXiv preprint arXiv:2003.09003 (2020)
25. Luiten, J., Osep, A., Dendorfer, P., et al.: HOTA: a higher order metric for evaluating multi-object tracking. Int. J. Comput. Vis. **129**, 548–578 (2021)
26. Kesa, O., Styles, O., Sanchez, V.: Multiple object tracking and forecasting: jointly predicting current and future object locations. In: IEEE Winter Conference on Applications of Computer Vision, pp. 560–569 (2022)
27. Dai, P., Weng, R., Choi, W., et al.: Learning a proposal classifier for multiple object tracking. In: CVPR, pp. 2443–2452 (2021)
28. Zeng, F., Dong, B., Zhang, Y., et al.: MOTR: end-to-end multiple-object tracking with transformer. In: Avidan, S., Brostow, G., Cissé, M., Farinella, G.M., Hassner, T. (eds.) ECCV 2022. LNCS, vol. 13687, pp. 23–27. Springer, Cham (2022)
29. Zhou, X., Yin, T., Koltun, V., et al.: Global tracking transformers. In: CVPR, pp. 8771–8780 (2022)
30. Aharon, N., Orfaig, R., Bobrovsky, B Z.: BoT-SORT: robust associations multi-pedestrian tracking. arXiv preprint arXiv:2206.14651 (2022)
31. Kuhn, H.W.: The Hungarian method for the assignment problem. Nav. Res. Logist. Q. **2**, 83–97 (1955)

Multi-relation Identification for Few-Shot Document-Level Relation Extraction

Dazhuang Wang, Shaojuan Wu, Xiaowang Zhang[✉], and Zhiyong Feng

College of Intelligence and Computing, Tianjin University, Tianjin 300350, China
{wdz,shaojuanwu,xiaowangzhang,zyfeng}@tju.edu.cn

Abstract. Document-level relation extraction aims to extract relations between entities mentioned in the given text. Existing approaches characterize relations by concatenating the representation of entities from numerous instances for each relation. However, it fails to identify multiple relations that may be expressed by the same entity pair in few-shot scenarios, since there may be only one instance for some relations. In this paper, we propose a Context-aware Hybrid Attention Network (CHAN) for few-shot document-level relation extraction to identify multi-relation. Specifically, we design instance-specific attention to localize the relevant context for each entity pair and capture keywords associated with different relations. In addition, we introduce a contrastive prototypical network to further distinguish the subtle difference between multiple relations. Experimental results show that CHAN achieved the best performance compared to previous methods, especially the F1 of the multi-relation identification is improved by 17.94% under 1-doc setting in FREDo benchmark.

Keywords: few-shot learning · document-level relation extraction · multi-relation · context-aware mechanism

1 Introduction

The goal of document-level relation extraction(DocRE) is to detect relations between entities spanning multiple sentences within a given document. Specifically, given a set of predefined relation types and two entities mentioned in the document, the goal is to determine the correct relations between them. DocRE is important for improving the ability of natural language processing systems to understand and analyze the content of documents. Most previous DocRE methods rely heavily on supervised learning with large annotated corpora, which leads to poor performance when limited data is available. Motivated by the achievements of few-shot learning methods in the few-shot sentence-level relation extraction [4,6,12], Popovic et al. [11] first proposed the task of few-shot document-level relation extraction(FSDLRE) and proposed the FREDo benchmark for evaluating the few-shot performance of DocRE models.

One of the major challenges in FSDLRE is the identification of multi-relation from a document. The overlap of entity pairs between different relations is a

L. Iliadis et al. (Eds.): ICANN 2023, LNCS 14262, pp. 52–64, 2023.
https://doi.org/10.1007/978-3-031-44201-8_5

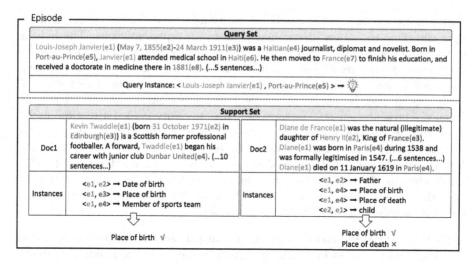

Fig. 1. Illustration of the 1-doc episode in FSDLRE setting. Given a support set consisting of one document with labeled relation examples, the task is then to identify and return all instances of the same relation types for the query document. Colored content represents given entities, entities excluded from the query instance are highlighted in grey. For a query instance "Louis-Joseph Janvier" and "Port-au-Prince", their relation is correctly predicted with Doc1 as a support set but not with Doc2. In Doc2, both "place of birth" and "place of death" relations only exist in the same entity pair "Diane de France" and "Paris". Existing methods only consider the entity pair of an instance, thus treating these two relations as a single relation. This leads to confusion in identifying the relations for the query instance. (Color figure online)

significant obstacle to this task, making those relations indistinguishable. Existing methods for DocRE [18,21] focus on explicitly representing entity pairs for instances while ignoring the relation difference between them. As a result, it becomes difficult to identify multi-relation that share the same entity pair. For instance, as illustrated in Fig. 1, the entity pair "Diane de France" and "Paris" exists in both the "place of birth" and "place of death" relation in Doc2, which leads to confusion when extracting the relations between "Louis-Joseph Janvier" and "Port-au-Prince" in the query set by referring to Doc2. In contrast, the relation can be correctly identified when referring to Doc1 because there are no multiple confusing relations.

In practical applications, it is common for a pair of entities to express multiple relations. For example, our analysis of the FREDo dataset shows that 19.25% of documents contain multi-relational entity pairs. Though important, it is a difficult task to correctly categorize multiple confusing relations expressed by the same entity pairs, which is more pronounced in few-shot scenarios because of the scarcity of relation instances.

To tackle this issue, we propose a new method, Context-aware Hybrid Attention Network (CHAN), for FSDLRE that takes inspiration from meta-learning, as shown in Fig. 2. CHAN combines entity-level and context-level instance representations to obtain discriminative instance representations. The hybrid attention mechanism in CHAN consists of instance-general and instance-specific attention that captures essential contextual information in the context encoder. The instance-general attention learns the general importance distribution of words. As the words related to entities are more likely to be informative in instance representation [21], we have designed an entity-guided attention mechanism that learns the importance of words related to entities. Additionally, to distinguish between multiple relations expressed by the same entity pair, we design a relation-guided attention that captures corresponding keywords for different relations. Additionally, we incorporate a contrastive loss to a prototypical network in the training strategy to boost the ability to identify multi-relation. The key contributions of this work are summarized as:

- We propose CHAN, an effective model that captures useful context for identifying multi-relation in FSDLRE. This is achieved by designing a context-aware hybrid attention mechanism that produces multi-level instance features and more distinctive representations.
- We introduce a contrastive prototypical network that utilizes two contrastive losses to better differentiate between multiple confusing relations with subtle distinctions.
- We evaluate our method on the novel benchmark FREDo and the results demonstrate that CHAN outperforms the baseline, especially in identifying multi-relation. The F1 score for multi-relation identification is improved by 17.94% under 1-doc in FREDo.

2   Related Work

2.1   Few-Shot Relation Extraction

Most existing few-shot relation extraction(FSRE) methods focus on the sentence level. Metric-based methods, which use similarity measures between examples to detect new classes given only a few samples, are thought to be more useful in FSRE [6]. As a strong correlation exists between the context information and relation in a single sentence, many models attempt to enhance critical contextual feature [3,5]. For example, some models incorporate local content words to acquire fine-grained information [15]. Although using explicit context information may achieve remarkable results in few-shot sentence level relation extraction, it may introduce noise in FSDLRE since only a few parts of the context in the document are related to the relation instances.

2.2   Document-Level Relation Extraction

Most existing methods for DocRE focus on representing and combining entities to learn the relations between them, which can be grouped into graph-based methods and sequence-based methods. Graph-based methods construct a document graph to model the interactions between different words, entities and sentences [8,10,20]. With the proposal of Transformer [17], word interactions can be learned directly. Consequently, sentence-based methods represent relations by directly aggregating entity representations obtained from Transformer-based pre-trained language models [7,16,21]. However, those methods treat different instances for each entity pair equally, which is counterintuitive because the same entity pairs can convey multiple relations within a given document.

2.3   Multiple Relations Extraction

In information extraction, extracting multiple relations is useful but challenging. One common strategy is to treat multiple relation extraction as a multi-label classification task, where a binary classifier is used for each relation type [1,18, 19,21]. However, such an approach needs to be provided with adequate training to recognize novel classes, which is difficult to achieve in few-shot scenarios.

3   Approach

3.1   Task Definition

FSDLRE is to predict relations between each entity pair (h, t) mentioned in the query document d (i.e., a document containing some entities) based on an episode. Specifically, an episode consists of a support set $\mathcal{S}$ and query set $\mathcal{Q}$. The support set consists of documents with annotated relations between each entity pair, formalized as $\mathcal{S} = \left\{ \left(d_i, h_i^k, t_i^k, y_i^k \right), i = 1, \ldots, N; k = 1, \ldots, K \right\}$ and the relation set $\mathcal{R} = \bigcup_{i=1}^{N} \bigcup_{k=1}^{K} y_i^k$, where $\left(d_i, h_i^k, t_i^k, y_i^k \right)$ means that there is a relation y_i^k between the entity pair $\left(h_i^k, t_i^k \right)$ in the document d_i. N and K denote the number of documents and relation instances, respectively. In FSDLRE, the relation between entities could be NOTA (None-of-the-above), indicating the given entity pair does not hold any relation defined in $\mathcal{R}$. Moreover, documents in the query set are unlabeled that are used to evaluate the ability of models in identifying new relations.

3.2   Overall Framework

As shown in Fig. 2, the overall framework of our model consists of three parts: 1) entity encoder, aiming to obtain the instance representation based on entities; 2) context encoder, used to capture a fine-grained instance representation related to instances and 3) contrastive prototypical network, further distinguishing the subtle difference between confusing relations.

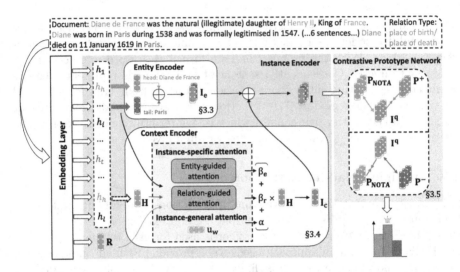

Fig. 2. The overall framework of Context-aware Hybrid Attention Network (CHAN).
§ denotes the section where the module is described.

3.3 Entity Encoder

We employ an entity encoder to generate instance representation based on the entity pair. Before introducing our proposed encoder, we introduce the entity marker symbol "*" before and after the entity mentions according to [13] and apply BERT [2] as the encoder to get corresponding contextualized embedding $\mathbf{H} = \{h_1, \ldots, h_l\} \in \mathbb{R}^{l \times d}$, where $h_i \in \mathbb{R}^d$ is the word embedding and d is the dimension of embedding.

We concatenate corresponding hidden states of head entity marker start h_h and tail entity marker start h_t as the basic representation of instance due to its effectiveness [13]:

$$\mathbf{I_e} = [h_h; h_t] \in \mathbb{R}^{2d} \tag{1}$$

where $[;]$ denotes concatenation operation. To address cases in which an entity appears more than once in a document, we compute the average embedding of all the mentions of this entity.

3.4 Context Encoder

Our context encoder is based on two kinds of context-aware attention. First, we utilize instance-general attention to estimate the general importance distribution of each word in the document. Additionally, we leverage instance-specific attention to learn context importance distribution specific to the corresponding instance.

Instance-General Attention. According to [15], we use a memory network [14] denoted as u_w to select the important words in each document. The instance-general attention α is computed as follows:

$$\alpha = softmax\left(\mathbf{H}u_w\right) \tag{2}$$

Instance-Specific Attention. To capture context importance that varies by instance, we introduce instance-specific attention consisting of two attention mechanisms: entity-guided attention and relation-guided attention.

First, we learn entity-guided attention to capture important words related to the entity pair, which helps reduce noise introduced by the context. This attention is transferred from a pre-trained language model with a well-learned multi-head self-attention matrix $A \in \mathbb{R}^{H \times l \times l}$. We use the entity markers positions of the head and tail entities as indexes and multiply the resulting entity attentions for the head and tail entities. By doing so, we locate words important to both head and tail entities. The entity-guided attention β_e is calculated as follows:

$$\beta_e = \left[\frac{1}{H}\sum_{i=1}^{H}[A]_i\right]_{I_h} \cdot \left[\frac{1}{H}\sum_{i=1}^{H}[A]_i\right]_{I_t} \tag{3}$$

where H represents the number of heads in the pre-trained language model, I_h and I_t represent the entity marker's position.

Second, we introduce a relation-guided attention mechanism to differentiate between various relations expressed by the same entity pair. We start with obtaining the relation type embedding $R \in \mathbb{R}^{l \times d}$ by feeding the relation type of instance into BERT. Then the relation-guided attention β_r is computed as follows:

$$\beta_r = softmax\left(sum\left(\mathbf{H}\left(\mathbf{R}\right)^{\top}\right)\right) \tag{4}$$

where $sum\left(\cdot\right)$ means a sum operation of all elements in the vector.

Since the relation type of the instance in query documents is unknown, it cannot be used to calculate relation-guided attention in the same way as support instances. Similar to the entity-guided attention computing mechanism, we rely on a pre-trained multi-head attention matrix A and obtain the relation-guided attention β_r^q for query instance as follows:

$$\beta_r^q = \left[\frac{1}{H}\sum_{i=1}^{H}[A]_i\right]_{I} \tag{5}$$

$$I = max\left(sum\left(\frac{1}{H}\sum_{i=1}^{H}[A]_i\right)\right) \tag{6}$$

where $max\left(\cdot\right)$ means to get the index of the largest attention keyword as a relation type in support documents.

Finally, the context instance representation is computed as follows:

$$\mathbf{I_c} = \left(\alpha + \beta_e + \beta_r\right)\mathbf{H} \in \mathbb{R}^d \tag{7}$$

3.5   Contrastive Prototypical Network

In this module, the entity and context instance representation are combined to obtain a multi-level instance representation $\mathbf{I}$. Then, the instance representation of K supporting instances is averaged to form a prototype representation $\mathbf{P}$ for each relation, following the approach of [21]:

$$\mathbf{P} = \frac{1}{K} \sum_{k=1}^{K} \mathbf{I^k} \in \mathbb{R}^{3d} \tag{8}$$

$$\mathbf{I^k} = \left[\mathbf{I_e^k}; \mathbf{I_c^k}\right] \tag{9}$$

where K represents the number of instances in an episode for the corresponding relation. Specially, the NOTA prototype is a learnable vector initialized by sampling the representation of 20 NOTA instances, following [11].

Finally, the probability of the relations for the query instance based on the similarity between the query instance representation $\mathbf{I^q}$ and the prototypes of each relation r_i is computed as follows:

$$logit_i = \frac{\exp\left(\mathbf{I^q} \cdot \mathbf{P^i}\right)}{\sum_{n=1}^{N} \exp\left(\mathbf{I^q} \cdot \mathbf{P^n}\right)} \tag{10}$$

where N represents the number of relation types the current episode contained.

Considering a threshold is needed to convert probability to relation labels, we use the max similarity score between query instance and NOTA as a threshold according to [11]. Then We incorporate a contrastive loss function to distinguish among the positive, the NOTA and negative classes and thus the difference between multiple confusing relations according to [21], which consists of two parts as shown below:

$$\mathcal{L}_1 = -\sum_{i \in \mathcal{P}_r} \log\left(\frac{\exp\left(logit_i\right)}{\sum_{i' \in \mathcal{P}_r \cup \{\text{NOTA}\}} \exp\left(logit_{i'}\right)}\right) \tag{11}$$

$$\mathcal{L}_2 = -\log\left(\frac{\exp\left(logit_{\text{NOTA}}\right)}{\sum_{i' \in \mathcal{N}_r \cup \{\text{NOTA}\}} \exp\left(logit_{i'}\right)}\right) \tag{12}$$

where $\mathcal{P}_r$ and $\mathcal{N}_r$ represent the sets of positive and negative relation classes for the current instance, respectively.

Finally, taking Eq. (11) and Eq. (12) into account, the final loss is the sum of the two losses:

$$\mathcal{L} = \mathcal{L}_1 + \mathcal{L}_2 \tag{13}$$

where $\mathcal{L}_1$ aims to increase the probability of all positive classes relative to the NOTA class and $\mathcal{L}_2$ is designed to decrease the probability of all negative classes relative to the NOTA class.

4 Experiments

4.1 Dataset and Settings

We conduct experiments on FREDo [11], a new benchmark for few-shot document-level relation extraction that includes in-domain and cross-domain tasks. The in-domain task contains 96 relations and 4051 documents, which are split into 62 classes for training, 16 for validation, and 16 for testing. The in-domain task is trained and tested on the DocRED [19]. The cross-domain task is trained on the DocRED but tested on the sciERC [9] domain, where the test set contains 7 scientific relations and 500 documents.

We evaluate our model using the 1-doc and 3-doc settings as defined in [11], indicating that each episode contained either 1 or 3 support documents. We utilize macro F1 score as the evaluation metric, i.e., the mean F1 score across the different relation types, as well as precision and recall. We utilize the base-cased version of BERT as basic encoder, which has 768 dimensions. To tackle the limitation of the maximum input length of 512 in BERT, we adopt a long text processing approach, following [21]. This allows us to encode inputs of up to 1024 lengths. We use AdamW as our optimizer, the learning rate of which is set to 1×10^{-5} and a linear warmup strategy for the first 1k steps is applied.

4.2 Baselines

We compare CHAN with various relation extraction methods: **ATLOP** [21], using attention directly from pre-trained language models to identify the related context of the entities for DocRE. **HCRP** [5], utilizing relation description files as clues to capture useful context from sentences for FSRE. **DL-MNAV** [11], aggregating entity representations as instance representations and representing NOTA class as learned vectors based on the prototypical network for FSDLRE. **DL-MNAV**$_{SIE}$, **DL-MNAV**$_{SIE+SBN}$ [11], where SIE means using all support instances instead of prototype for each relation when computing the probability of the relations and SBN means sampling most 5 similar NOTA instance as NOTA for each relation prototype instead of the learned vectors to adapt to the cross-domain task.

4.3 Results

Performance on FSDLRE. Table 1 and Table 2 show the in-domain and cross-domain results respectively. Our method achieves the best performance in the in-domain task, especially in 1-doc setting. Specifically, we improve 1-doc and 3-doc by 12.04% and 2.66% in terms of F1 than DL-MNAV, the next best FSDLRE model, demonstrating the effectiveness of the explicit introduction of the context feature. Compared to the 1-doc setting, each relation has more instances in the 3-doc setting, which weakens the impact of entity pair overlap in different relations. Although ATLOP considers the context related to entities, the instance is still represented based on the fusion of entities, which leads

Table 1. Performance (%) on FREDo in-domain test set. * denote our reproduced results in few-shot setting and ⋆ are reported by [11]. The underline denotes the next best results.

Model	1-Doc			3-Doc		
	Precision	Recall	F1	Precision	Recall	F1
ATLOP* [21]	5.71	20.46	6.33	6.58	21.47	7.08
HCRP* [5]	6.76	16.13	6.41	6.44	15.21	6.22
DL-MNAV⋆ [11]	6.26	21.08	7.05	7.71	22.80	8.42
DL-MNAV$_{SIE}$⋆ [11]	5.57	23.12	7.06	5.16	33.61	6.77
DL-MNAV$_{SIE+SBN}$⋆ [11]	1.02	22.94	1.71	1.75	23.41	2.79
CHAN(ours)	7.09	21.47	**7.91**	8.80	21.58	**8.65**

Table 2. Performance (%) on FREDo cross-domain test set.

Model	1-Doc			3-Doc		
	Precision	Recall	F1	Precision	Recall	F1
ATLOP [21]	1.72	3.77	1.66	2.09	1.62	1.42
HCRP [5]	1.76	3.62	1.71	2.51	2.24	1.50
DL-MNAV [11]	2.30	0.58	0.84	3.02	0.29	0.48
DL-MNAV$_{SIE}$ [11]	1.77	2.08	1.77	2.51	2.52	2.51
DL-MNAV$_{SIE+SBN}$ [11]	2.26	4.37	2.85	3.47	4.24	3.72
Ours	2.12	3.45	1.95	2.15	4.23	2.78
Ours$_{SIE+SBN}$	2.71	3.89	**3.12**	3.88	4.35	**4.04**

to poor performance. HCRP introduces noise while introducing local features because documents contain more irrelevant information than sentences. Our method improves F1 by 19.97% and 18.96% respectively, compared to ATLOP and HCRP in 1-doc setting, demonstrating the significance of our hybrid attention mechanism. In the cross-domain task, although our source model does not outperform DL-MNAV$_{SIE+SBN}$, our model with SIE and SBN achieves the best results, indicating that our approach has good adaptability.

Performance on Multi-relation Identification. To further exhibit the effectiveness of our model for identifying multi-relation, we evaluate our models on the FREDo in-domain test set under two scenarios, as presented in Table 3. We trained our models using a general training setting and evaluated them under two different settings: "Single" and "Multi". The Single setting evaluates the model's ability to classify single relations expressed by entity pair, while the Multi setting evaluates the model's performance in classifying multiple relations expressed by entity pair. As we can see, the performance of our baseline models dropped significantly from the Single setting to the Multi setting, especially around 25.36% in the 1-doc scenario, indicating that identifying multi-relation

Table 3. Macro-F1 (%) and the rate of change of two scenarios on FREDo in-domain test set. "Single" stands for evaluating only relations expressed by different entity pairs and "Multi" stands for evaluating including two or more relations expressed by the same entity pair. The Macro-F1 score excludes those relations that appear either only in the Single setting or only in the Multi setting.

Model	1-Doc	3-Doc
	Single → Multi	Single → Multi
ATLOP [21]	8.54 → 6.57 (↓ 23.07%)	9.38 → 8.18 (↓ 12.79%)
HCRP [5]	8.67 → 6.89 (↓ 20.53%)	8.79 → 7.84 (↓ 10.81%)
DL-MNAV [11]	9.11 → 6.80 (↓ 25.36%)	9.92 → 9.03 (↓ 8.18%)
Ours	**9.17 → 8.02 (↓ 12.54%)**	**9.96 → 9.25 (↓ 7.13%)**

is challenging. In contrast, our proposed CHAN model outperforms previous methods and drops less under the Multi setting, demonstrating its ability to distinguish between multiple confusing relations expressed by the same entity pair.

4.4   Ablation Study

To further validate the effect of the different submodules in our proposed CHAN model, we design an ablation study. As shown in Table 4, removing the context encoder completely, the performance severely decreases by 12.14%, indicating the explicit instance-related context is essential to represent instances. Furthermore, the performance has different degrees of decline without instance-general and instance-specific attention. The latter drops by 8.22%, more than the drop of 5.06% in the former, illustrating that instance-specific attention plays a more important role in capturing useful context. F1 drops by 4.17% and 3.03% when we remove the entity-guided and relation-guided attention respectively, which proves that it is beneficial to attend to context related to entities and relations jointly. In addition, we also observe that F1 drops by 6.19% when we use a binary

Table 4. Ablation study on FREDo in-domain test set showing F1(%).

Model	1-Doc	3-Doc
Ours	**7.91**	**8.65**
w/o context encoder	6.95	8.00
w/o instance-general attention	7.51	8.45
w/o instance-specific attention	7.26	8.08
w/o relation-guided attention	7.58	8.15
w/o entity-guided attention	7.67	8.24
w/o contrastive loss	7.42	8.31

cross entropy loss instead of contrastive loss, demonstrating the effectiveness of the contrastive prototypical network.

4.5 Qualitative Analysis

We visualize the context weight of an example introduced before in DL-MNAV and CHAN to better understand the role of our hybrid attention mechanism, as shown in the upper of Fig. 3. Our model attends to different keywords, such as "born" and "died", to distinguish between the relations "place of birth" and "place of death" respectively, that are expressed by the same entity pair "Diane de France" and "Paris". However, DL-MNAV attends to the same words for multi-relational entity pairs, leading to incorrect predictions. Moreover, we have visualized the relation prototype representation distributions using the t-SNE tool in DL-MNAV and CHAN, as shown in the lower of Fig. 3. Since "place of birth" and "place of death" are expressed by the same entity pair, DL-MNAV regards the two relations as single, resulting in the same predicted probability for the query instance on both relations. In contrast, our model can distinguish between the two relations in the embedding space and thus make the correct classification.

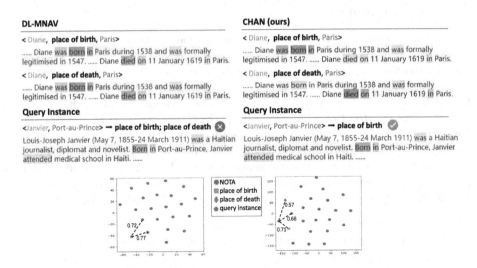

Fig. 3. A qualitative example from our model compared to the baseline DL-MNAV model. The upper visualizes the attention of each word by DL-MNAV and CHAN. A darker color indicates a higher value. The lower shows T-SNE plots of relation prototype embeddings of "NOTA", "place of birth", "place of death" and query instance, where "NOTA" consists of 20 vectors. The numbers shown in the T-SNE plots indicate the similarity between query instance and three relations. Only the max similarity score between query instance and 20 NOTA instances is notated as a threshold, where any relation with a higher similarity than NOTA is considered a positive class, and any relation with a lower similarity score is considered a negative class.

4.6 Limitations

Despite improving the performance of multi-relation identification for few-shot document-level relation extraction, our model still faces two challenges: (1) the lack of information available to identify relations between entities, which causes relations to be often classified as NOTA; (2) the serious imbalance of positive and negative instances. There are only a few instances containing relations in an episode of FREDo, leading to a performance bottleneck.

5 Conclusion

In the paper, we present CHAN model that effectively captures context information by attending to the words related to entities and relations and focus on identifying multi-relation in FSDLRE by capturing useful fine-grained information on the context related to relations. Our experimental results demonstrate that CHAN performs well on two tasks on the FREDo benchmark, especially in identifying multi-relation. In future research, we will focus on creating a generalized multi-label identification backbone network for various NLP few-shot tasks, such as few-shot document-level event argument extraction.

References

1. Chen, J., Yuan, C., Wang, X., Bai, Z.: MrMep: joint extraction of multiple relations and multiple entity pairs based on triplet attention. In: Proceedings of the 23rd Conference on Computational Natural Language Learning, pp. 593–602 (2019)
2. Devlin, J., Chang, M., Lee, K., Toutanova, K.: BERT: pre-training of deep bidirectional transformers for language understanding. In: Proceedings of the 2019 Conference of the North American Chapter of the Association for Computational Linguistics: Human Language Technologies, pp. 4171–4186 (2019)
3. Dou, C., Wu, S., Zhang, X., Feng, Z., Wang, K.: Function-words adaptively enhanced attention networks for few-shot inverse relation classification. In: Proceedings of the Thirty-First International Joint Conference on Artificial Intelligence, pp. 2937–2943 (2022)
4. Gao, T., et al.: Fewrel 2.0: towards more challenging few-shot relation classification. In: Proceedings of the 2019 Conference on Empirical Methods in Natural Language Processing and the 9th International Joint Conference on Natural Language Processing, pp. 6249–6254 (2019)
5. Han, J., Cheng, B., Lu, W.: Exploring task difficulty for few-shot relation extraction. In: Proceedings of the 2021 Conference on Empirical Methods in Natural Language Processing, pp. 2605–2616 (2021)
6. Han, X., et al.: Fewrel: a large-scale supervised few-shot relation classification dataset with state-of-the-art evaluation. In: Proceedings of the 2018 Conference on Empirical Methods in Natural Language Processing, pp. 4803–4809 (2018)
7. Jiang, F., Niu, J., Mo, S., Fan, S.: Key mention pairs guided document-level relation extraction. In: Proceedings of the 29th International Conference on Computational Linguistics, pp. 1904–1914 (2022)

8. Li, B., Ye, W., Sheng, Z., Xie, R., Xi, X., Zhang, S.: Graph enhanced dual attention network for document-level relation extraction. In: Proceedings of the 28th International Conference on Computational Linguistics, pp. 1551–1560 (2020)

9. Luan, Y., He, L., Ostendorf, M., Hajishirzi, H.: Multi-task identification of entities, relations, and coreference for scientific knowledge graph construction. In: Proceedings of the 2018 Conference on Empirical Methods in Natural Language Processing, pp. 3219–3232 (2018)

10. Peng, X., Zhang, C., Xu, K.: Document-level relation extraction via subgraph reasoning. In: Proceedings of the Thirty-First International Joint Conference on Artificial Intelligence, pp. 4331–4337 (2022)

11. Popovic, N., Färber, M.: Few-shot document-level relation extraction. In: Carpuat, M., de Marneffe, M., Ruíz, I.V.M. (eds.) Proceedings of the 2022 Conference of the North American Chapter of the Association for Computational Linguistics: Human Language Technologies, pp. 5733–5746 (2022)

12. Sabo, O., Elazar, Y., Goldberg, Y., Dagan, I.: Revisiting few-shot relation classification: evaluation data and classification schemes. Trans. Assoc. Comput. Linguistics **9**, 691–706 (2021)

13. Soares, L.B., FitzGerald, N., Ling, J., Kwiatkowski, T.: Matching the blanks: Distributional similarity for relation learning. In: Proceedings of the 57th Conference of the Association for Computational Linguistics, pp. 2895–2905 (2019)

14. Sukhbaatar, S., Szlam, A., Weston, J., Fergus, R.: End-to-end memory networks. In: Advances in Neural Information Processing Systems 28: Annual Conference on Neural Information Processing Systems 2015, pp. 2440–2448 (2015)

15. Sun, S., Sun, Q., Zhou, K., Lv, T.: Hierarchical attention prototypical networks for few-shot text classification. In: Proceedings of the 2019 Conference on Empirical Methods in Natural Language Processing and the 9th International Joint Conference on Natural Language Processing, pp. 476–485 (2019)

16. Tang, H., et al.: HIN: hierarchical inference network for document-level relation extraction. In: Lauw, H.W., Wong, R.C.-W., Ntoulas, A., Lim, E.-P., Ng, S.-K., Pan, S.J. (eds.) PAKDD 2020. LNCS (LNAI), vol. 12084, pp. 197–209. Springer, Cham (2020). https://doi.org/10.1007/978-3-030-47426-3_16

17. Vaswani, A., et al.: Attention is all you need. In: Advances in Neural Information Processing Systems 30: Annual Conference on Neural Information Processing Systems 2017, pp. 5998–6008 (2017)

18. Wang, H., et al.: Extracting multiple-relations in one-pass with pre-trained transformers. In: Proceedings of the 57th Conference of the Association for Computational Linguistics, pp. 1371–1377 (2019)

19. Yao, Y., et al.: Docred: a large-scale document-level relation extraction dataset. In: Proceedings of the 57th Conference of the Association for Computational Linguistics, pp. 764–777 (2019)

20. Zhang, Z., et al.: Document-level relation extraction with dual-tier heterogeneous graph. In: Scott, D., Bel, N., Zong, C. (eds.) Proceedings of the 28th International Conference on Computational Linguistics, pp. 1630–1641 (2020)

21. Zhou, W., Huang, K., Ma, T., Huang, J.: Document-level relation extraction with adaptive thresholding and localized context pooling. In: Thirty-Fifth AAAI Conference on Artificial Intelligence, pp. 14612–14620 (2021)

Multi-task Learning for Mongolian Morphological Analysis

Na Liu[1]⑩, Ren Qing-Dao-Er-Ji[1]⑩, Xiangdong Su[2](✉)⑩, Yatu Ji[1]⑩,
Aodengbala[3]⑩, and Guiping Liu[4]⑩

[1] School of Information Engineering, Inner Mongolia University of Technology, 49
Aimin Street Xincheng District, Hohhot 010051, People's Republic of China
[2] College of Computer Science Inner Mongolia University, 235 West University Road
Saihan District, Hohhot 010021, People's Republic of China
cssxd@imu.edu.cn
[3] Inner Mongolia Regional Language Research and Application Center, Huhhot
010010, People's Republic of China
[4] Department of Mathematics and Computer Science Hetao College, Yunzhong Road
Linhe District, Bayannur 015000, People's Republic of China

Abstract. Mongolian morphological analysis (MMA) includes two sub-
tasks: morphological segmentation and morphological tagging. It is a crucial preprocessing step in many Mongolian NLP applications. Recently,
end-to-end neural approaches have achieved excellent results in the
MMA task. However, these approaches handle morphological segmentation and morphological tagging independently, and ignore the relationship between the two subtasks. In this paper, we propose a multi-
task sequence-to-sequence model for the MMA task that learns Mongolian morphological segmentation and tagging jointly. The proposed
neural model introduces a shared morphological feature encoder to learn
character-level and context-level word information. Besides, we design a
flat joint attention decoder and a hierarchical joint attention decoder to
generate Mongolian segmentation and tagging results, respectively. We
employ the dynamic weight scheme to optimize and balance the weights
between the two subtasks in MMA. We compare the proposed model
with the baselines and evaluate the effectiveness of the sub-modules in
the experiment. The result suggests that the proposed MMA model outperformed the state-of-the-art baselines.

Keywords: Mongolian morphological segmentation · Mongolian
morphological tagging · Flat joint attention · Hierarchical joint
attention

1 Introduction

Mongolian is a morphologically rich language with complex word-formation,
derivation and inflection [1]. Mongolian natural language processing (NLP)
still faces many challenges and the most significant one is data sparseness [2].

L. Iliadis et al. (Eds.): ICANN 2023, LNCS 14262, pp. 65–77, 2023.
https://doi.org/10.1007/978-3-031-44201-8_6

In Mongolian NLP tasks, there is a tendency to process Mongolian text with morphemes rather than words, such as machine translation [3], speech synthesis [4] and named entity recognition [5]. Mongolian morphological tags are progressively used as abstract representations of words in several NLP tasks, such as Mongolian constituent parsing [6] and fixed phrase recognition [7]. Therefore, MMA is an essential preprocessing step in Mongolian NLP tasks.

# Sentence_id = 4003							
# text = ᠲᠤᠷᠰᠢᠯᠲᠠ ᠢᠨ ᠲᠤᠷᠰᠢ ᠬᠡ ᠰᠤᠳᠤᠯ ᠬᠡᠷᠡᠭᠲᠡᠢ᠃ ··							
1	ᠲᠤᠷᠰᠢᠯᠲᠠ ᠢᠨ ᠲᠤᠷᠰᠢᠯᠲᠠ+ᠢ+ ᠢᠨ	_	_	Ne2;Zx;Fc12	_	_
2	ᠲᠤᠷᠰᠢ ᠬᠡ ᠲᠤᠷᠰᠢ+ ᠬᠡ	_	_	Ne2;Fc31	_	_
3	ᠰᠤᠳᠤᠯ ᠰᠤᠳᠤᠯ	_	_	Ve1	_	_
4	ᠬᠡᠷᠡᠭᠲᠡᠢ᠃ ᠬᠡᠷᠡᠭ+ᠲᠡᠢ+ᠤ+ᠢ᠃	_	_	Ve2;Fe11;Zv1;Fs21	_	_
5	·· ··	_	_	Wp1	_	_

The meaning of the morphological labels:

Ne2	uncountable noun	**Zx**	dynamic suffix
Fc12	case category, genitive case 2	**Fc31**	case category, accusative case 1
Ve1	transitive verb	**Ve2**	intransitive verb
Fe11	voice category, causative voice 1	**Zv1**	connecting letter, connecting voice
Fs21	declarative, future tense 1	**Wp1**	punctuation

Fig. 1. Example sentence, annotated with morphological segmentation and morphological labels. The meaning of the sentence is "The service industry needs to be developed rapidly."

MMA includes morphological segmentation and tagging. Morphological segmentation divides the words in a sentence into the root and suffixes to form a morpheme sequence. Morphological tagging assigns root and suffixes to a series of morphological labels. Generally, Mongolian suffixes contain abstract information such as mood, case, tense and aspect [1,8], which are regarded as the surface realization of those underlying abstract information. Morphological labels are annotations of this abstract information in the form of specified character labels [9]. For most Mongolian words, each of them corresponds to only one segmentation result and tagging result. For example, the target the word "ᠬᠡᠷᠡᠭᠲᠡᠢ᠃", which means "need to be developed" is annotated with morphological segmentation "ᠬᠡᠷᠡᠭ+ᠲᠡᠢ+ᠤ+ᠢ᠃" and morphological tag set of {Ve2;Fe11;Zv1;Fs21}, in the example sentence (shown in the Fig. 1). Assuming that the MMA system provides us with the morphological segmentation "ᠬᠡᠷᠡᠭ+ᠲᠡ " and the morphological tag set {Ve2;Fc11} of the new word "ᠬᠡᠷᠡᠭᠲᠡ ", we can easily infer that the meaning of "ᠬᠡᠷᠡᠭᠲᠡ " is "make something develop". Therefore, MMA is very beneficial for Mongolian natural language processing, which is used to deal with rich morphology and data sparseness. However, some Mongolian words correspond to different MMA results according to the context where they appear. For example, while the word "ᠣᠴᠢ (means: went to)" is segmented to "ᠣᠴ+ᠢ " and tagged with {Ve1;Fn2} (meaning of the morphological labels:transitive verb;

suffix, separate adverb) in sentence "ᠠᠷᠠᠢ ᠲᠠᠷᠢ ᠣᠢᠨᠠᠢ ᠷᠠᠬᠤ᠊ " " (means:He went to work.), it is segmented to "ᠠᠢᠨᠠᠢ " (means:and) and tagged with {Cj} (meaning of the morphological label:conjunction) in sentence "ᠠᠷᠠᠢ ᠲᠣᠢ ᠣᠢᠨᠠᠢ ᠠᠷᠠᠷᠠᠢ ᠷᠣ ᠷᠠᠬᠤ᠊ " " (means:He took the book and pencil.). This further makes the MMA more difficult. In summary, the MMA remains an open challenge [10].

Obviously, MMA tasks are quite nuanced, and there is a clear relationship between segmentation and tagging, both of which are dependent on the words themselves and their contexts. In order to deal with these complex and delicate relationships, we propose a multi-task learning model in this paper. We focus on two key challenges of multi-task learning for MMA: (1) How to design a good share network that can extract morphological information well? (2) How can we optimize and balance the weights of the two subtasks in MMA to achieve better performance? We introduce a shared encoder to learn character-level and context-level morphological features. For the second challenge, we design a flat joint attention decoder and a hierarchical joint attention decoder to generate Mongolian segmentation and tagging results, respectively, and introduce the dynamic weight scheme to make the performance of MMA better. The results show that the proposed approach significantly outperforms the baselines. Our contributions are summarized as follows:

(1) We propose a multi-task sequence to sequence neural networks to learn Mongolian morphological segmentation and tagging jointly.
(2) We designed two types of decoders to generate Mongolian segmentation and tagging results, including flat joint attention decoder and hierarchical joint attention decoder.
(3) We introduce a dynamic weight scheme to optimize and balance the weights of the two subtasks in MMA, and prove that our approach is better than other methods.

2 Approach

2.1 Architecture Design

As mentioned, we proposed a multi-task learning architecture to perform Mongolian word segmentation and tagging, as shown in Fig. 2. The proposed architecture uses a sequence-to-sequence backbone network, which includes (1) shared feature encoder, (2) segmentation decoder and (3) tagging decoder. The shared features encoder takes input data and extracts the morphological features. The segmentation decoder and the tagging decoder learn the task-specific features by applying a dynamic weighting scheme and multiple attention mechanisms jointly. The details of each module are shown in the Fig. 3.

2.2 Shared Features Encoder

The lower-left of Fig. 3 is the shared morphological feature encoder, which shows an overview of morphological feature embedding. There are two types of morphological embedding: character-level embedding and context-level embedding.

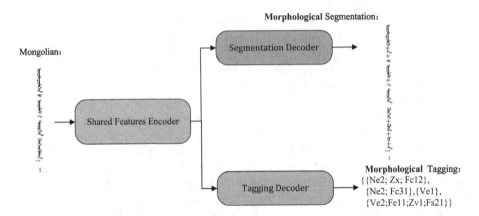

Fig. 2. Overview of our proposal architecture.

Character-level Embedding. We treat the word as a character sequence and pass them into BiLSTM. In order to characterize Mongolian words better, in the implementation, we use the attention mechanism in the character-level word embedding layer. A character representation lookup table is initialized at random, it contains a vector for every character. After that, an BiLSTM is used to learn the character-level embedding. Let w_i represents the ith word in the sentence, l_t represents the tth character in w_i. The BiLSTM processes characters in both directions and concatenate the hidden states. We obtain the character hidden states $\overleftrightarrow{h_t} = [\overrightarrow{h_T}; \overleftarrow{h_1}]$ from BiLSTM, where $\overrightarrow{h_T}$ comes from the forward LSTM, $\overrightarrow{h_T} = LSTM_{\text{forward}}\left(\overrightarrow{h_{T-1}}, l_T\right)$, $\overleftarrow{h_1}$ comes from backward LSTM $\overleftarrow{h_1} = LSTM_{\text{backward}}\left(\overleftarrow{h_2}, l_1\right)$, and T represents the length of the word w_i.

Character-level Attention. The character hidden state $\overleftrightarrow{h_t}$ is fed into an attention layer to generate the character-level word embedding $e_i{}^l$. The $e_i{}^l$ is calculated as, $e_i^l = \sum_{t=1}^{m} a_t^l \overleftrightarrow{h_t}$, where a_t^l are the attention weights. Note that we use global attention [17] in this paper.

Context-level Embedding. We adopt another BiLSTM as the context-level encoder to generate the context-level word embedding. One motivation of our contextualized representation approach is maintaining the MMA model simplicity in the low resource settings. Thus we employ the character-level word embedding as the input, avoiding relying on external resources. Like the character-level embedding, we leverage another BiLSTM to generate context vector $e_i^c = \left[\overrightarrow{h_i}; \overleftarrow{h_i}\right]$.

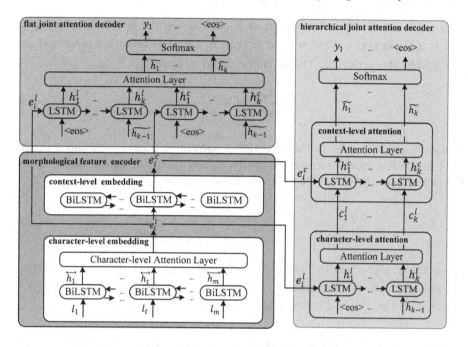

Fig. 3. The detail of our proposal architecture.

2.3 Mongolian Morphological Decoders

In this work, we propose two separate decoders for Mongolian morphological segmentation and morphological tagging. The decoding framework of the two subtasks are the same, and they are both fed with the same character-level word embedding e_i^l and context-level word embedding e_i^c. The difference is that their parameters are not shared. Take the Mongolian morphological tagging, for example. The decoder formalized formula as follows:

$$\widetilde{h}_t = tag\_decoder(h_t, h_t^l, h_t^c) \tag{1}$$

$$p(tag_{i,t} \mid \widetilde{h}_t) = softmax(\widetilde{h}_t) \tag{2}$$

where $\widetilde{h}_t$ is the final hidden states of the $tag\_decoder$, which is computed through LSTM networks and the joint attention mechanism. We design two different joint attention mechanisms: flat joint attention and hierarchical joint attention. Therefore, there are two types of decoders, flat joint attention decoder and hierarchical joint attention decoder.

Flat Joint Attention Decoder. The upper-left of Fig. 3 is the flat joint attention decoder. The flat joint attention mechanism allows the decoder to simultaneously focus on character-level and context-level features. In the flat joint attention decoder, the attention weights control the individual contribution of each hidden state, h^l_j and h^c_j. Both of h^l_j and h^c_j are the final hidden states of two LSTM networks. Than we put h^l_j and h^c_j into the attention layer and get the final hidden states $\tilde{h}_t$. The $\tilde{h}_t$ is calculated as formula:

$$\tilde{h}_t = \sum_{j=1}^{t} a^l_j h^l_j + \sum_{j=1}^{t} a^c_j h^c_j \tag{3}$$

where a^l_j and a^c_j represent the attention weight of character-level and context-level in the flat joint attention, respectively, and their calculation methods are the same. Take the character-level attention weight a^l_j as an example:

$$a^l_j = \frac{exp(u^{l\,T}_j u^l)}{\sum_{j=1}^{t} exp(u^{l\,T}_j u^l_j) + \sum_{j=1}^{t} exp(u^{c\,T}_j u^c_j)} \tag{4}$$

where the u^l_j and u^c_j are the new hidden states depending on h^l_j and h^c_j, and their calculation methods are the same. Take u^l_j as an example, $u^l_j = tanh(w^l h^l_j + b^l)$, where w^l is the weight matrix and b^l is the bias.

Hierarchical Joint Attention Decoder. The right part of Fig. 3 is the hierarchical joint attention decoder. The hierarchical joint attention mechanism considers the hierarchical structure of words (characters and context). It includes two attention modules: character-level attention focusing on the critical characters in each word and context-level attention identifying the important contextual words in the sentence. The structure of character-level and context-level attention modules are similar. The final hidden state $\tilde{h}_t$ of hierarchical joint attention decoder is calculated as:

$$\tilde{h}_t = \sum_{j=1}^{t} a^c_j h^c_j \tag{5}$$

where a^c_j is the context-level attention weight, and h^c_j is the output of LSTM decoding network in the context-level attention module, which calculated as formula:

$$h^c_j = LSTM(h^c_{j-1}, c^l_j) \tag{6}$$

and c^l_j is the output of the character-level attention module, $c^l_j = \sum_{k=1}^{j} a^l_k h^l_k$, where h^l_k is the input of the character-level attention module. The a^l_k is the character-level attention weight, and its calculation process is same as the context-level attention weight a^c_j. Take character-level attention weight a^l_k as example in detail:

$$a^l_k = \frac{exp(u^{l\,T}_k u^l_k)}{\sum_{k=1}^{j} exp(u^{l\,T}_k u^l_k)} \tag{7}$$

where the u^l_j is the new hidden state depending on h^l_j, $u^l_k = tanh(w^l h^l_k + b^l)$, and w^l is the weight matrix and b^l is the bias.

2.4   Learning Objective

When related tasks are processed jointly in multi-task learning, they share inductive bias. In the general multi-task learning with T tasks, the whole network is
trained by back propagating the sum of losses. The learning objective is defined
as:

$$\min \sum_{t=1}^{T} \lambda_t \mathcal{L}_t(\theta) \quad s.t. \quad \begin{matrix} \sum_{t=1}^{T} \lambda_t = 1 \\ \lambda_t \in \{0,1\} \end{matrix} \tag{8}$$

where the learning objective is a linear combination of the empirical loss $\mathcal{L}_t(\theta)$
for multiple tasks,λ is the weight coefficient for each subtask and θ represents
the parameters of a neural network instance. In general, every subtask task t
has a statically equal weight, $t = 1/T$. However, this solution is valid only when
the tasks do not compete, which rarely occurs. We will consider two sub-tasks,
segmentation and tagging, as an example, where there are two solutions θ_a and θ_b
such that $\mathcal{L}_{seg}(\theta_a) < \mathcal{L}_{seg}(\theta_b)$ and $\mathcal{L}_{tag}(\theta_a) > \mathcal{L}_{tag}(\theta_b)$. In other words, solution
θ_a is better for task segmentation where as θ_b is better for tagging. Without
pairwise importance of tasks, which is typically not available, it is impossible to
compare these two solutions. Although the weight summation formulation (8) is
simple and straightforward, searching for a proper weight vector is very difficult
and expensive [16]. A variety of optimization algorithms have been proposed to
balance subtasks in Multi-task learning, including gradient normalization [12],
dynamic weight averaging [13], and uncertainty weighting [14]. In our dynamic
weighting scheme, we create weights for each subtask using a "softmax" output
layer, just as neural networks generate class probabilities with a "softmax". In
the ith iteration, the weight coefficient $\lambda_{tag}(i)$ of subtask tagging is:

$$\lambda_{tag}(i) = \frac{exp(w_{tag}(i-1)/\alpha)}{exp(w_{tag}(i-1)/\alpha) + exp(w_{seg}(i-1)/\alpha)} \tag{9}$$

$$w_{tag}(i-1) = \frac{\mathcal{L}_{tag}(\theta_{i-1})}{\mathcal{L}_{tag}(\theta_{i-2})} \tag{10}$$

$$w_{seg}(i-1) = \frac{\mathcal{L}_{seg}(\theta_{i-1})}{\mathcal{L}_{seg}(\theta_{i-2})} \tag{11}$$

where $w_t(i-1) \in (0, +\infty)$ calculates the relative descending rate, and α represents a constant that controls the softness of task weighting. The weight coefficient $\lambda_t(i)$ of each subtask will equal as $1/T$ that α is large enough. In the
experiment, we set α to 2 and use cross entropy loss as the loss function. The
loss value of subtask t, $\mathcal{L}_t(\theta_{i-1})$, is calculated as the average loss in each epoch
over multiple iterations. This reduces the uncertainty of random training data
selection and stochastic gradient descent.

3   Experiments

3.1   Dataset and Experiment Setting

Nowadays, there is no open source Mongolian corpus with morphological information. We annotated a Mongolian morphological dataset by a group of Mongolian native speakers for this target. The dataset includes 5,000 Mongolian sentences, whose length varies from 2 to 37. The average length is 17.76. There are 88,793 words and 9,419 different words in total. We split it into training dataset (4,000 sentences, 80%), development dataset (500 sentences, 10%) and test (500 sentences, 10%).

We use 10-fold validation to determine the optimal parameters and an early stop mechanism in model training which stops the training after 10 consecutive epochs (patience) without improvement on the developing dataset. Note: The Mongolian morphological segmentation decoder uses the Limited Search Strategy (LSS) [10] for decoding.

3.2   Baselines

We select three single-task models based on BiLSTM neural network as baselines:

- **BiLa, Single-Task with Attention**: BiLa [11] model is an BiLSTM-based approach for morphological segmentation. In addition to adding the attention mechanism, this model is similar BiLSTM model. We reimplemented the model for Mongolian morphological segmentation and tagging and keep its default parameters unchanged.
- **BiLSTM-CRF*, Single-Task**: the BiLSTM-CRF [18] model is a sequence labeling model that implements MMA in two steps. Firstly, the morphological segmentation task is completed, and then converts morphemes into morphological tagging sequence. Due to the differences in experimental hardware and software environments and data resources, we reimplemented the model with the experimental data and evaluation metrics in this paper.
- **SAN+BiLSTM-DAD, Single-Task**: SAN+BiLSTM-DAD model was proposed by Na et al. [19], an effective method for Mongolian morphological segmentation. This model is based on the self-attention mechanism and uses the double attention decoder to fuse character-level and context-level information. We use the same hyperparameters as that in [19].

4   Results and Discussion

4.1   Comparison with Baselines

Table 1 shows the evaluation results of all baselines and our model. As one can observe that our proposed model achieves the best performance on both morphological segmentation and tagging. On the test dataset, we achieve 97.42% precision, 97.56% recall, and 97.49% $F1$ for segmentation and 96.16% precision, 95.67% recall, and 95.91% $F1$ for tagging. We discuss the effectiveness of our model as follows:

Table 1. Comparative results with our model and baseline approaches.

model	Segmentation			Tagging		
	P(%)	R(%)	$F1(\%)$	P(%)	R(%)	$F1(\%)$
BiLa	89.04	88.23	88.63	–	–	–
BiLSTM-CRF*	90.49	90.67	90.58	88.68	87.02	87.85
SAN+BiLSTM-DAD [19]	93.11	93.39	93.24	–	–	–
Ours	**97.42**	**97.56**	**97.49**	**96.16**	**95.67**	**95.91**

- Among those baseline models, the advantage of SAN+BiLSTM-DAD [19] model which incorporates contextual features is more significant than other methods. This can be attributed to the contextualized embedding of Mongolian words. Once Mongolian words are correctly contextualized, the subtle ambiguities between words can be distinguished and predicted correctly.
- Our proposed multi-task model outperforms all the other single-task methods with significant margins. These results indicate that the Mongolian morphological segmentation task and Mongolian morphological tagging task can promote each other, learn together, and achieve performance improvements under the framework of multi-task learning.

4.2 The Effect of the Different Decoders

To observe the applicability of the two decoders, we experiment on different combinations of the two decoders and report the results in Table 2. The conclusions are as follows:

Table 2. Comparisons of decoders.

Decoder		Segmentation			Tagging		
Segmentation	Tagging	P(%)	R(%)	$F1(\%)$	P(%)	R(%)	$F1(\%)$
FJAD	FJAD	96.47	95.63	96.05	94.92	93.89	94.40
FJAD	HJAD	**97.42**	**97.56**	**97.49**	**96.16**	**95.67**	**95.91**
HJAD	FJAD	95.05	94.16	94.60	93.72	92.11	92.91
HJAD	HJAD	96.03	94.61	95.31	95.68	93.47	94.56

As shown in Table 2, our model achieves the best performance by employing FJAD for segmentation and HJAD for tagging. Our model reaches 97.49 and 95.91% $F1$ in segmentation and tagging. We find that these two subtasks are interdependent, showing almost similar performance trends when subtasks are in different combinations. That is once again proved the necessity and the importance of using multi-task learning in MMA. Furthermore, we can see that FJAD has a clear and even significant advantage over HJAD for segmentation.

Decoding character-level and context-level features on the same layer, balancing two information levels to find the morpheme boundaries better. HJAD for the tagging is as remarkable as FJAD for the segmentation. This may benefit from the fact that the context features most relevant to tagging are at the top layer of the HJAD.

4.3   The Effect of Different-level Features

We conducted extensive analyses to understand better the efficacy of different-level features. Both character-level only and context-level only models are with the same decoder. The "only" means that we input one kind of character-level or context-level embedding at the decoding step.

Table 3. Comparisons of different-level features.

model	Segmentation			Tagging		
	P(%)	R(%)	$F1$(%)	P(%)	R(%)	$F1$(%)
character-level only	93.21	92.86	93.03	91.34	88.79	90.05
context-level only	94.62	92.17	93.38	93.64	91.31	92.46
Our	**97.42**	**97.56**	**97.49**	**96.16**	**95.67**	**95.91**

As shown in Table 3, the results demonstrate the importance of modeling contextual features for MMA task again. Compared with the character-level model, the context-level model improved the $F1$ of segmentation from 93.03 to 93.38% and tagging from 90.05 to 92.46%. Furthermore, the improvements are remarkable: FJAD and HJAD to fuse the character-level and context-level features lead to superior performance.

4.4   Effect of the Dynamic Weighting Scheme

Table 4. Comparative results of three weighting methods.

Weigthting Scheme	Segmentation			Tagging		
	P(%)	R(%)	$F1$(%)	P(%)	R(%)	$F1$(%)
equal weighting	97.06	96.70	96.83	95.15	95.11	95.13
weight uncertainty [14]	97.44	97.28	97.36	95.62	95.31	95.46
dynamic weighting scheme(**Our**)	**97.42**	**97.56**	**97.49**	**96.16**	**95.67**	**95.91**

We conduct experiments with three weighting methods to verify the effect of the objective function on the model: equal weighting, weight uncertainty [14] and

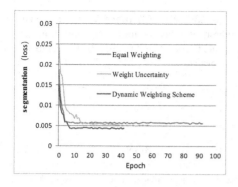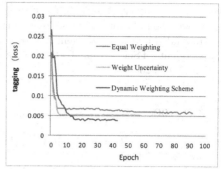

Fig. 4. The *Loss* for two tasks on the developing dataset with different weighting schemes.

the dynamic weighting scheme (2.4). Table 4 displays the experimental results. We find that our dynamic weighting scheme maintains a good advantage in performance. Compared with equal weighting and weight uncertainty [14] weighting methods, our dynamic weighting scheme improved the $F1$ of segmentation from 97.36% to 97.49% and tagging from 95.46 to 95.91%. In experiments, we find that our dynamic weighting scheme is more effective in convergence property, and is more robust and converges rapidly. In the setting of our early stopping mechanism (mentioned in Sect. 3.1), we conduct 10 experiments for each weighting scheme, and the average number of iterations for he equal weighting, weight uncertainty [14] and the dynamic weighting scheme was 96.7, 64.2, and 45.6, respectively. We selected the best model from each scheme and drew the validation loss curves for the two tasks on the developing set, as shown in Fig. 4. We can clearly see that our model follows a similar loss trend in different weighting schemes, and the dynamic weighting scheme is more advantageous.

5 Conclusions

This paper proposes a multi-task neural network for Mongolian morphological analysis. The proposed model consists of a shared morphological features encoder and two separate decoders for Mongolian morphological segmentation and morphological tagging. Specifically, we use an unsupervised approach to adaptively embed character-level and context-level representations. We input these two-level word representations into two different types of decoders, flat joint attention decoder and layered joint attention decoder. Then, the network is trained by the dynamic weighting scheme and attention mechanism jointly. Our experiment results show that the proposed model outperforms is competitive with baselines, and also show efficiency to the dynamic weighting scheme.

Acknowledgments. This work was funded by research program of science and technology at Universities of Inner Mongolia Autonomous Region (Grant No. NJZZ22251),

2022 Inner Mongolia Talent Support Project(DC2300001440), Inner Mongolia Natural Science Foundation (2022MS06013), Universities directly under the autonomous region Funded by the Fundamental Research Fund Project (JY20220122), Program for Young Talents of Science and Technology in Universities of Inner Mongolia Autonomous Region (NJYT23059).

References

1. Kullmann, R., Tserenpil, D.: Mongolian Gramma. ADMON Co., Ltd, Mongolia, pp. 33–72 (2008)
2. Na, L.: Mongolian Morphological Analysis and Application Research. Inner Mongolia University, Hohhot (2022)
3. Yatu, J., Lei, S., Yila, S., et al.: A strategy for referential problem in low-resource neural machine translation. In: International Conference of Artificial Neural Networks and Machine Learning (2021)
4. Rui, L., Sisman., Haizhou, L.: GraphSpeech: syntax-aware graph attention network for neural speech synthesis. In: Proceedings of the IEEE International Conference on Acoustics, Speech and Signal Processing, pp. 6059–6063 (2021)
5. Wang, W., Bao, F., Gao, G.: Learning morpheme representation for mongolian named entity recognition. Neural Process. Lett. **50**(2), 2647–2664 (2019)
6. Liu, N., Su, X., Gao, G., Bao, F., Lu, M.: Morphological knowledge guided Mongolian constituent parsing. In: Gedeon, T., Wong, K.W., Lee, M. (eds.) ICONIP 2019. LNCS, vol. 11955, pp. 363–375. Springer, Cham (2019). https://doi.org/10.1007/978-3-030-36718-3_31
7. Loglo, S.: Design and implementation of Mongolian fixed phrase recognition algorithm. J. Chin. Inf. Process. **31**, 85–91 (2017)
8. Sorokin, A.: Convolutional neural networks for low-resource morpheme segmentation: baseline or state-of-the-art?. In: Proceedings of the 2019 Conference of the North American Chapter of the Association for Computational Linguistics, pp. 154–159 (2019)
9. Ertai, Q.: Mongolian Gramma (2010)
10. Na, L., Xiangdong, S., Guanglai, G., et al.: Mongolian word segmentation based on three character level seq2seq models. In: 25th International Conference. Proceedings of the 25th International Conference, pp. 558–569 (2018)
11. Shunle, Z.: A neural attention based model for morphological segmentation. Wireless Pers. Commun. **102**(4), 2527–2534 (2011)
12. Chen, Z., Badrinarayanan., V., et al.: GradNorm: gradient normalization for adaptive loss balancing in deep multitask networks (2017)
13. Shikun, L., Johns, E., Davison, A.: Research on slavic Mongolian word segmentation based on dictionary and rule. J. Chin. Inf. Process. (2019). https://doi.org/10.1109/CVPR.2019.00197
14. Kendall, A., Gal, Y., Cipolla, R. Multi-task learning using uncertainty to weigh losses for scene geometry and semantics. In: Proceedings of the 2018 IEEE/CVF Conference on Computer Vision and Pattern Recognition (CVPR), pp. 7482–7491 (2018)
15. Mekala., Dheeraj., Jingbo, S.: Contextualized weak supervision for text classification. In: Proceedings of the 58th Annual Meeting of the Association for Computational Linguistics, pp. 323–333 (2020)
16. Lin, X., Huiling, Z., Zhehua, Z., et al.: Pareto multi-task learning (2020)

17. Luong, M.T., Pham, H., Manning, C.D.: Effective approaches to attention-based neural machine translation. In: Proceedings of the Conference on Empirical Methods in Natural Language Processing (2015)
18. Shengai, C.: Research on Mongolian Morphological Analysis Using Deep Neural Network. Beijing Jiaotong University, Beijing (2019)
19. Na, L., Xiangdong, S., Haoran, Z., et al.: Incorporating inner-word and out-word features for Mongolian morphological segmentation. In: Proceedings of the 28th International Conference on Computational Linguistics, pp. 4638–4648 (2020)

Multi-task Pre-training for Lhasa-Tibetan Speech Recognition

Yigang Liu[1,2], Yue Zhao[1,2(✉)], Xiaona Xu[1,2], Liang Xu[1,2], and Xubei Zhang[3]

[1] School of Information Engineering, Minzu University of China, Beijing, China
zhaoyueso@muc.edu.cn
[2] Key Laboratory of Ethnic Language Intelligent Analysis and Security Governance
of MOE, Minzu University of China, Beijing, China
[3] Boston University, Boston, USA

Abstract. Compared to mainstream languages such as Chinese and English, Tibetan speech corpus is limited. Pre-training technology can improve the speech recognition performance for low-resource language by using multiple languages corpus, which involves initially training a neural network on the multi-language dataset, followed by fine-tuning the trained model on low-resource language. In this paper, a multi-task serial pre-training method is proposed to address the limited resources in Tibetan speech recognition. By designing the number and order of tasks in the pre-training process, better recognition performance can be achieved. The experiments on the Lhasa-Tibetan speech recognition task show that our proposed method is significantly superior to the baseline model, achieving a Tibetan word error rate of 4.12%, which is a 9.34% reduction compared to the baseline model and 1.06% lower compared to the existing pre-training model.

Keywords: Lhasa-Tibetan speech recognition · Multi-task · Serial Pre-training

1 Introduction

The development of deep learning has resulted in neural network models with an immense number of parameters. This conveys that the model's training necessitates an extensive corpus of data. Nonetheless, when it comes to minority languages like Tibetan, constructing a sizable labeled corpus proves to be an expensive and time-intensive endeavor. It often requires numerous professionals to dedicate significant time to its completion. In light of this challenge, the pre-training technique offers a solution. By initially training the model on high-resource data and subsequently fine-tuning it for the target task, this method can yield optimal results. Pre-training serves as a means to compensate for the aforementioned limitation, enabling the model to leverage available resources and achieve superior performance.

This research was funded by National Natural Science Foundation of China, grant number 61976236.

L. Iliadis et al. (Eds.): ICANN 2023, LNCS 14262, pp. 78–90, 2023.
https://doi.org/10.1007/978-3-031-44201-8_7

Hendrycks et al. [1] conducted extensive training of the model using the 1000-class ImageNet dataset, followed by fine-tuning it on two different datasets, namely CIFAR-10 and CIFAR-100. The experimental result showed that pre-training enhances the model's robustness. Fan et al. [2] applied the pre-trained model in the domain of sequence-to-sequence speech recognition by separately pre-training the encoder and decoder with non-paired Chinese corpus. Subsequently, through fine-tuning on diverse language datasets, they observed a significant reduction in error rates when compared to models lacking pre-training. Moreover, the versatility and adaptability of pre-trained models across disparate tasks were exemplified by Lech et al. [3]. They leveraged a pre-trained image classification network to achieve real-time speech-emotion recognition. The results of their study showed the potential applicability of pre-trained models beyond their original domain, paving the way for novel interdisciplinary research. Bansal et al. [4] and Zhang et al. [5] used the pre-trained model trained on high-resource language speech recognition tasks for speech-to-text translation in low-resource languages. Their work shows that the pre-training process can address the problem of insufficient data in the target task.

Pan Lixin [6] harnessed the potential of pre-training models in tackling the Lhasa-Tibetan speech recognition, where Chinese, Nepali, Sinhalese, and Bengali were used as the source languages. The transformer model was pre-trained using each source language. The four different pre-trained models were fine-tuned on the Lhasa-Tibetan corpus. The lowest recognition error rate of the models was 33.64%. To further enhance the accuracy of Lhasa-Tibetan speech recognition, this paper introduces a novel method: the multi-task serial pre-training method. This method capitalizes on the power of continuous acquisition of knowledge during the pre-training process by incorporating different speech recognition tasks into the model's training process. Finally, the pre-trained model is fine-tuned on a small amount of Lhasa-Tibetan speech data.

The structure of this paper is as follows: Sect. 2 introduces related work, including an overview of pre-training techniques and the current research works of Lhasa-Tibetan speech recognition. Section 3 presents our pre-training method and the baseline model. Section 4 discusses the experimental data, setting, and results. Section 5 offers a discussion and summary of this work.

2   Related Work

Traditional speech recognition methods, which heavily rely on large amounts of prior knowledge and labeled data, have proven to be less suitable for Lhasa-Tibetan speech recognition tasks due to the inherent scarcity of resources in this domain. In recent years, the emergence of end-to-end models has heralded a new era in speech recognition. These models present a more fitting solution for Lhasa-Tibetan speech recognition, as they obviate the need for arduous training processes, while also alleviating the demand for extensive prior language knowledge. However, a direct application of end-to-end model to Tibetan speech recognition is suboptimal.

In 2017, Wang Qingnan et al. [7] conducted research to enhance the performance of the Connectionist Temporal Classification (CTC) network in Tibetan speech recognition. Through pre-training of the CTC network using Chinese speech data, they successfully integrated the trained end-to-end model into Tibetan speech recognition. The experimental results showed the effectiveness of pre-training in improving the recognition performance of the model. In 2018, Yan et al. [8] harnessed the power of pre-trained models to further augment Lhasa-Tibetan speech recognition. Their method was to train a Time Delay Neural Network (TDNN) on a Chinese corpus and then fine-tuned the TDNN with Lhasa-Tibetan corpus. The experimental results showed a significant reduction in error rates. The error rate decreased from 40.85% to 34.29%. In the year 2022, Qin et al. [9] proposed an innovative combination of Tibetan characters and Tibetan radicals as modeling units. The model was trained on Chinese corpus. They used the trained model for Tibetan speech recognition, the error rate was 29.61%. Wang Zhijie et al. [10] presented an effective method of Tibetan end-to-end speech recognition via cross-language transfer learning from three aspects: modeling unit selection, transfer learning method, and source language selection. Experimental results show that the Chinese-Tibetan multi-language learning method using multi-language character set as the modeling unit yields the best performance on the error rate (CER) at 27.3%.

The aforementioned pre-training methods in Tibetan speech recognition models rely on a single task for the initial learning phase of the model, which results in the "knowledge" acquired by the model through this method being too limited to provide general information to the target task. By enabling the model to engage in a continuous learning process that involves new tasks, it emphasizes the significance of continuous knowledge acquisition from some different tasks, so that it becomes capable of expanding its knowledge base and capturing more general information. This makes the model adapt more effectively to the target task, even when only a limited amount of data is available. Within the ERNIE 2.0 [11]framework, a serial incremental pre-training method is introduced. This method is a progressive training process, whereby the model is initially trained on task 1 and its knowledge is then saved. Subsequently, the model is reloaded and further trained on both task 1 and task 2, repeating this process until seven tasks have been included into the model's training. This incremental method ensures that the model continually expands its knowledge base, capturing more general information from each.

To further improve the accuracy of Tibetan speech recognition, we draw inspiration from the ERNIE 2.0 language model and propose a novel method: multi-task serial pre-training. The method is to first train serially the model with speech recognition tasks in different high-resource languages and then fine-tune it on the target task. Our target task is Lhasa-Tibetan speech recognition. Consequently, within the model pre-training phase, we serially train the tasks of "Chinese speech-to-Chinese character recognition," "Chinese speech-to-pinyin recognition," and "English speech-to-word recognition." The pre-trained model is fine-tuned with a small account of Lhasa-Tibetan speech data. The serial pre-training method contributes to enable the model to continuously acquire general knowledge from different speech recognition tasks. This knowledge acquisition enables the model to achieve a more robust adaptation to downstream tasks. Through this serial pre-training framework, we aim to improve the accuracy of Lhasa-Tibetan speech recognition models by leveraging the general knowledge derived from different speech recognition tasks.

3   Method

3.1   Multi-task Serial Pre-training Method

Pre-training involves the initial training of a model on a large-scale dataset, followed by fine-tuning on the target task. This method circumvents the need to train the model from scratch and significantly reduces the demand for labeled data. The choice of training parameters profoundly impacts the experimental outcomes. The primary objective of pre-training is to acquire a relatively reasonable set of training parameters. For neural networks, knowledge and judgments are retained within the weights. By retaining these weights during the pre-training process, the model retains its acquired knowledge. During the subsequent training of the target task, the pre-trained model's weights can be utilized as initial weights, which provides the model with a clear path rather than starting from a blindly initialized state. This initial strategy significantly reduces training costs. For successful pre-training, it is crucial to ensure that the pre-training task and the target task have sufficient similarities. The transferability of knowledge between tasks is directly proportional to their similarity. In some cases, tasks may require minimal modifications, such as changing only the output layer. It effectively eliminates the need for redundant training and improves overall training efficiency.

The focus of this paper is Lhasa-Tibetan speech recognition. In order to ensure the similarity between the pre-training task and the target task, our method involves the selection of multiple speech recognition tasks in high-resource languages. Specifically, we select three different tasks that form the backbone of our pre-training framework: "Chinese Speech-to-Chinese Character Recognition" (referred to as "ch"), "Chinese Speech-to-Pinyin Recognition" (referred to as "py"), and "English Speech-to-Word Recognition" (referred to as "en"). In the pre-training phase, our paper adopts the proposed method of multi-task serial pre-training. This method trains one task based on the pre-trained model obtained from another task. The number and order of tasks in the pre-training process can significantly influence the accuracy of the model's recognition. Hence, to provide a comprehensive evaluation, we compare the impact of different combinations of pre-training tasks on the performance of the target task.

In the fine-tuning phase, because of the strong similarities between the pre-training task and the target task, the model is designed to solely inherit the training parameters of the pre-trained model, except for the output layer. Through

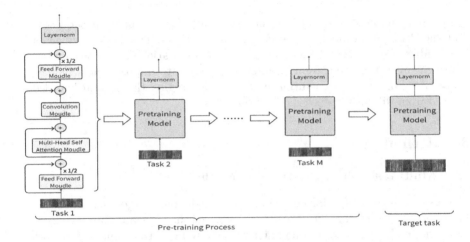

Fig. 1. Multi-task serial pre-training process

this pre-training and fine-tuning framework, we aim to leverage the shared speech and linguistic knowledge between the pre-training task and the target task.

Figure 1 shows the framework of Lhasa-Tibetan speech recognition based on multi-task serial pre-training. To discuss the impact of the number and order of pre-training tasks on the target task, we design five different training methods, namely the baseline model, single-task pre-training, two-task serial pre-training, three-task serial pre-training, and three-task serial incremental pre-training. By considering these different training methods, we aim to explore the impact of various combinations and sequences of pre-training tasks on the performance of the models in Lhasa-Tibetan speech recognition.

(1) Baseline model: we train the model directly using the Lhasa-Tibetan corpus without using any form of pre-training, denoted as model 1.
(2) Single-task pre-training: The pre-training process, as showed in Fig. 2, is designed to focus on a single task, which allows us to evaluate the performance of each pre-training model on the subsequent target task. In this process, the initial parameters of the pre-training model are randomly initialized. We proceed to fine-tune each of the three trained models using the Lhasa-Tibetan corpus and then compare the error rates of these models with that of the baseline model.

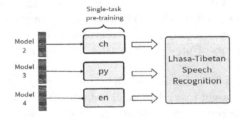

Fig. 2. Single-task pre-training model

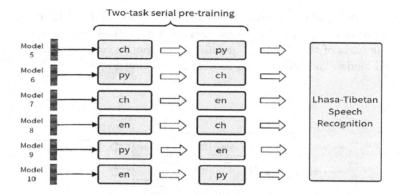

Fig. 3. Two-task serial pre-training model

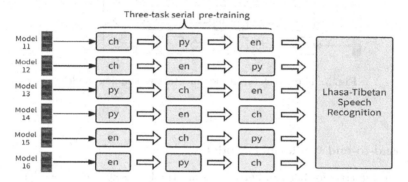

Fig. 4. Three-task serial pre-training model

(3) Two-task serial pre-training: This method has six different pre-training models, as illustrated in Fig. 3. Each model represents a unique combination of pre-training tasks. Notably, the initial parameters of the first pre-training stage for all six models are set to random initialization. The initial parameters of the second pre-training are designed to inherit all parameters from the first pre-training, except for the output layer. This method not only saves valuable training time but also facilitates rapid convergence of the models.

(4) Three-task serial pre-training: This pre-training method likewise yields six different models, as illustrated in Fig. 4. In this method, the initial parameters for the first pre-training of each model are randomly initialized. The initial parameters of the subsequent pre-training inherit all the learned parameters from the previous pre-training, except for the output layer.

(5) Three-task serial incremental pre-training: Inspired by the ERNIE 2.0 language model, the three-task serial incremental pre-training is implemented on the basis of the three-task serial pre-training to compare with our proposed model, and the training process is shown in Fig. 5.

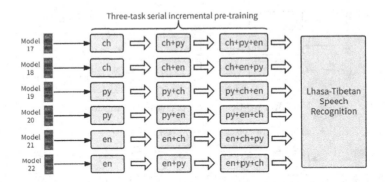

Fig. 5. Three-task serial incremental pre-training model

3.2   End-to-end Conformer Model

Although the transformer can better capture the long sequence dependencies in speech, it is relatively weak in extracting fine-grained local features. The convolutional neural network (CNN) has a good performance in extracting fine-grained local features. So, by combining the strengths of CNN and the transformer, Conformer, a convolution-enhanced transformer, was created. The conformer is composed of encoder and decoder, and the CNN is used to modify the encoder part. The overall architecture of the encoder is shown in Fig. 6 [13]. The conformer block is composed of three modules: the feed-forward module, the multi-head self-attention module, and the convolution module. Each module uses residual connections. The convolution and attention are concatenated to achieve an enhanced effect.

The conformer block contains two feed-forward modules. Between the two feed-forward modules are the multi-head self-attention module and the convolution module. This sandwich structure is inspired by the Macaron Net [12], which proposes to replace the original feed-forward layer in the transformer with two half-step feed-forward layers, one before the attention layer and one after the attention layer.

Similar to Macaron Net, the residual weight in the FFN module is set to 1/2 to reduce the size of the residual and avoid unstable training caused by large residual changes. In residual networks, the existence of residual connections can enhance the propagation of gradients, but it may also lead to gradient explosion or vanishing. By setting the residual weight to 1/2, the gradient propagation can

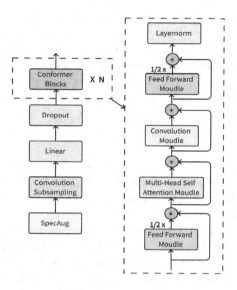

Fig. 6. The model structure of Encoder

be smoother while the residual connection remains effective, which is beneficial for model training and optimization. The calculation process of the output yi from the i-th input xi of the Conformer block is shown in Eqs. 1, 2, 3, and 4 [13], where FFN represents the feed-forward module, MHSA represents the multi-head self-attention module, and Conv represents the convolution module.

$$\widetilde{x}_i = x_i + \frac{1}{2} FFN\left(x_i\right) \tag{1}$$

$$x'_i = \widetilde{x}_i + MHSA\left(\widetilde{x}_i\right) \tag{2}$$

$$x''_i = x'_i + \text{Conv}\left(x'_i\right) \tag{3}$$

$$y_i = \text{Layernorm}\left(x''_i + \frac{1}{2} FNN\left(x''_i\right)\right) \tag{4}$$

4   Experiment

4.1   Experimental Data

The experimental data sets in this paper are obtained from the Open Speech and Language Resources (OpenSLR), as shown in Table 1.

The first data set comes from the Aishell-1 Chinese data set [14]. It is a Chinese speech corpus covering 11 fields such as smart homes, autonomous driving, and industrial production. We select 80,604 sentences with a total duration of 100.42 h. The audio files are converted into Windows Audio Volume (WAV) format with 16KHz sampling rate and 16-bit quantization accuracy.

Table 1. The statistics of data set

Data set	Speech Utterances		Duration		Size	
	Training data	Test data	Training data	Test data	Training data	Test data
Chinese	80604	–	100.42 h	–	10.7 GB	–
English	28539	–	100.59 h	–	6.21 GB	–
Tibetan	18738	4874	24.33 h	6.41 h	14.3 GB	3.79 GB

The second data set is the LibriSpeech English data set [15]. We select 28,539 sentences with a total duration of 100.59 h. The audio files are converted into Windows Audio Volume (WAV) format with 16KHz sampling rate and 16-bit quantization accuracy.

The third data set is the TIBMD@MUC Tibetan data set [16]. It is a multi-dialect Tibetan data set. We select 18,738 Lhasa-Tibetan sentences as the training set, with a total duration of 24.33 h. We select 4,874 Lhasa-Tibetan sentences as the test set, with a total duration of 6.41 h. The audio files are converted into Windows Audio Volume (WAV) format with 16KHz sampling rate and 16-bit quantization accuracy.

4.2   Experimental Results and Analysis

The indicator for evaluating experimental results in this paper is Tibetan word error rate (WER). The method of calculating WER is shown in Formula (5).

$$\text{Word Error Rate} = \frac{\text{Insertions + Substitutions + Deletions}}{\text{Total Words}} \times 100\% \quad (5)$$

The error rates of the five models on Lhasa-Tibetan speech recognition are shown as follows.

(1) Baseline model (Model 1): Without pre-training, the error rate of Lhasa-Tibetan speech recognition is 13.46% (Table 2).

Table 2. The experimental results of baseline model

Model	Pre-training Task	Lhasa-Tibetan Speech Recognition WER
Model 1	None	13.46%

(2) Single-task pre-training: After single-task pre-training, the experimental results of fine-tuning on the Lhasa-Tibetan corpus are shown in Table 3.

In direct comparison to the baseline model (Model 1), the results obtained after undergoing the single-task pre-training show a reduction in the recognition error rate. Among them, the model has the best recognition performance when the pre-training task is "py". The error rate of fine-tuning on the Lhasa-Tibetan corpus is 5.03%. This outcome reflects an impressive 8.43% decrease in error rate when contrasted with the baseline model.

Table 3. The experimental results of single-task pre-training

Model	Pre-training Task	Lhasa-Tibetan Speech Recognition WER
Model 2	ch	6.41%
Model 3	py	**5.03%**
Model 4	en	9.79%

(3) Two-task serial pre-training: After two-task serial pre-training, the experimental results of fine-tuning on the Lhasa-Tibetan corpus are shown in Table 4.

Table 4. The experimental results of two-task serial pre-training

Model	Order of Pre-training Tasks	Lhasa-Tibetan Speech Recognition WER
Model 5	ch→py	**4.52%**
Model 6	Py→ch	4.68%
Model 7	ch→en	5.44%
Model 8	en→ch	4.89%
Model 9	py→en	4.97%
Model 10	en→py	4.79%

Overall, this method can acquire more general "knowledge". These models show better recognition performance compared to single-task pre-training.

Notably, Models 5 and 6 stand out due to their exclusion of the "en" pre-training task. They have lower error rates than the remaining four models. These results show that Chinese, as a pre-training language, holds greater suitability for improving the accuracy of Lhasa-Tibetan speech recognition than English.

Comparing Model 5 with Model 6 and Model 9 with Model 10 longitudinally, it is observed that the "py" of Model 5 and Model 10 is closer to the target task. Remarkably, this proximity is reflected in their lower error rates compared to Models 6 and Model 9. Consequently, it can be inferred that the "py" pre-training task makes a more significant contribution to the overall performance of the target task.

After two-task serial pre-training, Model 5 has the best recognition performance. Its error rate is 4.52%. Compared to Model 3 (the best model in single-task pre-training), the error rate is reduced by 0.51%. It shows that increasing the number of pre-training tasks can reduce the error rate. Compared to Model 6, the error rate of Model 5 is reduced by 0.16%. It shows that an appropriate pre-training order can reduce the error rate.

(4) Three-task serial pre-training: After three-task serial pre-training, the experimental results of fine-tuning on the Lhasa-Tibetan corpus are shown in Table 5.

Table 5. The experimental results of three-task serial pre-training

Model	Order of Pre-training Tasks	Lhasa-Tibetan Speech Recognition WER
Model 11	ch→py→en	4.94%
Model 12	ch→en→py	**4.12%**
Model 13	py→ch→en	4.86%
Model 14	py→en→ch	4.64%
Model 15	en→ch→py	4.45%
Model 16	en→py→ch	4.55%

Overall, this method has better recognition performance compared to single-task pre-training and two-task serial pre-training.

When the last task of the pre-training process is "en", the error rate is higher. When the last task of the pre-training process is "py", the error rate is lower. The results show that the recognition performance of the model is better when the high contribution training corpus is closer to the Tibetan speech recognition.

After three-task serial pre-training, the recognition performance of Model 12 is the best. Its error rate is 4.12%. Compared to Model 5 (the best model in two-task serial pre-training), the error rate is reduced by 0.4%. It also shows that increasing the number of pre-training tasks can reduce the error rate. Compared to Model 12, the error rate is reduced by 0.82%. It also shows that an appropriate pre-training order can reduce the error rate.

(5) Three-task serial incremental pre-training: Drawing inspiration from the ERNIE 2.0 language model, the serial pre-training method is proposed in this paper. To provide a comprehensive comparison, we add experiments of the serial incremental pre-training method of ERNIE 2.0. To maintain the integrity and fairness of this comparison, each subtask within the pre-training process has been trained for the same number of epochs. The comparative results, showing the error rates (WER) of both the serial pre-training and serial incremental pre-training methods on the Lhasa-Tibetan speech recognition, are meticulously shown in Table 6.

Comparing the results of the six groups of models shows that the superiority and lower error rates achieved by our proposed multi-task serial pre-training method. In contrast, the serial incremental pre-training method, despite its advantages of augmenting the training data as the number of tasks increases, exposes a disadvantage: the gradual increase in training tasks adversely affects the convergence rate of the model, posing challenges to its overall convergence.

Table 6. The experimental results of three-task serial pre-training and serial incremental pre-training

Serial pre-training	WER	Serial incremental pre-training	WER
ch→py→en	4.94%	ch→ch+py→ch+py+en	5.04%
ch→en→py	**4.12%**	ch→ch+en→ch+en+py	5.18%
py→ch→en	4.86%	py→py+ch→py+ch+en	4.83%
py→en→ch	4.64%	py→py+en→py+en+ch	4.95%
en→ch→py	4.45%	en→en+ch→en+ch+py	5.22%
en→py→ch	4.55%	en→en+py→en+py+ch	5.12%

These results highlight the inherent limitations of the serial incremental pre-training method, further reinforcing the effectiveness and accuracy of our proposed multi-task serial pre-training method.

5 Conclusion

Compared to conventional speech recognition methods, the application of end-to-end models in Tibetan speech recognition tasks effectively addresses the challenge of limited prior knowledge of the Tibetan language. However, given the scarcity of data, enhancing the recognition performance of the end-to-end model becomes a crucial research focus. In this paper, we adopt the pre-training method to obtain more favorable initialization weights for the end-to-end model, which significantly influences the final model performance. By changing the number and order of pre-training tasks, the results show the effectiveness of our proposed multi-task serial pre-training method in enhancing model recognition. Remarkably, when serially pre-trained with three different tasks, our model achieves a WER of 4.12% for Lhasa-Tibetan speech recognition, showing a 9.34% improvement over the baseline model and a 1.06% improvement over existing pre-trained models. Notably, among the three tasks, the "py" task in Chinese speech has the highest contribution to Tibetan speech recognition. Moreover, compared to the ERNIE2.0 language model, our proposed multi-task serial pre-training method yields faster model convergence. Future research endeavors could leverage the pre-trained model for speech recognition in other Tibetan dialects or minority languages, thereby expanding its applicability and impact.

References

1. Hendrycks, D., Lee, K., Mazeika, M.: Using pre-training can improve model robustness and uncertainty. In: International Conference on Machine Learning, pp. 2712–2721. PMLR (2019)
2. Fan, Z., Zhou, S., Xu, B. Unsupervised pre-training for sequence to sequence speech recognition (2019)

3. Lech, M., Stolar, M., Best, C., Bolia, R.: Real-Time speech emotion recognition using a pre-trained image classification network: effects of bandwidth reduction and companding. Front. Comput. Sci. **2**, 14 (2020). https://doi.org/10.3389/fcomp.2020.00014
4. Bansal, S., Kamper, H., Livescu, K., et al.: Pre-training on high-resource speech recognition improves low-resource speech-to-text translation. arXiv preprint arXiv:1809.01431 (2018)
5. Zhang, W., Li, X., Yang, Y., Dong, R.: Pre-training on mixed data for low-resource neural machine translation. Information **12**, 133 (2021)
6. Pan, L.: Research on low resource multilingual speech recognition based on transfer learning. Tianjin University (2019). gtjdu.2019.004688. https://doi.org/10.27356/d.cnki
7. Wang, Q., Guo, W., Xie, C.: Tibetan speech recognition based on end-to-end technology. Pattern Recogn. Artif. Intell. **30**(04), 359–364 (2017). https://doi.org/10.16451/j.cnki.issn1003-6059.201704008
8. Yan, J., Lv, Z., Huang, S., et al.: Low-resource tibetan dialect acoustic modeling based on transfer learning. In: SLTU, pp. 6–10 (2018)
9. Qin, S., Wang, L., Li, S., et al.: Improving low-resource Tibetan end-to-end ASR by multilingual and multilevel unit modeling. J. Audio Speech Music Proc. **2022**, 2 (2022)
10. Wang, Z., Zhao, Y., Wu, L., et al.: Cross-language transfer learning-based Lhasa-Tibetan speech recognition. CMC-Comput. Mater. Continua **73**(1), 629–639 (2022)
11. Sun, Y., Wang, S., Li, Y., et al.: Ernie 2.0: a continual pre-training framework for language understanding. In: Proceedings of the AAAI Conference on Artificial Intelligence, vol. 34, no. 05, pp. 8968–8975 (2020)
12. Lu, Y., Li, Z., He, D., et al.: Understanding and improving transformer from a multi-particle dynamic system point of view. arXiv preprint arXiv:1906.02762 (2019)
13. Gulati, A., Qin, J., Chiu, C.C., et al.: Conformer: convolution-augmented transformer for speech recognition (2020)
14. Bu, H., Du, J., Na, X., et al.: Aishell-1: an open-source mandarin speech corpus and a speech recognition baseline. In: 2017 20th Conference of the Oriental Chapter of the International Coordinating Committee on Speech Databases and Speech I/O Systems and Assessment (O-COCOSDA), pp. 1–5. IEEE (2017)
15. Panayotov, V., Chen, G., Povey, D., et al.: Librispeech: an ASR corpus based on public domain audio books. In: 2015 IEEE International Conference on Acoustics, Speech and Signal Processing (ICASSP), pp. 5206–5210. IEEE (2015)
16. Zhao, Y., Xu, X., Yue, J., et al.: An open speech resource for Tibetan multi-dialect and multitask recognition. Int. J. Comput. Sci. Eng. **22**(2–3), 297–304 (2020)

Mutual Information Dropout: Mutual Information Can Be All You Need

Zichen Song$^{(\boxtimes)}$ ⓘ and Shan Ma

Lanzhou University, Lanzhou 730000, China
songzch21@lzu.edu.cn

Abstract. Dropout is a powerful way for preventing model overfitting. However, it is inefficient due to it randomly ignoring some neurons. Although there are many ways on Dropout, they are still either inefficient on improving generalization ability or not effective enough. In this paper, we propose Mutual Information Dropout, which is an efficient Dropout based on dropping neurons with low mutual information. In Mutual Information Dropout, instead of randomly ignoring some neurons, we first evaluated the mutual information of neurons to dropout with mutual information below a certain threshold. In this way, Mutual Information Dropout can achieve effective improving generalization ability with evaluate neurons. Extensive experiments on Three datasets show that Mutual Information Dropout is much more efficient than many existing Dropout and can meanwhile achieve comparable or even better generalization ability.

Keywords: Dropout · Mutual Information · Generalization Ability

1 Introduction

Dropout and their variants have achieved great success in many fields. For example, preventing overfitting in neural networks, improving model accuracy in image classification, balancing exploration and exploitation in reinforcement learning and so on. The core of a dropout is randomly ignoring some neurons, which allows the dropout to improving generalization ability. However, since dropout discards some useful information during the training process. Thus, it is difficult for standard dropout to efficiently improve generalization ability.

There are many ways to improve the generalization ability of neural networks, such as Drop-Connect, which sets each weight of the network to 0 with a certain probability during each training iteration. However, this way incurs significant computational overhead, and it can be difficult to select an appropriate dropout rate. Another way, Inverted Dropout, sets each neuron to zero with probability p and then divides its output by p during training. However, it can also be difficult to select an appropriate dropout rate, and these ways may not be efficient if an inappropriate dropout rate is chosen.

In this paper we propose Mutual Information Dropout, which is an efficient Dropout variant based on dropping neurons with low mutual information that can achieve effective

The code: https://github.com/shjdjjfi/MI-Dropout.git.

L. Iliadis et al. (Eds.): ICANN 2023, LNCS 14262, pp. 91–101, 2023.
https://doi.org/10.1007/978-3-031-44201-8_8

generalization ability. In Mutual Information Dropout, we first use mutual information to evaluate the usefulness of neurons. Next, we set an appropriate mutual information threshold. Finally, we perform neuron dropout on those neurons that fall below a certain threshold. We conduct extensive experiments on three benchmark datasets in various tasks. The results demonstrate that Mutual Information Dropout is much more efficient than many Dropout ways and can achieve improving the generalization ability.

The contributions of this paper are summarized as follows:

- We propose a Dropout based on dropping neurons with low mutual information. And we discussed the feasibility of applying mutual information to Dropout.
- We propose a method to explore the performance of neural networks and demonstrate this idea in experiments.
- Extensive experiments on three datasets show that Mutual Information Dropout is much more efficient than many Dropout ways and can achieve competitive performance.
- In addition, we found that the method always outperformed the original model and that the improvement was greater on difficult datasets.

2   Related Work

2.1   Dropout

The technique of dropout was first introduced by Hinton et al. (2012) as a form of regularization. Its purpose is to prevent overfitting during training by randomly setting a subset of neurons in a neural network to zero, thereby dropping them out. This compels the remaining neurons to learn more resilient and diverse representations as they have to handle the input data without the support of the dropped-out neurons. Dropout has been demonstrated to be highly effective in enhancing the generalization performance of neural networks across a broad spectrum of applications, including image classification, natural language processing, and speech recognition. A range of extensions and variations of dropout has been proposed, such as Drop Connect [9] and Spatial Dropout [4], which implement the dropout technique on different segments of the network. It is desirable to maintain low redundancy in the content.

2.2   Mutual Information

Mutual information is a crucial concept within information theory, as it quantifies the degree of information that two random variables share. Recently, mutual information has emerged as a potent tool for unsupervised and semi-supervised representation learning. One popular approach involves using mutual information as an objective function for training generative models, such as variational autoencoders (VAEs) and adversarial autoencoders (AAEs). By maximizing the mutual information between the input and latent variables, these models are encouraged to learn a compact and informative representation of the input data. In addition, mutual information has also found applications in feature selection and learning for supervised learning settings. For instance, the MICNN [10] method proposes maximizing the mutual information between the input and output of a neural network [11] to enable the network to learn discriminative features relevant to the target task. [12] Mutual information has also been widely used in other domains [13], including convolutional neural networks and signal processing. [14] Overall, minimizing the level of redundancy in content is desirable. [15].

2.3 Mutual Information and Dropout

Several recent studies have explored the use of mutual information (MI) in Dropout to automate the selection of the dropout rate. For example, Louizos et al. proposed the "Probabilistic Dropout" method [16], which uses the MI between the output and the weights of the network to dynamically adjust the dropout rate during training. The method was shown to improve the performance of deep learning models on various benchmark datasets, while reducing the need for manual tuning of the dropout rate. Similarly, Sun et al. proposed a method called "Info-Drop" [17] that uses the MI between the activations of the network layers and the output to adjust the dropout rate. The method was shown to outperform standard Dropout and other state-of-the-art regularization techniques on several benchmark datasets, including CIFAR-10, CIFAR-100, and SVHN. Moreover, Zhou et al. proposed a method called "ML-Dropout," [18] which uses the MI between the output and the weights to determine the optimal dropout rate for each layer of the network. The method was shown to improve the performance of deep learning models on several benchmark datasets, including MNIST, CIFAR-10, and ImageNet.

3   Mutual Information Dropout

In this section, we introduce our Mutual Information Dropout approach based on dropping neurons with low mutual information. The architecture of Mutual Information Dropout is shown in Fig. 1. It first uses mutual information to evaluate the usefulness of neurons, next set an appropriate mutual information threshold, and finally perform neuron dropout on those neurons that fall below a certain threshold. In this way, the test performance of the recompiled model was significantly better than that of the previously trained model and have effective generalization ability. Next, we introduce the details of Mutual Information Dropout in the following section.

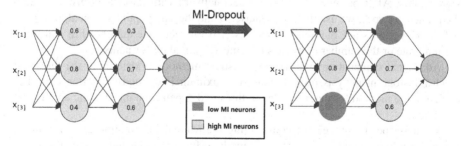

Fig. 1. The architecture of Mutual Information Dropout.

3.1 Architecture

Our neural network consists of fully connected layers, denoted as L_j. A vector X of size N is the input to the network and a vector y of size M is the output. The first layer L_1 has K_1 neurons, the second layer L_2 has K_2 neurons, and the j layer L_j has K_j neurons. The output of the neuron that number of i in layer L_j is denoted as a_{ij}, where j = 1, 2...L_j and i = 1, 2... K_j. During training the fully connected network, we use a labeled dataset D = $\{(x_1, y_1), (x_2, y_2)...(x_n, y_n)\}$, where N is the size of the dataset. We use mutual information function to measure the difference between the predicted output and the true label. Specifically, the loss function for a single (x_i, y_i) is given by:

$$L(x_i, y_i) = -\log\left(\text{SoftMax}(f(x_i))y_i\right) \tag{1}$$

where $f(x_i)$ is the output of the final layer of the neural network, SoftMax is the SoftMax function, and y_i is the true label of the input x_i. To optimize the loss function, we use the stochastic gradient descent (SGD) algorithm with a fixed learning rate. After training, we obtain the output of each layer for each input in the dataset.

Next, we aim to remove the neurons whose output is less relevant to the true label. To quantify the relevance, we use the concept of mutual information (MI). MI measures the amount of information that one random variable (in this case, the output of a neuron) contains about another random variable (in this case, the true label). For a given neuron i in layer L_j, we calculate the MI between its output a_{ij} and the true label y_i as follows:

$$MI\left(a_{ij}, y_i\right) = H\left(a_{ij}\right) - H\left(a_{ij}|y_i\right) \tag{2}$$

where H (a_{ij}) is the entropy of a_{ij}, and H $(a_{ij}|y_i)$ is the conditional entropy of a_{ij} given y_i. We calculate the average MI for all neurons in each layer as follows where j = 1, 2, 3:

$$MI_{avg}(j) = \frac{1}{k_j} \sum_{i=1}^{k_j} MI(a_{ji}, y) \tag{3}$$

Finally, we select a suitable MI threshold t such that all neurons with MI(a_{ij}, y) < t are pruned. We empirically determine the value of t by evaluating the performance of the pruned network on a validation set. Specifically, we start with a high value of t (e.g. 2.0) and gradually decrease it until the performance on the validation set drops significantly. After pruning, we obtain a new network with fewer neurons. To retrain the pruned network, we use the same dataset D and the same optimization algorithm as before. However, since the network has fewer parameters, we may need to adjust the learning rate or the number of epochs to achieve optimal performance.

Additional explanation: We utilize statistical methods to determine the threshold (such as histogram analysis, quartile analysis, maximum likelihood estimation, etc.). The choice of the method for determining the threshold depends on the specific application scenario.

We describe the process of constructing the Mutual Information Dropout model using algorithmic pseudo code, including modules for compiling and training the model without Dropout, calculating the mutual information of neurons, and performing Dropout operations on neurons using mutual information. The algorithmic procedure is as follows:

Algorithm 1 Main algorithm of MI-Dropout

```
Input: X represents the input random variable, Y repre-
sents the output random variable, H(X) represents en-
tropy, and H(X|Y) represents conditional entropy.
# Initialization
Randomly initialize data space X
Randomly initialize data label Y
# Create the ANN
input = Image (X, Y)
for each layer in the neural network do
    output = multiplication (input, weights) + biases
    output = activation-function(output)
    input = output
end for
output = input
# Use MI-Dropout cut the network
for each layer in the neural network do
    for each neuron in the layer do
        calculate the mutual information I (X; Y) of
        the neuron.
        # I (X; Y) = H(X) - H(X|Y)
        if I (X; Y) < threshold then
            with probability p, set the output of the
            neuron to 0
        end if
    end for
end for
```

3.2 Complexity Analysis

In this section, we analyze the computational complexity of Mutual Information Dropout. For the Dropout networks to discard neurons with mutual information below the threshold, their time and memory cost are both $O(N \cdot i \cdot j)$, and their total number of additional parameters is $2ij$ (i is the Layer number, j is the number of neurons for each Layer). In addition, the time cost and memory cost is also $O(N \cdot i \cdot j)$, the total complexity is $O(N \cdot i \cdot j)$, which is much more efficient than the standard Dropout with $O(\sum_{j=1}^{j} \sum_{i=1}^{i} n_{ij}^2)$ complexity. These analysis results demonstrate the theoretical efficiency of Mutual Information Dropout..

4 Experiments

4.1 Datasets and Experimental Settings

We conduct extensive experiments on three benchmark datasets for different tasks. Their details are introduced as follows.

Table 1. Statistics of image classification datasets.

Dataset	Training Samples	Test Samples	Input Dimension
MNIST	60,000	10,000	28×28
CIFAR-10	50,000	10,000	$32 \times 32 \times 3$
CIFAR-100	50,000	10,000	$32 \times 32 \times 3$

The first one is MNIST [1], which is a widely used dataset for handwritten digit recognition. The second one is CIFAR-10 [2]. It is a benchmark dataset for image classification tasks. The third one is CIFAR-100, which is a large-scale image classification dataset, consisting of 100 classes. We perform two tasks on this dataset, i.e., the digit recognition task based on handwritten digit dataset and image classification for limited set of categories task based on the RGB images. The detailed statistical information of the datasets introduced above are shown in Table 1.

Our experiments were conducted on an NVIDIA A100-SXM4-80GB machine equipped with 80 GB memory. We repeated each experiment five times to ensure statistical validity and reported both the average performance and standard deviations. We evaluated the classification tasks based on accuracy and loss performance metrics.

This experiment has high memory requirements for CPU. If you run the code on a computer with a small amount of memory, it may encounter out-of-memory errors when processing CIFAR100. Therefore, we recommend using a computer with larger memory or adjusting the batch size (though this may result in reduced performance).

4.2 Effectiveness Comparison

First, we compare the performance of Mutual Information Dropout with many baseline methods, including: (1) Dropout [3], the basic Dropout; (2) SpatialDropout2D [4], a Dropout variant with image datasets; (3) Alpha Dropout [5], an extension of Dropout, which can prevent neuron deactivation completely and maintain the mean and variance of input values during training; (4) Gaussian Dropout [6], a Dropout variant with lower complexity, which randomly perturbs input data instead of setting it to zero directly, it can increase the robustness and generalization ability of the model, and is suitable for situations where there is a small amount of noise in the input data.

The performance of these methods on the three classification datasets are compared in Table 2. Results indicate that efficient Dropout variants may not surpass the standard Dropout model due to different probability distributions and uniform dropout probabilities across all layers, restricting the model's potential. Mutual Information Dropout,

Table 2. The results of different methods in the image classification tasks. Best average scores are highlighted.

Model	MNIST		CIFAR-10		CIFAR-100	
	Accuracy	Loss	Accuracy	Loss	Accuracy	Loss
Dropout	0.9694	0.0972	0.2862	1.9093	0.0474	4.2141
Alpha-Dropout	0.9008	0.3279	0.3221	1.8531	0.0370	4.3159
Gaussian-Dropout	0.9680	0.1035	0.3204	1.8731	0.0574	4.1533
MI-Dropout	**0.9973**	**0.0091**	**0.5706**	**1.2062**	**0.3124**	**2.7232**

however, can achieve better performance than other efficient Dropout variants because it evaluates the mutual information between a neuron's output and the true output, leading to the removal of low mutual information neurons and improved generalization ability. MI-Dropout outperforms other methods in most metrics, highlighting its advantage in image classification.

4.3 Why is MI-Dropout Effective?

Based on experimental results on three datasets, Mutual Information Dropout consistently exhibits excellent performance. Recent research on the application of Mutual Information to evaluate the performance and interpretability of neural network models suggests that:

Mutual Information can accurately assess the generalization ability of neurons. Figure 2 shows that for datasets that are difficult to learn to generalize, the number of neurons with Mutual Information below the threshold significantly increases. This indicates that as the generalization ability of the neural network decreases, so does the Mutual Information.

The evolution of Mutual Information conforms to the learning principles of neural networks. The average Mutual Information of deep neural networks is often higher than that of shallow neural networks, which is consistent with the observation that deep networks often have better generalization ability than shallow networks. Therefore, Mutual Information can effectively evaluate the generalization ability of neural networks.

Since Mutual Information can effectively assess the generalization ability of neural networks, pruning neurons with Mutual Information below the threshold can effectively improve the model's generalization ability [7] and reduce its complexity [8].

To validate the effectiveness of our proposed MI-Dropout in improving generalization performance, we compiled the model after applying MI-Dropout and trained the recompiled model under the same environment and parameters. We calculated the average MI for each layer of the recompiled model and compared it with the average MI for each layer of the model without MI-Dropout in three different datasets. The results are shown in Fig. 3.

Note that the Mutual Information baseline of the two graphs is different. The Mutual Information baseline of the model without MI-Dropout on the left is 0.2, while the Mutual Information baseline of the model after MI-Dropout on the right is 0.3.

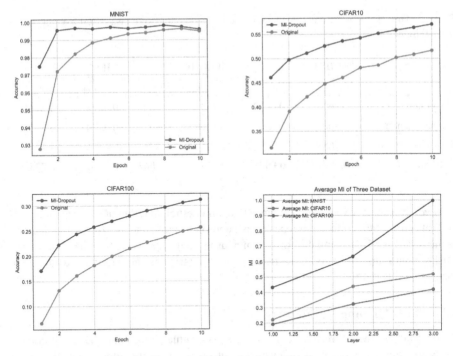

Fig. 2. The result of Mutual Information Dropout.

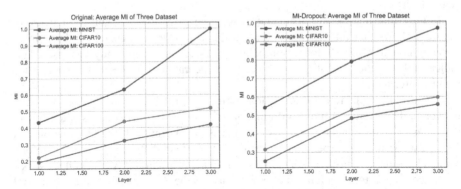

Fig. 3. Comparison of Mutual Information before and after MI-Dropout Operation.

From Fig. 3, it can be observed that the average Mutual Information for each layer of the model after MI-Dropout operation and retraining has increased, especially in the middle layers. This phenomenon is interesting because it not only indicates that the MI-Dropout operation itself discards neurons with lower generalization ability, but also suggests that the retained neurons continue to improve their generalization ability during training. Therefore, MI-Dropout operation can be performed after pre-training in large models, which can effectively improve the generalization ability of the model and reduce training costs.

The reason for this phenomenon is that the middle layer is a crucial layer for learning and generalization in neural network models. Therefore, the MI-Dropout operation effectively enhances the learning ability of the middle layer, resulting in a significant increase in the average performance of the middle layer. This also effectively improves the generalization ability of the neural network model.

4.4 Comparison with Other MI-Based Dropout Methods

According to our investigation of recent papers on MI-based Dropout variants, the currently popular methods include Probabilistic Dropout, Info-Drop, and ML-Dropout. To test the performance gap between our proposed MI-Dropout and these methods, we conducted two experiments: one using neural network models with MI Dropout variants and the other using neural network models with MI-Dropout. The experiments were conducted in a different environment (V100-32GB) and with an increased batch size. The average results were computed over five runs.

The experimental results, shown in Fig. 4, clearly demonstrate that our proposed MI-Dropout outperforms Probabilistic Dropout, Info-Drop, and ML-Dropout from the second epoch onwards. Specifically, MI-Dropout exhibits faster accuracy improvement and more stable accuracy increase without overfitting in the later stages.

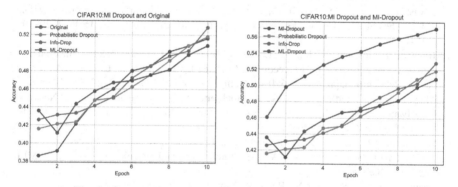

Fig. 4. Comparison between MI-based Dropout and MI-Dropout.

Figure 4 shows the comparison of results between the model without Dropout and the model with Dropout based on MI (Mutual Information) in the left panel, and the comparison between the MI-Dropout and the model with Dropout based on MI in the right panel.

5   Conclusion and Future Work

In this paper, we propose Mutual Information Dropout, which is a Dropout variant based on dropping neurons with low mutual information that can achieve effective generalization ability. In Mutual Information Dropout, we use mutual information to evaluate the usefulness of neurons. Next, set an appropriate mutual information threshold. Finally, we perform neuron dropout on those neurons that fall below a certain threshold. Extensive experiments on three benchmark datasets show that Mutual Information Dropout is much more efficient than many Dropout ways and can achieve improving the generalization ability.

In our future work, we plan to explore the combination of mutual information with other regularization techniques to further improve model performance by applying the mutual information between the normalized output of the batch normalization layer in neural networks and the normalized ground truth. Additionally, developing more efficient and scalable methods for estimating mutual information is also a crucial future direction, as current estimation methods can be computationally expensive and require large amounts of data. These improvements would make mutual information more accessible for use in a wider range of applications.

References

1. LeCun, Y., Cortes, C., Burges, C.: The MNIST database of handwritten digits. In: International Conference on Pattern Recognition (ICPR), pp. 545–548. IEEE Computer Society, Washington, DC (1998)
2. Krizhevsky, A.: Learning Multiple Layers of Features from Tiny Images. In: Technical Report, University of Toronto, pp. 1–60 (2009)
3. Srivastava, N., Hinton, G., Krizhevsky, A., Sutskever, I., Salakhutdinov, R.: Dropout: a simple way to prevent neural networks from overfitting. J. Mach. Learn. Res. 15(1), 1929–1958 (2014)
4. Tompson, J., Goroshin, R., Jain, A., LeCun, Y., Bregler, C.: Efficient object localization using convolutional networks. In: Proceedings of the IEEE Conference on Computer Vision and Pattern Recognition, pp. 648–656. IEEE Computer Society, Boston, MA, USA (2015)
5. Klambauer, G., Unterthiner, T., Mayr, A., Hochreiter, S.: Self-Normalizing Neural Networks. In: Advances in Neural Information Processing Systems 30, pp. 971–980. Curran Associates, Inc., Red Hook, NY, USA (2017)
6. Srivastava, R.K., Greff, K., Schmidhuber, J.: Highway networks. In: Proceedings of the 17th International Conference on Artificial Intelligence and Statistics, pp. 646–654. PMLR, Reykjavik, Iceland (2014)
7. Zhang, C., Bengio, S., Hardt, M., Recht, B., Vinyals, O.: Understanding deep learning requires rethinking generalization. In: Proceedings of the International Conference on Learning Representations (ICLR), pp. 1–14 (2017)
8. Ethayarajh, K., Choi, Y., Swayamdipta, S.: Information-Theoretic Measures of Dataset Difficulty. CoRR, abs/2110.08420 (2021)
9. Wan, L., Zeiler, M., Zhang, S., Cun, Y.L., Fergus, R.: Regularization of Neural Networks using DropConnect. In: Proceedings of the 30th International Conference on Machine Learning, pp. 1058–1066. JMLR.org, Atlanta, GA, USA (2013)
10. Zhang, Y., Zhang, L., Yang, J.: A novel deep learning framework for imbalanced multi-class classification problems. IEEE Trans. Neural Networks Learn. Syst. 29(8), 3573–3584 (2018)
11. Belghazi, M.I., Baratin, A., Rajeswaran, A., Ozair, S., Bengio, Y., Courville, A.: Mine: Mutual information neural estimation. In: International Conference on Machine Learning, vol. 80, pp. 409–418. PMLR (2018)
12. Oord, A.V.D., Li, Y., Vinyals, O.: Representation learning with contrastive predictive coding. arXiv preprint arXiv:1807.03748 (2019)

13. Poole, B., Lahiri, S., Raghu, M., Sohl-Dickstein, J., Ganguli, S.: On variational bounds of mutual information. arXiv preprint arXiv:1905.06922 (2019)
14. Han, Y., Liu, Z., Zhang, H., Yang, M., Zhu, S.C.: An efficient framework for mutual information estimation with improved optimization. In: Proceedings of the IEEE/CVF Conference on Computer Vision and Pattern Recognition, pp. 3083–3092 (2021)
15. Liu, Z., Han, Y., Zhang, H., Yang, M., Zhu, S.C.: MIE: Mutual information estimation under distributional shift. arXiv preprint arXiv:2102.08584 (2021)
16. Bishop, D., et al.: Spatial mapping of local density variations in two-dimensional electron systems using scanning photoluminescence. Phys. Rev. Lett. **119**, 136801 (2017)
17. Shao, W., Wang, B., Shen, Y., Liu, T., Yu, K.: Informative dropout for robust representation learning: a shape-bias perspective. In: Proceedings of the IEEE/CVF Conference on Computer Vision and Pattern Recognition (CVPR), pp. 6027–6036 (2021)
18. Wang, Y., Lin, Z., Wang, X., and Qian, C.: Multi-sample dropout for accelerated training and better generalization. In: Proceedings of the IEEE/CVF Conference on Computer Vision and Pattern Recognition, pp. 2766–2775 (2021)

Non-Outlier Pseudo-Labeling for Short Text Clustering

Fangquan Zhou and Shenglin Gui[✉]

School of Computer Science and Engineering,
University of Electronic Science and Technology of China, Chengdu 611731, China
shenglin_gui@uestc.edu.cn

Abstract. Instance-level correlation and cluster-level discrepancy of data are two crucial aspects of short text clustering. Current deep clustering methods, however, suffer from inaccurate estimation of either instance-level correlation or cluster-level discrepancy of data and strongly relay on the quality of the initial text representation. In this paper, we propose a Non-outlier Pseudo-labeling-based Short Text Clustering (NPLC) method, which consists of two parts. In the first part, we use Mask Language Model (MLM) to pre-train the feature model on a given dataset to enhance the initial text representation. The second part based on non-outlier pseudo-labeling is a joint training in which we first cluster the dataset and select cluster labels of outlier-free data in each cluster as pseudo labels for the next joint training based on a novel framework. The novel framework makes use of a contrastive loss to gain excellent inter-cluster separation by minimizing similarity between outlier-free and outlier data and a clustering loss to narrow intra-cluster distances by maximizing similarity among outlier-free data. Extensive experimental results demonstrate that NPLC achieves significant improvements over existing methods and advances the state-of-the-art results on most benchmark datasets with 1%–12% improvement on Accuracy and 1%–6% improvement on Normalized Mutual Information.

Keywords: Short text clustering · Deep clustering · Text representation · Outlier-free data

1 Introduction

Short text clustering (STC), as a essential task in unsupervised learning, aims to group short texts into different clusters without any label information. With the popularity of social media, short texts, like tweets, search inquiries, online reviews, etc., have increased significantly and rapidly [1]. Therefore, organizing these short texts (e.g., grouping them by event or topic) is an important step for many data mining tasks, such as data summarization [11], public opinion analysis [7] and event detection [10].

However, owing to high sparsity, high noise and high dimensionality of short texts, shallow clustering methods, relying on distance measured in the data

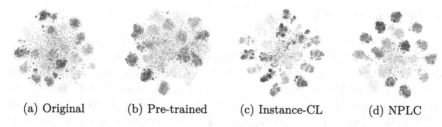

(a) Original   (b) Pre-trained   (c) Instance-CL   (d) NPLC

Fig. 1. TSNE visualization of the embedding space learned on StackOverflow using SentenceBERT [14] as backbone. Each color indicates a ground truth semantic category.

space, perform poorly on short texts. To solve the problem, deep clustering utilizes neural networks to enrich the sparse representations and gain promising improvements [6,19]. But the clustering performance is still inadequate when dealing with dataset with many clusters. As illustrated in Fig. 1, original text representation based on SentenceBERT [14] has poor purity and significant overlap across categories. After pre-trained by Mask Language Model (MLM) [4], text representation purity could get improved to some extent, but overlap across categories still needs to be further improved.

On the other hand, instance-wise contrastive learning (Instance-CL) has recently become prominent in self-supervised learning [19], which can make samples distribution scattered and alleviate data overlap (see Fig. 1(c)). The basic idea is to pull positive pairs augmented from the same original instance close while pushing negative pairs apart as long as they are from different original instances. Based on Instance-CL, SCCL [19] gains excellent clustering performance over earlier works. However, its intrinsic false-negative pairs whose original instances are in the same semantic cluster make Instance-CL less stable and more data-dependent.

To address the above problems, we propose a Non-outlier Pseudo-labeling-based Short Text Clustering, referred to as NPLC[1] Our main contributions are as follows: (a) We find pre-training the feature model over MLM could help greatly enhance the quality of initial short text representation for short text clustering, especially performing better on our framework. (b) We introduce outlier-free pseudo labels to help generate higher-quality negative pairs for self-supervised learning compared with [19]. (c) In our novel framework, self-training iterates with soft cluster assignment over the outlier-free pseudo labels, achieving the state-of-the-art on most of the mainstream datasets in terms of two popular metrics.

2   Related Work

In this section, we will provide a briefly introduction to recent developments in two related topics: self-supervised learning and short text clustering.

---

[1] Our code is available at https://github.com/zhoufangquan/NPLC.

2.1 Self-supervised Learning

Recent years have witnessed the rapid development of self-supervised learning, which provides effective representations for many downstream tasks. Early research concentrates on addressing various artificially designed pretext tasks to improve the quality of text representation. For example, BERT [4] uses two pre-training tasks: Mask Language Model and Next Sentence Prediction. Based on BERT, SentenceBERT [14] designs a task to improve text semantic similarity of sentence pairs which is conducted by a Siamese bert-networks.

On the other hand, Instance-CL promoted the development of self-supervised learning and gained many successes [5,8,16]. Importantly, constructing effective positive pairs is crucial for Instance-CL. SimCSE [5] directly utilizes the dropout in BERT as noise to create positive pairs by encoding an instance twice, resulting in better performance compared to SentenceBERT. The two instances of positive pair conducted in this way have the same length, which tends to make sentences of the same or similar length more similar in semantics. To alleviate this problem, ESimCSE [16] applies a repetition operation to modify the input sentence, then the two instances of positive pair have different lengths. Based on the powerful potential of BERT, PromptBERT [8] finds prompts can provide a better way to generate positive pairs by different viewpoints from different templates.

2.2 Short Text Clustering

As we mentioned before, short texts often lack context and can be ambiguous, making it difficult to identify their meanings and relationships accurately. Therefore, methods based on BoW and TF-IDF often add external knowledge resources to enrich the very sparse representation vectors that lack expressive ability [12], and then apply K-means to gain the cluster assignment.

In addition, neural networks can be used to enrich the text representation and clustering, where various word embeddings are used to boost performance. STCC [17] pre-trains word embedding on a large in-domain corpus using the Word2Vec method, then optimizes a CNN to enrich the representations further. Self-Train [6] uses Smooth Inverse Frequency (SIF) [2] to gain the text vectors, then leverages an autoencoder to pre-train the encoder by reconstructing these vectors. Finally, the pre-trained encoder is fine-tuned by minimizing the distance between the clustering probability distribution and an auxiliary target distribution. SCCL [19] leverages contrastive learning to improve representation learning and a clustering objective same as Self-Train for clustering learning. By optimizing the contrastive loss and clustering loss jointly, SCCL achieves better separated text representation. HAC-SD [13] proposes an iterative classification method to enhance the effect of initial clustering.

Although SCCL and HAC-SD have achieved good results, they both strongly rely on the initial short text representation. In this paper, before joint training, we first leverage MLM to pre-train SentenceBERT [14] to improve the quality of initial short text representation. Different from SCCL, we utilize the pseudo-labels from non-outliers in each cluster to alleviate the influence of intrinsic

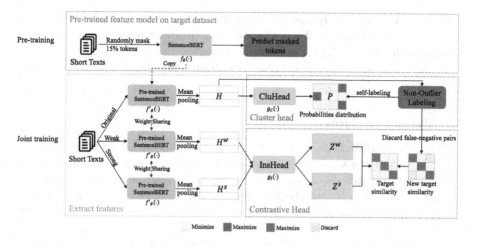

Fig. 2. The pipeline of our method

false-negative pairs, which can make the grouping effect of contrastive learning better and more stable. What's more, our pseudo-labels are obtained from the entire dataset, which contributes to our superior cluster performance.

3   Method

We aim to cluster a set of N short texts $\mathcal{X} = \{x_j\}_{j=1}^{N}$ into K classes by training our model without using any annotations. As illustrated in Fig 2, we use SentenceBERT as our feature model and our method consists of two parts: (1) We first use MLM to pre-train SentenceBERT on dataset $\mathcal{X}$; (2) we utilize the pre-trained SentenceBERT for a joint training, and the framework of this part comprises three components: a pre-trained SentenceBERT that extracts feature vectors from original texts and their augmentations, a cluster head that projects feature vectors to the probabilities over K classes, and a contrastive head that maps feature vectors to a 128-dimensional subspace. In the following subsections, we will elaborate on the two parts in turn.

3.1   Pre-train

Though SentenceBERT is effective for short text representation, it still has problems of poor purity and significant overlap across categories when clustering a given dataset. To this end, we use MLM to pre-train SentenceBERT and enhance the quality of short text representation on a specified dataset. As illustrated in Fig. 1(a) and Fig. 1(b), after pre-training, the purity of text representation on StackOverflow is higher. Following BERT [4], we randomly mask 15% of the input tokens, then use SentenceBERT $f_\theta(\cdot)$ to predict the original vocabulary id of the masked word based only on the input context. When the loss value is less than 0.055, we stop pre-training and use the pre-trained SentenceBERT $f'_\theta(\cdot)$ for the next joint training. When the loss value is about 0.055, we get the best average results on the eight benchmark datasets.

In the following three subsections, we will give the details about framework in the second part.

3.2 Extract Features

We select a minibatch $\mathcal{B} = \{x_i\}_{i=1}^M$ from the whole dataset $\mathcal{X}$ at random, and then generate a weak augmented minibatch $\mathcal{B}^w = \{x_i^w\}_{i=1}^M$ and a strong augmented minibatch $\mathcal{B}^s = \{x_i^s\}_{i=1}^M$, where M is batch size. In Sect. 4.2, we will detail how to generate the two augmentations. The aforementioned pre-trained SentenceBERT $f'_\theta(\cdot)$ is used to extract features from $\mathcal{B}$, $\mathcal{B}^w$ and $\mathcal{B}^s$ by $h_i = f'_\theta(x_i)$, $h_i^w = f'_\theta(x_i^w)$ and $h_i^s = f'_\theta(x_i^s)$.

As we don't have ground truth labels to train the clustering head and help the contrastive head to alleviate the influence of false-negative pairs, we introduce a non-outlier pseudo-labeling algorithm to generate pseudo labels to solve the two problems. Specifically, we get cluster labels $\mathcal{Y}' = \{y'_j\}_{j=1}^N$ by clustering $\mathcal{X}$ into K clusters. Then we apply an outlier detection algorithm called Isolation Forest [3] to select outliers in each cluster and set their cluster labels to -1. We use the cluster labels as pseudo labels to help train the two heads. It is worth noting that as the training goes on, we will update the pseudo labels every 50 mini-batches.

3.3 Compute Clustering Loss with Non-Outlier Pseudo-Labeling

The Clustering head includes a two-layer nonlinear MLP $g_C(\cdot)$, which maps feature vector h_i into a K-dimension vector p_i. The k-th element of p_i, $p_i[k]$, represents the probability of belonging to the k-th cluster. Formally, given the feature matrix $H = \{h_i\}_{i=1}^M$, we use clustering head to project it into probability matrix $P = \{p_i\}_{i=1}^M \in \mathbb{R}^{M \times K}$ via $p_i = g_C(h_i)$. We aim to train the clustering head only for predicting the cluster labels.

Based on the pseudo labels $\mathcal{Y}'$ of $\mathcal{X}$, we optimize the parameters of pre-trained SentenceBERT and clustering head by the following weighted cross-entropy loss function:

$$\mathcal{L}_1 = -\frac{1}{|\mathbf{S}|} \sum_{i \in \mathbf{S}} w_{y'_i} \log \left(\frac{\exp(p_i[y'_i])}{\sum_{k=0}^{K-1} \exp(p_i[k])} \right) \tag{1}$$

where $\mathbf{S} \equiv \{i | y'_i \neq -1, x_i \in \mathcal{B}\}$ is the index set of non-outliers in $\mathcal{B}$, and $w_k \propto 1/N_k$ is the weight parameter for cluster k whose size is N_k and can prevent large clusters from distorting the hidden feature space.

3.4 Compute Contrastive Loss with Non-Outlier Pseudo-Labeling

The objective of contrastive head is to maximize the similarities of positive pairs and minimize negative pairs. To improve the quality of negative pairs, we

---

Algorithm 1 . Non-outlier Pseudo-Labeling for Short Text Clustering

---

Input: dataset $\mathcal{X}$, cluster number K, SentenceBERT $f_\theta(\cdot)$, contrastive head $g_I(\cdot)$, cluster head $g_C(\cdot)$, batch size M, temperature parameter τ, iteration number L.

Output: cluster assignments

1: // pre-training part
2: pre-training $f_\theta(\cdot)$ on $\mathcal{X}$ by MLM until loss value is less than 0.055
3: get pre-trained SentenceBERT $f'_\theta(\cdot)$
4: // training part
5: compute pseudo labels $\mathcal{Y}'$ with pre-trained SentenceBERT $f'_\theta(\cdot)$
6: **for** $l = 1 \rightarrow L$ **do**
7:      randomly select a mini-batch $\mathcal{B}$ from $\mathcal{X}$
8:      get two augmentations $\mathcal{B}^w$ and $\mathcal{B}^s$
9:      extract feature vectors H, H^w, H^s
10:     compute clustering loss $\mathcal{L}_1$ and contrastive loss $\mathcal{L}_2$ by Eq.(1) and Eq.(3)
11:     compute total loss $\mathcal{L}$ by Eq.(4) and Eq.5
12:     update f_θ', g_I, g_C by minimizing $\mathcal{L}$
13:     **if** l mod 50 == 0 **then**
14:         update pseudo labels $\mathcal{Y}'$ with current SentenceBERT $f'_\theta(\cdot)$
15:     **end if**
16: **end for**
17: // test part
18: **for** x in $\mathcal{X}$ **do**
19:     extract features through $h = f_\theta'(x)$
20:     compute cluster assignment through $c = \arg\max_k(g_C(h))$
21: **end for**
22: **return** $C = \{c_i\}_{i=1}^N$

---

use aforementioned pseudo labels $\mathcal{Y}'$ to alleviate the influence of intrinsic false-negative pairs. Formally, the contrastive head is also a two-layer nonlinear MLP $g_I(\cdot)$, which projects feature vectors h_i^w and h_i^s into 128-dimension vectors z_i^w and z_i^s via $z_i^{w,s} = g_I(x_i^{w,s})$. We then minimize the following for x_i^w,

$$l_i^w = -\log \frac{e^{s(z_i^w, z_i^s)/\tau}}{\sum_{j \in \mathbf{N}_i}(e^{s(z_i^w, z_j^w)/\tau} + e^{s(z_i^w, z_j^s)/\tau}) + e^{s(z_i^w, z_i^s)/\tau}} \quad (2)$$

Here $\mathbf{N}_i \equiv \{j | x_j^w \in \mathcal{B}^w, y_i' \neq y_j' \ or \ y_j' = -1\}$ is the index set that does not belong to the same cluster as x_i, $s(z_1, z_2) = z_1^\top z_2 / \|z_1\|_2 \|z_2\|_2$ is a dot product between a pair of normalized outputs and τ is the temperature parameter which is set as 0.5. The computation method of l_i^s is similar to that of l_i^w.

The contrastive loss is averaged over all insrances in $\mathcal{B}^w$ and $\mathcal{B}^s$,

$$\mathcal{L}_2 = \frac{1}{2M} \sum_{i=1}^M (l_i^w + l_i^s) \quad (3)$$

We use a adjustment function λ to dynamically adjust the weight of contrastive loss $\mathcal{L}_2$. In summary, the overall objective loss function is,

$$\mathcal{L} = \mathcal{L}_1 + \lambda \mathcal{L}_2 \quad (4)$$

where the adjustment function is a monotonic decreasing function with a value interval of $[5, 15]$, namely,

$$\lambda(l) = 10 + 5 \cos\left(\frac{l}{L}\pi\right), l \in [0, L] \tag{5}$$

where l is the current iteration number and L is the expected total iteration number.

The total process is summarized in Algorithm 1.

4   Experiments

4.1   Datasets and Evaluation Metrics

We evaluate the effectiveness of NPLC method on eight widely-used datasets for clustering short texts. The left part of Table 1 shows a summary of the main statistics for all 8 datasets. AgNews is a subset of news titles [20], which contains 4 topics selected by [13]. StackOverflow is a collection of posts from question and answer site stackoverflow, published by Kaggle. This subset contains question titles from 20 different categories are selected by [17]. SearchSnippets is a text collection comprising web search snippets whose texts represent sets of keywords, rather than being coherent texts. Biomedical is a subset of the PubMed data distributed by BioASQ, which contains many special terms from biology and medicine [17]. The GoogleNewsTS, GoogleNewsT, GoogleNewsS and Tweet sets were exactly those datasets which are used in [18]. The first four datasets contain relatively low cluster counts ranging from 4 to 20, while the last four datasets have greater cluster counts ranging from 89 to 152.

Table 1. The left part is a summary of datasets used for evaluations (**N**: sample count; **Len**: average word count per sample; **K**: cluster count; **L**: the largest cluster; **S**: the smallest cluster). The right part are results of pre-trained SentenceBERT evaluated with two clustering algorithms: K-means and HAC.

Dataset	Documents		Clusters			K-means		HAC	
	N	Len	K	L	S	ACC	NMI	ACC	NMI
AgNews	8000	23	4	2K	2K	**80.6**	**57.8**	75.1	50.2
StackOverflow	20000	8	20	1K	1K	**79.8**	**75.3**	65.2	63.8
Biomedical	20000	13	20	1K	1K	**45.2**	**39.3**	38.9	33.2
SearchSnippets	12340	18	8	2.66K	0.37K	**75.1**	**60.2**	60.9	56.5
GooglenewsTS	11109	28	152	430	3	65.5	84.5	**83.5**	**92.8**
GooglenewsS	11109	22	152	430	3	64.0	81.4	**79.3**	**90.1**
GooglenewsT	11109	6	152	430	3	62.9	75.9	**77.5**	**89.3**
Tweet	2472	8	89	249	1	56.4	82.1	**82.0**	**91.3**

Following the previous works [6, 17, 19], two widely-used clustering metrics Accuracy (ACC) and Normalized Mutual Information (NMI) are adopt to evaluate our method.

4.2   Implementation Details

For pre-training, we choose distilbert-base-nli-stsb-mean-tokens in Sentence-BERT library [14] as feature model and use MLM to pre-train it on the target dataset.

For generating pseudo labels, compared with Hierarchical Agglomerative Clustering (HAC), K-means exhibits better clustering performance in terms of the former four datasets with fewer clusters, while HAC outperforms K-means in terms of the latter four datasets with more clusters (see the right part of Table 1).

For the joint training, we use the pre-trained SentenceBERT as the backbone, followed by two heads which are both two-layer nonlinear MLPs. One is the clustering head with one hidden layer of size 768, and output vectors of size K, where K is predefined as the class count on the target dataset as shown in Table 1; the other one is contrastive head with one hidden layer of size 768, and output vectors of size 128. The learning rate of the feature extractor is 5e-6, and that of two heads are 5e-4. We set the batch size to 800, the total number of iterations to 1000, the temperature parameter $\tau = 0.5$.

For augmented data, following the SCCL setting [19], we perform weak augmentation by randomly substituting 20% of the words in each text with their top-N appropriate words obtained from the pre-trained Roberta model in the Contextual Augmenter Library [9]; we employ four strong augmentation operations proposed by EDA [15] with a probability of 0.2 each, namely SynonymReplacement, RandomInsertion, RandomSwap, and RandomDeletion.

4.3   Results

We evaluate the proposed NPLC on 8 challenging short text datasets and compare it with 6 representative state-of-the-art clustering approaches, including Bow, TF-IDF, STCC [17], Self-Train [6], HAC-SD [13], SCCL [19]. Following the SCCL [19], we do not apply any pre-processing procedures on any of the 8 datasets either. However, STCC [17] & Self-Train [6] preprocessed Biomedical dataset and HAC-SD [13] preprocessed all 8 datasets by removing the stop words, punctuation, and converting the text to lower case.

The clustering results on 8 datasets shown in Table 2 demonstrate the promising performance of NPLC. It is worth noting that our method outperforms all baselines by a large margin on StackOverflow and performs best on the last four datasets in terms of NMI. Due to pre-training word embeddings on a large in-domain biomedical corpus, Self-Train [6] outperforms our method on Biomedical. SCCL [19] or HAC-SD [13] show better Accuracy on Tweet and GoogleNews than our method, for which we hypothesize three reasons: 1) both Tweet and GoogleNews have fewer training samples and more clusters, while contrastive learning requires a large training samples to guarantee its performance; 2) cluster head exhibits performance degradation when the cluster count is large; 3) due to applying agglomerative cluster on carefully selected pairwise similarities of preprocessed data, HAC-SD [13] can achieve better performance when text

Table 2. Clustering results for 8 short text datasets. Performance results are averaged over 5 random runs.

	AgNews		StackOverflow		Biomedical		SearchSnippets	
	ACC	NMI	ACC	NMI	ACC	NMI	ACC	NMI
Bow	27.6	2.6	18.5	14.0	14.3	9.2	24.3	9.3
TF-IDF	34.5	11.9	58.4	58.7	28.3	23.2	31.5	19.2
STCC	–	–	51.1	49.0	43.6	38.1	77.0	63.2
Self-Train	–	–	59.8	54.8	**54.8**	**47.1**	77.1	56.7
HAC-SD	81.8	54.6	64.8	59.5	40.1	33.5	82.7	63.8
SCCL	88.2	68.2	75.5	74.5	46.2	41.5	85.2	**71.1**
NPLC	**88.7**	**68.5**	**88.1**	**80.9**	48.9	42.6	**85.4**	69.0

	GooglenewsTS		GooglenewsT		GooglenewsS		Tweet	
	ACC	NMI	ACC	NMI	ACC	NMI	ACC	NMI
Bow	57.5	81.9	49.8	73.2	49.0	73.5	49.7	73.6
TF-IDF	68.0	88.9	58.9	79.3	61.9	83.0	57.0	80.7
STCC	–	–	–	–	–	–	–	–
Self-Train	–	–	–	–	–	–	–	–
HAC-SD	85.8	88.0	**81.8**	84.2	80.6	83.5	**89.6**	85.2
SCCL	89.8	94.9	75.2	88.3	**83.1**	90.4	78.2	89.2
NPLC	87.5	**95.5**	78.3	**90.8**	82.3	**91.8**	89.4	**93.5**

instances are very short and few. SCCL [19] performs better NMI than NPLC on SearchSnippets, for which we hypothesize that texts in SearchSnippets are incoherent, thus the pre-training strategy do not perform as well as expected.

We track the inter-cluster distance and inter-cluster distance evaluated in the feature space in the process of joint training. As shown in Fig. 3, with the progress of training, inter-cluster distance is getting bigger and bigger and intra-cluster distance is getting smaller and smaller as a whole. The contrastive loss domi-

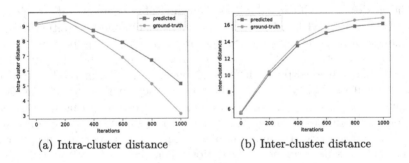

(a) Intra-cluster distance   (b) Inter-cluster distance

Fig. 3. Cluster-level evaluation on StackOverflow

nates in early training phase and samples are initially scattered in the feature space, hence the initial intra-cluster distance is big. Later, as training progresses, the training focus on clustering loss and the outlier-free samples are gradually clustered together.

4.4 Ablation Study

In this subsection, we conduct two ablation experiments to better validate our method.

Effectiveness of the Pre-training Strategy: To verify the effectiveness of pre-training strategy on NPLC and SCCL, we apply the pre-trained Sentence-BERT to SCCL [19], and conduct our NPLC without pre-training on StackOverflow, Tweet and Biomedical. As shown in Table 3, our NPLC and SCCL [19] both perform better on ACC and NMI after using pre-trained SentenceBERT. Moreover, our method can gain a greater margin for improvement based on pre-trained SentenceBERT. After using pre-trained SentenceBERT, our method achieves a maximum improvement of 12.9% (8.6%) on ACC (NMI), surpassing the maximum improvement of 10.1% (2.3%) achieved by SCCL.

Table 3. Effectiveness of the pre-training strategy. "SCCL^{+}" refers to results by reproducting SCCL with pre-trained SentenceBERT. "NPLC^{-}" refers to results by conducting our NPLC without pre-trained SentenceBERT.

	StackOverflow		Tweet		Biomedical	
	ACC	NMI	ACC	NMI	ACC	NMI
SCCL	75.5	74.5	78.2	89.2	46.2	41.5
SCCL^{+}	85.6 (+10.1)	76.6 (+2.1)	83.1 (+4.9)	91.5 (+2.3)	47.7 (+1.5)	42.0 (+0.5)
NPLC^{-}	75.2	74.1	77.6	88.3	40.3	39.9
NPLC	**88.1** (+12.9)	**80.9** (+6.8)	**89.4** (+11.8)	**93.5** (+5.2)	**48.9** (+8.6)	**42.6** (+2.7)

Effectiveness of Joint Training and Pseudo Labels: To verify the effectiveness of joint training, we evaluate NPLC on StackOverflow, Tweet and Biomedical against its fixed weight version, which fixes the weights of contrastive loss during joint training and its sequential version where we first train the contrastive head well and then train the other clustering head. For all three versions, we evaluate contrastive loss $\mathcal{L}_2$ against the loss where $\mathcal{L}_2$ doesn't leverage pseudo labels to filter out potential false-negative pairs, i.e. substituting $\mathbf{N}_i$ in Eq. (2) with $\mathbf{N}_i' \equiv \{j | x_j^w \in \mathcal{B}^w, i \neq j\}$. As shown in Table 4, the performance of clustering is improved after using pseudo labels to relieve the influence of intrinsic false-negative pairs. $\mathcal{L}_1 + \lambda \mathcal{L}_2$ outperforms its fixed weight version ($\mathcal{L}_1 + \mathcal{L}_2$) and sequential version (seq($\mathcal{L}_2$, $\mathcal{L}_1$)) on both $\mathbf{N}_i$ and $\mathbf{N}_i'$. We make two conjectures for our success: a) the two loss functions in NPLC could keep mutually promoting each other as the training goes on; b) by gradually decreasing the weight of contrastive loss, the focus of training shifts to clustering loss so that outlier-free samples gradually become closer.

Table 4. Effectiveness of joint training and pseudo labels

pseudo labels	Training model	Tweet		StackOverflow		Biomedical	
		ACC	NMI	ACC	NMI	ACC	NMI
$\mathbf{N}_i'$	$\mathrm{seq}(\mathcal{L}_2, \mathcal{L}_1)$	80.5	90.2	81.5	75.9	45.1	38.9
	$\mathcal{L}_1 + \mathcal{L}_2$	83.9	91.6	84.9	77.1	45.9	39.1
	$\mathcal{L}_1 + \lambda\mathcal{L}_2$	86.3	92.4	86.3	78.4	46.3	40.4
$\mathbf{N}_i$	$\mathrm{seq}(\mathcal{L}_2, \mathcal{L}_1)$	81.4	91.2	83.6	76.8	45.8	39.8
	$\mathcal{L}_1 + \mathcal{L}_2$	86.9	92.6	86.9	79.1	47.1	41.1
	$\mathcal{L}_1 + \lambda\mathcal{L}_2$	**89.4**	**93.5**	**88.1**	**80.9**	**48.9**	**42.6**

5 Conclusion

In this paper, we propose a method named NPLC, which leverages MLM to enhance the quality of initial text representation and introduce outlier-free pseudo labels to combine contrastive loss with clustering loss to learn instance-level correlation and cluster-level discrepancy of data. We evaluate our method on eight short text clustering datasets and achieved comparable results than state-of-the-art methods. In addition, we conduct two ablation experiments to verify the validity of our method. The first ablation experiment demonstrates that the pre-training strategy effectively improves clustering performance and can also work well in combination with other methods. The second ablation experiment demonstrates that filtering out potential false-negative pairs based on non-outlier pseudo labels can alleviate the influence of intrinsic false-negative pairs in contrastive loss. In the future, we will conduct more tests on clustering wild datasets from social media, making NPLC more practical.

Acknowledgements. This work is supported by the Fundamental Research Funds for the Central Universities under Grants XGBDFZ04 and ZYGX2019F005, and Sichuan Provincial Social Science Programs Project under Grants SC22EZD065.

References

1. Ahmed, M.H., Tiun, S., Omar, N., Sani, N.S.: Short text clustering algorithms, application and challenges: a survey. Appl. Sci. **13**(1), 342 (2023)
2. Arora, S., Liang, Y., Ma, T.: A simple but tough-to-beat baseline for sentence embeddings. In: International Conference on Learning Representations (2017)
3. Cheng, Z., Zou, C., Dong, J.: Outlier detection using isolation forest and local outlier factor. In: Proceedings of the Conference on Research in Adaptive and Convergent Systems, pp. 161–168 (2019)
4. Devlin, J., Chang, M., Lee, K., Toutanova, K.: BERT: pre-training of deep bidirectional transformers for language understanding. In: Burstein, J., Doran, C., Solorio, T. (eds.) Proceedings of the 2019 Conference of the North American Chapter of the Association for Computational Linguistics: Human Language Technologies, NAACL-HLT 2019, Minneapolis, MN, USA, 2–7 June 2019, Volume 1 (Long and Short Papers), pp. 4171–4186 (2019)

5. Gao, T., Yao, X., Chen, D.: SimCSE: simple contrastive learning of sentence embeddings. In: Proceedings of the 2021 Conference on Empirical Methods in Natural Language Processing, pp. 6894–6910. Online and Punta Cana, Dominican Republic, November 2021

6. Hadifar, A., Sterckx, L., Demeester, T., Develder, C.: A self-training approach for short text clustering. In: Proceedings of the 4th Workshop on Representation Learning for NLP (RepL4NLP-2019), pp. 194–199. Florence, Italy, August 2019

7. He, M., Ma, C., Wang, R.: A data-driven approach for university public opinion analysis and its applications. Appl. Sci. **12**(18), 9136 (2022)

8. Jiang, T., et al.: PromptBERT: improving BERT sentence embeddings with prompts. In: Proceedings of the 2022 Conference on Empirical Methods in Natural Language Processing, pp. 8826–8837. Abu Dhabi, United Arab Emirates, December 2022

9. Ma, E.: Nlp augmentation. https://github.com/makcedward/nlpaug (2019)

10. Mredula, M.S., Dey, N., Rahman, M.S., Mahmud, I., Cho, Y.Z.: A review on the trends in event detection by analyzing social media platforms & data. Sensors **22**(12), 4531 (2022)

11. Orǎsan, C.: Automatic summarisation: 25 years on. Natural Lang. Eng. **25**(6), 735–751 (2019)

12. Radford, A., Wu, J., Child, R., Luan, D., Amodei, D., Sutskever, I., et al.: Language models are unsupervised multitask learners. OpenAI blog **1**(8), 9 (2019)

13. Rashadul Hasan Rakib, M., Zeh, N., Jankowska, M., Milios, E.: Enhancement of short text clustering by iterative classification. arXiv e-prints pp. arXiv-2001 (2020)

14. Reimers, N., Gurevych, I.: Sentence-bert: Sentence embeddings using siamese bert-networks. In: Proceedings of the 2019 Conference on Empirical Methods in Natural Language Processing, November 2019

15. Wei, J., Zou, K.: EDA: easy data augmentation techniques for boosting performance on text classification tasks. In: Proceedings of the 2019 Conference on Empirical Methods in Natural Language Processing and the 9th International Joint Conference on Natural Language Processing (EMNLP-IJCNLP), pp. 6382–6388. Hong Kong, China, November 2019

16. Wu, X., Gao, C., Zang, L., Han, J., Wang, Z., Hu, S.: ESimCSE: enhanced sample building method for contrastive learning of unsupervised sentence embedding. In: Proceedings of the 29th International Conference on Computational Linguistics, pp. 3898–3907. Gyeongju, Republic of Korea, October 2022

17. Xu, J., Xu, B., Wang, P., Zheng, S., Tian, G., Zhao, J.: Self-taught convolutional neural networks for short text clustering. Neural Netw. **88**, 22–31 (2017)

18. Yin, J., Wang, J.: A model-based approach for text clustering with outlier detection. In: 2016 IEEE 32nd International Conference on Data Engineering (ICDE), pp. 625–636. Los Alamitos, CA, USA, May 2016

19. Zhang, D., et al.: Supporting clustering with contrastive learning. In: Proceedings of the 2021 Conference of the North American Chapter of the Association for Computational Linguistics: Human Language Technologies, pp. 5419–5430, June 2021

20. Zhang, X., LeCun, Y.: Text understanding from scratch. arXiv preprint arXiv:1502.01710 (2015)

Optimal Node Embedding Dimension
Selection Using Overall Entropy

Xinrun Xu[1,2], Zhiming Ding[1], Yurong Wu[1,2], Jin Yan[1,2], Shan Jiang[3(✉)],
and Qinglong Cui[4]

[1] Institute of Software Chinese Academy of Science, Beijing, China
[2] University of Chinese Academy of Sciences, Beijing, China
[3] Advanced Institute of Big Data, Beijing, China
`jiangshan@alumni.nudt.edu.cn`
[4] Beijing Institute of Control Engineering, Beijing, China

Abstract. Graph node embedding learning has gained significant attention with the advancement of graph neural networks (GNNs). The essential purpose of graph node embedding is down-scaling high-dimensional graph features to a lower-dimensional space while maximizing the retention of original structural information. This paper focuses on selecting the appropriate graph node embedding dimension for hidden layers, ensuring the effective representation of node information and preventing overfitting. We propose an algorithm based on the entropy minimization principle, called Minimum Overall Entropy (MOE), which combines graph node structural information and attribute information. We refer to one-dimensional and multi-dimensional structural entropy (MDSE) as a graph's structural entropy. A novel algorithm combines graph Shannon entropy, MDSE, and prior knowledge for faster convergence of optimal MDSE. We introduce an inner product-based metric, attribute entropy, to quantify node characteristics and simplify its calculation. Extensive experiments on Cora, Citeseer, and Pubmed datasets reveal that MOE, requiring just one computation round, surpasses baseline GNNs.

Keywords: Graph Neural Networks (GNNs) · Graph node embedding dimension · Structural entropy

1 Introduction

GNNs are a practical approach for learning graph representation, replacing network embeddings in graph ML [14]. GNNs have been successful in CV and NLP [34] but can lose graph structure information due to dimensionality reduction. Graph embedding algorithms, developed to address these challenges, map high-dimensional graph data to low-dimensional vectors while preserving structural information and features [15,36]. Graph embedding allows efficient integration of graph data into machine learning algorithms. The main challenges include selecting appropriate distance metrics and node properties, scalability, and determining

Supported by the National Key R&D Program of China (No. 2022YFF0503900) and Key R&D Program of Shandong Province (No. 2021CXGC010104).

L. Iliadis et al. (Eds.): ICANN 2023, LNCS 14262, pp. 114–127, 2023.
https://doi.org/10.1007/978-3-031-44201-8_10

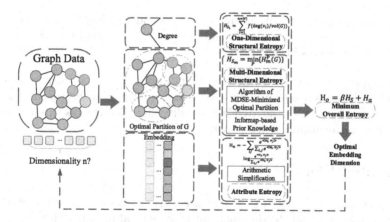

Fig. 1. The Minimum Overall Entropy (MOE) framework applies the principle of entropy reduction to determine optimal node embedding dimension (ONED). It establishes a connection between structural entropy, attribute entropy. MOE efficiently preserves a significant amount of graph's information while selecting an appropriate embedding dimension.

optimal embedding dimension. Over the past decade, embedding algorithms have evolved into three categories: (1) decomposition-based methods like HOPE [18], (2) random walk-based methods such as node2vec [8], and (3) deep learning-based methods including GCN [7,12]. Finding the optimal dimensionality is challenging as higher dimension improve accuracy but increase complexity, while lower dimension reduce complexity but sacrifice essential information. In this paper, we propose a novel method inspired by multi-dimensional structural information metric for graphs [13] and paired inner products for word embedding dimension [38]. We define the graph's overall entropy and relate it to structural entropy (including one-dimensional structural entropy (ODSE), multi-dimensional structural entropy (MDSE)) and attribute entropy. To tackle large graph MDSE computation, we propose a new algorithm and demonstrate its feasibility. We introduce the Informap-based PK approach, using prior knowledge (PK) [24] to reduce MDSE time complexity. Our approach utilizes attribute entropy from node pair inner products for computing graph features and introduces a simplified calculation method for computational efficiency. We also develop a new algorithm, MOE, following the entropy minimization principle to determine ONED. The algorithm flowchart is depicted in Fig. 1. The contributions of our paper are as follows:

1. We present a minimum entropy-based algorithm for ONED and preserving essential information by analyzing graph features, structural and attribute information.
2. We create and validate a PK-based algorithm to reduce MDSE time complexity for large graphs.
3. We suggest attribute entropy to measure graph node characteristics, utilizing node pair inner products to determine ONED. Our streamlined method significantly lowers time complexity.

4. We conduct extensive experiments on GNNs and benchmark datasets, evaluating MOE's generality and efficiency in downstream tasks like link prediction (LP) and node classification (NC).

The paper is structured as follows: Sect. 2 reviews related work on optimal embedding dimension selection and structural information. Section 3 describes MOE. Section 4 evaluates the MOE's generality and effectiveness through experiments. Section 5 concludes this paper.

2 Related Work

In this section, we provide a review of previous studies on optimal embedding dimension selection and the development of structural information theory.

Selecting an appropriate embedding dimension is critical for accurately capturing semantic and structural relationships in entity geometry, which significantly impacts the performance of downstream deep learning tasks [20,31]. Typically, default dimensional parameters (e.g., 100, 200, 300) are chosen for word embeddings to balance model performance and parameter count due to limited semantic space variation [9,11,19]. Yin et al. [38] compared embeddings of different dimension using a loss function based on the pairwise inner product between entities. However, complex and variable graph data structures necessitate adjusting dimensional parameters for different graphs. Graph embedding techniques map nodes to vectors by capturing a graph's structural information [8,10,12,21]. GNNs are popular for graph-based tasks such as LP and NC due to their robust representation capabilities [33,34]. To minimize noise and redundancy, previous studies have focused on dimensionality reduction [15,16,30,35,40]. However, these methods may not accurately capture a graph's structure, leading to information loss [28]. GNNs often select hyperparameters based on downstream task performance rather than the relationship between embedding dimension and graph links, even though the total information in graph data may not be relevant to the task.

Quantifying structural information has been a significant challenge in computer and information science for over half a century, originating from Shannon's 1953 proposal [29], and is considered one of the three main challenges in these fields [3]. Early attempts include Rashevsky's graph entropy [22], and Bonchev and Trinajsti's distance-based graph entropy measure, with varying results due to different distance calculation methods [2]. Raychaudhury et al. developed the first local graph entropy measure based on vertex complexity [23]. Bianconi et al. employed an exponential function based on Shannon entropy to capture the relationship between network structure and node semantics [1]. Choi and Szpankowski defined structural entropy for network models [5], and Li and Pan introduced structural information measure and the MDSE method for detecting complexity in fundamental structures and dynamic networks [13]. Yi et al. proposed a graph-based dimensionality reduction framework for graph optimization and low-dimensional feature extraction [37], while Fang et al. developed an entropy-driven graph embedding method using two heuristics to determine random walk length and walks per node [6].

3   MOE

Shannon defined the information entropy of a probability distribution $\mathbf{p} = (p_1, p_2, ...p_n)$ as: $H(p_1, p_2, ...p_n) = -\sum_i^n p_i \log p_i$. This formula measures the uncertainty or randomness of a probability distribution $\mathbf{p} = (p_1, p_2, ...p_n)$. Lower entropy values indicate higher confidence in the information contained, suggesting its usefulness. However, when dealing with graph data containing rich network structures, relying solely on information entropy is insufficient. To address this limitation, we propose a comprehensive entropy measure that considers both node attributes and network structure, as defined in Definition 1 - 8 in this paper.

Definition 1. *(Overall Entropy of A Graph): Given the structural entropy H_S and attribute entropy H_a of a graph, the overall entropy H_o of this graph can be defined as $H_o = \beta H_S + H_a$, where β is a hyperparameter that controls the ratio of structural entropy for embedding dimension selection.*

Structural entropy can be categorized into ODSE and MDSE, while attribute entropy links node attributes with the ideal dimension n_{ideal}. By employing the minimum entropy principle [39] to determine the minimum value of H_o, we can directly compute ONED.

3.1   Structural Entropy

Structural entropy is the sum of ODSE and MDSE. ODSE quantifies the inherent uncertainty in a graph, while Optimal MDSE [13] assesses the uncertainty embedded in the graph under the optimal coding tree. The optimal coding tree represents an abstract hierarchical mathematical model and data structure of the graph. Its uncertainty magnitude influences the entropy of the MDSE.

Definition 2. *(Structural Entropy):We define structural entropy as follows:*

$$H_S = H_{S_1} + H_{S_m} \tag{1}$$

where H_{S_1}, H_{S_m} represent the ODSE and MDSE respectively.

Shannon entropy and structural entropy, although related, are distinct concepts. Shannon entropy quantifies the information in a probability distribution, while structural entropy measures the complexity of structures in real-world systems, accounting for uncertainty and assisting in system semantics and functional analysis. Therefore, structural entropy offers a more direct and meaningful approach to quantifying information in complex systems.

Definition 3. *(One-Dimensional Structural Entropy, ODSE): The ODSE of an undirected graph $G(V, E, W)$ is defined as follows:*

$$H_{S_1} = \sum_{i=1}^{n=|V|} f(\deg(v_i)/\mathrm{vol}(G)) \tag{2}$$

where $v_i \in V$ is the vertex of G, $\deg(v_i)$ is the degree of a vertex v_i, and $\mathrm{vol}(G) = \sum_{i=1}^{n=|V|} \deg(v_i)$ is the volume of G. Usually, the mathematical expression of $f(*)$ is defined as $f(x) = -x\log_2 x$, where $x \in [0,1]$ and $f(0) = f(1) = 0$. For graph with empty edge sets, $\mathrm{vol}(G) = 0$.

The ODSE principle involves extracting a probability distribution from a graph's structure to measure its information. Specifically, the graph's degree distribution's Shannon entropy serves as the ODSE of the graph, representing its static information encoded in a single dimension. In contrast, the MDSE captures the graph's dynamic information.

Definition 4. *(Multi-Dimensional Structural Entropy, MDSE). Given set $P = \{V_1, V_2, \cdots, V_L\}$ where $|P| = L$, $\sum_{i=1}^{L} |V_i| = |V|$, $V_i \in V$, $\cap V_i = \emptyset$ and $\cup V_i = V$, the MDSE [13] of an undirected graph $G(V, E, W)$ is defined as: $H_m^p(G) = \sum_{j=1}^{L}[\frac{\mathrm{vol}(V_j)}{\mathrm{vol}(G)} * \sum_{i=1}^{N_i} f(\deg(v_i^i)/\mathrm{vol}(V_j)) + \frac{g_j}{\mathrm{vol}(V_j)} * f(\mathrm{vol}(V_j)/\mathrm{vol}(G))]$, where g_i is the number of edges from V_i to nodes outside of V_i.*

When the starting point of a random walk is known, $H_m^p(G)$ represents the information conveyed by the codeword generated by the coding tree to identify the vertex that the random walk reaches in the graph G.

Definition 5. *(Optimal MDSE): The optimal MDSE of an undirected graph $G(V, E, W)$ is defined as: $H_{S_m} = \min_P \{H_m^P(G)\}$, where P runs over all partitions of G, i.e. P takes all encoding trees of G.*

H_{S_m} decodes a coding tree that minimizes uncertainty in codewords for vertices visited by random walks in a graph G, thereby reducing dynamic uncertainty in G. This method identifies the significant structure in G by generating the best encoding of G with minimal uncertainty during random walks. The resulting coding tree decodes the information stored in G, enabling the identification of regular structure, random variation, and noise. [13] found that the optimal encoding tree of a graph G correlates with the minimum MDSE. This is because H_{S_m} encodes the optimal priority tree P for G, reducing uncertainty in identifying random walks in G. P determines the substantive structure of G, which is also the least uncertain. The ODSE and MDSE can measure the depth of information in a graph and decode its significant structure, facilitating semantic analysis of the graph's structural information.

Definition 6. *(The Change of MDSE): We describe* $\Delta^p_{i,j}$ *as the change of MDSE when partition* V_i *and partition* V_j *are combined into one partition.*

$$\begin{aligned}
\Delta^p_{i,j}(G) = & H^P_m(V_i) + H^P_m(V_j) - H^P_m(V_i + V_j) = \frac{\text{vol}(V_i) - g_i}{\text{vol}(G)} \log_2 \frac{\text{vol}(V_i)}{\text{vol}(G)} \\
& + \frac{\text{vol}(V_j) - g_j}{\text{vol}(G)} \log_2 \frac{\text{vol}(V_j)}{\text{vol}(G)} - \frac{\text{vol}(V_{ij}) - g_{ij}}{\text{vol}(G)} \log_2 \frac{\text{vol}(V_{ij})}{\text{vol}(G)}
\end{aligned} \tag{3}$$

where $V_i \cup V_j = V_{ij}$, g_{ij} *is the number of edges from* V_{ij} *to nodes outside of* V_{ij}.

Theorem 1. *For nodes set* $V_i \in V$ *and* $V_j \in V$, *where* $V_i \cap V_j = \emptyset$. *If there is no edge between* V_i *and* V_j, $\Delta^p_{(i,j)}(G) \leq 0$ *is satisfied.*

Proof (Proof of Theorem 1). By definition of MDSE, for the partition P, if there is no edge between V_i and V_j, then $\text{vol}(V_i) + \text{vol}(V_j) = \text{vol}(V_{ij})$, $g_i + g_j = g_{ij}$. To simplify the notations, we relabel $\text{vol}(V_i) \rightarrow V_i$, and then

$$\begin{aligned}
\text{vol}(G) \cdot \Delta^p_{(i,j)}(G) = & \text{vol}(G) \cdot (H^P_m(V_i) + H^P_m(V_j) - H^P_m(V_i + V_j)) \\
= & (V_i - g_i) \log_2 \frac{V_i}{\text{vol}(G)} + (V_j - g_j) \log_2 \frac{V_j}{\text{vol}(G)} - (V_{ij} - g_{ij}) \log_2 \frac{V_{ij}}{\text{vol}(G)} \\
= & (V_i - g_i) \log_2 V_i + (V_j - g_j) \log_2 V_j - (V_{ij} - g_{ij}) \log_2 V_{ij} \\
& - (V_i + V_j - V_{ij} - g_i - g_j + g_{ij}) \log_2 \text{vol}(G) \\
= & (V_i - g_i) \log_2 (\frac{V_i}{V_i + V_j}) + (V_j - g_j) \log_2 (\frac{V_j}{V_i + V_j}) \leq 0
\end{aligned}$$

Finally, $\Delta^p_{(i,j)}(G) \leq 0$ holds in the Theorem 1.

This work presents an algorithm for approximating the optimal partition of a graph using the MDSE-minimized strategy, described in Algorithm 1. MMOP consists of three steps: first, singleton $P_i = v_i$ is partitioned from V; next, the minimized $\Delta^p_{(i,j)}(G)$ is found for all pairs P_i, P_j until no (P_i, P_j) satisfies $\Delta^p_{(i,j)}(P_i, P_j) < 0$; and finally, the partition is sorted by the node order in V. MMOP is a greedy algorithm that approximates optimal graph partitions by dividing nodes into clusters. To improve the time efficiency of MMOP, a Informap-based PK [24] mechanism is proposed, which partitions the graph in advance to reduce the number of comparison operations needed by MMOP. Section 4 demonstrates the efficiency of Informap-based PK through comparative experiments with other mainstream PK-based clustering algorithms.

3.2 Attribute Entropy

We have developed a novel approach that employs inner product of node pairs as basic unit, under the premise that embeddings of neighboring nodes are likely to be more similar.

Algorithm 1: MDSE-Minimized Optimal Partition (MMOP)

Input: $G(V, E, W)$ - The extracted structure from data points where $|V| = n$,
  $|E| = m$, and $W \in R^{n \times n}$ is adjacency weights matrix.

Output: $P = \{P_1, P_2, \cdots, P_L\}$ - Graph partition where $P_i \cap P_j = \varnothing$ and
  $\cup P_i = V$.

1   $\{P_1, P_2, \cdots, P_n\} \leftarrow CutVertex(V)$ where $P_i \cap P_j = \varnothing$, $\cup P_i = V$, and $|P_i| = 1$.

2   $\mathbf{P}_0 \leftarrow \{P_1, P_2, \cdots, P_n\}$.

3 **repeat**

4    $\delta_{max} \leftarrow 0.0, P_{min} \leftarrow \varnothing$.

5   **for** P_i in P_0 **do**

6      $P'_0 \leftarrow P_0 - P_i$.

7   **for** P_j in P'_0 **do**

8        $\Delta^P_{(i,j)} \leftarrow \Delta^P_{(i,j)}(P_i, /P_j).$ //Eq. (3).

9   **if** $\Delta^P_{(i,j)} < 0$ and $\Delta^P_{(i,j)} < \delta_{max}$ **then**

10          $\delta_{max} \leftarrow \Delta^P_{(i,j)}$.

11          $P_{min} \leftarrow P_j$.

12   **end**

13   **end**

14   **if** $P_{min} \neq \varnothing$ And $P_{min} \in P'_0$ **then**

15        $P'_0 \leftarrow P'_0 - P_{min}$.

16        $P'_0 \cdot Insert(\{P_i + P_j\})$.

17   **else**

18        $P'_0 \cdot Insert(\{P_i\})$.

19   **end**

20      $P_0 \leftarrow P'_0$.

21   **end**

22 **until** there is no (P_i, P_j) such that $\Delta^P_{(i,j)}(P_i, P_j) < 0$;

23 $P \leftarrow SortByOrder(P_0)$.

24 **return** P and Optimal MDSE H_{S_m}.

Definition 7. *(Probability of A Node Pair): Given a graph $G = (V, E)$, V and E denote graph's node and edge set, respectively. Given a pair of corresponding node embedding v_i and v_j, $\langle *, * \rangle$ is inner product operation. We define the probability of a node pair as:* $Q(v_i, v_j) = \dfrac{e^{\langle v_i, v_j \rangle}}{\sum_{i,j} e^{\langle v_i, v_j \rangle}}$. *It's simple to obtain, that* $0 \leq Q(v_i, v_j) \leq 1$ *and* $\sum_{ij} Q(v_i, v_j) = 1$.

Definition 8. *(Attribute Entropy): Given the probability of node pairs. The attribute entropy of graph data can be defined as follows:*

$$
\begin{aligned}
H_a &= -\sum_{ij} Q(v_i, v_j) \log Q(v_i, v_j) = -\sum_{ij} \frac{e^{\langle v_i, v_j \rangle}}{\sum_{i,j} e^{\langle v_i, v_j \rangle}} \log \frac{e^{\langle v_i, v_j \rangle}}{\sum_{i,j} e^{\langle v_i, v_j \rangle}} \\
&= \log \sum_{i,j} e^{\langle v_i, v_j \rangle} - \frac{\sum_{ij} e^{\langle v_i, v_j \rangle} \langle v_i, v_j \rangle}{\sum_{i,j} e^{\langle v_i, v_j \rangle}} \\
&= \log(N^2 \frac{1}{N^2} \sum_{ij} e^{\langle v_i, v_j \rangle}) - \frac{N^2 \frac{1}{N^2} \sum_{ij} e^{\langle v_i, v_j \rangle} \langle v_i, v_j \rangle}{N^2 \frac{1}{N^2} \sum_{ij} e^{\langle v_i, v_j \rangle}} \\
&\approx \log N^2 + \log E_{v_i, v_j}(e^{\langle v_i, v_j \rangle}) - \frac{E_{v_i, v_j}(e^{\langle v_i, v_j \rangle} \langle v_i, v_j \rangle)}{E_{v_i, v_j}(e^{\langle v_i, v_j \rangle})}
\end{aligned}
\tag{4}
$$

where E is expectation operation, and N is the total number of nodes for graph.

Building upon [17], we have derived a mathematical expression for the correlation between ONED (n_{ideal}) and inner product, presented as: $x = \langle v_i, v_j \rangle = n * \cos\theta$. The computation of expectation is demonstrated as: $E(f(\theta)) = \int_0^\pi f(\theta) P_n(\theta) d\theta$, where $P_n(\theta) = \frac{\Gamma(\frac{n}{2})}{\Gamma(\frac{n-1}{2})\sqrt{\pi}} \sin^{n-2}\theta$. Plugging Taylor's formula, we get final result:

$$
H_a = \log N^2 + \log \int_0^\pi \sum_{i=0}^{+\infty} \frac{x^i}{i!} P_n(\theta) d\theta - \frac{\int_0^\pi \sum_{i=0}^{+\infty} \frac{x^i}{i!} x P_n(\theta) d\theta}{\log \int_0^\pi \sum_{i=0}^{+\infty} \frac{x^i}{i!} P_n(\theta) d\theta}
\tag{5}
$$

3.3 Algorithm of MOE

Finally, the overall entropy can be described as follows:

$$
\begin{aligned}
H_o &= \beta H_S + H_a \\
&= \beta\left(\sum_{i=1}^{n=|V|} f(\deg(v_i)/\operatorname{vol}(G)) + H_{S_m} \right) + \\
&\quad \log N^2 + \log \int_0^\pi \sum_{i=0}^{+\infty} \frac{x^i}{i!} P_n(\theta) d\theta - \frac{\int_0^\pi \sum_{i=0}^{+\infty} \frac{x^i}{i!} x P_n(\theta) d\theta}{\log \int_0^\pi \sum_{i=0}^{+\infty} \frac{x^i}{i!} P_n(\theta) d\theta}
\end{aligned}
\tag{6}
$$

The measure of structural uncertainty in a graph is represented by structural entropy (H_S), which can be reduced through hierarchical abstraction. Minimizing the MDSE yields the inherent structure of system components, allowing for a deeper exploration of data space. On the other hand, attribute entropy (H_a) quantifies the correlation between node pairs and ONED (n_{ideal}). The MOE algorithm for solving the multi-objective optimization problem is presented in Algorithm 2, with its time complexity discussed in Sect. 4.

Algorithm 2: Minimum Overall Entropy (MOE)

Input: $G(V, E)$ - The extracted structure from data points where $|V| = n$, $|E| = m$; Hyperparameter β.

Output: The ideal node embedding dimension n_{ideal} of graph G.

1 Calculate the adjacency matrix W of the graph dataset G.

2 Calculate the ODSE $H_{S_1} \leftarrow$ Eq. (2).

3 Use Informap-based PK to pre-partition the graph.

4 Calculate the optimal MDSE H_{S_m} using PK information $\leftarrow$ Algorithm 1.

5 Calculate the structural entropy $H_S \leftarrow$ Eq. (1).

6 Estimate the attribute entropy $H_a \leftarrow$ Eq. (5).

7 Calculate the overall entropy $H_o \leftarrow$ Eq. (6).

8 Obtain the ideal node embedding dimension $n_{ideal} \leftarrow$ Minimum (H_o).

---

4   Experiments

4.1   Datasets and Baselines

This section aims to demonstrate the effectiveness of MOE on benchmark datasets, using standard GNNs. We evaluated MOE on two types of tasks, namely LP and NC, utilizing reputable benchmark datasets commonly used in GNN research, such as Cora, Citeseer, and Pubmed [27].

Our evaluation encompassed popular GNNs, including GCN [12], GAT [32], and GCNII [4], to test the generalizability and efficiency of MOE. For NC, we adopted dataset partition outlined in Table 1. For LP, we randomly divided the edges into training, validation, and test sets at a ratio of 85%, 5%, and 10%, respectively. To ensure a fair comparison, GNNs were set to a dimensional interval of 64 for both tasks. All experiments utilized an early stopping strategy on validation set, with patience of 100 epochs. The reported results are the average of 10 runs, and unless otherwise noted, the original paper's optimal protocol and hyperparameters were maintained.

Table 1. Overview of benchmark datasets in GNNs. Where * denotes the optimal dimension in our experiments.

Dataset	# Nodes	# Edges	# Features	# Classes	# Training Nodes	# Validation Nodes	# Test Nodes	*
Cora	2708	5429	1433	7	120	500	1000	91
Citeseer	3327	4732	3703	6	140	500	1000	112
Pubmed	19717	44338	4500	3	2000	500	1000	115

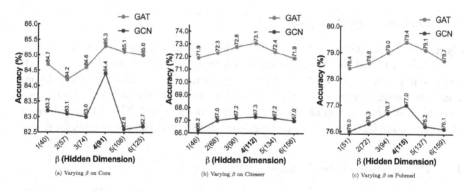

Fig. 2. Performance on NC with varying β, where horizontal axis is value of β and the number in brackets represents dimension of the last hidden layer.

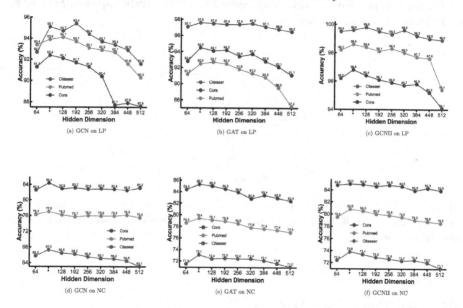

Fig. 3. Performance of MOE. Where * denotes ONED calculated by MOE.

4.2 Hyper-parameters Analysis

MOE uses a single hyperparameter β, to control the weight of structural entropy. By analyzing benchmark datasets with GCN and GAT, we found that setting $\beta = 4$ consistently results in peak accuracy for GNNs, as shown in Fig. 2. This is because structural entropy is a more significant factor than attribute entropy in MOE, as it decodes the underlying structure and supports semantic and functional analysis. For Cora, Citeseer, and Pubmed datasets, MOE computed ONED of 91, 112, and 115, respectively, in the last hidden layer of GNNs.

4.3 Performance Analysis

Figure 3 depicts the results of GNNs with different dimensions on benchmark datasets for LP and NC. GNNs with an appropriate dimension selected by MOE consistently achieve the best or near-best performance compared to other dimensions, demonstrating the effectiveness and generalizability of MOE. MOE measures both structural and attribute entropy to determine ONED of each dataset, capturing node features and link structures and leading to superior performance.

4.4 Prior Knowledge Analysis

We assess the efficiency of three clustering-based approaches for PK, specifically MiniBatch-K-Means [26], DBSCAN [25], and Informap [24]. Figure 4 illustrates that using PK, particularly Informap-based PK, significantly improves MMOP's performance and convergence speed.

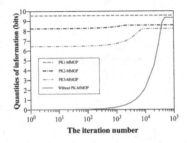

Fig. 4. The MMOP state updation with or without different PK initialization. Informap, MiniBatch-K-Means, and DBSCAN-based PK are represented as PK1, PK2, and PK3, respectively.

4.5 Time Complexity Analysis

In Fig. 4, we observe the complexity of Informap-based PK is significantly lower than DBSCAN-based PK, with the latter having a complexity of $O(n \log n)$, where n represents the number of graph nodes. The time complexity of MOE primarily depends on Informap-based PK (line 3 in Algorithm 2) and MMOP (line 4 in Algorithm 2), as other steps exhibit linear complexity. The time complexity of MMOP can be calculated as $O(k!)$, where k denotes the number of graph partitions after applying Informap-based PK. Given the sparse graph structures in our experiments, $O(k!) \ll O(n \log n)$, leading to an overall time complexity of MOE at $O(n \log n)$. It is worth noting that MOE requires a single execution on different datasets, whereas identifying ONED using traversal search necessitates multiple GNN runs, increasing computational burden and time.

5 Conclusion

We introduce MOE, an algorithm that integrates structural and attribute entropy to identify the optimal node embedding dimension for GNNs. Distinct from prior methods, MOE necessitates only a single calculation using the adjacency matrix, thereby eliminating repeated parameter adjustments. We evaluate MOE on widely-used GNNs and benchmark datasets, demonstrating its generality and efficiency. Furthermore, we propose an innovative algorithm for efficiently computing multidimensional structural entropy in large graphs. Our findings suggest that MOE is applicable to diverse GNNs, tasks, and datasets, as it successfully captures crucial graph properties and structural information.

References

1. Bianconi, G., Pin, P., Marsili, M.: Assessing the relevance of node features for network structure. Proc. Natl. Acad. Sci. **106**(28), 11433–11438 (2009)
2. Bonchev, D., Trinajstić, N.: Information theory, distance matrix, and molecular branching. J. Chem. Phys. **67**(10), 4517–4533 (1977)
3. Brooks, F.P., Jr.: Three great challenges for half-century-old computer science. J. ACM (JACM) **50**(1), 25–26 (2003)
4. Chen, M., Wei, Z., Huang, Z., Ding, B., Li, Y.: Simple and deep graph convolutional networks. In: International Conference on Machine Learning, pp. 1725–1735. PMLR (2020)
5. Choi, Y., Szpankowski, W.: Compression of graphical structures: fundamental limits, algorithms, and experiments. IEEE Trans. Inf. Theory **58**(2), 620–638 (2012)
6. Fang, P., et al.: How to realize efficient and scalable graph embeddings via an entropy-driven mechanism. IEEE Trans. Big Data **9**(1), 358–371 (2022)
7. Goyal, P., Ferrara, E.: Graph embedding techniques, applications, and performance: a survey. Knowl.-Based Syst. **151**, 78–94 (2018)
8. Grover, A., Leskovec, J.: node2vec: scalable feature learning for networks. In: Proceedings of the 22nd ACM SIGKDD International Conference on Knowledge Discovery and Data Mining, pp. 855–864 (2016)
9. Hamilton, W.L., Ying, R., Leskovec, J.: Inductive representation learning on large graphs. In: Proceedings of the 31st International Conference on Neural Information Processing Systems, pp. 1025–1035 (2017)
10. Hamilton, W.L., Ying, R., Leskovec, J.: Representation learning on graphs: methods and applications. In: Proceedings of the IEEE Data Engineering Bulletin, September 2017 (2017). http://sites.computer.org/debull/A17sept/p52.pdf
11. Huang, X., Song, Q., Li, Y., Hu, X.: Graph recurrent networks with attributed random walks. In: Proceedings of the 25th ACM SIGKDD International Conference on Knowledge Discovery & Data Mining, pp. 732–740 (2019)
12. Kipf, T.N., Welling, M.: Semi-supervised classification with graph convolutional networks. In: 5th International Conference on Learning Representations, ICLR 2017, Toulon, France, 24–26 April 2017, Conference Track Proceedings. OpenReview.net (2017). https://openreview.net/forum?id=SJU4ayYgl
13. Li, A., Pan, Y.: Structural information and dynamical complexity of networks. IEEE Trans. Inf. Theor. **62**(6), 3290–3339 (2016)
14. Li, C., Jia, K., Shen, D., Shi, C.J.R., Yang, H.: Hierarchical representation learning for bipartite graphs. In: IJCAI, vol. 19, pp. 2873–2879 (2019)

15. Liu, Z., Shi, K., Zhang, K., Ou, W., Wang, L.: Discriminative sparse embedding based on adaptive graph for dimension reduction. Eng. Appl. Artif. Intell. **94**, 103758 (2020)

16. Luo, G., et al.: Dynamically constructed network with error correction for accurate ventricle volume estimation. Med. Image Anal. **64**, 101723 (2020)

17. Luo, G., et al.: Graph entropy guided node embedding dimension selection for graph neural networks. In: Zhou, Z.H. (ed.) Proceedings of the Thirtieth International Joint Conference on Artificial Intelligence, IJCAI-21, pp. 2767–2774. International Joint Conferences on Artificial Intelligence Organization, August 2021. https://doi.org/10.24963/ijcai.2021/381. Main Track

18. Ou, M., Cui, P., Pei, J., Zhang, Z., Zhu, W.: Asymmetric transitivity preserving graph embedding. In: Proceedings of the 22nd ACM SIGKDD International Conference on Knowledge Discovery and Data Mining, pp. 1105–1114 (2016)

19. Pan, S., Hu, R., Long, G., Jiang, J., Yao, L., Zhang, C.: Adversarially regularized graph autoencoder for graph embedding. In: Proceedings of the Twenty-Seventh International Joint Conference on Artificial Intelligence, IJCAI-18, pp. 2609–2615. International Joint Conferences on Artificial Intelligence Organization, July 2018. https://doi.org/10.24963/ijcai.2018/362

20. Peng, H., et al.: Hierarchical taxonomy-aware and attentional graph capsule RCNNs for large-scale multi-label text classification. IEEE Trans. Knowl. Data Eng. **33**(6), 2505–2519 (2019)

21. Perozzi, B., Al-Rfou, R., Skiena, S.: DeepWalk: online learning of social representations. In: Proceedings of the 20th ACM SIGKDD International Conference on Knowledge Discovery and Data Mining, pp. 701–710 (2014)

22. Rashevsky, N.: Life, information theory, and topology. Bull. Math. Biophys. **17**(3), 229–235 (1955)

23. Raychaudhury, C., Ray, S., Ghosh, J., Roy, A., Basak, S.: Discrimination of isomeric structures using information theoretic topological indices. J. Comput. Chem. **5**(6), 581–588 (1984)

24. Rosvall, M., Bergstrom, C.T.: Maps of random walks on complex networks reveal community structure. Proc. Natl. Acad. Sci. **105**(4), 1118–1123 (2008)

25. Schubert, E., Sander, J., Ester, M., Kriegel, H., Xu, X.: DBSCAN revisited, revisited: why and how you should (still) use DBSCAN. ACM Trans. Database Syst. **42**(3), 19:1–19:21 (2017). https://doi.org/10.1145/3068335

26. Sculley, D.: Web-scale k-means clustering. In: Rappa, M., Jones, P., Freire, J., Chakrabarti, S. (eds.) Proceedings of the 19th International Conference on World Wide Web, WWW 2010, Raleigh, North Carolina, USA, 26–30 April 2010, pp. 1177–1178. ACM (2010). https://doi.org/10.1145/1772690.1772862

27. Sen, P., Namata, G., Bilgic, M., Getoor, L., Galligher, B., Eliassi-Rad, T.: Collective classification in network data. AI Mag. **29**(3), 93 (2008)

28. Seshadhri, C., Sharma, A., Stolman, A., Goel, A.: The impossibility of low-rank representations for triangle-rich complex networks. Proc. Natl. Acad. Sci. **117**(11), 5631–5637 (2020)

29. Shannon, C.: The lattice theory of information. Trans. IRE Prof. Group Inf. Theor. **1**(1), 105–107 (1953)

30. Shen, X.J., Liu, S.X., Bao, B.K., Pan, C.H., Zha, Z.J., Fan, J.: A generalized least-squares approach regularized with graph embedding for dimensionality reduction. Pattern Recogn. **98**, 107023 (2020)

31. Sun, Q., et al.: Sugar: subgraph neural network with reinforcement pooling and self-supervised mutual information mechanism. In: Proceedings of the Web Conference 2021, pp. 2081–2091 (2021)

32. Veličković, P., Cucurull, G., Casanova, A., Romero, A., Lio, P., Bengio, Y.: Graph attention networks (2018). https://iclr.cc/Conferences/2018/Schedule? showEvent=299
33. Wu, Z., Pan, S., Chen, F., Long, G., Zhang, C., Philip, S.Y.: A comprehensive survey on graph neural networks. IEEE Trans. Neural Netw. Learn. Syst. **32**(1), 4–24 (2020)
34. Xie, Y., Li, S., Yang, C., Wong, R.C.W., Han, J.: When do GNNs work: understanding and improving neighborhood aggregation. In: IJCAI, pp. 1303–1309 (2020)
35. Xiong, K., Nie, F., Han, J.: Linear manifold regularization with adaptive graph for semi-supervised dimensionality reduction. In: IJCAI, pp. 3147–3153 (2017)
36. Yan, S., Xu, D., Zhang, B., Zhang, H.J.: Graph embedding: a general framework for dimensionality reduction. In: 2005 IEEE Computer Society Conference on Computer Vision and Pattern Recognition (CVPR 2005), vol. 2, pp. 830–837. IEEE (2005)
37. Yi, Y., Wang, J., Zhou, W., Fang, Y., Kong, J., Lu, Y.: Joint graph optimization and projection learning for dimensionality reduction. Pattern Recogn. **92**, 258–273 (2019)
38. Yin, Z., Shen, Y.: On the dimensionality of word embedding. In: Bengio, S., Wallach, H., Larochelle, H., Grauman, K., Cesa-Bianchi, N., Garnett, R. (eds.) Advances in Neural Information Processing Systems, vol. 31. Curran Associates, Inc. (2018). https://proceedings.neurips.cc/paper/2018/file/b534ba68236ba543ae44b22bd110a1d6-Paper.pdf
39. Zhu, S.C., Wu, Y.N., Mumford, D.: Minimax entropy principle and its application to texture modeling. Neural Comput. **9**(8), 1627–1660 (1997). https://doi.org/10.1162/neco.1997.9.8.1627
40. Zhu, X., Lei, C., Yu, H., Li, Y., Gan, J., Zhang, S.: Robust graph dimensionality reduction. In: IJCAI, pp. 3257–3263 (2018)

PairEE: A Novel Pairing-Scoring Approach for Better Overlapping Event Extraction

Zetai Jiang[1,2] and Fang Kong[1,2(✉)]

[1] Laboratory for Natural Language Processing, Soochow University, Suzhou, China
20215227035@stu.suda.edu.cn
[2] School of Computer Science and Technology, Soochow University, Suzhou, China
kongfang@suda.edu.cn

Abstract. Event Extraction (EE) is a fundamental task and has achieved much success in the past few years. However, the overlap between the event elements has been largely ignored in most previous studies. In this paper, we propose a novel pairing-scoring approach to better solve the overlapping problem. In particular, we firstly extract all event triggers and arguments simultaneously. Then we cast the acquisition of the complete event as an assembly task. By pairing and scoring all possible event triggers and arguments, we group event elements into different events to get the list of complete events. In addition, we design a type-aware fusion layer to improve the extraction of event elements by explicitly exploiting predefined event type and argument role label information. Experiments on the FewFC demonstrate that our proposed model can significantly improve the performance of overlapping EE.

Keywords: Event extraction · Overlapped event · Pairing task

1 Introduction

Event Extraction (EE) is a fundamental task in natural language processing (NLP), which aims to extract concise, structured information from a large number of documents based on predefined event templates. Figure 1(a) illustrates a traditional event example. The given `Share Reduction` event is triggered by "reduced". Its `subject` argument is "Lugutong", and the `object` argument is "Kweichow Moutai". However, the phenomenon is more complicated in reality, even a single sentence may contain multiple events or overlapped events. In example (b), there are two events driven by different triggers (i.e., "acquire" and "litigation"). They share two arguments (i.e., "TSMC" and "SMIC"). What's more, "TSMC" acts as the same argument role `subject`, while "SMIC" acts as different roles `target` and `object`. In example (c), there are two different events driven by the same trigger "purchased". One event is `Investment` type, it has two arguments, i.e., Yunnan Tourism Corporation (`subject`) and Wenhua Technology (`object`). The other is `Share Transfer` type, it has three arguments, i.e., Yunnan Tourism Corporation (`subject`), Wenhua Technology (`object`), and 100% (`proportion`). They share two arguments and the trigger. From example

L. Iliadis et al. (Eds.): ICANN 2023, LNCS 14262, pp. 128–139, 2023.
https://doi.org/10.1007/978-3-031-44201-8_11

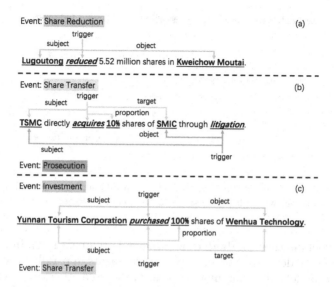

Fig. 1. Examples of events: (a) a normal event; (b) two overlapped events with different triggers; (c) two overlapped events with the same trigger.

(b) and (c), we can conclude that, not only do the event triggers overlap, but the arguments overlap between the two different events.

Although current studies on EE have achieved much success, the overlap between the event elements has been largely ignored. In this paper, we cast overlapping EE as a pairing task. Differing from other EE approaches, instead of considering the predefined relationships between triggers and arguments in the beginning, we firstly view both trigger and argument as spans, and extract them simultaneously. The obtained spans and their type labels are presented in the form of (*span, label*) tuples. For each span, multiple labels can make up multiple tuples, and thus we can solve the overlapping problem of one span acting as multiple roles. After that, we pair all possible trigger spans and argument spans. By calculating the pairing score between them, we can get the complete events and also solve the problem of overlapping the same tuple in multiple events. Figure 2 illustrates the detail of our pairing scheme using an example. We can find that, six spans and their corresponding labels are firstly extracted. Referring to the obtained labels, the six spans can be grouped into two triggers and four arguments. Then we pair all possible assemblies to get eight trigger-argument pairs. Finally, we calculate pairing score for each pair and filter out impossible ones. In this way, we end up with two complete events.

According to the above discussion, we propose a novel joint event extraction framework, named PairEE. Specifically, in the encoding phase, PairEE adopts a pre-trained BERT model [2] as the encoder to get the contextual representation of each token. In order to achieve event type aware and argument role aware representations, we design an information fusion layer to explicitly exploit

Fig. 2. Illustration of our pairing scheme. The example sentence from Fig. 1(b). For ease of understanding, we replace the spans with specific tokens.

predefined label information (both event type and argument role). In the extraction phase, the model extracts all triggers or arguments in parallel way by equipping a dual channel extraction module. And in the prediction phase, our framework builds a relative position based relation scorer to generate a score matrix of the pair-wise relations between extracted triggers and arguments, which can effectively integrate the distance information. The contributions of this paper are as follows:

- We propose PairEE, a novel joint event extraction framework, which treats EE as a pairing task for the first time and can effectively solve the overlapping problem in EE.
- We investigate the impact of predefined label information in EE and design an information fusion layer to implement event type aware and argument role aware representations for downstream subtasks.
- We conduct experiments to demonstrate that PairEE achieves significant improvements on overlapping EE compared with several competitive baselines.

2   Related Work

Most EE approaches can be divided into pipeline or joint approaches. Pipeline approaches [1,5,12,13] divide a complete EE into multiple independent subtasks, which greatly simplifies the complexity of EE but suffers from error propagation problem and neglects associations between different subtasks. Joint approaches [4,7,9–11] have been proposed as a promising alternative to alleviate error propagation by optimizing sharing parameters simultaneously. In this paper, our proposed framework adopts joint approach.

Despite the advances in EE, the existing research on overlapping problems is insufficient. On one hand, traditional sequence labeling based approaches [1,7,9,10] can quickly identify triggers and arguments with corresponding labels but have obvious difficulty to resolve overlapping problem due to label conflicts. On the other hand, question answering based approaches [3,5,6] need to customize more complex and differentiated questions so that the model may understand the differences and relations between overlapped triggers and arguments, which is time-consuming and labor-intensive. Recently, Yang et al. [13] tried to solve the overlapped argument problem by using the pre-trained language model, but they ignored the event trigger overlap cases. Sheng et al. [11] systematically investigated the overlapping problem in EE and proposed a joint framework CasEE to solve the overlapping problem. But they suffered from the error propagation problem in the cascade decoding paradigm and didn't make full use of argument information to assist with the extraction subtask.

3   Methodology

3.1   Problem Definition

To address the overlapping problem, we formulate EE into pairing task. Given an input segment $S = \{w_1, w_2, ..., w_n\}$ with n words, event types $\mathcal{C}$ and argument roles $\mathcal{R}$, we aim to extract all possible triggers $T_\mathcal{C} = \{t_1, t_2, ..., t_i\}$ and arguments $A_\mathcal{R} = \{a_1, a_2, ..., a_j\}$ in segment S (note that elements in $T_\mathcal{C}$ and $A_\mathcal{R}$ can be a single word or a phrase with the corresponding event type or argument role labels), and pair them into $O = \{(t_n, a_m), ...\}$. Thus, our objective is to maximize the following joint likelihood:

$$P(O|S) = P(A_\mathcal{R}, T_\mathcal{C}|S) \times P(O|A_\mathcal{R}, T_\mathcal{C})$$

$$= \prod_{a \in A_\mathcal{R}} P(a|S) \prod_{t \in T_\mathcal{C}} P(t|S) \prod_{a \in A_\mathcal{R}, t \in T_\mathcal{C}} P((a,t)|a,t) \qquad (1)$$

Based on Eq. (1), we design the model PairEE, the overall architecture is demonstrated in Fig. 3. There are three main components in our model, i.e., (1) Encoding fusion module adopts BERT encoder to get contextual representations and fuses the predefined label information through a fusion layer. (2) Dual channel extraction module $P(A_\mathcal{R}, T_\mathcal{C}|S)$ extracts triggers and arguments in parallel and generates a representation matrix for them respectively. (3) Pairing module $P(O|A_\mathcal{R}, T_\mathcal{C})$ calculates the scores between candidate triggers and arguments by a distance aware relation scorer.

3.2   Encoding Fusion Module

BERT Encoder. BERT [2] has been proven to be able to capture contextual representation effectively in various NLP tasks. Thus, we leverage BERT as the encoder in our model. Assume $BERT(\cdot)$ denotes the BERT encoder, the hidden representations $\mathbf{H} = \{\mathbf{h}_1, \mathbf{h}_2, ..., \mathbf{h}_n\} \in \mathbb{R}^{n \times d_h}$ of sentence $S = \{w_1, w_2, ..., w_n\}$ can be obtained by the following:

$$\{\mathbf{h}_1, \mathbf{h}_2, ..., \mathbf{h}_n\} = BERT(\{w_1, w_2, ..., w_n\}) \qquad (2)$$

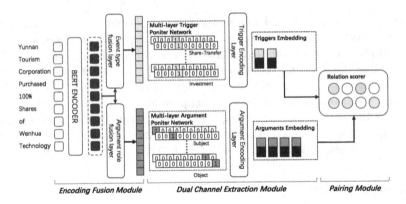

Fig. 3. The overall architecture of our framework.

Information Fusion Layer. In this layer, we aim to explicitly integrate pre-defined label information into $\mathbf{H}$ to generate event type aware and argument role aware representations for subsequent subtasks. To achieve this goal, we first randomly initialize label embedding matrices $\mathbf{C} = \{\mathbf{c}_1, \mathbf{c}_2, ..., \mathbf{c}_{|\mathcal{C}|}\} \in \mathbb{R}^{|\mathcal{C}| \times d_h}$ and $\mathbf{R} = \{\mathbf{r}_1, \mathbf{r}_2, ..., \mathbf{r}_{|\mathcal{R}|}\} \in \mathbb{R}^{|\mathcal{R}| \times d_h}$ for event types and argument roles, where $|\mathcal{C}|$ and $|\mathcal{R}|$ represent the number of predefined types and roles. To enable hidden representations $\mathbf{H}$ to detect the potential relationship with the label embedding matrices, we utilize the self-attention mechanism, which can obtain similarity weight distribution of values by calculating the dot product:

$$Attention\left(\mathbf{Q}, \mathbf{K}, \mathbf{V}\right) = softmax\left(\frac{\mathbf{Q}\mathbf{K}^T}{\sqrt{d_k}}\right)\mathbf{V} \qquad (3)$$

where $\mathbf{Q}$, $\mathbf{K}$ and $\mathbf{V}$ represent query, key and value, and $\sqrt{d_k}$ is the scaling factor.

Since we have observed that arguments and triggers have certain differences in semantics and part of speech, so we regard $\mathbf{H}$ as the query, $\mathbf{C}$ and $\mathbf{R}$ as different key and value separately. The formulas are as follows:

$$\begin{aligned}
\mathbf{E}^C &= Attention\left(\mathbf{H}\mathbf{W}_q^C, \mathbf{C}\mathbf{W}_k^C, \mathbf{C}\mathbf{W}_v^C\right) \\
\mathbf{E}^R &= Attention\left(\mathbf{H}\mathbf{W}_q^R, \mathbf{R}\mathbf{W}_k^R, \mathbf{R}\mathbf{W}_v^R\right)
\end{aligned} \qquad (4)$$

where $\mathbf{W}_q^C, \mathbf{W}_k^C, \mathbf{W}_v^C, \mathbf{W}_q^R, \mathbf{W}_k^R, \mathbf{W}_v^R \in \mathbb{R}^{d_h \times d_h}$ are the projections parameter matrices, and $\mathbf{E}^C, \mathbf{E}^R \in \mathbb{R}^{n \times d_h}$ are the output of self-attention. Then we preliminarily integrate $\mathbf{E}^C$ and $\mathbf{E}^R$ with $\mathbf{H}$ through Eq. (5) and get $\overline{\mathbf{E}}^C, \overline{\mathbf{E}}^R \in \mathbb{R}^{n \times 4d_h}$:

$$\begin{aligned}
\overline{\mathbf{E}}^C &= \left[\mathbf{H}; \mathbf{E}^C; \left|\mathbf{H} - \mathbf{E}^C\right|; \mathbf{H} \odot \mathbf{E}^C\right] \\
\overline{\mathbf{E}}^R &= \left[\mathbf{H}; \mathbf{E}^R; \left|\mathbf{H} - \mathbf{E}^R\right|; \mathbf{H} \odot \mathbf{E}^R\right]
\end{aligned} \qquad (5)$$

where $[\cdot; \cdot]$ denotes concatenation, $|\cdot|$ denotes an absolute value operator, $\odot$ denotes the element-wise production.

To avoid the harm of direct fusion to context representations $\mathbf{H}$, we designed a gate mechanism to calculate the retention ratio between $\mathbf{H}$ and $\overline{\mathbf{E}}^C$, $\overline{\mathbf{E}}^R$. Based on these ratios, we can generate complementary representations between $\mathbf{H}$ and $\mathbf{E}^C$, $\mathbf{E}^R$, which can effectively achieve event type awareness and argument role awareness. The gate mechanism is formulated as:

$$\mathbf{P} = \sigma\left(\mathbf{H}\mathbf{W}_p^H + \overline{\mathbf{E}}^C \mathbf{W}_p^C\right)$$
$$\mathbf{Q} = \sigma\left(\mathbf{H}\mathbf{W}_q^H + \overline{\mathbf{E}}^R \mathbf{W}_q^R\right) \tag{6}$$

$$\mathbf{H}^C = \mathbf{P} \odot \mathbf{H} + (1 - \mathbf{P}) \odot \overline{\mathbf{E}}^C$$
$$\mathbf{H}^R = \mathbf{Q} \odot \mathbf{H} + (1 - \mathbf{Q}) \odot \overline{\mathbf{E}}^R \tag{7}$$

where $\mathbf{W}_p^H, \mathbf{W}_q^H \in \mathbb{R}^{d_h \times 4d_h}$ and $\mathbf{W}_p^C, \mathbf{W}_q^R \in \mathbb{R}^{4d_h \times 4d_h}$ are trainable parameters, which map matrices to the same feature space, $\sigma(\cdot)$ denotes sigmoid function. $\mathbf{H}^C, \mathbf{H}^R \in \mathbb{R}^{n \times 4d_h}$ are event type aware and argument role aware representations, respectively.

3.3   Dual Channel Extraction Module

In this module, we extract triggers and arguments in the form of (span, label) by leveraging the embeddings $\mathbf{H}^C$ and $\mathbf{H}^R$ from the previous module. As illustrated in Fig. 3, in view of the discrepancy between triggers and arguments, we adopt a dual channel method to extract them in parallel. Each channel is equipped with a multi-layer label pointer network, which is composed of multiple groups of binary classifiers. Each group represents a particular label and consists of a start pointer classifier and an end pointer classifier, which can determine the span of triggers or arguments. Therefore, we can calculate the probability that a token w_i is the start position or the end position of $c \in \mathcal{C}$ or $r \in \mathcal{R}$:

$$t_i^{cs} = p\left(t_s^c | w_i\right) = \sigma\left(\mathbf{w}_{t_s}^c \mathbf{h}_i^C + \mathbf{b}_{t_s}^c\right)$$
$$t_i^{ce} = p\left(t_e^c | w_i\right) = \sigma\left(\mathbf{w}_{t_e}^c \mathbf{h}_i^C + \mathbf{b}_{t_e}^c\right) \tag{8}$$

$$a_i^{rs} = p\left(a_s^r | w_i\right) = \sigma\left(\mathbf{w}_{a_s}^r \mathbf{h}_i^R + \mathbf{b}_{a_s}^r\right)$$
$$a_i^{re} = p\left(a_e^r | w_i\right) = \sigma\left(\mathbf{w}_{a_e}^r \mathbf{h}_i^R + \mathbf{b}_{a_e}^r\right) \tag{9}$$

where $\mathbf{w}_{t_s}^c$, $\mathbf{w}_{t_e}^c$, $\mathbf{b}_{t_s}^c$, $\mathbf{b}_{t_e}^c$ and $\mathbf{w}_{a_s}^r$, $\mathbf{w}_{a_e}^r$, $\mathbf{b}_{a_s}^r$, $\mathbf{b}_{a_e}^r$ are learnable weights and bias, $\mathbf{h}_i^C$ and $\mathbf{h}_i^R$ are i-th embedding in $\mathbf{H}^C$ and $\mathbf{H}^R$.

We follow Sheng et al. [11], set a threshold $\delta_1 \in (0, 1)$ to filter invalid candidates, when the probability exceeds δ_1, the current token is the desired result. In this way, we can obtain all possible start and end positions of triggers and arguments, we enumerate over all the start positions, and match the nearest following end position as the span of the trigger or argument.

Then, we encode each trigger and argument according to their span and label for later pairing tasks. We concatenate the start and end token embeddings from $\mathbf{H}$ and the label embedding from $\mathbf{C}$ or $\mathbf{R}$ to represent a whole trigger or argument. Thus, for any $\mathbf{t}_n$ and $\mathbf{a}_m$ can be expressed as:

$$
\begin{aligned}
\mathbf{t}_n &= \mathbf{mlp}_t \left(\left[\mathbf{h}_{start(n)}; \mathbf{h}_{end(n)}; \mathbf{c}_{label(n)} \right] \right) \\
\mathbf{a}_m &= \mathbf{mlp}_a \left(\left[\mathbf{h}_{start(m)}; \mathbf{h}_{end(m)}; \mathbf{r}_{label(m)} \right] \right)
\end{aligned}
\tag{10}
$$

where $\mathbf{mlp}_t(\cdot)$, $\mathbf{mlp}_a(\cdot)$ are multi-layer perceptron. Ultimately we can generate the triggers embedding matrix $\mathbf{T} = \{\mathbf{t}_1, \mathbf{t}_2, ..., \mathbf{t}_i\} \in \mathbb{R}^{i \times d_h}$ and arguments embedding matrix $\mathbf{A} = \{\mathbf{a}_1, \mathbf{a}_2, ..., \mathbf{a}_j\} \in \mathbb{R}^{j \times d_h}$.

3.4   Pairing Module

To explore whether a trigger and an argument are in the same event, we pair each other of them and calculate their relation score. Because relative position can effectively help identify relationships in many pairing tasks, we also introduce the relative position embedding to our model. We feed all triggers and arguments into the relation scorer and generate the score matrix $\mathbf{S} \in \mathbb{R}^{i \times j}$, the pair-wise relation score $s_{nm} \in \mathbf{S}$ between trigger $\mathbf{t}_n \in \mathbf{T}$ and argument $\mathbf{a}_m \in \mathbf{R}$ is calculated as follows:

$$
\begin{aligned}
s_{nm} &= p\left((t_n, a_m)|t_n, a_m\right) = \\
&\sigma \left(\mathbf{w}_{nm}^s \left[\mathbf{t}_n; \mathbf{a}_m; \mathbf{t}_n \odot \mathbf{a}_m; \mathbf{p}_{i-j} \right] + \mathbf{b}_{nm}^s \right)
\end{aligned}
\tag{11}
$$

where $\mathbf{w}_{nm}^s$ and $\mathbf{b}_{nm}^s$ are learnable weights and bias, $\mathbf{p}_{i-j} \in \mathbb{R}^{d_p}$ denotes the randomly initialize relative position embedding.

We determine whether a trigger and an argument are related by setting a threshold $\delta_2 \in (0, 1)$, when $s_{nm} > \delta_2$, we assume that the current trigger and argument belong to the same event.

3.5   Model Training

The overall loss function $\mathcal{L}$ of our model is divided into $\mathcal{L}_T$, $\mathcal{L}_A$, and $\mathcal{L}_P$, corresponding to the extraction task and the pairing task described above. We use cross-entropy to formulate the loss function. The formulas are as follows:

$$
\mathcal{L} = \lambda_1 \mathcal{L}_T + \lambda_2 \mathcal{L}_A + \lambda_3 \mathcal{L}_P
\tag{12}
$$

$$
\mathcal{L}_T = \sum_{c=0}^{|\mathcal{C}|} \sum_{i=0}^{n} -\log p\left(t_s^c | w_i\right) + \sum_{c=0}^{|\mathcal{C}|} \sum_{i=0}^{n} -\log p\left(t_e^c | w_i\right)
\tag{13}
$$

$$
\mathcal{L}_A = \sum_{c=0}^{|\mathcal{R}|} \sum_{i=0}^{n} -\log p\left(a_s^c | w_i\right) + \sum_{r=0}^{|\mathcal{R}|} \sum_{i=0}^{n} -\log p\left(a_e^c | w_i\right)
\tag{14}
$$

$$
\mathcal{L}_P = \sum_{n=0}^{i} \sum_{m=0}^{j} -\log p\left((t_n, a_m)|t_n, a_m\right)
\tag{15}
$$

where λ_1, λ_2 and λ_3 are hyper-parameters.

4 Experiments

4.1 Experimental Settings

To assess the performance of our model in overlapping EE, we adopt a Chinese financial event extraction dataset FewFC [14] as the benchmark dataset, which contains a total of 8,982 sentences with 12,890 events, and nearly 22% sentences with the overlapping problem. We partitioned the dataset into training, validation, and testing sets according to an 8:1:1 ratio.

For fair evaluation, we also follow the metrics of previous works [1,3,11]: Trigger Identification (TI), Trigger Classification (TC), Argument Identification (AI),and Argument Classification (AC). We present each of the four metrics by Precision (P), Recall (R), and F measure (F1).

We adopt Bert-base-Chinese as the encoder, which has 768 hidden units and 512 maximum lengths. We utilize AdamW [8] to optimize the parameters of our model. We set the learning rate to $2e - 5$ for BERT encoder and $1e - 4$ for other modules. We also adopt the warming up and set the proportion to 10%. In the training stage, the max epoch is set to 50 and the batch size is set to 8. The thresholds δ_1 and δ_2 are all tuned to 0.1, and the dimensions of relative position embedding d_p are tuned to 128. To pursue the balance of each module, we set λ_1, λ_2, and λ_3 to 1. The hyper-parameters are all tuned based on the development dataset. In addition, the label embedding matrices and relative position embedding matrix are all trained from scratch.

4.2 Baselines

The baselines can be grouped into two groups, i.e., methods without considering overlapping, and methods for overlapping EE.

Methods without considering overlapping are mainly based on sequence labeling and assume that there are no overlapping problems in the sentence.**BERT-softmax** uses BERT to get the contextual representations and classifies event triggers and arguments directly. **BERT-CRF** adds a conditional random field (CRF) based on BERT-softmax, which can capture label dependencies by calculating transition probability. **BERT-CRF-joint** adopts joint labels of the type and role as B/I/O-type-role to joint extraction of entity and relation.

Methods for overlapping EE attempt to solve the overlapping problem. **PL-MEE** [13] solves the overlapped role problem by separating the argument predictions in terms of roles. **MQAEE** [5] adopts a multi-span extraction method that sequentially predicts triggers with types and then predicts overlapped arguments according to the typed triggers. **CasEE** [11] decomposes the complete EE task into type detection, trigger extraction, and argument extraction, where the overlapped targets are separately extracted conditioned on former predictions.

4.3 Experiment Results

Overall Performance. Table 1 shows the results, we can observe that: In comparison with the systems without considering overlapping, PairEE can achieve much better performance. The average F1 scores of our model on all four metrics

Table 1. Overall performance of all methods on FewFC.

	TI(%)			TC(%)			AI(%)			AC(%)		
	P	R	F1	P	R	F1	P	R	F1	P	R	F1
BERT-softmax	89.8	79.0	84.0	80.2	61.8	69.8	74.6	62.8	68.2	72.5	60.2	65.8
BERT-CRF	**90.8**	80.8	85.5	**81.7**	63.6	71.5	75.1	64.3	69.3	72.9	61.8	66.9
BERT-CRF-joint	89.5	79.8	84.4	80.7	63.0	70.8	**76.1**	63.5	69.2	**74.2**	61.2	67.1
PLMEE	83.7	85.8	84.7	75.6	74.5	75.1	74.3	67.3	70.6	72.5	65.5	68.8
MQAEE	89.1	85.5	87.4	79.7	76.1	77.8	70.3	68.3	69.3	68.2	66.5	67.3
CasEE	89.4	87.7	88.6	77.9	78.5	78.2	72.8	73.1	72.9	71.3	71.5	71.4
PairEE	87.7	**90.1**	**88.9**	77.4	**82.7**	**80.0**	72.0	**77.0**	**74.4**	69.8	**75.0**	**72.3**

outperform BERT-softmax, BERT-CRF, and BERT-CRF-joint by 6.9%, 5.6%, and 6.0%, respectively. It indicates the necessity of solving overlapping problem.

In comparison with the systems attempting to solve the overlapping problem, our model also achieves performance improvement, it indicates the effectiveness of our model on addressing overlapping problem. Comparing with MQAEE, our PairEE achieves better performance on all metrics. Even comparing with the state-of-the-art (SoTA) model, CasEE, the F1 score of PairEE on TI, TC, AI, and AC are better by 0.3%, 1.8%, 1.5%, and 0.9% respectively. Cascade decoding helps CasEE simplify the difficulty of triggers extraction, so it has achieved a pretty good result in TI, but also suffers from error propagation. PairEE takes full advantage of label information in the extraction stage, and extracts all triggers and arguments at once without error propagation, this is why the F1 score of PairEE is substantially leading on the three remaining metrics than CasEE.

Results on Overlapped and Normal Data. To further validate our model's ability to identify overlapped events and figure out how PairEE performs in normal data, we continue our experiments on the testing set that contains only overlapped or normal sentences.

As shown in Table 2, our model outperforms other methods in overlapped sentences and achieves acceptable results in normal sentences. PairEE has a very balanced performance in both cases. From dealing with normal sentences to dealing with overlapped sentences, our model has almost no significant performance degradation compared with other methods. The reasons are as follows: 1) PairEE is a general model that incorporates the ability to extract events in both situations. 2) The dual channel extraction module avoids label conflicts and error propagation problems, which occur frequently in other methods. 3) Even in more complex situations, our pairing scheme can still effectively discover potential relations between triggers and arguments.

Table 2. Performance on overlapped sentences(left) and normal sentences(right) in testing. We report F1 scores for each evaluation metric.

	Overlapped Sentences				Normal Sentences			
	TI(%)	TC(%)	AI(%)	AC(%)	TI(%)	TC(%)	AI(%)	AC(%)
BERT-softmax	76.5	49.0	56.1	53.5	86.9	79.9	**76.2**	**74.1**
BERT-CRF	77.9	52.4	61.0	58.4	88.4	80.8	74.9	72.8
BERT-CRF-joint	77.8	52.0	58.8	56.8	86.9	79.9	76.1	74.0
PLMEE	80.7	66.6	63.2	61.4	86.4	79.7	75.7	74.0
MQAEE	83.6	70.4	62.1	60.1	89.0	**82.0**	74.2	72.3
CasEE	**89.0**	74.9	71.5	70.3	88.4	80.2	74.0	72.3
PairEE	88.7	**78.6**	**73.6**	**72.0**	**89.1**	80.9	75.0	72.6

Ablation Study. We conduct ablation experiments for PairEE to evaluate the effectiveness of each component in our method. The experimental results are shown in Table 3. We first replace the gate mechanism by adding the two embeddings directly, the performance of our model has become worse. It suggests the usefulness of the gate mechanism. When we replace the information fusion layer with concatenation operation, the results decreased significantly, and the performance on the four metrics drops by 1.0%, 2.0%, 0.9%, and 0.9%, which suggests the fusion layer can effectively integrate contextual representations with label embeddings for subtasks. There is also a drop when we remove the relative position embeddings, the performance drops by 1.0%, 1.1%, 0.7%, and 0.7%, which indicates the relative position is critical for pairing tasks. Furthermore, when we remove the whole label embeddings, and the experimental results show a sharp decline on all metrics, the F1 scores decrease by 2.3%, 1.5%, 2.3%, and 2.4% respectively.

Analysis of Label Embeddings. To further verify the impact of label embeddings on experimental performance, we made a series of adjustments to the dimensions of the label embeddings. We center on the hidden layer dimensions 768 and gradually increase or decrease the dimensions, the changes of experimen-

Table 3. Results of ablation experiments on FewFC.

	TI(%)	TC(%)	AI(%)	AC(%)
PairEE	**88.9**	**80.0**	**74.4**	**72.3**
w/o Gate	88.6	79.5	74.0	72.0
w/o Fusion Layer	87.9	78.0	73.5	71.4
w/o Position Emb	87.9	78.9	73.7	71.6
w/o Label Emb	87.6	78.5	72.1	69.9

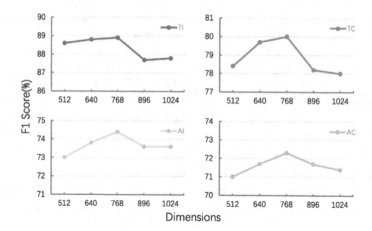

Fig. 4. Performance with different dimensions.

tal results on the four metrics are shown in Fig. 4. Combined with the previous results of removing label embeddings, it is not difficult to find that label embeddings are essential to our model, too long or too short dimensions can make the performance poor, and the length of the label embedding equals to the length of the contextual representation embedding seems to be a good choice. Meanwhile, TI, TC, and AI, AC are all sensitive to changes of dimensions according to experimental results. We consider the main reason is from the architecture of our model, which relies heavily on label embeddings. In extraction stage, we combine the label embeddings with contextual representations to identify the spans and categories of triggers and arguments, and in pairing stage, label embeddings are the clue to judge their relations. Thus, using high-quality label embeddings can effectively improve the performance of our model.

5   Conclusion

In this paper, we propose a novel joint framework based on pairing scheme, named PairEE, for overlapping EE. PairEE decomposes the complete EE into encoding, extraction, and pairing stage, which greatly simplifies the complexity of EE and effectively solves the overlapping problem. In addition, by equipping an information fusion layer, PairEE can enrich the contextual representations with label information. We conduct extensive experiments to demonstrate the effectiveness of our proposed model. In the future, we may further explore how to capture potential relations between triggers and arguments, and utilize pairing scheme to address other problems in EE.

Acknowledgements. This work was supported by Projects 62276178 under the National Natural Science Foundation of China, the National Key RD Program of China under Grant No.2020AAA0108600 and the Priority Academic Program Development of Jiangsu Higher Education Institutions.

References

1. Chen, Y., Xu, L., Liu, K., Zeng, D., Zhao, J.: Event extraction via dynamic multipooling convolutional neural networks. In: Proceedings of the Annual Meeting of the Association for Computational Linguistics, pp. 167–176 (2015)
2. Devlin, J., Chang, M.W., Lee, K., Toutanova, K.: BERT: pre-training of deep bidirectional transformers for language understanding. In: Proceedings of the Conference of the North American Chapter of the Association for Computational Linguistics: Human Language Technologies, pp. 4171–4186 (2019)
3. Du, X., Cardie, C.: Event extraction by answering (almost) natural questions. In: Proceedings of the Conference on Empirical Methods in Natural Language Processing (EMNLP), pp. 671–683 (2020)
4. Feng, Y., Li, C., Ng, V.: Legal judgment prediction via event extraction with constraints. In: Proceedings of the Annual Meeting of the Association for Computational Linguistics, pp. 648–664 (2022)
5. Li, F., et al.: Event extraction as multi-turn question answering. In: Findings of the Association for Computational Linguistics: EMNLP, pp. 829–838 (2020)
6. Liu, J., Chen, Y., Liu, K., Bi, W., Liu, X.: Event extraction as machine reading comprehension. In: Proceedings of the Conference on Empirical Methods in Natural Language Processing (EMNLP), pp. 1641–1651 (2020)
7. Liu, X., Luo, Z., Huang, H.: Jointly multiple events extraction via attention-based graph information aggregation. In: Proceedings of the Conference on Empirical Methods in Natural Language Processing (EMNLP), pp. 1247–1256 (2018)
8. Loshchilov, I., Hutter, F.: Decoupled weight decay regularization. In: Proceedings of the International Conference on Learning Representations. (2019)
9. Nguyen, T.H., Cho, K., Grishman, R.: Joint event extraction via recurrent neural networks. In: Proceedings of the Conference of the North American Chapter of the Association for Computational Linguistics: Human Language Technologies, pp. 300–309 (2016)
10. Nguyen, T.M., Nguyen, T.H.: One for all: neural joint modeling of entities and events. In: Proceedings of the AAAI Conference on Artificial Intelligence, pp. 6861–6858 (2019)
11. Sheng, J., et al.: CasEE: a joint learning framework with cascade decoding for overlapping event extraction. In: Proceedings of the Annual Meeting of the Association for Computational Linguistics, pp. 164–174 (2021)
12. Wang, S., Yu, M., Chang, S., Sun, L., Huang, L.: Query and extract: refining event extraction as type-oriented binary decoding. In: Findings of the Association for Computational Linguistics: ACL, pp. 169–182 (2022)
13. Yang, S., Feng, D., Qiao, L., Kan, Z., Li, D.: Exploring pre-trained language models for event extraction and generation. In: Proceedings of the Annual Meeting of the Association for Computational Linguistics, pp. 5284–5294 (2019)
14. Zhou, Y., Chen, Y., Zhao, J., Wu, Y., Xu, J., Li, J.: What the role is vs. what plays the role: semi-supervised event argument extraction via dual question answering. In: Proceedings of the AAAI Conference on Artificial Intelligence, pp. 14638–14646 (2021)

PCB Component Rotation Detection Based on Polarity Identifier Attention

Haoming Ma[1,3] and Hongjie Zhang[2,3](✉)

[1] School of Computer Science and Engineering,
Sun Yat-sen University, Guangzhou, China
mahm7@mail2.sysu.edu.cn
[2] College of Computer Science, Sichuan Normal University, Chengdu, China
[3] Sichuan Yuanzhigu Technology Co., Ltd., Chengdu, China
zhanghongjie@sicnu.edu.cn

Abstract. Accurate detection of component rotation is a critical task in the production of printed circuit boards (PCBs). However, with the rapid development of integrated circuits, manually labeling large datasets of all kinds of components for training machine learning models is time-consuming and impractical. To address this challenge, we propose a novel one-shot conditional component rotation detection framework, PolarNet. Given a standard image of the target component, a query image, and a polar indicator image as input, PolarNet can detect the rotation angle of the component in the query image. PolarNet comprises a Siamese network, an Indicator Attention Generator, and a Rotation Detector. The Indicator Attention Generator takes the polar indicator image as heuristic knowledge to help the Rotation Detector. Once trained, PolarNet can detect component rotation in both seen and unseen classes without further training. Our experiments on our own dataset demonstrate that PolarNet achieves good performance for one-shot rotation detection in both accuracy and scalability.

Keywords: Rotation Detection · One-shot Learning · Polar Component

1 Introduction

Component placement is a critical step in the manufacturing process of printed circuit boards (PCBs) as any misalignment can result in circuit errors and device malfunction or failure. To address this issue, automated optical inspection (AOI) systems and computer vision algorithms have been developed to detect errors in component orientation during the assembly process. AOI systems use advanced cameras and image recognition software to detect and verify the orientation of components on the PCB. Computer vision algorithms can process images of the PCB to identify and verify the orientation of components. These techniques have gained significant attention in the manufacturing industry as they help improve the accuracy and efficiency of the assembly process. However in practice, the use

L. Iliadis et al. (Eds.): ICANN 2023, LNCS 14262, pp. 140–151, 2023.
https://doi.org/10.1007/978-3-031-44201-8_12

of AOI is limited due to the low accuracy, difficulties with tuning parameters and strict environmental requirement such as illumination.

In recent years, the wide use of deep convolutional neural networks(CNN) in computer vision has made a huge progress in the field. Specifically, CNN has been used in various tasks including object detecting [1], visual tracking [2], similarity comparing [3] and rotation detection [4–6] recently. This method has also been used in PCB production assurance [7]. However, these methods' performances are closely associated with the scale of labeled data set, which have the inherent shortcomings in practice. For example, in object detecting tasks, a large number of manually labeled samples is often needed to tuning the parameters in the network, which is both consuming and unscalable with large amount of visual data which is accessible today. Moreover, these fully supervised models often have problems when extend to new classes. If we want to detect a new type of component we usually have to retrain the whole model, or at least a part of model to detect that kind of objects.

Recent researches on few-shot and one-shot image classification and detection start to appear [8,9]. The purpose of one- or few-shot learning is to learn rapidly from few new data. Few-shot learning approaches can be divided into three categories: Model-Based [10,11], Metric-Based [12,13] and Optimization-Based [14]. These approaches have shown promising results on various datasets, including image classification, object detection, and natural language processing. However, few works focus on object rotation detection, which is needed in PCB production process and quality inspection. Previous studies [4,5] mixed object detection and rotation detection together, making it hard to do one-shot rotation detection. Because these methods can only applied to objects in the training set, but cannot be used when detecting new kinds of objects. Therefore, we propose PolarNet, a self-supervised one-shot conditional rotation detection framework with generalization capability.

In this work, we find that most polar integrated components have polar indicators to denote direction, which is crucial for human recognition of orientation. Motivated by this finding, we design a framework to take this as heuristic knowledge to enhance the performance. The proposed PolarNet takes a standard image of the target component, a query image and a polar indicator image as input to detect the rotation angle of the query image. A Siamese network is first employed to extract features and map the images into a common embedding space. Then Indicator Attention Generator will work to generate attention to help Rotation Detector focus on the polar indicators. Lastly, Rotation Detector will predict the rotation angle of the query image based on features and attention.

Our contributions are summarized as follows:

1. We build and publish the first data set of polar circuit components to spur the research of implementing deep learning methods on circuit boards testing.
2. We propose a self-supervised one-shot rotation detection algorithm, PolarNet, with the heuristic information from polarity indicators.
3. We show that on our data set, PolarNet significantly outperforms traditional algorithms both accuracy and scalability.

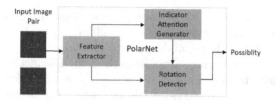

Fig. 1. PolarNet: the proposed one-shot conditional rotation detection scheme with Siamese feature extractor, Indicator Attention Generator and Rotation Detector.

2   Methodology

2.1   Overview

Our work is to learn ConvNet to detect the rotation angle of components on PCBs comparing the standard image and the under test PCB image (query image). To achieve that goal we propose a PolarNet to predict the component rotation angels. Specifically, we define the rotation transformation as $g(.)$. When the transformation is applied to image X with label y, which indicating the rotation angels, we get the transformed image $X^y = g(X, y)$.

The PolarNet get a pair of images of components, including the standard one and the query one, and output probabilities of certain rotation angels (e.g. 4 directions for rotating $0°$, $90°$, $180°$, $270°$).

Therefore, given a set of N training images $D = \{X_i\}_{i=1}^{N}$, the training objective that PolarNet must learn to solve is:

$$min_{\theta}(-\frac{1}{N}\sum_{i=1}^{N}\sum_{c=1}^{k} y_{ic}log(p_{ic})) \tag{1}$$

Here, k is the number of angels to detect, p_{ic} is the predicted probability for input X_i rotating angle c, y_{ic} is the ground-truth label for input X_i rotating angle c.

Figure 1 shows the basic framework of PolarNet. In the following subsection, we describe each part of PolarNet design in details and methods to enhance the performances of PolarNet.

2.2   Training Set Preprocessing

Since our task is to detect rotation, the manual labeled dataset is not always needed. Our dataset is based on a set of component images.

Firstly we rotate the image to y angles (depending on how much angles you want to classify). In our task, y = 4. Then by arranging the rotated images, we can get y^2 pairs of training data from one single component image, significantly increasing the scale of training set.

Secondly, several random data enhancement methods are applied to each of the image to improve interference immunity and avoid overfitting. Those methods include saturation transformation, image resizing and slightly rotation.

Indicator

Component

Fig. 2. Some components with indicators. The component images are in the upper part. The corresponding indicator images are in the lower part.

Fig. 3. One example in pretraining. The background is pure colored, with several randomly transformed irrelevant indicators. The relevant polarity indicator is pasted onto the image. In figure, the polarity indicator is boxed.

2.3 Pretraining

When human try to recognize the direction of components, we will find the certain kinds of polarity indicators on the components. As shown in Fig. 2, the indicator image can help us to find the rotation angle of component. We regard this as an heuristic information and use it to train our PolarNet.

To force PolarNet to focus on the indicators, we add a pretraining step. In this step, the training data is pairs of random images (background) with indicators pasted on the image. Only indicators are relevant to the label. One example of pretraining figure is shown in Fig. 3.

2.4 Rotation Detector Based on Similarity Comparing

In previous work [15], the ConvNet is used directly to classify the directions of images. But the same method doesn't perform well in our task. From our point of view, this is partly because of the traits of convolutional layers. The convolutional layers and pooling layers will extract features of image and keep them in spatial order. So the classification to multi classes depends on the final fully connected layers. The parameters of the final fully connected layers can be represented as W, which is a $n \times y$ matrix. Parameter n stands for the output dimension of last layer, and y stands for the classes.

In our work, we instead propose a method based on similarity comparing to detect the rotation. The input image pair includes a rotated image and an original image. The rotated image will be rotated for k times, compared with the original image and get k possibilities. These possibilities are inputted into a softmax layer and get the probability. The output of PolarNet for each input pairs of images is a probability, indicating the possibility of those two images are in the same direction. And to classify all the directions, the transformed image in the input pair will be rotated for y times, and each is put into the PolarNet with the original image and get an output respectively. We put these outputs into a softmax layer and get the final result. Therefore, the parameters W' for the last fully connected layer has been reduced to $n \times 1$, and all the training data can be used to tune these parameters. To illustrate, one original image with k different rotation angles can be used as one positive sample and (k - 1) negative samples. As a result, all the training data has been fully used to train the PolarNet, and the numbers of parameters has been reduced.

2.5   Network Design

A Siamese network [2] is a promising approach to develop a scalable rotation detector. The detection process can be divided into two steps: feature extraction and rotation angle prediction. In the first step, the same convolutional network is used to extract features from a pair of input images. In the second step, the feature maps are concatenated and fed into a fully connected layer for rotation angle prediction. However, this process does not take polar indicators into account as heuristic information, which can significantly improve the accuracy of the rotation detector.

Inspired by [1], we propose an Indicator Attention to help the PolarNet to focus on the indicators to detect rotation. Figure 1 shows the structure of Polar-Net.

Siamese Feature Extractor. We use a Siamese network as a feature extracting network to extract features from original images. Parameters in the Siamese network are shared in all branches. Let ψ to represent the Siamese network. When one group of images, including an original image I_o, an transformed image I_t and an indicator image I_i, is inputted into the network $\psi(.)$, the Siamese network is applied to each of the image, and we get features $(\psi(I_o), \psi(I_t), \psi(I_i))$. These features are used in the following process of rotation detection. Once we have these features, the following two-stage detection model will learn to use them and implement one-shot conditional detection.

Indicator Attention Generator. Indicator Attention generator aims to generate attention on both original image I_o and transformed image I_t to help the ConvNet to focus on polarity identifier and other helpful regions. Rotation angles are predicted on the combination of features $(\psi(I_o), \psi(I_t), \psi(I_i))$ generated by Siamese feature extractor. In this phase, Global Feature Extracting is applied to $\psi(I_i)$ to get salient indicator features. Then we scan the entire original image and transformed image and compare salient indicator features with local indicator features in each position.

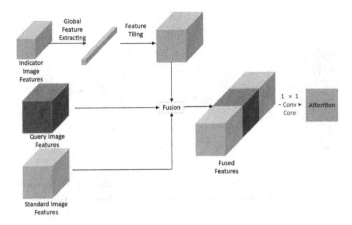

Fig. 4. Indicator Attention generator: Global Feature Extracting operation concatenates global average- and max-pooling features of indicator image, and halve the dimensions by an 1×1 convolutional layer. Feature Tiling tile the global feature to get the same size feature map as the original image features and transformed image features. Then, the global image feature is fused with original image features and transformed image feature by an 1×1 convolutional core to get the attention map.

Figure 4 shows the detailed structure of Indicator Attention Generator. Global Feature Extracting aims to get salient indicator features, and may have several types of implementation. In our network, we get global max and global average pooling, concatenate them into a $1 \times 1 \times 2k$ vector, where k is the dimension of Siamese network's output, and then use 1×1 convolutional kernels to reduce half of the dimensions. Then, in order to concatenate the indicator features with the original image feature and the transformed image feature, we use Feature tiling to make the tiled indicator features have the same spatial size as original and transformed image. Then the tiled indicator features, the original features and the transformed features are fused together and processed by a 1×1 convolutional layer to generate an attention matrix.

Rotation Detector. Based on the attention generated by the Indicator Attention generator, we can get potential region which may help with detecting rotation. Rotation Detector multiply the attention map with the original image features and transformed image features, then put them into a series of fully connected layers, which work as classifier to predict the probability of rotation. The network architecture is shown in Fig. 5.

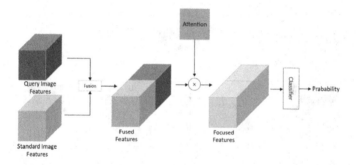

Fig. 5. Rotation Detector: the attention is applied to the fused feature to get the focused feature, then a classifier is used to get the probability of rotation.

3   Experiments

3.1   Dataset

Previous datasets have serveral printed circuit board (PCB) images. These images are labeled with location of each component. However, there is no indicator classification and no image of indicators. In our work, we build and publish the first dataset of polar circuit components to spur the research of implementing deep learning methods on circuit boards testing.

Our dataset[1] is based on PCB DSLR DATASET. The PCB DSLR dataset contains images of PCBs from a recycling facility, captured under representative conditions using a professional DSLR camera. We performed selective cropping on component regions from the original images and classified those components according to the indicators. There are seven kinds of indicators in our dataset, including arc, circle, groove, half, line, multiple lines and rectangular. There are several images of polarity component in each kind, and an indicator image, as shown in Fig. 2. In total, there are 671 images. In our experiment, the components with groove indicator are separated from the training set to test the scalability of models. The rest of images is divided into training set and validating set with the ratio of 19 : 1.

3.2   Baselines

Previous works [16,17] on rotation detection have primarily focused on denoising and detecting specific classes of objects, which is not scalable and limited to one-shot conditional detection. In our experiment, we have chosen methods based on Siamese networks as baselines, which are more scalable and applicable to a wider range of objects.

---

[1] https://github.com/ma-h-m/Polar-Component-with-Indicator-Image-Dataset.

Siamese Network. Siamese network get input as a pair of images. After using convolutional layers to extract features from the images, those features are inputted into a series of FC layers and output the probabilities of different rotation angles.

Siamese Network with Spatial Attention. Based on the features extracted by Siamese network, the Spatial Attention is generated using convolutional layers to fuse the information in different channels. Then, the Spatial Attention is applied to the features.

Siamese Network and GAM [18]. Global Attention Mechanism (GAM) uses both channel attention and spatial attention to generate attention for the network. GAM first uses an encoder-decoder structure to generate channel attention, and apply it to the feature F_0 and get feature F_1. Then, it use spatial attention, which has been described above, to attention F_1, and get F_2. And put F_2 into classifier.

3.3 Implementation Details

We resizes the input image to 224×224. The images will undergo a serious of random transformation to enhance the anti-interference ability, including rotation with in $15°C$, saturation adjustment, scaling and color changing. AlexNet [19] is chosen as the Siamese network to extract features. The classifier is three layers of FC with ReLU activation function. Each has 4096 neurons. Values of hyperparameters are shown in Table 1.

Table 1. Hyperparameters in Implementation

Hyperparameter	Value
Learning Rate	10^{-4}
Learning Rate Decay Rate per iteration	0.99
Training Iteration	100
Pretraining Iteration	30

3.4 Performance

Table 2 shows the performance of different rotation detectors on the our dataset. The proposed Indicator Attention yields 95.32% accuracy on validation set, and 94.70% accuracy on test set. Compared with other detectors, Indicator Attention network gains an improvement in performance, and remains the size of parameters.

In addition, to test the scalability and generalization ability, we test our network on unseen data set. In this dataset, the classes of indicators and component are both not used in training, so problem becomes one-shot problem. The proposed Indicator Attention yields 94.70% accuracy on seen classes (validation set), and 92.92% accuracy on unseen classes (test set). Compared with other detectors, Indicator Attention network are more generalizable (Table 3).

Table 2. Performance of different Rotation Detectors

Detector	Parameter Size	Validation Set Accuracy	Testing Set accuracy
Siamese network (4 class classification)	59.49M	83.76%	80.68%
Siamese network (similarity comparing)	59.48M	90.45%	91.60%
Spatial Attention	61.76M	93.32%	91.77%
GAM	62.69M	93.56%	92.92 %
PolarNet	61.95M	**95.32%**	**94.70%**

Table 3. Scalability of different Rotation Detectors

Detector	Seen Classes accuracy	Unseen Classes accuracy
Siamese network (4 class classification)	80.68%	82.45%
Siamese network (similarity comparing)	91.60%	86.32%
Spatial Attention	91.77%	90.26%
GAM	92.92%	92.86%
Indicator Attention	**94.70%**	**92.92%**

3.5 Visualization

In Fig. 6, we visualize some attention generated by Indicator Attention generator. At the left side, there are input images including original image, transformed image and the indicator image. At the right side, there are attention applied to the input. The brightness of each part of image represents the attention the network applied to that region.

In these examples, the Indicator Attention generator successfully focuses on the indicators in the image and detect the rotation correctly, while the Siamese network cannot correctly detect the rotation angles of them. This can partly explain the performance improvement of our network compared to the baselines.

3.6 Ablation Study

Similarity Comparing. We employ a rotation detection based on similarity comparing. The network only have to output a probability of whether rotation or not each time and do not have to predict the rotation angle. The transformed image is rotated for k times and inputted with the original image to detect each

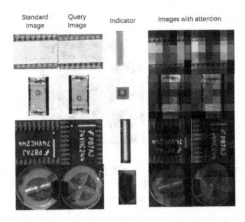

Fig. 6. Attention examples generated by the indicator attention generator. The brightness of the region indicates how much attention it pays to the region.

time. k is all the possible rotation angles. In our experiment, k = 4. Finally, we put all the probabilities into a softmax function and get the output. However, rotation detection can also be implied with a direct k-class classification. We demonstrate the effectiveness of our similarity comparing methods in Table 4.

On our dataset, similarity comparing achieves much better performance on both validation(seen) classes and testing(unseen) classes. Similarity comparing has an extra 18.25% and 20.46% accuracy improvement on seen and unseen classes. This experiment proves the effectiveness of our similarity comparing method in rotation detection.

Table 4. Comparison of similarity comparing and 4-class classification

Detector	Seen classes accuracy	Unseen classes accuracy
Indicator (4 class classification)	76.45%	72.46%
Indicator (similarity comparing)	**94.70%**	**92.92%**

Pretraining. In our first 30 epochs of training period, we employ a pretraining method described in Sect. 2.2 to help the whole network to focus on the indicator. We also tests these two implementation on our dataset. The result is shown in Table 5.

On our dataset, similarity comparing achieves better performance on both validation(seen) classes and testing(unseen) classes. Similarity comparing has an extra 1.29% and 3.73% accuracy improvement on seen and unseen classes.

Figure 7 shows an example of attention generated by network with and without pretraining. The brightness of each part indicates how much attention the

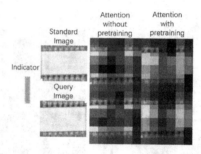

Fig. 7. Attention example of with and without pretraining. Input image pair is at left. Attention without pretraining is at middle. Attention with pretraining is at right. The brightness indicates how much attenton the network pays to the region.

network pays to that part when classification. We can see that the attention where the indicator is generated by network with pretraining is much higher than the attention generated by network without pretraining.

This experiment proves the effectiveness of pretraining in our experiment.

Table 5. Comparison of with pretraining and without pretraining

Detector	Seen classes	Unseen classes
Indicator Attention without pretraining	93.41%	89.19%
Indicator Attention with pretraining	**94.70%**	**92.92%**

4   Conclusion

This paper proposes a novel one-shot conditional component rotation detection framework, which aims to detect rotation of integrated components in PCB production from unseen classes without further training on these newly interested classes. We use a Siamese network to extract features from standard and query image. Indicator attention generator has been applied to evaluate the importance of each region in the image features. After applying the attention to the features, a similarity-comparing-based rotation detector has been implemented to predict the possibility of rotation. Experiments on our dataset verify that our method achieves good performance for one-shot rotation detection in both accuracy and scalability.

There are still some limitations: the performance gap between our model and the traditional rotation detectors, the strict requirement of physical environmental conditions. We will continue to improve the framework, such as exploring better Siamese networks and utilizing triplet loss to extract more expressive deep features. Additionally, we will device a more suitable dataset for PCB component rotation detection with more samples categories to promote the development of practice of deep learning in PCB production.

References

1. Fu, K., et al.: OSCD: a one-shot conditional object detection framework. Neurocomputing **425**, 243–255 (2020)
2. Bertinetto, L., Valmadre, J., Henriques, J.F., Vedaldi, A., Torr, P.H.S.: Fully-Convolutional Siamese Networks for Object Tracking. CoRR 2016, abs/1606.09549
3. Bromley, J.A.N.E., et al.: Signature verification using a "SIAMESE" time delay neural network. Int. J. Pattern Recogn. Artif. Intell. **7**(4), 669–688 (1993)
4. Yang, X., Yang, J., Yan, J., et al.: SCRDet: towards more robust detection for small, cluttered and rotated objects. In: 2019 IEEE/CVF International Conference on Computer Vision (ICCV), Computer Vision (ICCV), 2019 IEEE/CVF International Conference, pp. 8231–8240 (2019). https://doi.org/10.1109/ICCV.2019.00832
5. Yang, X., Zhang, G., Li, W., Wang, X., Zhou, Y., Yan, J.: H2RBox: Horizontal Box Annotation is All You Need for Oriented Object Detection (2022)
6. Jiang, Y., et al.: R2CNN: Rotational Region CNN for Orientation Robust Scene Text Detection (2017)
7. Zhao, W., Gurudu, S.R., Taheri, S., Ghosh, S., Mallaiyan Sathiaseelan, M.A., Asadizanjani, N.: PCB component detection using computer vision for hardware assurance. Big Data Cogn. Comput. **6**(2), 39 (2022). https://doi.org/10.3390/bdcc6020039
8. Finn, C., Abbeel, P., Levine, S.: Model-agnostic meta-learning for fast adaptation of deep networks. In: ICML2017, Proceedings of the 34th International Conference on Machine Learning. vol. 70 (2017)
9. Vinyals, O., Blundell, C., Lillicrap, T., Kavukcuoglu, K., Wierstra, D.: Matching networks for one shot learning. In: Advance Neural Information Processing System. vol. 29 (NeurIPS) (2016)
10. Santoro, A., Bartunov, S., Botvinick, M., et al.: One-shot learning with memory-augmented neural networks. arXiv preprint arXiv:1605.06065 (2016)
11. Tsendsuren, M., Yu, H.: Meta networks. In: Proceedings of the 34th International Conference on Machine Learning. vol. 70. JMLR (2017)
12. Vinyals, O., Blundell, C., Lillicrap, T., Wierstra, D., et al.: Matching networks for one shot learning. In: Advances in Neural Information Processing Systems, pp. 3630–3638 (2016)
13. Gregory, K., Zemel, R., Salakhutdinov, R.: Siamese neural networks for one-shot image recognition. In: ICML Deep Learning Workshop. vol. 2 (2015)
14. Sachin, R., Larochelle, H.: Optimization as a model for few-shot learning (2016)
15. Gidaris, S., Singh, P., Komodakis, N.: Unsupervised Representation Learning by Predicting Image Rotations (2018)
16. Yang, X., Yan, J., Liao, W., Tang, J., He, T.: SCRDet++: detecting small, cluttered and rotated objects via instance-level feature denoising and rotation loss smoothing. IEEE Trans. Pattern Anal. Mach. Intell. **45**(2), 2384–2399 (2023). https://doi.org/10.1109/TPAMI.2022.3166956
17. Yang, X., Yan, J.: Arbitrary-oriented object detection with circular smooth label. Lect. Notes Comput. Sci. **12353**, 677–694 (2020)
18. Liu, Y., Shao, Z., Hoffmann, N.: Global Attention Mechanism: Retain Information to Enhance Channel-Spatial Interactions (2021)
19. Krizhevsky, A., Sutskever, I., Hinton, G.E.: ImageNet classification with deep convolutional neural networks. Commun. ACM **60**(6), 84–90 (2017). https://doi.org/10.1145/3065386

PCDialogEval: Persona and Context Aware Emotional Dialogue Evaluation

Yuxi Feng[1], Linlin Wang[1,2(✉)], Zhu Cao[3], and Liang He[1]

[1] East China Normal University, Shanghai, China
51215901010@stu.ecnu.edu.cn, {llwang,lhe}@cs.ecnu.edu.cn
[2] Shanghai Artificial Intelligence Laboratory, Shanghai, China
[3] East China University of Science and Technology, Shanghai, China
caozhu@ecust.edu.cn

Abstract. Endowing dialogue systems with emotional intelligence is an essential strategy for machines to achieve deep social interaction with users, for which effective evaluation metrics for emotional dialogue are in urgent need. However, most existing evaluation methods ignore the impact of users' individual differences and situational contexts on emotional expressions, which poses a significant challenge in assessing the emotional expression capabilities of dialogue models. To address these issues, we propose a novel evaluation model that incorporates personality into evaluation metrics for dialogue systems. Our model quantifies the influence of human personality on emotional expressions and simulates the emotional transfer during conversations to calculate the intensity of emotional expressions in candidate sentences. To accomplish this calculation, we first incorporates "Big Five Personality" traits for personality analysis, and subsequently modify the emotion vector in a Valence-Arousal-Dominance (VAD) space. Furthermore, we construct mood transfer equations to simulate the impact of the conversational context on emotional expressions. Additionally, we propose an additional assessment at both sentence and session-levels to evaluate the fluency and coherence of the generated dialogue. Experimental results on two datasets demonstrate the effectiveness of the proposed evaluation model in accurately assessing the emotional expression capabilities of dialogue systems.

Keywords: Emotiona Dialogue Evaluation · Psychological Theory Application · Persona-Aware Modeling

1 Introduction

Due to the advance in neural models and the accessibility of massive datasets, open-domain dialog systems have made great progress in imitating human-like responses. In recent years, we have witnessed the rapid development of empathetic dialogue systems in endowing machines with emotional intelligence, which enables conversational models to better understand users' emotions, empathize with interlocutors, and achieve in-depth social interaction.

© The Author(s), under exclusive license to Springer Nature Switzerland AG 2023
L. Iliadis et al. (Eds.): ICANN 2023, LNCS 14262, pp. 152–165, 2023.
https://doi.org/10.1007/978-3-031-44201-8_13

An essential step in building an empathetic dialogue system is to evaluate the quality of the generated dialogue from the perspective of human emotions. Traditional evaluation metrics have the drawback of simply assessing the semantic equivalence instead of emotional-related characteristics. For instance, the BLEU [1] score, compares the candidate sentences with annotated references by calculating the n-gram overlap. Although it provides a simple and universal measurement method, this metric is insufficient to reflect the diversity of sentence composition and the amount of emotional information in generated responses. In recent years, the way to evaluate the fluency of statements has been constantly developed, such as BertScore [2], BartScore [3], etc. However, these evaluation method mainly focus on the assessment of sentence coherence, ignoring other significant aspects including emotional intensity. At present, the most reliable evaluation of dialog systems is still based on manual evaluation, which is time- and cost-intensive, and is not suitable for large-scale applications in scientific research.

In addition, how to evaluate the performance of an empathetic dialogue system is also an urgent problem. Train on conversations from different speakers, existing empathetic dialogue systems ignore the individual differences of expressing emotions, which may lead to inconsistent emotional interactions and disinterest users, because they may still feel that they are talking with a cold machine [4]. Mehrabian [5] showed that personality, such as the "Big Five personality" model [6], can also be expressed as temperament in the Valence-Arousal-Dominance (VAD) space for emotions [7]. This finding shows that different personalities have different effects on emotional expressions. For example, when feeling happy, extroverts may shout out, while introverts may only smile; At the same time, emotional expressions will also be affected by the Context. If a person's mood is very happy, the negative emotional response generated in the process of talking with others will be weakened, while the positive emotional response will be enhanced. Inspired by these works and phenomena, we propose a dialogue emotion evaluation method which is affected by personality. The sentence is modified by personality and Context, so that it can judge the emotional expression intensity of the sentence when it can perceive personality and context.

To be specific, our evaluation method analyzes the speaker's personality firstly, modifies the utterances based on personality, then models the emotional state in the conversation, considers the speaker's emotional change in the conversation, and finally calculates the intensity of emotional expressions. In addition to the assessment of emotional intensity, we also put forward the assessment of the fluency and coherence of dialogues at the sentence and session levels.

To sum up, the main contributions of our paper are as follows: (1) We propose **PCDialogEval**, a dialogue evaluation method that incorporates psychological concepts to measure the intensity of emotional expression and contextual awareness of personality. The method accounts for the speaker's personality and simulates the mood state of the conversation context to calculate the emotional expression intensity of the utterance. (2) Additionally, it evaluate dialogue fluency and coherence at both the independent sentence and session level.

(3) Experiments on the MELD and PERSONA-CHAT datasets demonstrate the effectiveness of our evaluation method, highlighting its superiority over traditional approaches in measuring the quality of emotional dialogue with respect to multiple aspects of personality and context.

2   Related Work

2.1   Dialogue Evaluation

Evaluating dialogue systems is a challenging task that has received significant attention in research. Evaluation is a crucial aspect of dialogue system development, aiming to provide an automated and repeatable process that can distinguish various dialogue strategies and identify critical features of the system [8]. Traditional evaluation methods involving human assessments and questionnaires are time-consuming and costly, thus necessitating the development of automatic dialogue evaluation. Existing automatic evaluation metrics, such as BLEU [1], mainly focus on comparing the similarity between candidate and reference sentences but fail to capture the diversity of words and structures that convey meaning. Therefore, there is a need for developing a reference-free automatic evaluation metric that aligns well with human intuition.

2.2   Emotion Model

Two main categories of models have been proposed to simulate the relationship between different emotions: Dimensional Affective Models and Discrete Affective Methods. Dimensional models are based on the assumption that affect has inherent continuity and project emotions onto several dimensions for representation. The widely used VAD affective model represents Valence (pleasure), Arousal (emotional intensity), and Dominance (control). Dimensional models emphasize conscious experience or emotional phenomenology, whereas there are hypotheses that there are patterns of discrete or interactive emotions in the conscious brain [9–11]. Discrete models propose several basic discrete emotions on which complex emotions form [12], of which the most universal six items [13,14] include anger, aversion, fear, happiness, sadness, and surprise. However, there are many types of discrete models, including those with eight, five, or ten basic emotions. A hybrid model also exists that combines discrete emotions with positive and negative dimensions to represent emotion intensity.

3   Methodology

In this paper, we propose a novel dialogue evaluation method to assess the quality of dialogue in multiple dimensions, including the influence of persona and contexts, the intensity of emotional expression, and the coherence. We will start with the preliminary knowledge of personality and the impact of personality on emotional expression, and subsequently provide the technical details of the evaluation method that we propose.

3.1 Preliminaries

Personality. Personality is a synthesis of all the traits -behavioral, disposi- tional, emotional, and spiritual -that characterize a unique individual. As we all know, in addition to the semantic content, speech also conveys a lot of informa- tion about the speaker, including the speaker's personality characteristics, which is one of the most basic differences between people. In recent years, researchers have formed a relatively consistent consensus on the personality description model, and the "Big Five" model of personality (OCEAN) is called a revolution in personality psychology. Using lexicographic methods, five traits were found to cover all aspects of personality description:

Openness: Openminded, imaginative, and sensitive.
Conscientiousness: Scrupulous, well-organized.
Extraversion: The tendency to experience positive emotions.
Agreeableness: Trusting, sympathetic, and cooperative.
Neuroticism: The tendency to experience psychological distress.

The "Big Five" model has become a standard in psychology over the past 50 years. There is evidence that personality interacts with and influences other aspects of language production. Compared with pragmatic phenomena such as emotions and opinions, personality is usually considered as a more long-term and stable individual factor [15].

Personalities in the VAD Space. The "Big Five" personality characteristics are widely used in psychological analysis. Mehrabiana [5]uses the temperament model fitted by statistical analysis to represent the corresponding relationship between the "Big Five" personality characteristics O, C, E, A, N and VAD emotional dimensions:

$$V = 0.21E + 0.59A + 0.19N,$$
$$A = 0.30A - 0.56N + 0.15O, \tag{1}$$
$$D = 0.60E - 0.32A + 0.25O + 0.17C.$$

Emotions in the VAD Space. Our evaluation method uses six basic emo- tions: **surprise, fear, sadness, joy, disgust** and **anger**. Referring to the pre- vious research results [16], the basic emotions can be projected into the Valence- Arousal-Dominance (VAD) space, as shown in Table 1. The VAD space indicates emotion intensity in three dimensions, in which the valence represents positiv- ity/negativity, arousal represents excitement/calmness, and dominance repre- sents powerfulness/weakness. As for the utterances without obvious emotion, we use **neutral** with (0.00,0.00,0.00) as the VAD vector.

Personality Effects on Emotions. Emotions reflect an individual's psycho- logical state when interacting with people or environment [17], which is a com- plex psychological experience. The VAD emotional model uses three dimensions

Table 1. Emotions in the VAD space

Basic Emotions	(Valence, Arousal, Dominance)
Surprise	(0.40,0.67,−0.13)
Fear	(−0.62,0.82,−0.43)
Sadness	(−0.63,−0.27,−0.33)
Joy	(0.81,0.51,0.46)
Disgust	(−0.60,0.35,0.11)
Anger	(−0.51,0.59,0.25)
Neutral	(0.00,0.00,0.00)

to provide a comprehensive description of emotional states. In the past, some psychologists have studied the relationship between human affective factors and personality factors, but most of them are rule-based and probability-based models. Mehrabian [5] used the "Big Five" Personality Theory [18] to derive a VAD emotional model through linear regression analysis. Since then, VAD models have been widely used to design emotional interaction robots [17,19], where predefined personality of the robot affects its propensity to simulate emotional switching.

Based on the theories analyzed above, Ball [20] uses Bayesian network to encode emotional and personality models to generate empathetic behaviors or verbal responses in conversations. Han et al. [17] applies the five personality factors to a 2D model (pleasure-wake) to represent the emotional model of a robot. Masuyama et al. [19] use an affective associative memory model to allow the robot to express emotions. Although there have been some studies in the field of natural language processing using VAD space to simulate emotions [21–23], the impact of personality on emotions in conversation still needs to be further explored.

3.2   Our Methods

Personality Analysis. With the help of previous work, we use the personality recognition model [26] to analyze and calculate the speaker's "Big Five" personality vector. The model uses the word features marked in the LIWC dictionary [27] and the MRC language psychology database [28] to conduct a preliminary assessment of the five dimensions of personality characteristics in the word-segmented text, and then uses regression and ranking models to evaluate the accuracy of personality recognition. After optimization, a five-dimensional OCEAN vector is finally obtained as a personality feature. The approach to the model can be summarized in four steps:

Step 1: To collect personal corpus.

Step 2: To collect relevant personality ratings for each participant.

Step 3: To extract relevant features from the text, find and calculate LIWC and MRC features of sentences and words.

Step 4: To construct a statistical model of personality score based on characteristics, the input is the linguistic psychological characteristics of the text, and the output is personality score.

The output recognizes the personality as a five-dimensional vector, and obtains a score in the interval $(0, 7)$ for each dimension.

Sentence-Level Emotional Expression Intensity. Personality affects how people express themselves and experience emotions. Different personalities respond differently to the same thing, with varying emotional expression. Researchers study the relationship between personality traits and emotional responses to better understand this. By incorporating personality into emotional response modeling, we can gain insights into how people with different personalities react to the same thing. Mehrabiana used statistical analysis and fitting to obtain the corresponding relationship between the emotional dimension of VAD and different personality traits [5] as Eq. (1).

The average score of each dimension of the population obtained from the "Big Five" personality scale is used as the reference point of each dimension, the position of the reference point is taken as the neutral point, and the part beyond the neutral point is taken as the factor affecting the VAD emotion. The emotional corresponding vector formula after personality modification is:

$$\hat{e}_p = \hat{e} + \hat{e}_p^*,\tag{2}$$

$$[\Delta E, \Delta A, \Delta N, \Delta O, \Delta C] = [E, A, N, O, C] - [\bar{E}, \bar{A}, \bar{N}, \bar{O}, \bar{C}]\tag{3}$$

$$\hat{e}_p^* = \begin{bmatrix} 0.21 & 0.59 & 0.19 & 0 & 0 \\ 0 & 0.30 & -0.56 & 0.15 & 0 \\ 0.60 & -0.32 & 0 & 0.25 & 0.17 \end{bmatrix} \cdot \begin{bmatrix} \Delta E \\ \Delta A \\ \Delta N \\ \Delta O \\ \Delta C \end{bmatrix}\tag{4}$$

where $\hat{e}_p$ is the emotional response vector obtained after the correction of the "Big Five" personality factors; $\hat{e}_p^*$ is the modification value of the "Big Five" personality factors in the three dimensions of V, A, and D; $\bar{O}$, $\bar{C}$, $\bar{E}$, $\bar{A}$, $\bar{N}$ represent the average scores of the population on the five dimensions obtained from the "Big Five" personality scale, which are 0.70, 0.73, 0.61, 0.60, and 0.60, respectively. Take these as a neutral level of human personality.

Next, the calculation of emotional expression intensity is carried out. Since the VAD emotional space is not a uniform Euclidean space, the Euclidean distance cannot be directly used to measure the intensity of emotion. Therefore, a calculation formula of emotional intensity suitable for VAD emotional space is proposed:

$$\hat{E}_p = \begin{cases} \|\hat{e}_p\| \, |\cos\theta| / \|\hat{e}_s\|, & \hat{E} > 0 \\ 0, & \hat{E} \leqslant 0 \end{cases}\tag{5}$$

where $\hat{E}_p$ is the emotional intensity that corresponds to $\hat{e}_p$, $\hat{e}_s$ is the reference emotional vector, and $\cos\theta$ is the cosine value of the angle between $\hat{e}_p$ and $\hat{e}_s$.

Session-Level Emotional Expression Intensity. In everyday life, people's moods can impact how they react emotionally to external stimuli. Emotions accumulate and affect one's overall state of mind. We have explored using mood state to modify emotional vectors and incorporating personality information. By doing so, we can better understand how personality and mood can interact with emotional states to impact overall emotional experience. We define the update state equation of the mood as follows:

$$\hat{e}_{\mathrm{pm}} = \varphi m_k + \hat{e}_{\mathrm{p}} \tag{6}$$

$$m_{k+1} = \begin{cases} m_0, & k = 0 \\ \frac{\gamma}{e^{\|m_0\|}} \hat{e}_{\mathrm{p}} + \left(1 - \frac{\gamma}{e^{\|m_0\|}}\right) m_k, & k > 0 \end{cases} \tag{7}$$

where γ is the influence coefficient of e_p on m_k, $\gamma = 0.2$.

Similarly, after modifying the emotion vectors using contextual information, the following formula is used to calculate the emotion intensity calculation formula of the VAD emotion space:

$$\hat{E}_{\mathrm{pm}} = \begin{cases} \|\hat{e}_{\mathrm{pm}}\| \, |\cos\theta| / \|\hat{e}_{\mathrm{s}}\|, & \hat{E} > 0 \\ 0, & \hat{E} \leqslant 0 \end{cases} \tag{8}$$

where $\hat{E}_{\mathrm{pm}}$ is the emotional intensity corresponding to $\hat{e}_{\mathrm{pm}}$, $\hat{e}_{\mathrm{s}}$ is the reference emotional vector, and $\cos\theta$ is the cosine value of the angle between $\hat{e}_{\mathrm{pm}}$ and $\hat{e}_{\mathrm{s}}$.

Sentence-Level Coherence Evaluation. In some natural language generation tasks, assessing the quality of generated responses using the BLUE score is not possible due to the lack of reference sentences. To overcome this, we use an automatic scoring method to measure the fluency of generated sentences. This method is similar to the perplexity and BARTScore evaluations [3], providing a more reliable means of evaluating the performance of natural language generation models:

$$S = -\sum_{i=1}^{L} \frac{1}{L} \log p\left(y_i \mid y_{<i}, \theta\right) \tag{9}$$

where y_i denotes the ith token in the generated response, θ stands for the language model, which is a fine-tuned GPT-2 [24] in our experiments; L is the sequence length.

With such a score, we can properly measure the response quality when BLEU score [1] is no longer applicable as the metric for evaluating dialogue response quality.

Session-Level Coherence Evaluation. In addition to sentence-level response quality, it is also important to measure the coherence of sentences throughout the session. Therefore, we use the session-level score to explore inter-sentence coherence in the whole dialogue.

Inspired by the next sentence prediction task [25], we construct a binary classification model to predict whether the interactions between adjacent sentences in a dialogue are coherent or not. Consider a continuous session consisting of the sentence u_t and its corresponding response r_t, and the next sentence u_{t+1}. We suppose the dialogue turns such as $[u_t, r_t]$ and $[r_t, u_{t+1}]$ are coherent in nature. We randomly select a response r^* to construct negative samples to train a binary classification to evaluate session-level correlations. After building the binary classifier, we use the average score (softmaxed confidence) of all $[u_t, r_t]$ and $[r_t, u_{t+1}]$ pairs in a session as the session-level score.

The session-level score can be used as an evaluator to measure the fluency of the whole session, that is, the session-level score evaluates the overall quality of sentences and responses at each turn. Therefore, such a score can be used to evaluate the performance of dialogue systems.

4   Experiments

4.1   Datasets

PERSONA-CHAT is a dataset consisting of conversations between randomly paired crowdworkers, each of whom is asked to play a given role (created by another group of crowdworkers), communicate naturally in the conversation, and get to know each other, resulting in interesting and engaging dialogue. The PERSONA-CHAT dataset contains 10,981 dialogues and 164,356 sentences. Each character in the dataset has a personality description (persona) of more than five sentences for personalized dialogue generation.
MELD is a collection of scripts from the TV series "Friends", containing daily dialogues with rich themes. The emotion labels include neutrality and Ekman's six basic emotions [29], namely happiness, surprise, sadness, anger, disgust, and fear.

4.2   Implementations

Baseline Models. A variety of excellent models were selected as baseline models: (1) **Seq-2Seq** [30] is a simple generation-based method that has been widely used in dialogue generation tasks. (2) **HRED** [31], a hierarchical encoder-decoder network, performs well due to its context modeling capability. (3) **ReCoSa** [32] employs self-attention to measure the correlation between response and dialogue history and achieves state-of-the-art performance on benchmark datasets. (4) **TTransfo** [33], proposed by the Huggingface team, is the first-place solution for automatic evaluation in the ConvAI2 competition, obtained by fine-tuning a pre-trained language model GPT on personalized dialogue data. (5) **LIC** [34], proposed by the Lost in Conversation team, is the first-place solution for human evaluation in the same competition, using a multi-input model that utilizes the encoder-decoder structure with GPT initialization parameters. (6) **AR** [35] is an encoder-decoder architecture similar to the full version of the

Transformer architecture. It incorporates context and persona embeddings of the corresponding speaker and concatenates persona key-value pairs of the target sequence into another sequence, which are then fed into the same encoder and decoder.

Automatic Metrics. (1) **PPL** is a language model quality metric that estimates the probability of a sentence based on each word and normalizes it by sentence length. Lower values indicate more coherent sentences. (2) **BLEU** [1] is used to calculate the similarity between generated responses and gold responses, commonly used in NLP tasks. Higher values indicate better results. (3) **Dist-n** [36] measures text diversity by the proportion of non-repeated n-grams to total n-grams. This paper employs Distinct-2 (Dist-2) to assess model diversity.

Proposed Evaluation. For **Emotional Expression Intensity**, we first calculate Sentence-level Emotional Expression Intensity and Session-level Emotional Expression Intensity on MELD and PERSONA-CHAT data sets respectively. After completing the calculation, we count their average and maximum emotional expression intensity, and conduct extensive case studies, which will be discussed in detail later. For the **sentence-level score**, we use a GPT-2 model and fine-tune the model using the dataset to be tested for special token learning. For the **session-level score**, we use a BERT-base model as the binary classification model and use the average softmax logits. For the sentence-level scores, we use a GPT-2 model and fine-tune the model using the data set to be tested for special token learning. In the implementation, we set the batch size to 32, trained the score model for 10 epochs with the learning rate of 1e-4, and added early stopping to prevent over-fitting.

Human Evaluation. For metrics without references, human evaluation is still the most reliable. Therefore, we designed corresponding human evaluation for emotional expression intensity and fluency evaluation respectively. Five human annotators are employed to score 100 test examples for each dataset from five aspects:

Sentence-level Emotional Expression Intensity: annotators need to observe separated utterances and, based on the speaker's personality, give a sense of how emotionally intense the utterance is.

Session-level Emotional Expression Intensity: annotators read the entire conversations and give the intensity of emotional expression they feel for each utterance based on the personalities and interactions of the speakers.

Fluency: measures whether the response is fluent and human-like, to match our sentence-level coherence evaluation, the rating scale ranges from 0 to 4 (higher scores indicating better results);

Coherency: measures whether the response is coherent with the dialogue context; to match our session-level coherence evaluation, the rating scale ranges from 0 to 1;

Consistency: measures whether the response is consistent with the target persona, rating scale ranges from 0 to 5.

4.3   Result Analysis

Automatic Evaluation. We calculate the automatic metrics on the baseline models for two datasets, PERSONA-CHAT and MELD, respectively. The results are shown in Table 2.

Table 2. Results of automatic metrics

PERSONA-CHAT				MELD			
Models	PPL	BLEU	Dist-2	Models	PPL	BLEU	Dist-2
LIC	–	1.97	0.248	Seq2Seq	108.29	1.34	2.13
TTransfo	17.87	2.08	0.273	HRED	121.51	1.17	1.55
AR	15.84	2.15	0.270	ReCoSa	114.19	2.11	2.57

From the results in Table 2, the BLEU scores of the baseline models on the two datasets are relatively close, while the PPL scores and Dist-2 scores of the PERSONA-CHAT based model are generally lower than those of the MELD-based model. This is most likely due to the source of the dataset, PERSONA-CHAT is crowdsourced by humans, and the generated sentences are more mundane and homogeneous in composition than the MELD extracted from the TV series.

Proposed Evaluation. We calculate the average and maximum emotional expression intensity on MELD and PERSONA-CHAT, as for human evaluation, annotators rate the emotional intensity of separated sentences, or sentences in a whole conversation, and the average of all annotators' scores are used as Sentence-Avg. and Session-Avg., the results are shown in Table 3.

Table 3. Statistical data of emotional expression intensity

Datasets		MELD	PERSONA-CHAT
Sentence-level	Avg.	**2.36**	1.06
	Max	13.41	9.60
Session-level	Avg.	**10.44**	1.46
	Max	119.26	40.71
Human Evaluation	Sentence-Avg.	**2.77**	1.35
	Session-Avg.	**16.53**	1.57

As seen in Table 3, the emotional expression intensity of MELD is higher than that of PERSONA-CHAT. The possible reason is that MELD is collected from the comedy "The Big Bang Theory", in which the dialogue emotions are rich and the expressions are exaggerated. While PERSONA-CHAT comes from the chit-chat of crowdsourcing workers, there are no fixed topics and emotions, so the overall emotional expression intensities are relatively low.

The sentence-coherence and session-coherence scores of MELD and PERSONA-CHAT, as well as the relative human evaluation scores are shown in Table 4. In this part, human annotators rate the extracted dialogues on Fluency, Coherency, and Consistency. We collect all human ratings and take the average as the final result of human evaluation.

Table 4. Results of different datasets under sentence-score and session-score

Metrics		MELD	PERSONA-CHAT
Our Evaluation	Sentence-Score	2.80	**3.35**
	Session-Score	0.72	**0.94**
Human Evaluation	Flu.	2.77	**3.27**
	Coh.	0.72	**0.92**
	Con.	**4.23**	3.9

As seen in Table 4, the sentence coherence score of PERSONA-CHAT is 3.35, 0.55 higher than MELD, and the session coherence score is 0.94, 0.22 higher than MELD. PERSONA-CHAT performs better than MELD in both metrics, with more fluent sentences and more coherent sessions.

We calculate the Pearson correlation between the above metrics and the human evaluation. Since the scale of each metric is different, we use the Avg./Max of each metric as the attribute value to measure the correlation, and the results are shown in Table 5.

Table 5. Pearson correlation with human judgments on PERSONA-CHAT and MELD datasets

Metrics	PERSONA-CHAT	MELD
PPL	0.81	0.75
BLEU	0.78	0.68
Dist-2	0.84	0.87
Our Evaluation	**0.95**	**0.91**

The results show that the Pearson correlation coefficient between the proposed metric and human evaluation is 0.91 on the MELD dataset, and 0.95 on the PERSONA-CHAT dataset, both higher than the automatic metrics on the baseline models. The correlation coefficients show that our methods are highly correlated with human evaluation results.

5   Conclusion

In this paper, we propose PCDialogEval, an innovative evaluation model for assessing the quality of generated conversations. Our approach incorporates psychological concepts to evaluate dialogue systems, leveraging the speaker's persona to modify the emotion vector in the Valence-Arousal-Dominance (VAD) space and employing the mood transfer equation to model the conversation context to measure the intensity of emotional expression in the conversation. Moreover, PCDialogEval assesses fluency and coherence at both the sentence and session levels, based on the dialogue itself. Through experiments conducted on two datasets, our method demonstrates significant effectiveness in terms of persona and contextual awareness, offering a novel and efficient evaluation approach for emotional dialogue.

Acknowledgments. This work was supported by National Natural Science Foundation of China (No. 62006077).

References

1. Papineni, K., Roukos, S., Ward, T., Zhu, W.J.: BLEU: a method for automatic evaluation of machine translation. In: Proceedings of the 40th Annual Meeting of the Association for Computational Linguistics, pp. 311–318 (2002)
2. Zhang, T., Kishore, V., Wu, F., Weinberger, K.Q., Artzi, Y.: BERTScore: Evaluating text generation with bert. In: arXiv preprint arXiv:1904.09675 (2019)
3. Yuan, W., Neubig, G., Liu, P.: BARTScore: evaluating generated text as text generation. In: Neural Information Processing Systems, pp. 27263–27277 (2021)
4. Wen, Z., Cao, J., Yang, R., Liu, S., Shen, J.: Automatically select emotion for response via personality-affected emotion transition. In: Findings of the Association for Computational Linguistics: ACL-IJCNLP, pp. 5010–5020 (2021)
5. Mehrabian, A.: Analysis of the big-five personality factors in terms of the PAD temperament model. Aust. J. Psychol. **48**, 86–92 (1996)
6. Costa, P.T., McCrae, R.R.: Normal personality assessment in clinical practice: the NEO personality inventory. In: Psychological assessment, pp. 5 (1992)
7. Mehrabian, A.: Pleasure-arousal-dominance: a general framework for describing and measuring individual differences in temperament. In: Current Psychology, pp. 261–292 (1996)
8. Deriu, J., et al.: Survey on evaluation methods for dialogue systems. In: Artificial Intelligence Review, pp. 755–810 (2021)
9. Izard, C.E.: Human emotions. In: Springer Science & Business Media, pp. 1–54 (2013)
10. Izard, C.E.: Basic emotions, natural kinds, emotion schemas, and a new paradigm. In: Perspectives on Psychological Science, pp. 260–280 (2007)
11. Izard, C.E.: Levels of emotion and levels of consciousness. In: Behavioral and Brain Sciences, pp. 96–98 (2007)
12. Russell, J.A.: Is there universal recognition of emotion from facial expression? A review of the cross-cultural studies. In: Psychological Bulletin, pp. 102 (1994)
13. Ekman, P., Friesen, W.V., O'sullivan, M., Chan, A., Diacoyanni-Tarlatzis, I., et al.: Universals and cultural differences in the judgments of facial expressions of emotion. In: Journal of Personality and Social Psychology, pp. 712 (1987)

14. Ekmann, P.: Universal facial expressions in emotion. In: Studia Psychologica, pp. 140 (1973)
15. Scherer, K.R.: Vocal communication of emotion: a review of research paradigms. In: Speech Communication, pp. 227–256 (2003)
16. Russell, J.A., Mehrabian, A.: Evidence for a three-factor theory of emotions. In: Journal of Research in Personality, pp. 273–294 (1977)
17. Han, M.J., Lin, C.H., Song, K.T.: Robotic emotional expression generation based on mood transition and personality model. In: IEEE Transactions on Cybernetics, pp. 1290–1303 (2012)
18. Costa, P.T., McCrae, R.R.: Normal personality assessment in clinical practice: the NEO personality inventory. In: Psychological Assessment, pp. 5 (1992)
19. Masuyama, N., Loo, C.K., Seera, M.: Personality affected robotic emotional model with associative memory for human-robot interaction. In: Neurocomputing, pp. 213–225 (2018)
20. Ball, G., Breese, J.: Emotion and personality in a conversational agent. In: Embodied Conversational Agents, pp. 189 (2000)
21. Mohammad, S.: Obtaining reliable human ratings of valence, arousal, and dominance for 20,000 English words. In: Proceedings of the 56th Annual Meeting of the Association for Computational Linguistics, pp. 174–184 (2018)
22. Colombo, P., Witon, W., Modi, A., Kennedy, J., Kapadia, M.: Affect-driven dialog generation. In: arXiv preprint arXiv:1904.02793 (2019)
23. Asghar, N., Poupart, P., Hoey, J., Jiang, X., Mou, L.: Affective neural response generation. In: European Conference on Information Retrieval, pp. 154–166 (2018)
24. Radford, A., Wu, J., Child, R., Luan, D., Amodei, D., Sutskever, I.: Language models are unsupervised multitask learner. In: OpenAI blog, pp. 9 (2019)
25. Devlin, J., Chang, M.W., Lee, K., Toutanova, K.: BERT: pre-training of deep bidirectional transformers for language understanding. In: North American Chapter of the Association for Computational Linguistics (NAACL) (2018)
26. Mairesse, F., Walker, M.A., Mehl, M.R., Moore, R.K.: Using linguistic cues for the automatic recognition of personality in conversation and text. In: Journal of Artificial Intelligence Research, pp. 457–500 (2007)
27. Pennebaker, J.W., Francis, M.E., Booth, R.J.: Linguistic inquiry and word count: LIWC 2001. In: Mahway: Lawrence Erlbaum Associates (2001)
28. Coltheart, M.: The MRC psycholinguistic database. In: The Quarterly Journal of Experimental Psychology Section A, pp. 497–505 (1981)
29. Poria, S., Hazarika, D., Majumder, N., Naik, G., Cambria, E., Mihalcea, R.: MELD: a multimodal multi-party dataset for emotion recognition in conversations. In: Proceedings of the 57th Annual Meeting of the Association for Computational Linguistics, pp. 527–536 (2019)
30. Sutskever, I., Vinyals, O., Le, Q.V.: Sequence to sequence learning with neural networks. In: Advances in Neural Information Processing Systems (2014)
31. Serban, I., Sordoni, A., Bengio, Y., Courville, A., Pineau, J.: Building end-to-end dialogue systems using generative hierarchical neural network models. In: AAAI (2016)
32. Zhang, H., Lan, Y., Pang, L., Guo, J., Cheng, X.: ReCoSa: detecting the relevant contexts with self-attention for multi-turn dialogue generation. In: Proceedings of the 57th Annual Meeting of the Association for Computational Linguistics, pp. 3721–3730 (2019)
33. Wolf, T., Sanh, V., Chaumond, J., Delangue, C.: TransferTransfo: A transfer learning approach for neural network based conversational agents. In: arXiv preprint arXiv:1901.08149 (2019)

34. Golovanov, S., Kurbanov, R., Nikolenko, S., Truskovskyi, K., Tselousov, A., Wolf, T.: Large-scale transfer learning for natural language generation. In: Proceedings of the 57th Annual Meeting of the Association for Computational Linguistics, pp. 6053–6058 (2019)
35. Zheng, Y., Zhang, R., Huang, M., Mao, X.: A pre-training based personalized dialogue generation model with persona-sparse data. In: Proceedings of the AAAI Conference on Artificial Intelligence, pp. 9693–9700 (2020)
36. Li, J., Galley, M., Brockett, C., Gao, J., Dolan, B.: A diversity-promoting objective function for neural conversation models. In: Proceedings of the 2016 Conference of the North American. Chapter of the Association for Computational Linguistics: Human Language Technologies, 2016, pp. 110–119 (2016)

PlantDet: A Benchmark for Plant Detection in the Three-Rivers-Source Region

Huanhuan Li[1], Yu-an Zhang[1]([✉]), Xuechao Zou[1], Zhiyong Li[1], Jiangcai Zhaba[2], Guomei Li[2], and Lamao Yongga[2]

[1] Department of Computer Technology and Applications, Qinghai University, Xining, China
2011990029@qhu.edu.cn
[2] Forestry and Grassland Comprehensive Service Center of Yushu Prefecture, Yushu, China
https://www.qhu.edu.cn/

Abstract. The Three-River-Source region is a highly significant natural reserve in China that harbors a plethora of botanical resources. To meet the practical requirements of botanical research and intelligent plant management, we construct a dataset for **P**lant detection in the **T**hree-**R**iver-**S**ource region (PTRS). It comprises 21 types, 6965 high-resolution images of 2160 × 3840 pixels, captured by diverse sensors and platforms, and featuring objects of varying shapes and sizes. The PTRS presents us with challenges such as dense occlusion, varying leaf resolutions, and high feature similarity among plants, prompting us to develop a novel object detection network named PlantDet. This network employs a window-based efficient self-attention module (ST block) to generate robust feature representation at multiple scales, improving the detection efficiency for small and densely-occluded objects. Our experimental results validate the efficacy of our proposed plant detection benchmark, with a precision of 88.1%, a mean average precision (mAP) of 77.6%, and a higher recall compared to the baseline. Additionally, our method effectively overcomes the issue of missing small objects.

Keywords: Object Detection · Plant Recognition · Transformer

1 Introduction

The Three-Rivers-Source region is located in the hinterland of the Qinghai-Tibet Plateau, in the southern part of Qinghai Province. It is the largest nature reserve in China, containing extremely rich wild plant resources. In recent years, the conservation of flora and fauna in the Three-Rivers-Source region has become a focus of attention. However, due to its remote geographical location, underdeveloped information technology, people's awareness of vegetation protection in the Three-Rivers-Source region is relatively low. Therefore, conducting a survey of plant resources in the Three-Rivers-Source region, especially in plant detection, is of great significance for achieving intelligent plant management and protection.

© The Author(s), under exclusive license to Springer Nature Switzerland AG 2023
L. Iliadis et al. (Eds.): ICANN 2023, LNCS 14262, pp. 166–177, 2023.
https://doi.org/10.1007/978-3-031-44201-8_14

In recent years, with the rapid development of artificial intelligence and computer vision, many convolutional neural network models based on deep learning,such as AlexNet [1], ResNet [2], and VGGNet [3], have emerged. They have propelled the development of object detection algorithms. The introduction of algorithms such as SSD [4], YOLO series [5–10], and the algorithms based on the R-CNN [11], has expanded the promotion and application of object detection in the agricultural field. Numerous experimental results have shown that algorithmic models based on convolutional neural networks perform well in plant recognition research. Therefore, utilizing artificial intelligence and deep learning technology to detect plants in the Three-Rivers-Source region is feasible.

In essence, we have made the following contributions:

- We collected 6965 plant images of 21 categories from the Three-River-Source region, and manually annotated them to establish a large-scale dataset called PTRS for plant detection. This dataset lays the foundation for precise and modern plant detection in the Three-River-Source region.
- We proposed a novel object detection benchmark called PlantDet on PTRS to tackle the challenges of uneven leaf sizes and high feature similarity of diverse plant species. This method consists of three parts: Backbone, Neck, and Head. We introduced an efficient self-attention module based on sliding windows to enhance the feature extraction ability of the backbone and obtained robust feature representation of different scales through efficient feature fusion strategies.
- Experimental results on PTRS demonstrated that our benchmark (PlantDet) surpasses the baseline (YOLOv5), achieves a precision of 88.1% and mAP of 77.6%, and mitigates the problem of missed detection and false positives for small objects.

2   Related Work

2.1   Object Detection

Compared to image classification, object detection not only identifies the category of various objects in the image but also determines their location. Object detection can be divided into two types: one is the two-stage algorithm represented by R-CNN [11]. The principle of such methods is to generate candidate boxes, search for prospects, and adjust bounding boxes through specialized modules. Although this candidate region-based detection method has relatively high accuracy, it runs slowly and does not meet the demand for real-time detection.

To tackle the crucial issue of slow detection speed, one-stage object detection algorithms such as SSD and YOLO series algorithms have emerged. They consider the detection task as a regression problem and directly classify and locate objects in the image through a single neural network. Due to the usage of a single network, they are relatively faster and can meet the real-time detection requirements in the industry. The YOLO series of algorithms have been widely applied in the agricultural field such as detecting diseases and pests [12], maturity [13], and growth stages [14], among others.

2.2   Visual Transformer

In 2017, the Google research team proposed the transformer architecture based on the self-attention mechanism, which achieved tremendous success in the field of natural language processing. The rapid development of the transformer in natural language processing has attracted widespread attention in the field of computer vision. The advantage of a transformer lies in its explicit modeling of long-range dependencies between contextual information, so many researchers have attempted to apply the transformer to computer vision in order to enhance the overall perceptual ability of images. In 2020 Carion et al. [15] proposed the first end-to-end transformer-based object detection model. That same year, the proposal of the image classification model ViT [16] led to the rapid development of visual transformers.

Today, the visual transformer is widely used in various computer vision fields, such as image classification, object detection, image segmentation, and object tracking. So far, many algorithm models based on the visual transformer have emerged: 1) Transformer-based object detection and segmentation models, such as Swin Transformer [17] and Focal Transformer [18] which replace CNN-based backbone networks for feature extraction and combine classic object detection and segmentation networks to complete detection and segmentation tasks; 2) Transformer-based object tracking tasks, such as TrSiam [19] for single-object tracking tasks, TransTrack [20] for multi-object tracking. The rapid development of the transformer in computer vision is mainly due to its ability to extract the relevance of contextual information to obtain global receptive fields, which improves the performance of the model compared to CNN-based models.

3   Method

3.1   Overall Pipeline

Plant detection is an application of object detection technology in botany. A deep learning-based task takes an image with plants as input and outputs the plant's category and bounding box location of its leaves. The Three-River-Source region has diverse flora, to achieve real-time detection, we use YOLOv5 as the baseline for the plant detection pipeline.

Having an efficient model structure is one of the most critical issues in designing a real-time object detector. Our proposed method, PlantDet, uses CSPDark-Net and CSPPAFPN composed of the same building units for multi-scale feature fusion, and finally inputs the features into different detection heads. The overall model structure of PlantDet is shown in Fig. 1. PlantDet consists of three parts: 1) Backbone: it mainly performs feature extraction in the main part and effectively extracts crucial feature information of the feature map through downsampling; 2) Neck: this part consists of FPN [21] and PAN [22], respectively performing upsampling and downsampling to achieve the transmission of object feature vectors of different scales and fusion of multiple feature layers; 3) Head: which is made up of three multi-scale detectors and performs object detection on feature maps of different scales using grid-based anchors.

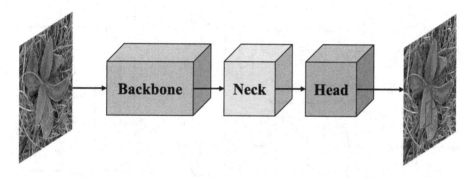

Fig. 1. A pipeline of our one-stage plant detection methods (like the Y0LO series).

3.2 Detection Backbone

We use YOLOv5 as the baseline for the plant detection pipeline. YOLOv5 consists of Input, Backbone, Neck and Head. The backbone (refer to Fig. 2(a)) mainly includes C3 and SPPF, where C3 consists of a CBS layer with x residual connections for Concat operation, which improves the feature extraction ability and retains more feature information. SPPF first performs the extracted feature map for multiple maximum pooling operations, and then the results after each maximum pooling are summed for Contact operation, i.e., feature fusion.

In response to the issue of difficult detection caused by varying distributions of leaf sizes in different plants, severe occlusion, and high feature overlap, we have introduced a sliding window module based on self-attention and embedded it into the backbone (refer to Fig. 2) to obtain a robust feature representation with multi-scale resolution.

Specifically, we have re-designed the C3 module in the YOLOv5 backbone, which has the most significant impact on feature extraction. The C3 module primarily acquires feature representation through two parallel convolution branches and introduces residual connections, but does not consider modeling global contextual information. Therefore, we have introduced a self-attention module named "ST block" (refer to Fig. 2(c)) to obtain a global receptive field and more robust representation.

The ST block includes sliding window operation with hierarchical design. It consists of LayerNorm and a shifted window-based MSA with two layers of MLP. Firstly, input features are normalized using Layer Normalization (LN) to expedite model convergence. Subsequently, global feature representation is obtained through the multi-head self-attention mechanism. Furthermore, the features are further enhanced and their expression ability is strengthened through the use of MLP. Finally, residual connection is employed for feature reuse. In addition, a window mechanism is utilized to reduce the additional overhead resulting from the calculation of self-attention matrices.

As is well known, Convolutional Neural Networks (CNNs) perform exceptionally well in local feature extraction due to their inductive bias, while transformer networks based on self-attention mechanisms are effective in modeling long-range

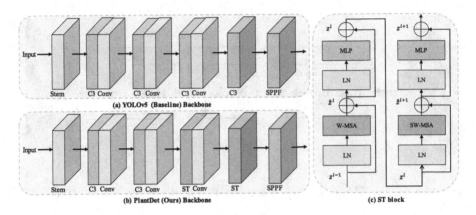

Fig. 2. Backbone of our proposed PlantDet and details of the ST block. (a) Structure of the original YOLOv5's backbone. (b) Structure of our proposed PlantDet's backbone. (c) Details of the ST block in PlantDet. The specially designed ST block is used for extracting global contextual information, mainly composed of W-MSA and SW-MSA, for information exchange within and between windows, respectively.

global contextual information. Taking into account the superiority of both convolutional and self-attention mechanisms, we have designed a robust backbone feature extractor for plant detection, as shown in Fig. 2(b). It consists of two C3 modules for local feature extraction and two ST blocks for global feature extraction. Finally, the SPPF module fuses the features extracted by both modules to obtain a robust feature representation.

3.3 Loss Function

The task of object detection involves the regression of bounding boxes in addition to classification. Consequently, the training loss function comprises three parts: 1) bounding box regression loss; 2) confidence prediction loss; 3) category prediction loss. These three loss functions are jointly optimized to achieve the goal of object detection

$$\mathcal{L} = \lambda_1 \mathcal{L}_{reg} + \lambda_2 \mathcal{L}_{obj} + \lambda_3 \mathcal{L}_{cls}, \tag{1}$$

where $\lambda_1, \lambda_2, \lambda_3$ represent the weights of the three loss functions, respectively.

Bounding Box Regression Loss. To account for the large variation in scale among different plant leaves and to balance the impact of objects of different sizes on detection performance, we use the Complete-IoU(CIoU) [23] to calculate the bounding box regression loss

$$\mathcal{L}_{reg} = CIoU = IoU - \frac{\rho^2}{c^2} - \alpha v, \tag{2}$$

where ρ, c, and v respectively represent the distance, the diagonal length and the similarity of aspect ratio between the centers of the predicted and ground-truth bounding boxes, and α represents the impact factor of v.

Confidence Loss. The loss function for confidence prediction is computed by matching positive and negative samples. Firstly, it involves the predicted confidence within the bounding box. Secondly, it uses the Intersection over Union (IoU) value between the predicted bounding box and its corresponding ground-truth bounding box as the ground-truth value. These two values are then used to calculate the final loss for the confidence prediction, which is obtained through binary cross-entropy

$$\mathcal{L}_{obj}(p_o, p_{iou}) = BCE_{obj}^{sig}(p_o, p_{iou}; w_{obj}), \tag{3}$$

where p_o and p_{iou} represent the predicted confidence and ground truth confidence, respectively, w_{obj} demonstrates the weight of positive samples.

Classification Loss. The category prediction loss is similar to the confidence loss. It involves predicting the category score within the bounding box and using the ground-truth one-hot encoding of the category for the corresponding ground-truth bounding box. The category prediction loss is computed using the following formula

$$\mathcal{L}_{cls}(c_p, c_{gt}) = BCE_{cls}^{sig}(c_p, c_{gt}; w_{cls}), \tag{4}$$

where c_p and c_{gt} represent the predicted values for the corresponding categories.

4 Experiments

4.1 Dataset

Data Collection. The research object of this experiment is the vegetation in the grassland plots distributed in the Three-River-Source region. The plant species image data were taken between July and August 2022 using a handheld camera, approximately 20 cm away from the plot, and recorded at a certain speed. After processing, 6965 grassland images were obtained, involving 21 plant species. The plant images involved in the experiment and their corresponding Latin names are shown in Fig. 3. These plants were all identified by experienced experts in the field.

Data Annotations. 6965 images of 21 plant species involved in this experiment were annotated by experienced experts in the field. Initially, the Make Sense(https://www.makesense.ai/) labeling tool provided by YOLO was utilized to generate label files containing information about plant categories and target plant coordinates. Subsequently, the above data was organized into VOC format datasets for **P**lant detection in the **T**hree-**R**iver-**S**ource region (PTRS). Finally, PTRS was divided into training, validation, and testing sets in an 8:1:1 ratio. In addition, comparing our dataset PTRS with other plant detection datasets, the detailed comparison results of these existing datasets are shown in Table 1.

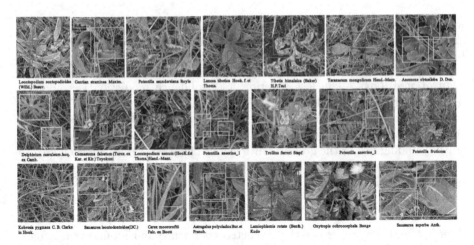

Fig. 3. Samples and corresponding Latin names of our dataset for Plant detection in the Three-River-Source region (PTRS).

Table 1. Comparison among PTRS (Ours) and other plant detection datasets in agriculture. "-" indicates that this metric is not revealed in the original paper.

Dataset	Annotation way	Classes	Instances	Images	Image Size
AT [24]	Oriented Bounding Box	1	1000	1000	410*410
GHLD [25]	Horizontal Bounding Box	1	-	300	416*416
TDAP [26]	Horizontal Bounding Box	1	-	5000	-
TFP [27]	Oriented Bounding Box	1	-	814	-
GPSD [28]	Horizontal Bounding Box	4	-	1200	-
PTRS (Ours)	Horizontal Bounding Box	**21**	**122300**	**6965**	**2160*3840**

4.2 Implementation Details

Training Settings. The important training parameters for the model in this experiment were set as follows: training epoch of 300, uniform resizing of input images to 640 × 640 resolution, training batch-size of 32, an initial learning rate of 0.01 with Stochastic Gradient Descent (SGD) optimizer. The model was trained on a device with a GPU of 1xNVIDIA A100 and 80GB memory, and the deep learning framework PyTorch was used for implementation.

Evaluation Metrics. In these experiments, Precision (P), Recall (R), and mean of Average Precision (mAP@0.5) are used as evaluation metrics.

4.3 Ablation Studies

Transformer Backbone. To investigate the efficacy of self-attention mechanisms and determine the optimal mechanism applicable to plant detection, we conducted experiments using YOLOv5 as the baseline as shown in Table 2.

Table 2. Ablation experiments of self-attention mechanisms.

Self-Attention	Precision	Recall	mAP@0.5
Baseline	88.0	71.9	76.6
Baseline+MSA	86.1	66.2	72.1
Baseline+W-MSA	**88.1**	**72.9**	**77.6**

The MSA represents the original implementation of self-attention, whereas the W-MSA is a window-based self-attention mechanism. The experimental results demonstrate that compared to the model combined with MSA, the combination of W-MSA module yields better results on the PTRS dataset. Specifically, the Precision, Recall, and mAP were improved by 2.0%, 6.7%, and 5.5%, respectively. This improvement is attributed to the fact that the W-MSA is constructed based on the image resolution hierarchy, which not only achieves feature connections across different windows but also enhances information exchange among different windows, allowing for the extraction of more effective multi-scale feature information to exhibit superior detection performance.

Strategy for Combining Global and Local Modules. In the original YOLOv5, the feature extraction network of the backbone consists of four C3 modules. We conducted ablation experiments to explore the impact of different module combination strategies (C3 and ST block) on the detection results, and the results are shown in Table 3.

Table 3. Ablation experiments of module combination strategies.

Number of Module		Precision	Recall	mAP@0.5
C3	ST block			
0	4	87.3	70.8	75.9
1	3	84.3	72.5	75.8
2	**2**	**88.1**	**72.9**	**77.6**
3	1	85.7	72.3	76.0
4	0	88.0	71.9	76.6

The results indicate that the best performance in feature extraction is achieved by using two C3 modules and two ST blocks in the backbone. This is because the C3 module based on the convolutional network can extract local features, while the ST block based on self-attention can extract global features, and the fusion of the two types of features can obtain a more robust feature representation. Therefore, we use two C3 modules and two ST blocks for feature extraction, aiming to improve model performance while minimizing model parameters and computation time complexity.

5   Comparison with the State-of-the-Arts

Quantitative Comparison. We conducted experiments to quantitatively compare PlantDet with currently popular object detection algorithms on our self-made PTRS dataset. The results are shown in Table 4. The results indicate that comparing to the baseline YOLOv5, the Recall and mAP of PlantDet increased by 1%, and achieves SOTA results. The outstanding performance of PlantDet is due to the robust detection backbone we have proposed, which integrates global and local information to obtain a more robust multi-scale feature representation. In addition, the numerical evaluation results of Precision, Recall and mAP of baseline (YOLOv5) and PlantDet on the PTRS dataset are shown in Table 5.

Table 4. Quantitative comparison between our and existing models on the dat-aset.

Mothods	Precision	Recall	mAP@0.5
SSD [4]	46.6	18.6	48.9
FCOS [29]	–	71.8	57.4
CornerNet [30]	11.0	51.9	38.1
Fast R-CNN [31]	–	40.0	56.3
YOLOF [32]	–	69.7	54.6
YOLOv7 [10]	84.9	72.7	76.0
YOLOv5	88.0	71.9	76.6
PlantDet (Ours)	**88.1**	**72.9**	**77.6**

Qualitative Comparison. In order to further verify the superiority of our proposed PlantDet for plant detection, we conducted qualitative experiments to compare the detection performance of PlantDet and other models (FCOS, YOLOv5 and YOLOv7). The specific visualization results are shown in Fig. 4.

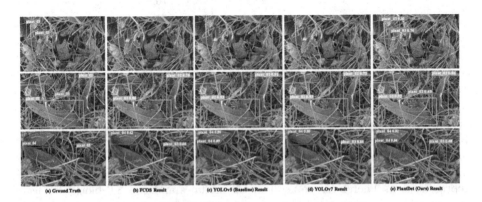

Fig. 4. Visualization results on our PTRS dataset.

Table 5. Numerical results of YOLOv5 and our PlantDet in 21 categories of our PTRS dataset. Size represents the size of plant leaves, obtained by calculating the bounding box size of all class instances. It can be easily observed that PlantDet enhances the detection performance of small and medium-sized targets, and has a superior effect.

Plant	Size	YOLOv5 (Baseline)			PlantDet (Ours)		
		Precision	Recall	mAP@0.5	Precision	Recall	mAP@0.5
01	Small	86.9	66.6	73.6	85.4	**65.4**	72.8
02	Medium	88.9	77.1	82.3	88.9	76.7	82.1
03	Medium	89.2	74.9	80.8	**89.5**	**74.9**	**80.8**
04	Large	90.7	75.7	81.5	88.6	**76.3**	**81.8**
05	Medium	85.5	66.4	70.3	82.4	63.8	70.2
06	Medium	87.7	73.6	78.0	82.5	**74.3**	77.2
07	Small	90.0	73.3	77.8	**92.9**	68.0	75.0
08	Large	95.5	77.9	81.1	**96.2**	77.0	79.1
09	Small	82.8	67.2	69.8	**84.2**	**67.5**	**71.5**
10	Small	87.7	72.7	81.3	**98.8**	**90.9**	**90.6**
11	Medium	93.5	76.3	81.1	92.3	75.2	**81.9**
12	Small	89.7	76.0	84.5	89.5	**84.0**	**88.2**
13	Medium	86.8	69.7	74.6	85.0	69.7	73.8
14	Medium	91.1	77.1	81.0	90.0	**77.9**	**81.8**
15	Small	77.2	53.4	57.6	73.2	**55.1**	**59.6**
16	Small	93.7	77.4	81.4	93.6	**80.2**	**85.4**
17	Small	82.6	68.2	69.7	81.7	68.1	**70.7**
18	Small	85.7	69.7	73.7	**86.1**	69.7	**75.0**
19	Large	79.8	66.7	66.0	80.4	61.9	63.7
20	Medium	93.3	86.0	92.7	**97.3**	86.0	89.7
21	Large	88.9	63.0	70.3	**91.8**	**68.5**	**79.6**
Avg	–	88.0	71.9	76.6	**88.1**	**72.9**	**77.6**

The visualization results show that compering with other models, our Plant-Det can effectively prevent the occurrence of missed inspections and reduce the false detection rate while ensuring detection accuracy. In summary, our PlantDet has better performance for plant detection in the Three-River-Source region, and can meets the needs of botanical Studies and intelligent plant management.

6   Conclusion

To address the problem of varying leaf resolution, severe occlusion, and high feature similarity in plant species, we proposed a novel object detection benchmark called PlantDet. Experimental results show that our PlantDet achieves SOTA detection performance and effectively prevents false detection and missed detection. In addition, we construct a large-scale dataset for plant detection in the Three-River-Source region, which provides data foundation and technical support for the informatization of grassland resources and the construction of a smart ecological animal husbandry new model of "reducing pressure and increasing efficiency" for ecological protection of the Three-Rivers-Source region.

Acknowledgments. This study is supported by the Science and Technology Plan of Qinghai Province (2020-QY-218), and China Agriculture Research System of MOF and MARA (CARS-37).

References

1. Krizhevsky, A., Sutskever, I., Hinton, G.E.: Imagenet classification with deep convolutional neural networks. Commun. ACM **60**(6), 84–90 (2017)
2. He, K., Zhang, X., Ren, S., Sun, J.: Deep residual learning for image recognition. In: Proceedings of the IEEE Conference on Computer Vision and Pattern Recognition, pp. 770–778 (2016)
3. Simonyan, K., Zisserman, A.: Very deep convolutional networks for large-scale image recognition. arXiv preprint arXiv:1409.1556 (2014)
4. Liu, W., Anguelov, D., Erhan, D., Szegedy, C., Reed, S., Fu, C.-Y., Berg, A.C.: SSD: single shot multibox detector. In: Leibe, B., Matas, J., Sebe, N., Welling, M. (eds.) ECCV 2016. LNCS, vol. 9905, pp. 21–37. Springer, Cham (2016). https://doi.org/10.1007/978-3-319-46448-0_2
5. Redmon, J., Divvala, S., Girshick, R., Farhadi, A.: You only look once: unified, real-time object detection. In: Proceedings of the IEEE Conference on Computer Vision and Pattern Recognition, pp. 779–788 (2016)
6. Redmon, J., Farhadi, A.: Yolo9000: better, faster, stronger. In: Proceedings of the IEEE Conference on Computer Vision and Pattern Recognition, pp. 7263–7271 (2017)
7. Redmon, J., Farhadi, A.: Yolov3: an incremental improvement. arXiv preprint arXiv:1804.02767 (2018)
8. Bochkovskiy, A., Wang, C.Y., Liao, H.Y.M.: Yolov4: optimal speed and accuracy of object detection. arXiv preprint arXiv:2004.10934 (2020)
9. Li, C., et al.: Yolov6: a single-stage object detection framework for industrial applications. arXiv preprint arXiv:2209.02976 (2022)
10. Wang, C.Y., Bochkovskiy, A., Liao, H.Y.M.: Yolov7: trainable bag-of-freebies sets new state-of-the-art for real-time object detectors. arXiv preprint arXiv:2207.02696 (2022)
11. Girshick, R., Donahue, J., Darrell, T., Malik, J.: Rich feature hierarchies for accurate object detection and semantic segmentation. In: Proceedings of the IEEE Conference on Computer Vision and Pattern Recognition, pp. 580–587 (2014)
12. Liu, J., Wang, X.: Plant diseases and pests detection based on deep learning: a review. Plant Methods **17**, 1–18 (2021)
13. Mohammadi, V., Kheiralipour, K., Ghasemi-Varnamkhasti, M.: Detecting maturity of persimmon fruit based on image processing technique. Scientia Horticulturae **184**, 123–128 (2015)
14. Tian, Y., Yang, G., Wang, Z., Wang, H., Li, E., Liang, Z.: Apple detection during different growth stages in orchards using the improved yolo-v3 model. Comput. Electron. Agric. **157**, 417–426 (2019)

15. Carion, N., Massa, F., Synnaeve, G., Usunier, N., Kirillov, A., Zagoruyko, S.: End-to-end object detection with transformers. In: Vedaldi, A., Bischof, H., Brox, T., Frahm, J.-M. (eds.) ECCV 2020. LNCS, vol. 12346, pp. 213–229. Springer, Cham (2020). https://doi.org/10.1007/978-3-030-58452-8_13

16. Dosovitskiy, A., et al.: An image is worth 16x16 words: transformers for image recognition at scale. arXiv preprint arXiv:2010.11929 (2020)

17. Liu, Z., et al.: Swin transformer: Hierarchical vision transformer using shifted windows. In: Proceedings of the IEEE/CVF International Conference on Computer Vision, pp. 10012–10022 (2021)

18. Yang, J., et al.: Focal self-attention for local-global interactions in vision transformers. arXiv preprint arXiv:2107.00641 (2021)

19. Wang, N., Zhou, W., Wang, J., Li, H.: Transformer meets tracker: Exploiting temporal context for robust visual tracking. In: Proceedings of the IEEE/CVF Conference on Computer Vision and Pattern Recognition, pp. 1571–1580 (2021)

20. Sun, P., et al.: TransTrack: multiple object tracking with transformer. arXiv preprint arXiv:2012.15460 (2020)

21. Lin, T.Y., Dollár, P., Girshick, R., He, K., Hariharan, B., Belongie, S.: Feature pyramid networks for object detection. In: Proceedings of the IEEE Conference on Computer Vision and Pattern Recognition, pp. 2117–2125 (2017)

22. Wang, W., et al.: Efficient and accurate arbitrary-shaped text detection with pixel aggregation network. In: Proceedings of the IEEE/CVF International Conference on Computer Vision, pp. 8440–8449 (2019)

23. Zheng, Z., Wang, P., Liu, W., Li, J., Ye, R., Ren, D.: Distance-IOU loss: Faster and better learning for bounding box regression. In: Proceedings of the AAAI Conference on Artificial Intelligence, vol. 34, pp. 12993–13000 (2020)

24. Buzzy, M., Thesma, V., Davoodi, M., Mohammadpour Velni, J.: Real-time plant leaf counting using deep object detection networks. Sensors **20**(23), 6896 (2020)

25. Oh, S., et al.: Plant counting of cotton from UAS imagery using deep learning-based object detection framework. Remote Sens. **12**(18), 2981 (2020)

26. Fuentes, A., Yoon, S., Kim, S.C., Park, D.S.: A robust deep-learning-based detector for real-time tomato plant diseases and pests recognition. Sensors **17**(9), 2022 (2017)

27. Reckling, W., Mitasova, H., Wegmann, K., Kauffman, G., Reid, R.: Efficient drone-based rare plant monitoring using a species distribution model and AI-based object detection. Drones **5**(4), 110 (2021)

28. Basavegowda, D.H., Mosebach, P., Schleip, I., Weltzien, C.: Indicator plant species detection in grassland using efficientdet object detector. 42. GIL-Jahrestagung, Künstliche Intelligenz in der Agrar-und Ernährungswirtschaft (2022)

29. Tian, Z., Shen, C., Chen, H., He, T.: FCOS: fully convolutional one-stage object detection. In: Proceedings of the IEEE/CVF International Conference on Computer Vision, pp. 9627–9636 (2019)

30. Law, H., Deng, J.: CornerNet: detecting objects as paired keypoints. In: Proceedings of the European Conference on Computer Vision (ECCV), pp. 734–750 (2018)

31. Girshick, R.: Fast R-CNN. In: Proceedings of the IEEE International Conference on Computer Vision, pp. 1440–1448 (2015)

32. Chen, Q., Wang, Y., Yang, T., Zhang, X., Cheng, J., Sun, J.: You only look one-level feature. In: Proceedings of the IEEE/CVF Conference on Computer Vision and Pattern Recognition, pp. 13039–13048 (2021)

PO-DARTS: Post-optimizing the Architectures Searched by Differentiable Architecture Search Algorithms

Debei Hao and Songwei Pei[✉]

School of Computer Science (National Pilot Software Engineering School), Beijing University of Posts and Telecommunications, Beijing 100876, China
peisongwei@bupt.edu.cn

Abstract. In neural architecture search, differentiable architecture search algorithm has become one of the mainstream methods. However, no matter in the search or evaluation stage, the architecture is repeatedly stacked by two kinds of Cells, namely Normal Cell and Reduction Cell, respectively. This undoubtedly limits the performance of the evaluation architecture to a large extent due to the architecture restriction, resulting in sub-optimal performance. In order to alleviate the impact of architecture restriction on network performance, this paper proposes to post-optimize the architecture searched by differentiable architecture search algorithms by freezing the architecture parameters of partial Cells and further searching other Cells to bring more diversity into the stacked Cells. The proposed post-optimizing methods consist of the global post-optimizing search method and the local post-optimizing search method, respectively. The performance of the evaluation architecture can benefit from the diverse stacked Cells with less architecture restriction. In the experiments, the proposed post-optimizing method is applied to the mainstream differentiable architecture search algorithms such as DARTS and P-DARTS, and superior results have been achieved on CIFAR-10 and CIFAR-100 datasets. Moreover, the proposed method can obtain the post-optimized architecture with limited computing resources.

Keywords: Deep Learning · Image Classification · Differentiable Architecture Search · Neural Network Optimization

1 Introduction

Currently, neural architecture search (NAS) technology has been paid attention to the fields of computer vision [1], speech recognition [2], etc. Among them, the architecture search based on differentiable strategies stands out from various search algorithms by virtue of the advantages of low search cost and easy implementation. The goal of the NAS based on differentiable strategies is to search for two kinds of Cells, namely Normal Cell and Reduction Cell, from the search space composed of various candidate operations, and then generate the evaluation architecture by repeatedly stacking the searched Cells [3]. Compared with the search algorithms of other strategies [4–6], the NAS based on differentiable strategies can search for a more excellent architecture in a short time.

© The Author(s), under exclusive license to Springer Nature Switzerland AG 2023
L. Iliadis et al. (Eds.): ICANN 2023, LNCS 14262, pp. 178–190, 2023.
https://doi.org/10.1007/978-3-031-44201-8_15

Although differentiable architecture search has the advantage of low search time cost, there are also some shortcomings that limit the performance of this method. The obvious disadvantage is that the architecture can only be generated by repeatedly stacking the searched Normal Cell and Reduction Cell, thereby bringing the reduction of network performance caused by the serious architecture restriction.

In order to improve the shortcomings mentioned above, this paper proposes to post -optimize the evaluation architecture searched by the differentiable architecture search algorithms. The evaluation architecture built by the searched Cells is further post-optimized by re-searching Cells with different structures, and then an evaluation architecture formed by a variety of Cells can be generated. The proposed post-optimizing method can not only alleviate the gap in the architecture search and evaluation stages, but also break through the limitation that the evaluation architecture can only be stacked repeatedly by Cells, making the searched architecture perform better.

The main contributions of the paper are as follows:

1. In order to alleviate the impact of repeatedly stacking of Normal Cell and Reduction Cell on network performance, post-optimizing algorithms are proposed in this paper, which can be further divided into the global post-optimizing algorithm and the local post-optimizing algorithm. Among them, the global post-optimizing algorithm can find a more optimized architecture, and the local post-optimizing algorithm can get a better architecture in a short time.
2. In this paper, the global post-optimizing algorithm is performed based on the evaluation architecture searched by DARTS (first-order and second-order). Experiments show that the test errors on CIFAR-10 are reduced from 3.03% and 3.06% to 2.54% and 2.58%, respectively, and the test errors on CIFAR-100 are reduced from 17.76% and 17.54 to 15.68% and 15.73%, respectively.
3. In this paper, the local post-optimizing algorithm is performed based on the architecture searched by DARTS (first-order and second-order) and P-DARTS, respectively. Experiments show that the test errors on CIFAR-10 are reduced to 2.66%, 2.63%, and 2.43%, respectively, and the test errors on CIFAR-100 are reduced to 16.06%, 15.83%, and 15.66%, respectively.

The paper is organized as follows: Sect. 2 introduces related works. Section 3 introduces the proposed post-optimization method. In Sect. 4, the post-optimization strategies proposed in this paper are experimentally verified. This paper is concluded in Sect. 5.

2 Related Work

In recent years, NAS has gradually received more attention as a new research direction. Its goal is to find a way to automatically design the architecture to replace the original human manual design method. Currently, the main popular neural architecture search methods can be roughly divided into three categories, including reinforcement learning based architecture search [4], evolutionary algorithm based architecture search [5] and differentiable architecture search [3]. Among them, the first two methods dominated the field of neural architecture search in the early days, but the search cost was extremely high. This was followed by the method of differentiable architecture search, in which the seminal work is DARTS [3].

The contribution of DARTS is significant, and there also exists a series of improved algorithms on the basis of DARTS. For example, to address the depth gap between the architecture search and evaluation, P-DARTS [7] proposes to progressively increase the depth of stacked Cells to alleviate this gap. In order to further reduce the computational overhead of DARTS, PC-DARTS [8] designs a channel-based sampling mechanism. There are also many redesigns of the search space to reduce the amount of calculation, such as GOLD-NAS [9], etc.

In addition, FairDARTS [10] reveals the reason why large amounts skip connections prone to occur, and proposes to replace the Softmax with the Sigmoid function to transform the candidate operation in the search stage from a competitive relationship to a cooperative relationship. NoisyDARTS [11] injects noise into skip connections to alleviate the enrichment of skip connections and poor architectural performance caused by unfair competition to a certain extent. DARTS+ [12] found that early stopping can be used to prevent excessive skip-connects, and proposed two early stopping strategies.

3   The Proposed Method

In the DARTS algorithm, the architecture under search is formed by stacking 8 Cells consisting of Normal Cell and Reduction Cell. After the end of search process, the searched Normal Cell and Reduction Cell are repeatedly stacked to form the evaluation architecture. It is worth noting that both the search and evaluation architectures are built by repeatedly stacking the Normal Cell and Reduction Cell in a series of DARTS derived algorithms. Although the composition of this architecture is simple, it will limit the performance of the network to a certain extent due to the architecture restriction. This paper proposes to post-optimize the evaluation architecture searched by differentiable architecture search algorithms to bring more diversity into the stacked Cells. In this work, we propose two post-optimizing methods, called global post-optimizing search and local post-optimizing search, respectively.

3.1   Global Post-optimizing Search

The goal of the global post-optimizing search is to search for a better architecture on the basis of the evaluation architecture obtained by the differentiable architecture search algorithm. In this section, we verified the proposed global post-optimizing search algorithm by leveraging the evaluation architecture generated by the DARTS algorithm. To bring more diversity into the stacked Cells, the global post-optimizing gradually re-search the Cell from the beginning to the end of the evaluation architecture while freezing the architecture parameters of other Cells of the architecture. The compositions of the evaluation architectures before and after post-optimizing are shown in Fig. 1.

Figure 1(A) shows the architecture under search and evaluation in DARTS, and Fig. 1(B) shows the architecture to be post-optimized and after post-optimization. Compared with the way of repeatedly stacking Cells, the post-optimized architecture is composed of Cells with different structures, and the architecture is more diverse. In short, the global post-optimizing search proposed in this section is firstly to use the evaluation architecture generated by existed differentiable architecture search algorithm as the target to be post-optimized, and then gradually re-search the Cell in the target to obtain a new architecture by further applying the search strategy on a pre-set search space, so as to elevate the performance of the evaluation architecture.

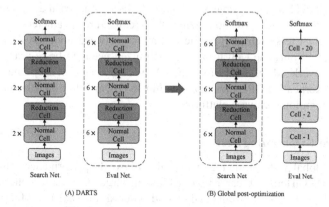

Fig. 1. The global post-optimizing search.

It is worth noting that the depth and width of the architecture to be post-optimized are set to the same settings as the final evaluation architecture. Based on the DARTS algorithm, the depth of the network to be post-optimized consists of 20 Cells, and the number of initial-channel of the network is 36. Since the architecture to be post-optimized is already consistent with that of the evaluation architecture, this approach can further bridge the gap between the architecture search and evaluation as known in the original DARTS architecture search method.

Table 1. Algorithmic process of global post-optimizing search.

Global Post-Optimizing Search Algorithm
1. Obtain Cells searched by DARTS
2. Built the evaluation network with the searched Cells.
3. *for* first Cell *to* last Cell *do*:
4.   Freeze the architecture parameters of other Cells except for the post-optimized Cell.
5.   *while* not converge *do*:
6.   update network weights and architecture parameters.
7.   *end while*
8.   /*Complete the optimization of the current Cell*/
9. *end for*

When post-optimizing, the architecture parameter of most Cells in the architecture will be frozen, and only the specific Cell will be further post-optimized. By re-searching the specific Cell, the new Cell obtained by the latest search will replace the original Cell at the same position. In this way, each Cell that constitutes the evaluation architecture is post-optimized from the beginning to the end, which is called the global post-optimizing search. The global post-optimization algorithm is shown in Table 1.

It is worth mentioning that when using the global post-optimization algorithm, there is no need to worry about the pressure on computing resources. Also take the architecture generated by DARTS as an example, although 20 Cells are stacked and the initial channel number is set to 36 when post-optimizing, the architecture parameters of most Cells are frozen at each re-search, that is, the operations between nodes in these Cells are deterministic, and only the Cell to be post-optimized needs to be re-searched, so the GPU memory overhead will not be too much. When only one Cell is optimally searched at a time, the overhead of GPU memory is within 16 GB, and the algorithm can be easily deployed on common hardware platforms.

3.2 Local Post-Optimizing Search

Although the global post-optimizing search can improve the performance of the architecture, the overhead in terms of search time is relatively large. We leveraged the architecture searched by the DARTS (first-order and second-order) as the start-point for global post-optimization, and collected the time overheads by conducting the global post-optimizing search algorithm on NVIDIA GeForce RTX 3090 GPU twice. The time overheads are shown in Table 2.

Table 2. The time overhead for global post-optimizing search.

Search Algorithm	DARTSv1	DARTSv2
Total optimization time (GPU-hours)	8.5	8.0
	8.9	7.6

Among them, DARTSv1 and DARTSv2 mean that we use DARTS first-order search algorithm and DARTS second-order search algorithm for re-searching the specific Cell in the global post-optimizing search, respectively. It can be seen that if the global post-optimizing search is adopted, it means that the user needs to invest more additional post-optimizing search time. Therefore, in order to post-optimize the architecture more efficiently, a local post-optimizing search algorithm which only re-searches a very small number of Cells is proposed in this section, and the architecture performance can also be improved but requires a much shorter time. However, the local post-optimization needs to consider which part of the architecture should be post-optimized to better improve the network performance. To this end, this paper explores the Cell locations that are in the front, middle, and rare of the architecture to determine which Cells are suitable for post-optimization on the basis of the DARTS algorithm. To pursuit the efficiency, we only re-search two Cells in the local post-optimizing search. The exploited locations are shown in Fig. 2, in which the first two Cells of the extracted image features are called the front (denoted as f2), the middle two Cells are called the middle (denoted as m2), and the last two Cells are called the rear (denoted as r2).

To verify which Cells after post-optimization can improve the performance of the architecture more effectively, this paper sets up experiments for post-optimizing the front, middle and rear Cells, respectively. Local post-optimizing search is firstly to freeze the architecture parameters of other parts of the architecture other than the Cell to be post-optimized, and then perform re-search for the specific Cells. The difference between the local post-optimizing search and the global post-optimizing search is that the local post-optimizing search does not need to re-search every Cell in the architecture, but only post-optimizes the Cells in the front, the middle, or the rear of the evaluation architecture. In the experiments, we found it better to post-optimize the Cells in the front mainly due to the vital role in the feature extraction at the early layer, and we call it front local post-optimizing algorithm. By local post-optimizing, the search time can be shortened to a large extent, and the performance of the optimized architecture is comparable to the global optimization in accuracy.

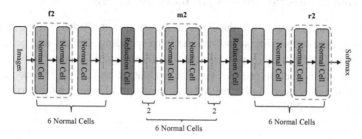

Fig. 2. Post-optimizing exploration for Cells in the front, middle, and rare of the architecture.

4 Experiments

In this section, we first introduce the experimental setup, then verify the effectiveness of the global post-optimizing search and the local post-optimizing search, and finally compare with the state-of-the-art methods on CIFAR-10 and CIFAR-100 datasets.

4.1 Experimental Setup

In order to verify the effectiveness of the proposed method, the datasets used in the experiment are CIFAR image classification datasets, including CIFAR-10 and CIFAR-100, and the differentiable architecture search algorithms used are DARTS and P-DARTS. It is consistent with DARTS and P-DARTS in terms of dataset processing. Whether searching on CIFAR-10 or CIFAR-100, the training set is equally divided into two subsets, one for optimizing network parameters and the other for optimizing architecture parameters.

In the post-optimizing search algorithms, the candidate operation category is consistent with DARTS and P-DARTS, and there are a total of 8 candidate operations including zero operation. In terms of network configuration, the architecture consists of 20 Cells, and the initial number of channels is set to 36. The neural architecture parameters use the Adam optimizer with learning rate = 0.0006, weight decay = 0.001, and momentum =

(0.5,0.999). During the global post-optimizing search, we performed the post-optimizing search on each of the Normal Cells from the beginning to the end. When performing the local post-optimizing search experiments, we conduct post-optimizing searches for different partition Cells of the architecture. For the post-optimizing search of Cells, we set the epoch to 15 and the batch size to 96. Furthermore, in order to accelerate the post-optimization, we use the first-order approximation for parameter optimization.

When evaluating the architecture on CIFAR-10 or CIFAR-100, we use the standard training set/test set split for the dataset. The evaluation architecture consists of 20 Cells, the number of initial-channels is set to 36, the batch size is 128, and the standard SGD optimizer is used. For CIFAR-10 and CIFAR-100, the weight decay is set to 0.0003 and 0.0005 respectively, the momentum is 0.9, the initial learning rate is 0.025 and decays to 0 according to the cosine rule, and a total of 600 epochs are trained from scratch.

4.2 Experimental Results and Analysis Based on DARTS

For the architecture searched by the DARTS algorithm on CIFAR-10, we perform a further global post-optimizing search on the corresponding dataset, and generate the evaluation architecture. In order to verify the transferability of the post-optimized architecture during the evaluation process, we also evaluate it on CIFAR-100, and compare the test error of the architecture before and after post-optimization on the corresponding dataset, as shown in Table 3.

Table 3. Comparison of the evaluation results before and after the global post-optimizing search (GOS) of the architecture searched by DARTS.

Architecture	Test Err. (%)		Params (M)
	CIFAR-10	CIFAR-100	
DARTS (first order)	3.03	17.76	3.16
DARTS (second order)	3.06	17.54	3.36
DARTS (first order) + GOS	**2.54**	**15.68**	**3.37**
DARTS (second order) + GOS	**2.58**	**15.73**	**3.20**

Among them, GOS represents the global post-optimizing search algorithm proposed in this paper. On the NVIDIA GeForce RTX 3090 GPU, the total search time cost of the global post-optimizing search algorithm is within 9 h. From the results in Table 3, it can be concluded that the test errors of the obtained architectures on CIFAR-10 can be reduced to 2.54% and 2.58% by applying the global post-optimizing search algorithm based on the DARTS first-order and DARTS second-order methods, respectively. In order to verify the transferability of the post-optimized architecture, we evaluated it on CIFAR-100, and the test errors can be reduced to 15.68% and 15.73%, respectively. It can be seen that the global post-optimizing algorithm proposed in this paper can greatly improve the performance of the evaluation architecture.

In order to illustrate the difference between the evaluation architecture before and after the global post-optimization, we draw a schematic diagram of the Normal Cell obtained by the DARTS (first-order) search algorithm and partial re-searched Cells after the global post-optimization. Among them, Fig. 3(A) is the Normal Cell obtained by DARTS (first-order) search, and Fig. 3(B) shows partial post-optimized Cells after the global post-optimization. Due to the limited space, here we only draw two post-optimized Cells for comparison. By comparing Cells before and after post-optimization, it can be found that the connections in the post-optimized Cells are deeper than those before post-optimization, and the operations between nodes are more complex and diverse. In terms of the performance, the accuracy of the post-optimized evaluation architecture is much higher.

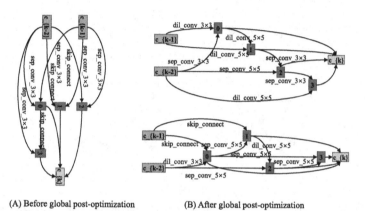

(A) Before global post-optimization   (B) After global post-optimization

Fig. 3. The schematic diagram of Cells before and after the global post-optimization on the basis of the DARTS (first-order).

In addition, in order to shorten the post-optimization time of the architecture, this paper validates the local post-optimizing search algorithm through experiments. After we obtained the architecture by using the DARTS (first-order) on CIFAR-10, we only post-optimized the Cells in the front, middle, and rear of the architecture, and then evaluated it on CIFAR-10 and CIFAR-100, respectively. The results are shown in Fig. 4.

Among them, Fig. 4(A) and Fig. 4(B) show the evaluation results of the architecture by applying the local post-optimizing the Cells in the front, middle, and rear of the architecture based on the first-order and second-order search algorithms of DARTS, respectively. The blue histogram represents the performance of the architecture on CIFAR-10 before and after local post-optimization of different parts of Cells. The orange histogram is to verify the transferability of the post-optimized architecture, that is, the performance on CIFAR-100. On an NVIDIA GeForce RTX 3090 GPU, the local post-optimization search time overhead is within one hour.

By comparing the experimental results of the global post-optimization and the local post-optimization, it can be found that when post-optimizing the same architecture, the accuracy of the architecture after global post-optimizing is higher. Although it is more likely to obtain a better architecture through the global post-optimization, the global post-optimizing algorithm is relatively unstable, and the reason for the instability is related to the approximate optimization algorithm when post-optimizing the architecture. When continuing to post-optimize the next Cell, it will depend on the last post-optimized Cell to a certain extent. Therefore, the global post-optimizing search algorithm is less stable, but more likely to discover novel architectures. For practical applications, from the perspective of time-saving or algorithm stability, the local post-optimizing search algorithm is a good choice.

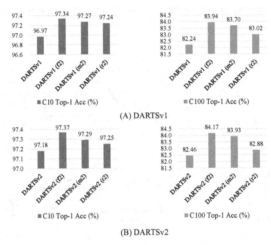

Fig. 4. The performance of the architecture before and after the local post-optimizing search on CIFAR-10 and CIFAR-100.

According to the results, it can be seen that when post-optimizing the front Cells of the architecture, the result is better than that of other parts. We believe that after post-optimization for the front Cells, the architecture can better extract image features. If the Cells in the front are not good enough and the extracted features are not sufficient, then even if the Cells in the back are excellent, the performance of the entire architecture is still limited. Therefore, we encourage to consider the front local post-optimizing search when conducting the local post-optimization, and we will only conduct post-optimizing with the front local post-optimizing search algorithm later.

4.3   Experimental Results and Analysis Based on P-DARTS

P-DARTS [7] is an improved algorithm for DARTS to alleviate the depth gap. In the field of NAS, P-DARTS and DARTS are also widely concerned. Due to the advantage of front local post-optimizing search, we apply it on the architecture searched by P-DARTS to further verify the effectiveness of proposed post-optimization. First, the P-DARTS algorithm is used to search for the architecture on CIFAR-10 and CIFAR-100, and then front local post-optimizing is used to update the architecture. On CIFAR-10, the Cells obtained before and after front local post-optimization are shown in Fig. 5.

Among them, Fig. 5(A) shows the Normal Cell searched on CIFAR-10 by using P-DARTS. Figure 5(B) and Fig. 5(C) show the Cell structure after applying the front local post-optimizing search, Cell-1 and Cell-2 represent the first and second Cell in the post-optimized architecture, respectively. By comparing the structure before and after post-optimization, it can be easily found that the post-optimized Cells will contain more convolutions with larger convolution kernels. These convolutions have a larger receptive field, which facilitates the extraction of more image features.

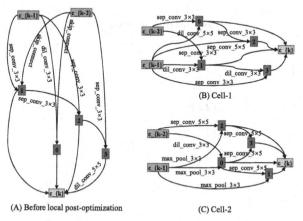

(A) Before local post-optimization   (C) Cell-2

Fig. 5. The Schematic diagram of Cells before and after front local post-optimizing search on the basis of P-DARTS.

Table 4. The evaluation results before and after post-optimization of the front Cells of the architecture searched by P-DARTS.

Architecture	Test Err. (%)		Params (M)
	CIFAR-10	CIFAR-100	
P-DARTS CIFAR10	2.55	16.40	3.4
P-DARTS CIFAR100	2.66	16.26	3.7
P-DARTS CIFAR10 + LOS	**2.43**	**15.66**	**3.4**
P-DARTS CIFAR100 + LOS	**2.55**	**15.86**	**3.7**

We evaluated the post-optimized architecture and compared the results of performance with that of the P-DATS, as shown in Table 4. It is marked with LOS to indicate that the front local post-optimizing algorithm is adopted to optimize the architecture searched by P-DARTS, that is, only the two Cells in the front part of the architecture are optimized. "P-DARTS CIFAR10" and "P-DARTS CIFAR100" represent the architectures searched on CIFAR-10 and CIFAR-100 using the P-DARTS, respectively. The local post-optimizing search process takes only one hour on an NVIDIA GeForce RTX 3090. It can be seen from Table 4 that the proposed local post-optimizing search algorithm can greatly improve the performance of the architecture in a short time.

4.4 Comparison with State-of-the-Art

In order to better illustrate the effectiveness of the proposed method in this paper, Table 5 lists the comparison between the results of the post-optimization of P-DARTS and some other mainstream NAS methods.

Table 5. Comparison with state-of-the-arts on CIFAR-10 and CIFAR-100.

Architecture	Test Err. (%)		Params (M)	Method
	CIFAR-10	CIFAR-100		
DenseNet-BC [13]	3.46	17.17	25.6	manual
AmoebaNet-B [5]	2.55	–	2.8	evolution
PNAS [14]	3.41	–	3.2	SMBO
ENAS [15]	2.89	–	4.6	RL
PC-DARTS [8]	2.57	–	3.6	gradient
R-DARTS [16]	2.95	18.01	–	gradient
FairDARTS [10]	2.59	–	3.8	gradient
NoisyDARTS-b [11]	2.47	–	3.0	gradient
SDARTS-ADV [17]	2.61	–	3.3	gradient
DARTS- [18]	2.50	–	3.5	gradient
β-DARTS [19]	2.53	16.24	3.8	gradient
P-DARTS CIFAR10 + LOS	**2.43**	**15.66**	**3.4**	**gradient**
P-DARTS CIFAR100 + LOS	**2.55**	**15.86**	**3.7**	**gradient**

By using the post-optimizing search algorithm, we reduce the test error on CIFAR-10 and CIFAR-100 to 2.43% and 15.66%, respectively. It can be seen from Table 5 that when the post-optimizing search algorithm proposed in this paper is used, the obtained architecture is superior to many current mainstream NAS methods in terms of performance.

5 Conclusions

This paper proposes effective post-optimizing methods based on the differentiable architecture search algorithm. The evaluation architecture formed by repeatedly stacking the Normal Cell and Reduction Cell searched by differentiable architecture search algorithms is regarded as the network to be post-optimized, and then the specific Cell can be re-searched through the global post-optimizing and local post-optimizing search methods, respectively. By post-optimizing the Cells, the final evaluation architecture will be composed of Cells with more diverse structures, which lightens the architecture restriction and performs better. Experimental results show that the proposed method achieves superior performance on both CIFAR-10 and CIFAR-100.

Acknowledgement. This work was supported in part by National Natural Science Foundation of China (NSFC) under Grant No.61772061.

References

1. Wang, C.Y., Bochkovskiy, A., Liao, H.Y.M.: Scaled-yolov4: scaling cross stage partial network. In: Proceedings of the IEEE/CVF Conference on Computer Vision and Pattern Recognition, pp. 13029–13038 (2021)
2. Dong, L., Xu, B.: Cif: continuous integrate-and-fire for end-to-end speech recognition. In: ICASSP 2020–2020 IEEE International Conference on Acoustics, Speech and Signal Processing, pp. 6079–6083, IEEE (2020)
3. Liu, H., Simonyan, K., Yang, Y.: DARTS: differentiable architecture search. In: 7th International Conference on Learning Representations. (2019)
4. Zoph, B., Vasudevan, V., Shlens, J., Le, Q.V.: Learning transferable architectures for scalable image recognition. In: 2018 IEEE Conference on Computer Vision and Pattern Recognition, pp. 8697–8710 (2018)
5. Real, E., Aggarwal, A., Huang, Y., Le, Q.V.: Regularized evolution for image classifier architecture search. In: The Thirty-Third AAAI Conference on Artificial Intelligence, pp. 4780–4789 (2019)
6. Zoph, B., Le, Q.V.: Neural architecture search with reinforcement learning. In: 5th International Conference on Learning Representations (2017)
7. Chen, X., Xie, L., Wu, J., Tian, Q.: Progressive differentiable architecture search: Bridging the depth gap between search and evaluation. In: 2019 IEEE/CVF International Conference on Computer Vision, pp. 1294–1303 (2019)
8. Xu, Y., et al.: PC-DARTS: partial channel connections for memory efficient architecture search. In: 8th International Conference on Learning Representations (2020)
9. Bi, K., Xie, L., Chen, X., Wei, L., Tian, Q., "Gold-nas: gradual, one-level, differentiable". arXiv preprint arXiv:2007.03331 (2020)
10. Chu, X., Zhou, T., Zhang, B., Li, J.: Fair DARTS: eliminating unfair advantages in differentiable architecture search. Comput. Vis. ECCV **12360**, 465–480 (2020)
11. Chu, X., Zhang, B.: Noisy differentiable architecture search. In: 32nd British Machine Vision Conference, p. 217 (2021)
12. Liang, H., et al.: Darts+: improved differentiable architecture search with early stopping. arXiv preprint arXiv:1909.06035 (2019)
13. Huang, G., Liu, Z., Van Der Maaten, L., Weinberger, K.Q.: Densely connected convolutional networks. In: 2017 IEEE Conference on Computer Vision and Pattern Recognition, pp. 2261–2269 (2017)
14. Liu, C., Zoph, B., Neumann, M., Shlens, J.: Progressive neural architecture search. Comput. Vis. ECCV **11205**, 19–35 (2018)
15. Pham, H., Guan, M., Zoph, B., Le, Q., Dean, J.: Efficient neural architecture search via parameter sharing. In: Proceedings of the 35th International Conference on Machine Learning, vol. 80, pp. 4092–4101 (2018)
16. Zela, A., Elsken, T., Saikia, T., Marrakchi, Y., Brox, T., Hutter, F.: Understanding and robustifying differentiable architecture search. In: 8th International Conference on Learning Representations (2020)
17. Chen, X., Hsieh, C.J.: Stabilizing differentiable architecture search via perturbation-based regularization. In: Proceedings of the 37th International Conference on Machine Learning, vol. 119, pp. 1554–1565 (2020)

18. Chu, X., Wang, X., Zhang, B., Lu, S., Wei, X., Yan, J.: DARTS-: robustly stepping out of performance collapse without indicators. In: 9th International Conference on Learning Representations (2021)
19. Ye, P., Li, B., Li, Y., Chen, T., Fan, J., Ouyang, W.: β-darts: Beta-decay regularization for differentiable architecture search. In: IEEE/CVF Conference on Computer Vision and Pattern Recognition, pp. 10864–10873 (2022)

Predicting High vs Low Mother-Baby Synchrony with GRU-Based Ensemble Models

Daniel Stamate[1,2(⊠)], Riya Haran[1], Karolina Rutkowska[1], Pradyumna Davuloori[1], Evelyne Mercure[3], Caspar Addyman[4], and Mark Tomlinson[4]

[1] Data Science and Soft Computing Lab, Department of Computing, Goldsmiths, University of London, London, UK
d.stamate@gold.ac.uk
[2] School of Health Sciences, University of Manchester, Manchester, UK
[3] Department of Psychology, Goldsmiths, University of London, London, UK
[4] Department of Global Health, Stellenbosch University, Stellenbosch, South Africa

Abstract. The early stages of life are paramount for the baby's brain and emotional development, and the quality of interaction between mother and baby - measured as a dyadic synchrony score, is critical in that period. This study proposes the first machine learning prediction modelling approach, based on Gated Recurrent Unit - GRU ensemble models, to automatically differentiate high from low dyadic synchrony between mother and baby, using a dataset of videos capturing this interaction. The GRU ensemble models which were post-processed by maximising the Youden statistic in a ROC analysis procedure, show a good prediction capability on test samples, including a mean AUC of 0.79, a mean accuracy of 0.72, a mean precision of 0.87, a mean sensitivity of 0.64, a mean f1 performance of 0.72, and a mean specificity of 0.83. In particular the latter performance represents an 83% detection rate of the mother-baby dyads with low synchrony, suggesting these models' high capability for automatically flagging such cases that may be clinically relevant for further investigation and potential intervention. A Monte Carlo validation procedure was conducted to accurately estimate the above mean performance levels, and to assess the proposed models' stability. The statistical significance of the prediction ability of the models was also evaluated, i.e. mean AUC > 0.5 (p-value < 9.82×10^{-19}), and future research directions were discussed.

Keywords: Automating mother-baby synchrony detection · Gated Recurrent Units - GRU · Ensemble learning · ROC analysis · Monte Carlo validation

1 Introduction

The early stages of life are paramount for babies' brain and emotional development, and the quality of interaction between mother and baby is critical in that period. If a baby is denied the attention and a positive interaction, they can struggle in later life with forming relationships, education and functioning in society [1]. An increasing body of research shows that babies who were neglected from the early stages of development face

L. Iliadis et al. (Eds.): ICANN 2023, LNCS 14262, pp. 191–199, 2023.
https://doi.org/10.1007/978-3-031-44201-8_16

further social development difficulties [2]. In particular, research suggests that synchrony between the infant's behaviour and their caregivers play many functions in the infants' development, from co-regulations of exchanges in interactions to language acquisition [3]. A functional interaction between mother and baby is one in which the mother focuses her attention on the child and responds to their behaviour in a short time. Such an interaction can be described as synchronous. According to [4] synchrony between two people is defined as a state where they move together in the same or almost the same time with one another. Research suggests that synchrony in group interactions can have a later positive influence on forming social actions [5]. Synchrony is used to find patterns in movements of positive and negative interactions between mother and baby. Developing new methods for finding synchrony patterns can help to automate the process of assessing the mother-baby interaction quality.

Due to its vital role in the early stages of baby's development, expert assessment of the synchrony between mother and baby in videos capturing this interaction, is an important research question. Moreover, there is value in automating this assessment process using machine learning, as such automation could flag those videos which are more likely to capture a negative, lower synchrony between mother and baby, allowing early specialist intervention in problematic mother-baby interactions.

Predicting synchrony between participants in videos using machine learning models, was previously tackled in literature including works such as [6], in which the authors successfully trained a model based on Long Short-Term Memory (LSTM) recurrent neural networks [13, 14], on facial expressions data that had been extracted from pre-recorded videos representing a group of three interacting people. The proposed approach was used to predict synchrony score on a scale of 1 to 5, and the recurrent neural model's predictions were validated by comparison with predictions based on a random permutations baseline. In another machine learning study proposing the prediction of synchrony between a human arm and a robot arm, the final position of the human arm was predicted also with recurrent neural networks based on LSTM models [7].

In the present study we propose an innovative machine learning approach to predicting the categorical level of dyadic synchrony – high versus low, for 58 mother-baby dyads, based on a dataset comprising 58 records with body part coordinates extracted from 58 videos capturing the interaction of these dyads. Our approach is based on Gated Recurrent Unit (GRU) recurrent neural networks [8, 13] as baseline models, with a focus on ensembles of such models – with the purpose to enhance the models' prediction and stability on a relatively small number of record dataset. GRUs are similar to but involve a lesser complexity in training than LSTM models [13, 14] since they are able to store and filter the information using only two gates - *reset* and *update*, as opposed to three gates – *input*, *output* and *forget*, for LSTMs, respectively. GRU models are often capable of performance levels comparable to SLTM models, and due to their reduced relative complexity are preferred in this preliminary study on a dataset comprising a relatively small number of records. However, the volume of data extracted from videos is relatively large, overall, leading to a substantial computational cost.

The rest of the paper is organised as follows: Sect. 2 introduces our proposed prediction modelling approach's methodology, including data description and pre-processing, and model development, evaluation, and Monte Carlo validation. Section 3 presents and discusses our results, and Sect. 4 concludes the paper and outlines future research directions.

2   Methodology

2.1   Data Description and Pre-Processing

This work was based on a sample of 60 videos from the SPEAKNSIGN dataset [20], each lasting more than 10 min with 25 frames per second, capturing a session of free-play between 4–7-month-old infants and their mothers. The videos were scored by experts with a dyadic synchrony score ranging from 2 (low) to 14 (high).

OpenPose library [19] was used to extract a 5D array based on coordinates of body part keypoints from each video. In particular, for the purpose of this analysis, data representation was adapted and simplified by extracting, for each frame, pairs of x and y coordinates for 25 body keypoints for each mother and her baby. Figure 1 illustrates the body part keypoints extracted by OpenPose from a single frame of the interaction video. 3D arrays were finally obtained for the analysis, comprising the record number corresponding to each video, the frame number, and the sum aggregation of the x and y coordinates. Two records were discarded as they did not meet the data quality requirements, leading to a dataset of 58 records in all. Records were categorized in two classes by using the dyadic synchrony scores: class 1 – high synchrony, and class 0 – low synchrony, containing the highest 60% scores and the lowest 40% scores in the dataset, respectively.

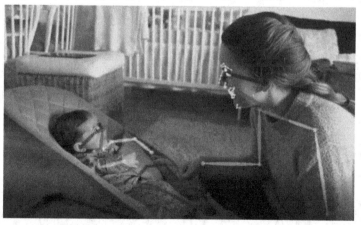

Fig. 1. Body part keypoints extracted by OpenPose from a single frame of the interaction video.

The dataset was cleaned with respect to missing values which were imputed with linear interpolation, and outliers were detected using criteria based on the range of 0.025 or 0.975 quantiles, and discarded. Data was normalised.

Figure 2 illustrates, in a preliminary exploratory data analysis conducted in [20], a partial correlation between mother and baby as reflected by the whole body movement index aggregating differences in body coordinates in the frame sequence [20]. We note various levels of correlation of the body movement index between mother and baby, and these go as high as 0.84 in the four examples of mother-baby dyads illustrated here (see second plot).

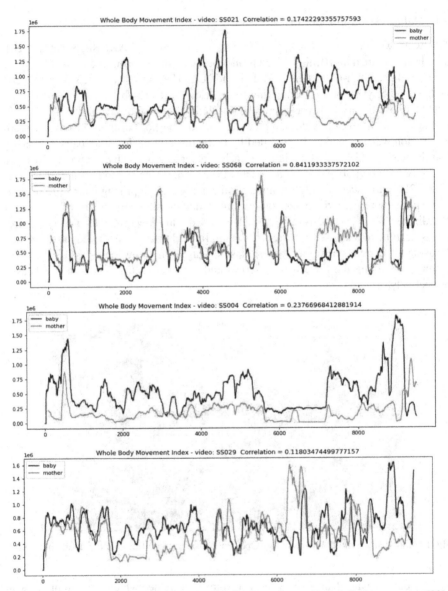

Fig. 2. Body movement index capturing a correlation in mother and baby's body movement [20].

2.2 Model Development, Evaluation and Monte Carlo Validation

The baseline GRU neural network architectures [8, 13] used in this work comprised 2 and 3 GRU layers with 200, 256, 300 nodes, and 1 hidden dense layer with 50, 64, 70 nodes, implemented in Keras and TensorFlow. As activation functions we employed *relu, prelu, elu, selu, softplus* for the hidden dense layer and *sigmoid* for the output layer, while for the GRU layers we used *tanh* as activation function and *sigmoid* as recurrent activation. As loss functions we employed *Binary crossentropy* and *binary focal crossentropy* (for the moderate data imbalance 60:40 present in the data). The constant learning rate of 0.001, and the exponential learning rate scheduling were used, together with *adam*, and *nadam* optimisers. To prevent overfitting, an early stopping with 4, 5, 7, 10 *patience*, and *L2 regularization* for the dense layer, were explored.

Due to the relatively small number of records available in the dataset, i.e. 58, which may increase the variance of the model performance and hence negatively affect the model stability, we built ensembles of 10 and 20 GRU models whose predicted probabilities were averaged. After splitting the dataset into a test set and a non-test set, the GRU models in each ensemble were obtained by repeatedly further splitting the non-test set into validation and train set, for 10 and 20 times, and training the models in each case. The ensemble of 10 and 20 models was then evaluated on the test set. Data splitting was stratified, and the following proportions were used for the test, validation, and training set, respectively: (0.3, 0.3, 0.4), (0.25, 0.3, 0.45), (0.25, 0.25, 0.5).

For this binary classification problem with a moderately imbalanced dataset, the primary performance in evaluating the models was the ROC Area Under Curve, denoted *AUC*. We utilised the *Youden statistic* maximisation method in a ROC analysis procedure [18] for estimating the optimal probability threshold on the non-test (i.e. training and validation) set of records, in order to apply this threshold on the test set to predict the high and low synchrony classes. With this optimal threshold we computed *accuracy, precision, sensitivity, specificity,* and *f1* performances.

Moreover, for each model, we computed the *Cohen's kappa statistic* and *MCC* (*Matthews correlation coefficient*) whose positive values, when sufficiently far from 0, suggest the existence of predictive pattern in the data that is captured by models. Model predictiveness was established also by running a one-side T-test, inferring statistically that the model's AUC is significantly larger than 0.5 which corresponds to a random prediction model.

Such evaluations are useful also when working with a relatively small number of records, which usually increases the range of variation of models' performance at the point of overlapping with the performance range of a random prediction. With the same rationale in mind, we conducted a Monte Carlo validation (MCV) based on 30 experiments, each of which consisting of: (a) a test/non-test data set split; and (b) building the ensemble model as explained above in this subsection, and then evaluating it on the test set using the performances mentioned above.

Building a GRU ensemble model especially on a large data volume extracted from videos is a computationally expensive procedure (even if the number of records is relatively small as in our approach). Moreover, an MCV multiplies this computational cost by the number of experiments (i.e. 30). However, this is beneficial in our case to reliably assess the model prediction performances and stability, given the relatively small number of records at our disposal in this study (i.e. 58).

2.3 Software and Hardware

The data analysis was conducted using Python, with libraries Numpy, Pandas, TensorFlow, Keras, Sklearn and Seaborn. Videos were initially processed with OpenPose library to detect the body, hand, facial, and foot keypoints coordinates.

The hardware consisted of 3 Linux servers with Xeon 6-cores processors and 96 GB RAM each, for data exploration and pre-processing, and for code prototyping, and 2 Linux servers with Intel 9 10-cores and AMD Ryzen 16-cores with 128 GB RAM each, and Titan RTX 24GB and 3090 RTX 24 GB GPUs, for GRU and ensemble model training and MCV intensive computation procedures for building and assessing the models' performances and stability.

3   Results and Discussion

The results in the Monte Carlo validation (MCV) illustrated in Fig. 3, reveal the following aspects:

a) The mean AUC of 0.79 of the GRU ensemble models (ens_auc_test) shows a good prediction level for the relatively small number of records in the dataset.
b) The ROC analysis estimating optimal probability thresholds for classification by maximising the Youden statistic [18], led to good levels of mean accuracy (acc_test) 0.72, mean precision (prec_test) 0.87, mean f1 performance (f1_test) 0.72, as well as positive, far from 0, mean Mathews correlation coefficient (mcc_test) 0.48 and mean Kappa coefficient (kappa_test) 0.44.
c) Given the mean precision (prec_test), mean sensitivity (sens_test), and mean specificity (spec_test) levels achieved by the models, we can infer that 87% of mother-infant dyads predicted as being in the high synchrony class, were predicted correctly by the ensemble models, and that these ensemble models detected 64% of the high synchrony cases; More importantly, these ensemble models detected also 83% of mother-infant dyads with low synchrony. This suggests our models' capability for automatically flagging such cases that may be clinically relevant for further investigation and potential intervention.

The performance values in Fig. 3 are means computed in the Monte Carlo validation on 30 test sets randomly sampled from the dataset (more precisely, via random training, validation, test stratified splits). Due to the relatively small number of records and the data splitting required for building and evaluating the models, which make the training and test sets even smaller, the model stability has some expected limitations as suggested by the various performance boxplots illustrated in Fig. 3 and by the AUC performance histogram depicted in Fig. 4, both of which showing a significant variation of such performances across the Monte Carlo validation procedure.

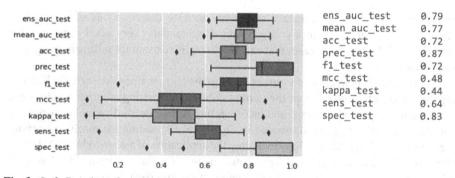

ens_auc_test	0.79
mean_auc_test	0.77
acc_test	0.72
prec_test	0.87
f1_test	0.72
mcc_test	0.48
kappa_test	0.44
sens_test	0.64
spec_test	0.83

Fig. 3. Left: Boxplots of ensemble model performances on 30 test sets in Monte Carlo validation. Right: mean performances in Monte Carlo validation.

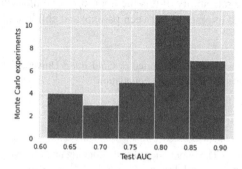

Fig. 4. Histogram of AUC performances on 30 test sets in Monte Carlo validation.

We also conducted a T-Test based on the AUC results obtained in the 30 experiments in the Monte Carlo validation, which led to establishing, with a significant p-value $< 9.82 \times 10^{-19}$, the alternative hypothesis that mean AUC > 0.5. This proves also statistically that the models proposed in this approach predict better than chance.

4 Conclusion and Future Research Directions

To our knowledge, this work represents the first machine learning based approach in literature, predicting the categorical level of dyadic synchrony – high versus low, in mother-baby interactions captured in a dataset of videos. We processed the videos with OpenPose library for extracting coordinates from the mother and baby body movements, expected to inform mother-baby dyadic synchrony. Using the dataset of extracted coordinates, this work proposed a novel and substantially high-performing prediction modelling approach, by developing GRU models and ensembles of such models, which were studied in terms of exploring various model architectures, and of assessing prediction performances and model stability with a Monte Carlo Validation procedure.

The GRU ensemble models showed a good prediction capability on test samples, including a mean AUC of 0.79, a mean accuracy of 0.72, a mean precision of 0.87, a mean sensitivity of 0.64, a mean f1 performance of 0.72, and a mean specificity of 0.83.

In particular the latter performance represents an 83% detection rate of the mother-baby dyads with low synchrony, suggesting these models' very good capability for automatically flagging such cases that may be clinically relevant for further investigation and potential intervention.

Future research directions to further develop the current study concern: (a) Extending the analysis to a superset of the current dataset, comprising additional videos not available in the present analysis, and incorporating further derived variables exploiting correlations similar to those illustrated in Fig. 1; (b) Expanding the machine learning prediction modelling methodology including the application of autoencoders [13, 14] for alternative feature extraction and representation, and of transfer learning [17] based on other similar datasets, as further enhancements of the approach proposed in this study; (c) Developing explanatory models for getting insights of the prediction, and for performance comparison with the black-box models presented in this study; (d) Expanding and evaluating the generalisability of this methodology by employing alternative video based data capturing the interaction between parents and children in other various joint activities.

Acknowledgements. This work was supported by Goldsmiths University of London, and Global Parenting Initiative (Funded by The LEGO Foundation).

References

1. Winston, R., Chicot, R.: The importance of early bonding on the long-term mental health and resilience of children. London J. Primary Care **8**(1), 12–14 (2016)
2. Feldman, R.: The relational basis of adolescent adjustment: Trajectories of mother–child interactive behaviors from infancy to adolescence shape adolescents' adaptation. Attach. Hum. Develop. **12**(1–2), 2010
3. Delaherche, E., Chetouani, M., et al.: Interpersonal synchrony: A survey of evaluation methods across disciplines. IEEE Trans. Affective Comput. **3**(3) (2012)
4. Merriam-Webster. (n.d.). Synchrony. In Merriam-Webster.com dictionary
5. Wiltermuth, S., Heath, C.: Synchrony and cooperation. Psychol. Sci. **20**(1) (2009)
6. Watkins, N., Nwogu, I.: Computational Social Dynamics: Analyzing the Face-level Interactions in a Group. arXiv preprint arXiv:1807.06124. (2018)
7. Chellali, R., Li, Z.: Predicting arm movements a multi-variate LSTM based approach for human-robot hand clapping games. In: Proceedings of 27th IEEE International Symposium on Robot and Human Interactive Communication (2018)
8. Cho, K., van Merrienboer, B., et al.: Learning phrase representations using RNN encoder-decoder for statistical machine translation. In: Proceedings of the 2014 Conference on Empirical Methods in Natural Language Processing (2014)
9. Leclère, C., Avril, M., Viaux-Savelon, S., Bodeau, N., Achard, C., Missonnier, S., et al.: Interaction and behaviour imaging: a novel method to measure mother–infant interaction using video 3D reconstruction. Transl. Psych. **6**(5) (2016)
10. Guedeney, A., Matthey, S., Puura, K.: Social withdrawal behavior in infancy: a history of the concept and a review of published studies using the Alarm Distress baby scale. Infant Ment. Health J. **34**(6), 516–531 (2013)
11. Noor, M.N., Yahaya, A.S., Ramli, N.A., Al Bakri, A.M.M.: Filling missing data using interpolation methods: study on the effect of fitting distribution. Key Eng. Mater. 594–595 (2013)

12. Dey, R., Salem, F.M.: Gate-variants of Gated Recurrent Unit (GRU) neural networks. In: Proceedings of IEEE 60th International Midwest Symposium on Circuits and Systems (2017)
13. Aggarwal, C.: Neural networks and deep learning: A textbook. Springer (2018)
14. Goodfellow, I., Bengio, Y., Courville, A.: Deep Learning, MIT Press (2016)
15. Bishop, C.: Pattern Recognition and Machine Learning, Springer (2006)
16. Hastie, T., Tibshirani, R., Friedman, J.: The Elements of Statistical Learning: Data Mining, Inference, and Prediction. Springer (2009)
17. Geron, A.: Hands-on Machine Learning with Scikit-Learn, Keras, and TensorFlow: Concepts, Tools, and Techniques to Build Intelligent Systems, O'Reilly (2019)
18. Unal, I.: Defining an optimal cut-point value in ROC analysis: an alternative approach. J. Comput. Math. Meth. Med. **2017** (2017)
19. Cao, Z., Hidalgo, G., Simon, T., Wei, S.-E., Sheikh, Y.; OpenPose: realtime multi-person 2d pose estimation using part affinity fields. J. IEEE Trans. Pattern Anal. Mach. Intell. **43** (2021)
20. Rutkowska, K.: Automated measurement of nonverbal synchrony in infant-mother interaction using machine learning, MSc dissertation, supervisors D. Stamate, C. Addyman, Data Science & Soft Computing Lab and Computing Department, Goldsmiths College, University of London (2020)

Properties of the Weighted and Robust Implicitly Weighted Correlation Coefficients

Jan Kalina and Petra Vidnerová[(✉)]

The Czech Academy of Sciences, Institute of Computer Science,
Pod Vodárenskou věží 2, 182 07 Prague 8, Czech Republic
kalina@cs.cas.cz, petra@cs.cas.cz
http://www.cs.cas.cz/staff/kalina/en

Abstract. Pearson product-moment correlation coefficient represents a fundamental measure of similarity between two data vectors. In various applications, it is meaningful to consider its weighted version known as the weighted Pearson correlation coefficient. Its properties are studied in this theoretical paper; these include the robustness to rounding, as it is an important issue in approximate neurocomputing, or specific robustness properties for the context of template matching in image analysis. For a highly robust correlation coefficient inspired by the least weighted estimator, properties are derived and novel hypothesis tests are proposed. This robust measure is recommendable particularly for data contaminated by outliers (not only) in the context of image analysis.

Keywords: Correlation coefficient · Outliers · Robustness · Image analysis · Approximate computing

1 Introduction

Pearson product-moment correlation coefficient r represents a notoriously well known measure of similarity between two data vectors. It has been widely used e.g. in very recent deep learning applications. Most recently, the coefficient r was successfully used in nonlinear regression applications with the aims to compare the results of predictions of a continuous response given by two deep networks [17] or to compare the predictions with the ground truth [12]. Also in the context of time series, r has commonly been used to measure the quality of predictions reported by deep networks [10].

In image analysis, Pearson correlation coefficient is habitually used as a similarity measure in object detection by centroid-based methods (template matching) or landmark localization [4]. Template matching is commonly performed by comparing a template with every candidate area in the image [3]. The theory of

The research was supported by the grant 22-02067S "Approximate Neurocomputing" of the Czech Science Foundation.

L. Iliadis et al. (Eds.): ICANN 2023, LNCS 14262, pp. 200–212, 2023.
https://doi.org/10.1007/978-3-031-44201-8_17

centroids (prototypes, ideal simplified objects, typical forms with ideal appearance) and centroid-based object detection in images was developed in [8]. In some applications such as in image analysis, it is meaningful to consider the weighted Pearson correlation coefficient r_w as a natural weighted version of r. A sophisticated procedure for the optimal construction of centroids for template matching was suggested in [15], where r_w was used as the similarity measure between the centroid and a given image. For optimal centroids, robustness against outlying values turns out to be interconnected with sparsity [13]; the optimal centroids are sparse trimming away not only irrelevant pixels but also those pixels that violate the robustness [15].

Because both r and r_w are vulnerable to the presence of outliers in the data, robust measures may be more appropriate to evaluate the correlation for contaminated data [19]. The correlation coefficient r_{LWS} based on the highly robust LWS (least weighted squares) estimator [7] seems to represent an especially perspective alternative to r. It was shown to be highly robust for contaminated data as well as highly efficient for non-contaminated data in [14], where however other useful properties were not studied. The robust correlation coefficient has the potential to be routinely used in various deep learning applications, where r remains to represent the most fundamental measure, e.g. in template matching within deep learning or within (modified) convolutional networks.

This paper is focused on deriving properties of r_w and r_{LWS}. The weighted correlation coefficient is investigated in Sect. 2, where the effect of rounding the data (i.e. the trade-off between the energetic demands and the performance) is evaluated in a context of approximate neurocomputing. Also, the effect in the context of applying the weighted correlation coefficient to images within template matching is quantified there. Properties of the robust correlation coefficient based on the least weighted squares (LWS) estimator are investigated in Sect. 3, where a novel hypothesis test about the population correlation coefficient based on the robust estimator is also proposed. Section 4 concludes the paper and recommends r_{LWS} for contaminated data (not only) in image analysis tasks.

2 Weighted Correlation Coefficient

Let us consider two data vectors

$$x = (x_1, \ldots, x_n)^T \in \mathbb{R}^n \quad \text{and} \quad y = (y_1, \ldots, y_n)^T \in \mathbb{R}^n. \tag{1}$$

In some applications, weights may be naturally assigned to each of the pairs $(x_1, y_1)^T, \ldots, (x_n, y_n)^T$. Such situation may occur e.g. if each of the pairs corresponds to a measurement obtained under different conditions with different (known or estimated) measurement errors; in image processing, the weights may be assigned to pixels according to their positions within the image [15]. Thus, the correlation between x and y may be in many applications naturally measured by means of r_w with given non-negative weights $w = (w_1, \ldots, w_n)^T \in \mathbb{R}^n$ fulfilling the assumption $\sum_{i=1}^{n} w_i = 1$. We may recall r_w to be defined by

$$r_w(x, y; w) = \frac{\sum_{i=1}^{n} w_i(x_i - \bar{x}_w)(y_i - \bar{y}_w)}{\sqrt{\sum_{i=1}^{n}[w_i(x_i - \bar{x}_w)^2]\sum_{i=1}^{n}[w_i(y_i - \bar{y}_w)^2]}}, \tag{2}$$

where $\bar{x}_w = \sum_{i=1}^{n} w_i x_i \in \mathbb{R}$ denotes the weighted mean of x. A template matching study of [15] revealed the superior performance of r_w if suitable weights were used; the study considered mouth localization in facial images and constructed optimal weights maximizing the localization performance. Generally valid properties of r_w were investigated in [14] and additional specific purpose properties for the context of template matching will be derived in this section.

2.1   Energetic Demands

In various machine learning tasks, recent attention has been paid to the task to reduce tedious computations that are energetically demanding (energy-hungry) and researchers attempted to formulate low-energetic alternatives within the field of approximate neurocomputing [22]. This subsection is focused on reducing the energetic demands in the context of template matching. The vector playing the role of a template will be denoted as $c \in \mathbb{R}^n$, where $c_1, \ldots, c_n$ are grey values for the individual coordinates. The centroid c, which is ideally obtained by some sophisticated (optimization) procedure, is assumed here not to be known precisely. Instead, an approximate version denoted as $\tilde{c}$ is available. This may be obtained by rounding of the precise (ideal) c or by some approximate training procedure following the recent paradigm of approximate computation [2]. The task now is to study the effect of replacing c by $\tilde{c}$ within the weighted correlation coefficient, i.e. the effect of replacing $r_w(x, c)$ by $r_w(x, \tilde{c})$. We can say this corresponds to the effect of replacing the original centroid by a low-energy version.

We consider two n-variate vectors according to (1). In order to stress that the approach is tailor-made for templates (centroids), the data vectors will be denoted as x and c. The vector $\tilde{c}$ is replaced by

$$\tilde{c} = c + e, \quad \text{where } e \in \mathbb{R}^n, \quad -\varepsilon \leq e_i \leq \varepsilon, \quad i = 1, \ldots, n. \tag{3}$$

It is meaningful to interpret ε as a very small positive number. A formulation of an upper and lower bounds on $r_w(\tilde{c}, x)$ is now presented. The lower and upper bounds for $r_w(\tilde{c}, x)$ are much simplified here thanks to the assumption that x and c contain only non-negative values.

Lemma 1. *Let us have data vectors (1) and a centroid c with its modification according to (3). It is further assumed that $x_i \geq 0$ for every $i = 1, \ldots, n$ and also $c_i \geq 0$ for every $i = 1, \ldots, n$. Then, it holds that*

$$L(x, c, w, \varepsilon) \leq r_w(\tilde{c}, x) \leq U(x, c, w, \varepsilon), \tag{4}$$

where

$$L(x, c, w, \varepsilon) = \frac{\sum_{i=1}^{n}(x_i - \bar{x}_w)(c_i - \bar{c}_w) - 2\varepsilon\sum_{i=1}^{n} w_i x_i}{\sqrt{\sum_{i=1}^{n} w_i x_i^2 - \bar{x}_w^2}\sqrt{\sum_{i=1}^{n} w_i c_i^2 - (\bar{c}_w)^2 + 2\varepsilon(1 - \bar{c}_w)}} \tag{5}$$

and

$$U(x, c, w, \varepsilon) = \frac{\sum_{i=1}^{n}(x_i - \bar{x}_w)(c_i - \bar{c}_w) + 2\varepsilon \sum_{i=1}^{n} w_i x_i}{\sqrt{\sum_{i=1}^{n} w_i x_i^2 - \bar{x}_w^2} \sqrt{\sum_{i=1}^{n} w_i c_i^2 - (\bar{c}_w)^2 - 2\varepsilon(1 - \bar{c}_w)}}. \tag{6}$$

Proof. Let us start by finding lower and upper bounds separately for the numerator (say ξ) and for the denominator (say η) of $r_w(\tilde{c}, w)$ evaluated for the version $\tilde{c}$ considered in the approximate neurocomputing setup. Recalling (3) to have $\tilde{c} = c + e$, we now consider partial derivatives of ξ and η with respect to individual coordinates of e. Particularly, the derivative of the numerator

$$\frac{\partial \xi}{\partial e_i} = 2w_i(1 + e_i) - 4w_i \sum_{j=1}^{n} w_j c_j, \quad i = 1, \ldots, n, \tag{7}$$

reveals the numerator to be a monotone function of e_i for every $i = 1, \ldots, n$ so that the upper bound is obtained for $e_i = \varepsilon$ for every i. Thus, we obtain

$$\xi_0 - 2\varepsilon(1 - \bar{c}_w) \leq \xi \leq \xi_0 + 2\varepsilon(1 - \bar{c}_w), \tag{8}$$

where

$$\xi_0 = \sum_{i=1}^{n} w_i c_i^2 - \bar{c}_w^2. \tag{9}$$

In an analogous way, derivatives of the denominator in the form

$$\frac{\partial \eta}{\partial e_i} = w_i \left(x_i - \sum_{j=1}^{n} w_j x_j \right), \quad i = 1, \ldots, n, \tag{10}$$

reveal the upper bound to be obtained for $e_i = \varepsilon$ for every i. We get

$$\eta_0 - 2\varepsilon \bar{x}_w \leq \eta \leq \eta_0 + 2\varepsilon \bar{x}_w, \tag{11}$$

where

$$\eta_0 = \sum_{i=1}^{n} w_i x_i y_i - \bar{x}_w \bar{y}_w. \tag{12}$$

A suitable combination of (8) and (11) gives the formulas (5) and (6).

2.2   Formulas for a Modified Image

Our aim now is to express the effect (influence) of modifying the image on the resulting values of r_w in the context of template matching. Formulas for the effect of some selected modifications of the images will now be presented for 3 situations in centroid-based object localization with asymmetric illumination (in 2 different versions) or rotation of the image. While the centroid and candidate areas are matrices of size (say) $I \times J$ pixels, it is natural to use them in computations after being transformed to vectors of length IJ, where we denote $n = IJ$. Nevertheless, it will be more convenient to use here the following notation.

Model $\mathcal{M}$: We assume the centroid $c = (c)_{i,j}$ with $i = 1, \ldots, I$ and $j = 1, \ldots, J$ to be a matrix of size $I \times J$ pixels. A candidate area x and non-negative weights w with $\sum_i \sum_j w_{ij} = 1$ are assumed to be matrices of the same size as c.

Asymmetric illumination I. In the first situation, let us consider a selected candidate area x to be divided to three parts denoted as $x = (x_1^T, x_2^T, x_3^T)^T \in \mathbb{R}^n$. Let $\sum_{II}$ and $\sum_{III}$ denote the sum over the pixels of the second or third part, respectively. The modified image corresponds e.g. to the situation when grey values on one side of the image (in a rectangular area) are additively modified by $a \in \mathbb{R}$ and the grey values of the background on one side of the axis are modified by $b \in \mathbb{R}$.

Lemma 2. *Let us consider Model $\mathcal{M}$. For*

$$x = (x_1, x_2, x_3)^T \quad and \quad x^* = (x_1, x_2 + a, x_3 + b)^T \quad with \quad a \in \mathbb{R}, \; b \in \mathbb{R}, \quad (13)$$

it holds

$$r_w(x^*, c) = r_w(x, c)\frac{S_w(x)}{S_w^*(x)} + \frac{a\sum_{II} w_i(c_i - \bar{c}) + b\sum_{III} w_i(c_i - \bar{c})}{S_w(c)S_w^*(x)}, \quad (14)$$

where $(S_w^*(x))^2 =$

$$S_w^2(x) + 2a\sum_{II} w_i(x_i - \bar{x}) + 2b\sum_{III} w_i(x_i - \bar{x}) + a^2(1 - a)\sum_{II} w_i + b^2(1 - b)\sum_{III} w_i. \quad (15)$$

Asymmetric illumination II. The next lemma may be used for evaluating the effect of illumination from aside that is proportional to the distance of columns of the image from one side. There, the choice $k > 0$ grants columns with a large j to be lighter compared to those with a smaller j.

Lemma 3. *Let us consider Model $\mathcal{M}$. For* $x^* = (x_{ij}^*)_{i,j}$ *defined by* $x_{ij}^* = x_{ij} + kj$ *for* $i = 1, \ldots, I$, $j = 1, \ldots, J$, *and for* $k > 0$, *it holds that*

$$r_w(x^*, c) = r_w(x, c)\frac{S_w(x)}{\sqrt{S_w^{*2}(x)}} + \frac{k\sum_{i=1}^I \sum_{j=1}^J w_{ij}j(c_{ij} - \bar{c}_w)}{S_w(t)\sqrt{S_w^{*2}(x)}} \quad (16)$$

with

$$S_w^{*2}(x) = S_w^2(x) + 2k\sum_{i,j} w_{ij}jx_{ij} - k\bar{x}_w J(J + 1)$$

$$+ \frac{1}{6}k^2 IJ(J + 1)(2J + 1) + \frac{1}{4n}k^2 I(I - 2)J^2(J + 1)^2. \quad (17)$$

Rotated image. Further, it is shown that centroid-based object localization can be expected to be robust only to a very small rotation of the image. Here, $[a]$ denotes the integer value that is the closest to $a \in \mathbb{R}$.

Lemma 4. *Let us consider Model $\mathcal{M}$. Without loss of generality, let us assume both c and x to be standardized to zero mean and unit variance. By rotating the candidate area x by angle $\theta \in [-\pi, \pi)$ around a given the center of rotation $[i_0, j_0]$, the rotated area x^* of size $I \times J$ pixels is obtained. Let us assume that all pixels after the rotation still belong to the original image. For particular values of i and j, let us consider the angle φ and the radius r defined as*

$$\varphi = \arctan(i/j) \quad and \quad r = \sqrt{(i-i_0)^2 + (j-j_0)^2}. \tag{18}$$

Then, it holds

$$r_w(x^*, c) = \sum_{i=1}^{I} \sum_{j=1}^{J} w_{ij} c_{ij} x_{[i-r\theta \sin \varphi],[j+r\theta \cos \varphi]} + o(\theta). \tag{19}$$

Proof. For an infinitesimal rotation $\theta \to 0$, we may use Taylor's expansion of $\sin \theta$ and $\cos \theta$ of the first order to obtain the approximation of $r_w(x^*, c)$. The expansion is applied to the following considerations. If the image x was continuous (defined not only in individual discretized pixels), the expressions

$$r_w(x^*, c) = \sum_{i=1}^{I} \sum_{j=1}^{J} w_{ij} c_{ij} x_{r \cos(\varphi+\theta), r \sin(\varphi+\theta)}$$

$$= \sum_{i=1}^{I} \sum_{j=1}^{J} w_{ij} c_{ij} x_{r(\cos\varphi - \theta \sin \varphi), r(\sin \varphi + \theta \cos \varphi)} \tag{20}$$

would hold exactly. Because the coordinates have to be integers, the real (non-integer) numbers are rounded in (20); the effect of rounding is negligible for $\theta \to 0$ so that the statement remains to be approximately valid.

The assumption that all pixels after the rotation belong to the image makes the lemma applicable for candidate areas not at the very boundary of the image. The idea of the proof is formulated in the appendix.

3   LWS-Based Robust Correlation Coefficient

The highly robust correlation coefficient r_{LWS} based on the least weighted squares (LWS) estimator will now be recalled and its properties will be studied. These include two novel r_{LWS}-based methods for hypothesis testing about the significance of the population correlation coefficient.

3.1   Definition

First, we recall the least weighted squares (LWS) estimator with fixed magnitudes of the weights. This is formulated for the standard linear regression model

$$y_i = \beta_1 x_{i1} + \cdots + \beta_p x_{ip} + e_i, \quad i = 1, \ldots, n, \tag{21}$$

where the vector $x_i = (x_{i1}, \ldots, x_{ip})^T$ corresponds to the i-th observation for $i = 1, \ldots, n$. Let us also consider a particular weight function, which represents a non-increasing and continuous function $\psi : [0,1] \to [0,1]$ with $\psi(0) = 1$ and $\psi(1) = 0$. The residual for any (fixed) $b = (b_1, \ldots, b_p)^T \in \mathbb{R}^p$ will be denoted as

$$u_i(b) = y_i - b_1 x_{i1} - \cdots - b_p x_{ip} = y_i - x_i^T b, \quad i = 1, \ldots, n. \tag{22}$$

The LWS estimator [7] of the parameters $(\beta_1, \ldots, \beta_p)^T$ in (21) is defined as

$$\arg\min_{b \in \mathbb{R}^d} \sum_{i=1}^{n} \psi\left(\frac{i - 1/2}{n}\right) u_{(i)}^2(b). \tag{23}$$

Let us further denote the squared residuals arranged in ascending order as $u_{(1)}^2(b) \leq \cdots \leq u_{(n)}^2(b)$. We can alternatively express (23) as

$$\arg\min_{b \in \mathbb{R}^d} \sum_{i=1}^{n} w_i u_{(i)}^2(b), \tag{24}$$

where given magnitudes of weights $w_1, \ldots, w_n$ are assigned to individual observations after the optimal permutation. The magnitudes $w_1, \ldots, w_n$ should be non-increasing and a simple choice is to take linearly decreasing weights [16]. More suitable data-dependent (adaptive) weights were proposed by [7] based on comparing the empirical distribution of the squared residuals with the expected counterpart under normally distributed errors; other choices were compared in [14]. The appealing properties of the LWS are ensured by the ranking of residuals, which has been repeatedly exploited e.g. to construct estimators that are robust to measurement errors [20].

   Correlation analysis is connected to a regression model with $p = 1$. For the data (1), let us consider the model (21) in the form

$$y_i = \beta_0 + \beta_1 x_i + e_i, \quad i = 1, \ldots, n, \tag{25}$$

with $x_i \in \mathbb{R}$. Then, $r_{LWS}(x, y)$ is defined as $r_w(x, y; \tilde{w})$ with the permutation of the weights that is found as the optimal permutation given by the LWS estimator [16]. The weights after the optimal permutation will be denoted as $\tilde{w} = (\tilde{w}_1, \ldots, \tilde{w}_n)^T$.

3.2   Properties of r_{LWS}

Some properties of r_{LWS} were investigated already in [14]. These include the asymptotic distribution of r_{LWS} under normality (without outliers in the data).

Moreover, the LWS-based robust correlation coefficient r_{LWS} is known to be a highly robust alternative to standard r in terms of the breakdown point [14]. It will be convenient to use the notation for the weighted mean of x and weighted variance of $x \in \mathbb{R}^n$ with given weights $w_1, \ldots, w_n$ in the form

$$\bar{x}(w) = \sum_{i=1}^{n} w_i x_i \in \mathbb{R} \quad \text{and} \quad S^2(x; w) = \sum_{i=1}^{n} w_i (x_i - \bar{x}(w))^2 \in \mathbb{R}. \tag{26}$$

The linear model (25) will be symbolically denoted as $y \sim x$ here.

Lemma 5. *Let us assume* $x \in \mathbb{R}^n$, $y \in \mathbb{R}^n$, *and* $z \in \mathbb{R}^n$. *Let us select fixed magnitudes of non-negative weights. Let the optimal permutation of the weights in the model* $x \sim z$ *be denoted as* $\tilde{w}_1^I, \ldots, \tilde{w}_n^I$. *Let the optimal permutation of the weights in the model* $y \sim z$ *be denoted as* $\tilde{w}_1^{II}, \ldots, \tilde{w}_n^{II}$. *Let the optimal permutation of the weights in the model* $(x - y) \sim z$ *be denoted as* $\tilde{w}_1^{III}, \ldots, \tilde{w}_n^{III}$. *Let us introduce the notation*

$$x^* = \left(\sqrt{\tilde{w}_1^I} x_1, \ldots, \sqrt{\tilde{w}_n^{II}} x_n \right)^T, \quad y^* = \left(\sqrt{\tilde{w}_1^{II}} y_1, \ldots, \sqrt{\tilde{w}_n^{II}} y_n \right)^T, \tag{27}$$

and

$$\tilde{x} - \tilde{y} = \left(\sqrt{\tilde{w}_1^{III}} (x_1 - y_1), \ldots, \sqrt{\tilde{w}_n^{III}} (x_n - y_n) \right)^T. \tag{28}$$

Then, it holds that

-
$$r_{LWS}(x, z; \tilde{w}^I) \geq r_{LWS}(y, z; \tilde{w}^{II}) \quad \Longleftrightarrow \quad r(x^*, z) \geq r(y^*, z), \tag{29}$$

-
$$r_{LWS}(x - y, z; \tilde{w}^{III}) \geq 0 \quad \Longleftrightarrow \quad r(\tilde{x} - \tilde{y}, z) \geq 0. \tag{30}$$

Lemma 5 represents an extension of Lemma 2 of [14], where the latter was formulated for r_w.

3.3   A Hypothesis Test Based on r_{LWS}

In this section, hypothesis tests about the population correlation coefficient are formulated. For this task, we need to assume the data to come from a bivariate normal distribution and the population correlation coefficient between the first and the second coordinate will be denoted as ρ. We are interested in testing the null hypothesis $H_0 : \rho = 0$ against the general alternative hypothesis $H_1 : \rho \neq 0$ based on r_{LWS}. First, a theorem from [14] is recalled, which holds under general (and rather technical) assumptions on the distribution of the random errors.

Theorem 1. *Let us assume a random sample* $(x_1, y_1)^T, \ldots, (x_n, y_n)^T$ *from a bivariate normal distribution with correlation coefficient* ρ. *The variances of both marginal distributions are assumed to be positive and* $\rho \in (-1, 1)$ *is assumed.*

We will denote $x = (x_1, \ldots, x_n)^T$ *and* $y = (y_1, \ldots, y_n)^T$. *It holds under* H_0 *and under Assumptions* $\mathcal{A}$ *of* [23] *that*

$$T_{LWS} = \frac{r_{LWS}(x,y)}{\sqrt{1 - r_{LWS}^2(x,y)}} \sqrt{n-2} \overset{D}{\to} Z \tag{31}$$

for $n \to \infty$, *where* Z *is a random variable with normal* $\mathsf{N}(0,1)$ *distribution.*

As a novelty, we now suggest to perform the test of H_0 against H_1 based on Theorem 1 according to the decision rule

$$H_0 \text{ is rejected} \iff |T_{LWS}| \geq z_{1-\alpha/2}, \tag{32}$$

where $z_{1-\alpha/2}$ is the $(1 - \alpha/2)$-quantile of $\mathsf{N}(0,1)$ distribution.

Note 1. The test (32) represents an extension of a standard test of H_0 based on r for bivariate normal distribution. To recall, the test statistic

$$T = \frac{r}{\sqrt{1 - r^2}} \sqrt{n - 2} \tag{33}$$

has Student's t_{n-2} distribution for normally distributed errors as formulated in [18]. Let us also recall that an equivalent test based directly on r is presented in more traditional literature; tables of critical values of r based on the monotone transform (33) of r depending on n and α have namely been available.

Note 2. Constructing a Wald-type test based on r_{LWS} is not meaningful, because asymptotic normality of r_{LWS} does not hold. In the test statistics, although one can exploit approximate theoretical results

$$\mathsf{E}\, r \doteq \rho - \frac{1 - \rho^2}{n} \quad \text{and} \quad \text{var}\, r \doteq \frac{(1 - \rho^2)^2}{n} \tag{34}$$

for bivariate normal distribution [18], replacing ρ by r much deteriorates the resulting null distribution of the test statistic (see e.g. Chap. 6 of [5]). This is fact motivates us to consider the Fisher transform and to apply it to r_{LWS}, because it is well known to be stable (to keep the asymptotic distribution) in such a situation.

3.4   A Hypothesis Test Based on r_{LWS} Based on the Fisher Transform

We will now propose another novel approach for testing H_0 against H_1 exploiting the Fisher transform applied to r_{LWS}. Such test is based on the test statistic

$$Z_{LWS} = \frac{1}{2} \log \frac{1 + r_{LWS}}{1 - r_{LWS}} \tag{35}$$
$$= \text{arctanh}(r_{LWS}).$$

The Fisher transform used in (38) is one of variance stabilization transforms making the variances of r to be independent of the correlation magnitudes. The transform is also popular for constructing confidence intervals for ρ [15], thanks to its reliability also for values of ρ close to -1 or 1 (which is a property not needed for testing of $H_0 : \rho = 0$).

The test of H_0 against H_1 based on (35) is based on the decision rule

$$H_0 \text{ is rejected} \iff Z_{LWS}/SD(Z_{LWS}) \geq z_{1-\alpha/2}. \tag{36}$$

Bootstrapping can be used to estimate the standard deviation of Z_{LWS} denoted here as $SD(Z_{LWS})$.

Note 3. Specifically, if r_{LWS} is computed with the adaptive weights of [7], it is possible to express an explicit approximate formula for $SD(Z_{LWS})$ in the form

$$SD(Z_{LWS}) \doteq \sqrt{\frac{1}{n-3}}, \tag{37}$$

which requires the assumptions of Theorem 3 of [7]. This is in fact the approximate standard deviation of

$$Z = \frac{1}{2} \log \frac{1+r}{1-r}, \tag{38}$$

as can be derived by considering Taylor's series approximation [5]. If Z_{LWS} considered with adaptive weights under the given assumptions (i.e. for the non-contaminated case), one obtains the very same standard deviation (37) thanks to the fact that the weights converge to 1 in probability for the adaptive weights.

Theorem 2. *Under the assumptions of Theorem 1, the test statistics T_{LWS} (31) and Z_{LWS} (35) are first-order equivalent under H_0.*

Proof. Let us understand

$$T(r_{LWS}) = \sqrt{n-2}\frac{r_{LWS}}{\sqrt{1-r_{LWS}^2}} \quad \text{and} \quad Z(r_{LWS}) = \frac{1}{2} \log \frac{1+r_{LWS}}{1-r_{LWS}} \tag{39}$$

as functions of the argument r_{LWS}. We need to express the derivatives

$$T'(r_{LWS}) = \sqrt{n-2} \left(\frac{1}{\sqrt{1-r_{LWS}^2}} - \frac{r_{LWS}}{2}(1-r_{LWS}^2)^{-3/2} \right) \tag{40}$$

and

$$Z'(r_{LWS}) = \frac{1+r_{LWS}}{(1-r_{LWS})^3}. \tag{41}$$

Now, using Taylor's approximation for $r \to 0$ leads to proving the theorem thanks to

$$T(r) = T(0) + rT'(0) + o(r) \quad \text{and} \quad Z(r) = Z(0) + rZ'(0) + o(r). \tag{42}$$

Numerical experiments will be needed to compare the performance of the test (32) and the test (36). Let us at least recall that numerical evidence showed the test based on (33) to be superior to the test based on (38), especially because of a quicker convergence to the normal distribution.

4   Conclusion

Properties of r_w are derived here as tailor-made expressions for a particular context of template matching. The study of r_w in Sect. 2.1 is applicable for performing template matching on specific devices such as cell phones (mobile devices with limited memory and powered by a battery); this result may find applications within approximate neurocomputing. Should a more intensive acceleration of the computation be desirable, it remains possible to resort to using sparse (compressed) centroids. The much more specific results on r_w in Sect. 2.2 are tailor-made for template matching and reveal r_w to be vulnerable to modified illumination or rotation of the images.

The properties of r_{LWS} derived here with deterministic as well as probabilistic tools are generally valid results not connected to the context of image analysis. The robust r_{LWS} inherits some properties of r_w and the hypothesis tests proposed here represents the first available tests about the population correlation coefficient based on r_{LWS}, which are useful for image analysis tasks with the need to evaluate the significance of the correlation coefficient [6]. Extensive numerical experiments related to the performance of r_w and r_{LWS} in object localization tasks in images have already been performed. The performance of both r_w and r_{LWS} is superior to that obtained with r [15] and r_w yields quite good results also for data with a moderate contamination by outliers [15].

For severe contamination of the data, r_{LWS} may be recommended as a similarity measure for various following applications. Methods based on centroids may be used for object localization in images within deep learning procedures. Particularly, the weighted and the robust correlation coefficients studied in this paper may be used to replace convolutions within deep networks [1]. Also template matching may be transferred into a deep-feature space provided by a deep convolutional network. For these possible applications, we find the derived properties to be very useful. In [24], template matching was exploited withing a deep learning procedure for ship identification in underwater sound waves. Using centroids within deep learning may be expected to be more tolerant to changes in appearance (such as lighting conditions or partial occlusion) and may benefit from combining features from different network layers [9, 11, 21].

Acknowledgements. The authors are grateful to Jakub Krett for numerical experiments motivating this work and to Jiří Šíma and Václav Šmídl for discussion about Sect. 2.

References

1. Alsahafi, Y.S., Kassem, M.A., Hosny, K.M.: Skin-Net: a novel deep residual network for skin lesions classification using multilevel feature extraction and cross-channel correlation with detection of outlier. J. Big Data **10**, 105 (2023)
2. Azar, J., Makhoul, A., Barhamgi, M., Couturier, R.: An energy efficient IoT data compression approach for edge machine learning. Futur. Gener. Comput. Syst. **96**, 168–175 (2019)

3. Bilan, S., Yuzhakov, S.: Pattern Recognition Based on Parallel Shift Technology. CRC Press, Boca Raton (2018)

4. Böhringer, S., de Jong, M.A.: Quantification of facial traits. Front. Genet. **10**, 397 (2019)

5. Borenstein, M., Hedges, L.V., Higgins, J.P.T., Rothstein, H.R.: Introduction to Meta-analysis, 2nd edn. Wiley, Chichester (2021)

6. Botvinik-Nezer, R., Holzmeister, F., Camerer, C.F., Dreber, A., Huber, J., et al.: Variability in the analysis of a single neuroimaging dataset by many teams. Nature **582**, 84–88 (2020)

7. Čížek, P.: Semiparametrically weighted robust estimation of regression models. Comput. Stat. Data Anal. **55**, 774–788 (2011)

8. Delaigle, A., Hall, P.: Achieving near perfect classification for functional data. J. Roy. Stat. Soc. **74**, 267–286 (2012)

9. Ferrari, C., Berretti, S., Bimbo, A.D.: Discovering identity specific activation patterns in deep descriptors for template based face recognition. 14th IEEE International Conference on Automatic Face & Gesture Recognition (FG 2019), pp. 1–5 (2019)

10. Gamel, S.A., Hassan, E., El-Rashidy, N., Talaat, F.M.: Exploring the effects of pandemics on transportation through correlations and deep learning techniques. Multimed. Tools Appl. (2023)

11. Gao, B., Spratling, M.W.: Robust template matching via hierarchical convolutional features from a shape biased CNN. In: Yao, J., Xiao, Y., You, P., Sun, G. (eds.) The International Conference on Image, Vision and Intelligent Systems (ICIVIS 2021). LNEE, vol. 813, pp. 333–344. Springer, Singapore (2022). https://doi.org/10.1007/978-981-16-6963-7_31

12. Guyll, M., Madon, S., Yang, Y., Wells, G.: Validity of forensic cartridge-case comparisons. Psychol. Cogn. Sci. **120**, e2210428120 (2023)

13. Jurečková, J., Picek, J., Schindler, M.: Robust Statistical Methods with R, 2nd edn. CRC Press, Boca Raton (2019)

14. Kalina, J.: Robust coefficients of correlation or spatial autocorrelation based on implicit weighting. J. Korean Stat. Soc. **51**, 1247–1267 (2022)

15. Kalina, J., Matonoha, C.: A sparse pair-preserving centroid-based supervised learning method for high-dimensional biomedical data or images. Biocybern. Biomed. Eng. **40**, 774–786 (2020)

16. Kalina, J., Tichavský, J.: On robust estimation of error variance in (highly) robust regression. Meas. Sci. Rev. **20**, 6–14 (2020)

17. Naeem, A., Anees, T., Ahmed, K.T., Naqvi, R.A., Ahmad, S., Whangbo, T.: Deep learned vectors formation using auto-correlation, scaling, and derivations with CNN for complex and huge image retrieval. Complex Intell. Syst. **9**, 1729–1751 (2023)

18. Rao, C.R.: Linear Statistical Inference and Its Applications. Wiley, New York (2002)

19. Rather, A.A., Chachoo, M.A.: Robust correlation estimation and UMAP assisted topological analysis of omics data for disease subtyping. Comput. Biol. Med. **155**, 106640 (2023)

20. Saleh, A.K.M.E., Picek, J., Kalina, J.: R-estimation of the parameters of a multiple regression model with measurement errors. Metrika **75**, 311–328 (2012)

21. Sun, L., Sun, H., Wang, J., Wu, S., Zhao, Y., Xu, Y.: Breast mass detection in mammography based on image template matching and CNN. Sensors **2021**, 2855 (2021)

22. Sze, V., Chen, Y.H., Yang, T.J., Emer, J.S.: Efficient Processing of Deep Neural Networks. Morgan & Claypool Publishers, San Rafael (2020)
23. Víšek, J.Á.: Consistency of the least weighted squares under heteroscedasticity. Kybernetika **47**, 179–206 (2011)
24. Yang, H., Zheng, K., Li, J.: Open set recognition of underwater acoustic targets based on GRU-CAE collaborative deep learning network. Appl. Acoust. **193**, 108774 (2022)

PSML: Prototype-Based OSSL Framework for Multi-information Mining

YiYong Xiao[✉], GuiMei Ying, and YongCan Fu

TaiYuan Normal University, Jinzhong, China
291832548@qq.com

Abstract. Openset semi-supervised learning (OSSL) has been mainly used in recent years to address the negative impact of out-of-distribution (OOD) unlabeled data on semi-supervised learning. However, current openset semi-supervised learning approaches directly discard the identified ood data, while ignoring the positive impact of ood data similar to in-distribution (ID) data on semi-supervised learning. And the method based on learnable parameters is prone to overfitting ood unlabeled data. Therefore, we propose a prototype-based OSSL framework for multi-information mining (PSML) to better mine ood unlabeled data and improve the classification performance of ID data. Specifically, we detect the multi-level information density of unlabeled data by a learnable OOD detector and a non-learnable prototype similarity detector. Then we perform different degrees of prototype based information mining on the data with different information densities (ID data, similar data, and dissimilar data). As a result, PSML is able to perform better information mining in ood unlabeled data, and thus it achieves a significant performance improvement relative to previous work, as demonstrated in experiments on multiple benchmark datasets.

Keywords: Semi-Supervised Learning · Class Mismatch · Prototypical Network

1 Introduction

Semi-supervised learning (SSL) [6,28,29] as an efficient machine learning paradigm has achieved remarkable progress with limited labeled data available, contributing to its superiority in harvesting information from a large amount of unlabeled data. Most existing works [5,8,14,15] on SSL assume that the categories of unlabeled data are identical with with the categories of labeled data, both unlabeled and labeled data belong to the same class distribution (ID). However, this assumption hinders the application of semi-supervised learning in more practical scenarios. To tackle with this issue, most recently, open-set semi-supervised learning (OSSL) [4,21,26] is proposed to broaden the application scenarios by allowing the inclusion of out-of-distribution unlabeled data.

Recently, many OSSL modeling approaches [11,18,21,26] have emerged, which usually mine the information difference between ID data and OOD data

© The Author(s), under exclusive license to Springer Nature Switzerland AG 2023
L. Iliadis et al. (Eds.): ICANN 2023, LNCS 14262, pp. 213–224, 2023.
https://doi.org/10.1007/978-3-031-44201-8_18

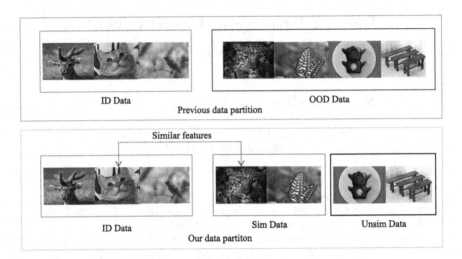

Fig. 1. Data partiton compared

using labeled data and noise learning. The ID data is separated from the OOD data by fitting an energy function or training a detector. The ID data detected in the unlabeled data is then used for semi-supervised learning to improve the classification performance of the ID data. These methods all perform well in semi-supervised learning of open sets, however, they may incur two major challenges: Firstly, previous methods [2,10,18] discarding the OOD data directly may cause a waste of information. Most of the current OSSL methods learn to identify between OOD data and ID data for semi-supervised learning, while the OOD data are usually ignored in the training of categories. We consider that, some of the OOD data can be helpful for the category training of the model, especially on the data with similar categories as in Fig. 1, where learning some of the tiger's features can be beneficial to train a superior SSL model. Moreover, parametric models are more likely to be overfitted in SSL. These methods usually use learnable parametric methods such as fully connected layers as the solution dock for ID data classification. In semi-supervised scenarios where labeled data are missing, this parametric decoding approach requiring data redundancy is not conducive to the classification of ID data. Due to the experimental setup of OpenSet, these approach will fit the noisy-OOD data in the unlabeled data. Therefore, a more robust, structurally simple way of decoding feature classification is needed for the semi-supervised learning scenario of OpenSet.

In OSSL, the classification performance of ID data can be improved when the open set contains OOD data (sim data) that are similar to ID data [1,12,26]. The inclusion of sim data can help the model to learn the features of ID data because of the similarity of the features of sim data and ID data. Meanwhile, prototype learning has been used in many classification works [17,20,25] with a limited number of labeled samples due to its efficient use of data and robustness properties. In OSSL, OOD data are easily introduced as noise in the classification learning of ID data due to the error of OOD detector. And the property that prototype learning is not easy to overfit can mitigate the negative impact of these noises on the classification effect of ID data. Therefore, to address the above challenges, we design a new framework for OSSL– Prototype based Multi-information mining OSSL (PMSL). PMSL Based on prototype learning by using a prototype approach to measure the beneficial information density of OOD data, and accordingly perform different levels of information mining on OOD data. Specifically, we simultaneously evaluate the multi-level information density of unlabeled data by a learnable OOD detector and a non-learnable prototype similarity detector. Then based on the data with different information densities (ID data, similar data, and dissimilar data), different degrees of information mining and learning are performed on different data by different loss functions to reduce the waste of information. Since the classification head of parametric approach tends to overfit a small amount of labeled data in semi-supervised learning, We adobt the prototype learning approach to train the model for classification and utilize the prototype to perform similarity data information mining on the data.

The main contributions of our work are summarized as follows:

1. In this work, we design prototype based multi-information mining OSSL as a new framework to improving OSSL performance.
2. By using a prototype approach to measure the useful information density of OOD data, and accordingly perform different levels of information mining on OOD data.
3. The validity of the method was verified by comparing it with state-of-the-art methods on various public datasets.

2   Related Work

2.1   Semi-Supervised Learning

Semi-Supervised Learning (SSL) has led to remarkable progress in diverse machine learning problems. This success can be attributed to advancements in learning algorithms and the utilization of large amounts of unlabeled data. Three main categories of Deep SSL methods exist, namely consistency regularization, pseudo-labeling, and hybrid methods.

Consistency regularization methods, as proposed in [14,19], make use of unlabeled data by assuming that the model should output similar predictions for any image and its perturbed version. Pseudo-labeling methods, as proposed in [5,15,24,28], utilize the model to generate artificial labels for unlabeled data. Hybrid methods, as proposed in [2,3], combine both consistency regularization and pseudo-labeling and also make use of data augmentation techniques, such as those proposed in [8,9,23], to further enhance performance.

However, the effectiveness of these methods depends on the assumption that all labeled and unlabeled data originate from the same distribution. Once this assumption is violated, the performance of seen-class classification may degrade and even fall below the performance of supervised learning methods, as reported in [4,10,16].

2.2 Openset Semi-Supervised Learning

The concept of Openset SSL methods refers to situations where the labeled and unlabeled datasets have different class sets. This issue was first addressed by Laine and Aila [14] and Oliver et al. [16]. Since then, several approaches have been proposed to tackle this problem. One such approach is Uncertainty Aware Self-Distillation (UASD) [7], which uses historical predictions to identify out-of-distribution (OOD) data and applies a self-distillation method to filter out potentially OOD data. Another approach is Safe Deep Semi-Supervised Learning (DS3L) [10], which employs a meta-learning scheme to automatically reduce the impact of OOD data. Multi-Task Curriculum Framework (MTC) [26] treats ID and OOD data as separate domains and employs curriculum learning to distinguish between them. These methods have made significant strides towards resolving the class-mismatch problem. OpenMatch [18] unifies FixMatch with novelty detection based on one-vs-all (OVA) classifiers.

However, the current methods all default OOD data as harmful data, which may miss the beneficial information.

3 Method

3.1 Overview

In Fig. 2, assuming a collection of labeled images $\{X_l, Y_l\}$ and an unlabeled collection $\{X_u\}$, the features extracted from the labeled data with the number of categories C are averaged to obtain the prototype $V_p = \{V_0, V_1 \dots V_c\} \in \mathbb{R}^{C \times M}$, while the data are classified into ID data X_{ID} and OOD data X_{OOD} using an OOD detector F. We aim to train a SSL model using labeled and unlabeled data via prototype-based loss L_l and hard pseudo-labeled loss L_{hard}. And the classification probability function of model prediction is set to $p_m(y \mid x)$. The OOD data are then classified into similar data and dissimilar data by the distance between the OOD data features and the prototype V_p. We leverage soft pseudo-labeled label loss L_{soft} for similar data to train the model. And we adopt uniform class distribution loss L_{ucd} for dissimilar data.

3.2 Preliminary

The proposed framework is flexible to multiple SSL baselines, and in this paper we use the FixMatch [21]. PMSL trains the data by augmenting the data with strong $A(\cdot)$ and weak $a(\cdot)$ data, via supervised loss L_l with unsupervised loss L_{hard}. First, the weakly supervised labeled data $a(X_u)$ are trained using the standard cross-entropy loss $CE(p,q)$. The unlabeled data are subjected to strong augmentation and weak data augmentation $A(\cdot), a(\cdot)$ here we set to and then the weakly augmented predictions p_u with higher probability confidence are used as the pseudo-label $\hat{Y}_u = argmax(p_u)$ for the strongly augmented predictions. Finally the unlabeled data are trained with consistent regularization via cross entropy.

$$L_l = \frac{1}{X_l} CE\left(Y_l, p_m\left(y \mid a\left(X_l\right)\right)\right) \tag{1}$$

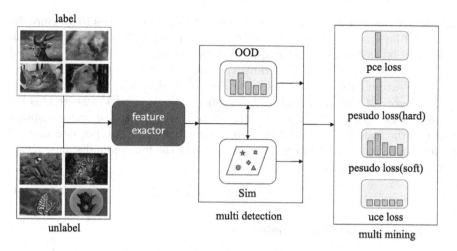

Fig. 2. PSML framework

$$L_{hard} = \frac{1}{X_u}\mathbb{I}(max(p_u) \geq \gamma)CE(\hat{Y}_u, p_m(y|A(X_u))) \qquad (2)$$

3.3 Multi Detection

Since some OOD data may contain beneficial information for OSSL, detecting only the OOD score of the data is more homogeneous and lacks the exploration of the beneficial information density of OOD data. To this end, we propose the Multi detection method by using a learnable OOD detector with a prototypical similarity detector for multi-perspective information detection of unlabeled data.

To detect OOD scores for unlabeled data, we need to train an OOD detector. To optimize the OOD detector using noise labels so that it can predict the OOD scores of the data. First, we initialize the OOD scores for all data. For labeled data, the score S_l is initialized to 0, and for unlabeled data, 0 is used as the initialized score S_u. Since a faster learning rate reduces the model's fit to noisy data, the initialized OOD scores are trained as the labels for OOD detection in the first round. The labels are then updated in a momentum fashion using the predicted OOD scores from each round. Where the parameters of the OOD detector can be updated by the following equation.

$$L_{ood} = \frac{1}{|X_l|}CE(S_l', S_l) + \frac{1}{|X_u|}CE(S_u', S_u) \qquad (3)$$

where S_l^u, S_u' denotes the X_l, X_u prediction results of OOD detector and CE is the cross entropy.

In the training phase, the network usually learns how to extract discriminative features from the data, and similar data are prone to extract similar features. The features from some categories that share similar patterns may be beneficial to each other. Thus, propose to adopt to use prototypes to measure the beneficial information density of OOD data, and obtain the similarity of unlabeled and labeled data by comparing the distribution of features of unlabeled data with the distribution of features (prototypes) of labeled data. First, features are extracted from the labeled data by the backbone network F, and then each category of features are averaged to obtain a prototype V_p, where C is the number of categories and M denotes the feature dimension. The vector distance between the features extracted by F and the category prototypes is compared with a function as shown in Eq. Then the value at the maximum distance $d(p, q)$ is taken as the similarity score:

$$Sim = max(d(F(X_{ood}), V_{ood}))$$ (4)

3.4   Multi Knowledge Minging

When performing information mining, since the use of fully-connected layers as classification prediction does not directly train the feature representation of the feature network. This can affect the accuracy of measuring the representation of the prototype versus the distance between the data and the prototype during prototype similarity detection. Also, the fully-connected layer tends to overfit the features on a small amount of labeled data. Therefore, we propose to utilize prototype to train the OSSL model. The classification probability p_m is obtained based on the softmax of the distance between the features and the corresponding prototypes of each category, as shown in Eq.

$$p_m(y = k|x) = \frac{exp(-d(F(X)), V_k)}{\sum_{k'} exp(-d(F(X)), V_{k'})}$$ (5)

After determining the implementation of classification probabilities p_m, we divide the data into several data domains based on the results of Multi detection scores and use different losses to mine them for different levels of information. We set thresholds ∂_{ood} and ∂_{sim} for OOD scores and Sim scores, using OSTU method[ref]. Moreover the unlabeled data are divided into ID data X_{id} and OOD data X_{ood} based on OOD score . The similar data X_{sim} and dissimilar data X_{unsim} are obtained based on the division with sim scores.

For X_{id} data, we adopt supervised loss L_l and unsupervised loss L_{hard} for information mining. In this manner, the framework is more robust to information mining of ID data of unlabeled data by strong and weak consistency regularization, which is a better performing learning framework in semi-supervised learning.

For similar OOD data X_{sim}, it may often have different degrees of similarity to different classes of data in some aspects (a deer can have the body shape of a dog while having the tail of a rabbit). To this end, we expect that these OOD data, close to ID data in the feature domain, will have a consistent classification probability distribution under strong and weak data augmentation both with the distance distribution of the prototype with the same strong and weak augmentation. To achieve this, we design the loss function L_{soft} in a soft way to train the ID similar part of the X_{sim} data for information mining. As shown in L_{soft}. we computed the probabilities of the strongly and weakly enhanced distributions separately and supervised the consistency of these two probability distributions via the cross-entropy loss function CE:

$$L_{soft} = \frac{1}{|X_{sim}|} CE(p_m(y|a(X_{sim})), p_m(y|A(X_{sim}))) \tag{6}$$

At the same time, these dissimilar data we want to reduce the bias learning of the model discriminator for these dissimilar data by training their probability distributions to average probability distributions. As shown in Eq. Here, both the strong and weak enhanced probability distributions are added to the average class distribution loss.

$$L_{aug()} = CE(p_{us}, p_m(y|aug(X_{us}))) \tag{7}$$

$$L_{ucd} = \frac{1}{|X_{unsim}|}(L_{a()} + L_{A()}) \tag{8}$$

3.5   Trainning and Inference

We divide the training process of PSML into two stages: pre-training and formal training. Firstly, in the pre-training stage, we use labeled data to train the backbone network of the model and the ood detection of the Multi-detection module. Among them, the backbone network is trained through prototype classification tasks with labeled data. Through pre-training, the ood detector can preliminarily have ood detection functions, and the backbone network can also extract data features to some extent. We extract features from all labeled data, and average the features by category to obtain the most initial prototype. This step will be performed before each epoch of formal training and remain fixed within the epoch.

In the formal training stage, we jointly train labeled and unlabeled data. Firstly, the Multi-detection is performed on the input unlabeled data. The ood score and sim score of the predicted and trained data are predicted and trained through the ood detector and sim detector. Then, the Multi-mining module divides the data into labeled data, unlabeled ID data, sim ood data, and unsim ood data according to the predicted information of Multi-detection, and uses different loss functions to mine information of different data to varying degrees.

For the overall training loss L_{all} of each batch of PSML in the training, it is jointly calculated by labeled data and unlabeled data as shown in the formula.

$$L_{all} = L_l + \lambda_{ood}L_{ood} + \lambda_{hard}L_{hard} + \lambda_{soft}L_{soft} + \lambda_{ucd}L_{ucd} \tag{9}$$

4   Experiment

4.1   Experimental Settings and Evaluation

We validated the PSML method on multiple SSL benchmarks. Among them, we divided the categories of datasets such as cifra10/cira100 [13] and imagenet30 [22] into known and unknown categories to construct the OSSL task, and conducted experiments and parameter adjustments based on parameters such as labeled data quantity and known/unknown category ratio.

In the experiments, we used multiple hyperparameters in the training loss to balance the weights of different losses. In the pre-training stage, we set λ_{ood} to 0.3, while setting the values of λ_{hard}, λ_{soft}, and λ_{ucd} to 0, so that only the classification loss of labeled data and the ood detector were trained in this stage. In the formal training stage, λ_{ood} was set to 0.2, while λ_{hard} and λ_{soft} were both 0.5, and λ_{ucd} was set to 0.1 at the end. We set the pre-training stage to train for the first 100 epochs, and then train for 400 epochs in the formal training stage. We used wideresent [27] as the backbone network for all methods to extract features. For each experiment, only one NVIDIA 3090 GPU was used for training.

For testing the dataset, we only used the known categories for in-domain classification results testing. Then, we mainly used classification accuracy (%) as the result indicator for testing the model on different datasets.

4.2   CIFRA10 and CIFRA100

To validate the feasibility of our method, we need to artificially construct semantic correlations between known and unknown categories in the experiments. Specifically, we extracted 4 animal categories from the 6 animal categories in CIFRA10, and took 2 non-animal categories to form the known categories of the CIFRA10 dataset, while the remaining 4 categories were unknown categories. Similarly, for CIFRA100, we divided the categories according to coares labels. In this experiment, we set two partition parameters following previous work: 80 known categories (20 unknown categories) and 55 known categories (44 unknown categories).

In both of these partition parameters, we still followed the principle that there is partial correlation between known and unknown categories. At the same time, we also compared the performance of the methods under different numbers of class labels (the number of labeled samples of each class).

Table 1 and Table 2 describes the validation set classification accuracy of different methods under different experimental settings (dataset, number of class labels, and category ratio). It can be seen that the PSML method performs better than other methods in different settings. PSML improves the ability of feature extraction and class clustering of ID data by detecting and mining useful information from OOD data at multiple levels. Specifically, when the number of labeled data is 50, PSML is significantly better than other methods. This is because the prototype classification feature in PSML can efficiently utilize limited labeled data and reduce overfitting to noise.

4.3   ImageNet

To further validate the performance of POML in the OSSL scenario, we compared the effectiveness of different methods on ImageNet. As the cost of training

Table 1. Results of CIFRA10.

CIFRA10 (6/4)			
Method	50	100	400
FixMatch	58.2 ± 0.23	68.5 ± 0.25	77.1 ± 0.17
MTC	78.0 ± 0.19	85.9 ± 0.14	90.7 ± 0.13
OpenMatch	83.2 ± 0.21	88.1 ± 0.12	92.3 ± 0.11
PSML	$\mathbf{86.1} \pm 0.13$	$\mathbf{90.6} \pm 0.09$	$\mathbf{94.3} \pm 0.10$

Table 2. Results of CIFRA100.

Method	CIFRA100 (55/45)		CIFRA100 (80/20)	
	50	100	50	100
FixMatch	63.7 ± 0.29	72.4 ± 0.35	58.0 ± 0.22	65.1 ± 0.46
MTC	68.2 ± 0.18	73.8 ± 0.67	60.2 ± 0.44	67.4 ± 0.12
OpenMatch	71.2 ± 0.21	76.9 ± 0.34	63.4 ± 0.29	70.5 ± 0.12
PSML	$\mathbf{74.6} \pm 0.15$	$\mathbf{79.3} \pm 0.26$	$\mathbf{66.2} \pm 0.42$	$\mathbf{73.8} \pm 0.32$

Table 3. Results of IMAGENET30.

ImageNet30 (20/10)		
Method	2%	10%
FixMatch	82.3 ± 0.14	87.5 ± 0.09
MTC	83.6 ± 0.12	88.1 ± 0.02
OpenMatch	84.9 ± 0.08	90.3 ± 0.11
PSML	$\mathbf{86.2} \pm 0.13$	$\mathbf{91.2} \pm 0.09$

and validating on the full ImageNet dataset is relatively high (in terms of time and computation power), we conducted experiments on the ImageNet30 subset. This dataset includes 30 different categories of images and is easier to validate and compare than the complete ImageNet dataset. Similarly, we divided the 30 categories into 20 visible categories and 10 invisible categories, and set different labeled data quantities (2% and 10% of each category) for multiple experiments.

Table 3 describes the performance of different methods in different experimental settings in ImageNet30. Similarly, PSML outperforms other methods in different settings.

4.4   Ablation Study

In this section, we will carry out the ablation experiment analysis of the information mining part and the prototype classification part of the OOD data to verify the validity of our viewpoint. In this ablation experiment, we will remove

Table 4. Results of IMAGENET30.

ImageNet30 (20/10)		
method	2%	10%
baseline	84.7 ± 0.12	88.5 ± 0.08
PSML	$\mathbf{86.2} \pm 0.13$	$\mathbf{91.2} \pm 0.09$

Table 5. Results of IMAGENET30.

ImageNet30 (20/10)		
method	2%	10%
baseline	85.3 ± 0.23	89.6 ± 0.14
PSML	$\mathbf{86.2} \pm 0.13$	$\mathbf{91.2} \pm 0.09$

some modules in POSL as the baseline for effect comparison and compare with the complete POSL method under ImagetNet30 (2%) dataset.

OOD Information Mining. In the baseline method, we will remove the Sim score calculation module of the data in the multi detection module and the information mining of the OOD data part in the multi knowledge mining module (L_{soft}, L_{ucd}) (Table 4).

Prototype Classification. In the baseline method, we change the classification method in the model to a learnable fully connected layer, and directly input the sample features to regress its category probability (Table 5).

5   Conclusion

This paper design a new framework for OSSL– Prototype based Multi-information mining OSSL (PMSL) to better mine the information of OOD data in unlabeled data, thereby improving the classification performance of ID data. PMSL uses the prototype-based Multi detection method to calculate the active knowledge capacity of the OOD Sample, and based on this, different degrees of information mining are carried out on the data.The validity of the method was verified by comparing it with state-of-the-art methods on various public datasets.

References

1. Banitalebi-Dehkordi, A., Gujjar, P., Zhang, Y.: AuxMix: semi-supervised learning with unconstrained unlabeled data. In: Proceedings of the IEEE/CVF Conference on Computer Vision and Pattern Recognition, pp. 3999–4006 (2022)
2. Berthelot, D., et al.: RemixMatch: semi-supervised learning with distribution alignment and augmentation anchoring. arXiv preprint arXiv:1911.09785 (2019)

3. Berthelot, D., Carlini, N., Goodfellow, I., Papernot, N., Oliver, A., Raffel, C.A.: MixMatch: a holistic approach to semi-supervised learning. In: Advances in Neural Information Processing Systems, vol. 32 (2019)

4. Calderon-Ramirez, S., Yang, S., Elizondo, D.: Semisupervised deep learning for image classification with distribution mismatch: a survey. IEEE Trans. Artif. Intell. **3**(6), 1015–1029 (2022)

5. Cascante-Bonilla, P., Tan, F., Qi, Y., Ordonez, V.: Curriculum labeling: revisiting pseudo-labeling for semi-supervised learning. In: Proceedings of the AAAI Conference on Artificial Intelligence, vol. 35, no. 8, pp. 6912–6920 (2021)

6. Chapelle, O., Scholkopf, B., Zien, A.: Semi-supervised learning (Chapelle, O. et al., eds.; 2006) [book reviews]. IEEE Trans. Neural Netw. **20**(3), 542 (2009) (2006)

7. Chen, Y., Zhu, X., Li, W., Gong, S.: Semi-supervised learning under class distribution mismatch. In: Proceedings of the AAAI Conference on Artificial Intelligence, vol. 34, no. 04, pp. 3569–3576 (2020)

8. Cubuk, E.D., Zoph, B., Mane, D., Vasudevan, V., Le, Q.V.: AutoAugment: learning augmentation strategies from data. In: Proceedings of the IEEE/CVF Conference on Computer Vision and Pattern Recognition, pp. 113–123 (2019)

9. DeVries, T., Taylor, G.W.: Improved regularization of convolutional neural networks with cutout. arXiv preprint arXiv:1708.04552 (2017)

10. Guo, L.Z., Zhang, Z.Y., Jiang, Y., Li, Y.F., Zhou, Z.H.: Safe deep semi-supervised learning for unseen-class unlabeled data. In: International Conference on Machine Learning, pp. 3897–3906. PMLR (2020)

11. He, R., Han, Z., Lu, X., Yin, Y.: Safe-student for safe deep semi-supervised learning with unseen-class unlabeled data. In: Proceedings of the IEEE/CVF Conference on Computer Vision and Pattern Recognition, pp. 14585–14594 (2022)

12. Huang, Z., Yang, J., Gong, C.: They are not completely useless: towards recycling transferable unlabeled data for class-mismatched semi-supervised learning. IEEE Trans. Multimed. (2022)

13. Krizhevsky, A., Hinton, G., et al.: Learning multiple layers of features from tiny images (2009)

14. Laine, S., Aila, T.: Temporal ensembling for semi-supervised learning. arXiv preprint arXiv:1610.02242 (2016)

15. Lee, D.H., et al.: Pseudo-label: the simple and efficient semi-supervised learning method for deep neural networks. In: Workshop on challenges in representation learning, ICML, vol. 3, p. 896 (2013)

16. Oliver, A., Odena, A., Raffel, C.A., Cubuk, E.D., Goodfellow, I.: Realistic evaluation of deep semi-supervised learning algorithms. In: Advances in Neural Information Processing Systems, vol. 31 (2018)

17. Rosch, E.: Prototype classification and logical classification: the two systems. New Trends in Conceptual Representation: Challenges to Piaget's Theory, pp. 73–86. Lawrence Erlbaum Associates, New Jersey (1983)

18. Saito, K., Kim, D., Saenko, K.: OpenMatch: open-set semi-supervised learning with open-set consistency regularization. In: Advances in Neural Information Processing Systems, vol. 34, pp. 25956–25967 (2021)

19. Sajjadi, M., Javanmardi, M., Tasdizen, T.: Regularization with stochastic transformations and perturbations for deep semi-supervised learning. In: Advances in Neural Information Processing Systems, vol. 29 (2016)

20. Snell, J., Swersky, K., Zemel, R.: Prototypical networks for few-shot learning. In: Advances in Neural Information Processing Systems, vol. 30 (2017)

21. Sohn, K., et al.: FixMatch: simplifying semi-supervised learning with consistency and confidence. In: Advances in Neural Information Processing Systems, vol. 33, pp. 596–608 (2020)
22. Wah, C., Branson, S., Welinder, P., Perona, P., Belongie, S.: The caltech-UCSD birds-200-2011 dataset (2011)
23. Xie, Q., Dai, Z., Hovy, E., Luong, T., Le, Q.: Unsupervised data augmentation for consistency training. In: Advances in Neural Information Processing Systems, vol. 33, pp. 6256–6268 (2020)
24. Xie, Q., Luong, M.T., Hovy, E., Le, Q.V.: Self-training with noisy student improves ImageNet classification. In: Proceedings of the IEEE/CVF Conference on Computer Vision and Pattern Recognition, pp. 10687–10698 (2020)
25. Yang, H.M., Zhang, X.Y., Yin, F., Liu, C.L.: Robust classification with convolutional prototype learning. In: Proceedings of the IEEE Conference on Computer Vision and Pattern Recognition, pp. 3474–3482 (2018)
26. Yu, Q., Ikami, D., Irie, G., Aizawa, K.: Multi-task curriculum framework for open-set semi-supervised learning. In: Vedaldi, A., Bischof, H., Brox, T., Frahm, J.-M. (eds.) ECCV 2020. LNCS, vol. 12357, pp. 438–454. Springer, Cham (2020). https://doi.org/10.1007/978-3-030-58610-2_26
27. Zagoruyko, S., Komodakis, N.: Wide residual networks. arXiv preprint arXiv:1605.07146 (2016)
28. Zhu, X., Goldberg, A.B.: Introduction to semi-supervised learning. Synthesis Lect. Artif. Intell. Mach. Learn. 3(1), 1–130 (2009)
29. Zhu, X.J.: Semi-supervised learning literature survey (2005)

Pure Physics-Informed Echo State Network
of ODE Solution Replicator

Dong Keun Oh$^{(\boxtimes)}$ (iD)

Korea Institute of Fusion Energy, Daejeon 34133, South Korea
`spinhalf@kfe.re.kr`

Abstract. Inspired by recent arguments to the echo state neurons, a reservoir model of sequential data is polished to replicate the solution of given ODEs (Ordinary Differential Equations). By training with the differential equation itself, a pure physics-informed echo state network (ESN) is firstly introduced based on the loss function as consistent with the general invariance of differential equations, in which the actual training scheme is implemented as a regression in two stages. On such a physics-informed model of recurrent neurons, some dynamical problems are explored by means of sequential generation of the ODE solution as drawn from the nonlinear trajectories of hidden state in the reservoir model.

Keywords: Echo State Network · Physics-informed Neural Network · Neural ODE approximator

1 Introduction

Echo state property is a fundamental concept to support the reservoir computing (RC) paradigm as a necessary condition for the "trainable readout mechanism" from the already configured recurrent neurons [1–3]. In such a neural model, the neurons are initially created at random, and stay fixed, potentially being independent of the training process. To secure the desired output from a given input sequence, each evolution of the reservoir has to be at the state of "echoing" memory [1, 4, 5]. This property just claims a passive state of the neurons accumulating the input history in a certain period to the past [1].

On many insights to the neurobiological system [6, 7], for instance, to cerebral cognitive processes [8, 9], the idea of echo state network (ESN) has proven itself outperforming in supervised learning problems for the complicated dynamic patterns. In practice, it has achieved great success in nonlinear system modeling, specifically, for generation [10] and prediction [11, 12] of nonlinearly evolving sequences. At the same time, this approach has been recognized as a breakthrough to the difficulty in training of recurrent networks [1–3]. Hence, particularly related to the echo state property, reservoir models have led specific interests in how the neural memory of fading out surely assimilates the given nonlinear behavior, or what conditions make such a chaotic data systematically lead the trained readout. Thus, in a number of different aspects, theoretical deductions have been calling out stochastic viewpoint on the driving inputs as a matter of probabilistic behavior. For instance, a stricter definition of the echo state was proposed relying on non-autonomous input-driven dynamics [4], and a stronger inference is attained assuming the target system as an ergodic source [4, 13, 14]. On this ground, the efficacy of ESN is ensured in terms of universal approximation [15]. Furthermore, as a complement of this argument, it was also discussed that an ESN surely embeds a structurally stable dynamical system [13, 14]. In those theoretical developments, the dynamical behavior was proven to be imposed by an L2 approximation, and it is possible to reproduce the future observation by means of regularized least square regression [14].

While the recent arguments are quite evident how an ESN model works to secure the chaotic trajectories, the actual inference about "learning dynamical behaviors" has an inherent limitation so far, because the main idea just relies on a sampled sequence, eventually, without the dynamics (physical information) itself into the learning process. As a shortcoming on the attempt of theoretical demonstration, it was already indicated that the underlying dynamics of the target system has been ignored in ESN models [14]. Then, any alternative development is critically recommendable to integrate the input driver's dynamics into the reservoir training scheme. Hence, attention has to be paid to the recent studies [16–23] on the echo state memory consolidated with physical information [13, 14].

However, no meaningful development has not been made yet, not only to activate any theoretical demonstration of the embedding (or approximation) to the dynamical behaviors, but also to establish a pure physics-informed reservoir model in which the underlying dynamics is assimilated by the recurrent neurons. In this study, an ESN-based ODE solution replicator is introduced as the first realization of a reservoir model trained absolutely in physics-informed manner, because a differential equation itself is solely attributed to the information for training without supervision of data, to generate the solution in sequence. Namely, the echo state of recurrent neurons is invoked in the attempt of "training by pure physical information" by the simple type of differential equation $\dot{y} = f(y)$, as described in the rest of this article.

2   Background - A Neural ODE Approximator as a Physics-Informed ESN

Since the emergence of physic-informed neural network, common efforts have been made on the physics-driven models of machine learning, mostly, applied to the feedforward neural networks [16–20]. They have emerged on the aim of "learning analytic relations instead of data", and just derived a recent activity as a notion of "physics-informed neural network (PINN)" [17]. As shown in the studies such as a neural approximator of differential equation [19, 20], their learning process is a regression on the error of outputs deviated from the causal relations, namely, of the governing equations or its underlying principles.

As an extension of feedforward PINN, some pilot studies of "physics-informed ESN" have been also found [21–23] incorporated with the physical error terms like any other feed forward PINN. Nonetheless, the physical information was employed only in part, i.e., as a complement of the supervision by prerequisite data (solutions) [21, 22]. In practice, pure physics-informed ESN is challenging indeed, as it is easy to point out that the piecewise recurrence of reservoir neurons is inevitably prone to be deviated from the target system's dynamical behavior. Hence, care must be taken to keep up the basic invariance of differential equations, in particular, between the sequential steps of recurrent generation of reservoir model.

3   Outline - ESN-Based ODE Model

An ESN model of ODE solution is conceived on to the sequential nature of recurrent evaluation. In order to represent such a recurrence, the readout has to follow discrete steps of the given ODE on the independent variable t getting forward to $t+\tau$ in sequence. Thus, by means of a simple modification from the standard layout of reservoir models, it is possible to take an idea to update the $(n + 1)^{\text{th}}$ recurrent state h^{n+1} following the independent variable t^n. In Eq. 1, the recurrent state is represented for the input vector (y^n, τ^n) in case of $\dot{y} = f(y)$, or (y^n, t^n, τ^n) in case of $\dot{y} = f(y, t)$,

$$
\begin{aligned}
h^{n+1} &= \sigma\left(M \cdot h^n + V \cdot y_0^n + b\tau^n + c\right) \\
\text{or } h^{n+1} &= \sigma\left(M \cdot h^n + V \cdot y_0^n + at^n + b\tau^n + c\right)
\end{aligned}
\tag{1}
$$

where σ means element-wise operation of the nonlinear activation, and the fixed variables M, V, a, b and c are the weight matrices and vectors of the hidden layer's (the reservoir's) connection randomly configured in the beginning [1–3]. Then, the readout y^{n+1} comes out of the update of hidden state as the following,

$$
y^{n+1} = y_0^n + \tau^n W \cdot h^{n+1}
\tag{2}
$$

where W is the readout matrix of weights to be determined by means of regression, i.e., in the training process.

Indeed, Eq. 2 describes an incremental update, just conforming to the integral of ODE along the interval of $[t^n, t^n + \tau^n]$. Thus, it is suitable to express the solution after τ^n, namely at $t^n + \tau^n$, where the initial condition is given by the nth input y_0^n. For simplicity, the intervals are applied to be constant. Following up of the layout (Eqs. 1 and 2), one has to get into the details of regression process to the solution. Namely, the matrix W will be determined to get to the solutions in step. Of course, $\dot{y}$ is what is to be informed to learn the physical system, and the proposed layout (Eqs. 1 and 2) is possible to provide such a differential to τ^n explicitly. Hence, the ESN-based ODE replicator is drawn on the ground of such an outline.

In spite of the minor modification, the training process is different a lot, when compared with other cases of regularized linear regression. That is to say, an intrinsic difficulty will be brought, whenever nonlinearity on the right-hand-side of $f(y)$ or $f(y, t)$ is involved into the least square terms, while solving a linear system is enough [1–3] just for the regression to the sampled data y_{target}^n. Just at a glance to a particular formula

$|\dot{y} -f|^2$ after the causality directly from the ODE, it is simple to notice that, even to be straightforward to the physical information [17, 19–22], nonlinearity out of $f(y)$ or $f(y, t)$ has to invoke an essential measures of iterative regression which is not avoidable in case of the nonlinear least square minimization. Thus, it is a critical to develop the training scheme in this work. On the other hand, any attempt on this study has to respect the sense of sampling, regarding the sequential outputs. Namely, the y^n just represents a numerical approximation to the solution for each period. Ultimately, the reservoir model works in autonomous mode to generate the solution in sequence. Thus, all readouts are to be connected in series with each other as an approximation to the solution. In other words, at each initial condition given by y_0^n of the nth input, the incremental part of the readout Δy^n is to be consistent with the solution of $\dot{y} = f(y)$ with respect to each initial condition y_0^n.

$$\Delta y^{n+1} = \tau^n \mathbf{W} \cdot h^{n+1}(\tau^n, y_0^n, h^n) \tag{3}$$

In consequence, the readout can be described as a series of previous Δy according to the recurrent evaluation, when the nth readout y^n is transferred to the next step as an input y_0^n, i.e., in recurrence.

$$y^{n+1} = y^n + \Delta y^{n+1}$$
$$\Rightarrow y^{n+1} = y^{n-n_0} + \Delta y^{n+1} + \Delta y^n + \cdots + \Delta y^{n-n_0+1}(n \geq n_0 \geq 0) \tag{4}$$

Meanwhile, the fundamental logic of differential equation is always satisfied in the flashback (Eq. 4) to the point n_0 shifted backward. Namely, the output y^n is also the same solution regardless of what n_0 is selected for the initial state. Hence, one must take into account such a nature of the solution as an important consideration to establish the details. Actually, it is noted as the most particular idea in this study of physics-informed ESN, to take care of such a consistency in the sequential readouts regarding the general principle of differential equations; it is described in the next section.

3.1 Solution in Recurrence - How to Constrain the Neural Output

The Lie invariance is the neatest idea to consider a solution in the form of recurrent sequence, which is the fundamental idea about general invariance (symmetry) of differential equations, particularly, with respect to the arbitrary shifts by a certain parameter [24, 25]. Into a step further about the loss function, it is natural to consider the $|\dot{y} -f|^2$ term for the causality at each prompt response "on the steps". At the same time, such an invariance on the recurrent evaluation just inspires to bring an essential idea of "constraint between the steps".

$$y^* = Y(y, t; \tau), t^* = T(y, t; \tau) = t + \tau$$
$$\Xi = f(y, t) \cdot \tfrac{\partial}{\partial y} + \tfrac{\partial}{\partial t} \tag{5}$$

To describe the particular idea, every readout of the reservoir can be denoted by y^* as a solution of $dy^*/dt^* = f(y^*, t^*)$ on the evolution toward $t^* = t + \tau$ from the moment t with the initial value y. Then, the Lie transformation is naturally brought to correspond (y, t) to (y^*, t^*), i.e., for the both of independent and dependent variables. As written in Eq. 5, the transformation is ruled by the parameter τ, and the logical layout is supported by the infinitesimal evolution operator Ξ. Namely, as a special case of the general transformation, $T(y, t; \tau) = t + \tau$ is able to be applied, and $Y(y, t; \tau)$ is represented as $y + \tau(\Xi \cdot y) + O(\tau^2) \approx y + \tau f(y, t)$ in terms of infinitesimal evolution of τ [28, 29]. Thus, the constraint equation (Eq. 6) is derived as a differential formula in the Lie's theory of differential equation, where Eq. 5 is proposed to make it conform to the evolution getting to y^* over the period of τ [27, 28].

$$\frac{dy^*}{dt^*} = \frac{D_t Y}{D_t T} = \frac{\left(\frac{\partial}{\partial t} + \dot{y} \cdot \frac{\partial}{\partial y}\right) Y}{\left(\frac{\partial}{\partial t} + \dot{y} \cdot \frac{\partial}{\partial y}\right) T}$$

$$\Rightarrow f(y^*, t^*) = \left(\frac{\partial}{\partial t} + f(y, t) \cdot \frac{\partial}{\partial y}\right) y^* \tag{6}$$

In accordance with the idea, the formulation in Eq. 7 just fits to the sequential output. Indeed, it is introduced as a solution virtually evolving along the period of τ^n, where (y^n, t^n) is given to be the initial state.

$$\begin{cases} y^{n+1} = y^n + \tau^n \Delta^{n+1}(y^n, t^n; \tau^n) \\ t^{n+1} = t^n + \tau^n \end{cases} \tag{7}$$

To be consistent with the equation $dy/dt = f(y, t)$ the essential constraint on y^{n+1}, which is ruled by Δ^{n+1}, should be applied above all in terms of the τ-derivative; see the first formula in Eq. 8. In addition, another essential constraint, as the last formula in Eq. 8, should be taken following the invariance principle represented in Eq. 6, for the recurrence between the output and the input (or the previous output) of the reservoir.

$$\Delta^{n+1}(y^n, t^n; \tau^n) + \tau^n \frac{\partial}{\partial \tau} \Delta^{n+1}(y^n, t^n; \tau^n) = f(y^{n+1}, t^{n+1})$$

$$\Delta^{n+1}(y^n, t^n; \tau = 0) = f(y^n, t^n) \tag{8}$$

$$\left(f(y^n, t^n) \cdot \frac{\partial}{\partial y^n} + \frac{\partial}{\partial t^n}\right) y^{n+1} = f(y^{n+1}, t^{n+1})$$

As a result, the constraint equations (Eq. 8) are obtained to make the readout tight enough to the sequential solution getting into step with its recurrent evaluation. From the Eq. 8, the error terms will be derived for a loss function to be applied to the actual process of training.

3.2 Regression Strategy in Two Steps - the Actual Training Scheme

In case of ODE approximator based on the recurrent layout in Eq. 1–4, the input sequence is unknown, in principle, to be determined as an accurate solution. Thus, it does not makes sense either to prepare a proper input at one go, or to keep up with the approximation without spoiling the straightforwardness of regression. On such a ground, an idea of training scheme "in two stage" just emerges leading a kind of pre-casting from a trial solution. Once an accurate approximation is secured based on the trial solution at the first stage, it is possible to prepare the input sequence for the next stage on the ultimate purpose to generate the solution in recurrent manner. Thus, it is possible to actualize the two-pass regression scheme in terms of least square minimization for given ODEs.

Once the solution strategy is established, each stage of regression is implemented to minimize the sum of square errors which indicate how much the approximation deviates regarding the causality from the differential equations as described by some constraints. To build such a function of square errors, the error vectors are formulated with respect to Eq. 8 not only for each step (the first two formulae in Eq. 8), but also between the contiguous evaluations (the last formula in Eq. 8). Actually, one is able to regard the constraint equations as a general formulation, and the t-derivative term is neglected just because of the equations in the form of $dy/dt = f(y)$; however, the formulation is easy to extend to the cases of absolute t-dependence in f.

At the first stage, the trial solution is denoted by y_0^n. Then, to obtain the neural approximation in sequence, $\bar{y}^n$ is supposed to be the reservoir's readout in the next step evolving from $\bar{y}^n$ at present. Thus, one has to take into account the previous readout as the initial value of the next step, whereas the second stage, even at the same logic, must bring the input sequence instead.

$$
\bar{y}^{n+1} = \bar{y}^n + \tau^n \overline{\mathbf{W}} \cdot \bar{h}^{n+1}
$$
$$
\text{where} \begin{cases} \bar{h}^{n+1} = \sigma\left(\bar{z}^{n+1}\right) \\ \bar{z}^{n+1} = \mathbf{b}\tau^n + \mathbf{M} \cdot \bar{h}^n + \mathbf{V} \cdot y_0^n + \mathbf{c} \end{cases} \tag{9}
$$

Thus, the second stage output y^n is represented in terms of $\bar{y}^n$ out of the first stage.

$$
y^{n+1} = \bar{y}^n + \tau^n \mathbf{W} \cdot h^{n+1}
$$
$$
\text{where} \begin{cases} h^{n+1} = \sigma\left(z^{n+1}\right) \\ z^{n+1} = \mathbf{b}\tau^n + \mathbf{M} \cdot h^n + \mathbf{V} \cdot \bar{y}^n + \mathbf{c} \end{cases} \tag{10}
$$

Hence, the error vectors of the first stage is defined, according to the three constraint equations in Eq. 8, and the second stage also goes in the similar manner, where $\bar{z}_0^{n+1}$ is $\mathbf{M} \cdot \bar{h}^n + \mathbf{V} \cdot y_0^n + \mathbf{c}$, and z_0^{n+1} is $\mathbf{M} \cdot h^n + \mathbf{V} \cdot \bar{y}^n + \mathbf{c}$ meaning $\tau = 0$ on the second constraint formula of Eq. 8. Being notable to the first stage, the third constraint (Eq. 8) requires the derivative by $\bar{y}^n$ on which the hidden state $\bar{h}^{n+1}$ doesn't have any explicit dependence. Thus, care has to be taken of the $\bar{y}^n$-derivative term $\partial \bar{y}^{n+1}/\partial \bar{y}^n$ to be imbedded into the error vector $\bar{e}_3$ in an implicit manner by means of the identities of $\partial \bar{y}^{n+1}/\partial \bar{h}^n = (\partial \bar{y}^{n+1}/\partial \bar{y}^n) \cdot (\partial \bar{y}^n/\partial \bar{h}^n)$ and $\partial \bar{y}^{n+1}/\partial \bar{h}^n = \mathbf{W}$. After all, the error vectors are written just in code-ready form, where $\odot$ is element-wise multiplication of two vectors (Eq. 11). Now, one is able to introduce the loss functions of square error $\bar{L} = \bar{e}_1^T \cdot \bar{e}_1 + \bar{e}_2^T \cdot \bar{e}_2 + \bar{e}_3^T \cdot \bar{e}_3$ for the first stage, and $L = e_1^T \cdot e_1 + e_2^T \cdot e_2 + e_3^T \cdot e_3$ for the second stage.

$$
\begin{cases}
\bar{e}_1^{n+1} = \mathbf{f}\left(\bar{y}^{n+1}\right) - \overline{\mathbf{W}} \cdot \left\{\sigma\left(\bar{z}^{n+1}\right) + \tau^n \mathbf{b} \odot \dot{\sigma}\left(\bar{z}^{n+1}\right)\right\} \\
\bar{e}_2^{n+1} = \mathbf{f}\left(\bar{y}^n\right) - \overline{\mathbf{W}} \cdot \sigma\left(\bar{z}_0^{n+1}\right) \\
\bar{e}_3^{n+1} = \left(\mathbf{f}\left(\bar{y}^n\right) \cdot \frac{\partial}{\partial \bar{y}^n}\right) \bar{y}^{n+1} - \mathbf{f}\left(\bar{y}^{n+1}\right) \\
e_1^{n+1} = \mathbf{f}\left(y^{n+1}\right) - \mathbf{W} \cdot \left\{\sigma\left(z^{n+1}\right) + \tau^n \mathbf{b} \odot \dot{\sigma}\left(z^{n+1}\right)\right\} \\
e_2^{n+1} = \mathbf{f}\left(y^n\right) - \mathbf{W} \cdot \sigma\left(z_0^{n+1}\right) \\
e_3^{n+1} = \left(\mathbf{f}\left(y^n\right) \cdot \frac{\partial}{\partial y^n}\right) y^{n+1} - \mathbf{f}\left(y^{n+1}\right)
\end{cases} \tag{11}
$$

As a result, each stage of least square regression is ready in action relying on the loss function, to determine the weight matrices $\overline{\mathbf{W}}$ and $\mathbf{W}$ for each stage in turn. Solving regularized linear equations based the Gauss-Newton method, the local minimum of each loss function is obtained from the iterative process updating the weight matrix $\overline{\mathbf{W}}$ or $\mathbf{W}$ [26] applying the Tikhonov regularization [27] whose parameter is adjusted to be small enough.

4 Implementation - A Test of Harmonic Oscillator

As the details of regression are arranged, it is tested above all whether the implemented approximator works as planned. Namely, a pilot program is carried out to get a solution of the simple harmonic oscillator, i.e., $\dot{y}_1 = y_2$ and $\dot{y}_2 = -y_1$. The reservoir neurons are just built based on the custom class, importing the Tensorflow library, with respect to the proposed structure. Setting up the ESN model, 200 neurons of the hidden (recurrent) layer are configured at random connection whose connectivity is 0.01–0.1, and the spectral width of the hidden connection's weight $\mathbf{W}$ is controlled by its 2-norm to be 10.0, as the 2-norm is the upper bound of the spectral radius of $\mathbf{W}$. Notably, the large spectral radius doesn't belong to the sufficient condition for echo state in the conventional setup ($\rho(\mathbf{W}) < 1$) [1], but just selected to be good enough for this special modification. For the main part of regression, a trial solution is prepared, by means of the Euler method, on the sequential steps of $\tau = 0.05$, and is cropped to get 500 points on the span of neural solution. In this course, 150 points of the leading part are dropped to wash out the initial transient of reservoir [3]. Then, the regression process of the first stage is invoked to carry out the Gauss-Newton iteration which needs the initial guess of $\overline{\mathbf{W}}$. Finding nothing for alternative, the initial guess is selected just to replicate the trial solution, i.e., to make $\mathbf{y}_0 = \tau^n \overline{\mathbf{W}}^n \cdot \overline{\boldsymbol{h}}^{n+1}$ equal to $\mathbf{y}_0^{n+1}$. As obtained in a different context from the actual formulation (Eq. 9), the first stage output with the initial guess of $\overline{\mathbf{W}}$ can be far from the expectation as demonstrated in Fig. 1.

After the iterations, the final $\overline{\mathbf{y}}^n$ comes out to be accurate enough. Then, the result is transferred to the second stage of regression. Because the harmonic oscillator is a linear equation, it is easy to converge so that only a few iterations are enough to stabilize the relative change of total loss $|\Delta L/L|$ to be less than 10^{-5} in the both stages. Eventually, the demonstration is completed to verify the regression process was a training scheme of the ESN-based ODE solution replicator.

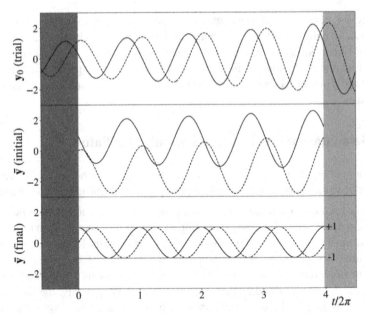

Fig. 1. Training by the harmonic oscillator equation in the first stage: the trial solution is prepared by the explicit Euler method (upper). Then, the initial state for the regression process is presented as an initial guess (middle).The finial state of regression is converged to the accurate sinusoidal waves (lower).

5 Result - Demonstrations of Nonlinear Dynamic Problem

As the verification is successful, the cases of nonlinear equation are attempted as presented in this section; one is the van der Pol oscillator [28], and the other is the Lorentz chaotic system [29].

5.1 Case 1: The van der Pol Oscillator

The van der Pol equation can be written in the form of $\dot{y} = f(y)$, where $f(y) = (y_2, y_2 - y_1 - y_1^2 y_2)$ for $y = (y_1, y_2)$ [28]. The reservoir of 300 neurons are configured in the same manner of the previous verification with a simple harmonic oscillator. For the evolution span of 500 points, the input sequence is prepared by the trial solution with $\tau = 0.1$. In the both stages of regression, the regularization parameter $\lambda = 10^{-7}$ is assigned, and the iterations are carried out as presented in Fig. 2. As a result, the neural solution is obtained comparing with the trial solution for the first stage (Fig. 3).

5.2 Case 2: The Lorenz Equations

The Lorenz equations are well-known as a nonlinear system of chaotic behavior. The system of differential equations, which are $\dot{y}_1 = \sigma(y_2 - y_1)$, $\dot{y}_2 = y_1(\rho - y_3) - y_2$ and $\dot{y}_3 = y_1 y_2 - \beta y_3$, exhibit chaotic attractors, which Lorenz discovered with the

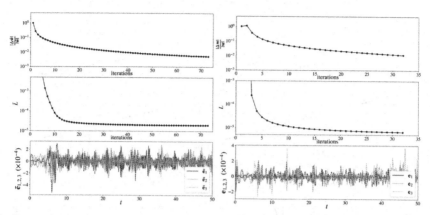

Fig. 2. The first stage regression process for the van der Pol oscillator (left); the relative change of the weight matrix versus the number of iterations (left upper), the amount of error versus the number of iterations (left middle), and the final error vectors (left lower). The second stage regression process (right) for the van der Pol oscillator; the relative change of the weight matrix versus the number of iterations (right upper), the amount of error versus the number of iterations (right middle), and the final error vectors (right lower).

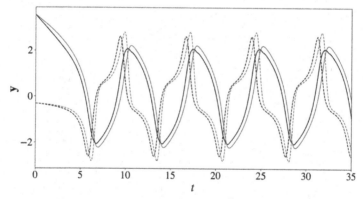

Fig. 3. The result of the van der Pol Oscillator; y_1 is plotted in solid line, and y_2 is in dotted line; the trial solution is plotted in gray color just for comparison.

parameters $\sigma = 10$, $\rho = 28$, and $\beta = 8/3$ [29]. To generate the 200 sequential solutions on the intervals of $\tau = 0.03$, the ESN-based ODE approximator is configured with 1500 hidden neurons which is large amount selected in reason after many efforts to make the regression converged. To prepare the trial solution, the time interval $\tau/20$ is applied to the Euler method, and the original period τ is recovered by means of downsampling; it is required to make the Euler step sufficiently fine. After then, the regression is done for each stage, and its progress in detail is described in Fig. 4 respectively per stage. Eventually, the neural solution is obtained, as shown in Fig. 5.

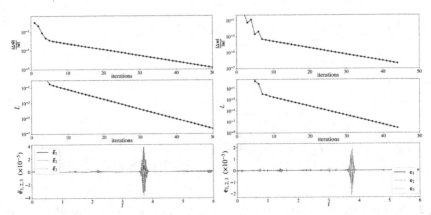

Fig. 4. The first stage regression process for the Lorenz system (left), and the second stage (right); the relative change of the weight matrix versus the number of iteration (upper), the amount of error versus the number of iteration (middle), and the final error vectors (lower).

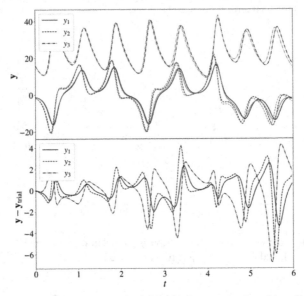

Fig. 5. The result of the Lorenz system; the final neural output is plotted in solid line as well as the trial solution in grey color just for comparison (upper), and the difference between the result and the trial solution is presented (lower).

6   Conclusion

As already recognized, the feedforward PINN are just supposed to learn the solution at a specified condition of initial or boundary constraints, which means that one has to do training again whenever those conditions are changed. Thus, it is not suitable to replicate the target system's behavior under the various conditions in practice. In such a point of view, the ESN-based replicator is important in favor of the recurrent architecture based on the reservoir neurons, where it is expected to assimilate the nonlinear (chaotic) trajectories [13–15]. On the other hand, its power of insight is possibly extended to the theoretical discussions on the dynamical behavior hidden in the reservoir-based model of nonlinear trajectories. Paying attention to the logical layout to be consistent with the theory of differential equations, this study just implements the neural ODE replicator, in particular, evaluating in step respecting the integration along each interval of the dynamical interactions. What is the most remarkable is that the physical information is imposed in terms of the invariant principle as a special constraint between the recurrent steps. For a practical activity, the idea of this study is possible to enhance the previous attempts [21–23] of the physics-informed ESN which extracts the hidden states' behavior as constrained by the Lie invariance.

References

1. Jaeger, H.: "The "echo state" approach to analyzing and training recurrent neural networks." Technical Report GMD Report 148, German National Research Center for Information Technology (2001)
2. Sun, C., Song, M., Cai, D., Zhang, B., Hong, S., Li, H.: A systematic review of echo state networks from design to application. IEEE Transactions on Artificial Intelligence (2022) early access
3. Lukoševičius, M.: A practical guide to applying echo state networks." Neural Networks: Tricks of the Trade, pp. 659–686. Springer (2012)
4. Manjunath, G., Jaeger, H.: Echo state property linked to an input: exploring a fundamental characteristic of recurrent neural networks. Neural Comput. $25(3)$, 671–696 (2013)
5. Yildiz, I.B., Jaeger, H., Kiebel, S.J.: Re-visiting the echo state property. Neural Netw. 35, 1–9 (2012)
6. Tanaka, G., et al.: Recent advances in physical reservoir computing: a review. Neural Netw. 115, 100–123 (2019)
7. Gürel, T., Rotter, S., Egert, U.: Functional identification of biological neural networks using reservoir adaptation for point processes. J. Comput. Neurosci. $29(1–2)$, 279–299 (2010)
8. Dominey, P.: Recurrent temporal networks and language acquisition—from corticostriatal neurophysiology to reservoir computing. Front. Psychol. 4, 500 (2013)
9. Dominey, P., Arbib M., Joseph J.-P.: A model of corticostriatal plasticity for learning oculomotor associations and sequences. J. Cogn. Neurosci. 7, 311–336 (1995)
10. Freyberg, S., Hauser, H.: The morphological paradigm in robotics. Stud. Hist. Philos. Sci. 100, 1–11 (2023)
11. Pathak, J., Hunt, B., Girvan, M., Lu, Z., Ott, E.: Model-free prediction of large spatiotemporally chaotic systems from data: a reservoir computing approach. Phys. Rev. Lett. $120(2)$, 024102 (2018)
12. Chen, P., Liu, R., Aihara, K., Chen, L.: Autoreservoir computing for multistep ahead prediction based on the spatiotemporal information transformation. Nat. Commun. $11(1)$, 4568 (2020)
13. Hart, A., Hook, J., Dawes, J.: Embedding and approximation theorems for echo state networks. Neural Netw. 128, 234–247 (2020)
14. Hart, A.G., Hook, J.L., Dawes, J.H.: Echo State Networks trained by Tikhonov least squares are L^2 approximators of ergodic dynamical systems. arXiv preprint arXiv:2005.06967 (2020)
15. Grigoryeva, L., Ortega, J.P.: Echo state networks are universal. Neural Netw. 108, 495–508 (2018)

16. King, R., Hennigh, O., Mohan, A., Chertkov, M.: From deep to physics-informed learning of turbulence: Diagnostics. arXiv preprint arXiv:1810.07785 (2018)
17. Raissi, M., Perdikaris, P., Karniadakis, G.E.: Physics-informed neural networks: A deep learning framework for solving forward and inverse problems involving nonlinear partial differential equations. J. Comput. Phys. **378**, 686–707 (2019)
18. Tartakovsky, A.M., Marrero, C.O., Perdikaris, P., Tartakovsky, G.D., Barajas-Solano, D.: Physics-informed deep neural networks for learning parameters and constitutive relationships in subsurface flow problems. Water Resources Res. **56**(5), e2019WR026731 (2020)
19. Filici, C.: On a neural approximator to ODEs. IEEE Trans. Neural Networks **19**(3), 539–543 (2008)
20. Lagaris, I.E., Likas, A., Fotiadis, D.I.: Artificial neural networks for solving ordinary and partial differential equations. IEEE Trans. Neural Networks **9**(5), 987–1000 (1998)
21. Doan, N.A.K., Polifke, W., Magri, L.: Physics-informed echo state networks for chaotic systems forecasting. In: Rodrigues, J.M.F., Cardoso, Pedro J S., Monteiro, Jânio., Lam, Roberto, Krzhizhanovskaya, Valeria V., Lees, Michael H., Dongarra, Jack J., Sloot, Peter M A. (eds.) ICCS 2019. LNCS, vol. 11539, pp. 192–198. Springer, Cham (2019). https://doi.org/10.1007/978-3-030-22747-0_15
22. Doan, N.A.K., Polifke, W., Magri, L.: Learning hidden states in a chaotic system: A physics-informed echo state network approach. arXiv preprint arXiv:2001.02982 (2020)
23. Huhn, F., Magri, L.: Learning ergodic averages in chaotic systems. arXiv preprint arXiv:2001.04027 (2020)
24. Oliveri, F.: Lie symmetries of differential equations: classical results and recent contributions. Symmetry **2**(2), 658–706 (2010)
25. Ibragimov, N.K.: Group analysis of ordinary differential equations and the invariance principle in mathematical physics (for the 150th anniversary of Sophus Lie). Russ. Math. Surv. **47**(4), 89 (1992)
26. Nocedal, J., Wright, S.: Numerical optimization. Springer Science & Business Media (2006)
27. Tikhonov, A.N., Goncharsky, A.V., Stepanov, V.V., Yagola, A.G.: Numerical methods for the solution of ill-posed problems, vol. 328. Springer Science & Business Media (2013)
28. "Van der Pol equation", Encyclopedia of Mathematics, EMS Press (2001)
29. Lorenz, E.N.: Deterministic nonperiodic flow. J. Atmos. Sci. **20**(2), 130–141 (1963)

RegionRel: A Framework for Jointly Extracting Relational Triplets by Performing Sub-tasks by Region

Zihao Li and Qun Mo[✉]

Zhejiang University, Hangzhou, China
moqun@zju.edu.cn

Abstract. Extraction of the relation triple is a fundamental work for the construction of knowledge graph. Since extraction of the relation triple can be divided into two sub-tasks: entity recognition and relation classification, most existing models conduct these sub-tasks jointly. However, most models suffer from the problem that the information of two sub-tasks can't be interacted with. To this end, we propose a new joint model named RegionRel, which conducts two sub-tasks in one module at the same time instead of several separate modules, a unified label space is designed for unifying the learning of two sub-tasks. By doing so, the problem mentioned above can be alleviated. Experiment on two widely used datasets has proved that our proposed model performs better than most of the state-of-the-art baselines.

Keywords: Relation triple · Joint model · Unified label space

1 Introduction

Extracting the relation triple in the form of triplet like (subject, relation, object) or (s,r,o) is a fundamental work for the construction of knowledge graph. Traditional pipeline methods treat it as two separate tasks:(1)*Extraction of entities*;(2)*Relation classification between entities*. This is concise and easy to understand but the result of the second step depends on the first step, which causes the problem of error accumulation [1]. To solve this problem, most recent studies focus on extracting relation triples jointly through an end-to-end model named the joint approach. Some works [2,3] have proved that the joint model performs better than the pipeline model due to the alleviation of error accumulation.

Most existing joint models divide relation triple extraction into several sub-tasks. ETL [4] and CasRel [5] first extract head entities, then extract relation and tail entities according to the head entities. Some methods [6,7] use graph neural networks to extract entities and relations.

Sequence tagging methods [2,3] use various tagging methods to mark relation triple but still suffer from the problem of overlapping patterns. Apart from that, most tagging strategies employ BIO annotation which is complex when

© The Author(s), under exclusive license to Springer Nature Switzerland AG 2023
L. Iliadis et al. (Eds.): ICANN 2023, LNCS 14262, pp. 237–248, 2023.
https://doi.org/10.1007/978-3-031-44201-8_20

handling long entities. Generation methods [8] treat the triple extraction task as a generation task that considers triple as a sequence that can be generated employing an encoder-decoder framework.

TPLinker [9] divides the task into two sub-tasks:(1)*Alignment of subject-object* and (2)*Entity recognition*, these two sub-tasks are conducted jointly. An additional relation judgment module that aims to identify potential relations in a sentence is added to PRGC [10] based on the two sub-tasks of TPLinker, the sub-tasks are conducted jointly and alleviates the problem of error accumulation to some extent.

By summarizing the above models, we can observe that some models with multiple modules split the task into sub-tasks and conduct sub-tasks separately in different modules instead of one module, resulting in the information of different modules not getting interacted which hinders better extractions. One reason for not conducting sub-tasks in one module is that it is generally acknowledged that the label space of different sub-tasks is difficult to be unified.

UniRE [11] takes the lead to break this conventional thought, it designs a token pair matrix to represent both the entity and the relationship between entities. However, due to its special tagging schema and decoding strategy, some special patterns of relation triples are unable for extraction such as subject-object overlap(SOO) and entity pair overlap(EPO). For example, the entity pair("Leborn", first name, "Leborn James") is unable to be extracted because the subject and object overlap. Inspired by it, we propose a new model named RegionRel to divide the task into two sub-tasks: entity recognition and subject-object alignment, it conducts different sub-tasks in the same module and can deal with different patterns of relation triples. Specifically, given a sentence, we first use the biaffine attention mechanism [12] to construct a token pair matrix, then use start-end annotation to recognize entities. Considering the start position of the entity always appears before the end position of the entity, the label space of the entity recognition task is always distributed in the upper triangular region of the matrix. Therefore, the lower triangular region of the matrix is applied for the subject-object alignment task. In this way, the training of two sub-tasks is unified in the same module. Experimental result has proved that our model performs better than most of the state-of-the-art baselines.

In summary, the main contributions of this paper are as follows:

- We propose a new joint model named RegionRel which tackles the problem in a novel perspective that decomposes the relation triple extraction task into two sub-tasks in one module. The experiment has proved that our method effectively makes the information of two sub-tasks interact and successfully deals with different special patterns.
- Experiment has proved that our proposed model shows a better F1-score in most datasets compared with other state-of-the-art baselines. In addition, our model is robust enough for different overlapping patterns of relation triple extraction.

2   Related Work

Traditional pipeline methods [13,14] mainly consider the task as two sub-tasks: *Entity recognition* and *Relation classification*. These methods are intuitive but fails to focus on the intrinsic relevance between the two sub-tasks. To handle it, many researchers focus on joint models, early joint models such as [15,16] require a complex process of feature engineering and many NLP tools.

To address the problem, neural network-based joint models have attracted the attention of researchers. Some researchers used the traditional sequence tagging method [3] to extract the triple jointly but failed to handle the problem of overlapping patterns. RSAN [2] used a set of tagging sequences for each relationship between entities to address the problem of overlapping patterns. ETL [4] and CasRel [5] used a novel sequence tagging method to extract head entities first, then extract tail entities and relations based on the result of the early step. However, these methods neglect the relevance between two sub-tasks and lead to redundancy in relation classification.

TPLinker [9] employs two modules to conduct sub-tasks jointly. However, this method needs $2 * R + 1(R$ denotes pre-defined relations) token pair matrices which still leads to the problem of redundancy of parameters and complexity of decoding. PRGC [10] used a module for potential relation judgment to reduce the parameter redundancy caused by pre-defined relations, but it still suffers from the problem that the information of modules doesn't get interacted.UniRE [11] conducts two sub-tasks in one module by which the information between two sub-tasks has interacted, but due to its special way of table-filling, it suffers from overlapping patterns.

3   Methodology

3.1   Task Definition

The goal of relation triple extraction is to identify all possible triples like (subject, relation, object) from a given sentence. The input of our model is a sentence with n tokens $S = \{\omega_1, \omega_2, ..., \omega_n\}$. The output of the model is a set of triples $\tau = \{(s, r, o)|s, o \in E, r \in R\}$, where E and R denotes the entity set and relation set.

3.2   Encoder

Given a sentence with n tokens $S = \{\omega_1, \omega_2, ..., \omega_n\}$, we first employ a pre-trained BERT [17] as sentence encoder to obtain contextual representation as follows:

$$\{h_1, h_2, ..., h_n\} = BERT(\{\omega_1, \omega_2, ..., \omega_n\}) \tag{1}$$

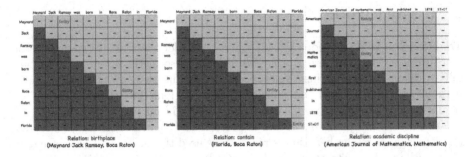

Fig. 1. The decode framework of our model. The left and middle matrices represent the decoding situation of RegionRel of different relations respectively. The upper triangle region in light yellow of the matrix is used for named entity recognition and the lower triangle region in dark yellow of the matrix is used for alignment of subject-object. The right matrix represents the decoding situation of RegionRel Plus, the grey and white region represents the extra region compared with RegionRel. **ST-OT** represents the end position of subject to the end position of object. Similarly, **OT-ST** represents the end position of object to the end position of subject, **T-T** represents the same end position of both subject and object. (Color figure online)

3.3 Construction of Token Pair Matrix

We employ biaffine attention mechanism [12] to generate $h_{i,j}^{span}$ as representation of the token pair(ω_i, ω_j) for each index pair (i, j) in following way:

$$head_i = MLP_{head}(h_i) \tag{2}$$

$$tail_j = MLP_{tail}(h_j) \tag{3}$$

$$h_{i,j}^{span} = head_i^T U tail_j + W(head_i \oplus tail_j) + b \tag{4}$$

According to [18], the experiment has proved that two separate MLPs project encoded text to different feature spaces which leads to worse performance. We employ a single MLP to project text for the above reason.

In this way, if the length of the sentence is L, we can obtain the vector representation $h_{i,j}^{span}$ of all L^2 token pairs. We arrange these vectors by row and column index (i, j) to get the token pair matrix $\mathcal{R}$. the shape of $\mathcal{R}$ is $L * L * N$, where L denotes the length of the given sentence, and N denotes the dimension of the vector representation $h_{i,j}^{span}$.

3.4 Tagging Strategy

Motivation. Biaffine attention [12] was proposed to address the problem of long entity recognition. This method constructs the token pair matrix which is mentioned above to calculate the score for each position(i, j), the index of the row i denotes the start position of the entity, and the index of the column j denotes the end position of the entity. Since the start of the entity always appears before the end of the entity, the lower triangular region of the matrix is not utilized.

For this reason, the task of relation triple extraction can be divided into two sub-tasks: *Entity recognition* and *Alignment of subject-object*. We apply Biaffine attention mechanism to these two sub-tasks. Especially, the first sub-task of entity recognition is conducted in the upper region of the token pair matrix; the second sub-task of subject-object alignment is conducted in the lower region which is not utilized in named entity recognition. Different regions have been differentiated by color in Fig. 1.

Strategy. In this section, we will give an introduction to the tagging strategy of the token pair matrix $\mathcal{R}$ which is derived according to Sect. 3.3.

We name these two sub-tasks mentioned above as task A: **Entity recognition** and task B: **Alignment of subject-object**. In task A, there are two labels: {Entity Type, None}.In this way, by using biaffine attention mechanism [12], we can identify the start position and the end positions of each entity in the upper region of the token pair matrix.

After getting all possible entities of one sentence, we need to determine the correct pairs of the subjects and objects for which we focus on subject-object alignment in Task B. In Task B we need to choose a suitable link scheme first. Here we choose the end position of the subject to the end position of the object(ST-OT) as our links of subject and object, in this way, all correct entity pairs are detected. For example, for the relation triple("Maynard Jack Ramsay", birthplace, "Boca Raton"), the position of the token pair("Ramsay", "Raton") is assigned with ST-OT to identify the relation triple. For the lower triangular region of the matrix which is colored with dark yellow in Fig. 1, the index of rows is always greater than the index of columns, ST-OT can't be tagged here when the end position of the subject appears before the end position of the object, we need to tag it conversely as OT-ST in this situation. In this way, there are three labels for Task B:{ST-OT, OT-ST, None}.

From the above discussion, in order to achieve the goal of joint learning of two sub-tasks, we unify the label spaces of the two sub-tasks. As a result, there are four labels {*Entity Type, ST-OT, OT-ST, None*} to identify all relation triples. The last dimension of matrix $\mathcal{R}$ is 4.

3.5 Decoding

In this section, we will give a detailed introduction to the decoding of triplets. In the left matrix of Fig. 1, the example sentence is "Maynard Jack Ramsay was born in Boca Raton in Florida" in which there are two relation triples:("Maynard Jack", birthplace, "Boca Raton") and ("Florida", contains, "Boca Raton"). The whole matrix is split by different colors corresponding to different sub-tasks.

For the entity recognition, the position of the token pair ("Maynard", "Ramsay") and ("Boca", "Raton")are tagged as "Entity Type" which means that both "Maynard Jack Ramsay" and "Boca Raton" is the entity in the relationship of "birthplace". For the alignment of subject-object, the token pair of ("Raton", "Ramsay") is tagged as "OT-ST" which means the subject of the triple ends with "Ramsay" and the object of the triple ends with "Raton". Therefore a triple ("Maynard Jack Ramsay", birthplace, "Boca Raton") is extracted, as same as talked about above, ("Florida", contains, "Boca Raton") is another triple.

3.6   RegionRel Plus

From the discussion above we know that most triplets can be predicted by RegionRel. However, the diagonal of the matrix is used to identify entities, which means that the token pair in the diagonal can't be tagged as ST-OT or OT-ST. This flaw of the decoding strategy leads to the problem that some relation triples with the end position of the subject is the same as the end position of the object are unable to be predicted.

The core of the flaw is that the region of two sub-tasks overlaps. To solve this problem, the labeled region of the matrix should be expanded.

To this end, we add an extra special token to the end of the sentence named "[ST=OT]". As is shown in the right sub-figure of Fig. 1, the number of token pairs has increased from L^2 to $(L+1)^2$ after adding "[ST=OT]", the extra region of the token pair matrix is marked with grey and white. As we mentioned above, for the triplet whose end position of the subject is the same as the end position of the object, subject-object alignment can't be tagged in the original matrix. However, the last row of the matrix can be tagged for subject-object alignment after adding an extra token to the sentence. For example, the sentence in the right sub-figure is "American Journal of Mathematics was first published in 1878", ("American Journal of Mathematics", academic discipline, "Mathematics") is one relation triplet with entity pair overlaps, therefore, the position of the token pair ("ST=OT", "Mathematics") is tagged as "tail-to-tail"(T-T) which means that "Mathematics" is both the end position of the subject and the end position of the object.

In this way, some special triplets which can't be extracted in RegionRel are extracted by the new model named RegionRel Plus. Compared with the original model, there is a new label in the label space called "T-T" which means the end position of the subject is the same as the end position of the object. In the experiment process, we use "ST-OT" to replace "T-T" because the label distribution will be unbalanced if "T-T" is added to our label space.

3.7   Loss Function

Classification Loss. From the discussion above, the task is abstracted into a multi-label classification problem, so the loss function of our model is defined as follow:

$$\mathscr{L}_{cls} = -\frac{1}{L \times L \times R} \times$$
$$\sum_{i=1}^{L}\sum_{j=1}^{L}\sum_{k=1}^{R}(y_{ijk}\log{(\mathcal{R}_{i,j,:}^k)} + (1 - y_{ijk})\log{(1 - \mathcal{R}_{i,j,:}^k)}) \tag{5}$$

where L is the length of sentence, R is the number of relations, y_{ijk} is the gold label of the token pair(h_i, h_j) and kth relation, $\mathcal{R}^k_{i,j,:}$ is the score of the token pair matrix $\mathcal{R}$ with the token pair(h_i, h_j) and kth relation.

Constraint Loss. Based on our assumptions about the model, the distribution of label space is not dependent. Labels of entity recognition tend to be distributed in the upper triangle region while labels of subject-object alignment tend to be distributed in the lower triangle region. Therefore, it's necessary to add some constraints to the model which helps the model learn the label distribution better.

Specifically, After we derive $\mathcal{R}$, distribution probability is achieved by follows which is noted as $\mathcal{P}$:

$$\mathcal{P}^k_{i,j,:} = Softmax(\mathcal{R}^k_{i,j,:}) \tag{6}$$

We denote positive labels belong to the sub-task of entities recognition as $\mathcal{Y}_e$ and positive labels belong to the sub-task of subject-object alignment as $\mathcal{Y}_a$, that is, $\mathcal{Y}_e = \{Entity\ Type\}$ and $\mathcal{Y}_a = \{ST - OT, OT - ST\}$. We want the sum of the probability scores belonging to $\mathcal{Y}_e$ to be greater than the sum of the probability scores belonging to $\mathcal{Y}_a$ for the upper triangle region, and conversely for the lower triangle region. We formulate this constraint loss as follows, $Relu(x)$ means $max(0, x)$.

$$\mathcal{L}_{con} = \frac{1}{L \times L \times R} \times \sum_{k=1}^{R}$$
$$(\sum_{(i,j)\in up} ReLu(\sum_{y\in\mathcal{Y}_a} \mathcal{P}^k_{i,j,y} - \sum_{y\in\mathcal{Y}_e} \mathcal{P}^k_{i,j,y}) +$$
$$\sum_{(i,j)\in low} ReLu(\sum_{y\in\mathcal{Y}_e} \mathcal{P}^k_{i,j,y} - \sum_{y\in\mathcal{Y}_a} \mathcal{P}^k_{i,j,y})) \tag{7}$$

Finally, the final loss is derived as $\mathcal{L} = \mathcal{L}_{cls} + \mathcal{L}_{con}$.

4   Experiment

4.1   Datasets

To compare with previous work, we conduct our experiment on two public datasets NYT [20] and WebNLG [21]. Both of which have two versions, we denote these datasets as **NYT,NYT*** and **WebNLG** and **WebNLG***. The difference between them is that NYT* and WebNLG* annotate the last token of entities, NYT and WebNLG annotate the whole span of the entity. The details of the datasets are shown in Table 1.

In Table 1, **SEO** is short for Single Entity Overlap which means the same subject or object corresponding to different relations like ("James", live in, **"USA"**) and ("Davis", live in, **"USA"**).**EPO** is short for Entity Pair Overlap which

Table 1. Details of four Datasets and numbers of different patterns in the test set. **Train, Valid, Test** means the number of sentences in the train set, dev set and test set.

Dataset	Train	Valid	Test	Relations	Normal	SEO	EPO	SOO
NYT*	56195	4999	5000	24	3266	1297	978	45
NYT	56196	5000	5000	24	3071	1273	1168	117
WebNLG*	5019	500	703	171	245	457	26	84
WebNLG	5019	500	703	216	239	448	6	85

means the same entity pair corresponding to different relations like(**"China"**, the capital city,**"Beijing"**) and (**"China"**, contains,**"Beijing"**).**SOO** is short for Subject Object Overlap like (**"Leborn James"**, first name,**"Leborn"**)

We report the standard micro Precision(Prec.), Recall(Rec.), and F1-score for all baselines in our experiments. Following previous work, we use *Partial Match* for NYT* and WebNLG* which means an extracted triple is predicted correctly only if the relation and the last word of both subject and object are all predicted correctly, and use *Exact Match* for NYT and WebNLG which means an extracted triple is predicted correctly only if the relation and the whole span of both subject and object are all predicted correctly.

4.2 Experiment Settings

We use bert-base-cased which contains 12 Transformer blocks with 768 dimensions of hidden layer as our pre-trained encoder, the pre-trained model is available on Huggingface. The batch size is 8/3 for NYT, NYT*/WebNLG, WebNLG*. The accumulation step is 1/2 correspondingly. The dimension of MLP in biaffine attention is 100. The max length of the sentence is 200. The dropout probability is set to 0.5. All parameters are optimized by Adam [22] with a learning rate of 1e-5. The training epoch is set to 400.

Table 2. Comparison between our model with previous models.

Model	NYT*			WebNLG*			NYT			WebNLG		
	Prec	Rec	F1.	Prec	Rec	F1.	Prec	Rec	F1.	Prec	Rec	F1
GraphRel [6]	63.9	60.0	61.9	44.7	41.1	42.9	–	–	–	–	–	–
ETL-span [4]	84.9	72.3	78.1	84.0	91.5	87.6	85.5	71.7	78.0	84.3	82.0	83.1
RSAN [2]	–	–	–	–	–	–	85.7	83.6	84.6	80.5	83.8	82.1
CasRel [5]	89.7	89.5	89.6	93.4	90.1	91.8	–	–	–	–	–	–
TPLinker [9]	91.3	**92.5**	91.9	91.8	92.0	91.9	91.4	92.6	92.0	88.9	84.5	86.7
PRGC [10]	93.3	91.9	92.6	94.0	92.1	93.0	**93.5**	91.9	92.7	89.9	87.2	88.5
EmRel [19]	91.7	92.5	92.1	92.7	**93.0**	92.9	92.6	92.7	92.6	90.2	**87.4**	88.7
RegionRel	93.5	91.6	92.5	94.6	87.5	90.9	93.4	91.8	92.6	**92.0**	85.9	88.9
RegionRel Plus	**93.5**	92.3	**92.9**	**94.9**	92.4	**93.6**	93.1	**92.8**	**93.0**	91.5	87.1	**89.2**

4.3 Main Result

Table 2 shows the result of our model compared with other baselines on four public datasets. From the result, we can observe that our model outperforms most of the baselines in terms of precision and F1-score. Both CasRel and TPLinker are methods that split tasks into several sub-tasks performed in different modules. Our model outperforms CasRel by 3.3 and 1.8 in F1-score on NYT* and WebNLG*, and outperforms TPLinker by 1.0,1.7, 1.0, and 2.5 in F1-score on NYT*, WebNLG*, NYT and WebNLG. It can be obtained that our model alleviates the problem of error accumulation.

However, it is worth noting that the recall of RegionRel is generally poor compared with most baselines. The main reason for this phenomenon is that our model can't recognize some specific triples due to the flaws of the model structure which we mentioned above. RegionRel Plus solved this problem, so we can observe that the recall returned to normal levels, especially outperforming RegionRel by 4.9 in WebNLG*.The precision of our model is better than most models. It can be mainly attributed to the following two reasons: first, the decoding method prevents wrong triplets as much as possible; second, the relation-specific decoding method improves the precision of our models.

To sum up, our model achieves satisfying results compared with other baselines. The results of F1-score and Precision are better than most previous sota baselines

4.4 Detailed Result

We also conduct further experiments to test our model when handling different overlapping patterns and different numbers of triples on the test set of NYT* and WebNLG*.

Table 3. Detail result of different patterns on test set of NYT* and WebNLG*. **SEO, EPO, SOO** means different overlapping patterns mentioned in Table 1, and **N** means the number of triples in one example.

Model	NYT*									WebNLG*								
	Normal	SEO	EPO	SOO	$N=1$	$N=2$	$N=3$	$N=4$	$N \geq 5$	Normal	SEO	EPO	SOO	N=1	N=2	N=3	N=4	$N \geq 5$
ETL-Span	88.5	87.6	60.3	-	88.5	82.1	74.7	75.6	76.9	87.3	91.5	80.5	-	82.1	86.5	91.4	89.5	91.1
CasRel	87.3	91.4	92.0	77.0	88.2	90.3	91.9	94.2	83.7	89.4	92.2	94.7	90.4	89.3	90.8	94.2	92.4	90.9
TPLinker	90.1	93.4	94.0	**90.1**	90.0	92.8	93.1	96.1	90.0	87.9	92.5	**95.3**	86.0	88.0	90.1	94.6	93.3	91.6
RegionRel	**91.7**	92.8	94.0	82.3	**91.3**	92.8	92.7	95.8	90.3	90.2	91.5	89.4	83.4	86.2	90.6	94.8	92.4	90.4
Region Plus	91.1	**94.0**	**94.5**	82.9	90.4	**93.0**	**93.5**	**96.4**	**92.7**	**92.7**	**94.1**	94.2	**94.3**	**91.3**	**92.0**	**96.0**	**95.0**	**92.6**

As shown in Table 3, it can be observed that our model performs well in most scenarios. It obtains the best F1-score on 14 of 18 subsets. Our model achieves better results compared with other baselines when handling different numbers of triples. Compared with RegionRel, RegionRel Plus improves performance about SOO, increasing by 0.6% and 10.9% on NYT* and WebNLG*, it can be attributed to the extra regions added by RegionRel Plus by which model can predict most special patterns, especially SOO. This result shows that our model has advantages in dealing with complex scenarios.

4.5   Result on Sub-task

In this subsection, we will conduct experiments to compare the performance of entity recognition with other models. Considering the entity in the task is divided into subject and object, we decide to take the entity pair (subject, object) as our target to compare with other models. The result is shown in Table 4, from the result we can observe that our model performs better than most baselines in entity recognition, especially compared with PRGC which conducts sub-tasks separately, our model outperforms PRGC in all instances except the precision of NYT*. This result proves that integrating entity recognition and subject-object alignment into one module can effectively improve the effect of the model.

Table 4. The performance of entity pair(subject, object) on test set of NYT* and WebNLG*

Model	NYT*			WebNLG*		
	Prec.	Rec.	F1.	Prec.	Rec.	F1
CasRel	89.2	90.1	89.7	95.3	91.7	93.5
PRGC	**94.0**	92.3	93.1	96.0	93.4	94.7
RegionRel Plus	93.7	**92.7**	**93.2**	**96.8**	**94.0**	**95.4**

5   Ablation Study

In this section, we will conduct several ablation experiments to explain the interaction between sub-tasks and analyze the effects of the loss function. The result is reported in Tables 5 and 6.

Table 5. Ablation study on the dev set of NYT.

entity recognition	Prec.	Rec.	F1
+ subject-object alignment	**0.960**	**0.950**	**0.955**
- subject-object alignment	0.942	0.945	0.943

From Table 5, we can observe that the performance of entity recognition with subject-object alignment increase Precision, Recall, and F1-score by 1.8%,0.5%, and 1.2% compared with conducting entity recognition task only. This result proves that our proposed model can make information of two sub-tasks interact which contributes to better performance of relation triple extraction.

The result of Table 6 shows us the fact that adding constraint loss will significantly improve the effectiveness of the model. This is because the distribution of label space will approach the ideal distribution by adding constraint loss which helps the model converge better.

Table 6. Model performance with/without constraint loss on the test set of WebNLG*.

method	Prec.	Rec.	F1
with constraint	**94.9**	**92.4**	**93.6**
without constraint	94.4	92.2	93.3

6   Conclusion

In this paper, we propose a new joint model named RegionRel Plus for relation triple extraction. It splits the task into two sub-tasks and conducts them in one module which successfully alleviates the problem of error accumulation. More importantly, this method successfully conducts two sub-tasks in one module and shows that the label space of different sub-tasks can be unified. As a result, the information of different sub-tasks is interacted which contributes to better performance of our model.

In the future, we would like to improve the generalization of our model in low-resource scenarios.

Acknowledgments. This work is supported by the NSFC grant (11871481,11971427) and STI2030-Major Project 2021ZD0204105.

References

1. Li, Q., Ji, H.: Incremental joint extraction of entity mentions and relations. In: ACL, vol. 1, pp. 402–412 (2014)
2. Yuan, Y., Zhou, X., Pan, S., Zhu, Q., Song, Z., Guo, L.: A relation-specific attention network for joint entity and relation extraction. In: IJCAI, vol. 2020, pp. 4054–4060 (2020)
3. Zheng, S., Wang, F., Bao, H., Hao, Y., Zhou, P., Xu, B.: Joint extraction of entities and relations based on a novel tagging scheme. arXiv preprint arXiv:1706.05075 (2017)
4. Yu, B., et al.: Joint extraction of entities and relations based on a novel decomposition strategy. arXiv preprint arXiv:1909.04273 (2019)
5. Wei, Z., Su, J., Wang, Y., Tian, Y., Chang, Y.: A novel cascade binary tagging framework for relational triple extraction. arXiv preprint arXiv:1909.03227 (2019)
6. Fu, T.J., Li, P.H., Ma, W.Y.: GraphRel: modeling text as relational graphs for joint entity and relation extraction. In: Proceedings of the 57th Annual Meeting of the Association for Computational Linguistics, pp. 1409–1418 (2019)
7. Sun, C., et al.: Joint type inference on entities and relations via graph convolutional networks. In: Proceedings of the 57th Annual Meeting of the Association for Computational Linguistics, pp. 1361–1370 (2019)
8. Zeng, X., Zeng, D., He, S., Liu, K., Zhao, J.: Extracting relational facts by an end-to-end neural model with copy mechanism. In: Proceedings of the 56th Annual Meeting of the Association for Computational Linguistics (vol. 1: Long Papers), pp. 506–514 (2018)

9. Wang, Y., Yu, B., Zhang, Y., Liu, T., Zhu, H., Sun, L.: TPLinker: single-stage joint extraction of entities and relations through token pair linking. arXiv preprint arXiv:2010.13415 (2020)

10. Zheng, H., et al.: PRGC: potential relation and global correspondence based joint relational triple extraction. arXiv preprint arXiv:2106.09895 (2021)

11. Wang, Y., Sun, C., Wu, Y., Zhou, H., Li, L., Yan, J.: UniRE: a unified label space for entity relation extraction. arXiv preprint arXiv:2107.04292 (2021)

12. Yu, J., Bohnet, B., Poesio, M.: Named entity recognition as dependency parsing. arXiv preprint arXiv:2005.07150 (2020)

13. Chan, Y.S., Roth, D.: Exploiting syntactico-semantic structures for relation extraction. In: Proceedings of the 49th Annual Meeting of the Association for Computational Linguistics: Human Language Technologies, pp. 551–560 (2011)

14. Zelenko, D., Aone, C., Richardella, A.: Kernel methods for relation extraction. J. Mach. Learn. Res. **3**(Feb), 1083–1106 (2003)

15. Yu, X., Lam, W.: Jointly identifying entities and extracting relations in encyclopedia text via a graphical model approach. In: Coling 2010: Posters, pp. 1399–1407 (2010)

16. Miwa, M., Sasaki, Y.: Modeling joint entity and relation extraction with table representation. In: Proceedings of the 2014 Conference on Empirical Methods in Natural Language Processing (EMNLP), pp. 1858–1869 (2014)

17. Devlin, J., Chang, M.W., Lee, K., Toutanova, K.: . BERT: pre-training of deep bidirectional transformers for language understanding. arXiv preprint arXiv:1810.04805 (2018)

18. Gu, Y., Qu, X., Wang, Z., Zheng, Y., Huai, B., Yuan, N.J.: Delving deep into regularity: a simple but effective method for Chinese named entity recognition. arXiv preprint arXiv:2204.05544 (2022)

19. Xu, B., et al.: EmRel: joint representation of entities and embedded relations for multi-triple extraction. In: Proceedings of the 2022 Conference of the North American Chapter of the Association for Computational Linguistics: Human Language Technologies, pp. 659–665 (2022)

20. Riedel, S., Yao, L., McCallum, A.: Modeling relations and their mentions without labeled text. In: Balcázar, J.L., Bonchi, F., Gionis, A., Sebag, M. (eds.) ECML PKDD 2010. LNCS (LNAI), vol. 6323, pp. 148–163. Springer, Heidelberg (2010). https://doi.org/10.1007/978-3-642-15939-8_10

21. Gardent, C., Shimorina, A., Narayan, S., Perez-Beltrachini, L.: Creating training corpora for NLG micro-planning. In: 55th Annual Meeting of the Association for Computational Linguistics (ACL) (2017)

22. Kingma, D.P., Ba, J.: Adam: a method for stochastic optimization. arXiv preprint arXiv:1412.6980 (2014)

Robustness to Variability and Asymmetry of In-Memory On-Chip Training

Rohit K. Vartak[1]($\boxtimes$) (iD), Vivek Saraswat[1] (iD), and Udayan Ganguly[1,2] (iD)

[1] Indian Institute of Technology Bombay, Mumbai 400076, India
`rohitkvartak4@gmail.com`
[2] IITB Centre for Semiconductor Technologies (SEMIX), Mumbai 400076, India

Abstract. In-memory on-chip learning is crucial for low-power, in-field training capabilities at the edge. We demonstrate the robustness of on-chip back-propagation to hardware variability in terms of bit-cell transistor V_T variability ($2.5\times$ more robust than off-chip training). We use perturbation schemes, asymmetry variations and variability-aware update schemes to identify the relative contribution of different on-chip operations: forward pass, backward pass and weight updates to Fashion-MNIST classification performance degradation with variations. It is revealed that variability during the weight update step is crucial while accuracy of backward pass or gradient calculation is not critical. We promote weight perturbation scheme over back-propagation as the choice for on-chip in-memory training with reduced points of failure and low cost of hardware.

Keywords: In-memory · Variability · Back-propagation · Perturbation

1 Introduction

Hardware acceleration of artificial neural network (ANN) operations is crucial for widespread deployment in high-throughput applications. Further, the explosion of data at the edge and concerns of personal data privacy require on-chip learning capabilities for low-power devices [9,17,18]. Learning at the edge has the potential to relieve communication bandwidth and promote decentralised edge computing rather than centralised cloud computing. However, learning is typically an expensive operation with high data movement resulting in high energy and latency requirements [8,15].

In-memory computing using conventional (Static Random Access Memory or SRAM, Dynamic Random Access Memory or DRAM, Flash) or emerging memories (Resistive Random Access Memory of RRAM, Magneto-resistive Random Access Memory or MRAM, Ferroelectric Random Access Memory or FeRAM) provides an alternative architecture for high-speed, low-power operations using device physics and circuit laws for partially analogous computing [14]. Specifically, vector-matrix inner product and vector-vector outer product operations have been accelerated in-memory to demonstrate on-chip learning for

L. Iliadis et al. (Eds.): ICANN 2023, LNCS 14262, pp. 249–257, 2023.
https://doi.org/10.1007/978-3-031-44201-8_21

ANNs [1,5,6]. However, hardware non-idealities like quantization and variability pose a challenge to accuracy [4,16].

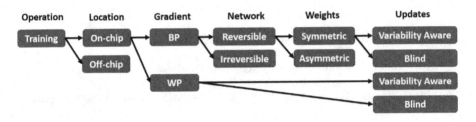

Fig. 1. Comparison of the decisions involved in the BP and WP pathways for in-memory on-chip training

Backpropagation (BP) is a powerful learning algorithm employing forward pass for loss, backward pass for gradients and weight update computations as the fundamental operations [13]. In-memory implementation of BP incurs errors in these operations owing to hardware non-idealities. Further, on-chip implementation of BP requires reversibility of network hardware to allow bidirectional passes [8] along with the assumption of availability of exactly transpose weights (i.e., no asymmetry variation) for backward pass. In this work, we motivate the robustness of "on-chip learning" vis-à-vis "offline learning followed by on-chip inference" to hardware variability. Next, we use a weight perturbation (WP) scheme to identify the primary operation in BP that is affected by variability while training on-chip [15]. Finally, we test the robustness of on-chip BP to the extent of asymmetry in forward and backward passes weights of the network. These requirements for a successful on-chip BP implementation namely reversibility in hardware puts BP at a disadvantage when compared to more generally applicable perturbation schemes (Fig. 1).

2   Related Work

Due to the adverse effects of variability on-chip on the performance of ANNs trained using the Back Propagation algorithm, researchers have suggested several ways to improve model performance, for example - [2,7,10].

[3] develops quantization-aware and variability-aware training or QAVAT, improving performance of models on computer vision datasets like CIFAR100. To make the network robust to variability, QAVAT, introduces variability during training and attempts to find the unbiased estimator for the gradients. [12] develops a Weight Variation Aware Training or WVAT for Spiking Neural Networks (SNNs) and ANNs. WVAT aims to find model parameters which are resilient to small changes.

While all these developments propose techniques that show improvements in model performance, none attempt to answer which step in the training process of ANNs is the most affected by variability. Thus, in addition to having a variability-aware weight update algorithm, which shows improvement in model performance, we fundamentally answer the question - which step in our training process is the most affected by on-chip non-idealities?

3   Methods

3.1   Modelling Hardware Non-Idealities

We assume the weights of the network are implemented using multi-bit digital arrays of memories with capability of in-memory vector-matrix multiplications ($w_{ij,Q} = \sum_{k=0}^{N-1} b_k.2^k$). Each bit of each weight has the capability of an analog readout current using a transistor depending on the bit value (1/0) (Fig. 2(a),(b)). The effective weight ($w_{ij,eff}$) that participates in multiply and accumulate (MAC) during forward/backward passes is then computed as a summation of the bit-wise currents scaled according to their significance:

$$w_{ij,eff} = \frac{1}{I_1} \sum_{k=0}^{N-1} I_{ij,k}(b_k).2^k \tag{1}$$

where $[b_{N-1}, \cdots, b_1, b_0]$ is the bit-pattern for the specific weight, I_1 is the nominal ON current for bit '1' and $I_{ij,k}$ is the instance of current readout from the kth bit of ij^{th} weight. $I_{ij,k}$ are variable bit to bit, weight to weight due to transistor threshold (V_T) variability and sampled from the distribution:

$$I_{ij,k}(b_k) = I_x \exp \frac{\Delta V_T}{\eta V_{th}} \tag{2}$$

where $x \in \{0,1\}$ gives the nominal OFF (I_0) or ON (I_1) current depending on value of b_k ($I_1/I_0 \sim 10^4$), ΔV_T **is sampled from a normal distribution with zero mean and** σ_{V_T} **standard deviation,** η (~ 1.5) is the transistor sub-threshold non-ideality factor and V_{th} (26 mV) is the thermal voltage at room temperature. These effective weights, with quantization and variability, affect the MAC and weight update operations and hence, the on-chip learning and inference performance. In this work, only the weights and weight updates are considered non-ideal during operation since these consume the maximum area on-chip and undergo an aggressively scaled implementation, and are thus vulnerable to variations.

3.2   Weight Perturbation Scheme

Weight Perturbation (WP) is an alternative of BP, an approximate method to calculate the gradients that does not involve backward pass through the network. In this scheme, the weights of the network are perturbed one by one. After perturbing a weight, a forward pass is done and the new output loss is observed, then:

$$\frac{\partial L}{\partial w_{ij}} \sim \frac{\Delta L}{\Delta w_{ij,eff}} \tag{3}$$

Here $\Delta w_{ij,eff}$ is the change in the effective weight when perturbed by 1 bit value from its current bit-pattern.

3.3 Blind Updates Vs. Variability Aware Updates

Once the gradients and hence the desired weight updates are calculated using BP or WP, we need to update the $w_{ij,Q}$. We can quantize the obtained updates and add it to previous bit-pattern of the weights digitally. This method is termed as a blind update as it is blind to the variability of the effective weight of the new bit-pattern. On the other hand, we can find a new effective weight which results in an effective weight update closest to the calculated update. This method is termed as a variability aware update. It is important to note here that typically the user only has access to the $w_{ij,Q}$. However, variability aware updates assume a knowledge of available $w_{ij,eff}$ corresponding to different quantized levels $W_{ij,Q}$ can take, and hence it will require specialized hardware to implement. Currently, we generate a lookup table of effective weights for all bit-patterns of each weight to enable variability aware updates (Fig. 2(c)).

3.4 Asymmetry in Forward and Backward V_T

Backpropagation assumes reversible network hardware for forward and backward passes with symmetric forward and backward effective weights for transposed weight multiplication operations (Fig. 2(a),(b)). However, when implemented in technology using transistors, the source to drain and drain to source current at appropriately reversed biasing may result in different current flows (Fig. 2(d)). This effectively means that the forward $V_{T,F}$ and backward $V_{T,B}$ may not be identical. We consider the scenario where the $V_{T,F}$ and $V_{T,B}$ are sampled from a bi-variate normal distribution with same σ_{V_T} and different amounts of correlation ρ between $V_{T,F}$ and $V_{T,B}$. Typical measurements conducted on 6 Metal-Oxide-Semiconductor Field-Effect Transistor (MOSFET) devices in 32 nm Partially Depleted Silicon On Insulator (PDSOI) technology ($W = 450$ nm and $L_G = 40$ nm) and distributions reported earlier in 65 nm Complementary Metal-Oxide-Semiconductor or CMOS [11] for extracted V_T for forward and backward bit-cell currents are shown in (Fig. 2(d),(inset)). The experimental data suggests prevalence of high $\rho \sim 0.9$.

4 Results and Discussions

All experiments are performed for the training and testing of Fashion-MNIST dataset (90% - 10% training-testing split) using a fully connected layered network ($784 \times 10 \times 10$). We use only one hidden layer to keep the number of learn-able parameters in our network small as Weight perturbation is slow to train the network since the gradient computation for each weight is performed sequentially.

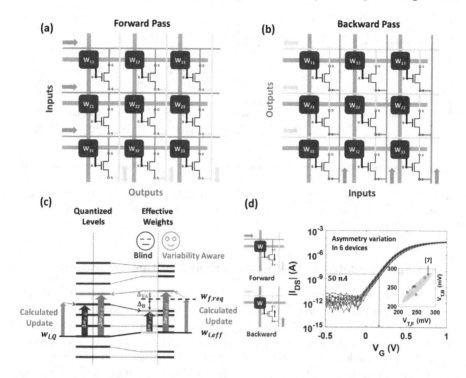

Fig. 2. (a) Forward and (b) Backward pass in-memory MAC scheme for the special case of 1-bit weights, (c) Blind vs. variability aware updates, (d) Measured asymmetry variations for 6 devices, (inset) Extracted $V_{T,B}$ vs. $V_{T,F}$ along with distributions reported earlier [11]

We use ReLU activations in the hidden layer and softmax activations in the output layer with categorical cross entropy loss for training. A batch-size of 630 samples is used with a fixed learning rate of 0.1. We use a quantization of 12 bits per weight and sweep the amount of variability per bit (σ_{V_T}). Each variability experiment is run for 5 instances to obtain statistical data and the mean (markers) and standard deviation (shaded) of test accuracy are reported for the following experiments.

4.1   Robustness of On-Chip Learning to Variability

We consider two scenarios. (1) Ideal weights trained off-chip in software are transferred on-chip for inference, (2) Training is performed on-chip with variability inflicted but symmetric weights and blind updates. We see that case (2), i.e., calculation of loss and gradients on-chip through effective weights (Sect. 3.1) grants the system significantly higher robustness (2.5× higher) against variability (Fig. 3(a)).

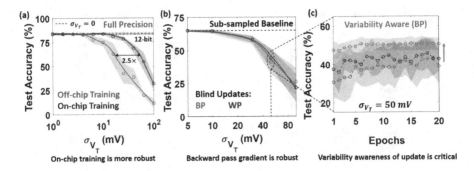

Fig. 3. (a) Test accuracy vs. σ_{V_T} for off-chip and on-chip training, (b) Overlapping test accuracy for WP and BP blind updates, (c) Test accuracy vs. epochs and improvement due to variability awareness

4.2   Weight Updates as the Fundamental Limiting Operation

In this Section, we sub-sample inputs to reduce network size to $16 \times 10 \times 10$ and use a fixed learning rate of 1. The weights are symmetric and the updates are blind. We compare on-chip BP and WP (Sect. 3.2) based accuracies to determine the limiting operation out of forward pass, backward pass and weight updates. WP requires no backward pass but overlaps in performance with BP (Fig. 3(b)). This indicates that on-chip backward pass for gradients calculation is not responsible factor for performance degradation with variations. This also implies that it is the blind weight update step that is the performance defining critical operation during learning on-chip. Further, adding variability awareness (Sect. 3.3) to updates enhances the performance significantly reinforcing the role of update step as the fundamental limiting operation (Fig. 3(c)).

4.3   Impact of Asymmetric V_T on Performance

We perform blind updates based BP for the asymmetric V_T scenarios (Sect. 3.4). Asymmetry variations in V_T translate to different forward and backward weights (W_F and W_B). This experiment provides a method to resolve the importance of exact transpose weights multiplication during backward pass. For $\rho = 0$, we observe that the performance is similar to the symmetric V_T case (Fig. 4(a)) for different amounts of σ_{V_T}. An instance of $V_{T,F}$ and $V_{T,B}$ sampling for the uncorrelated case and the corresponding asymmetry in W_F and W_B is shown in Fig. 4(b),(c). Next, we fix $\sigma_{V_T} = 30\ mV$, and sweep the correlation ρ from -1 to 1 (Fig. 4(d)). Again, a correlation insensitive test accuracy is observed. An instance of $V_{T,F}$ and $V_{T,B}$ sampling for $\rho \sim 0.9$ case and the corresponding asymmetry in W_F and W_B is shown in Fig. 4(e),(f). These experiments suggest that the asymmetry in W_F and W_B caused due to hardware asymmetry variations in $V_{T,F}$ and $V_{T,B}$ is not a critical factor in backpropagation accuracy. This again reinforces the conclusion that the accuracy of backward pass or gradients calculation is not the performance limiting operation.

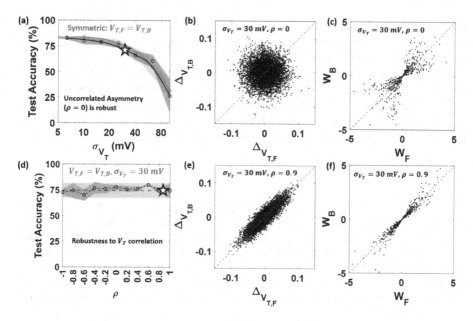

Fig. 4. (a) Test accuracy for uncorrelated asymmetry case, Distribution for forward and backward (b) Δ_{V_T} and (c) W for $\rho = 0$ and $\sigma_{V_T} = 30\ mV$, (d) Test accuracy for different V_T correlation case, Distribution for forward and backward (e) Δ_{V_T} and (f) W for $\rho = 0.9$ and $\sigma_{V_T} = 30\ mV$, Typical hardware σ_{V_T} and ρ are star-marked

4.4 Benefits of Weight Perturbation

Clearly, it is beneficial to have an on-chip in-memory training capability (Sect. 4.1. Further, the critical operations are the loss calculation (forward pass) and weight updates on-chip for robustness to variability. However, if we choose to develop hardware for BP, there is increased cost of reversible hardware capable of forward and backward pass in the same memory array along with the peripherals needed to enable that. In contrast, WP requires much simple hardware. The network does not need to be reversible. It does not need to be compatible with backpropagating gradients and hence asymmetry is immaterial. The network can be fully connected sequential layers or recurrent. WP would function agnostic to network architecture and is thus more generally applicable with reduced number of potential failures and low cost of implementation. However, WP is expected to run slower, polling through the weights, as compared to BP. If the frequency of re-learning weights is low, WP is an excellent choice for in-memory on-chip learning hardware.

5 Conclusion

We have analysed the impact of V_T variability and asymmetry variations in weights on the performance of backpropagation on-chip using an in-memory implementation. On-chip training is more robust (2.5× higher) to hardware variability. It is critical to implement on-chip loss calculation (forward pass) and variability-awareness in weight update step while the accuracy of backward pass and gradients calculation on-chip shows low significance to performance degradation with variability. Backpropagation requires reversible hardware in order to calculate gradients on-chip increasing the cost of hardware implementation. Weight perturbation on the other hand does not depend on reversibility and hence, is more generally applicable with reduced hardware cost.

References

1. Ali, M., Jaiswal, A., Kodge, S., Agrawal, A., Chakraborty, I., Roy, K.: IMAC: In-memory multi-bit multiplication and accumulation in 6T SRAM array. IEEE Trans. Circuit. Syst. I: Regular Papers **67**(8), 2521–2531 (2020). https://doi.org/10.1109/TCSI.2020.2981901. https://ieeexplore.ieee.org/document/9050543/. Publisher: IEEE

2. Chang, C.C., et al.: Device quantization policy in variation-aware in-memory computing design. Sci. Rep. **12**, 112 (2022). https://doi.org/10.1038/s41598-021-04159-x

3. Deng, Z., Orshansky, M.: Variability-aware training and self-tuning of highly quantized DNNs for analog PIM. CoRR abs/2111.06457 (2021). arxiv.org/abs/2111.06457

4. Doevenspeck, J., et al.: OxRRAM-based analog in-memory computing for deep neural network inference: a conductance variability study. IEEE Trans. Electr. Devices **68**(5), 2301–2305 (2021). https://doi.org/10.1109/TED.2021.3068696. https://ieeexplore.ieee.org/document/9405305/

5. Fumarola, A., et al.: Bidirectional non-filamentary RRAM as an analog neuromorphic synapse, Part II: impact of Al/Mo/Pr 0.7 Ca 0.3 MnO 3 device characteristics on neural network training accuracy. IEEE J. Electr. Devices Soc. **6**(1), 169–178 (2018). https://doi.org/10.1109/JEDS.2017.2782184. Publisher: Institute of Electrical and Electronics Engineers Inc

6. Gokmen, T., Vlasov, Y.: Acceleration of deep neural network training with resistive cross-point devices: design considerations. Front. Neurosci. **10**, 333 (2016). https://doi.org/10.3389/fnins.2016.00333. https://journal.frontiersin.org/Article/10.3389/fnins.2016.00333/abstract

7. Gonugondla, S.K., Kang, M., Shanbhag, N.R.: A variation-tolerant in-memory machine learning classifier via on-chip training. IEEE J. Solid-State Circuits **53**(11), 3163–3173 (2018). https://doi.org/10.1109/JSSC.2018.2867275

8. Jiang, H., Peng, X., Huang, S., Yu, S.: CIMAT: a compute-in-memory architecture for on-chip training based on transpose SRAM arrays. IEEE Trans. Comput. **69**, 944–954 (2020). https://doi.org/10.1109/TC.2020.2980533. https://ieeexplore.ieee.org/document/9035482

9. Kim, S., Gokmen, T., Lee, H.M., Haensch, W.E.: Analog CMOS-based resistive processing unit for deep neural network training. In: 2017 IEEE 60th International Midwest Symposium on Circuits and Systems (MWSCAS), pp. 422–425. IEEE, Boston, MA, USA (2017). https://doi.org/10.1109/MWSCAS.2017.8052950. https://ieeexplore.ieee.org/document/8052950/

10. Long, Y., She, X., Mukhopadhyay, S.: Design of reliable DNN accelerator with un-reliable ReRam. In: 2019 Design, Automation & Test in Europe Conference & Exhibition (DATE), pp. 1769–1774 (2019). https://doi.org/10.23919/DATE.2019. 8715178

11. Miyamura, M., Nagumo, T., Takeuchi, K., Takeda, K., Hane, M.: Effects of drain bias on threshold voltage fluctuation and its impact on circuit characteristics. In: 2008 IEEE International Electron Devices Meeting, pp. 1–4. IEEE, San Francisco, CA, USA (2008). https://doi.org/10.1109/IEDM.2008.4796721. https:// ieeexplore.ieee.org/document/4796721/

12. Oh, M.H.: A weight variation-aware training method for hardware neuromorphic chips (2023). https://openreview.net/forum?id=3urtgEaXCA9

13. Rumelhart, D.E., Hinton, G.E., Williams, R.J.: Learning representations by back-propagating errors. Nature **323**(6088), 533–536 (1986). https://doi.org/10.1038/ 323533a0

14. Sebastian, A., Le Gallo, M., Khaddam-Aljameh, R., Eleftheriou, E.: Memory devices and applications for in-memory computing. Nat. Nanotechnol. **15**(7), 529–544 (2020). https://doi.org/10.1038/s41565-020-0655-z. https://www.nature.com/ articles/s41565-020-0655-z

15. Valle, M.: Analog VLSI implementation of artificial neural networks with supervised on-chip learning. Analog Integr. Circ. Sig. Process **33**(3), 263–287 (2002). https://doi.org/10.1023/A:1020717929709

16. Wang, Q., Park, Y., Lu, W.D.: Device variation effects on neural network inference accuracy in analog in-memory computing systems. Adv. Intell. Syst. **4**(8), 2100199 (2022). https://doi.org/10.1002/aisy.202100199. https://onlinelibrary.wiley.com/ doi/10.1002/aisy.202100199

17. Xiao, T.P., Bennett, C.H., Feinberg, B., Agarwal, S., Marinella, M.J.: Analog architectures for neural network acceleration based on non-volatile memory. Appl. Phys. Rev. **7**(3), 031301 (2020). https://doi.org/10.1063/1.5143815. https://aip. scitation.org/doi/10.1063/1.5143815

18. Zhao, J., et al.: CORK: a privacy-preserving and lossless federated learning scheme for deep neural network. Inf. Sci. **603**, 190–209 (2022). https://doi.org/10.1016/j. ins.2022.04.052. https://linkinghub.elsevier.com/retrieve/pii/S0020025522004042

Selecting Distinctive-Variant Training Samples Base on Intra-class Similarity

Hang Diao[1], Zhengchang Liu[2], Fan Zhang[1(✉)], Jiaqing Huang[3], Feiyu Zhou[3], and Samee U. Khan[4]

[1] Ocean College, Zhejiang University, Zhoushan, China
`f.zhang@zju.edu.cn`
[2] Computer Science and Technology, Nanjing Tech University, Nanjing, China
[3] Shaoxing Lanhung Intelligent Technology Co., Ltd., Shaoxing, China
[4] Mississippi State University, Starkville, Mississippi State, MS, USA

Abstract. Deep learning models often require a significant amount of data, which can be computationally intensive and architecturally complex. Efforts to address the challenge of handling large amounts of data in high-resolution scenarios have led to the development of techniques like data pruning and data diet approaches. We present a novel approach called *Select Base on Intra-Class Similarity* (SICS), distinguishes itself by measuring the similarity of samples within the same class and identifies the most informative samples that are most dissimilar from others, and introducing the novel concept of a *distinctive-variant sample*, vital for enhancing deep-learning classification tasks. We evaluated our method on several image classification benchmarks and compared it with existing techniques. Our results show that in high-resolution images and many class scenarios, $SICS$ can achieve the same level of accuracy as the full data while using only about 80% of the training data, outperforming the $ForgettingScore$ method by 20% to 90%. Additionally, our method maintains its robustness when switching to different training models. Our source code is publicly available at https://github.com/Gusicun/SICS.

Keywords: Data pruning · Data diet · Intra-class similarity · Important samples · Distinctive-variant samples

1 Introduction

Deep learning has achieved remarkable success in various domains. However, deep learning faces significant challenges due to its models and datasets' increasing scale and complexity. For example, GPT-3 (Generative Pre-training Transformer) [2], one of the most significant language models, has over 175 billion parameters and requires hundreds of gigabytes of data to train. Similarly, ImageNet [5], a classic dataset for image recognition, contains over one billion images and takes up over 300 GB of storage. This poses several challenges: (1) Collecting and annotating large-scale datasets is expensive and time-consuming; (2)

L. Iliadis et al. (Eds.): ICANN 2023, LNCS 14262, pp. 258–269, 2023.
https://doi.org/10.1007/978-3-031-44201-8_22

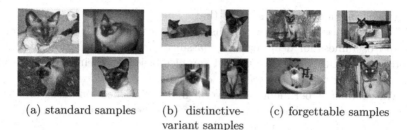

(a) standard samples   (b) distinctive-   (c) forgettable samples
                             variant samples

Fig. 1. Differences in selecting samples using $SICS$**(Ours) and Forgetting Score(baseline)** Fig. 1a shows the most standard samples of the Siamese Cat category in the Oxford Pets dataset; Fig. 1b shows the most distinctive-variant samples we choose by the $SICS$ method; Fig. 1c shows the most forgettable samples chosen by the $ForgettingScore$ method.

Training on large-scale datasets requires huge computational resources and long training time; (3) Large-scale datasets contain redundant or noisy samples that degrade the model performance.

In response to those challenges, the concepts of data pruning and data diet have been proposed in online and active learning, as discussed in references [3,12]. One possible solution is to select a subset of essential training samples that can effectively represent the characteristics and diversity of the full dataset. This reduces the data size and complexity, saves computational costs and time, and improves model performance and robustness. However, selecting essential training samples is not a trivial task.

Inspired by the established research on human perception and performance, we extend the concept of *variations* to deep learning classification tasks. Variations refer to the degree of deviation among samples within a category. For example, in human perception, Nosofsky's seminal study [10] showed that people could accurately identify and categorize new stimuli if they were exposed to diverse examples from each category rather than just prototypes or averages. Similarly, variations can help capture more salient or distinctive features and reduce redundancy among samples within a category. We provide empirical evidence to support this claim in our experiments.

We focus on a specific type of training sample that we call *distinctive-variant sample*. These samples deviate from the majority of others within their category in some specific features but still share salient features with other samples in the same category. We argue that selecting distinctive-variant samples can improve the performance and robustness of deep learning models for classification tasks. Existing methods for data pruning are either based on random sampling or inter-class similarity, which does not capture the intra-class similarity. Therefore, we propose a novel method to bridge the gap. We named our method *Select Base on Intra-Class Similarity* (SICS). SICS aims to select a subset of samples that effectively represent the full dataset while eliminating redundant samples.

Our experimental findings suggest that:

1) We introduce the concept of a distinctive-variant sample, show its importance and usefulness for deep learning classification tasks, and propose a novel method for selecting distinctive-variant samples based on their intra-class similarity. We call our method *Select Base on Intra-Class Similarity* (SICS).

2) We conduct experiments on several image classification tasks and show that our method can achieve comparable or even better results than using the full dataset or other data pruning methods.

3) We show that our method excels when the pruning ratio is high and when the original dataset is complex. We demonstrate that our method can improve the robustness and generalization of the model by transferring distinctive-variant samples between different DNN architectures.

2   Related Work

We have conducted a comprehensive evaluation of various techniques employed for data pruning and data diet and have compared them with our own novel approach. Cody et al. [4] proposed a method called *selection via proxy* (SVP), which selects the samples that have the highest loss on the proxy model. Pruthi et al. [8] proposed a method that uses influence functions to estimate the change in test loss when a training sample is removed. Zhu et al. [15] proposed a method that defines two scoring metrics: Gradient Normed (GraNd) score and Error L2-Norm (EL2N) score.

Inspired by Zhu's work, Toneva et al. [14] defined a training sample that is characterized as *forgettable* if the model keeps wrongly predicting it over the course of multiple epochs during the training process. On the contrary, a training sample that is *unforgettable* if it remains correctly predicted on the training process. *Unforgettable samples* can be eliminated from the training set without affecting the performance of the network. Paul et al. [11] proposed a method that cherrypicks the important samples in early training. They used the Gradient Normed (GraNd) score and the Error L2-Norm (EL2N) score, which are computed from the initial loss gradient norm and the normed error of each training sample over multiple weight initializations, to identify a subset of important training data.

Our proposed method *Select Base on Intra-Class Similarity* (SICS) differs from these existing methods in several aspects. We introduce the concept of a distinctive-variant sample and show its importance and usefulness for deep-learning classification tasks.

3   Methodology

3.1   Definition and Methodology

Our proposed method consists of two main steps: feature extraction and sample selection. In the feature extraction step, we use a pre-trained model or a self-defined Convolutional Neural Network (CNN) model as the backbone to extract

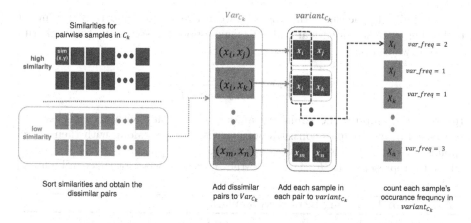

Fig. 2. The *Select Base on Intra-Class Similarity* (SICS) method follows a well-defined workflow. Through intra-class similarity computation, the least similar pairs populate Var_{C_k}, and training samples with the highest occurrence rate, embodying distinctness, are chosen.

features from each sample. In the sample selection step, we calculate the pairwise similarity between each pair of samples using the extracted features and rank them accordingly. We then select a subset of samples that have high intraclass similarity as the distinctive-variant samples we desired. Formally, let $D = \{D^{train}, D^{test}\}$ be a given dataset that comprises of N distinct classes $C = \{C_1, C_2, \ldots, C_N\}$. Let x be a training sample and x' be a test sample.

In our approach, we calculate intra-class pairwise similarity, relocate the least similar half to Var_{C_k}, tally sample occurrence, and retain those with top frequencies, arguing their distinctness due to maximal dissimilarity. Further subsections delve into specifics of our approach (Fig. 2).

3.2 Getting Intra-class Similarity

First, we extract features from each training sample using a pre-trained model or a self-defined Convolutional Neural Network (CNN) model. The extracted features are used to measure the similarity among samples within each class. We use pre-trained models as the backbone because they have been shown to be efficient for various image classification tasks [7,13]. We use ResNet [6] as our default pre-trained model, but other models are also used depending on the dataset and task. For some intricate datasets, we design custom convolutional layers to capture the specific characteristics of each training sample.

Let $backbone(x)$ be a function that extracts features from sample x using the pre-trained or self-defined CNN model. We define the feature extracted from sample x as f_x:

$$f_x = backbone(x) \tag{1}$$

To measure the degree of similarity between samples within class C_k, we compute the pairwise similarity between all samples in class C_k using cosine similarity [9].

Cosine similarity measures the angle between two vectors and ranges from -1 to 1, where 1 means identical and -1 means opposite. We define the similarity between two samples x_i and x_j as:

$$sim(x_i, x_j) = \frac{f_{x_i} \cdot f_{x_j}}{||f_{x_i}|| \times ||f_{x_j}||} \tag{2}$$

In order to compute the similarity among all samples within each class, we proceeded to form tuples consisting of pairwise samples along with their corresponding similarity values. These tuples were then appended to the $sim_l list_{C_k}$, where C_k represents the K class. The step-by-step process for this can be found in Algorithm 1.

Algorithm 1: Getting Intra-class Similarity

    Input: Train dataset: D^{train}, all classes: C, a model for feature
             extraction: *backbone*, function to compute the degree of similarity
             between two samples: $sim(x_i, x_j)$
    Output: The list of tuples that contains each pairwise sample and their
              similarity for each class: $sim\_list_{C_k}$

  1 **foreach** *class C_k in C* **do**
  2   f_list = empty list ;
  3     $sim\_list_{C_k}$ = empty list ;
  4   **foreach** *sample $x \in D^{train}$* **do**
  5   **if** $x \in C_k$ **then**
  6             $f_x = backbone(x)$;
  7   add f_x to f_list ;
  8   **end**
  9   **end**
10   **foreach** $f_{x_i}, f_{x_j} \in f\_list$ **do**
11   Initialize variable sim_{x_i,x_j} to store the result of $sim(x_i, x_j)$;
12         $sim_{x_i,x_j} \leftarrow sim(x_i, x_j)$;
13   add $((x_i, x_j), sim_{x_i,x_j})$ to $sim\_list_{C_k}$;
14   **end**
15 **end**
16 **return** $sim\_list_{C_k}$ for each class C_k in C

3.3 Select Distinctive-Variant Samples via Intra-class Similarity

Having identified the intra-class similarity, the subsequent step involves selecting the distinctive-variant samples within each class. To achieve this, we establish a threshold for each class based on the median similarities within that class. Our working hypothesis suggests that samples with a lower similarity value may exhibit unique features compared to other pairs, implying that they are distinctive-variant.

Assume that we have a list of thresholds defined as $Th = \{Th_{C_1}, Th_{C_2}, \ldots, Th_{C_N}\}$ for the N classes. For any two samples x_i and x_j in class C_k, we obtain the similarity value sim_{x_i,x_j}, as we gain from each tuple through $sim\_list_{C_k}$. The threshold of C_k is denoted as Th_{C_k}. Then, we can define the subsets for each class as Var_{C_k}, which contains pairs of samples with low similarity values.

In the context of Var_{C_k}, each sample in a sample pair is considered an individual sample. Thus, when a pairwise sample such as (x_i, x_j) and (x_i, x_k) appears in Var_{C_k}, both samples x_i, x_j, and x_k are added repeatedly to the list $variant_{C_k}$. In other words, each sample is treated independently and added to the list multiple times if it appears in multiple sample pairs.

$$Var_{C_k} = \{(x_i, x_j)|sim_{x_i,x_j} \geq Th_{C_k}, \forall x_i, x_j \in C_k, x_i \neq x_j\} \qquad (3)$$

$$variant_{C_k} = x_i \mid \exists x_j : (x_i, x_j) \in Var_{C_k} \cup x_j \mid \exists x_i : (x_i, x_j) \in Var_{C_k} \qquad (4)$$

Samples that appear at least once in $variant_{C_k}$ are identified as distinctive-variant, for we consider these samples to have unique characteristics that differentiate them from other samples. To measure the distinctiveness of these samples, we rank them based on their frequency in $variant_{C_k}$. Samples that occur more frequently are considered to have higher distinctive-variant features and therefore are given higher priority. Conversely, samples with low frequency are deemed not-salient-feature samples and can be removed. To denote the frequency of a particular sample x, we use the notation $var_freq(x, variant_{C_k})$ and sort the samples in descending order as $var_{des C_k}$. The Kronecker delta function [1] is utilized to indicate the number of times a sample x appears in $variant_{C_k}$.

$$var\_freq(x, variant_{C_k}) = \sum_{v \in variant_{C_k}} \delta_{v,x} \qquad (5)$$

Upon identifying distinctive-variant samples, we proceed with data pruning, utilizing a predetermined ratio. Suppose we aim to preserve a fraction of the original training dataset, denoted by R. In that case, we must choose $\lfloor |C_k| \times R \rfloor$ samples from each category C_k based on the priority we established earlier to construct the retention dataset. We repeat this iterative process until we reach the desired quota, resulting in a new dataset for each category, which we label $retention_{C_k}$. The retention procedure is visually presented in Fig. 3.

To provide a more comprehensive explanation of the process, we describe the discipline in greater detail in Algorithm 2. To demonstrate the distinctiveness of the most frequent occurrence of dissimilar samples, Fig. 4. illustrates the var_freq for samples obtained from Algorithm 2.

4   Experiments

In order to validate our hypothesis, we experimentally apply our methodology to multiple models and datasets.

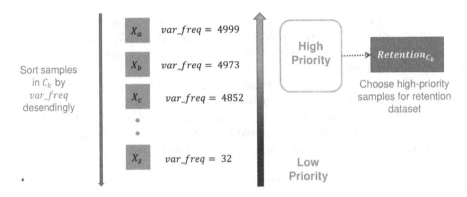

Fig. 3. Arrange the samples in descending order based on their *var_freq* values. During the dataset selection phase, we accord greater precedence to samples with higher *var_freq* values.

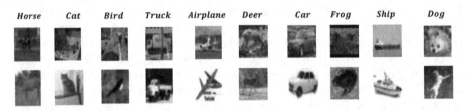

Fig. 4. A comparison between samples chosen through the *Select Base on Intra-Class Similarity* (SICS) approach from the CIFAR10 dataset. Specifically, the upper row displays the most distinctive-variant samples with high *var_freq* values, while the lower row showcases the samples with low *var_freq* values.

4.1   Experimental Setup

Opting for a custom two-layer CNN for MNIST's low-resolution data and a pretrained Resnet18 for other datasets, we applied the pruned dataset to the feature extraction model for generalization accuracy evaluation. The experiments were expedited on multiple 3080Ti GPUs for computational efficiency.

Datasets. Our experiments leveraged multiple benchmark datasets: MNIST with 70,000 28×28 grayscale digit images, CIFAR10 and CIFAR100 containing 60,000 32×32 color images across 10 and 100 classes respectively, STL10 comprising 96×96 color images across ten classes with an additional 100,000 unlabeled images for unsupervised learning, and the Oxford Pets dataset, featuring diverse pet images across 37 categories. We partitioned the Oxford Pets dataset into training and testing sets in an 8:2 ratio.

Backbones. In this experimental setup, we used various backbone networks to extract features. For ResNet18, we reduced the output dimension by 99.5%, from

---

Algorithm 2: Selecting Distinctive-variant Samples based on Intra-class Similarity

---

Input: List of tuples for each class we gain from last algorithm $sim\_list_{C_k}$, set of all classes C, set of thresholds Th

Output: Retention dataset for each class $retention_{C_k}$

1 **foreach** $C_k \in C$ **do**
2   Initialize empty set Var_{C_k}, list var_des to store samples on frequncy in descending order, variable R to store the retention ratio of dataset, variable $freq_x$ to count frequncy of sample x, and list of tuple var_list to store each sample and its frequncy ;
3   **foreach** $((x_i, x_j), sim_{x_i,x_j}) \in sim\_list_{C_k}$ **do**
4   **if** $sim_{x_i,x_j} \geq Th_{C_k}$ **then**
5               $Var_{C_k} \leftarrow Var_{C_k} \cup (x_i, x_j)$;
6   **end**
7   **end**
8   add each sample in each pairwise sample in Var_{C_k} to $variant_{C_k}$;
9   **foreach** $sample\ x \in C_k$ **do**
10          $freq_x \leftarrow var\_freq(x, variant_{C_k})$;
11   add $(x, freq_x)$ to var_list ;
12   **end**
13   Sort var_list on $freq_x$ for $\forall x \in C_k$ in descending order and store the sorted samples into $var\_des_{C_k}$ by same order;
14   Initialize empty set $retention_{C_k}$;
15   **foreach** $x \in var\_des_{C_k}$ **do**
16          $retention_{C_k} \leftarrow retention_{C_k} \cup x$;
17   **if** $|retention_{C_k}| = |C_k| \times R$ **then**
18   **break**;
19   **end**
20   **end**
21 **end**
22 **return** $retention_{C_k}$ for each class C_k in C

1000 to 5, and initialized it with a unit matrix. We also froze the parameters to avoid overfitting. For the customized CNN model, we only used the convolutional layers as features. This simplified the model and improved the feature quality.

Training Setup. Post-pruning, we retrained a model, assessing test accuracy across datasets to exhibit our method's generalization and competitive performance. Training involved 200 epochs for MNIST, CIFAR10, CIFAR100, and Oxford Pets, with STL10 at 100 epochs, utilizing SGD optimizer with momentum and suitable schedulers for optimization.

4.2   Results Analysis

Compare with Forgetting Score Method. Figure 5 presents the experimental results in comparison with the $ForgettingScore$ method [14]. The x-axis

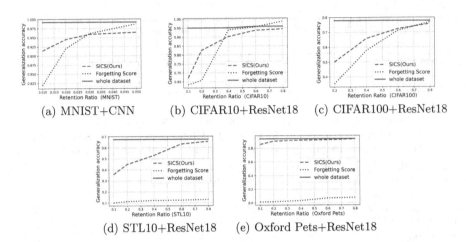

(a) MNIST+CNN   (b) CIFAR10+ResNet18   (c) CIFAR100+ResNet18

(d) STL10+ResNet18   (e) Oxford Pets+ResNet18

Fig. 5. Impact of pruning different percentages of the training data The horizontal red solid line represents training with the whole training data without data pruning; The horizontal blue dot represents a *ForgettingScore* pruning away of the same amount of data; The green dashed lines represent the results of using *SICS*(Our method) to prune the data.

represents the retention ratio, where a higher ratio indicates a lower percentage of pruned training samples, e.g., 80% retention ratio means 20% of samples are pruned. The y-axis represents the model accuracy achieved by training only on the retained data. The solid line in each figure represents the results obtained without data pruning, while our method is depicted by a dashed line and the forget method by a dotted line.

Our proposed SICS approach demonstrates significant performance improvements in Fig. 5a, achieving up to 10% higher accuracy on MNIST when the retention ratio is between 1% and 3%. On CIFAR10 in Fig. 5b, SICS achieves up to 17% higher accuracy with a 35% retention ratio. Similarly, on CIFAR100 in Fig. 5c, SCIS outperforms the *ForgettingScore* method by up to 15% accuracy under a 70% retention ratio. The performance gap is even more pronounced in Fig. 5d and Fig. 5e, with accuracy improvements of 56% and 80% across all retention ratios. These results highlight the significant advantage of our approach over the *ForgettingScore*, particularly at low retention ratios.

Our method achieves higher accuracy than the Forgetting Score on different datasets, especially when the original dataset has higher image resolution or more categories to be classified. This trend is highlighted in Table 1, where we compare our method with the Forgetting Score on various datasets with different characteristics.

Based on Table 1, it is evident that the Oxford Pets dataset and the STL10 dataset outshine the other datasets in terms of resolution. Moreover, the Oxford Pets dataset stands out with its larger number of categories compared to the other datasets. By employing our method, we were able to achieve a considerable

Table 1. A comparison of the generalization accuracy on $SICS$(Ours) and Forgetting Score when different datasets are used with different proportions of data retention. We bold the results that are better than the $ForgettingScore$.

Dataset	Resolution	Retention Ratio	SICS(Ours)	Forgetting Score
MNIST(CNN)	28×28	1%	**0.914**	**0.819**
		2%	**0.945**	**0.920**
		3%	0.959	0.961
		5%	0.964	0.987
CIFAR10(resnet18)	32×32	10%	**0.671**	**0.634**
		20%	**0.826**	**0.658**
		40%	0.903	0.940
		60%	0.937	0.956
		80%	0.944	0.959
CIFAR100(resnet18)	32×32	20%	**0.496**	**0.384**
		40%	**0.658**	**0.593**
		60%	**0.724**	**0.713**
		80%	0.758	0.769
STL10(resnet18)	96×96	10%	**0.357**	**0.101**
		20%	**0.448**	**0.112**
		40%	**0.529**	**0.121**
		60%	**0.632**	**0.123**
		80%	**0.655**	**0.129**
Oxford Pets(resnet18)	over 200×200	10%	**0.856**	**0.014**
		20%	**0.903**	**0.018**
		40%	**0.919**	**0.032**
		60%	**0.925**	**0.069**
		80%	**0.936**	**0.078**

improvement in generalization accuracy, which was almost 60% on STL10 and more than 90% on Oxford Pets when compared to the baseline. This remarkable improvement validates our hypothesis.

Generalization Capability on Different Models. The $SICS$ methodology entails the careful selection of critical training samples through a meticulous analysis of feature similarity within each class. As part of our ongoing research, we aim to further expand the scope of our experiments by leveraging the selected dataset to evaluate various models. Notably, our training process solely utilized distinctive-variant samples that were previously identified through the pre-trained ResNet18 model on the MobileNet-v2 model. The experiments were conducted on the CIFAR10 dataset, employing the forgetting-score and random approach as evaluation metrics. Table 2 showcases the comparative results, indicating that the *SICS* approach consistently maintains a substantial advantage of up to 25% over the forgetting-score method and up to 5% over the random approach. The experimental findings affirm that the *SICS* approach exhibits good generation capability when applied to diverse models.

Table 2. A comparison of the generalization accuracy on SICS(Ours) and Random-chose samples of CIFAR10 on MobileNet-v2 are used with different proportions of data retention.

Dataset	Retention Ratio	SICS(Ours)	Forgetting Score	Random
CIFAR10	10%	**0.357**	**0.233**	**0.313**
	20%	**0.576**	**0.329**	**0.525**
	40%	**0.753**	**0.603**	**0.748**
	60%	0.815	**0.784**	0.819
	80%	**0.840**	**0.831**	**0.832**

5   Conclusion and Future Work

In this study, we have introduced a novel approach called *Select Base on Intra-Class Similarity*, which leverages the concept of *distinctive-variant samples* to efficiently prune training data for classification tasks without compromising performance. Our experimental results on multiple datasets have demonstrated the effectiveness and robustness of our proposed method, particularly at high resolutions and across various model architectures. These findings have important implications for improving the efficiency and scalability of data-centric methods and offer a fresh perspective on data pruning and data diet.

In the future, we plan to: (1) use more diverse datasets due to limitations in our current datasets; (2) streamline the sample-selecting process to reduce the number of steps involved, and (3) explore data pruning and data diet applications in other domains.

References

1. Abramowitz, M., Stegun, I.A., Romer, R.H.: Handbook of Mathematical Functions with Formulas, Graphs, and Mathematical Tables (1988)
2. Brown, T., et al.: Language models are few-shot learners. Adv. Neural. Inf. Process. Syst. **33**, 1877–1901 (2020)
3. Castellani, A., Schmitt, S., Hammer, B.: Stream-based active learning with verification latency in non-stationary environments. In: Pimenidis, E., Angelov, P., Jayne, C., Papaleonidas, A., Aydin, M. (eds.) Artificial Neural Networks and Machine Learning–ICANN 2022. ICANN 2022. Lecture Notes in Computer Science, vol. 13532, pp. 260–272. Springer, Cham (2022). https://doi.org/10.1007/978-3-031-15937-4_22

4. Coleman, C., et al.: Selection via proxy: efficient data selection for deep learning. arXiv preprint arXiv:1906.11829 (2019)

5. Deng, J., Dong, W., Socher, R., Li, L.J., Li, K., Fei-Fei, L.: Imagenet: a large-scale hierarchical image database. In: 2009 IEEE Conference on Computer Vision and Pattern Recognition, pp. 248–255. IEEE (2009)

6. He, K., Zhang, X., Ren, S., Sun, J.: Deep residual learning for image recognition. In: Proceedings of the IEEE Conference on Computer Vision and Pattern Recognition, pp. 770–778 (2016)

7. Huang, G., Liu, Z., Van Der Maaten, L., Weinberger, K.Q.: Densely connected convolutional networks. In: Proceedings of the IEEE Conference on Computer Vision and Pattern Recognition, pp. 4700–4708 (2017)

8. Koh, P.W., Liang, P.: Understanding black-box predictions via influence functions. In: International Conference on Machine Learning, pp. 1885–1894. PMLR (2017)

9. Manwar, A., Mahalle, H.S., Chinchkhede, K., Chavan, V.: A vector space model for information retrieval: a Matlab approach. Indian J. Comput. Sci. Eng. $3(2)$, 222–229 (2012)

10. Nosofsky, R.M.: Attention, similarity, and the identification-categorization relationship. J. Exp. Psychol. Gen. $115(1)$, 39 (1986)

11. Paul, M., Ganguli, S., Dziugaite, G.K.: Deep learning on a data diet: finding important examples early in training. Adv. Neural. Inf. Process. Syst. 34, 20596–20607 (2021)

12. Settles, B.: Active learning literature survey (2009)

13. Simonyan, K., Zisserman, A.: Very deep convolutional networks for large-scale image recognition. arXiv preprint arXiv:1409.1556 (2014)

14. Toneva, M., Sordoni, A., Combes, R.T., Trischler, A., Bengio, Y., Gordon, G.J.: An empirical study of example forgetting during deep neural network learning. arXiv preprint arXiv:1812.05159 (2018)

15. Zhu, C., Chen, W., Peng, T., Wang, Y., Jin, M.: Hard sample aware noise robust learning for histopathology image classification. IEEE Trans. Med. Imaging $41(4)$, 881–894 (2021)

Semantic Information Mining and Fusion Method for Bot Detection

Lijia Liang[✉][ID], Xinzhong Wang[ID], and Gongshen Liu[ID]

School of Electronic Information and Electrical Engineering,
Shanghai Jiao Tong University, Shanghai 200240, China
{lianglijia,2046449167,lgshen}@sjtu.edu.cn

Abstract. Twitter bot detection is a crucial yet challenging task. The existing bot detection methods have limited semantic information mining ability for a large number of tweets posted by social media users. To address this challenge, we propose SIMF, which stands for Semantic Information Mining and Fusion. SIMF leverages a pre-training scorer to rank a large number of a user's tweets, and filters them based on specific rules. Additionally, SIMF preprocesses tweets and integrates multiple information encodings to obtain user representation, which enhances its ability to capture a diverse array of fake bots. Our comprehensive experiments on the benchmark TwiBot-20 demonstrate that SIMF outperforms other competitive algorithms.

Keywords: Twitter Bot Detection · Social Media · Semantic Information Mining

1 Introduction

With the rapid development of social networks, millions of users are active on social platforms such as Twitter, Weibo and so on. Nowadays, social networks have gradually become an important part of people's online life. But in addition to genuine users, social networks are also home to a large number of social bots, automated programs that mimic normal human behavior on social networks with a purpose. Some malicious bots will actively participate in online discussions of important events in an attempt to manipulate opinions, such as election intervention [1]. Malicious bots are also responsible for spreading low-credibility information [2] and extreme ideologies [3]. The appearance of malicious social bots has a bad effect on the order of social networks and is a serious threat to the security of cyberspace. Therefore, it is of great practical significance to detect bot accounts on social networks.

Twitter bots hide their automated nature by mimicking real users. Because identifying bots in social media is critical to maintaining the integrity of online discourse, much research work has been devoted to identifying bots active on Twitter. Over the past few years, a number of people have proposed machine learning frameworks for bot detection on Twitter (refer to the Related Work

L. Iliadis et al. (Eds.): ICANN 2023, LNCS 14262, pp. 270–282, 2023.
https://doi.org/10.1007/978-3-031-44201-8_23

section). But challenges remain due to the diversity and dynamic behavior of social bots. Most current methods try to identify bots by a user's property information, which means new bots can be specifically designed to evade existing detection systems.

However, Twitter bots often need to send tweets to achieve their purposes, such as influencing public opinion and promoting advertisements. The tweets they release are different from those of real users, which makes it possible to detect the bots through their tweets. At the same time, based on the Transformer [4], a variety of large-scale pre-training language models(PLM) have emerged and show strong performance in various natural language processing tasks, mainly because the large-scale PLM improves the semantic information encoding performance and enriches the semantic representation input. However, most of these methods do not carry out in-depth research on how to extract semantic information more effectively, but simply use PLM to encode semantic information which limits the final detection ability of the model.

In this article, we propose a framework to address this challenge. By mining semantic information, especially tweets, beyond a user's property information, our model can process richer information and is less likely to miss bots designed to evade existing systems. We first train a scorer to rank a user's tweets and filters tweets according to specific rules. Then, multiple information is fused to obtain user representation. Obviously, how to combine multiple twitter user information for next detection step is also a big challenge. In this paper, we study different ways of mining semantic information and integrating multiple information to address the challenge of bot disguise.

Our contributions are as follows:

- We propose a tweet filter that improves the efficiency of semantic representation. By applying specific rules and rankings from a pre-training scorer, we reduce a large number of tweets to the most critical ones.
- We design a bot detection model that can incorporate various user information with flexibility.
- Our model outperforms other baselines in terms of F1-Score and Accuracy. Furthermore, the comparison between the experimental groups demonstrates the effectiveness of our model design (Fig. 1).

2   Related Work

Most existing bot detection methods are based on supervised machine learning. An earlier Twitter bot detection scheme proposed by Lee *et al.* [5] focuses on feature engineering with user information. Yang *et al.* [6] design new features to counter the evolution of Twitter bots. Other features are also adopted, such as the information of a user's home page [7] and social networks [8]. Some methods also incorporate information from the content of tweets. For example, A recursive neural network proposed by Wei *et al.* [9] identifies bots with semantic information in tweets. Kudugunta *et al.* [10] develop a bot detector based on LSTM both considering user tweets and property information. Yang *et al.* [11] take a new

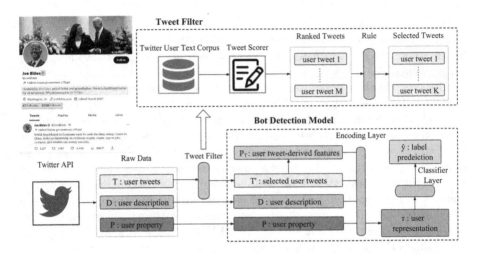

Fig. 1. Overall architecture of SIMF

perspective and minimize account metadata to scale and generalize social bot detection. Graphics-based bot detectors are also being developed, which consider social user's neighborhood information. Alhosseini *et al.* [12] regard Twitter as a user network and use graphical convolutional networks for bot detection. SATAR [13] proposes a task to learn the representation of the user and is fine-tuned for the robot detection task. BotRGCN [14] further constructs a heterogeneous information network to represent Twitter and uses relational graph convolutional networks for bot detection. Finally, RGT [15] constructs a heterogeneous information network with users as nodes and decentralized relationships as edges, and conducts heterogeneous sensing Twitter bot detection.

Large data sets are also essential for training and evaluating bot detection methods. The earliest bot detection data set is caverlee-2011 [7]. The bot accounts in the Cresci-17 [16] data set contain more granular breakdown: traditional spambots, social spambots, and fake followers. Recent data sets include verified-2019 [11], botwiki-2019 [11], cresci-rtbust-2019 [17], Astroturf [18]. In order to facilitate the use of multi-modal user information, Feng *et al.* [19] construct TwiBot-20 containing semantic, property and neighborhood information.

3   Problem Definition

Let $D = \{d_i\}_{i=1}^{L_D}$ represents a user's description with L_D words. Let $T = \{t_i\}_{i=1}^{M}$ represents a user's M tweets. And $t_i = \{w_1^i, \cdots, w_{Q_i}^i\}$ represents each tweet with Q_i words. Let $P = \{p_i\}_{i=1}^{N}$ represents a user's N property features. Let y represents a user's label, generally "0" represents a genuine user, and "1" represents a bot. The bot detection task through a user's information is to identify the label y with the help of the following information D, T, P.

4   Tweet Filter

How to filter more effective content from the mass of tweets sent by Twitter users is the problem of tweet filtering. We first use the user data (D, T, P) in the data set to construct a Twitter user text corpus, which will be used to train a scorer to evaluate the tendency of a tweet to be a bot. The scorer then calculates a score for each tweet that can be used to filter subsequent tweets. As we can see that certain rules are used to calculate scores in some competitions, for example, the highest and lowest scores are removed before the average score is calculated. So we propose some rules to be applied to tweet filtering, and their effectiveness will be investigated in later experiments. Besides, the tweet preprocessing method also should be taken into account.

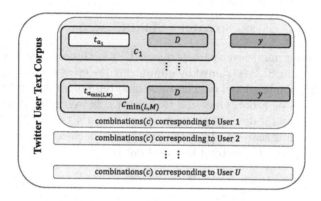

Fig. 2. The process of constructing the Twitter User Text Corpus

4.1   Twitter User Text Corpus

Figure 2 illustrates the process of constructing a Twitter user text corpus. To begin, we extract the tweets, descriptions, and labels of U users from the source dataset. Next, we select L tweets from each user's M tweets. If M is less than L, we take out all M tweets. The randomly selected i^{th} tweet is represented by t_{a_i}, then combined with the user's description D and label y to form $\min(L, M)$ pieces of data. Let c represents the combination of a single tweet and a single description. Therefore, each piece of data is composed of combination c and label y:

$$\{(t_{a_i}, D), y\}_{i=1}^{\min(L,M)} = \{c_i, y\}_{i=1}^{\min(L,M)} \tag{1}$$

Since a single user can generate multiple pieces of data in the Twitter user text corpus, we can easily create a larger corpus by including all user data from the source dataset.

4.2   Tweet Scorer

Based on the constructed Twitter user text corpus, We will then train a scorer to rate and filter a user's tweets.

Firstly, we define the feature extraction method of the combination of a tweet and a description, c. We use the large-scale PLM BERT [20] to extract features. Specifically we put tweets/descriptions into the BERT, and take the pooling average of the 12th layer as the feature extraction vector:

$$\text{BERT}(c) = [\text{BERT}(t); \text{BERT}(D)] \tag{2}$$

All input combinations of a tweet and a description, $\{c_1, c_2, \cdots, c_{|c|}\}$, receive the scores $\{s_1, s_2, \cdots, s_{|c|}\}$ by the tweet scorer, which includes the feature extractor and a single-layer perceptron (SLP):

$$s = \text{Scorer}(c) = \text{SLP}(\text{BERT}(c)) \tag{3}$$

We avoid using multi-layer perceptrons(MLP) in this scenario because MLP tends to overfit. The SLP is trained by minimizing the cross entropy loss between s_i and the corresponding label y_i. The value of s_i represents the likelihood of the combination c_i to be a bot. Once the tweet scorer is well trained, we associate corresponding a user's description with all of a user's tweets $T = \{t_i\}_{i=1}^{M}$ to obtain corresponding scores $\{s_i\}_{i=1}^{M}$. We can then rank each tweet by their scores from smallest to largest, resulting in a ranking $\{r_i\}_{i=1}^{M}$.

4.3   Rule

Due to the large number of tweets posted by users (usually $M \gg 100$), we will try to select K tweets by the ranking r. We want to find out which segment of the ranked tweets is best to distinguish between genuine users and bots.

- High: This rule assumes a significant difference between highly ranked tweets from bots and those from genuine users. It means selecting K tweets with the highest rating.
- Low: This rule assumes a gap between lowly ranked tweets from bots and those from genuine users. It means selecting K tweets with the lowest rating.
- Mid: This rule assumes that both overrated and underrated tweets are biased. It means choosing K tweets with a rating in the middle range.
- Rand: This rule assumes that the overall difference between bots and real users is most noticeable. It means K tweets are randomly chosen, and the first K tweets are chosen for simplicity.

4.4   Preprocessing

In general, a tweet can be divided into the following parts: the text posted by the user, other users mentioned in the tweet (users can use the "@user" format

Table 1. Tweet preprocesing example

Preprocesing	Tweet after preprocessing
Raw	@White: POTUS remarks at the 2020 Council https://www.xxx.com
Sub	@user POTUS remarks at the 2020 Council http
Del	POTUS remarks at the 2020 Council

to remind a specific user to follow the tweet), the topic of the tweet (users can use the "#topic" format to remind a specific user to follow the tweet), and the url of the tweet. Messy "@user" symbols and url links may reduce the feature extraction ability of PLM. In this part, we propose some preprocessing methods to solve this problem. Let $T = \{t_i\}_{i=1}^{M}$ represent a user's original M tweets. Three preprocessing methods are defined below. Table 1 shows an example of them.

- Raw: Nothing is done because it assumes preprocessing is not necessary.
- Sub: Replace words beginning with "@" with "@user", and replace words beginning with "http" with "http".
- Del: Delete words beginning with "@" or "http".

5 Bot Detection Model

5.1 User Representation

After getting selected tweets T', we combine user property information P and description D to classify users. In addition, We propose tweet-derived features to help bot detection.

Description Vector. We apply BERT to description feature extraction. Descriptions are input into the BERT model, and the pooling average of the 12th layer is used as the output of sentences:

$$r_D = \text{BERT}(D), \quad r_D \in \mathbb{R}^{D_{des} \times 1} \tag{4}$$

where D_{des} is equal to the dimension of the pooling average from BERT 12th layer.

Tweet Vector. We propose two tweet encoding methods to gain tweet vector. One is to concatenate K tweets and encode them by BERT at one time; the other is to encode K tweets separately and then average them. Following r_T^1 and r_T^2 are collectively referred to by tweet vector r_T.

- Concat: Use "[SEP]" symbol to concatenate K tweets, then use BERT to encode the whole concatenated tweet:

$$\hat{t} = [t_1; [SEP]; \cdots ; [SEP]; t_K], t_i \in T' \tag{5}$$

$$r_T^1 = BERT(\hat{t}), \quad r_T^1 \in \mathbb{R}^{D_{tweet} \times 1} \tag{6}$$

where D_{tweet} is equal to D_{des} for the same reason.

- Average: The second approach starts by encoding each tweet using BERT, then average all K vectors:

$$\overline{t_i} = BERT(t_i), \quad t_i \in T' \tag{7}$$

$$r_T^2 = \sum_{i=1}^{K} \overline{t_i}, \quad r_T^2 \in \mathbb{R}^{D_{tweet} \times 1} \tag{8}$$

Property Vector. Most methods attempt to identify bots by user property, which means that new bots can be specially designed to evade existing detection systems. Therefore, we only use the user property "verified" to assist our detection. This property "verified" indicates to others that the user has been verified by Twitter.

$$P = \begin{cases} 0 & , \text{ if verified} = \text{False} \\ 1 & , \text{ if verified} = \text{True} \end{cases} \tag{9}$$

Tweet-Derived Vector. We also attempt to extract a tweet-derived vector P_T from tweets. $Num_@, Num_\#, Num_{http}$ means the number of "@","#","http" symbols in T'. $Rate_@, Rate_\#, Rate_{http}$ represents the frequency of the corresponding symbols in T'. $Rate_{clean}$ means the ratio of the length of T' after Raw preprocesing to Del preprocessing.

$$P_T = [Num_@; Num_\#; Num_{http}; Rate_@; Rate_\#; Rate_{http}; Rate_{clean}], \quad P_T \in \mathbb{R}^{7 \times 1} \tag{10}$$

User Representation Vector. We can flexibly select the combination of the above vectors and then concatenate them to get the user representation vector r. For example, we use the concatenation of all the above vectors to get:

$$r = [r_D; r_T; P; P_T], \quad r \in \mathbb{R}^{D_{user} \times 1}$$

where D_{user} is the user representation vector dimension.

5.2   Classifier Layer

Let r_i represents the user representation vector of user i. We use a single-layer neural network with activation function for prediction.

$$\hat{y}_i = \text{softmax}(W_O \cdot r_i + b_O) \tag{11}$$

where W_O, b_O are learnable parameters.

The loss function is composed of supervised annotations and a regularization term, shown as follows:

$$\text{Loss} = -\sum_{i \in U} [y_i \log (\hat{y}_i) + (1 - y_i) \log (1 - \hat{y}_i)] + \lambda \sum_{w \in \theta} w^2 \qquad (12)$$

where U represents the set of labeled users, y_i is the label of the real user i, and θ is all the learnable parameters in the classifier.

6   Experiments

6.1   Experiment Settings

Data Set. TwiBot-20 [19] contains 229,573 Twitter users, 33,488,192 tweets, 8,723,736 user property items and 455,958 follow relationships. We apply our model in TwiBot-20 according to the classification of training, verification and test sets in the original benchmark.

Twitter User Text Corpus Details. For each user in the training set and verification set of TwiBot-20, we randomly select $L = 10$ tweets to form a Twitter user text corpus.

Hyperparameters. BERT-base is chosen when we need to use BERT to extract semantic features. In Tweet Filter, the optimizer and learning rate of SLP are SGD and 0.001. We train our SLP for 200 steps with the batch size as 200. In Bot Detection Model, the optimizer, learning rate, λ and dropout of the Classifier Layer are AdamW, 0.00001, 0.000001, 0.3. We train our Bot Detection Model for 3000 epochs with the batch size as 64.

Baseline Methods

– **Kudugunta** et al. [10]: Kudugunta et al. propose an architecture considering both user tweet and user property.
– **Yang** et al. [11]: Yang et al. attempt to find minimal account metadata and use random forest classifier.
– **Wei** et al. [9]: Wei et al. identify bots by a three-layer BiLSTM for bot detection with semantic information.
– **Lee** et al. [7]: Lee et al. focus on user engineering and use random forest to classify.
– **Miller** et al. [21]: Miller et al. detect bot by feature engineering of user information.
– **Alhosseini** et al. [12]: Alhosseini et al. regard Twitter as a user network and use graphical convolutional networks for bot detection.

Table 2. Bot Detection performance on TwiBot-20 benchmark. The letters **P**, **S**, and **N** in the "Type" column indicates whether a baseline is based on property information, semantic information, or neighborhood information.

Method	Type	F1-score	Acc
Kudugunta *et al.* [10]	P	0.8174	0.7517
Yang *et al.* [11]	P	0.8546	0.8191
Wei *et al.* [9]	S	0.7533	0.7126
SIMF(S)	S	**0.7842**	**0.7548**
Lee *et al.* [7]	PS	0.7823	0.7459
Miller *et al.* [21]	PS	0.6266	0.4801
SIMF(PS)	PS	**0.8857**	**0.8698**
Alhosseini *et al.* [12]	PSN	0.7318	0.6813
Botometer [22]	PSN	0.4892	0.5584
SATAR [13]	PSN	0.8642	0.8412
BotRGCN [14]	PSN	0.8707	0.8462
RGT [15]	PSN	0.8821	0.8664

- **Botometer** [22]: Botometer is a widely used service that leverages many features.
- **SATAR** [13]: SATAR does a task to learn the representation of the user and is fine-tuned for the robot detection task.
- **BotRGCN** [14]: BotRGCN develops a heterogeneous information network to represent Twitter and use relational GNN for bot detection.
- **RGT** [15]: RGT conducts heterogeneous sensing Twitter bot detection by constructing a heterogeneous information network with users as nodes and decentralized relationships as edges.

6.2   Bot Detection Performance

Table 2 shows the bot detection performance on TwiBot-20. The SIMF(S) method utilizes only semantic information, whereas the SIMF(PS) method combines both property and semantic information. The results indicate that SIMF(PS) achieves the best performance among all the methods, as it has strong semantic information extraction abilities. Additionally, SIMF(S), which only uses semantic information, outperforms other models that rely solely on semantic information. These findings demonstrate that SIMF can effectively utilize the semantic information of Twitter users.

6.3   Semantic Information Study

In semantic information extraction, selecting the appropriate K value, rules, and tweet encoding method is crucial. The performance of the SIMF model under

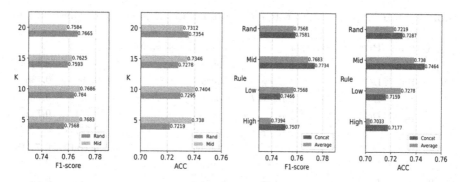

Fig. 3. The chart on the left shows SIMF(S) performance with different K while Preprocessing = Del, Tweet Encoding Method = Average; the right chart shows SIMF(S) performance with different Rule while $K = 5$, Preprocessing=Del.

different rules and tweet encoding methods when $K = 5$ is shown in the right chart of Fig. 3. The results indicate that both the "Mid" and "Rand" rules are effective, and the "Concat" tweet encoding method has a slightly better effect than the "Average" tweet encoding method when $K = 5$.

We also investigate whether the model's effectiveness changes with different values of K, as shown in the left chart of Fig. 3. When using the "Average" tweet encoding method, the "Mid" rule does not require a large K value, and its best effect is inferior to that of the "Concat" tweet encoding method with $K = 5$. Conversely, the "Rand" rule favors larger K values, as tweets encoded with larger K values tend to be more representative of a user's overall behavior.

In summary, based on the experiments conducted above, we have identified two optimal combinations of parameters for K, rule, and tweet encoding method: {5, "Mid", "Concat"} and {20, "Rand", "Average"}. Table 3 displays the model's performance for different preprocessing and user representation techniques, using these two combinations as the baseline. Our analysis reveals that the "Sub" preprocessing approach yields the best performance among the three methods tested. Additionally, we observed that P_T has a slightly negative effect on the results when only semantic information is considered.

6.4   Fusion Information Study

In the fusion information study, the semantic information extraction methods are the same combinations as above. The results in Table 4 demonstrate that incorporating property information significantly enhances the model's detection ability. Specifically, the inclusion of P_T results in a slight improvement when comparing experiments 1 and 2 to experiments 3 and 4. However, the inclusion of r_D has a negative impact on model performance, as seen in experiments 3–6.

It's worth noting that in experiments 3–10 as shown in Table 4, the combination of {5, "Mid", "Concat"} proves significantly more effective than {20, "Rand", "Average"}, underscoring the power of Tweet Filter. Moreover, the

Table 3. SIMF(S) performance with different preprocessings and user representations

No	K	Rule	Preprocessing	r	Tweet Encoding Method	F1-score	Acc
1	5	Mid	Del	$[r_D; r_T]$	Concat	0.7734	0.7464
2	20	Rand	Del	$[r_D; r_T]$	Average	0.7665	0.7354
3	5	Mid	Del	$[r_D; r_T; P_T]$	Concat	0.7705	0.7421
4	20	Rand	Del	$[r_D; r_T; P_T]$	Average	0.7712	0.7422
5	5	Mid	Sub	$[r_D; r_T]$	Concat	0.7771	0.7498
6	20	Rand	Sub	$[r_D; r_T]$	Average	**0.7842**	**0.7548**
7	5	Mid	Raw	$[r_D; r_T]$	Concat	0.7720	0.7439
8	20	Rand	Raw	$[r_D; r_T]$	Average	0.7713	0.7387
9	5	Mid	Sub	$[r_D; r_T; P_T]$	Concat	0.7744	0.7465
10	20	Rand	Sub	$[r_D; r_T; P_T]$	Average	0.7820	0.7540

Table 4. SIMF(PS) performance with different preprocessings and user representations

No	K	Rule	Preprocessing	r	Tweet Encoding Method	F1-score	Acc
1	5	Mid	Del	$[r_T; P]$	Concat	0.8769	0.8597
2	20	Rand	Del	$[r_T; P]$	Average	0.8800	0.8630
3	5	Mid	Del	$[r_T; P; P_T]$	Concat	0.8811	0.8648
4	20	Rand	Del	$[r_T; P; P_T]$	Average	0.8810	0.8648
5	5	Mid	Del	$[r_D; r_T; P; P_T]$	Concat	0.8805	0.8655
6	20	Rand	Del	$[r_D; r_T; P; P_T]$	Average	0.8771	0.8614
7	5	Mid	Sub	$[r_T; P; P_T]$	Concat	**0.8857**	**0.8698**
8	20	Rand	Sub	$[r_T; P; P_T]$	Average	0.8831	0.8672
9	5	Mid	Raw	$[r_T; P; P_T]$	Concat	0.8810	0.8655
10	20	Rand	Raw	$[r_T; P; P_T]$	Average	0.8798	0.8630

results from experiments 3, 4, and 7–10 reveal a notable variance across different preprocessing methods, with the "Sub" method outperforming the others.

7   Conclusion

Bot detection is an area of increasing interest. Our proposed method, SIMF, aims to improve the extraction ability of semantic information by filtering and encoding tweets, jointly encoding multiple user information, and constructing neural networks for classification. The SIMF approach is specifically designed to address the challenge of camouflaging bots. We conduct extensive experiments to demonstrate the effectiveness of SIMF compared to current state-of-the-art baseline methods. Further study has confirmed that SIMF offers significant advantages in bot detection by effectively mining and fusing semantic information.

Acknowledgment. This research work has been funded by Joint Funds of the National Natural Science Foundation of China (Grant No. U21B2020).

References

1. Deb, A., Luceri, L., Badaway, A., Ferrara, E.: Perils and challenges of social media and election manipulation analysis. In: Companion Proceedings of the 2019 World Wide Web Conference, pp. 237–247 (2019)
2. Shao, C., Ciampaglia, G.L., Varol, O., Yang, K.C., Flammini, A.: The spread of low-credibility content by social bots. Nat. Commun. 9(1), 1–9 (2018)
3. Berger, J. M., Morgan, J.: The ISIS Twitter census: defining and describing the population of ISIS supporters on Twitter. In: The Brookings project on US relations with the Islamic world 3, 20, 4–1 (2015)
4. Vaswani, A., Shazeer, N., Parmar, N., Uszkoreit, J.: Attention is all you need. In: Advances in Neural Information Processing Systems, vol. 30 (2017)
5. Lee, S., Kim, J.: WARNINGBIRD: a near real-time detection system for suspicious URLs in Twitter stream. IEEE Trans. Dependable Secur. Comput. 10(3), 183–195 (2013)
6. Yang, C., Harkreader, R., Gu, G.: Empirical evaluation and new design for fighting evolving Twitter spammers. IEEE Trans. Inf. Forensics Secur. 8(8), 1280–1293 (2013)
7. Lee, K., Eoff, B., Caverlee, J.: Seven months with the devils: a long-term study of content polluters on twitter. In: Proceedings of the International AAAI Conference on Web and Social Media, vol. 5, No. 1, pp. 185–192 (2011)
8. Minnich, A., Chavoshi, N., Koutra, D., Mueen, A.: BotWalk: efficient adaptive exploration of Twitter bot networks. In: Proceedings of the 2017 IEEE International Conference on Advances in Social Networks Analysis and Mining, pp. 467–474 (2017)
9. Wei, F., Nguyen, U.T.: Twitter bot detection using bidirectional long short-term memory neural networks and word embeddings. In: 2019 First IEEE International Conference on Trust, Privacy and Security in Intelligent Systems and Applications, pp. 101–109 (2019)
10. Kudugunta, S., Ferrara, E.: Deep neural networks for bot detection. Inf. Sci. 467, 312–322 (2018)
11. Yang, K.C., Varol, O., Hui, P.M., Menczer, F.: Scalable and generalizable social bot detection through data selection. In: Proceedings of the AAAI Conference on Artificial Intelligence, Vol. 34, No. 01, pp. 1096–1103 (2020)
12. Ali Alhosseini, S., Bin Tareaf, R., Najafi, P., Meinel, C.: Detect me if you can: spam bot detection using inductive representation learning. In: Companion Proceedings of the 2019 World Wide Web Conference, pp. 148–153 (2019)
13. Feng, S., Wan, H., Wang, N., Li, J., Luo, M.: Satar: a self-supervised approach to twitter account representation learning and its application in bot detection. In: Proceedings of the 30th ACM International Conference on Information & Knowledge Management, pp. 3808–3817 (2021)
14. Feng, S., Wan, H., Wang, N., Luo, M.: BotRGCN: Twitter bot detection with relational graph convolutional networks. In: Proceedings of the 2021 IEEE International Conference on Advances in Social Networks Analysis and Mining, pp. 236–239 (2021)
15. Feng, S., Tan, Z., Li, R., Luo, M.: Heterogeneity-aware twitter bot detection with relational graph transformers. In: Proceedings of the AAAI Conference on Artificial Intelligence, Vol. 36, No. 4, pp. 3977–3985 (2022)
16. Cresci, S., Di Pietro, R., Petrocchi, M., Spognardi, A.: The paradigm-shift of social spambots: evidence, theories, and tools for the arms race. In: Proceedings of the 26th International Conference on World Wide Web Companion, pp. 963–972 (2017)

17. Mazza, M., Cresci, S., Avvenuti, M., Quattrociocchi, W., Tesconi, M.: RTbust: exploiting temporal patterns for botnet detection on twitter. In: Proceedings of the 10th ACM Conference on Web Science, pp. 183–192 (2019)

18. Sayyadiharikandeh, M., Varol, O., Yang, K. C.: Detection of novel social bots by ensembles of specialized classifiers. In: Proceedings of the 29th ACM International Conference on Information & Knowledge Management, pp. 2725–2732 (2020)

19. Feng, S., Wan, H., Wang, N., Li, J., Luo, M.: TwiBot-20: a comprehensive twitter bot detection benchmark. In: Proceedings of the 30th ACM International Conference on Information & Knowledge Management, pp. 4485–4494 (2021)

20. Radford, A., Narasimhan, K., Salimans, T., Sutskever, I.: Improving language understanding by generative pre-training (2018)

21. Miller, Z., Dickinson, B., Deitrick, W., Hu, W., Wang, A.H.: Twitter spammer detection using data stream clustering. Inf. Sci. **260**, 64–73 (2014)

22. Davis, C. A., Varol, O., Ferrara, E., Flammini, A., Menczer, F.: BotOrNot: a system to evaluate social bots. In: Proceedings of the 25th International Conference Companion on World Wide Web, pp. 273–274 (2016)

Semilayer-Wise Partial Quantization Without Accuracy Degradation or Back Propagation

Tomoya Matsuda[1]([✉]), Kengo Matsumoto[1], Atsuki Inoue[1], Hiroshi Kawaguchi[1], and Yasufumi Sakai[2]

[1] Graduate School of Science, Technology and Innovation, Kobe University, 1-1 Rokkoudai, Nada, Kobe 657-8501, Hyogo, Japan
{matsuda.tomoya,matsumoto.kengo}@cs28.cs.kobe-u.ac.jp, {ainoue, kawapy}@godzilla.kobe-u.ac.jp
[2] Fujitsu Research, Fujitsu Limited, 4-1-1 Kamikodanaka, Nakahara, Kawasaki 211-8588, Kanagawa, Japan
sakaiyasufumi@fujitsu.com

Abstract. In edge AI technologies, reducing memory bandwidth and computational complexity without reducing inference accuracy is a key challenge. To address this difficulty, partial quantization has been proposed to reduce the number of bits in weight parameters of neural network models. However, existing techniques monotonically degrade accuracy with the compression ratio without retraining. In this paper, we propose an algorithm for semilayer-wise partial quantization without accuracy degradation or back-propagation retraining. Each layer is divided into two channel groups (semilayers): one being positive for loss degradation and the other negative. Each channel is classified as positive or negative in terms of cross-entropy loss and assigned to a semilayer accordingly. The evaluation was performed with validation data as input. Then, the quantization priority for every semilayer is determined based on the magnitude in the Kullback-Leibler divergence of the softmax output before and after quantization. We observed that ResNet models achieved no degradation in accuracy at certain parameter compression ratios (i.e., 79.43%, 78.01%, and 81.13% for ResNet-18, ResNet-34, and ResNet-50, respectively) in partial 6-bit quantization on classification tasks using the ImageNet dataset.

Keywords: Partial Quantization · Sensitivity Analysis · Image Classification

1 Introduction

Compression methods such as quantization [21], which reduces the number of bits, have been proposed to reduce the size and computational costs of neural network models. Quantization is an effective method of compressing learning models because it can reduce their size, memory requirements, and computational cost. Nonetheless, there is a tradeoff relation between the compression ratio and the accuracy of the compressed model; that is, quantization degrades accuracy. In previous studies on full quantization of neural networks, models were uniformly quantized with the same bit width [8, 16].

L. Iliadis et al. (Eds.): ICANN 2023, LNCS 14262, pp. 283–295, 2023.
https://doi.org/10.1007/978-3-031-44201-8_24

However, differing distributions of weights in each layer have been shown to exhibit different impacts on accuracy in quantization. Therefore, partial quantization, in which quantization is selectively performed for some parts of a model (e.g., layers), can be used to make a tradeoff between accuracy and size. Sensitivity analysis methods [20] have been proposed to answer the question of which layers and channels should be quantized; either accuracy or loss are used as measures of sensitivity. Layer-wise [18, 19] and channel-wise quantization [2, 11, 15] methods have been used to prioritize network regions where quantization should be performed. In these methods, quantization is performed on a layer-by-layer or channel-by-channel basis. Layer-wise quantization is more compatible with edge AI and is easy to handle for hardware owing to its larger granularity. In some earlier studies [7, 15, 18, 19], learning models were quantized without retraining. Naturally, quantized models must be created in a practical computation time. This approach also prevents the possible degradation of generalization performance owing to retraining. However, models quantized using these existing methods cannot be compressed sufficiently while maintaining accuracy.

In this study, to achieve compression of neural models while suppressing accuracy degradation resulting from quantization, we propose a new layer-wise partial quantization method. The proposed method examines the $\Delta loss$ of the entire model when quantizing only one channel for all convolutional layers of a pretrained neural network. The evaluation was performed with validation data as input. It then divides each convolutional layer into two channel groups according to the positive and negative values of $\Delta loss$ for all channels. These are referred to as "semilayers". The proposed method quantizes the model on a semilayer basis. We also incorporate Kullback-Leibler (KL) divergence in the sensitivity analysis. In fact, $\Delta loss$ includes more information than accuracy. Moreover, it is effective in terms of sensitivity [15]. However, the change compared to the original model cannot be considered by $\Delta loss$, whereas the KL divergence measures changes between models and tends to exhibit a large value when the absolute value of $\Delta loss$ is large. Thus, introducing KL divergence as a measure of sensitivity is effective in suppressing large model changes due to compression.

To evaluate the performance of the proposed method, we conducted experiments on standard image classification tasks using the ImageNet dataset [3] with various ResNet models [24] and the CIFAR-10 dataset [22] with a VGG-16-bn model [25]. The contributions of this study are summarized as follows:

- We propose a new quantization granularity for convolutional neural network (CNN) models, which considers "semilayers" as an alternative to layers and channels. A positive semilayer has positive channels in $\Delta loss$. A negative semilayer contains negative channels in $\Delta loss$. Consequently, the accuracy of this approach can be improved after priority quantization of the negative semilayers.
- For the sensitivity analysis, we consider KL divergence for each semilayer. Introducing KL divergence improves the tradeoff between accuracy and compression.
- We observed that the proposed semilayer-wise partial quantization exhibited maximum accuracy greater than that of baseline models, and that it caused no accuracy degradation at certain compression ratios in the image classification tasks of the ImageNet and CIFAR-10 datasets. For example, the proposed method maintained a 76.12% accuracy at a compression ratio of 81.13% for ResNet-50.

2   Related Work

Prior works have proposed a unified framework for CNNs, referred to as quantized CNNs (Q-CNNs) [21], which simultaneously accelerates and compresses CNN models with only slight performance degradation. The results indicate that Q-CNN models can perform especially fast computation in the testing phase and that they significantly reduce storage and memory requirements. Specifically, this approach can achieve 4–6× speedup and compress a model by a factor of 15–20 while decreasing classification accuracy by less than 1%. Furthermore, the Q-CNN models can be implemented on mobile devices and have been shown to classify images in less than one second. Quantization has also been widely adopted to assess compression methods. An earlier report [11] described that introducing channel-wise quantization instead of layer-wise quantization could reduce the degradation in accuracy after 8-bit quantization without finetuning. One study [2] indicated that a channel-wise quantization scheme that minimized the mean square error was effective for 4-bit quantization. In addition, a quantization step size designed to minimize cross-entropy loss has been used [14]. Another report [13] proposed the use of approximate loss functions to optimize rounding. As another approach, one study proposed performing partial quantization based on individually investigated layer sensitivities before employing quantization aware learning [20]. Reportedly, $\Delta loss$ analysis (DLA) [15], in which quantization is selectively performed depending on the parts of the model (e.g., layers), is useful to make a tradeoff between accuracy and model size. Along these lines, a sensitivity search method has also been proposed based on the idea that accuracy can be improved using $\Delta loss$, especially at the channel level of each convolutional layer. In other studies [18, 19], a deterministic greedy search algorithm (GSA) inspired by submodular optimization was used to derive a practical solution to the bit assignment problem without retraining. Another approach proposed a mixed hardware-friendly quantization (MXQN) method [7] that applies fixed-point quantization and logarithmic quantization without finetuning deep CNNs. Constrained-optimization-based algorithm for mixed-precision quantization (CQ) exploited Hessians [1], but it required retraining. In the present work, our proposed method allows sufficient quantization of the trained model without accuracy degradation or back-propagation retraining.

3   Proposed Method

For simplicity, the proposed method is described in this section using the case of a ResNet-18 model for the ImageNet dataset. We consider quantization for weights only and not for activation.

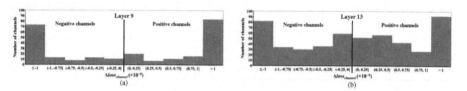

Fig. 1. Histograms of $\Delta loss_{channel}$ for all channels in layers (a) 9 and (b) 13 at 6-bit quantization.

3.1 Semilayer-Wise Quantization Using $\Delta loss$ per Channel

The ResNet-18 network has 16 convolutional layers. Here, we refer to these as layers 1, 2,..., 16, starting from the layer closest to the input. First, a pretrained model to be quantized[1] is prepared. Next, we perform a validation test on the trained model to check its baseline cross-entropy $loss_{before}$ as the classification error. The evaluation using ImageNet classification was performed with 50-k validation data as input. Then, only one of the first channels of the first layer is quantized, and a validation test is performed to obtain its cross-entropy loss $loss_{after-1,1}$. Similarly, after $loss_{after-i,j}$ is calculated for the i-th layer and the j-th channel, the difference between the loss functions $\Delta loss_{i,j}$ is calculated for every layer and every channel as

$$\Delta loss_{i,j} = loss_{after-i,j} - loss_{before}. \tag{1}$$

Some examples of the channel-wise distribution of $\Delta loss_{channel}$ for ImageNet classification when 6-bit quantization is applied in ResNet-18 are shown in Fig. 1. The horizontal axis represents the $\Delta loss_{channel}$ bins. Almost half of the channels have negative values in $\Delta loss_{channel}$. This may indicate that quantization of half of a pretrained model could improve its accuracy.

In quantization, a set of weights w are shifted by a quantization error Δw. In channel-wise quantization, the weights and quantization errors respectively have vectors with channel sizes w and Δw. In this case, $\Delta loss$ is approximated as a quadratic function [13]

$$\Delta loss \approx \Delta w^T \cdot g + 1/2\Delta w^T \cdot H \cdot \Delta w + \cdots, \tag{2}$$

where g and H denote the gradients and Hessians, respectively. Figure 2 shows the relationships between $\|\Delta w\|_1$ (an L1 norm for weights) and $\Delta loss$. Some channels apparently behave as quadratic functions; this phenomenon has been analyzed in [13]. In particular, some channels in the negative semilayer seem to have a minimum point in $\Delta loss$. That is, the 6-bit quantization is superior to others in this case. Therefore, we mainly chose 6-bit quantization.

We propose the division of each layer into two channel groups (semilayers) according to the positive and negative values of channel-wise $\Delta loss$. For example, if $\Delta loss$ of the first channel of layer 1 is negative, then it is assigned to the semilayer.

1-negative. The positive channel of layer 1 is assigned to the semilayer 1-positive. This process is performed for all channels in all layers. The purpose of this operation is to divide each layer into channels for which quantization is expected to improve accuracy and channels for which there is some possibility of decreasing accuracy.

---

[1] Note that the quantization method is the same approach as the "qint" cast in PyTorch [6].

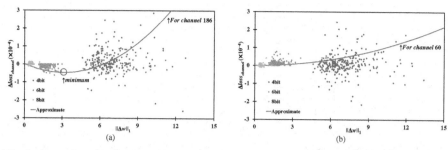

Fig. 2. Scattering plots of $\|\Delta w\|_1$ and $\Delta loss_{channel}$ for channels in layer 13 of a ResNet-18 model. (a) only channels with negative $\Delta loss_{channel}$ for 6-bit quantization and corresponding points for 4-bit and 8-bit quantizations are shown. (b) only channels with positive $\Delta loss_{channel}$ for 6-bit quantization and corresponding points for 4-bit and 8-bit quantizations are shown.

3.2 KL Divergence in Sensitivity Analysis

We calculated the KL divergence for all semilayers. The KL divergence DKL for a semilayer is calculated as follows.

$$D_{\mathrm{KL}}(P\|Q) = \sum\nolimits_{x \in X} P(x) \log \frac{P(x)}{Q(x)}, \tag{3}$$

where x is one of output, X is number of classifications (1000 for ImageNet classifications), $P(\cdot)$ denotes the softmax output of the pretrained model, and $Q(\cdot)$ denotes the softmax output of the model after quantization of all channels in a semilayer. The evaluation using ImageNet classification was performed with 50-k validation data as input. As described herein, KL divergence for each semilayer was calculated for all 50-k inputs individually. The average value of the 50-k data was taken as the KL divergence after quantization for that semilayer. This KL divergence was calculated for each of the 32 semilayers in ResNet-18 with 16 convolutional layers.

In the sensitivity analysis, KL divergence obtained using the operation above is normalized by the number of parameters in the semi-layer. In the proposed approach, KL divergence normalization is calculated as $KL_{parameterized}$

$$KL_{parameterized} = \frac{D_{\mathrm{KL}}(P\|Q)}{param(X)}, \tag{4}$$

where $param(\cdot)$ represents the number of parameters in the semilayer. In the case of a process that quantizes multiple parameters together, such as layer-wise quantization, a greater number of parameters quantized is associated with a greater effect on the output of the neural network. Therefore, to consider the number of parameters in a semilayer, we normalize KL divergence in Eq. (3) by the number of parameters in a given semilayer.

Actually, in sensitivity analysis, it might be seen that the $\Delta loss$ is more informative and effective for partial quantization [15]. However, the degree of change from the original model is not considered in $\Delta loss$ when it is used as a sensitivity. That is, a semilayer with larger absolute values of the $\Delta loss$ ($= \Delta loss_{semilayer}$) might incur greater model change. The large changes in weight prevent continuous compression without

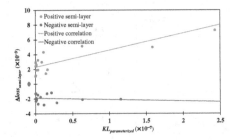

Fig. 3. Correlation between $KL_{parameterized}$ and $\Delta loss_{semilayer}$ with semilayers quantized.

accuracy degradation. Thus, we adopt the KL divergence to limit changes in the model or its weights to moderate levels. KL divergence tends to be smaller when the absolute values of the $\Delta loss_{semilayer}$ are smaller. Figure 3 shows the correlation between $KL_{parameterized}$ and $\Delta loss_{semilayer}$ for 6-bit quantization in ResNet-18 when each semilayer was quantized separately. The correlation coefficient of the negative semi-layer was -0.129. That of the positive semi-layer was 0.834. The figure shows that the absolute values of the $\Delta loss_{semilayer}$ with larger $KL_{parameterized}$ were larger. In fact, a more negative $\Delta loss_{semilayer}$ indicates good performance in terms of loss, but it is not effective as a measure of sensitivity owing to the large changes in the model. To suppress this shortcoming, the KL divergence is prioritized for the evaluation index.

3.3 Postponing Strategy after Sensitivity Analysis

For the $KL_{parameterized}$ obtained in the preceding subsection, all semilayers are quantized in order of decreasing value according to the sensitivity analysis findings. As an exception, we introduce "postponing" only once for each semilayer. This process ensures that the accuracy is improved and contributes to the efficiency of parameter compression. To perform this process within a practical computational time, we use semilayers, which is not a channel-wise approach, but rather is closer to layer-wise. In all, 32 semilayer-wise quantizations are performed on ResNet-18 models in order of decreasing $KL_{parameterized}$. In the postponing strategy, however, if the accuracy is lower than the state before semilayer-wise quantization, then the semilayer is not quantized at this time step, and is instead postponed. The next semilayer is examined and inference performed similarly, starting in the original sorted order. When all sorted semilayers have been examined, postponing the first trial is completed. An improvement in accuracy is expected in the first trial.

Next, the remaining semilayers that have not yet been quantized are quantized and inferred again as the second trial, according to the sensitivity analysis. The postponing strategy is not adopted in the second trial, where accuracy degradation is expected. Based on this tendency, by improving the accuracy in the first trial and slightly decreasing the accuracy in the second trial, accuracy and the parameter compression ratio are maximally improved without any reduction in accuracy, as shown by the results of the experiments described below. The pseudocode of the algorithm for the proposed semilayer-wise quantization is shown in Algorithm 1.

Algorithm 1: Proposed method

Input: Pre-trained FP32 model.

1: **for** $i = 1, 2, ..., I, j = 1, 2, ..., J$ **do**

2: $\quad \Delta loss_{i,j} = loss_{after-i,j} - loss_{before}$ (1)

3: **end for**

4: **for** $i = 1, 2, ..., I$ **do**

5: $\quad$ **semilayer_i-negative** $\leftarrow$ Index of channel with negative $\Delta loss_{i,j}$

6: $\quad$ **semilayer_i-positive** $\leftarrow$ Index of channel with positive $\Delta loss_{i,j}$

7: $\quad$ **semilayers** $\leftarrow$ **semilayer_i-negative, semilayer_i-positive**

8: **end for**

9: **for semilayers do**

10: $\quad D_{KL}(P||Q) = \sum_{x \in X} P(x) \log (\frac{P(x)}{Q(x)})$ (3)

11: $\quad KL_{parameterized} = \frac{D_{KL}(P||Q)}{param(x)}$ (4)

12: **end for**

13: **sorted_semilayers** $\leftarrow$ Index of $KL_{parameterized}$ sorted in decreasing order

14: **for** $s \in$ **sorted_semilayers do**

15: $\quad$ Quantize s and Inference model.

16: $\quad$ **if** the accuracy deteriorates when s is quantized

17: $\quad\quad$ Postpone quantization of s that was quantized.

18: $\quad\quad$ **skipped_semilayers** $\leftarrow s$

19: $\quad$ **end if**

20: **end for**

21: **for** $s \in$ **skipped_semilayers do**

22: $\quad$ Quantize s and Inference model.

23: **end for**

Output: Compressed model.

---

4 Experiments

4.1 ResNets for ImageNet

We used ResNet-18, ResNet-34, and ResNet-50 [24] in the experimental evaluation of the proposed approach. Figure 4 shows the results obtained from 6-bit and 4-bit quantizations using a pretrained ResNet-18 model as the ImageNet dataset. Our method compressed the number of parameters of the model by 79.43% in 6-bit quantization and by 33.82% for 4-bit quantization without degradation of accuracy. Figure 5 shows other results for the 6-bit and 4-bit quantizations on ResNet-34. Our method compressed the number of parameters by 78.01% for 6-bit quantization and by 38.05% compression for 4-bit quantization without degradation of accuracy. On ResNet-50, 6-bit quantization compressed the number of parameters by 81.13%, as shown in Fig. 6.

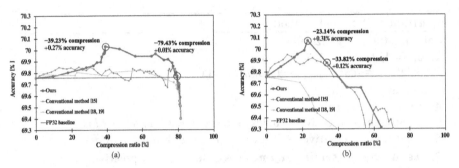

Fig. 4. Accuracies in (a) 6-bit quantization and (b) 4-bit quantization of a ResNet-18 model.

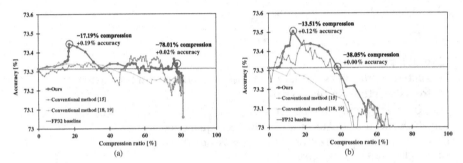

Fig. 5. Accuracies in (a) 6-bit quantization and (b) 4-bit quantization of a ResNet-34 model.

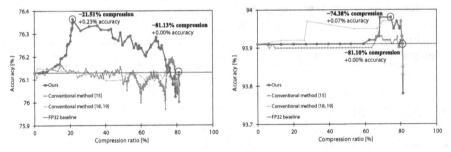

Fig. 6. Accuracies in 6-bit quantization of a ResNet-50 model.

Fig. 7. Accuracies in 6-bit quantization on a VGG-16-bn model for CIFAR-10 dataset.

4.2 VGG-16-bn for CIFAR-10

Figure 7 presents the results obtained for 6-bit quantization using VGG-16-bn as the trained model and a classification task on the CIFAR-10 evaluation dataset. Our method achieved 81.10% parameter compression with 6-bit quantization without accuracy degradation.

Table 1. Results for ImageNet dataset. The "*b*MP" refers to mixed-precision quantization, where *b* is the lowest bits used for weights.

Network	Method	Baseline	Quantization bit	Compression ratio	Top-1 /quant	Top-1 /rop	Retraining
ResNet-18	GSA [18, 19]	69.75%	4	±00.00%	69.75%	±0.00%	No
	GSA [18, 19]	69.75%	6	−64.34%	69.79%	+0.04%	No
	DLA [15]	69.75%	4	−35.23%	69.82%	+0.07%	No
	DLA [15]	69.75%	6	−79.06%	69.77%	+0.02%	No
	MXQN [7]	69.75%	8	−75.00%	67.61%	−2.14%	No
	CQ [1]	69.75%	3MP	−87.98%	69.66%	−0.09%	Yes
	CQ [1]	69.75%	2MP	−90.61%	69.39%	−0.36%	Yes
	Ours	69.75%	4	−33.82%	69.88%	+0.13%	No
	Ours	**69.75%**	**6**	**−79.43%**	**69.77%**	**+0.02%**	**No**
ResNet-34	GSA [18, 19]	73.31%	4	−12.23%	73.31%	±0.00%	No
	GSA [18, 19]	73.31%	6	−36.36%	73.33%	+0.02%	No
	DLA [15]	73.31%	4	− 34.26%	73.35%	+0.04%	No
	DLA [15]	73.31%	6	−69.88%	73.32%	+0.01%	No
	MXQN [7]	73.31%	8	−75.00%	71.43%	−1.88%	No
	Ours	73.31%	4	−38.05%	73.31%	±0.00%	No
	Ours	**73.31%**	**6**	**−78.01%**	**73.34%**	**+0.03%**	**No**
ResNet-50	GSA [18, 19]	76.12%	6	−73.45%	76.13%	+0.01%	No
	DLA [15]	76.12%	6	−79.36%	76.13%	+0.01%	No
	MXQN [7]	76.12%	8	−75.00%	74.06%	−2.06%	No
	CQ [1]	76.12%	2MP	−91.83%	75.28%	+0.16%	Yes
	Ours	**76.12%**	**6**	**− 81.13%**	**76.12%**	**±0.00%**	**No**

(*continued*)

Table 1. (*continued*)

Network	Method	Baseline	Quantization bit	Compression ratio	Top-1 /quant	Top-1 /rop	Retraining
VGG-16-bn	GSA [18, 19]	93.90%	6	− 81.03%	93.91%	+0.01%	No
	DLA [15]	93.90%	6	−80.83%	93.90%	±0.00%	No
	Ours	**93.90%**	**6**	**−81.10%**	**93.90%**	**±0.00%**	**No**

4.3 Comparison with Other Methods

Table 1 presents our experimental results. Compared with conventional methods, the proposed method provided sufficient compression without back-propagation retraining or accuracy degradation. The GSA and The DLA were ineffective because they achieved lower parameter compression values than the proposed method did. Mixed hardware-friendly quantization (MXQN) [7] and constrained optimization-based algorithm for mixed-precision quantization (CQ) [1] achieved a parameter compression ratio of 75.0% and 91.83%, respectively, in ResNet-50; especially, CQ was superior in terms of compression ratio. However, CQ was impractical because it required retraining and degraded the accuracy compared to the baseline.

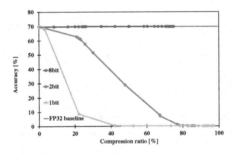

Fig. 8. Accuracies in 8-bit, 2-bit, and 1-bit quantizations.

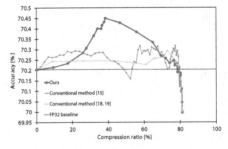

Fig. 9. Accuracies in 6-bit quantizations on 10 epochs trained ResNet-18.

4.4 Quantization with More and Fewer Bits

Here, we also provide experimental results obtained from 8-bit, 2-bit, and 1-bit quantizations of a ResNet-18 model. Figure 8 shows the results for 8-bit, 2-bit, and 1-bit quantization for the pretrained ResNet-18 model performing a classification task on the ImageNet evaluation dataset. The proposed method is not suitable for 8-bit quantization because the maximum compression ratio by bit reduction is lower than that of 6-bit quantization that can compress parameters efficiently. The 8-bit quantization is near the original pretrained model and far from the minimum point in $\Delta loss$ (see Fig. 2a). In the 2-bit and 1-bit quantizations, $\Delta loss$ seems to have reached a massive value, which cannot maintain accuracy.

4.5 Experiment with Another Trained Model

We ran the same experiment on another trained model under varying conditions to demonstrate the reproducibility of the proposed method. We experimented with a publicly available ResNet-18 model [24] that was retrained for 10 epochs by 1.2-M training data. Figure 9 shows the results obtained from 6-bit quantization using the retrained ResNet-18 model; we observed that the baseline was improved by 0.45% (compare to Fig. 4a). Even in such case, our method achieved 79.40% parameter compression for 6-bit quantization without accuracy degradation. These results show that the proposed method can provide efficient compression for models with different levels of training.

5 Conclusions

In this paper, we proposed a new method for the quantization of trained neural networks. This method enables more efficient compression without reduction of accuracy. The proposed method is a semilayer-wise quantization in which each layer is classified into two channel groups according to $\Delta loss$, in contrast to layer-wise quantization. The results of the experimental evaluation of the proposed method on classification tasks with the ImageNet dataset using various trained neural networks have shown that it can improve the tradeoff between reducing the size of a model and degrading its accuracy. Specifically, using a trained network as a starting point, the proposed method successfully compressed the number of parameters of a ResNet-18 model through 6-bit quantization by 79.43% without accuracy degradation, and by 78.01% and 81.13% for a ResNet-34 model with 6-bit quantization and a ResNet-50 model with 6-bit quantization, respectively.

References

1. Chen, W., Wang, P., Cheng, J.: Towards mixed-precision quantization of neural networks via constrained optimization. In: IEEE/CVF International Conference on Computer Vision (ICCV), pp. 5350–5359 (2021)
2. Choukroun, Y., Kravchik, E., Yang, F., Kisilev, P.: Low-bit Quantization of Neural Networks for Efficient Inference. arXiv preprint arXiv:1902.06822v2 (2019)

3. Deng, J., Dong, W., Socher, R., Li, L., Li, K., Fei-Fei, L.: Imagenet: a large-scale hierarchical image database. In: IEEE Conference on Computer Vision and Pattern Recognition (CVPR), pp. 248–255 (2009)
4. Girshick, R.: Fast R-CNN. In: IEEE International Conference on Computer Vision (ICCV), pp. 1440–1448 (2015)
5. Girshick, R., Donahue, J., Darrell, T., Malik, J.: Rich feature hierarchies for accurate object detection and semantic segmentation. In: IEEE Conference on Computer Vision and Pattern Recognition (CVPR), pp. 580–587 (2014)
6. He, K., Zhang, X., Ren, S, Sun, J.: Deep residual learning for image recognition. In: IEEE Conference on Computer Vision and Pattern Recognition (CVPR), pp. 770–778 (2016)
7. Huang, C., Liu, P., Fang, L.: MXQN: mixed quantization for reducing bit-width of weights and activations in deep convolutional neural networks. In: Applied Intelligence, vol. 51, pp. 1–14 (2021)
8. Jacob, B., et al.: Quantization and training of neural networks for efficient integer-arithmetic-only inference. In: IEEE Conference on Computer Vision and Pattern Recognition (CVPR), pp. 2704–2713 (2018)
9. Krizhevsky, A., Sutskever, I., Hinton, G.E.: Imagenet classification with deep convolutional neural networks. In: Neural Information Processing Systems (NIPS), pp. 1097–1105 (2012)
10. LeCun, Y., et al.: Backpropagation applied to handwritten zip code recognition. In: Neural Computation, vol. 1, pp. 541–551 (1989)
11. Lee, J.H., Ha, S., Choi, S., Lee, W., Lee, S.: Quantization for Rapid Deployment of Deep Neural Networks. arXiv:1810.05488 (2018)
12. Markidis, S., Chien, S.W.D., Laure, E., Peng, I.B., Vetter, J.S.: Nvidia Tensor Core Programmability, Performance Precision. arXiv:1803.04014v1 (2018)
13. Nagel, M., Amjad, R.A., Baalen, M.V., Louizos, C., Blankevoort, T.: Up or down? adaptive rounding for post-training quantization. In: International Conference on Machine Learning, PMLR, vol. 119, pp. 7197–7206 (2020)
14. Nahshan, Y., et al.: Loss aware post-training quantization. In: Machine Learning, vol. 110, pp. 3245–3262 (2021)
15. Ohkado, K., Matsumoto, K., Inoue, A., Kawaguchi, H., Sakai, Y.: Channel-wise quantization without accuracy degradation using $\Delta loss$ analysis. In: International Conference on Machine Learning Technologies (ICMLT), pp. 56–61 (2022)
16. Shuchang, Z., Yuxin, W., Zekun, N., Xinyu, Z., He, W., Yuheng. Z.: DoReFa-Net: Training Low Bitwidth Convolutional Neural Networks with Low Bitwidth Gradients. arXiv:1606.06160 (2016)
17. Simonyan, K., Zisserman, A.: Very deep convolutional networks for large-scale image recognition. In: IEEE Conference on Computer Vision and Pattern Recognition (CVPR), arXiv:1409.1556 (2015)
18. Tsuji, S., Yamada, F., Kawaguchi, H., Inoue, A., Sakai, Y.: Greedy search algorithm for partial quantization of convolutional neural networks inspired by submodular optimization. In: 2020 India International Congress on Computational Intelligence (2020)
19. Tsuji, S., Kawaguchi, H., Inoue, A., Sakai, Y., Yamada, F.: Greedy search algorithm for mixed precision in post-training quantization of convolutional neural network inspired by submodular optimization. In: Asian Conference on Machine Learning, PMLR, vol. 157, pp. 886–901 (2021)
20. Wu, H., Judd, P., Zhang, X., Isaev, M., Micikevicius, P.: Integer Quantization for Deep Learning Inference: Principles and Empirical Evaluation. arXiv:2004.09602 (2020)
21. Wu, J., Leng, C., Wang, Y., Hu, Q., Cheng, J.: Quantized convolutional neural networks for mobile devices. In: IEEE Conference on Computer Vision and Pattern Recognition (CVPR), pp. 4820–4828 (2016)

22. CIFAR-10. https://www.cs.toronto.edu/~kriz/cifar.html. Accessed 19 April 2023
23. PyTorch. https://pytorch.org. Accessed 19 April 2023
24. ResNet-18, https://download.pytorch.org/models/resnet18-5c106cde.pth. Accessed 19 April 2023
25. ResNet-34. https://download.pytorch.org/models/resnet34-333f7ec4.pth. Accessed 19 April 2023
26. ResNet-50. https://download.pytorch.org/models/resnet50-19c8e357.pth. Accessed 19 April 2023
27. VGG-16-bn. https://pytorch.org/vision/main/models/generated/torchvision.models.vgg16_bn.html. Accessed 19 April 2023

ShadowGAN for Line Drawings Shadow Generation

Huanhuan Xue and Chunmeng Kang[✉]

Shandong Normal University, Jinan, China
2986752830@qq.com, kcm89kimi@163.com

Abstract. Shadow performs an important role in the image, which can enhance the image effect and convey important visual clues. We propose a method based on deep learning to automatically generate stylized shadows for line drawings. Based on StarGAN, a shadow generation adversarial network (ShadowGAN) is designed, which can automate the creation of stylized shadows with different light directions. This method defines eight light directions. Users can select one of the eight light directions around the 2D image to specify the light source according to the encoding of the light direction, and generate the shadow corresponding to the light direction. We use a new dataset containing line drawings with shadows and label information corresponding to the light direction. Experiments show that our method can generate stylized shadows for line drawing with satisfactory quality, which can simplify the user's workflow, and save the time of drawing line drawing shadows.

Keywords: Stylized shadow · Line drawings · Deep learning · ShadowGAN

1 Introduction

The shadow is an important element in the drawing. Shadow can enhance the effect of image and convey important visual clues about scene depth, shape, motion and light [1]. Many artists paint shadows and lines to draw the outlines and express their ideas.

Stylized shadows are fundamentally different from physical shadows and realistic shadows. Stylized shadows are artistic and free, drawn by the artist to depict the mood of the character and express emotions and not limited by the structure of physical shadows. Artists adjust the position, proportion, shape, density and other characteristics of shadows to achieve different artistic purposes, such as magnification, exaggeration, contrast, silhouette, etc [2]. Shadow drawing is the basis for the further creation of various artistic works. When drawing shadows, the artist has to make constant adjustments according to the structure of the image and the direction of the light, which takes a lot of time and effort.

Nowadays, there are more and more applications and researches in the field of image using deep learning, such as IC-GAN [3], StarGAN [4], Pix2pix [5], Cycle-GAN [6], CGAN [7], etc. Some researchers have focused on using deep learning

L. Iliadis et al. (Eds.): ICANN 2023, LNCS 14262, pp. 296–307, 2023.
https://doi.org/10.1007/978-3-031-44201-8_25

to generate stylized shading for line drawings [2,8]. In this paper, we propose a method to generate stylized shadows using shadow generative adversarial network (ShadowGAN). The method in this paper does not require separate treatment of shadows and line drawings during training, and can be trained directly by inputting line drawings with shadows and label information corresponding to the light direction, which improves the processing efficiency and reduces the complexity of data for generating stylized shadows for line drawings based on deep learning methods.

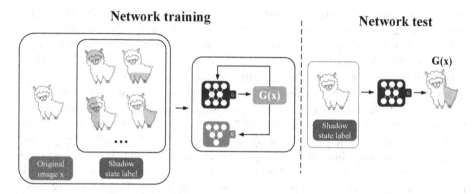

Fig. 1. Training and testing of our network. The network training consists of generator and discriminator, using the generator to produce images with shadows.

In our method, the stylized shadows are generated according to the line drawing and the specified light direction. These shadows can be used directly or modified by artists. We use the deep learning method to design a network model. Given a line drawing and light direction, the network automatically generates a shadow image. We divide the 2D image with shadows into 8 directions according to the light in 8 different directions. As shown in Fig. 1, the network consists of generator and discriminator, and generator G receives training data with multiple shadow states and converts the non-shadowed line drawings into multiple images with shadows in different directions. The generator takes the image and shadow state label information as input, and the training model flexibly converts the input image to the target shadow state. In this way, the image can be converted to any desired shadow image by controlling the shadow status label. The main contributions of our work:

1. In this paper, we propose a method based on deep learning to generate shadows for line drawings. This method can automatically generate stylized shadows in different light directions.
2. We design a deep learning network model ShadowGAN that can accurately identify the direction of shadows and light. ShadowGAN can learn shadow images directly, which improves the processing efficiency and reduces the

complexity of data for generating stylized shadows for line drawings based on deep learning methods.

3. The feasibility of the network model is verified on a new dataset. Experiments show that the method in this paper can generate excellent shadow effects for line drawing.

2   Related Work

Unlike real physical light and realistic rendering, the artistic creation of shadows is a perception-oriented process [2]. ShadeSketch [8] is the first time to use deep learning to automatically generate artistic shadows from line drawings and light directions. Hudon *et al.* [9] proposed a method to increase the global illumination effect for hand drawn objects. Zhang *et al.* [10] proposed a method based on stroke density to generate digital painting light effects for a single image. Hudon *et al.* [11] proposed a CNN-based method for predicting high-quality, high-resolution normal maps from single-line drawn character images that automatically generates shadow effects for hand-drawn characters. Petikam *et al.* [12] addressed the problem of dynamic stylized shadow editing by parameterizing individual edits, where the parametric model produces locally stylized shadow edited shapes. DeCoro *et al.* [13] proposed an algorithm to control stylized shadows based on four intuitive parameters: expansion, brightness, softness, and abstraction.

Generative adversarial networks (GAN) have been much studied in image translation and style transfer. The GAN consists of a generator, which generates samples that are as real as possible, and a discriminator, which distinguishes between real and fake samples. Zhang *et al.* [14] integrated residual U-net to apply the style to the grayscale sketch with auxiliary classifier generative adversarial network. Wei *et al.* [15] implemented image style translation based on cyclic consistent adversarial generative networks. In this paper, we propose a deep learning based shadow drawing method to generate stylized shadow effects for line drawings.

3   Method

In this paper, we train a shadow generative adversarial network (ShadowGAN) to draw shadows using the given line drawing and shadow state label information, and the network can complete the transition between multiple shadow states at the same time. In this section, we describe data preparation, network training and loss functions, and design of generator and discriminator networks.

3.1   Data Preparation

In this paper, we use a new shadow image dataset. Since the line drawing shadow dataset is small and the format of the existing data does not match our network, a line drawing shadow dataset is created in this paper. We collect a total of 18,208 line drawing images from the internet. The collected images are preprocessed into a unified format, and the standard size of each image is 256 × 256px. Then we manually mark the shadow corresponding to the light direction of the image to facilitate network training. This paper focuses on the attribute of shadow state. As shown in Fig. 2, eight light directions are defined and represented in the dataset by the numbers 1–8. It is intuitive for the user to specify the light source by selecting one of the 8 light directions around the 2D image. The network draws the stylized line drawing shadow according to the direction of light source.

Fig. 2. We define eight light directions in a two-dimensional plane. The shadow images of the 8 light directions were done in two parts during the training process.

3.2   Network Training and Loss Function

Based on the StarGAN which can realize the multi domain translation of images, this paper designs a new network model. The network consists of one generator and one discriminator. When the network is trained, images with different shadow states and corresponding labels are input. The Generator G can convert the input image x to a stylized shadow image under the condition of the target shadow state label c. As shown in Fig. 3, G receives an image and a target shadow state label as input and generates a fake image which can deceive the discriminator. G reconstructs the fake shadow image into the original image with the original shadow state label. The reconstructed image and the original image are constrained for consistency. These two parts use one generator. The training process makes G generate images that are indistinguishable from the real images. The discriminator D distinguishes between real and fake images and classifies the real image to the corresponding shadow state. In our experiments, the shadows of the eight light directions are trained in two parts for network performance and image generation results. Five directions of shadows are selected respectively, and eight styles of shadows in the corresponding direction of light are selected at least once. We use one-hot vectors to represent the attribute of

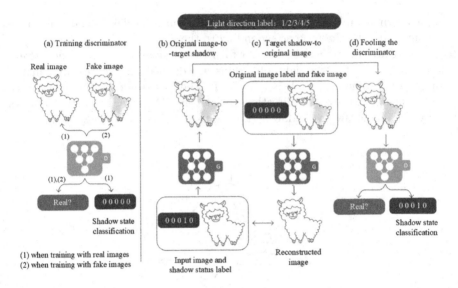

Fig. 3. Network training process.

the shadow state. In this vector, the bit corresponding to the light direction is set to 1, and the other bits are set to 0. For example, for a shadow style with light direction 4, the shadow status label is (0 0 0 1 0).

A. Adversarial loss. In order to generate the image which is indistinguishable from the real image, we use adversarial loss. The calculation method is

$$\mathcal{L}_{adv} = \mathbb{E}_x[\log D_{src}(x)] + \\ \mathbb{E}_{x,c}[\log(1 - D_{src}(G(x,c)))]. \tag{1}$$

Generator G generates a shadow style image $G(x,c)$ conditional on the input image x and the target shadow state label c. $D_{src}(x)$ represents the probability distribution of the input image on the shadow state given by the discriminator D. The G reduces the difference between the generated shadow image and the real image as much as possible, and make D cannot discriminate. The D identifies the real image and the generated shadow image as accurately as possible.

B. Shadow state classification loss. For a given input image x and shadow state label c, our goal is to convert x to an output image y with shadows and correctly classify it to the corresponding shadow state c. The discriminator D discriminates between the real shadow image and the fake image generated by generator. At the same time, we add an auxiliary classifier to D, and add shadow state classification loss when optimizing D and G. The shadow state classification loss of the real image used to optimize D is

$$\mathcal{L}_{cls}^r = \mathbb{E}_{x,c'}[-\log D_{cls}(c'|x)]. \tag{2}$$

$D_{cls}(c'|x)$ represents the probability distribution on the shadow state label c' of the corresponding image x calculated by discriminator D. By minimizing the target, D classifies the real shadow image x into its corresponding original shadow state c'. The generator G generates a fake image $G(x,c)$ based on the input image x and target shadow label c. The loss function of fake image shadow state classification is defined as

$$\mathcal{L}_{cls}^{f} = \mathbb{E}_{x,c}[-\log D_{cls}(c|G(\mathrm{x},c))]. \tag{3}$$

The generator G tries to minimize this target in order to generate shadow images that can be classified as target shadow states c.

C. Reconstruction loss. The generator generates realistic images and classifies them to the correct target shadow state. However, minimizing the above adversarial loss and classification losses does not guarantee that the translation of the shadow image only changes the shadow-related part of the input image while preserving the rest of its input image. Therefore, a cyclic consistency loss is introduced in the generator, that is the reconstruction loss. By using the generator twice, the first generated fake image and original image label are input to the generator again to generate the reconstructed image, and the reconstructed image and the original image are constrained for consistency. Then the reconstruction loss is

$$\mathcal{L}_{rec} = \mathbb{E}_{x,c,c'}[\||x - G(G(x,c),c')\||_1]. \tag{4}$$

where G receives the fake shadow image $G(x,c)$ and the shadow state label c' as input and reconstructs the original image x. In this paper, the $L1$ norm is used as the reconstruction loss.

D. Full Objective. The discriminator loss consists of two parts: the adversarial loss and the shadow state classification loss. The generator loss consists of three parts: the adversarial loss, the shadow state classification loss and the reconstruction loss. The full objectives are

$$\mathcal{L}_D = -\mathcal{L}_{adv} + \lambda_{cls}\mathcal{L}_{cls}^{r}, \tag{5}$$

$$\mathcal{L}_G = \mathcal{L}_{adv} + \lambda_{cls}\mathcal{L}_{cls}^{f} + \lambda_{rec}\mathcal{L}_{rec}. \tag{6}$$

λ_{cls} and λ_{rec} are hyper-parameters, which control the relative importance of shadow state classification and reconstruction loss relative respectively, compared to the adversarial loss. We use $\lambda_{cls}=1$ and $\lambda_{rec}=10$ in all of our experiments. To improve the stability of the network and the quality of shadow images, Eq. (1) is replaced by the Wasserstein-GAN [16,17] objective with gradient penalty

$$\mathcal{L}_{adv} = \mathbb{E}_x[D_{src}(x)] - \mathbb{E}_{x,c}[D_{src}(x,c)] \\ - \lambda_{gp}\mathbb{E}_{\hat{x}}[\||\nabla_{\hat{x}}D_{src}(\hat{x})\||_2 - 1)^2. \tag{7}$$

$\hat{x}$ is sampled uniformly between the real image and the generated image along a straight line. We use $\lambda_{gp} = 10$ for all experiments.

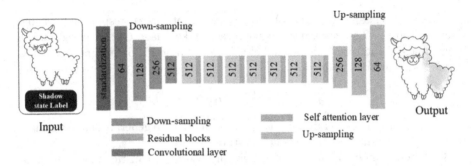

Fig. 4. Network architecture of the generator.

3.3 Network Structure

The structure of the generator network is shown in Fig. 4. The line drawings are normalized before input to unify the size, and then the network is trained. The 3-channel image and 5-channel label are used as input. Through a layer of convolution, the number of output channels is 64 and the convolution kernel size is 7 × 7. Except for the output layer, all layers use instance normalization to accelerate training and improve the stability of training. We use the ReLU function as the activation function. Three convolutional layers are used for downsampling, and the stride is two, which can better extract image features and decompose the input image. Seven residual blocks [18], which can identify the shadows of the images, train deeper networks, and ensure excellent performance. Self attention layer [19] is added to each residual block to strengthen shadow boundary and improve the quality of image shadow effect. Three transposed convolutional layers with stride of two are used for upsampling. The output layer uses the Tanh activation function to obtain a shadow image with an output dimension of 3.

The discriminator uses PatchGAN [5, 6, 20]. The discriminator is not normalized and uses Leaky ReLU as the activation function for all layers except the output layer. The output layer outputs the real or fake of the image and the shadow state label of the image.

4   Experiments and Evaluation

In this section, we evaluate the performance of ShadowGAN, show stylized shadows, and compare it to previous work. In this paper, ablation studies are done to show that each component of the network is essential.

4.1 Implementation Details

All images in the dataset are preprocessed to generate a standard data representation. There are 18208 images in the dataset, and each image has a shadow attribute. The entire dataset is used as the training data and 1000 original images are selected as the test set. The model is trained using Adam [21] with $\beta1=0.5$ and $\beta2=0.999$. For data augmentation, we flip the images horizontally with a probability of 0.5. A generator update is performed after five discriminator updates. For all experiments, the batch size is set to 8 and the learning rate is set to 0.00001. Both parts of the data are trained with 10 epochs, which takes about one day in total.

4.2 Shadow Effect Show

In this section, we show the shadow effects of line drawings generated by ShadowGAN. In this paper, we design a new network based on StarGAN with three convolutional layers for downsampling and three transposed convolutional layers for upsampling to extract image features and enhance the image shadow boundary effect. The residual layer and self-attention layer are added to improve the network performance, enhance the change of shadow details, improve the quality of shadows, accurately identify the direction of shadows and light, and generate usable shadows for users. As shown in Fig. 5, we show the generated shadow effects from different light directions.

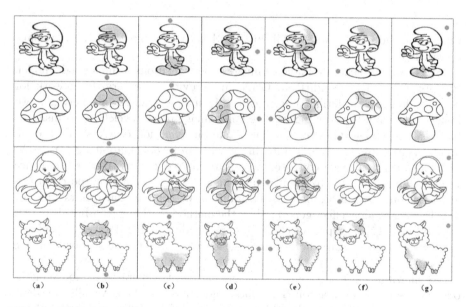

(a)   (b)   (c)   (d)   (e)   (f)   (g)

Fig. 5. The shadow effects are shown. (a) is the original images. In images (b)-(g), the yellow dots indicate the light direction. (Color figure online)

4.3 Comparison with Prior Work

To prove the effectiveness of the stylized shadow generation method proposed in this paper, we compare our network with the baseline models StarGAN [4],

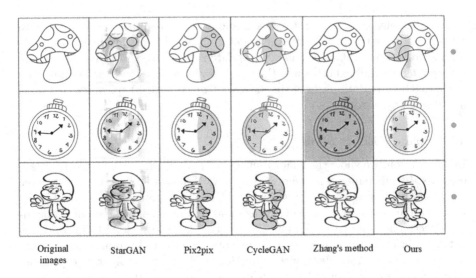

Original   StarGAN   Pix2pix   CycleGAN   Zhang's method   Ours
images

Fig. 6. Comparisons with prior works. The shadows generated by our method own good quality and accurate shadow direction.

Pix2pix [5] and CycleGAN [6]. All three models are proposed for image-to-image translation.

StarGAN can generate multiple image style transitions using a single model. Pix2pix is based on conditional GAN and provides a general framework for image-to-image translation, but it can only handle translations between two image styles, and the training data requires image pairs. CycleGAN transforms between two image types by learning a mapping relation $G : X \rightarrow Y$ through an adversarial loss function, combining it with an inverse mapping $F : Y \rightarrow X$, and introducing a cycle consistency loss to enforce $F(G(X)) \approx X$ (and vice versa). It does not need to input paired images, and is mainly composed of two generators and two discriminators. In addition, we compare our results with the line drawing shadow effect generated by the method of Zhang [15]. In this paper, we use StarGAN, Pix2pix, CycleGAN source code training dataset to generate shadows for comparison, and use Zhang's source code generate shadows for line drawings.

As shown in Fig. 6, we compare the shadow effects generated by above methods in the same light direction. The shadow generated by StarGAN fills the whole image, which is not beautiful and has no artistic effect. There are several places beyond the line drawings boundary. The shadows generated by Pix2pix do not conform to the light direction, and most of generate shadows is opposite to the light direction. The network cannot generate shadows in multiple directions. The shadow images generated by CycleGAN are blurred with redundant lines, and the shadows do not conform to the structure of line drawing. Zhang's method is to generate digital painting lighting effects for images, which can generate excellent lighting effects for some images with brilliant colors and more strokes, but it cannot generate lighting and shadows for line drawings. The experimental results show that the network in this paper performs well in generating line drawing shadows and can generate high-quality shadow effects.

(a)   (b)   (c)   (d)   (e)   (f)   (g)

Fig. 7. Ablation studies. The impact of each individual component is studied by removing the network components one by one.

4.4   Ablation Study

We performed seven ablation studies in this section. In Fig. 7(a), the generator network uses two convolutional layers for downsampling, six residual layers and two transposed convolutional layers for upsampling. The shadow images generated after network training are blurred, with poor shadow quality and unclear lines. In Fig. 7(b), the generator network uses two convolutional layers for downsampling, seven residual layers and two transposed convolutional layers for upsampling. The shadow shape generated after network training is out of control, shadow fills the whole image, and the shadow direction cannot be correctly recognized. In Fig. 7(c), the generator network uses three convolutional layers for downsampling, six residual layers and three transposed convolutional layers for upsampling. In Fig. 7(d), the generator network uses three convolutional layers for downsampling, seven residual layers and three transposed convolutional layers for upsampling. In Fig. 7(g), the generator network uses three convolutional layers for downsampling, six residual layers, each residual layer adds a self attention layer, and three transposed convolutional layers for upsampling. In (c)(d)(g), the shadows generated by the network are not evenly distributed and do not perform well in terms of detailing, with large gaps in the shadow range and shadow overflow, failing to achieve an aesthetically pleasing and balanced appearance. In Fig. 7(e), the generator network uses two convolution layers for downsampling and six residual layers, each residual layer adds a self attention layer, and two transposed convolutional layers for upsampling. The shadows generated after network training are distorted, without smooth boundaries, and the shadow shapes do not correspond to the light direction, and the shadows are extremely poor. In Fig. 7(f), the generator network uses two convolutional layers for downsampling, seven residual layers, each residual layer adds a self attention layer, and two transposed convolutional layers for upsampling. The shadows generated after network training appear blocky, with distorted shadow boundaries and no obvious shadow direction. The quality of the shadows generated by the network in Fig. 7(a)–Fig. 7(g) is lacking and cannot achieve the desired shadow appearance for the users. Overall, with 8 light directions, our network obtains the best results and can identify shadows in any light direction. Experiments show that every structure in this network is essential.

5   Conclusion

We propose a deep learning based method to automatically generate stylized shadows for line drawings. A new network model, ShadowGAN, is designed based on StarGAN to accurately identify the direction of light and generate usable shadows for users. We defined 8 light directions for the image to generate the corresponding stylized shadows. In the network, we use three convolutional layers for downsampling and three transposed convolutional layers for upsampling to extract image features and enhance image shadow boundary effects. Adding residual layers and self attention layers can improve the performance of the network, strengthen shadow detail processing, generate good shadow effects for the images, and improve the shadow quality. Experiments show that the method in this paper can generate stylized shadows for line drawings, and can greatly reduce the workload of users and saving the time of drawing image shadows.

References

1. Anjyo, K., Wemler, S., Baxter, W.: Tweakable light and shade for cartoon animation. In: Proceedings of the 4th International Symposium on Non-photorealistic Animation and Rendering, PP. 133–139 (2006)
2. Zhang, L., Jiang, J., Ji, Y., Liu, C.: SmartShadow: artistic shadow drawing tool for line drawings. In: Proceedings of the IEEE/CVF International Conference on Computer Vision, PP. 5391–5400 (2021)
3. Casanova, A., Careil, M., Verbeek, J., Drozdzal, M., Romero-Soriano, A.: Instance conditioned GAN. In: Advances in Neural Information Processing Systems, vol. 34, pp. 27517–27529 (2021)
4. Choi, Y., Choi, M., Kim, M., Ha, J.W., Kim, S., Choo, J.: StarGAN: unified generative adversarial networks for multi-domain image-to-image translation. In: Proceedings of the IEEE Conference on Computer Vision and Pattern Recognition, PP. 8789–8797 (2018)
5. Isola, P., Zhu, J.Y., Zhou, T., Efros, A.A.: Image-to-image translation with conditional adversarial networks. In: Proceedings of the IEEE Conference on Computer Vision and Pattern Recognition, PP. 1125–1134 (2017)
6. Zhu, J.Y., Park, T., Isola, P., Efros, A.A.: Unpaired image-to-image translation using cycle-consistent adversarial networks. In: Proceedings of the IEEE International Conference on Computer Vision, PP. 2223–2232 (2017)

7. Mirza, M., Osindero, S.: Conditional generative adversarial nets. arxiv.org/abs/1411.1784 (2014)
8. Zheng, Q., Li, Z., Bargteil, A.: Learning to shadow hand-drawn sketches. In: Proceedings of the IEEE/CVF Conference on Computer Vision and Pattern Recognition, PP. 7436–7445 (2020)
9. Hudon, M., Lutz, S., Pagés, R., Smolic, A.: Augmenting hand-drawn art with global illumination effects through surface inflation. In: Proceedings of the 16th ACM SIGGRAPH European Conference on Visual Media Production, PP. 1–9 (2019)
10. Zhang, L., Simo-Serra, E., Ji, Y., Liu, C.: Generating digital painting lighting effects via RGB-space geometry. ACM Trans. Graph. **39**(2), 1–13 (2020)
11. Hudon, M., Grogan, M., Pagés, R., Smolić, A.: Deep normal estimation for automatic shading of hand-drawn characters. In: Leal-Taixé, L., Roth, S. (eds.) ECCV 2018. LNCS, vol. 11131, pp. 246–262. Springer, Cham (2019). https://doi.org/10.1007/978-3-030-11015-4_20
12. Petikam, L., Anjyo, K., Rhee, T.: Shading rig: dynamic art-directable stylised shading for 3D characters. ACM Trans. Graph. (TOG) **40**(5), 1–14 (2021)
13. DeCoro, C., Cole, F., Finkelstein, A., Rusinkiewicz, S.: Stylized shadows. In: Proceedings of the 5th International Symposium on Nonphotorealistic Animation and Rendering, PP. 77–83 (2007)
14. Zhang, L., Ji, Y., Lin, X., Liu, C.: Style transfer for anime sketches with enhanced residual U-net and auxiliary classifier GAN. In: Proceedings of the 4th IAPR Asian Conference on Pattern Recognition, PP. 506–511 (2017)
15. Wei, T., Zhu, L.: Comic style transfer based on generative confrontation network. In: Proceedings of 2021 6th International Conference on Intelligent Computing and Signal Processing (ICSP), PP. 1011–1014. IEEE (2021)
16. Arjovsky, M., Chintala, S., Bottou, L.: Wasserstein generative adversarial networks. In: Proceedings of the 34th International Conference on Machine Learning (ICML), PP. 214–223 (2017)
17. Gulrajani, I., Ahmed, F., Arjovsky, M., Dumoulin, V., Courville, A.: Improved training of wasserstein GANs. (2017). arxiv.org/abs/1704.00028
18. He, K., Zhang, X., Ren, S., Sun, J.: Deep residual learning for image recognition. In: Proceedings of the IEEE Conference on Computer Vision and Pattern Recognition, PP. 770–778 (2016)
19. Zhang, H., Goodfellow, I., Metaxas, D., Odena, A.: Self-attention generative adversarial networks. In: Proceedings of the 36th International Conference on Machine Learning, PP. 7354–7363. PMLR (2019)
20. Li, C., Wand, M.: Precomputed real-time texture synthesis with Markovian generative adversarial networks. In: Leibe, B., Matas, J., Sebe, N., Welling, M. (eds.) ECCV 2016. LNCS, vol. 9907, pp. 702–716. Springer, Cham (2016). https://doi.org/10.1007/978-3-319-46487-9_43
21. Kingma, D., Ba, J.: Adam: a method for stochastic optimization. arxiv.org/abs/1412.6980 (2014)

Ship Attitude Prediction Based on Dynamic Sliding Window and EEMD-SSA-BiLSTM

Jiaqi Wang[1,2(✉)] and Yaojie Chen[1,2]

[1] Department of Computer Science and Technology, Wuhan University of Science and Technology, Wuhan, China
1411012563@qq.com
[2] Hubei Province Key Laboratory of Intelligent Information Processing and Real-time Industrial System, Wuhan, China

Abstract. A ship attitude prediction method is proposed in this paper, which combines dynamic sliding window, sparrow search algorithm (SSA), Ensemble Empirical Mode Decomposition (EEMD), and Bidirectional Long Short-Term Memory (BiLSTM). This method addresses the highly random, non-stationary, and non-linear characteristics of ship motion on the sea surface, making it difficult to accurately predict its motion state. Firstly, the EEMD method is used to decompose the ship attitude into several Intrinsic Mode Functions (IMF) and a Residual (Res) to reduce noise and non-smoothness in the ship attitude data. Secondly, the corresponding sliding window size and sliding step length are calculated for each IMF component, and the dynamic sliding window is used to extract the local features of the data, reducing the high randomness influence of the ship motion attitude. Finally, the SSA algorithm is used to find the optimal parameters in the BiLSTM network to improve the accuracy of the prediction method. The experimental results show that the EEMD-SSA-BiLSTM model incorporating dynamic sliding windows significantly improves prediction accuracy and generalization ability compared to other models.

Keywords: Ship attitude prediction · Neural Networks · Dynamic sliding window · Ensemble Empirical Mode Decomposition · Sparrow search algorithm

1 Introduction

Under the complex environment of the sea, the ship's navigation is affected by environmental factors such as sea wind and waves, resulting in changes in the ship's movement full of uncertainty, this uncertainty poses a safety hazard to the ship's operation at sea. Therefore, predicting the ship's attitude in advance during navigation is essential to ensure the stable use of shipboard equipment and navigation safety.

© The Author(s), under exclusive license to Springer Nature Switzerland AG 2023
L. Iliadis et al. (Eds.): ICANN 2023, LNCS 14262, pp. 308–319, 2023.
https://doi.org/10.1007/978-3-031-44201-8_26

In recent years, neural networks have been used as the main method for predicting the attitude of a ship. The biggest advantage of neural networks is that the process of data analysis and modelling is eliminated, making the problem processing process simple and more applicable to practical engineering problems. [11] Wei et al. used a bi-directional long and short-term memory (BiLSTM) network to predict ship motion with high accuracy. [14] Yin et al. constructed a variable radial basis function (RBF) network based on sliding data windows, [15] Zhang et al. used a combined CNN-LSTM model to predict the attitude of unmanned surface vehicles. Recurrent neural networks,particularly represented by BiLSTM, have achieved remarkable success in the field of time series prediction with the ability to capture the past and future context of the input elements. [5,6,8,17]

However, BiLSTM does not address the problem of random initialisation of neural network parameters, which can seriously affect the accuracy of prediction. To solve this problem, existing methods for optimising neural networks have mainly focused on improving the loss and activation functions, or optimising the initial parameters of the network using population intelligence optimisation algorithms [1,16]. In [7] Ren et al. applied the particle swarm algorithm Particle Swarm Optimization) to LSTM, and the experimental results showed that the root mean square error of prediction of the PSO-optimized LSTM model was reduced by 9%. Various optimization algorithms exist, [9,10,13] such as Particle Swarm Optimization (PSO), Grey Wolf Optimization (GWO), and Sparrow Search Algorithm (SSA), [3] and the SSA algorithm is widely used for the optimization of model parameters because of its powerful optimization-seeking capability.

There is also the problem of ignoring the possible noise in the data itself in ship attitude prediction, which makes the raw data have a greater impact on the prediction results. Therefore, signal decomposition techniques are often used to pre-process non-smooth time-series data such as ship attitude, thereby reducing the effect of noise in the data. In [18] Zheng et al. combined empirical mode decomposition (EMD) and long short-term memory (LSTM) neural networks to forecast electrical loads, and in [2] Hao et al. used EMD to process wave data and predicted the processed data using LSTM models. [4] Xiao et al. used EEMD to process ship attitude signals, which reduced their RMSE by 5.26% compared to a single model. [12] The EEMD algorithm is widely used to process non-smooth, non-linear signals as it solves the modal confounding problem that occurs during signal decomposition.

Therefore, we constructed a combined model in terms of both data pre-processing and optimisation of parameters related to the prediction algorithm, and proposed a combined model based on dynamic sliding windows and EEMD-SSA-BiLSTM. The ship attitude data is decomposed by EEMD to make the data smoother, and then the SSA-based optimised parametric BiLSTM model is used to predict the components. A comparison of our model with EEMD-BiLSTM and SSA-BiLSTM shows that our model can effectively improve the prediction accuracy of ship attitude.

2   Theoretical Foundations

2.1   Ensemble Empirical Modal Decomposition

To solve the problem of the influence of non-smoothness and non-linearity of ship motion attitude data on prediction accuracy, we use EEMD to process the raw ship data. The method is adapted to the needs of processing non-stationary signals by decomposing the signal into different basis functions according to the characteristics of the signal source itself. During processing, different scales of Gaussian white noise are introduced into the ship attitude data to compensate for the missing time scale in the attitude data. The following is the decomposition process for EEMD: White noise is added to the original signal.

$$X_m(t) = X(t) + kq_m(t), m = 1, 2, 3..   \tag{1}$$

where: $X(t)$ represents the original data sequence of the ship's attitude; m is the number of times white noise is added; $q_m(t)$ represents Gaussian white noise; represents the new power sequence. EMD decomposition of the new pose sequence $X_m(t)$ to obtain n IMF components and a residual component

$$X_m(t) = \sum_{i=1}^{n} IMF_{mi}(t) + r_m(t)   \tag{2}$$

where $IMF_{mi}(t)$ is the nth IMF component obtained from the mth decomposition; $r_m(t)$ is the residual component of the decomposition. Calculate the mean value of each decomposition quantity:

$$IMF_i(t) = \frac{1}{n} \sum_{i=1}^{n} IMF_{mi}(t)   \tag{3}$$

$$r_m(t) = \frac{1}{n} \sum_{i=1}^{n} r_{im}(t)   \tag{4}$$

The final output is a single decomposition component obtained by EEMD, which decomposes the attitude data into a number of intrinsic mode functions (IMFs), each representing a specific frequency component. These IMF components exhibit a greater degree of regularity and smoothness.

2.2   Bi-directional Long and Short-Term Memory Networks

BiLSTM is a further improvement on LSTM, which uses a combination of forward LSTM and reverse LSTM networks to combine the forward and reverse hidden states that are stitched together to capture more comprehensive time series information. As a result, the model can train the influence of future information on the current state compared to the LSTM, enhancing the model's ability to learn from data that exhibit both backward and forward dependencies, thus better reflecting the trend of the time series. The advantage of BiLSTM for introducing contextual information is due to the inherent periodic and recipro-cal nature of ship attitude, so a ship attitude prediction method using BiLSTM based on BiLSTM is proposed.

$$i_t = \sigma\left(w_{ki}x_t + w_{hi}h_{t-1} + b_i\right) \tag{5}$$

$$g_t = \sigma\left(w_{xg}x_t + w_{hg}h_{t-1} + b_g\right) \tag{6}$$

$$C_t = f_t C_{t-1} + i_t g_t \tag{7}$$

$$h_t = o_t \tanh\left(C_t\right) \tag{8}$$

$$f_t = \sigma\left(w_{kf}x_t + w_{hf}h_{t-1} + b_f\right) \tag{9}$$

where: x_t denotes the input to the neuron at moment t. The variable signifies the Sigmod number, while f_t, i_t denote the bias terms of the forgetting gate, input gate, respectively. Moreover, w_{kf}, w_{ki}, w_{k0} represent the weights of the forgetting gate, input gate, and output gate, respectively. of the network.

2.3 Sparrow Search Algorithm

The Sparrow Search Algorithm is a population-based intelligent optimization algorithm used to locate the global optimum. It simulates the foraging pro-cess of sparrows and is inspired by their behavior when foraging and evading predators. The algorithm involves coding and determining the adaptive value of each individual, mimicking the natural behavior of sparrows such as searching for food and escaping from predators, and ultimately selecting individuals that meet certain conditions.

3 Ship Attitude Prediction Model

3.1 Dynamic Siding Window Settings

The movement of ships on the sea surface exhibits a high degree of randomness and uncertainty. However, the actual situation shows that there are also periodic variations in the ship's motion. To read the periodic data in the highly random ship motion, this paper sets up a dynamic sliding window to read the decom-posed EEMD data a dynamically adjusted sliding window, which can adjust the window size according to the actual data changes.

The selection of the sliding window size usually requires consideration of several factors. This model takes the IMF component as a feature, the time-domain characteristics of the IMF component and the sampling rate of the data as considerations, and since the IMF component usually has a short mean period and time-varying energy distribution characteristics, the length of the window is set to half the mean period of the IMF component. The average period $T(k)$ is calculated as follows:

$$T(k) = 2\pi/\omega(k) \tag{10}$$

$$W(k) = \int_{-\infty}^{\infty} f(t)e^{-i\omega t}dt \qquad (11)$$

where (k) is the frequency of the IMF components, where the mean periods are all specific to each IMF component, i.e. there is a corresponding mean period for each IMF component, and the BiLSTM sliding window size is determined based on these characteristic parameters. The sliding step length is the length of each sliding window step forward, which is set to four-fifths of the sliding window size in this paper.

3.2   SSA Optimizes BiLSTM Parameters

To address the problem that individual BiLSTM neural networks in ship attitude prediction are greatly influenced by the initialization and hyperparameter values, we use SSA to determine the hyperparameters in BiLSTM. The SSA parameters are set as follows: the number of populations is 20, the maximum The four hyperparameter optimization intervals of the BiLSTM are as follows: numHiddenUnits1 and numHiddenUnits2 are $[1, 100]$, Iterations are $[1, 100]$, and learning rate is $[0.001, 0.1]$, and the search process is as follows: (1) Determine the parameters of the algorithm. In the sparrow search algorithm, the number of populations, the number of iterations, the ratio of predators and joiners, and the range interval for the speed-to-take values are initialized. For BiLSTM, on the other hand, the number of neuron nodes in each network layer, the number of hidden layer units, the learning rate, and the weight matrix are initialized. (2) Calculate the fitness value. In this paper, the mean square error function is chosen as the fitness function for this experiment, and the formula is as follows. The particle position that makes the smallest fitness function value corresponds to the best number of hidden layer nodes of the neural network, and the test set of experimental data is tested to construct the fitness function of SSA with the prediction value of BiLSTM algorithm and the root mean square error of the sample data to calculate the fitness value of each sparrow and solve for the best particle.

$$fit_{MSE} = \frac{1}{n}\sum_{i=1}^{n}(\hat{y}_i - y_i)^2 \qquad (12)$$

where n is the number of particles (population size), $\hat{y}_i$ is the predicted value and y_i is the actual value. (3) Finding the global optimal solution. The identity of the sparrow population is divided into discoverers and joiners, both of which change dynamically, but occupy a constant proportion of the population. The global optimal position of the population is constantly updated by the discoverer searching for areas with abundant food and the joiner following the discoverer to change its position. (4) Determine the termination condition. Repeat the above steps and if the number of iterations reaches the maximum, exit the iteration and save the optimal individual, i.e. the optimal parameters of the BiLSTM network. (5) Output the optimal solution. The optimal particles calculated by SSA are used as parameters of the BiLSTM.

3.3   EEMD-SSA-BiLSTM Ship Attitude Prediction Model

Our proposed EEMD-SSA-BiLSTM is shown in Fig. 1 and is built as follows:
(1)Collect ship attitude data. (2) Sequentially process each IMF component
obtained from the EEMD decomposition. Calculate the sliding window size, i.e.,
predict the next stage data using a historical period of data, and then slide to
read the corresponding historical sequence period decomposition data for each
IMF component. (3) Input the IMF components into a two-layer stacked BiL-
STM layer. With the first and second-layer neural dimensions set to 128 and
64, respectively. During the model training process, "mse" is used as the loss
function, and "$adam$" is used as the model optimizer. The EEMD decomposition feature modal components are mapped to higher dimensions through a
double-layer BiLSTM network for learning. (4) Use SSA to optimize several
hyperparameters of BiLSTM. (5) After the large amount of time series data collected by the inertial measurement unit is preprocessed by the EEMD algorithm.
Several feature variables highly correlated with the ship's motion attitude are
obtained. Select the time series data of the roll, pitch and yaw angles at time t
as the input of the neural network, and output the ship's roll, pitch, and yaw at
time $t + N$(N is a smaller period). (6) Output the prediction results.

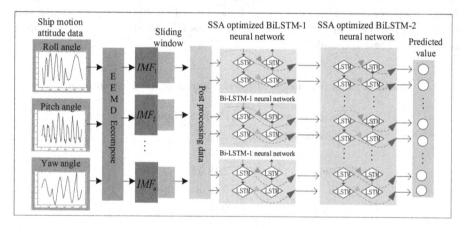

Fig. 1. Ship attitude prediction model based on dynamic sliding window and EEMD-
SSA-BiLSTM.

4   Experimental Results and Analysis

4.1   Platform Construction and Data Collection

In this paper, a six-degree-of-freedom platform is used to simulate the real-life
situation of a ship moving on the sea surface, and attitude data is collected
using an attitude sensor. The attitude sensor model is HWT905, which is a

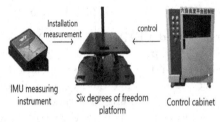

Fig. 2. Experimental site.   **Fig. 3.** Experimental equipment.

high-performance 3D motion attitude measurement unit based on MEMS technology, capable of collecting high accuracy, high dynamic, and real-time compensated 3- axis attitude angles. The six-degree-of-freedom platform model ACE6-16052008OF-07LM1 is capable of realistically simulating the rocking generated by a ship in the direction of six degrees of freedom while sailing on the sea. The longitudinal and transverse rocking angles of the attitude sensor are corresponding to the longitudinal and transverse rocking angles of the platform, and through calibration, the angle measured by the attitude sensor is the angle of change of the six degrees of freedom platform. The experimental site and equipment parameters are shown in Figs. 2, 3 and Table 1. 1000 bars of transverse and longitudinal rocking were measured under Class III waves as well as yaw angle, as shown in Figs. 4, 5 and 12.

Table 1. Main parameters of the six degrees of freedom platform.

Range of motion	Project parameters
Horizontal rocking	$\pm 15.0°$
Longitudinal rocking	$\pm 15.0°$
Yaw	$\pm 18.0°$
Lift	$0.16\,m$
Traverse	$0.19\,m$

4.2 Data Pre-processing

One of the characteristics of the EEMD method is that there is no unified expression for the basis functions, which depend on the signal source itself and can decompose different signals into different basis functions. Therefore, EEMD is suitable for processing and analyzing non-stationary signals such as ship motion attitude. 1000 posture data were decomposed using EEMD, the result of the decomposition is shown in Fig. 6. The ship attitude data were decomposed into an intrinsic mode function (IMF1−IMF10) component and a Res using EEMD. As shown in Fig. 6, the IMF1−IMF10 component exhibits overall similarities.

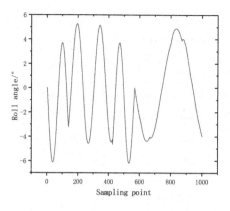

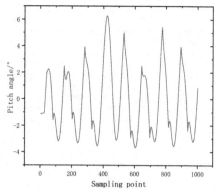

Fig. 4. Roll angle

Fig. 5. Pitch angle

Typically, the high-frequency IMF component is considered to be influenced by external factors, while the low-frequency component represents the trend of the ship motion. It can be seen that the IMF1–IMF6 components processed by EEMD consist of high frequency sinusoidal intermittent signals, and can be seen as small energy losses for the. When analyzing high-frequency signals, stacking these signals as reconstructed high-frequency signals can lead to better analysis results and effectively extract the low-frequency components in the signal.

4.3   Comparative Experiments

For ship attitude prediction accuracy, the choice of data pre-processing method and neural network model play a greater influence, so this paper mainly conducts comparisonexperiments from these two aspects, and the results are shown in Figs. 7, 8 and Table 2.

Table 2. Model prediction error results.

Modules	Models	RMSE	MAE
Neural network	LSTM	0.1158	0.0982
	GRU	0.1035	0.0712
	BiLSTM	0.0725	0.0623
Data preprocessing methods	EMD-BiLSTM	0.0595	0.0412
	VMD-BiLSTM	0.0513	0.0385
	EEMD-BiLSTM	0.0413	5.132

(1) To verify the superiority of the BiLSTM model in ship attitude prediction, the ship transverse rocking angle attitude data were predicted under three models, BiLSTM, LSTM, and GRU respectively. It can be seen that the ship

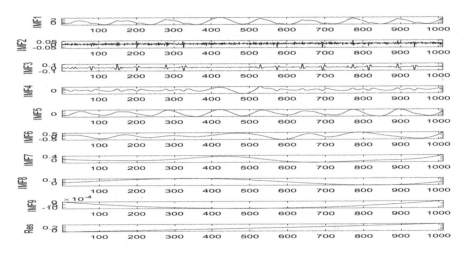

Fig. 6. IMF Restructuring Results.

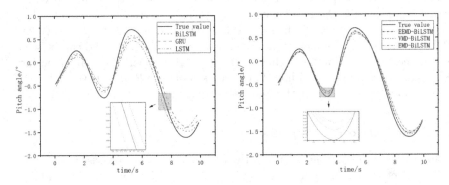

Fig. 7. Neural Network Comparative Experiment

Fig. 8. Comparative Experiment on Preprocessing Methods

transverse rocking attitude angle predicted by the BiLSTM model has the best fit between the real data, and the RMSE of BiLSTM is 0.0433 and 0.031 lower than that of LSTM and GRU respectively, and its MAE is 0.0359 and 0.0089 lower than that of LSTM and GRU respectively when predicting, which shows the BiLSTM has higher accuracy in ship attitude prediction compared with GRU and LSTM, and better reflects the trend of time series.

(2) To verify the superiority of EEMD in smoothing the ship attitude data, the ship transverse rocking angle attitude data were predicted under three models, EMD-BiLSTM, VMD-BiLSTM, and EEMD-BiLSTM, respectively. It can be seen that the ship transverse rocking attitude angle predicted by the EEMD-BiLSTM model has the best fit with the real data, with its MAE reduced by 0.0182 and 0.01 compared to EMD-BiLSTM and VMD-BiLSTM respectively, and its MAE reduced by 0.0116 compared to EMD-BiLSTM and VMD-

BiLSTM respectively and 0.0089, which shows that EEMD is better for ship attitude compared to EMD and VMD.

4.4 Ablation Experiment

To verify the role of each module in this model, the transverse and longitudinal rocking angles as well as the bow rocking angle were experimented with under the five models BiLSTM, SSA-BiLSTM, EEMD-BiLSTM, EEMD-SSA-BiLSTM and EEMD-SSA-BiLSTM based on sliding windows. The results are shown in Figs. 9, 10, 11 and Table 3.

(1)From the graphs and tables, it can be seen that the predicted RMSE and MAE were reduced by 0.0073 and 0.0114 on average after adding SSA, indicating that SSA solved the problem of random initialization assignment of the result parameters of the BiLSTM network and improved the prediction accuracy to a certain extent. (2)The predicted RMSE and MAE were reduced by 0.0304 and 0.0322 on average after the addition of EEMD, and the prediction accu-

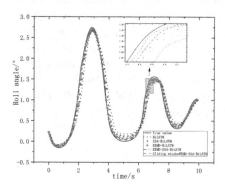

Fig. 9. Ablation experiment based on roll angle.

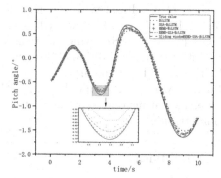

Fig. 10. Ablation experiment based on pitch angle.

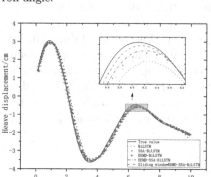

Fig. 11. Ablation experiment based on heave displacement.

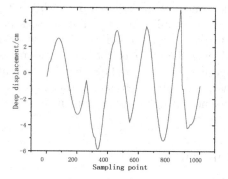

Fig. 12. Deep displacement.

Table 3. Model prediction error results.

Models	Roll angle		Pitch angle		Heave displacement	
	RMSE	MAE	RMSE	MAE	RMSE	MAE
BiLSTM	0.1112	0.1003	0.0725	0.0623	0.0625	0.0565
SSA-BiLSTM	0.1035	0.0912	0.0652	0.0525	0.0556	0.0412
EEMD-BiLSTM	0.0825	0.0654	0.0413	0.0296	0.0312	0.0276
EEMD-SSA- BiLSTM	0.0678	0.0541	0.0215	0.0196	0.0253	0.0233
Ours	0.0578	0.0423	0.0165	0.0152	0.0179	0.0154

racy was improved significantly. Although the prediction curves did not change much from the true values in the monotonically increasing and monotonically decreasing intervals, the degree of fit to the true values in the peaks and troughs was greatly better than that without the addition of EEMD, indicating that the EEMD method can adapt to the temporal and characteristic changes in the data. Sequence changes and feature changes in the data, effectively addressing the effects of non-linearity and non-smoothness in the ship's attitude. (3)The predicted RMSE and MAE are reduced by 0.0439 and 0.0407 on average after adding EEMD and SSA, which is a significant improvement in accuracy compared with the single addition of SSA, proving the superiority of combining SSA and EEMD. (4)The dynamic sliding window mechanism added to the EEMD-SSA-BiLSTM reduces the predicted RMSE, and MAE by 0.0539 and 0.0487 on average, indicating that it reduces the effect of high randomness in the ship motion attitude.

5   Conclusion

We propose a dynamic sliding window-based EEMD-SSA-BiLSTM prediction model for the non-smoothness and non-linearity of ship motion attitude. EEMD is used to pre-process and decompose the ship attitude data to reduce the non-smoothness of the original data while retaining the data features, while SSA is used to optimise the BiLSTM network parameters. A dynamic sliding window is used to read the IMF and pass it into the BiLSTM model for prediction, reducing the effect of the high randomness of the ship's motion attitude. The experimental results show that the ship attitude prediction model proposed in this paper effectively solves the non-smoothness of ship attitude, reduces the influence of high randomness and significantly improves the attitude prediction accuracy.

References

1. Cui, J., Zhang, M., Song, D., Shan, X., Wang, B.: MODIS land surface temperature product reconstruction based on the SSA-BiLSTM model. Remote Sens. **14**(4), 958 (2022)

2. Hao, W., Sun, X., Wang, C., Chen, H., Huang, L.: A hybrid EMD-LSTM model for non-stationary wave prediction in offshore China. Ocean Eng. **246**, 110566 (2022)
3. Huang, Z., Huang, J., Min, J.: SSA-LSTM: short-term photovoltaic power prediction based on feature matching. Energies **15**(20), 7806 (2022)
4. Li, C., Tao, Y., Ao, W., Yang, S., Bai, Y.: Improving forecasting accuracy of daily enterprise electricity consumption using a random forest based on ensemble empirical mode decomposition. Energy **165**, 1220–1227 (2018)
5. Lu, W., Li, J., Wang, J., Qin, L.: A CNN-BiLSTM-AM method for stock price prediction. Neural Comput. Appl. **33**, 4741–4753 (2021)
6. Peng, T., Zhang, C., Zhou, J., Nazir, M.S.: An integrated framework of Bi-directional long-short term memory (BiLSTM) based on sine cosine algorithm for hourly solar radiation forecasting. Energy **221**, 119887 (2021)
7. Ren, X., Liu, S., Yu, X., Dong, X.: A method for state-of-charge estimation of lithium-ion batteries based on PSO-LSTM. Energy **234**, 121236 (2021)
8. Siami-Namini, S., Tavakoli, N., Namin, A.S.: The performance of LSTM and BiL-STM in forecasting time series. In: 2019 IEEE International Conference on Big Data (Big Data), pp. 3285–3292. IEEE (2019)
9. Taorui, Z., Hongwei, J., Qingli, L., Kunlong, Y.: Landslide displacement prediction based on variational mode decomposition and MIC-GWO-LSTM model. Stoch. Env. Res. Risk Assess. **36**(5), 1353–1372 (2022)
10. Wang, P., Zhao, J., Gao, Y., Sotelo, M.A., Li, Z.: Lane work-schedule of toll station based on queuing theory and PSO-LSTM model. IEEE Access **8**, 84434–84443 (2020)
11. Wei, Y., Chen, Z., Zhao, C., Tu, Y., Chen, X., Yang, R.: A BiLSTM hybrid model for ship roll multi-step forecasting based on decomposition and hyperparameter optimization. Ocean Eng. **242**, 110138 (2021)
12. Wu, Z., Jiang, C., Conde, M., Deng, B., Chen, J.: Hybrid improved empirical mode decomposition and BP neural network model for the prediction of sea surface temperature. Ocean Sci. **15**(2), 349–360 (2019)
13. Yang, S., Jin, A., Nie, W., Liu, C., Li, Y.: Research on SSA-LSTM-based slope monitoring and early warning model. Sustainability **14**(16), 10246 (2022)
14. Yin, J.C., Zou, Z.J., Xu, F.: On-line prediction of ship roll motion during maneuvering using sequential learning RBF neuralnetworks. Ocean Eng. **61**, 139–147 (2013)
15. Zhang, W., Wu, P., Peng, Y., Liu, D.: Roll motion prediction of unmanned surface vehicle based on coupled CNN and LSTM. Future Internet **11**(11), 243 (2019)
16. Zhang, X., Jiang, X., Li, Y.: Prediction of air quality index based on the SSA-BiLSTM-LightGBM model. Sci. Rep. **13**(1), 5550 (2023)
17. Zhao, C., Huang, X., Li, Y., Yousaf Iqbal, M.: A double-channel hybrid deep neural network based on CNN and BiLSTM for remaining useful life prediction. Sensors **20**(24), 7109 (2020)
18. Zheng, H., Yuan, J., Chen, L.: Short-term load forecasting using EMD-LSTM neural networks with a Xgboost algorithm for feature importance evaluation. Energies **10**(8), 1168 (2017)

Solving Math Word Problem with External Knowledge and Entailment Loss

Rizhongtian Lu, Yongmei Tan[✉], Shaozhang Niu, and Yunze Lin

Beijing University of Posts and Telecommunications, Beijing, China
{lurizhongtian,ymtan,szniu,linyunze}@bupt.edu.cn

Abstract. Automatic math word problem(MWP) solving is an interesting task for NLP researchers in recent years. Over the last few years, a growing number of effective sequence-to-sequence deep learning-based model are proposed. However, these models do not efficiently consider factual errors as the sequence-to-sequence model can produce expressions that do not appear in the question. Additionally, these models neglect external knowledge information during the math word problem-solving process. To address these problems, we propose a model that can automatically solve math word problems with External Knowledge and Entailment Loss (MathEE). MathEE uses a Textual-Entailment auxiliary task to identify factual errors and introduces an entity graph based on external knowledge to model the highly relevant entity words in the question. Our experimental results on publicly available Chinese datasets Ape210K and Math23K show that MathEE achieves an accuracy rate of 74.43% and 78.7%, which is 2.08% and 1.6% higher than strong baseline models.

Keywords: math word problem · textual entailment · external knowledge aware

1 Introduction

Solving math word problems(MWPs) is a common challenge in daily life, and exploring ways to solve MWPs automatically is necessary. Early methods relied on either predefined rules or statistical methods to map problems into several predefined templates [1–3]. These methods required a large number of manually formulated features and could only be applied to small-scale MWP datasets. Recently, deep neural networks are used to solve MWPs [4–6], and promising results are reported on some datasets. These methods use end-to-end models to generate mathematical expressions directly from the question text.

Table 1 shows an example of the MWP. The crucial step in solving such a problem is to construct a mathematical expression. Wang et al. (2017) [5] proposes a sequence-to-sequence model to translate language text to a solution expression. Since then, many sequence-to-sequence models are proposed [6–10].

L. Iliadis et al. (Eds.): ICANN 2023, LNCS 14262, pp. 320–331, 2023.
https://doi.org/10.1007/978-3-031-44201-8_27

Although sequence-to-sequence models achieve promising results, several problems still need to be addressed.

The first is factual errors. We need to ensure that if a mathematical expression can be inferred from the question, the question must entail the mathematical expression. However, the sequence-to-sequence model sometimes can make factual errors, since it can produce expressions that do not appear in the question text.

The second is integrating external background knowledge. Humans are naturally aware of the background knowledge connected highly relevant entity words in the question text when they read the question. It is difficult for the model to get this information from question text without external background knowledge. As shown in Table 1, "weekly paper" and "evening paper" are different entities but they have the same hypernym.

To address these problems, we propose MathEE, a sequence-to-sequence model with Textual-Entailment and External Knowledge-Aware modules. The Textual-Entailment auxiliary task module can identify factual errors in the target sentence and provide feedback to train the model better. Meanwhile, MathEE can obtain representations of commonsense information and improve interactions between words by modeling highly relevant entity words in the question text.

The main contributions are as follows:

- We propose a Textual-Entailment auxiliary task module to address factual errors. To the best of our knowledge, this is the first time that factual errors are systematically discussed in the MWP solving task.
- We propose an External Knowledge-Aware module that includes an effective entity graph to model highly relevant entity words in the question text and incorporate external knowledge into math word problem-solving tasks.
- We conduct extensive experiments on Math23K and Ape210K [11] two Chinese benchmark datasets compared with strong baselines and the results confirm the effectiveness of the MathEE.

Table 1. An example of the math word problems from Ape210K dataset.

Problem	Grandpa Li's news-stand receives 230 yuan today, among them, weekly newspaper sells 85 copies, each weekly newspaper is 1.5 yuan, each evening paper is 0.5 yuan, how many evening papers does Grandpa Li sell today?
Equation	(230-1.5*85)/0.5
Answer	205

2 Related Work

Previous methods to automatic MWP solving involve incorporating additional features by creating fine-grained templates or defining math concepts [1-3], which are then used to generate the mathematical expression. Huang et al.

(2017) [12] proposed fine-grained templates and aligned numbers in MWPs with candidate templates. Roy and Roth (2018) [13] developed declarative rules to convert math concepts into mathematical expressions without relying on additional predefined templates. However, according to Huang et al. (2016) [15], these kinds of methods did not perform satisfactorily on a large dataset comprising more than 18,000 questions, as these methods require manually created features and may be challenging to apply to MWPs in various domains.

In recent years, deep learning models are used to solve MWPs automatically [4–6]. Wang et al. (2017) [5] proposed a sequence-to-sequence neural network model that achieved promising results in MWP solving, while Zou and Lu (2019) [27] parsed question text into math expressions using a sequence-to-sequence framework. Xie and Sun (2019) [28] proposed a sequence-to-tree model to generate expression tree in a goal-driven manner based on the parent node and left sibling tree of each node. Li et al. (2020) [22] proposed a graph-to-tree neural network model to generate expression tree. Qin et al. (2021) [23] proposed a neural network model to generate expression with four auxiliary tasks. Additionally, Lan et al. (2022) [25] used BERT and Roberta to solve MWP. Compared with traditional template or feature matching methods, the sequence-to-sequence model based on deep learning neural network does not require manually formulated features. However, these models ignore the external background knowledge, making it is necessary to incorporate such external knowledge into the MWP solving task.

Pre-training models have achieved significant success in various natural language processing tasks in recent years. Specifically, pre-training models like BERTGen [25] and RobertaGen [25] are utilized for automatic MWP solving with promising results. Additionally, other pre-trained language models such as Unified pre-trained Language Model (UniLM) [16] have demonstrated effectiveness in this task. The model is pre-trained using three types of language modeling tasks, and its ability to perform sequence-to-sequence predictions makes it suitable for fine-tuning in generation tasks, including MWP solving.

3   Model

The model incorporates the Textual-Entailment auxiliary task for truth checking and the External Knowledge-Aware module for modeling the highly relevant entity words in the question text. AS shown in Fig. 1, the input of this model is a MWP and the output is a mathematical expression.

3.1   Input Representation

AS shown in Fig. 1, for a MWP, the question and the mathematical expression can be expressed as $P = \{P_1, ..., P_m\}$ and $E = \{E_1, ..., E_n\}$, respectively. We always add a special token [CLS] at the beginning of the question and a [SEP] token at the end of each segment. The [SEP] token marks the sentence boundary. It is also used for the model to learn when to terminate the decoding process

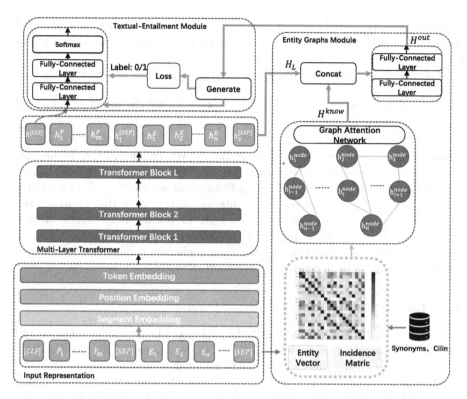

Fig. 1. An overview of the MathEE model includes Textual-Entailment module with automatic labeling ability and External Knowledge-Aware module.

in natural language generation tasks. Texts are tokenized to subword units by WordPiece. The representation of each token is computed by summing the corresponding token embedding, position embedding, and segment embedding.

3.2 Multi-layer Transformer

As shown in Fig. 1, The input sequence $< [CLS] ; P; [SEP] ; E; [SEP] >$ is first mapped into $H_0 = \left[h_0^{CLS}; H_0^P; h_{0_1}^{SEP}; H_0^E; h_{0_2}^{SEP}\right]$, and then encoded into contextual representations using a L-layer Transformer $H_l = Transformer_l (H_{l-1})$. In each Transformer block, multiple self-attention heads are used to aggregate information from the output vectors of the previous layer and produce a new set of features. For the l-th Transformer layer, the output of a self-attention head A_l is computed via:

$$A_l = softmax\left(\frac{QK^T}{\sqrt{d_k}} + M\right) V_l \qquad (1)$$

where $Q = H_{l-1}W_l^Q, K = H_{l-1}W_l^K, V = H_{l-1}W_l^V$. The previous layer's output H_{l-1} is linearly projected to a triple of queries, keys and values using parameter matrices W_l^Q, W_l^K, W_l^V respectively, and the self-attention mask matrix M determines whether a pair of tokens can attend to each other, the white squares denote 0 and black squares denote $-\infty$.

The above description can be abstracted into the following equations:

$$H_L = Multi\_Layer\_Transformer\,(< [CLS]; P; [SEP]; E; [SEP] >) \quad (2)$$

$$H_L = \left[h^{CLS}; H_L^P; h_1^{SEP}; H_L^E; h_2^{SEP} \right] \quad (3)$$

where H_L is the output of the last layer of the L-layer Transformer. h^{CLS} denotes the summary representation of the question and mathematical expression. This representation will be used in Textual-Entailment auxiliary task in Sect. 3.3. $H_L^P = \{h_1^P, ..., h_m^P\}$ denotes the representation of tokens in the question text. $H_L^E = \{h_1^E, ..., h_n^E\}$ enotes the representation of tokens in the mathematical expression. h_1^{SEP} and h_2^{SEP} represent the special token [SEP], with the h_2^{SEP} serving the additional function of determining when to terminate the decoding process. Notably, all representations are context-aware.

3.3 Textual-Entailment Module

We use Textual-Entailment to identify factual errors in the target sentence and provide feedback to the model. As shown in Fig. 1, we obtain the Textual-Entailment label using the loss value of the sequence generation task.

We use the [CLS] token, which contains contextual information, and design a Textual Entailment auxiliary task as a classification task in the training stage. The output from the L-th layer(the last layer) of the Multi-Layer Transformer is represented as $H_L = \left[h^{CLS}; H_L^P; h_1^{SEP}; H_L^E; h_2^{SEP} \right]$. H_L^E is used to calculate the loss of the target sequence, which represents the target mathematical expression, and cross-entropy is used to calculate the loss. After obtaining the loss value from the sequence generation task, we use it to automatically label the Textual Entailment auxiliary task. The h^{CLS} which represents the summary representation of the question and mathematical expression, is used as the input for the Textual Entailment auxiliary task. We pass the h^{CLS} through two fully connected layers, followed by a randomly initialized softmax-classifier:

$$TE = Softmax\left((h^{[CLS]}W \right) \quad (4)$$

where the W refers to a trainable parameter matrix and TE is the output of the softmax-classifier. We utilize the prediction results to fine-tune the parameters of the pre-trained model and train the classifier using mean squared error loss as the loss function.

3.4 Entity Graphs Module

Each MWP question text can be represented by an entity graph $G = (N, E)$, where N is the list of nodes and the E is the adjacent matrix of these nodes.

Nodes represent words in the MWP, and edges are retrieved from external knowledge bases as relationships between words. An edge is added between two words when they have similar semantic representations and are strongly related. With n words in the MWP, the corresponding entity graph will have a node list $N = \{x_1, x_2, ..., x_n\}$ with n nodes.

A two-layer Graph Attention Network (GAT) [18] is used to process word vectors and synonym correlation matrices after word embedding from the question text obtained in data preprocessing. This is done to obtain high-dimensional knowledge representation feature vectors of synonym entities. Using this method, we obtain the node initial vectors $h^{node} = \{h_1^{node}, h_2^{node}, ..., h_n^{node}\}$. We then use a two-layer GAT to obtain the hidden vectors $H^{know} = \{h_1^{know}, h_2^{know}, ..., h_n^{know}\}$ for these nodes. The GAT functions are defined as follows:

$$h_i^{know} = \|_{k=1,...K} \sigma \left(\sum_{A_{ij}=1} \alpha_{ij} W_k h_j^{node} \right) \tag{5}$$

$$\alpha_{ij} = \frac{exp(LRelu(w_s^T[W_h h_i^{node} \| W_h h_j^{node}]))}{\sum_{A_{ij}=1} exp(LRelu(w_s^T[W_h h_i^{node} \| W_h h_j^{node}]))} \tag{6}$$

where w_s^T, W_h, W_k represent the trainable weight vectors and matrices. The $\|$ represents the concatenation operation, and LRelu is a LeakyRelu activation function [19]. K represents the number of heads in the GAT, and $A_{ij} = 1$ means that there is an edge between the i-th and j-th node.

Then we concatenate the output from the L-th layer of the Multi-Layer Transformer H_L with the knowledge graph vectors H^{know} to obtain the output of the encoder H^{out}.

$$H^{out} = [H_L : H^{know}] \tag{7}$$

4   Experiments

4.1   Dataset

We evaluate MathEE on both Math23K and Ape210K two large-scale Chinese datasets. The Math23K and Ape210K datasets contain 24162 and 210488 elementary school MWPs respectively, each MWP originally associates with an expression and answer.

Table 2. The Statistics of MWPs in Ape210K and Math23K datasets.

		Train	Valid	Test
Ape210K	Before Preprocessing	200488	5000	5000
	After Preprocessing	200390	4999	4998
Math23K	Before Preprocessing	21162	1000	1000
	After Preprocessing	20657	972	980

Data Preprocessing. We use Cilin [20] and Synonyms as our external knowl-edge sources. Cilin is a synonym dictionary while Synonyms is a toolkit for natural language processing and understanding in Chinese. Both can be used to group words in the question text, and by using the Synonyms toolkit, we can obtain semantic units of entities in the question text. We use these word groups and semantic representations to construct the entity graph. Furthermore, to facil-itate the automatic calculation of mathematical expressions by the program and remove some MWPs with errors, we processed the mathematical expressions in the Ape210K dataset. We replace the percentage such as '$a\%$' with the fractional like '$a/100$', improper fractions such as '$a(b/c)$' with the form of '$(a+b/c)$', and the ':' which represents the proportion with '/'. Then we calculate the equation to obtain the final numerical answer and compare the result with the provided answer to remove MWPs with errors. Finally, the number of available MWPs in the Ape210K and Math23K datasets is shown in Table 2.

4.2   Implementation Details

Our code was implemented with Pytorch[1] and based on UniLM [16], with the hidden size of 768. We use the Adam optimizer with a learning rate of 2e-5 and a dropout rate of 0.1. To improve speed and reduce memory usage, we trim questions and mathematical equations to 256 and 40 tokens, respectively. We train the model for 20 epochs with a batch size of 8. During decoding, the beam size was set to 3.

4.3   Comparing Models

To evaluate the performance of MathEE, we compare it with the following mod-els:

StackDecoder. [21] is a neural sequence-to-sequence model where the encoder is designed to obtain the semantic embedding of the numbers in the question description, while the decoder is designed to construct the mathematical equa-tion in a suffix manner by applying stack actions to a stack.

GTS-model. [6] is a tree-structured neural model. The encoder is designed to encoder the question texts to contextual representations with a two-layer Bi-GRU, and the decoder is designed to construct the mathematical equation. Given a goal vector, the decoder predicts the token $\hat{y}$, if the predicted token $\hat{y}$ is a numeric value, the goal is marked as achieved. Otherwise, if the predicted token is an operator, the goal vector q will be split into a left sub-goal q_l and a right sub-goal q_r, respectively. The left sub-tree will be embedded via a recursive neural network and used when this model decodes the right sub-tree.

Feature-Enriched and Copy-Augmented LSTM. [11] follows the encoder-decoder approach with soft attention. There are five handcrafted features in the

---

[1] https://pytorch.org/.

word embedding layer: 1) the character of the current position; 2) the part-of-speech tag of the word in the current position; 3) the word of the current position; 4) whether the character of the current position is a number or not based on regular expression matching; and 5) sorting all the numbers in the question description in descending order and assigning each number an index starting from 0. The model uses a 4-layer Bi-LSTM as an encoder and a 2-layer Bi-LSTM as a decoder.

BERTGen. [25] is a Pre-trained model that uses BERT [17] as encoder and Transformer as the decoder to solve MWPs. Similarly, the **RobertaGen** uses Roberta [26] as the encoder and Transformer as the decoder to solve these problems.

4.4 Main Results

We use accuracy as the evaluation metric. For a given MWP, a predicted equation is considered correct if it produces the same numerical answer as the ground truth.

Result on Math23K Dataset. We compare MathEE with well-known MWP solvers from 2017 to the present on the Math23K dataset and present the results in Table 3. MathEE achieves an accuracy of 78.7% on the Math23K dataset, outperforming UniLM by 1.5%.

Table 3. The performance of models on Math23K test dataset.

Model	Accuracy
StackDecoder [21]	65.8%
GTS-model [6]	74.3%
Feature-enriched and Copy-augmented LSTM [11]	77.5%
BERTGen [25]	76.6%
RobertaGen [25]	76.9%
UniLM [16]	77.1%
MathEE	**78.7%**

Result on Ape210K Dataset. We choose three state-of-the-art open-source models: StackDecoder, GTS, UniLM, and the baseline of the Ape210K dataset to compare with MathEE on the Ape210K dataset. Table 4 shows the accuracy rates of MathEE and several other models on the Ape210K dataset. As we can see, MathEE outperforms all the models. Specifically, MathEE outperforms the Feature-enriched and Copy-augmented LSTM model, which is a strong baseline in the Ape210K dataset. Moreover, MathEE improves the accuracy rate of UniLM from 72.35% to 74.43%.

Table 4. The performance of models on Ape210K test dataset.

Model	Accuracy
StackDecoder [21]	52.28%
GTS-model [6]	56.56%
Feature-enriched and Copy-augmented LSTM [11]	70.20%
BERTGen [25]	70.91%
RobertaGen [25]	71.78%
UniLM [16]	72.35%
MathEE	74.43%

Model Performance on Different Length of the Expressions. We compare the MathEE model with the best-performing state-of-the-art model, UniLM, to investigate the performance of the models on expressions of different lengths.

As shown in Table 5, we divide the test dataset from Ape210K into four subsets according to the expression length. MathEE outperforms UniLM with respect to expressions of different lengths, especially those with a length of less than 5, which means that there is only one number in the expression and it is equal to the answer. One possible explanation for this is that such problems require the model to generate the answer directly, making UniLM more likely to make factual errors while MathEE can handle them with the Textual-Entailment module. These results further demonstrate the beneficial effect of the Textual-Entailment module in the MathEE model.

Table 5. The performance of models on Ape210K test dataset that was divided into 4 subsets according to the length of the expression

Expression Length	UniLM [16] Acc	MathEE Acc	Percent
length of expression<5	39.89%	**43.45%**	3.56%
5≤length of expression<10	73.39%	**75.44%**	23.45%
10≤length of expression<20	80.11%	**82.01%**	49.80%
20≤length of expression	59.62%	**61.97%**	23.19%

4.5 Ablation Study

As an ablation study, we compare our model with the models that without the modules we propose. The results of the ablation study on the Ape210K and Math23K datasets are shown in Table 6.

Table 6. The ablation study results of MathEE on Ape210K and Math23K.

Model	Ape210K	Math23K
Feature-enriched and Copy-augmented LSTM [11]	70.20%	77.50%
UniLM [16]	72.35%	77.10%
MathEE w/o Textual-Entailment	74.15%	78.29%
MathEE w/o External Knowledge-Aware module	73.73%	77.83%
MathEE	**74.43%**	**78.70%**

1) **Textual-Entailment Auxiliary Task:** We first investigate the effect of the Textual-Entailment auxiliary task on the results. As shown in Table 6, the model with the Textual-Entailment auxiliary task module outperformed the model without this module on Ape210K and Math23K by 1.38% and 0.73% accuracy rate, respectively. This shows that the Textual-Entailment auxiliary task module is important, as it can strengthen the relationship between the target sentence and the source sentence. In other words, it can strengthen the relationship between the mathematical expression and the question text, identify factual errors in the target sentence, provide feedback to the model, reduce the incidence of factual errors, and ultimately improve the performance of the model.

2) **External Knowledge-Aware Module:** We investigate the influence of the External Knowledge-Aware module on the results. The External Knowledge-Aware module makes the model capable of connecting highly relevant entity words in the question text and dynamically encoding external knowledge into the model, which improves the performance. As shown in Table 6, the model with the External Knowledge-Aware module outperformed the model without this module on Ape210K and Math23K by 1.80% and 1.19% accuracy rate, respectively.

4.6   Case Study

Table 7 shows an example generated by MathEE for comparison with UniLM [16]. In the first example, without the Textual-Entailment module and the External Knowledge-Aware module, UniLM does not realize that this question is asking about the weight of fruit instead of the weight of oranges. And it cannot aware the background information that apples, pears, and oranges are fruits, therefore it generates incorrect results. By incorporating the Textual-Entailment module and the External Knowledge-Aware module, MathEE can obtain this information and generate the correct expression.

In the second example, UniLM cannot combine the "news-stand total income" with the price of each "weekly newspaper" and "evening paper" without external knowledge, and it even ignores the existence of "weekly newspapers", resulting in incorrect results. By incorporating external knowledge and

Table 7. An example of expressions generated by MathEE compared with UniLM.

Example1	In a box of fruit, the weight of apples is 36KG, the weight of pears is (1/3) of apples, and the weight of oranges is (5/4) of pears. What is the weight of the box of fruit?
UniLM [16]	36*1/3*5/4 (Wrong)
MathEE	36+36*1/3+36*1/3*5/4 (Right)
Example2	Grandpa Li's news-stand receives 230 yuan today, among them, weekly newspaper sells 85 copies, each weekly newspaper is 1.5 yuan, each evening paper is 0.5 yuan, how many evening papers does Grandpa Li sell today?
UniLM [16]	230/0.5 (Wrong)
MathEE	(230-1.5*85)/0.5 (Right)

the External Knowledge-Aware module, MathEE is able to establish the relationship between these kinds of newspapers and generate correct expressions.

5   Conclusion

In this study, we propose a model that can automatically solve MWPs with External Knowledge and Entailment Loss (MathEE). We use an entity graph to model the highly relevant entity words in the question text and incorporate external knowledge into the model. Additionally, we propose a Textual-Entailment auxiliary task module with automatic labeling ability to reduce the incidence of factual errors. Our experimental results on Ape210K and Math23K confirm that our MathEE model outperforms other models.

References

1. Bakman, Y.: Robust understanding of word problems with extraneous information (2007)
2. Feigenbaum, E.A., et al.: Computers and Thought. McGraw-Hill, New York (1963)
3. Fletcher, C.R.: Understanding and solving arithmetic word problems: a computer simulation. Behav. Res. Methods Instrum. Comput. **17**(5), 565–571 (1985)
4. Wang, L., et al.: MathDQN: solving arithmetic word problems via deep reinforcement learning, vol. 32, no. 1 (2018)
5. Wang, Y., Liu, X., Shi, S.: Deep neural solver for math word problems, pp. 845–854 (2017)
6. Xie, Z., Sun, S.: A goal-driven tree-structured neural model for math word problems, pp. 5299–5305 (2019)
7. Wang, L., et al.: Translating a math word problem to a expression tree. In: EMNLP, pp. 1064–1069 (2018)
8. Chiang, T.R., Chen, Y N.: Semantically-aligned equation generation for solving and reasoning math word problems. In: NAACL-HLT, pp. 2656–2668 (2019)

9. Wang, L., et al.: Template-based math word problem solvers with recursive neural networks. In: AAAI (2019)
10. Liu, Q., et al.: Tree-structured decoding for solving math word problems. In: EMNLP-IJCNLP, pp. 2370–2379 (2019)
11. Zhao, W., et al.: Ape210k: a large-scale and template-rich dataset of math word problems. arXiv preprint: arXiv:2009.11506 (2020)
12. Huang, D., et al.: Learning fine-grained expressions to solve math word problems, pp. 805–814 (2017)
13. Roy, S., Roth, D.: Mapping to declarative knowledge for word problem solving. Trans. Assoc. Comput. Linguist. **6**, 159–172 (2018)
14. Lewis, A.B.: Training students to represent arithmetic word problems. **81**(4), 521 (1989). American Psychological Association
15. Huang, D., et al.: How well do computers solve math word problems? Large-scale dataset construction and evaluation, pp. 887–896 (2016)
16. Dong, L., et al.: Unified language model pre-training for natural language understanding and generation (2019)
17. Devlin, J., Chang, M.-W., Lee, K., Toutanova, K.: BERT: pre-training of deep bidirectional transformers for language understanding (2018)
18. Velickovic, P., et al.: Graph attention networks (2017)
19. Xu, B., Wang, N., Chen, T.: Empirical evaluation of rectified activations in convolutional network (2015)
20. Mei, J.: Tongyi ci cilin. Shanghai Cishu Chubanshe (1985)
21. Chiang, T.-R., Chen, Y.-N.: Semantically-aligned equation generation for solving and reasoning math word problems (2018)
22. Li, S., et al.: Graph-to-tree neural networks for learning structured input-output translation with applications to semantic parsing and math word problem. arXiv preprint: arXiv:2004.13781 (2020)
23. Qin, J., et al. Neural-symbolic solver for math word problems with auxiliary tasks. arXiv preprint: arXiv:2107.01431 (2021)
24. Liang, Z., Zhang, J., Shao, J., et al.: MWP-BERT: a strong baseline for math word problems (2021)
25. Lan, Y., et al.: MWPToolkit: an open-source framework for deep learning-based math word problem solvers. In: Proceedings of the AAAI Conference on Artificial Intelligence, vol. 36, no. 11, pp. 13188–13190 (2022)
26. Liu, Y., Ott, M., Goyal, N., et al.: RoBERTa: a robustly optimized BERT pre-training approach. arXiv preprint: arXiv:1907.11692 (2019)
27. Zou, Y., Lu, W.: Text2Math: end-to-end parsing text into math expressions. arXiv preprint: arXiv:1910.06571 (2019)
28. Xie, Z., Sun, S.: A goal-driven tree-structured neural model for math word problems. In: IJCAI, pp. 5299–5305 (2019)

Spatially Invariant and Frequency-Aware CycleGAN for Unsupervised MR-to-CT Synthesis

Shuang Song[1], Jun Zhang[2(✉)], Wenbin Hu[1], Yong Luo[1], and Xin Zhou[3]

[1] School of Computer Science and Hubei Key Laboratory of Multimedia and Network Communication Engineering, Wuhan University, Wuhan, China
{songshuang327,hwb,luoyong}@whu.edu.cn
[2] Department of Radiation and Medical Oncology, Hubei Key Laboratory of Tumor Biological Behaviors, Hubei Cancer Clinical Study Center, Zhongnan Hospital of Wuhan University, Wuhan, China
zhangjun110@whu.edu.cn
[3] Jiangxi Science and Technology Normal University, Nanchang, China
zhouxin@jxstnu.edu.cn

Abstract. Synthesis of computed tomography (CT) images from magnetic resonance (MR) images plays an important role in radiotherapy treatment planning. CycleGANs have achieved promising performance in unsupervised MR-to-CT synthesis. However, the inter-modality gap between the two modalities and the loss of high-frequency information in the synthetic CT images are still not well addressed. In this paper, we propose a spatially invariant and frequency-aware CycleGAN (SF-CycleGAN) to improve the performance of unsupervised MR-to-CT synthesis. Specifically, we introduce a translation-invariant generator to generate CT from MR images, while maintaining the invariance of spatial feature during translation for those positions having similar characteristics. Furthermore, we define a frequency-consistent loss to promote the consistency of the frequency between real and synthesized images and adaptively guide the model to pay more attention to synthesizing the harder-frequency (e.g., higher-frequency) parts. Intensive results in unpaired brain MR-to-CT image synthesis demonstrate that our method provides both quantitatively and qualitatively superior performance as compared to the baseline (CycleGAN) and other state-of-the-art approaches.

Keywords: MR-to-CT synthesis · unsupervised · CycleGAN

1 Introduction

Computed tomography (CT) and magnetic resonance (MR) images are two commonly-used medical imaging modalities, which are both important and widely applied in the treatment planning of radiotherapy [1]. MR images deliver

L. Iliadis et al. (Eds.): ICANN 2023, LNCS 14262, pp. 332–343, 2023.
https://doi.org/10.1007/978-3-031-44201-8_28

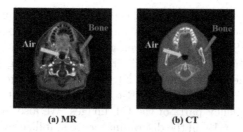

Fig. 1. Example of a pair of brain MR and CT images from the same patient.

excellent soft-tissue contrast that is useful for the delineation of gross tumors and organs at risk (OARs) [2], while CT images provide electron density information for dose calculation and reference images for pre-treatment positioning [3]. Due to their complementary characteristics, the acquisition of both CT and MR images of the patient has become part of the clinical workflow [4]. However, obtaining both CT and MR images is not only time-consuming and costly, but also leads to the nonrigid misalignment between the two modalities. In light of these challenges, MR-only treatment planning based on MR-to-CT synthesis has become an attractive alternative, which is valuable for both scientific research and clinical application.

Recently, since deep learning has shown great success in medical image analysis [5,6], many CNN-based architectures have been proposed for MR-to-CT synthesis, and the most popular ones are the U-nets [7] and generative adversarial networks (GANs) [8]. Although these approaches can produce promising synthetic images sometimes, most of them learn using paired MR and CT data, which are hard to acquire in practice. To relax the requirement of paired training data, some approaches based on CycleGAN [9] have been developed for unsupervised medical image translation [10–12].

Despite the certain success of existing approaches in CT synthesis, the following challenges still remain to be tackled: 1) there is a large inter-modality appearance gap between the MR and CT images, as shown in Fig. 1, and thus it is difficult to encode both the spatial and context information and learn accurate translation between the two modalities [13]. 2) the reconstruction error in CT images is crucial in the high-frequency components, where a lot of detailed information (*e.g.*, contours) is contained [14]. However, the existing loss function, such as the simple ℓ_1 loss, may lead to poor preservation of image details since it is minimized by averaging for all possible outputs [15]. Some researches [16] also reveal that deep neural networks (DNNs) tend to learn from low to high frequencies during training. That is, the low-frequency parts are learned faster, at the sacrifice of the high-frequency parts.

To tackle these challenges, we propose a spatially invariant and frequency-aware CycleGAN, termed SF-CycleGAN, for unsupervised MR-to-CT synthesis using unpaired training data. This method not only constrains translation-invariance of the spatial feature between the input MR and synthetic CT images without additional requirements on the training dataset, but also adaptively enforces the model to focus on synthesizing the frequency components that are hard to synthesize. Specifically, we leverage dynamic region-aware convolution [17], which can automatically assigns filters to corresponding spatial-dimension regions, as part of the image generator. Furthermore, we improve focal frequency loss [18] to make it better adapt to MR-to-CT synthesis, compensating for the loss of the high-frequency parts of the CT images. We also incorporate a spectral normalization step [19] in the discriminators to stabilize the training process. Our contributions can be summarized as follows:

- We propose a novel generator to dynamically learn the distribution of spacial semantics, which reduces the modality gap and well preserves the translation-invariance of spacial features during MR-to-CT synthesis.
- We define a frequency-consistent loss to maintain the frequency-consistency between the input and synthetic images, as well as adaptively focus the model on the frequency parts that are hard to synthesize.

Comprehensive experiments are performed for MR-to-CT synthesis, and the results indicate the superiority of our method over the state-of-the-art approaches.

2   Related Works

A variety of deep learning-based methods have been proposed to synthesize CT images from MR images. Generally, medical image synthesis methods can be roughly classified into supervised and unsupervised methods.

Supervised methods require non-rigidly aligned image pairs of the same patients during training. Han [20] proposed using Deep Convolutional Neural Networks (DCNN) to generate synthetic CT images, outperforming the traditional atlas-based approach. Cusumano [21] applied conditional generative adversarial networks (cGAN) [22] to generate pelvic and abdominal CT images from MR images. Despite the success of these methods in synthesizing medical images, they require a large number of pairwise aligned MR and CT training images of the same patient, which may not be easy to access in practice.

For the lack of paired MR and CT images, an increasing number of unsupervised methods have been developed to learn from unpaired MR and CT training data. Wolterink et al. [10] applied cycle generative adversarial network (CycleGAN) [9] with unpaired brain MR and CT images, to successfully generate high-quality synthetic CT images. Unfortunately, CycleGAN cannot guarantee the structure alignment between the input and synthetic images since there are no direct constraints between these two images. Some studies then added additional losses for improved performance of synthesized images. Hiasa et al. [11] utilized a gradient consistency loss to improve the boundary alignment between the input and synthesized images. Yang et al. [12] defined a cross-modality structure-consistency loss to provide structural consistency constraints.

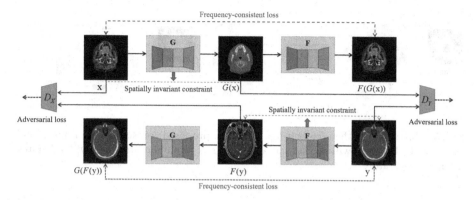

Fig. 2. Illustration of the framework of our proposed SF-CycleGAN. Two generators G and F learn the MR-to-CT and CT-to-MR mappings, respectively, where **spatially invariant constraint** is enforced to reduce the modality gap. Two discriminators D_X and D_Y distinguish between real and synthesized images in the MR and CT domain, respectively, and a **frequency-consistent loss** is added to make the generated image maximally preserve details.

3 Proposed Method

3.1 Model Overview

The ultimate goal of our proposed SF-CycleGAN is to obtain a mapping from the MR image to the CT image without using paired training data. We suppose that $X = \{x_i\}_{i=1}^{N}$ and $Y = \{y_j\}_{j=1}^{M}$ are the sets of MR and CT images, respectively. As shown in Fig. 2, based on CycleGAN [9], our SF-CycleGAN employs two generators $G : x \rightarrow \hat{y}$ and $F : y \rightarrow \hat{x}$ to learn the MR-to-CT and CT-to-MR mappings, respectively, where $\hat{y} = G(x)$ and $\hat{x} = F(y)$ represent synthesized CT and MR images. In addition, two generators D_X and D_Y are used to distinguish the synthetic and real images within the MR and CT domains, forcing the generators to synthesize more realistic images.

3.2 Translation-Invariant Generator

Due to the complex nonlinear mapping between MR and CT images, it's difficult to ensure the consistency of the spatial features during MR-to-CT translation and capture sufficient spatial semantic information that is significant for identifying the anatomical structure. Inspired by the observation that DRConv [17] is able to maintain the translation-invariance for the same objects, our goal is to develop a generator to extract plentiful semantic information and enforce the translation-invariance between the MR and CT domains, without using additional structural constraints. To achieve this, we incorporate DRConv into the generator, as shown in Fig. 3.

DRConv [17] can be divided into two modules: the learnable guided mask and the filter generator $g(X)$. The mask decides which filter will be assigned to

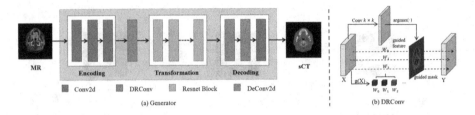

Fig. 3. Illustration of the architectures of (a) the proposed translation-invariant generator and (b) DRConv with kernel size $k \times k$ and region number m, where $g(X)$ denotes the filter generator.

which region by applying a $k \times k$ standard convolution to produce guided feature with m channels. The filter generator generates m filters, which will be assigned to the corresponding m spatial regions. Each region utilizes an individual filter and standard 2D convolution is performed using the corresponding filter in these regions to output Y.

Our proposed generator network mainly contains an encoder, a transformation module, and a decoder. The encoder extracts the knowledge of images from the original domain. The transformation module transforms the feature from the original domain to the target domain. And the decoder maps feature to the synthesized image. In the proposed network, DRConv is utilized in the generator, which takes the output vectors from the encoder as inputs, to maximally extract useful spatial features from the source domain, and further preserve spatial feature invariance for the positions that have similar characteristics.

3.3 Frequency-Consistent Loss

In the literature, the frequency domain gap between the real and fake images is a common issue for deep learning-based image reconstruction and synthesis models, since the DNNs tend to fit training data using a low-frequency function and hence, the high-frequency components cannot be well exploited [16]. In the MR-to-CT translation task, the lack of high-frequency information is reflected in the blurring of the synthesized CT images. This issue can be alleviated by utilizing the focal frequency loss (FFL) [18], which directly optimizes image synthesis approaches in the frequency domain. Given an image x of size $M \times N$, x is converted into its frequency representation using a 2D discrete Fourier transform, i.e.,

$$F_x(u, v) = \sum_{p=0}^{M-1} \sum_{q=0}^{N-1} f(p,q) \cdot e^{-i2\pi(\frac{up}{M} + \frac{vq}{N})}, \tag{1}$$

where (p, q) represents the spatial coordinate of an image pixel; $f(p, q)$ is the pixel value; e and i are Euler's number and the imaginary unit, respectively; $F(u, v)$ is the spatial frequency value at the spectrum coordinate (u, v) of the input image.

Let $F_x(u, v)$ be the spatial frequency value at the spectrum coordinate (u, v) of the real image x, and $F_{x'}(u, v)$ is of the reconstructed image x'. The focal frequency loss can be regarded as a weighted average of the frequency distance between the real and fake images, which can be defined by:

$$\mathcal{L}_{ff}(x, x') = \frac{1}{MN} \sum_{u=0}^{M-1} \sum_{v=0}^{N-1} w(u, v) |F_x(u, v) - F_{x'}(u, v)|^2, \tag{2}$$

where $w(u, v)$ denotes the weight of the spatial frequency at (u, v), which can be expressed as:

$$w(u, v) = |F_x(u, v) - F_{x'}(u, v)|^\alpha, \tag{3}$$

where α is the scaling factor of the spectrum weight matrix for flexibility and is set to 1 by default.

Following the above formulations, we improve FFL to make it adapt better for the unsupervised MR-to-CT synthesis task. Our frequency-consistent loss (FCL) is defined to encourage the synthesized images $G(F(x))$ and $F(G(y))$ to be frequency-identical to their inputs x and y, respectively, as well as make the model focus on synthesizing hard-frequency parts, $e.g.$, the edges and boundaries in CT images, adaptively. Our frequency-consistent loss is given by:

$$\mathcal{L}_{fc}(G, F, X, Y) = \mathbb{E}_{x \sim p_{data}(x)} \mathcal{L}_{ff}(x, F(G(x))) \\ + \mathbb{E}_{y \sim p_{data}(y)} \mathcal{L}_{ff}(y, G(F(y))), \tag{4}$$

The frequency-consistent loss calculates the weighted average of the frequency distance between the real and the cycle-reconstructed images in the same domain. It guides the model to pay more attention to synthesizing hard-frequency parts during training, by adaptively increasing the corresponding weights and progressively refining the synthesized images.

3.4   Training Objective

Our training loss consists of two terms: the standard adversarial loss [8] and our frequency-consistent loss presented in Eq. (4), and we introduce the adversarial loss function and the final objective as follows.

Adversarial Loss. The adversarial loss is applied to both mappings, as shown in Fig. 2. For the generator $G : X \to Y$ and its discriminator D_Y, the adversarial loss is:

$$\mathcal{L}_{adv}(G, D_Y, X, Y) = \mathbb{E}_{y \sim p_{data}(y)} [\log D_Y(y)] \\ + \mathbb{E}_{x \sim p_{data}(x)} [\log(1 - D_Y(G(x)))], \tag{5}$$

where x and y are the input MR and CT images, respectively. During training, the generator G generates images $G(x)$ that look as close as possible to the domain Y, while D_Y tries to distinguish the synthesized $G(x)$ from the real images y. The adversarial loss of generator $F : Y \to X$ and its discriminator D_X is defined similarly.

Final Objective. Given the adversarial loss and frequency-consistent loss mentioned above, the final training objective of our SF-CycleGAN is defined as:

$$\mathcal{L}(G, F, D_X, D_Y) = \mathcal{L}_{adv}(G, D_Y, X, Y)$$
$$+ \mathcal{L}_{adv}(F, D_X, Y, X) \qquad (6)$$
$$+ \lambda \mathcal{L}_{fc}(G, F, X, Y).$$

where λ is a trade-off hyper-parameter.

4   Experiment

4.1   Experiment Setup

Dataset. In this study, the GammaKnife-Hippocampal [23] dataset, which is provided by The Cancer Imaging Archive (TCIA) [24], is used for performance evaluation. The dataset contains high-resolution (1 mm slice thickness) T1 FLASH trans-axial MR imaging and their corresponding high-resolution CT image from 390 patients with brain diseases. The MRI volumes were rigidly registered and resized to the coordinate space and voxel dimensions of the CT volume ($0.5 \times 0.5 \times 1.0$ mm).

To perform experiments on 2D axial images, five axial slices from each MR and CT volume pair are extracted, which are then padded and randomly cropped to the resolution of 256×256. We randomly select 300 patients with $1,500$ image pairs for training and 40 patients with 200 image pairs for testing. To achieve unsupervised MR-to-CT synthesis, the paired brain CT and MR data are shuffled to create an unpaired training set. The intensity ranges are $[-700, 1300]$ HU for CT images and $[0, 1000]$ (arbitrary units) for MR images, both of which are linearly normalized to $[-1, 1]$ for training.

Evaluation Metrics. Three popular evaluation metrics, including mean absolute error (MAE), peak signal-to-noise ratio (PSNR), and structural similarity (SSIM) are used to quantitatively evaluate algorithm performance. For MAE, the lower the better; for PSNR and SSIM, higher values indicate better results.

4.2   Implementation Details

For the discriminator networks, 70×70 PatchGANs [22] is utilized to classify whether the overlapping image patches are realistic or synthetic. Additionally, we implement a spectral normalized (SN) convolutional layer [19] instead of the conventional one in the discriminators to stabilize the training process.

Our network implementation is based on Pytorch and all the experiments are performed on three NVIDIA Geforce RTX 3090 (24GB). All networks are optimized by the Adam solver with a learning rate of 0.0002 and coefficients of (0.5, 0.999), using a batch size of 16 and 200 epochs.

Table 1. Quantitative comparison in terms of CT synthesis quality evaluation metrics for various state-of-the-art image synthesis models. Both mean and standard deviation are reported.

Method	MAE	PSNR	SSIM
CycleGAN [9]	88.26 ± 14.64	26.05 ± 0.31	0.7478 ± 0.063
AttentionGAN [25]	88.51 ± 9.50	26.53 ± 0.59	0.8533 ± 0.035
CUT [26]	62.59 ± 13.68	26.31 ± 0.58	0.8444 ± 0.030
GCGAN [27]	60.20 ± 7.10	26.08 ± 0.35	0.9368 ± 0.027
DCLGAN [28]	45.42 ± 11.06	26.30 ± 0.47	0.9697 ± 0.031
SCC-CycleGAN [29]	117.14 ± 16.43	24.06 ± 0.15	0.5846 ± 0.073
Ours	**36.32 ± 8.43**	**27.55 ± 0.49**	**0.9771 ± 0.013**

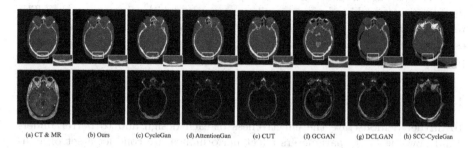

(a) CT & MR   (b) Ours   (c) CycleGan   (d) AttentionGan   (e) CUT   (f) GCGAN   (g) DCLGAN   (h) SCC-CycleGan

Fig. 4. Visualization of synthetic CT images using different methods. For one test subject, we show the ground-truth CT image and the input MR image, the synthetic CT images, and their difference from the ground-truth image.

4.3   Comparison Results

To verify the effectiveness of the proposed method, we conduct comprehensive comparisons between our SF-CycleGAN and other state-of-the-art unsupervised image-to-image synthesis approaches, including CycleGAN [9], AttentionGAN [25], CUT [26], GCGAN [27], DCLGAN [28], and SCC-CycleGan [29].

Table 1 reports the quantitative results of different methods on the test set. As can be seen, our model outperforms the other approaches in synthesizing CT images in terms of all metrics, which indicates that the synthesized CT images of our method are closer to the real CT images in both CT values and anatomical structure. Compared with the conventional CycleGAN, our model achieves 58.85%, 5.76%, and 30.66% improvements in MAE, PSNR, and SSIM, respectively, which indicates that the proposed method can better maintain the translation and frequency consistency between the source and target domains.

A visualization of the test results on a subject is shown in Fig. 4. The first column shows the ground-truth CT image and the input MR image. The second to the eighth columns show the synthesized CT images along with the difference images between the real and synthesized images by different methods. It

Table 2. Ablation study: CT synthesis quality under different conditions. Both mean and standard deviation are reported.

Method	MAE	PSNR	SSIM
CycleGan	88.26 ± 14.64	26.05 ± 0.31	0.7478 ± 0.063
Ours w/o TG & FCL	75.33 ± 12.53	26.39 ± 0.38	0.8344 ± 0.044
Ours w/o FCL	66.70 ± 12.61	26.60 ± 0.34	0.8550 ± 0.049
Ours w/o TG	48.29 ± 11.45	27.11 ± 0.47	0.9502 ± 0.023
Ours	**36.32 ± 8.43**	**27.55 ± 0.49**	**0.9771 ± 0.013**

can be seen that the synthesized images by our model are more identical to the real one, and the difference between the ground-truth and CT images produced by our model is relatively smaller as compared with other approaches. The red squares in Fig. 4 highlight our ability to better reduce synthesized errors, especially in high-frequency parts, which demonstrates the effectiveness of the proposed frequency-consistent loss in improving CT synthesis performance.

4.4 Ablation Study

To further demonstrate the effectiveness of each design and to better understand how the hyper-parameters affect performance, we conduct a set of ablation studies to systematically evaluate the importance of the main components in our model. As shown in Table 2, we can observe that all components play a vital role in improving our model's performance. Compared with the conventional CycleGAN, the CycleGAN with spectral normalization ("ours w/o TG & FCL") obtains better results in all metrics. Our proposed translation-invariant generator (TG) can help improve the quality of synthesized images. Besides, the frequency-consistent loss (FCL) has an outstanding contribution to explicitly enhance high-frequency MR-to-CT image synthesis. In summary, SF-CycleGAN with all its components achieves the best performance.

Impact of the Translation-Invariant Generator: To choose the optimal number of divided regions, *i.e.*, m introduced in Sect. 3.2, we vary the number from 2 to 8 in the proposed generator. The results in Table 3 show that applying DRConv in the generator achieves significantly better performance in terms of all metrics than the conventional CycleGAN (see "CycleGan" in Table 1). Besides, the performance reaches its peak when we divide the spatial dimension into 4 regions. Fewer divided regions cannot learn sufficient spatial semantics, while more regions may lead to filter assign error and optimization difficulty.

Impact of the Frequency-Consistent Loss: We study the influence of the frequency-consistent loss (FCL) by conducting experiments under different λ chosen from $\{1.0, 2.0, 5.0, 10.0, 20.0\}$ in Eq. (6). Results in Table 4 outperform

Table 3. CT synthesis quality for our model trained with different region numbers of DRConv in the generator. Both mean and standard deviation are reported.

Number	MAE	PSNR	SSIM
2	52.41 ± 10.19	26.77 ± 0.42	0.9580 ± 0.018
4	**36.32 ±8.43**	**27.55 ± 0.49**	**0.9771 ± 0.013**
8	53.59 ± 6.26	26.78 ± 0.28	0.9437 ± 0.016

Table 4. CT synthesis quality for our model trained under different choices of hyperparameter λ. Both mean and standard deviation are reported.

λ	MAE	PSNR	SSIM
1	45.36 ± 5.22	26.82 ± 0.31	**0.9782 ± 0.009**
2	41.11 ± 7.22	27.18 ± 0.42	0.9761 ± 0.011
5	**36.32 ± 8.43**	**27.55 ± 0.49**	0.9771 ± 0.013
10	37.71 ± 7.35	27.36 ± 0.41	0.9763± 0.012
20	61.95 ± 8.13	26.57 ± 0.28	0.9180 ± 0.022

those of the CycleGAN model in Table 1, which indicates the superiority of the proposed frequency-consistency loss over the cycle-consistency loss in improving image synthesis quality and semantic information alignment. The best MAE and PSNR are obtained when we set λ to be 5, while the highest SSIM appears when $\lambda = 1$. This is because when λ is too large, the model focuses too much on maintaining frequency consistency, leading to the ignorance of the pixel distance and style information learned from CycleGAN.

5   Conclusion

In this paper, we propose SF-CycleGAN, a spatially invariant and frequency-aware CycleGAN to reduce the modality gap and improve the details information for unsupervised MR-to-CT synthesis. The proposed translation-invariant generator synthesizes CT images from MR images, which not only extracts more plentiful spatial information but also preserves the invariance of spatial feature during translation. Moreover, we define a frequency-consistent loss to minimize the frequency distance between real and synthesized images and adaptively enforce the model to focus on the frequency parts that are hard to synthesize. Comprehensive experiments on unpaired brain MR and CT images show that our method can achieve better CT synthesis performance compared with the state-of-the-art approaches. In the future, we intend to develop 3D-based synthesis models to take full use of 3D spatial information of medical images.

Acknowledgements.. This work is supported by the Science and Technology Innovation Cultivation Foundation of Zhongnan Hospital of Wuhan University

(ZNPY2019095), the Medical Science and Technology Innovation Platform Project of Zhongnan Hospital of Wuhan University (PTXM2022033), the National Natural Science Foundation of China (No.62262026), the project of Jiangxi Education Department (No.GJJ211111), and the Fundamental Research Funds for the Central Universities (No. 2042023kf1033).

References

1. Chen, L., et al.: MRI-based treatment planning for radiotherapy dosimetric verification for prostate IMRT. Int. J.. Radiat. Oncol. * Biol.* Phys. **60**(2), 636–647 (2004)
2. Khoo, V., Joon, D.: New developments in MRI for target volume delineation in radiotherapy. Br. J. Radiol. **79**(special_issue_1), S2–S15 (2006)
3. Wang, T., et al.: A review on medical imaging synthesis using deep learning and its clinical applications. J. Appl. Clin. Med. Phys. **22**(1), 11–36 (2021)
4. Guerreiro, F., et al.: Evaluation of a multi-atlas CT synthesis approach for MRI-only radiotherapy treatment planning. Physica Med. **35**, 7–17 (2017)
5. Xu, R., et al.: SGDA: towards 3D universal pulmonary nodule detection via slice grouped domain attention. IEEE/ACM Trans. Comput. Biol. Bioinform. (2023)
6. Xu, R., Luo, Y., Du, B., Kuang, K., Yang, J.: LSSANet: a long short slice-aware network for pulmonary nodule detection. In: Wang, L., et al. (eds.) MICCAI 2022. Lecture Notes in Computer Science, vol. 13431, pp. 664–674. Springer, Cham (2022). https://doi.org/10.1007/978-3-031-16431-6_63
7. Ronneberger, O., Fischer, P., Brox, T.: U-Net: Convolutional networks for biomedical image segmentation. In: Navab, N., Hornegger, J., Wells, W.M., Frangi, A.F. (eds.) MICCAI 2015. LNCS, vol. 9351, pp. 234–241. Springer, Cham (2015). https://doi.org/10.1007/978-3-319-24574-4_28
8. Goodfellow, I., Pouget-Abadie, J., Mirza, M., Xu, B., Warde-Farley, D., Ozair, S., Courville, A., Bengio, Y.: Generative adversarial networks. Commun. ACM **63**(11), 139–144 (2020)
9. Zhu, J.Y., Park, T., Isola, P., Efros, A.A.: Unpaired image-to-image translation using cycle-consistent adversarial networks. In: Proceedings of the IEEE International Conference on Computer Vision, pp. 2223–2232 (2017)
10. Wolterink, J.M., Dinkla, A.M., Savenije, M.H.F., Seevinck, P.R., van den Berg, C.A.T., Išgum, I.: Deep MR to CT synthesis using unpaired data. In: Tsaftaris, S.A., Gooya, A., Frangi, A.F., Prince, J.L. (eds.) SASHIMI 2017. LNCS, vol. 10557, pp. 14–23. Springer, Cham (2017). https://doi.org/10.1007/978-3-319-68127-6_2
11. Hiasa, Y., et al.: Cross-modality image synthesis from unpaired data using Cycle-GAN. In: Gooya, A., Goksel, O., Oguz, I., Burgos, N. (eds.) SASHIMI 2018. LNCS, vol. 11037, pp. 31–41. Springer, Cham (2018). https://doi.org/10.1007/978-3-030-00536-8_4
12. Yang, H., et al.: Unsupervised MR-to-CT synthesis using structure-constrained CycleGAN. IEEE Trans. Med. Imaging **39**(12), 4249–4261 (2020)
13. Xiang, L., et al.: Deep embedding convolutional neural network for synthesizing CT image from T1-weighted MR image. Med. Image Anal. **47**, 31–44 (2018)
14. Shi, Z., Mettes, P., Zheng, G., Snoek, C.: Frequency-supervised MR-to-CT image synthesis. In: Engelhardt, S., et al. (eds.) DGM4MICCAI/DALI -2021. LNCS, vol. 13003, pp. 3–13. Springer, Cham (2021). https://doi.org/10.1007/978-3-030-88210-5_1

15. Mathieu, M., Couprie, C., LeCun, Y.: Deep multi-scale video prediction beyond mean square error. arXiv preprint: arXiv:1511.05440 (2015)

16. Xu, Z.J., Zhou, H.: Deep frequency principle towards understanding why deeper learning is faster. In: Proceedings of the AAAI Conference on Artificial Intelligence, vol. 35, pp. 10541–10550 (2021)

17. Chen, J., Wang, X., Guo, Z., Zhang, X., Sun, J.: Dynamic region-aware convolution. In: Proceedings of the IEEE/CVF Conference on Computer Vision and Pattern Recognition, pp. 8064–8073 (2021)

18. Jiang, L., Dai, B., Wu, W., Loy, C.C.: Focal frequency loss for image reconstruction and synthesis. In: Proceedings of the IEEE/CVF International Conference on Computer Vision, pp. 13919–13929 (2021)

19. Miyato, T., Kataoka, T., Koyama, M., Yoshida, Y.: Spectral normalization for generative adversarial networks. arXiv preprint: arXiv:1802.05957 (2018)

20. Han, X.: MR-based synthetic CT generation using a deep convolutional neural network method. Med. Phys. **44**(4), 1408–1419 (2017)

21. Cusumano, D., et al.: A deep learning approach to generate synthetic CT in low field MR-guided adaptive radiotherapy for abdominal and pelvic cases. Radiother. Oncol. **153**, 205–212 (2020)

22. Isola, P., Zhu, J.Y., Zhou, T., Efros, A.A.: Image-to-image translation with conditional adversarial networks. In: Proceedings of the IEEE Conference on Computer Vision and Pattern Recognition, pp. 1125–1134 (2017)

23. Porter, E., et al.: Gamma knife MR/CT/RTSTRUCT sets with hippocampal contours. Cancer Imaging Archive (2022)

24. Clark, K., et al.: The cancer imaging archive (TCIA): maintaining and operating a public information repository. J. Digit. Imaging **26**(6), 1045–1057 (2013)

25. Tang, H., Liu, H., Xu, D., Torr, P.H., Sebe, N.: AttentionGAN: unpaired image-to-image translation using attention-guided generative adversarial networks. IEEE Trans. Neural Netw. Learn. Syst. (2021)

26. Park, T., Efros, A.A., Zhang, R., Zhu, J.-Y.: Contrastive learning for unpaired image-to-image translation. In: Vedaldi, A., Bischof, H., Brox, T., Frahm, J.-M. (eds.) ECCV 2020. LNCS, vol. 12354, pp. 319–345. Springer, Cham (2020). https://doi.org/10.1007/978-3-030-58545-7_19

27. Fu, H., Gong, M., Wang, C., Batmanghelich, K., Zhang, K., Tao, D.: Geometry-consistent generative adversarial networks for one-sided unsupervised domain mapping. In: Proceedings of the IEEE/CVF Conference on Computer Vision and Pattern Recognition, pp. 2427–2436 (2019)

28. Han, J., Shoeiby, M., Petersson, L., Armin, M.A.: Dual contrastive learning for unsupervised image-to-image translation. In: Proceedings of the IEEE/CVF Conference on Computer Vision and Pattern Recognition, pp. 746–755 (2021)

29. Guo, J., Li, J., Fu, H., Gong, M., Zhang, K., Tao, D.: Alleviating semantics distortion in unsupervised low-level image-to-image translation via structure consistency constraint. In: Proceedings of the IEEE/CVF Conference on Computer Vision and Pattern Recognition, pp. 18249–18259 (2022)

Spatio-Temporal Attention Model with Prior Knowledge for Solar Wind Speed Prediction

Puguang Cai, Liu Yang$^{(\boxtimes)}$, and Yanru Sun

College of Intelligence and Computing, Tianjin University, Tianjin 300350, China
{pgcai,yangliuyl,syr}@tju.edu.cn

Abstract. Solar wind prediction is a critical aspect of space weather forecasting, and current research has primarily focused on feature extraction from historical wind speed or individual solar images. To enhance the quality of data and improve prediction accuracy, we propose a novel approach that leverages multi-modality, combining both temporal and spatial dimensions. Additionally, we utilize prior knowledge to guide model training, specifically in the image preprocessing and matrix multiplication stages, where prior knowledge constraints are applied. Our study introduces the spatio-temporal attention model (STA) for solar wind prediction, which comprises an image branch and a solar wind speed data branch. The image branch uses a shared-weight feature extraction network to extract features from EUV images, while the solar wind speed data branch models temporal dynamics with sequence networks. Furthermore, we incorporated an attention-based feature extraction module and a feature fusion module to enhance the model's performance. Our experimental results demonstrate that the proposed STA model outperforms existing state-of-the-art models.

Keywords: Solar Wind Forecast · Multimodal Learning · Prior Knowledge · Space Weather Forecast

1 Introduction

The solar wind is a dynamic and uninterrupted flow of charged particles emanating from the Sun's corona, the outermost layer of its atmosphere. Comprised mostly of electrons, protons, and alpha particles, this plasma exhibits a broad range of kinetic energies spanning from 0.5 to 10 keV. As the Earth is constantly exposed to the solar wind, any alterations to its conditions can result in widespread repercussions. Satellites may lose their ability to function, communication links can be disrupted, navigation systems may fail, and power grids can experience blackouts. To alleviate these risks, scientists closely monitor solar wind conditions utilizing satellites such as Advanced Composition Explorer(ACE), which can aid in predicting magnetic storms. Typically, solar wind speeds greater than 500 km/s is the conditions most likely to trigger magnetic storms. The interplanetary magnetic field is produced by the Sun and is

L. Iliadis et al. (Eds.): ICANN 2023, LNCS 14262, pp. 344–355, 2023.
https://doi.org/10.1007/978-3-031-44201-8_29

conveyed throughout the solar system by the solar wind. By continuously monitoring the solar wind and anticipating potential space weather events, we can enhance our readiness and minimize the impact on our technology and infrastructure.

High-speed solar wind streams (HSS) are a well-known phenomenon originating from coronal holes that exert a strong influence on the Earth's magnetosphere and affect various technological systems such as satellites. Although HSS-driven storms are typically weak, they can have long-lasting recovery phases that give rise to enhanced substorm activity. This poses a significant risk to satellites due to repeated injections of suprathermal electrons into the inner magnetosphere and substantial increases in the fluxes (Schrijver et al., 2015) [7]. Nevertheless, coronal holes are not the only source of high-speed solar wind. Coronal mass ejections (CMEs), which are large-scale explosions on the Sun that propel vast amounts of plasma into space, also generate high-speed solar wind. As the occurrence rate of CMEs peaks at solar maximum, most periods of high solar wind speed observed during these periods are usually CME-driven (St. Cyr et al., 2000) [8]. The range of speeds in interplanetary coronal mass ejections (ICMEs) and sheath regions linked with CMEs on the Sun spans from 250 to 950 kms^{-1} (Kilpua et al., 2017) [9]. Thus, it is crucial to consider both coronal holes and CMEs as potential sources of high-speed solar wind when predicting solar wind speed.

To date, deep learning techniques have been applied to solar EUV images to forecast or backcast solar wind speed. Upendran et al. (2020) [10] was the first to apply deep learning techniques to solar extreme ultraviolet(EUV) images for solar wind speed forecasting. They used images from both 193 and 211 A wavelengths to forecast the solar wind speed at a daily resolution. They extracted features from each image using GoogleNet (Szegedy et al., 2014) [11], which was pre-trained on the ImageNet data set (Deng et al., 2009) [12]. Then they fed the features into an LSTM Recurrent Neural Network (Hochreiter & Schmidhuber, 1997) [6] to generate the predicted solar wind speed. Their best model achieved a correlation of 0.55 and an RMSE of 80.28 kms^{-1} at a lag of three days and a history of four days. Raju and Das (2021) [4] have proposed a compact three-layer convolutional feature extractor, trained on solar EUV images at 193 A wavelength. Unlike Upendran(2020), their approach involves backcasting, rather than forecasting, solar wind speed. Specifically, the current solar wind speed is used to select the past image that is most likely to have caused it, which is then input into their model to reconstruct the observed solar wind speed. Raju and Das (2021) present findings for a fixed four-day forecast horizon model, yielding an RMSE of 78.3 km/s and a correlation of 0.55, using 2018 as a test set.

However, above approach utilized historical solar wind speed or integrated information from image sequences. In a separate study, Edward Brown and Svoboda (2021) [1] utilized an attention-based neural network architecture for predicting solar wind speed. However, their model was constrained by the use of single-frame images as input, which precluded the integration of information from image sequences. This limitation is especially critical as a single-frame image may not entirely capture the solar wind speed at a given moment. Notably, their also did not utilize historical solar wind speed, which is essential for accurate solar wind predictions, as it facilitates the integration of both temporal and spatial dimensions.

This study presents a novel approach for predicting solar wind speed by incorporating both spatial and temporal information, along with prior knowledge. Firstly, an attention mechanism that considers both spatial and temporal information is proposed. Secondly, prior knowledge is incorporated by multiplying a latitude-varying matrix with the solar image. Thirdly, an EfficientNet architecture is employed to extract features from the solar images, using multiple scales. The attention-based feature extraction module and feature fusion module are added for improving the model's accuracy and generalization ability. Solar images from the SDO/AIA dataset and solar wind speed data from the OMNI database are used for the experiments. The experimental results demonstrate that the proposed model outperforms the state-of-the-art models in terms of prediction accuracy and generalization ability. The effectiveness of incorporating prior knowledge and utilizing both spatial and temporal information for solar wind prediction is highlighted by the results.

2   Data Analysis and Processing

This section presents the methodology used to curate and preprocess the data for our study.

2.1   Solar Images

The image dataset used in this study was obtained from NASA's Solar Dynamics Observatory (SDO) and was captured by the Atmospheric Imaging Assembly (AIA). The dataset underwent a series of instrumental corrections to ensure its accuracy and quality. Additionally, the images were downsampled to enable spatial and temporal resolutions and were synchronized both spatially and temporally to form the SDOML dataset. The resulting dataset contains monochromatic images that provide information on the intensity of light. Specifically, this study utilizes the EUV images at 211 Angstroms, which allows for the detection of coronal loops and other solar structures are important for understanding solar activity.

Prior to model training, we preprocessed the input and output data to facilitate faster and more effective convergence of the model. Our image preprocessing approach not only accelerates model training, but also incorporates prior knowledge and introduces additional constraints, resulting in improved model performance. In the image preprocessing stage, we first cropped the solar images to remove irrelevant information and speed up model training. L. Zhao and R. T. Wicks(2016) [2] observed a negative correlation between the peak speed of the solar wind and the co-latitude of the corresponding solar source coronal hole. Specifically, their analysis showed that as the co-latitude of the coronal hole increases, the peak speed of the solar wind decreases accordingly. So we multiplied the images with a latitude-varying weight mask to incorporate prior knowledge that coronal holes at different latitudes have different effects on solar wind. Mathematically, let I be the original solar image and M be the weight mask, the preprocessed image I_p is computed as follows: $I_p = I \odot M$ where $\odot$ denotes element-wise multiplication (Fig. 1).

2.2   Solar Wind Speed

The solar wind speed data are taken from the OMNIWeb service. Specifically, we use the solar wind speed, measured in km/s, at a 1 min time resolution for the OMNI data set. The data comes from WIND and the Advanced Composition Explorer spacecraft, both positioned at the L1 point, about 1.5 million km from Earth.

The numerical magnitude and distribution of the initial values of the solar wind speed from OMNI are not suitable for the output of machine learning. Therefore, we normalized all solar wind speed values. $Label_i = (S_i - Min)/N$ where S_i is the speed value, Min and N are the minimum value for removing outliers and the value range of all data. $Label_i$ is the label value of our supervised model.

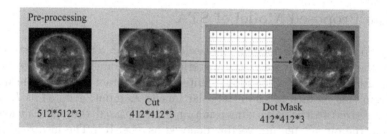

Fig. 1. In pre-processing, we crop to remove irrelevant information and speed up model training. Then, we multiply the mask with a weight varying with latitude to incorporate prior knowledge about the effects of coronal holes at different locations on the solar wind.

2.3   Training, Validation and Test Sets

In this research, we employed a 5-fold cross-validation technique to evaluate the models. Because the solar wind speed exhibits auto-correlation up to a period of approximately 4 days. Specifically, during the period from June 2010 to December 2018, the auto-correlation remains high at 0.70 for one day. As a result, the proximity of timestamps in the training, validation, and test sets can significantly impact the model's performance evaluation, as It doesn't reflect a fair representation of the Sun's changes in a short period of time.

2.4   Assessment Criteria

When making model predictions, it is important to establish performance metrics that can quantitatively evaluate the model's accuracy. To accomplish this, we use several metrics, including the root mean square error, and the Pearson correlation coefficient between predicted and observed values.

$$RMSE = \sqrt{\frac{\sum_{k=1}^{N}(o^k - p^k)^2}{N}} \tag{1}$$

$$CC = \frac{\sum_{k=1}^{N}(p^k - \bar{p})(o^k - \bar{o})}{\sqrt{\sum_{k=1}^{N}(p^k - \bar{p})^2}\sqrt{\sum_{k=1}^{N}(o^k - \bar{o})^2}} \tag{2}$$

where o^k is the observed speed value, p^k is the predicted speed value, $\bar{o}$ and $\bar{p}$ are the mean value, and N is the batch_size of data. RMSE uses the average error and is sensitive to both large and small errors within the set of measurements, making it a good indicator of the predicted value's accuracy. The Pearson correlation coefficient CC is used to measure the linear correlation between predicted and observed values. By using these metrics, we can better evaluate the accuracy of the model and eliminate the influence of sample size N and dimension.

3   The Proposed Model of STA

This section presents our model. The model is based on a two-branch structure, namely the image branch and the historical speed branch. The image branch uses the EfficientNet deep learning architecture to extract features from images of the Sun. The branch takes in the solar images as input, denoted as I, which are first resized to the same dimension and then passed through EfficientNet to obtain the output feature vector, denoted as $B \in \mathbf{R}^d$. The historical speed branch provides context for the model by incorporating information about the past speed of the solar wind. The Branch takes in the solar wind time series as input, denoted as $X = \{x_1, x_2, ..., x_T\}$, where T is the sequence length. It first passes X through A-RNN to obtain the output feature vector, denoted as $A \in \mathbf{R}^d$, where d is the dimensionality of A. The two branches are combined through a feature concatenation process denoted as $F = [A; B] \in \mathbf{R}^{2d}$. This F is then input into a Transformer module which consists of N identical layers. Each layer consists of a multi-head self-attention mechanism and a position-wise feedforward network. The input to each layer is F, denoted as F_0, and the output is $F_N \in \mathbf{R}^{2d}$. Then A, B, F_N are concatenated through the self-attention module, which is passed through a fully-connected layer to obtain the predicted solar wind speed, denoted as $\hat{y} \in \mathbf{R}$. The loss function used Huber loss.

Incorporating both time and spatial information into the design of the solar wind prediction model offers several advantages. Firstly, by utilizing image processing techniques, the model can take into account the visual characteristics of the Sun that are directly related to the speed of the solar wind. This can lead to more accurate predictions by capturing complex relationships between the Sun's appearance and the behavior of the solar wind. Secondly, incorporating historical speed information enables the model to account for the dynamic nature of the solar wind and understand how it evolves over time. Finally, using a Transformer module allows the model to handle both time and spatial information effectively, making more informed predictions. In conclusion, incorporating both time and spatial information into the design of the solar wind prediction model offers a comprehensive understanding of the solar wind, leading to more precise predictions (Fig. 2).

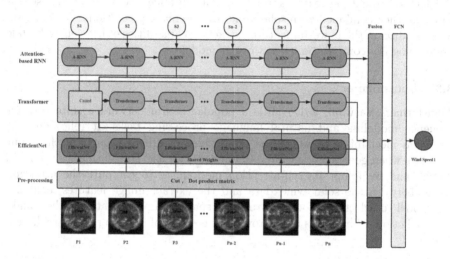

Fig. 2. Framework of the model. An image branch that uses a shared-weight Efficient-Net network to extract features from solar images, and a solar wind branch that uses an attention-based RNN to process historical solar wind data. The outputs of the two branches are then merged and fed into a fully connected layer for final prediction.

3.1 Attention-Based RNN

An attention-based RNN is a type of recurrent neural network that uses an attention mechanism to selectively focus on specific parts of the input sequence when making predictions. In our model, we used an attention-based RNN to process the solar wind data, with the goal of capturing the temporal dependencies and identifying important features in the time series data. Specifically, we used a self-attention mechanism to compute the importance of each time step in the input sequence and selectively attend to those time steps that are most relevant for making predictions. This approach allows our model to effectively capture the complex dynamics of the solar wind and make accurate predictions of the solar wind speed.

3.2   EfficientNet

We employ EfficientNet (Tan, 2019) [5] as our feature extraction backbone. EfficientNet is a convolutional neural network that comprises multiple layers of convolutional, activation, and pooling operations. The model aims to achieve a balance between network depth, width, and resolution, leading to improved accuracy and efficiency. EfficientNet employs the "compound scaling" technique to adjust these factors by scaling the network's parameters based on predefined ratios. This enables the network to handle high-resolution images while maintaining computational efficiency. Specifically, we utilize the shared weights of EfficientNet to extract features from the image branch of our model. These features are then combined with solar wind data to make predictions. By doing so, we capitalize on the powerful feature extraction capabilities of EfficientNet while minimizing the computational cost of our model.

3.3   Transformer

Transformer (Vaswani, 2017) [3] is a popular neural network architecture for sequence modeling and natural language processing tasks. It relies on self-attention mechanism to weigh the importance of different parts of the input sequence when generating outputs. In our task, we use Transformer as the main model, and we adopt its self-attention mechanism to compute the attention scores between the solar wind data and the extract image features, enabling the model to selectively focus on relevant spatio-temporal features when making predictions. This helps to improve the accuracy of our solar wind prediction model.

Multi-head Attention. In the Transformer architecture, Multi-Head attention is a key component that allows the model to selectively attend to different parts of the input sequence in a self-attention mechanism. Specifically, Multi-Head attention computes the dot-product of the queries and keys from different "heads" to obtain the attention weights, which are then used to compute the weighted sum of the values. This process is performed in parallel across multiple heads, and the outputs are concatenated and projected to obtain the final attention output. In Fig. 3, we give the structure of multi-head attention.

In our model, Multi-Head attention is applied to the features extracted from the low-dimensional features, allowing the model to capture complex temporal dependencies in the solar wind data. By selectively attending to different parts of the input sequence, the Multi-Head attention mechanism helps the model better distinguish relevant information from noise, leading to more accurate predictions.

Q, K, V transformation formula in Multi-Head Attention:

$$Query(Q) : \mathbf{Q} = \mathbf{W}_Q\mathbf{X}; Key(K) : \mathbf{K} = \mathbf{W}_K\mathbf{X}; Value(V) : \mathbf{V} = \mathbf{W}_V\mathbf{X} \qquad (3)$$

$$Attention(Q, K, V) = softmax\left(\frac{QK^T}{\sqrt{d_k}}\right)V \qquad (4)$$

Among them, the $\mathbf{W}_Q$, $\mathbf{W}_K$, $\mathbf{W}_V$ is weighting matrix, $\mathbf{X}$ as input characteristic matrix. Attention(Q, K, V) is the attention output of a head.

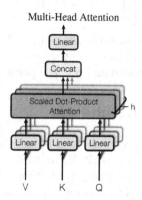

Fig. 3. Multi-head attention is implemented by projecting the input into multiple subspaces and performing separate scaled dot-product attention computations on each of them before concatenating and projecting the results.

3.4   Feature Fusion

We fuse the features from two branches, one for solar wind time series data and the other for solar images, to capture both temporal and spatial information. Specifically, the low-dimensional features A and B extracted from the A-RNN and EfficientNet, respectively, are concatenated to form a mid-level feature representation, which is then fused with the high-dimensional feature C extracted from the Transformer. The fusion mode is that we first concatenate the features ABC into matrix D, and then through the self-attention algorithm, output matrix E, the shape of matrix E. Features of different dimensions are given different weights. This fusion not only gives different features different weights but the combination of features from multiple levels enables the model to effectively capture both shallow and deep information. This fusion method improves the performance of the model in solar wind prediction by integrating complementary information from different sources.

3.5   Loss Function

Solar wind speed exhibits large fluctuations over time, and conventional loss functions such as MSE can be sensitive to large errors, resulting in models that are overly responsive to these fluctuations. Compared to MSE, Huber Loss has a lower sensitivity to outliers, using MSE for samples with small errors and MAE for samples with large errors. This loss function can be adjusted by controlling the hyperparameter δ to balance MSE and MAE. Specifically, when the absolute error is less than or equal to δ, MSE is used, and when the absolute error is greater than δ, MAE is used. The mathematical form of Huber Loss is given as:

$$L_\delta(y,\hat{y}) = \begin{cases} \frac{1}{2}(y-\hat{y})^2, & if \ |y-\hat{y}| \leq \delta \\ \delta|y-\hat{y}| - \frac{1}{2}\delta^2, & if \ |y-\hat{y}| > \delta \end{cases} \tag{5}$$

Among them, δ is a hyperparameter, indicating that when $|y-\hat{y}| \leq \delta$, use the mean square error as the loss function, otherwise use the linear function of the absolute error. y is the true value and $\hat{y}$ is the predicted value.

4   Experiments and Results

In this section, conducted experiments to compare the proposed model with the models developed by Raju and Das (2021) and Edward Brown & Filip Svoboda (2021) for solar wind prediction. The proposed model outperformed both of the existing models, achieving a 4.61% improvement in the RMSE metric. These results suggest that the proposed model can effectively predict solar wind values and may have practical applications in the field of space weather forecasting.

4.1   Benchmark Models

The proposed model was evaluated with a series of carefully selected and tuned parameters to ensure optimal performance. These parameters included a learning rate of 1e-5, a batch size of 32, a number of training epochs set to 100, a weight decay of 0.9, and the use of Adam as the optimizer. Through a series of experiments, these parameters were carefully tuned to achieve the best possible results. Our experimental results confirm the effectiveness of these settings.

Table 1. Performance of Our Solar Models Relative to (Raju and Das, 2021; Edward Brown 2021;) Predicting Solar Wind Speed Using Extreme Ultraviolet Data at a 4 Day Forecast Horizon in for the Year 2018.

Model	RMSE	%Improvement	Correlation	%Improvement
Persistence	118.76	−65.75%	−0.027	−104.2%
Raju and Das	78	−8.86%	0.55	−14.6%
Edward Brown	71.65	–	0.644	–
STA(Our)	**68.35**	4.61%	**0.677**	5.12%

We compare STA with Raju and Das (2021) and Edward Brown (2021). As shown in Table 1, we summarize the experimental results of our model and other benchmark models based on the performance indices: RMSE and CC. We can see that our model achieves the best performance, with the lowest RMSE and the highest CC. It can also be seen from Fig. 4 that our model achieves the best fitting of the observed values and better captures the upward and downward trend of the solar wind speed. The reason is that the STA learn the feature dimension and the time dimension automatically. And the addition of prior knowledge also plays a key role, which we'll talk about in the ablation experiment.

As illustrated in Fig. 5, our model effectively avoids overfitting on the training set, thereby demonstrating its aptitude in capturing the fluctuating trends of the solar wind speed and acquiring insightful information for predicting the same from solar observation images. This phenomenon can be attributed to the capacity of the STA to autonomously acquire various spatio-temporal feature dimensions.

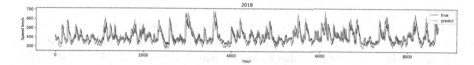

Fig. 4. Fitting curve of the predicted value of the STA model and the observed value of the verification set. The blue line is the observed value, and the red line is the predicted value of the STA model 96 h in advance. It is a good predictor of the upward and downward trends of observations, respectively. (Color figure online)

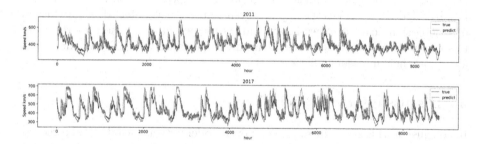

Fig. 5. STA model effectively avoids overfitting on the training set, thereby demonstrating its aptitude in capturing the fluctuating trends of the solar wind speed and acquiring insightful information for predicting the same from solar observation images. Space is limited, we only show 2011 and 2017.

4.2 Ablation Experiments

To investigate the importance of various components of the proposed model, ablative experiments were conducted. In this section, we present the results of removing each component from the model and report the corresponding changes in the model's performance. The experimental results are shown in Table 2.

Table 2. Ablation Experiments.

Model	Removing Module	RMSE	%Improvement	Correlation	%Improvement
Model-1	Dot-Mask	70.42	−3.02%	0.622	−3.27%
Model-2	A-RNN	72.93	−6.70%	0.614	−9.31%
Model-3	EfficientNet	69.17	−1.20%	0.625	−7.68%
Model-4	Transformer	72.68	−6.34%	0.539	−20.4%
Model-5	Attention Fusion	70.64	−3.35%	0.643	−5.02%
STA(Our)	−	**68.35**	−	**0.677**	−

This study analyzes the effectiveness of various components in our proposed solar wind prediction model. Experiment Model-1 compares model performance with and without prior knowledge mask, showing a decrease of 3.02% and 3.27% in RMSE and CC, respectively, indicating the benefit of using prior constraints. Model-2 assesses the contribution of A-RNN in capturing temporal dependencies, showing a significant decrease in performance when this component is removed. Model-3 investigates the role of the EfficientNet network in capturing spatial features, showing a noticeable but less critical impact. Model-4 explores the impact of transformer network and position encoding, emphasizing the importance of the transformer network in capturing complex relationships and position encoding in enabling the transformer network to capture sequential information. Finally, Model-5 examines the impact of removing attention-based feature fusion, observing significant declines in key indicators, emphasizing the importance of this fusion in extracting features of varying importance in both time and space, as well as their interdependence.

5   Discussion and Conclusion

In conclusion, this study introduces a novel model for solar wind speed forecasting that surpasses existing models. By employing an attention-based recurrent neural network on solar wind time-series data and a shared-weight EfficientNet on solar images, the model effectively captures the temporal and spatial characteristics, thereby enhancing the prediction task. The integration of information from both branches through a transformer further improves the combination of shallow and deep information, enabling the model to capture interdependencies among input features. However, the incorporation of prior knowledge in the model is relatively simplistic. To enhance accuracy and reliability in predicting solar wind speed, future work should focus on incorporating more comprehensive prior knowledge and leveraging deep learning techniques. This would enable a more sophisticated integration of prior knowledge into the forecasting process, holding great potential for further advancements in this field.

Acknowledgements. This work was supported in part by the National Natural Science Foundation of China under Grant 62076179.

References

1. Brown, J.E., Svoboda, E.: Attention-based machine vision models and techniques for solar wind speed forecasting using solar EUV images. Remote Sens. **13**(7), 1343 (2021)
2. Zhao, L., Wicks, R.T.: Negative correlation between the peak speed of the solar wind and the co-latitude of the corresponding solar source coronal hole. Astrophys. J. **830**(1), 56 (2016)
3. Vaswani, A., et al.: Attention is all you need. In: Advances in Neural Information Processing Systems, vol. 30, pp. 5998–6008 (2017)
4. Raju, S.S., Das, A.: Solar wind speed backcasting from solar EUV images using convolutional neural networks. Sol. Energy **220**, 183–193 (2021). https://doi.org/10.1016/j.solener.2021.01.014
5. Tan, M., Le, Q.: EfficientNet: rethinking model scaling for convolutional neural networks. arXiv preprint: arXiv:1905.11946 (2019)
6. Hochreiter, S., Schmidhuber, J.: Long short-term memory. Neural Comput. **9**(8), 1735–1780 (1997)
7. Schrijver, C.J., et al.: Understanding space weather to shield society: a global road map for 2025–2050 commissioned by COSPAR and ILWS. Adv. Space Res. **55**(12), 2745–2807 (2015)
8. St. Cyr, O.C., et al.: Coronal mass ejections and the solar wind. J. Geophys. Res.: Space Phys. **105**(A12), 27421–27438 (2000)
9. Kilpua, E.K., Koskinen, H.E.J., Pulkkinen, T.I., Vourlidas, A.: Introduction to ICMEs and space weather. In: ICMEs and Space Weather: Causes, Characteristics, and Consequences, pp. 1–26. Springer, Cham (2017)
10. Upendran, L., Kwon, H.D., Kang, S.B., Park, H., Moon, Y.J.: Solar wind forecasting using deep learning techniques with solar EUV images. Astron. Astrophys. **642**, A26 (2020)
11. Szegedy, C., et al.: Going deeper with convolutions. In: Proceedings of the IEEE Conference on Computer Vision and Pattern Recognition, pp. 1–9 (2014)
12. Deng, J., Dong, W., Socher, R., Li, L.J., Li, K., Fei-Fei, L.: ImageNet: a large-scale hierarchical image database. In: 2009 IEEE Conference on Computer Vision and Pattern Recognition, pp. 248–255. IEEE (2009)

Spatiotemporal Model with Attention Mechanism for ENSO Predictions

Wei Fang[1,2,3(✉)], Yu Sha[1], and Xiaozhi Zhang[1]

[1] School of Computer and Software, Engineering Research Center of Digital Forensics, Ministry of Education, Nanjing University of Information Science and Technology, Nanjing 210044, China
hsfangwei@sina.com
[2] Jiangsu Collaborative Innovation Center of Atmospheric Environment and Equipment Technology (CICAEET), Nanjing University of Information Science and Technology, Nanjing 210044, China
[3] Provincial Key Laboratory for Computer Information Processing Technology, Soochow University, Suzhou 215000, China

Abstract. Climate disasters such as floods and droughts often cause significant losses to human life, national economy, and public safety. The El Niño Southern Oscillation (ENSO) is one of the most important interannual climate signals in tropical regions, and has a global impact on atmospheric circulation and precipitation. Accurate ENSO predictions can help prevent related climate disasters. Recently, convolutional neural networks (CNNs) have shown the best techniques for ENSO prediction. However, it is difficult for convolutional kernels to capture the long-distance features of ENSO due to the locality of convolution itself. We regard ENSO prediction as a spatiotemporal series prediction problem, and propose an ENSO non-stationary spatiotemporal prediction deep learning model based on a new attention mechanism and a recurrent neural network, called ENSOMIM. The model expands the Receptive field of the network to achieve the learning space characteristics of local and global interaction, and uses high-order nonlinear spatiotemporal neural networks to encode long-term time series features. In order to adequate training the model, we also add historical simulation data to the training set and conduct transfer learning. The experimental results indicate that ENSOMIM is more suitable for large-scale and long-term prediction. During the testing period from 2015 to 2023, ENSOMIM's Niño3.4 index's all-season correlation skill improved by 11% compared to classical CNNs, and the root mean square error decreased by 29%. It can provide effective predictions for a lead time of up to 20 months. Therefore, ENSOMIM can serve as a powerful tool for predicting ENSO events.

Keywords: Climate Disasters · ENSO · Long Term Prediction · Spatiotemporal Series Prediction · Deep Learning

L. Iliadis et al. (Eds.): ICANN 2023, LNCS 14262, pp. 356–373, 2023.
https://doi.org/10.1007/978-3-031-44201-8_30

1 Introduction

Climate change is currently a difficult problem facing the world, affecting people's lives to a large extent. The most significant El Niño Southern Oscillation (ENSO) phenomenon is the most important interannual signal of short-term climate change on the earth [1], which has a great impact on global climate, environment and socioeconomic.

ENSO is the wind field and sea surface temperature oscillation in the equatorial eastern Pacific region. In 1969, Bjerknes [2] proposed that El Niño and Southern Oscillation are two different manifestations of the same physical phenomenon in nature, which are reflected in the sea as El Niño phenomenon and in the atmosphere as Southern Oscillation phenomenon. El Niño refers to the phenomenon that the equatorial eastern Pacific Ocean warms abnormally every two to seven years (every four years on average). The opposite cold phenomenon is called La Niña phenomenon [3]. Due to ENSO being a global ocean atmosphere interaction, it has significant impacts on global weather, climate, and ultimately agriculture. In 1997–1998, fires caused by the abnormal drought caused by ENSO destroyed large areas of tropical rainforest worldwide [4]. In ENSO, almost half of the basins across the earth's surface had abnormal flood risk [5]. In order to cope with the threat of such climate disasters, making effective ENSO prediction in advance is essential to reduce disaster losses around the world.

Since the 1980s, scientists from all countries have been committed to the prediction research of ENSO [6]. Because the relevant time scale of sea surface temperature variability in most of the tropical Pacific is about 1 year, and the ENSO event dominates the sea surface temperature variability [7], the occurrence of ENSO phenomenon is reflected by sea surface temperature anomaly (SSTA), so predicting ENSO phenomenon is equivalent to predicting SSTA. In addition, among all indexes, Niño3.4 index is the most commonly used to measure ENSO phenomenon, and Niño3.4 index is the average sea temperature in the range of $5°N \sim 5°S$ $170°W \sim 120°W$. The traditional ENSO prediction models are mainly divided into statistical models and dynamic models. Statistical models analyze and predict ENSO through a series of statistical methods, such as linear transposition model (LIM) [8], nonlinear canonical correlation analysis (NLCCA) [9], Markov model (MKV) [10], etc., but they do not make full use of physical laws. The dynamic model is mainly based on the dynamic theory of the interaction between the atmosphere and the ocean, such as the simple coupling model [11], the intermediate coupling model (ICM) [12], the mixed coupling model (HCM) [13] and the fully coupled circulation model (GCMs) [14]. The prediction has reached the reliable prediction of 6 to 12 months, which is successful in the short-term prediction, but does not make full use of the existing large amount of actual historical data. For the long-term prediction, the simple dynamic method is difficult to work. Practices have shown that both dynamic and statistical methods have certain accuracy, and both can reflect some laws of atmospheric motion [15–17]. However, due to the variability and diversity of ENSO space-time evolution, most of the traditional methods are difficult to generate sophisticated predictions with a longer lead time than 12 months [18]. Especially in the 21st century, the impact of the extratropical atmosphere on the tropical region is intensified, making ENSO more complex and difficult to predict.

With the advent of the era of big data, Artificial Intelligence (AI) has made breakthroughs in various fields. Recently, the deep learning model based on neural network has made some promising achievements in ENSO prediction, namely, artificial neural network [19], recurrent neural network [20], short-term and short-term memory neural network [21–23], convolutional long-short-term memory [24], CNNs [25] and graph neural network [26]. Among them, the depth CNN shows a reliable prediction of up to 16 months, which is superior to most classical models [27]. The remarkable performance mainly comes from the convolution kernel, which can learn local signals from ENSO precursors. However, according to some recent findings in the field of computer vision, convolution kernels are inherently inefficient in learning the long-term correlation of ENSO predictors. For example, based on the local convolution kernel, in order to calculate the relationship between the SSTA of the North Pacific and the South Atlantic, it is necessary to accumulate deep layers of small nuclei.

We use simulation data and reanalysis data to alleviate the problem of insufficient training sets, and introduces a spatiotemporal series prediction method to predict ENSO. The main contributions are as follows.

(1) We express ENSO prediction as a spatiotemporal prediction problem rather than a time series regression task. Using the spatiotemporal series (meteorological factors) of the past three months of T time, a deep learning model for predicting ENSO is constructed to predict the Niño3.4 index in the next 20 months. For meteorological data, we regard the distribution field of a certain element at a certain time as an image and take it as the input of the model.

(2) We propose a new channel spatial attention module BGAM, which combines MBConv, channel attention and spatial attention. Spatial attention includes local and global attention, which can better conduct spatial interaction.

(3) We design an ENSO unsteady spatiotemporal prediction model based on attention mechanism and recurrent neural network, ENSOMIM, and use this model to predict the monthly mean sea surface temperature anomaly distribution and the corresponding Niño3.4 index in the equatorial Pacific in the next two years. ENSOMIM is an improved encoder-decoder structure of MIM-Block. The encoder extracts spatial features through convolution layer and attention mechanism, ST-LSTM and stacked memory module capture temporal features and non-stationary state. The decoder predicts through three-layer memory module and convolution layer.

(4) The experimental results show that from 2015 to 2023, ENSOMIM outperforms existing models based on CNNs and recurrent neural networks (RNNs) in terms of long-term prediction over 20 months.

2   Related Work

2.1   Spatiotemporal Sequence Forecasting

The problem of spatiotemporal series prediction includes two factors: time and space. Here, time refers to the sequence before and after. Space refers to both the target in the picture and the spatial information of the target's movement and change, as well as the GPS data in the tabular data or the spatial information of longitude and latitude. The data predicted by ENSO is the spatial information of the longitude and latitude of the latter. The problem of spatiotemporal series prediction has been widely used in the fields of precipitation nowcasting, typhoon prediction, traffic flow prediction, video prediction, etc., and has innovatively developed many variant structures, which has become a research hotspot in depth learning. In 1997, Srivastava et al. [28] proposed the Long Short-Term Memory (LSTM) model, which improves the performance of RNN model by injecting forgetting gate to learn selective memory of important information and forgetting secondary information. In order to better apply the LSTM model to image sequences, Dr. Shi Xingjian [29] proposed a new network of Convolutional LSTM (ConvLSTM) that combines convolution structure with LSTM in 2015. This model can learn both spatial and temporal features. In 2016, Dr. Shi Xingjian continued to propose trajectory GRU to overcome the local in-variance of convolution structure. In 2017, Yunbo Wang et al. [30] improved the internal structure of ConvLSTM and proposed a "gzag" network PredRNN to effectively utilize horizontal and vertical information. In 2018, they further improved this model and proposed PredRNN++ [31]. There is an adaptive connection between each time step and each layer serving both long-term and short-term routes, and proposed the Gradient Highway Unit to prevent the gradient from disappearing for a long time. In 2019, Yunbo Wang et al. [32] continued to propose a Memory in Memory (MIM) network, which utilizes the differential signals between adjacent repeating states to potentially handle high-order non-stationary behavior by stacking multiple MIM blocks.

2.2 Deep Learning for ENSO Forecasting

With the rapid development of AI, prediction methods based on deep learning are widely used in various fields. Some scholars began to try to improve ENSO prediction skills by using deep learning. In 2019, Ham et al. [27] first proposed to use CNN for ENSO prediction. The research results show that when the prediction time is more than 6 months, the prediction ability of CNN method to Niño 3.4 index is significantly higher than the current international best dynamic prediction system. When testing the real data from 1984 to 2017, CNN can predict the El Niño event 18 months in advance. At that time, this research achievement was regarded as the pioneering work of in-depth learning in the field of meteorological prediction. In the same year, He Dandan et al. [33] established the deep learning ENSO prediction model (DLENSO) by using ConvLSTM to predict ENSO by directly predicting the sea surface temperature (SST) in the tropical Pacific region. DLENSO is superior to LSTM model and deterministic prediction model, and is almost equal to integrated average prediction model in medium-long term prediction. In 2021, Hu et al. [34] used dropout and transfer learning to overcome the problem of insufficient data during model training, and proposed a model based on deep residual convolution neural network. The model effectively predicted the Niño 3.4 index with a lead time of 20 months during the evaluation period of 1984–2017. In the same year, Mu et al. [35] proposed a deep learning prediction model EN-SO-ASC based on a coupled model, which includes an encoder and decoder for capturing and restoring multi-scale spatiotemporal correlations, as well as two attention weights. During the validation period from 2014 to 2020, ENSO-ASC's Niño3.4 index had a higher seasonal correlation skill than existing dynamic models and re-current neural networks, and its prediction performance for a lead time of up to 20 months far exceeded [27]. In 2022, Feng et al. [36] applied Transformer to ENSO prediction, which can predict the monthly average Niño3.4 index for up to a year and a half, and can also predict strong El Niño phenomena more than a year in advance. In addition, with the increasing recognition of deep learning in various fields, more and more scholars have applied deep learning model prediction methods to ENSO prediction [25, 37, 38].

3 Method

We use pattern simulation data for pre-training of the model, then finetune the model through reanalysis of the data, and introduce an improved spatiotemporal prediction model ENSOMIM to predict SSTA in the Niño3.4 region. From the perspective of feature pre-extraction, we select the leading and most stable model for improvement and propose ENSOMIM. ENSOMIM is an Encoder-Decoder structure that integrates convolutional modules, attention modules, ST-LSTM, and uses MIM as a recurrent unit to improve the accuracy of model prediction, alleviate the problem of neglecting spatial information, forgetting too much long-term information, and the high order non-stationary features of ENSO data in spatiotemporal sequence prediction, resulting in limited prediction time and low accuracy.

3.1 Modeling ENSO Prediction Problems

The Pacific region where ENSO occurs is divided into a uniform grid by longitude and latitude, with each grid point having multiple meteorological element values at each time step, such as SST, sea surface wind speed, seawater velocity, etc. These elements are horizontally distributed in two-dimensional (2D). Therefore, after adding time dimension, for some time, SST data is three-dimensional (3D), which are time, longitude, and latitude, respectively. We use meteorological factors from the past 3 months (including time T), including global sea surface temperature and upper 300m ocean heat content, to construct a deep learning model for predicting ENSO and predict the Niño 3.4 index for the next 20 months.

The basic data predicted by ENSO is the monthly seawater surface temperature. We treat it as the four-dimensional grid data of the moving average seawater surface temperature anomaly every three months. For meteorological data, we regard the distribution field of a certain element at a certain time as a frame image, and take it as the input of the model, and expressed by tensor $X \in R^{P \times M \times N}$, where $M \times N$ represents the spatial area, P represents the number of meteorological factors, and then the prediction of sea surface temperature anomalies is expressed as an unsupervised spatiotemporal prediction problem. The observation of T time steps with time changes forms a group of dynamic sequences, which are represented by a total of T frame data of matrix sequence $X_1, X_2 \cdots, X_T$. Given the previous S frame data, the most likely N frame data in the future can be predicted, which can be modeled as shown in formula (1). The sequence prediction process is shown in Fig. 1.

$$\widehat{X}_{T+1}, \cdots, \widehat{X}_{T+N} = \mathop{argmax}_{X_{t+1}, \cdots, X_{t+N}} p(X_{T+1}, \cdots, X_{T+N} | X_{T-S+1}, \cdots, X_T) \qquad (1)$$

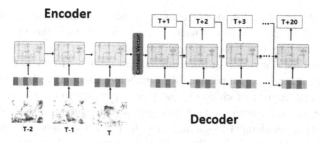

Fig. 1. The diagram of Series Forecast

3.2 BGAM

Considering that the ENSO prediction factors, namely the sea surface temperature and the ocean heat content, are greatly affected by the ocean internal dynamics and external environmental factors, the temperature change of a certain grid point in the same sea area can not only consider the influence of the surrounding grid points, but also need to consider the influence of the remote grid points, so we propose a new local global attention module BGAM combining MBConv, channel attention (CAM) and spatial attention (SAM), Among them, spatial attention includes local and global attention for better spatial interaction. The structure of attention module is shown in Fig. 2.

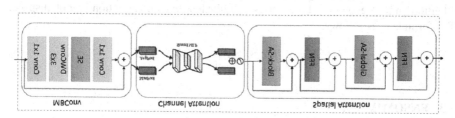

Fig. 2. Structure of BGAM.

MBConv and attention mechanism can be used together to improve the generalization ability and trainability of the network, and can also be replaced by other convolutions; CAM and SAM sub-modules are used for channel and spatial attention respectively, which not only save parameters and computing power, but also ensure that they can be integrated into the existing network architecture as plug-and-play modules. Input the characteristic $F \in R^{C*H*W}$, and then the channel attention module one-dimensional convolution $M_c \in R^{C*1*1}$, multiply the convolution result by the original image, take the CAM output result as input, and perform two-dimensional convolution M of the spatial attention module $M_s \in R^{1*H*W}$, and then multiply the output result with the original figure. The formula is as follows:

$$F' = M_c(F) * F \tag{2}$$

$$F'' = M_S(F') * F' \tag{3}$$

In CAM, the channel dimension remains unchanged and the space dimension is compressed. This module focuses on what information is useful in the input feature map. The input feature map first passes through two parallel MaxPool layers and AvgPool layers, changing the dimension of the feature map from C * H * W to C * 1 * 1, then through the MLP module, compressing the number of channels to 1/r (reduction rate) times the original number of channels, and then expanding to the original number of channels. After the ReLU activation function, the two activated results are obtained. Add the two output results element-by-element, and then use a sigmoid activation function to get the CAM output result. Finally, multiply the output result by the original image and change it back to the size of C * H * W, as shown in the following formula:

$$M_c(F) = \sigma(MLP(AvgPool(F)) + MLP(MaxPool(F))) = \sigma\left(W_1\left(W_0\left(F_{max}^c\right)\right)\right) \quad (4)$$

In SAM, the spatial dimension remains unchanged and the channel dimension is compressed. This module focuses on where the useful information is. First, change the output dimension of CAM into H * W * C, and divide the feature into shape tensor (H/P × W/P, P × P. C), indicating that the window is divided into non-overlapping windows, and the size of each window is P × P. Applying self-attention in the local spatial dimension is equivalent to paying attention in each small window after division. We use this block of attention for local interaction. Next, we use the fixed G × G Uniform mesh to transform tensor mesh into shape (G × G, H/G × W/G, C), instead of using a fixed window size to split the feature map, to generate an adaptive size H/G × W/G window. Using self-attention on the decomposed mesh axis is equivalent to using attention in global space. The formula is as follows.

$$M_S(F) = \sigma([Block\_SA(F); Global\_SA(F)]) \quad (5)$$

3.3 ENSOMIM

Aiming at the problem that the improved LSTM-based deep learning method cannot capture the spatiotemporal non-stationary characteristics of ENSO, we improved on the mature Memory in Memory (MIM) network, and designed two cascaded time memory multiplexing modules in MIM to replace the time forgetting gate. The first module (MIM-N) starts with H_{t-1}^1 is the input, which is used to capture non-stationary changes based on the difference between two consecutive hidden representations $(H_t^1 - H_{t-1}^1)$. The differential characteristic D of the other loop module (MIM-S) output by the MIM-N module D_t^l and external time memory cell C_{t-1}^l is used as the input to capture the nearly stable changes in the space-time series. This method, which combines stationary and non-stationary changes, can more effectively deal with complex dynamics in space-time series. The key calculation formulas in the MIM block are as follows. The structure of the two modules is shown in Fig. 3.

$$g_t = \tanh(W_{xg} * H_t^{l-1} + W_{hg} * H_{t-1}^l + b_g) \quad (6)$$

$$i_t = \sigma(W_{xi} * H_t^{l-1} + W_{hi} * H_{t-1}^l + b_i) \quad (7)$$

$$D_t^l = \text{MIM} - \text{N}(H_t^{l-1}, H_{t-1}^{l-1}, N_{t-1}^l) \tag{8}$$

$$T_t^l = \text{MIM} - \text{S}(D_t^l, C_{t-1}^l, S_{t-1}^l) \tag{9}$$

$$C_t^l = T_t^l + i_t \odot g_t \tag{10}$$

$$g_t' = \tanh(W'_{xg} * H_t^{l-1} + W_{mg} * M_t^{l-1} + b'_g) \tag{11}$$

$$i'_t = \sigma(W'_{xi} * H_t^{l-1} + W_{mg} * M_t^{l-1} + b'_g) \tag{12}$$

$$f'_t = \sigma(W'_{xf} * H_t^{l-1} + W_{mf} * M_t^{l-1} + b'_f) \tag{13}$$

$$M_t^l = f'_t \odot M_t^{l-1} + i'_t \odot g'_t \tag{14}$$

$$o_t = \sigma(W_{xo} * H_t^{l-1} + W_{ho} * H_{t-1}^l + W_{co} * C_t^l + W_{mo} * M_t^l + b_o) \tag{15}$$

$$H_t^l = o_t \odot \tanh(W_{1x1} * [C_t^l, M_t^l]) \tag{16}$$

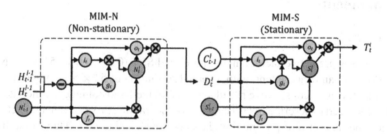

Fig. 3. Structure of MIM cell.

We build an encoder-decoder structure. In the encoder, we first use two layers of 3 × 3. The convolution extracts the underlying features, changes the number of channels, and makes the input data dimension adapt to the input of the attention module. Then, the attention module extracts the local and global features in space, and then uses the stacked three-layer MIM blocks to extract the temporal features and unsteady state. In the decoder, the three-layer MIM is simply used as a predictor, and the prediction results are input into the convolution layer, and the number of channels is combined into 1. At the end of the model, the output of the decoder is input into a convolution network composed of single-layer transposed convolution, and the predicted spatiotemporal sequence of the next 20 months will use longitude and latitude as the width and height of the image to form the size of the original image. Finally, through a full connection layer, the output sequence and label data set are arranged in the same way (channel number * 24 * 72,

1), which is convenient for later measurement of model performance. The overall model structure is shown in Fig. 4. The black arrow represents the transition path of state M, the red arrow represents the diagonal transition path of hidden state H, and the blue arrow represents the horizontal transition path of storage cells C, N, and S. Subscript represents time, superscript represents layer.

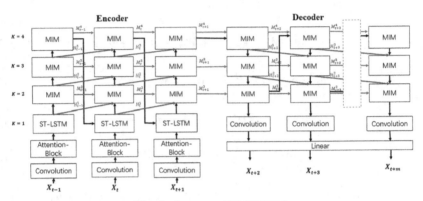

Fig. 4. Structure of ENSOMIM.

4 Experiments

4.1 Datasets

Our model uses predictive factors including global SST ($0° − 360°$E, $55°$S-$60°$N) and upper 300 m ocean heat content, with a spatial resolution of $5° × 5°$, using sea surface temperature for three consecutive months to predict the Niño 3.4 index, which is one of the indicators used to describe ENSO events. For the training process of neural networks, we divide the dataset into pre-training data and fine-training data. Due to the limited number of observation data samples, we are unable to meet the demand for sufficiently large data. We use coupled models from 1861 to 2013 to compare the simulation data of 15 climate models in the Coupled Model Intercomparison Project Phase 6 (CMIP6), and preliminarily trained the neural network model. However, the CMIP6 model has bias, which can affect the prediction accuracy of the constructed model. Therefore, we use the transfer learning method to further calibrate the pre-training model by using the simple ocean data assimilation (SODA) reanalysis data [39] in the transfer training from 1870 to 1973, which to some extent simulated the development of ENSO [40]. In addition, for cross validation analysis, we use the Global Ocean Data Assimilation System (GODAS) reanalysis data from 1984 to 2014 [41] as the validation set to evaluate prediction techniques. In order to eliminate the possible impact of ocean memory during the training period on the validation period ENSO, we leave a ten-year gap between the last year of the training set and the earliest year of the validation set. The dataset partitioning is shown in Table 1.

We preprocess the datasets. First, we aggregate the training data set to form a large data array. Then we unify the time range, calculate the moving average of three months, and then interpolate it into the required network. Finally, we calculate the SSTA and save the data set for training. We visualized the results of global seawater surface temperature interpolation from 1870 to 2023, as shown in Fig. 5. In addition, due to the large time scale of ENSO data, and the monthly scale data represented by each sample, the temperature difference will also be large, so it is difficult to accurately predict ENSO. We have visualized the SSTA from 1870 to 2023, as shown in Fig. 6.

Table 1. Datasets used to train and validate the ENSOMIM model.

	Data	Period
Training dataset	CMIP6 historical run	1861–2013
	Reanalysis(SODA)	1870–1973
Validation dataset	Reanalysis(GODAS)	1984–2014
Test dataset	Reanalysis(GODAS)	2015–2023

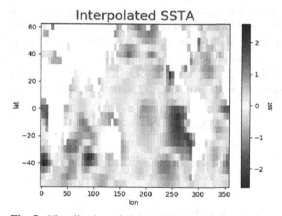

Fig. 5. Visualization of global SSTA after interpolation.

4.2 Experimental Designs

4.2.1 Experimental Details

We set up five sets of experiments to verify the performance of our model. The first group of experiments is to explore the effectiveness of the embedded position of attention module. The second group of experiments is to explore the effectiveness of MIM layers and structures. The third group of experiments evaluated the performance of the proposed attention mechanism. The fourth group of experiments is to verify the prediction ability of ENSOMIM model in the long term through evaluation indicators. The fifth group of

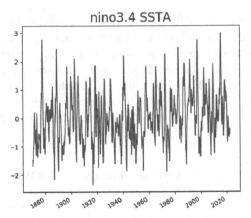

Fig. 6. Distribution of SSTA in Niño 3.4.

experiments is a comparison experiment between our proposed model and other dynamic models and deep learning models.

All our experiments are implemented on Pytorch, using the Adamw optimizer to train multiple models with a learning rate of 0.0003 and a batch size of 4. In addition, in order to further improve performance. We use the mean square error (MSE), root mean square error (RMSE), and mean absolute error (MAE) to evaluate the model's ability to predict changes in SSTA, and use the Pearson correlation coefficient PCC (the current month and the next two months) of the three-month moving average of the Niño3.4 index to evaluate the model's ability to predict ENSO. Low MAE and RMSE, high correlation skill PCC represent good predictive ability. The indicators are defined as follows:

$$\text{MAE} = \frac{1}{m} \sum_{i=1}^{m} |(y_i - \widehat{y_i})| \tag{17}$$

$$\text{MSE} = \frac{1}{m} \sum_{i=1}^{m} (y_i - \widehat{y_i})^2 \tag{18}$$

$$\text{RMSE} = \sqrt{\frac{1}{m} \sum_{i=1}^{m} (y_i - \widehat{y_i})^2} \tag{19}$$

$$p = \frac{\sum_{i=1}^{n} (x_i - \hat{x})(y_i - \hat{y})}{\sqrt{\sum_{i=1}^{n} (x_i - \hat{x})^2} \sqrt{\sum_{i=1}^{n} (y_i - \hat{y})^2}} \tag{20}$$

4.2.2 Optimization of Related Algorithms

When training the deep learning neural network, we usually hope to get the best generalization performance, that is, to fit the data well. However, all standard deep learning neural network structures are easy to over-fit, that is, when the network performs better and better in the training set and the error rate is lower and lower, in fact, at some point, its performance in the test set has begun to deteriorate. In order to make the model have better generalization ability and avoid over-fitting to achieve good equilibrium, we introduce the concept of early stop method. Early stop method is a widely used method, which is better than regularization method in many cases. The main steps are as follows: divide the original training data set into training set and verification set, and train only on the training set. Calculate the error of the model on the verification set for each period. Set a patient (patient ≤ epoch) in advance, which represents the maximum period that can tolerate generalization error. When the error of the model on the verification set is worse than the last training result, save the model parameters in the last iteration result, At the same time, the counter is increased by 1. When the counter and the patient are equal, the training is stopped. Assumption $E_{opt}(t)$ is the best validation set error obtained at the iteration number t, then $E_{opt}(t) = min_{t' \leq t} E_{va}(t')$, the growth rate of generalization error is shown in formula (21). See Fig. 7 for the effect of early stop.

$$GL(t) = 100 * (\frac{E_{va}(t)}{E_{opt}(t)} - 1) \qquad (21)$$

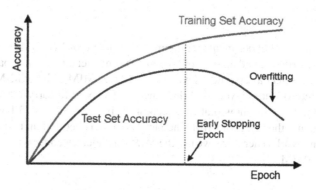

Fig. 7. Early Stopping Rendering.

In the subsequent network training process, the learning rate automatic attenuation strategy is adopted to accelerate the training speed. A large learning rate will achieve very fast convergence, so a larger value will be adopted at the initial stage, while avoiding falling into a local minimum; When the training reaches a certain level, the excessive learning rate may jump back and forth around the global minimum, resulting in the gradient swinging around the convergence. Therefore, a smaller learning rate can reduce the convergence pace and avoid the result swing. The learning rate decay strategy can be expressed as formula (22). When the number of training rounds reaches the set value, the learning rate will decrease a little. Wherein, *decay_rate* is the initial coefficient, *epoch*$_i$ means the ith training, α_0 is the initial learning rate.

$$\alpha_i = \frac{1}{1 + decay\_rate * epoch_i} * \alpha_0 \qquad (22)$$

4.3 Results

We first conduct experiments on the location of attention, aiming to find out where the attention module can be embedded in the encoder to better extract features. The experimental results are shown in Table 2. We conduct experiments on the classic MIM network, using ST-LSTM and three-layer MIM, respectively placing BGAM at the front and back ends of the MIM network. The experiments show that the location of the front and back has little impact on the experimental results, the error of extracting spatial features through attention is slightly small at the beginning.

Table 2. Error of different positions of BGAM.

Positions	MSE ↓	MAE ↓	RMSE ↓
Att-MIM	**0.1413**	**0.2660**	**0.3759**
MIM-Att	0.1444	0.2718	0.3800
Att-MIM-Att	0.1617	0.2945	0.4021

Then we carry out experiments on the model structure of ENSOMIM, as shown in Table 3. For the structure and number of layers of the encoder and decoder based on MIM in the model, we select a separate 3-layer MIM, 5-layer MIM, 7-layer MIM and coder-decoder structure of three layers of MIM-Encoder-Decoder to carry out experiments. The experimental results show that in a separate MIM network, the 3-layer MIM has the best effect, and the effect of MIM-Encoder-Decoder is better than that of a separate 3-layer MIM network. Therefore, we use the MIM-Encoder-Decoder with the best effect to build ENSOMIM.

Table 3. Comparative experimental results of different layers and structures of MIM.

Models	MSE ↓	PCC ↑
MIM7	0.1750	0.4210
MIM5	0.1566	0.4239
MIM3	0.1398	0.4329
MIM-Encoder-Decoder	**0.1384**	**0.4336**

In order to verify the effectiveness of the channel-space attention mechanism we proposed, we use the most popular channel-space attention module CBAM as the contrast object. On the basic of the previous two groups of experimental results, the location of embedded attention is selected as the starting position of the encoder, and the MIM-Encoder-Decoder is selected as the MIM structure. Under the same experimental conditions, the experimental effects of CBAM and BGAM are compared, the results as shown in Table 4.

Table 4. Comparative experimental results between CBAM and BGAM.

Models	MSE ↓	PCC ↑
MIM-Encoder-Decoder	0.1384	0.4336
With CBAM	0.1822	0.4285
With BGAM	**0.1359**	**0.4487**

Considering the large amount of data in pattern simulation and its bias, which can affect the prediction accuracy of the constructed model, we only use reanalysis data in the experiment of model structure exploration, which is the reason why the error of the experimental results is small but the correlation coefficient is low. In the training of the final model ENSOMIM, we use pattern simulation data for pre-training of the model, and then finetuning the model through reanalysis of the data. The ENSOMIM model predicts the MAE and RMSE of Niño3.4 SSTA during the 1 to 20 months lead time on the validation set, as shown in Fig. 8, demonstrating the long-term predictive ability of the ENSOMIM model. During a lead time of up to 14 months, the RMSE was all below 0.5, and during a lead time of 20 months, the MAE was all below 0.7. Overall, ENSOMIM is more suitable for long-term forecasting and has shown superiority in the prediction range of nearly two years. Figure 9 shows the difference between the predicted and true values of ENSOMIM's Niño3.4 index for each year during the 10-year period from 1984 to 1993. Figure 10 shows the difference between the predicted and true values of ENSOMIM's Niño3.4 index for each month on the test set. It can be seen that ENSOMIM can approximate the trend of the Niño3.4 index, but its predictions for certain extreme cases are too conservative.

We compare the test results of ENSOMIM with 8 deep learning models and 4 dynamic models, and the full season related techniques of each model are shown in Fig. 11. The results of 13 models are compared in the experiment, and the ENSOMIM model show a higher correlation in long-term prediction time over 15 months compared to other models' curves. The relevant skills within a lead time of 1–14 months also exceed most deep learning models and all dynamic models, achieving the best results in a prediction interval of 20 months in advance.

We also compare various evaluation indicators of different deep learning models, and Table 5 shows the MAE, RMSE, and PCC indicators of different deep learning models in the training set. Compared with 2D CNN that does not consider any temporal order of a given input, ENSOMIM uses 3D Receptive field blocks with 2D+ time convolution filters to learn spatiotemporal patterns from short-term inputs (three months), and uses MIM-Encoder-Decoder modules with attention mechanisms to learn the temporal order of long-term sequences. The Encoder Decoder structure constructed based on MIM modules can retain long-term contextual information in sequential input data even after small batch processing by maintaining its hidden and unit states. In addition, the attention mechanism allows the proposed model to process geophysical data and accurately focus on more relevant regions at specific time steps in prediction tasks, making the model more effective than simply using CNNs or RNNs.

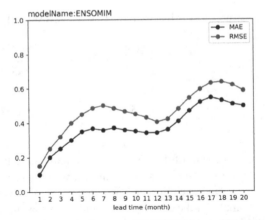

Fig. 8. Evaluation indicators of ENSOMIM in 1–20 lead times.

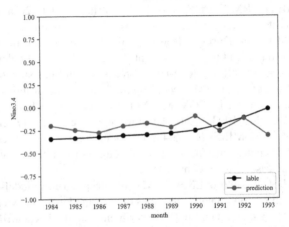

Fig. 9. Comparison of Predicted Values and Real Values from 1984 to 1993.

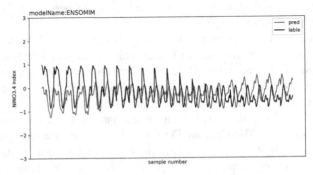

Fig. 10. Comparison of Predicted and Real Values on a test set.

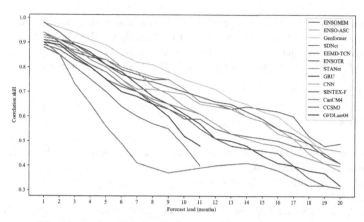

Fig. 11. Correlation skill for various lead times and methods.

Table 5. Evaluation indicators of different deep learning models at a lead time of 20 months.

Models	RMSE ↓	MAE ↓	PCC ↑
EEMD-TCN [25]	0.78	—	0.31
GRU [23]	0.87	—	0.32
CNN [27]	0.88	0.72	0.38
STANet [23]	0.85	—	0.40
ENSOTR [36]	—	—	0.41
SDNet [37]	0.75	—	0.41
GeoFormer [38]	0.86	0.69	0.41
ENSO-ASC [35]	—	—	0.46
ENSOMIM	**0.59**	**0.50**	**0.49**

5 Conclusion

At present, deep learning networks based on CNN can achieve the best results, but there are still shortcomings. We consider the ENSO prediction problem as a spatiotemporal prediction problem and design the ENSOMIM model. Compared with traditional dynamic methods and existing deep learning methods, ENSOMIM can provide more effective predictions, especially in long-term predictions lasting up to two years. This model exhibits superior potential. Considering the versatility of ENSOMIM and the high-order non-stationary nature of ENSO, we will also attempt to apply it to the prediction of radar echoes, precipitation, humidity, and other meteorological factors in the future. In addition, future work can combine other relevant climate variables with ENSOMIM or better architectures to further improve prediction results and provide new information on the relationships between global regions represented by the learned connectivity structures.

Acknowledgement. This work is supported by the National Natural Science Foundation of China (Grant No.42075007), the Open Grants of the State Key Laboratory of Severe Weather (No.2021LASW-B19), and the Open Project of Provincial Key Laboratory for Computer Information Processing Technology under Grant KJS2275, Soochow University.

References

1. McPhaden, M.J., Zebiak, S.E.: ENSO as an integrating concept in earth science. Science **314**(5806), 1740–1745 (2006)
2. Bjerknes, J.: Atmospheric teleconnections from the equatorial Pacific. Mon. Weather Rev. **97**(3), 163–172 (1969)
3. Lin, J., Qian, T.: Switch between el nino and la nina is caused by subsurface ocean waves likely driven by lunar tidal forcing. Sci. Rep. **9**(1), 1–10 (2019)
4. Siegert, F., Ruecker, G.: Increased damage from fires in logged forests during droughts caused by El Nino. Nature **414**(6862), 437–440 (2001)
5. Ward, P.J., Jongman, B.: Strong influence of El Niño Southern Oscillation on flood risk around the world. Proc. Natl. Acad. Sci. **111**(44), 15659–15664 (2014)
6. Tang, Y., Zhang, R.H.: Progress in ENSO prediction and predictability study. Natl. Sci. Rev. **5**(6), 826–839 (2018)
7. Masson, S., Terray, P.: Impact of intra-daily SST variability on ENSO characteristics in a coupled model. Clim. Dyn. **39**(3), 681–707 (2012)
8. Alexander, M.A., Matrosova, L.: Forecasting pacific SSTs: linear inverse model predictions of the PDO. J. Clim. **21**(2), 385–402 (2008). https://doi.org/10.1175/2007JCLI1849.1
9. Barnston, A.G., Van, den, Dool, H.M., Zebiak, S.E.: Long-lead seasonal forecasts—where do we stand. Bull. Am. Meteorol. Soc. **75**(11), 2097–2114 (1994)
10. Xue, Y., Leetmaa, A.: Forecasts of tropical Pacific SST and sea level using a Markov model. Geophys. **27**(2), 2701–2704 (2000)
11. Hirst, A.C.: Unstable and damped equatorial modes in simple coupled ocean-atmosphere models. J. Atmos. Sci. **43**(6), 606–632 (1986)
12. Zebiak, S.E., Cane, M.A.: A model el niño–southern oscillation. Mon. Weather Rev. **115**(10), 2262–2278 (1987)
13. Barnett, T.P., Graham, N.: ENSO and ENSO-related predictability. Part I: prediction of equatorial Pacific sea surface temperature with a hybrid coupled ocean–atmosphere model. J. Clim. **6**(8), 1545–1566 (1993)
14. Luo, J.J., Yuan, C.: Current status of intraseasonal–seasonal-to-interannual prediction of the Indo-Pacific climate. Indo-Pacific Climate variability and predictability. pp. 63–107 (2016)
15. Jin, E.K., Kinter, J.L.: Current status of ENSO prediction skill in coupled ocean–atmosphere models. Clim. Dyn. **31**(6), 647–664 (2008)
16. Ren, F.M., Yuan, Y.: Review of progress of ENSO studies in the past three decades. Adv. Meteorol. Sci. Technol. **2**(3), 17–24 (2012)
17. Clarke, A.J.: El Niño physics and El Niño predictability. Annu. **6**(1), 79–99 (2014)
18. Fang, X., Xie, R.: A brief review of ENSO theories and prediction. Sci. China Earth Sci. **63**, 476–491 (2020)
19. Petersik, P.J., Dijkstra, H.A.: Probabilistic forecasting of El Niño using neural network models. Geophys. Res. Lett. **47**(6), e2019GL086423 (2020)
20. Mahesh, A., Evans, M., Jain, G.: Forecasting El Niño with convolutional and recurrent neural networks. In: 33rd Conference on Neural Information Processing Systems (NIPS 2019), pp. 8–14. Vancouver, Canada (2019)

21. Broni-Bedaiko: El Niño-southern oscillation forecasting using complex networks analysis of LSTM neural networks. Life Robot. **24**(4), 445–451 (2019)

22. Yuan, Y., Lin, L., Huo, L.Z.: Using an attention-based LSTM encoder–decoder network for near real-time disturbance detection. IEEE J. Select. Top. Appl. Earth Observ. Remote Sens. **13**, 1819–1832 (2020)

23. Kim, J., Kwon, M., Kim, S.D.: Spatiotemporal neural network with attention mechanism for El Niño forecasts. Sci. Rep. **12**(1), 7204 (2022)

24. Gupta, M., Kodamana, H.: Prediction of ENSO beyond spring predictability barrier using deep convolutional LSTM networks. Remote Sense. **19**, 1–5 (2020)

25. Yan, J., Mu, L., Wang, L.: Temporal convolutional networks for the advance prediction of ENSO. Sci. Rep. **10**(1), 1–15 (2020)

26. Cachay, S.R., Erickson, E.: The World as a Graph: Improving El Ni\~ no Forecasts with Graph Neural Networks. arXiv pre-print arXiv:2104.05089 (2021)

27. Ham, Y.G., Kim, J.H.: Deep learning for multi-year ENSO forecasts. Nature **573**(7775), 568–572 (2019)

28. Srivastava, N., Mansimov, E., Salakhudinov, R.: Unsupervised learning of video representations using LSTMS. In: International Conference on Machine Learning, pp. 843–852. PMLR (2015)

29. Shi, X., Chen, Z., Wang, H.: Convolutional LSTM network: a machine learning approach for precipitation nowcasting. Adv. Neural. Inf. Process. Syst. **28**(3), 802–810 (2015)

30. Wang, Y., Long, M., Wang, J.: Predrnn: recurrent neural net-works for predictive learning using spatiotemporal LSTMS. Adv. Neural. Inf. Process. Syst. **30**(2), 879–888 (2017)

31. Wang, Y., Gao, Z., Long, M.: Predrnn++: Towards a resolution of the deep-in-time dilemma in spatiotemporal predictive learning. PMLR. **80**(5), 5123–5132 (2018)

32. Wang, Y., Zhang, J., Zhu, H.: Memory in memory: a predictive neural network for learning higher-order non-stationarity from spatiotemporal dynamics. In: Proceedings of the IEEE/CVF Conference on Computer Vision and Pattern Recognition, pp. 9154–9162 (2019)

33. He, D., Lin, P.: Dlenso: A deep learning enso forecasting model. In: Pacific Rim International Conference on Artificial Intelligence, pp. 12–23. Springer, Cham (2019)

34. Hu, J., Weng, B.: Deep residual convolutional neural network combining dropout and transfer learning for ENSO forecasting. Geophys. Res. Let. **48**, e2021GL093531 (2021)

35. Mu, B., Qin, B., Yuan, S.: ENSO-ASC 1.0. 0: ENSO deep learning forecast model with a multivariate air–sea coupler. Geoscientific Model Development. **14**(11), 6977–6999 (2021)

36. Ye, F., Hu, J., Huang, T.Q.: Transformer for El Niño-Southern oscillation prediction. IEEE Geosci. Remote Sens. Lett. **19**, 1–5 (2021)

37. Hai, L.L., Wei, G.S., Jia, K.Z.: Spatiotemporal semantic decoupling network for improved ENSO forecasting. CLIVAR Exch. **81**, 12–15 (2021)

38. Zhou, L., Zhang, R.H.: A self-attention–based neural network for three-dimensional multivariate modeling and its skillful ENSO predictions. Sci. Adv. **9**(10), eadf2827 (2023)

39. Carton, J.A., Giese, B.S.: A reanalysis of ocean climate using Simple Ocean Data Assimilation (SODA). Mon. Weather Rev. **136**(8), 2999–3017 (2008)

40. Tian-Jun, Z., Li-Wei, Z.O.U., Xiao-Long, C.: Commentary on the coupled model intercomparison project phase 6 (CMIP6). Adv. Clim. Chang. Res. **15**(5), 445 (2019)

41. Saha, S., Nadiga, S., Thiaw, C.: The NCEP climate forecast system. J. Clim. **19**(15), 3483–3517 (2006)

SPM-Diffusion for Temperature Prediction

Wei Fang[1,2,3($\boxtimes$)], Zhong Yuan[1], and Qiongying Xue[1]

[1] College of Computer and Software, Engineering Research Center of Digital Forensics Ministry of Education, Nanjing University of Information Science and Technology, Nanjing, China
[2] Jiangsu Collaborative Innovation Center of Atmospheric Environment and Equipment Technology (CICAEET), Nanjing University of Information Science and Technology, Nanjing, China
[3] Provincial Key Laboratory for Computer Information Processing Technology, Soochow University, Suzhou, China
hsfangwei@sina.com

Abstract. Temperature prediction is a critical component of weather forecasting, impacting human life, safety, and property. Compared to traditional numerical weather prediction models, data-driven deep learning methods have more advantages in terms of computational time and resource consumption. However, existing deep learning methods also have inherent drawbacks, such as producing more ambiguous and diffused forecast results. To address these limitations, we introduce a novel model composed of a Spatiotemporal Perception Module (SPM) and an enhanced diffusion model. The SPM captures the long-term dependency information, serving as the generation condition for the diffusion model, and thereby endowing it with forecasting capabilities. We also introduce a new equilibrium loss function that balances the generation abilities of the diffusion model and the spatiotemporal information extraction capabilities of the SPM. Our model demonstrates superior performance on Weatherbench temperature prediction. It achieves a 13.3%.

Keywords: Temperature Prediction · Deep Learning · Spatiotemporal Perception Module · Diffusion

1 Introduction

Machine learning methods have seen successful applications in the realm of climate and weather forecasting [1–3]. Extreme gradient boosting trees (EXtreme Gradient Boosting,XGBoost) have been utilized in near-term rainfall forecasting [4], whereas Quan et al. [5]employed support vector regression models and genetic algorithms to optimize parameters and predict water temperatures.

Supported by the National Natural Science Foundation of China (Grant No.42075007) and the Open Project of Provincial Key Laboratory for Computer Information Processing Technology under Grant KJS2275, Soochow University.

Deep learning has also started to make strides in weather forecasting. Ayzel et al. [6]used a fully stacked two-dimensional convolutional structure for radar-based precipitation forecasting, demonstrating that a straightforward deep learning model can predict short-term precipitation field evolution. Three-dimensional convolution, capable of extracting temporal information, has shown promise in accurately capturing precipitation trends over time [7]. In the realm of weather forecasting, which requires precise forecasts for each grid point, semantic segmentation algorithms like Unet have proven applicable [8], Trebing et al. [9]extended Unet to propose SmaAT-UNet, an algorithm that achieves short-term precipitation forecasting with less memory consumption. Xie et al. [10]used ConvLSTM for storm surge floodplain prediction, while Luo et al. [11]introduced a novel LSTM network capable of capturing both spatial and motion information, applying it to short-term precipitation forecasting. Deep generative models have been used to address short-term precipitation [12]and Xu et al. [13] employed generative adversarial networks for satellite image prediction.

The development of deep learning in computer science has led to an array of new models and ideas that can be integrated into weather forecasting. ConvLSTM [14]is a recurrent neural network (RNN) that extends a fully connected LSTM, using memory units to capture features of past input data and perform well in learning long-range dependencies. PredRNN [15]employs an Encoding-Forecasting structure that uses stacked structures to store spatiotemporal memories. MIM [16]takes into account nonstationary prediction, dividing information into stationary and nonstationary terms, introducing the concept of difference, and proposing the MIM mechanism to extract nonstationary information. E3D-LSTM [17] integrates 3D convolution into RNNs, and PhyDnet [18]learns the dynamics of partial differential equations in latent space, inspired by bias correction in meteorology. Self-Attention ConvLSTM [19]changes the way long-term spatial dependencies are captured through attention mechanisms. PredRNN++ [20]proposes Causal LSTM and a GHU structure to mitigate gradient vanishing, while CrevNet [21] suggests using CNN's normalized flow module to encode, decode, and save feature transformation information.

In the field of image generation, there have been significant developments in the use of variational autoencoders [22],generative adversarial networks [23], and diffusion models [24–26]These have made notable progress in static visual data, surpassing GAN in image synthesis [27].However, their application in weather forecasting remains largely unexplored. We, therefore, aim to incorporate diffusion models into temperature forecasting, marking the first instance of a diffusion model used in weather forecasting.

In conclusion, the advancements in deep learning have transformed many fields, and weather forecasting is ripe for such change. To simulate the spatiotemporal relationship, we propose SPM-Diffusion, which employs SPM to capture spatiotemporal information, grasp the high-order information of the input data, and harness the powerful generation abilities of diffusion models. The synergy between the SPM and the diffusion model allows our model to generate more accurate temperature predictions. We also introduce a new equilibrium loss function to balance the generation abilities of the diffusion model and the spatiotemporal information extraction capabilities of the SPM, improving the overall model performance.

The rest of this paper is organized as follows: Sect. 2 reviews related works. Section 3 introduces the model and the proposed loss function. Section 4 presents experimental results, and Sect. 5 discusses the results and gives conclusions.

2   Background

2.1   Diffusion Model

Denoising diffusion probabilistic models (DDPM) is a generative model that relies on the maximum likelihood training paradigm and has considerable image quality. Like VAE (Variational Autoencoder), it is a deep latent variable model, but unlike VAE, the dimension of each latent variable of DDPM is the same. Its main idea is to x_0 the initial data, continuously add Gaussian noise z, gradually destroy the structure of the initial data x_0 and finally x_0 will become a random noise after several steps, and then go through a denoising process to gradually generate the structure. For the process of forward noise, this is shown in Eq. (1).

$$q(\mathbf{x}_t \mid \mathbf{x}_{t-1}) = \mathcal{N}(\mathbf{x}_t; \sqrt{1 - \beta_t}\mathbf{x}_{t-1}, \beta_t\mathbf{I}) \tag{1}$$

In Equation (1), t represents the number of times noise is added, x_0 represents no noise added, x_t represents the addition of t noise, and $\{\beta_t\}_{t=1}^T$ is the variance used for each step, which is between 0–1. Each step of the diffusion process generates a noisy data, which is a Markaf chain as shown in Eqs. (2)(3).

$$q(\mathbf{x}_{1:T} \mid \mathbf{x}_0) = \prod_{t=1}^{T^1} q(\mathbf{x}_t \mid \mathbf{x}_{t-1}) \tag{2}$$

$$\mathbf{x}_t = \sqrt{\bar{\alpha}_t}\mathbf{x}_0 + \sqrt{1 - \bar{\alpha}_t}\epsilon \tag{3}$$

$$p_\theta(\mathbf{x}_{0:T}) = p(\mathbf{x}_T) \prod_{t=1} p_\theta(\mathbf{x}_{t-1} \mid \mathbf{x}_t)(\mathbf{x}_{t-1} \mid \mathbf{x}_t)$$
$$= \mathcal{N}(\mathbf{x}_{t-1}; \mathbf{p}_\theta(\mathbf{x}_t, t), \mathbf{x}_\theta(\mathbf{x}_t, t)) \tag{4}$$

The second process of the diffusion process is noise reduction process, as shown in formula (4), Here $p(\mathbf{x}_T) = \mathcal{N}(\mathbf{x}_t; 0, \mathbf{I})$, and $p_\theta(\mathbf{x}_{t-1}|\mathbf{x}_t)$, is a parameterized Gaussian distribution, and their means and variances are given by the trained networks $\boldsymbol{\mu}_\theta(x_t, t)$ and $\Sigma_\theta(x_t, t)$, since $p_\theta(x_{t-1}|x_t)$ cannot be processed directly, but can be obtained by taking advantage of the properties of Bayesian formula and Markov chains (5)(6).

$$(\mathbf{x}_{t-1} \mid \mathbf{x}_t, \mathbf{x}_0) = \mathcal{N}(\mathbf{x}_{t-1}; \widetilde{\mu}(\mathbf{x}_t, \mathbf{x}_0), \widetilde{\beta}_t\mathbf{I}). \tag{5}$$

$$\tilde{\beta}_t = \frac{\sqrt{\alpha_t}(1 - \bar{\alpha}_t - 1)}{1 - \bar{\alpha}_t}\mathbf{x}_t + \frac{\sqrt{\bar{\alpha}_t - 1}\beta_t}{1 - \bar{\alpha}_t}\mathbf{x}_0 \tag{6}$$

It can be seen that the variance is a fixed value, while the mean is a function of x_t, and x_0 can be derived from the formula of the noise process, so that the mean is a function of $f_\theta(\mathbf{x}_t, t)$ between x_t and t.

2.2   Recurrent Neural Networks

Recurrent neural networks (RNNs) are a class of neural networks that incorporate a hidden state h_t to capture higher-order representations of past data. This class includes LSTM and GRU, which can learn long-range dependencies and utilize memory gates, forget gates, output gates, and other mechanisms to capture important information and discard irrelevant information, thereby enriching the information encoded in h_t.

Shi et al. [14] leveraged the temporal modeling capabilities of LSTM and GRU and introduced convolutional operations to enable them to capture spatial correlations. They proposed ConvLSTM and ConvGRU, which extend the fully connected LSTM and GRU to have a convolutional structure that captures spatiotemporal dependencies. As a result, h_t not only encodes temporal information but also spatial information, as demonstrated in Eq. (7).

$$h_t = f_{rn}(v_n, v_{n-1}, \ldots, v_{n-i+1}) \tag{7}$$

The architecture of RNNs incorporates memory and forget units to jointly regulate the learning of higher-order features, with the learning process being akin to temperature evolution.

We present a temperature prediction model, named SPM-Diffusion (SPMD), which leverages both the generative capabilities of Diffusion and the contextual information extraction abilities of SPM. SPM extracts high-order information, such as representation, position, and motion information, from past data, and utilizes this information as the generation condition for the Diffusion generative model.

3   Approach

3.1   SPM-Diffusion

The SPM module comprises a three-layer RNN architecture, with each layer capable of extracting higher-order features. The deepest layer can capture more sophisticated features, such as motion information, while the shallower layers capture more elementary information, such as position information.

We utilize a slice operation on the RNN, where the slice size is p, and the original $V_i \in \mathbb{R}^{c,H,W}, i = 1 \ldots n + 1$ is sliced such that $V_i \in \mathbb{R}^{c*p*p,H/p,W/p}, i = 1 \ldots n + 1$. The higher-order features captured by the RNNs are denoted as $H_n \in \mathbb{R}^{3,c,H/p,W/p}$, where H and W are the spatial extent of meteorological elements, c is the number of channels, and the number of hidden layers in the network. To transform H_n to pp in the channel dimension, a new ResBlock is designed, resulting in $H'_n \in \mathbb{R}^{3,p*p,H/p,W/p}$. The output is then matched with

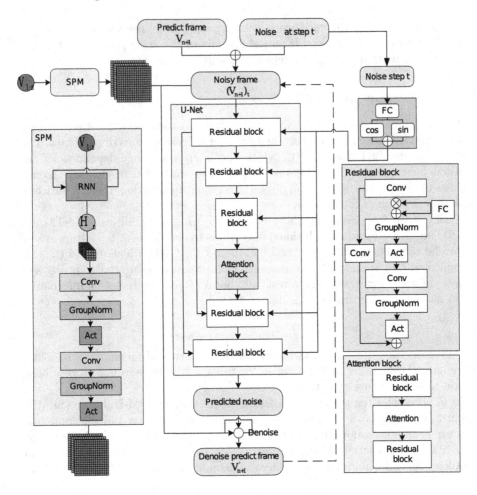

Fig. 1. SPM-Diffusion network architecture.

$(V_{n+1})_t \in \mathbb{R}^{1,H,W}$ in the last two dimensions by adding noise, enabling the re-extraction of H_n features.

The information captured by SPM is connected to the noised $(V_{n+1})_t$ in the channel dimension, providing the Diffusion model with predictive capabilities. To embed time-step information, we adopt a learnable method for each residual block, where the information about the time step t is embedded. Although heavy parameter techniques are used, the noise added at different time steps varies, which requires a focus on the information from different time steps.

Figure 1 illustrates the network architecture, where $V_{1:n}$ represents n frames from the past, and V_{n+1} represents the ground-truth frame to be predicted. During training, the input is the ground-truth value of the next time step V_{n+1}, which is continuously corrupted by adding noise. The value $(V_{n+1})t$ is obtained by adding noise at the t-th time step, and if t is sufficiently large, then $(Vn + 1)t \sim \mathcal{N}(0, \mathbf{I})$. In the testing phase, the input to the model is random noise generated by sampling from a Gaussian distribution. The noise is gradually removed through the $\epsilon\theta$ predicted by the network.

3.2 Equilibrium Loss Function

We propose a hybrid equilibrium loss function, which not only ensures the generation ability of Diffusion, but also protects the SPM's ability to grasp long-term dependent information, and the equilibrium loss function is shown in Eq. (8).

$$L(\theta) = \mathbb{E}_{\mathbf{x}_0, n, \epsilon} \|\epsilon - f_\theta(\mathbf{x}_n, n, h_t)\|^2 \times \lambda_t + \|g_{rnn}(\mathbf{x}_1, \mathbf{x}_2...\mathbf{x}_{n-1}) - \mathbf{x}_n\|^2 \times \beta \quad (8)$$

Here, $\lambda_t = (k + \bar{\alpha}_t/(1 - \bar{\alpha}t))^\gamma$ is a function of t, where γ is a hyperparameter that controls the weight reduction intensity, with no weight reduction when $\gamma = 0$ and the maximum reduction when $\gamma = 1$. The parameter k is also a hyperparameter used to prevent weight explosions caused by very small signal-to-noise ratios, and it determines the sharpness of the weighting scheme. $f_\theta(\mathbf{x}_n, n, h_t)$ is the noise predicted based on x_n, n, and h_t.

While H_t provides the high-level information required for Diffusion generation, it is critical to control the output of the RNNs in SPM to ensure the learned H_t captures remote dependency information effectively. Diffusion also needs to extract the necessary parts from this data. Therefore, an additional loss term $\|g_{rnn}(\mathbf{x}_1, \mathbf{x}_2 \dots \mathbf{x}_{n-1}) - \mathbf{x}_n\|^2$ is added, where $g_{rnn}(\mathbf{x}_1, \mathbf{x}_2...\mathbf{x}_{n-1})$ is the output of the RNN in the SPM module, and β is a hyperparameter used to balance the loss relationship with Diffusion.

4 Experiment

This section focuses on evaluating the performance and effectiveness of the SPM-Diffusion architecture for weather forecasting. To this end, we explore multiple options for RNN cells in SPM and propose two new variants of the model, SPMD-ConvLSTMcell and SPMD-ConvGRUcell. We then compare these variants with commonly used and state-of-the-art deep learning algorithms in meteorology to validate the effectiveness of the SPM-Diffusion architecture. Next, we evaluate the performance of the model using the publicly available weatherbench [29] dataset and compare it with that of physical models. Finally, we conduct ablation experiments to confirm the effectiveness of the equilibrium loss function used in the SPM-Diffusion architecture. Overall, this section provides a comprehensive evaluation of the proposed model and its performance in the context of weather forecasting.

4.1   Variant of SPM-Diffuison

Different RNNs possess varying abilities in feature extraction. In our experiment, we test two variants of SPMD, with a batch size of 32 and a patch size of 4, using three hidden layers, each with a dimension of 64. Figure 2 displays the output results of the two SPM-Diffusion variants at different iterations, allowing us to compare and select the most suitable RNN structure. The following steps outline the algorithm's execution.

Algorithm 1. SPMD train

Require: $\beta \leftarrow choice(0,1)$;

1: **while** not converged **do**
2:     Sample $x_n \sim p(x_n)$;
3:     $L = 0$;
4:     **for** t = 1 to n **do**
5:         $h_t, frames = f_{SPM}(x_t)$;
6:     **end for** $\epsilon \sim \mathcal{N}(0, I)$; $y_0^n = \left(x^t - \mu_\phi(h_t)\right)/\sigma$; $y_n^n = \sqrt{\overline{\alpha}_n} y_0^n + \sqrt{1 - \overline{\alpha}_n}\epsilon$; $L = \mathbb{E}_{x_n, n, \epsilon}\|\epsilon - f_\theta(y_n^n, n, h_t)\|^2 \times \lambda_t + \|\mathbf{frames} - \mathbf{x}_n\|^2 \times \beta$; $(\theta, \phi) \cong (\theta, \phi) - \nabla_{\theta, \phi} L$
7: **end while**

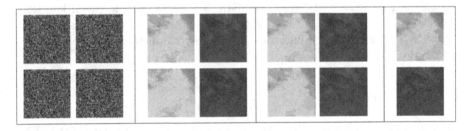

Fig. 2. SPMD-ConvLSTMcell (first row) and ConvGRUcell (second row) compared with four columns with 0, 20K and 40K training times and real values.

Figure 2 displays the experimental results, which consist of four blocks. The first block shows the output result when the number of iterations is 0. The second and third blocks show the output results at iterations 20K and 40K, respectively. The last block includes two images of the true values. We combine the structures of the two STMs and present the output results of the iterations at 0, 20K, and 40K. When the number of iterations is 0, both variants produce random noise and do not learn effective features. However, after 20K iterations, both variants learn basic features. Nevertheless, our experiments show that the ConvGRU unit fails to capture specific details effectively. The area with higher temperature is overly broad, and the overall trend of diffusion is not very accurate. In contrast, the ConvLSTM unit exhibits a better combined learning effect. After 40K iterations, both variants demonstrate good effects, accurately capturing the intensity of the range and temperature, thereby proving the feasibility of SPMD.

4.2   Comparison of Spatiotemporal Series Prediction Algorithms

In this section, we compare our model with the latest spatiotemporal sequence prediction algorithms. We split the dataset into three parts: 80% for training, 10% for validation, and 10% for testing. The meteorological values in the data change significantly in each three-hour interval, presenting a significant challenge for the model. Table 1 and Figure 3 display the performance of various models and the results of different evaluation metrics.

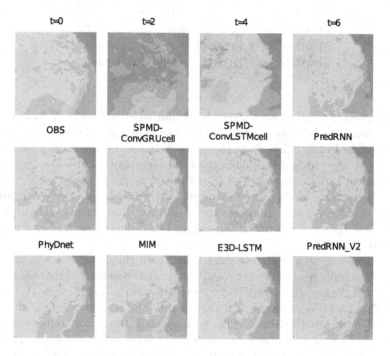

Fig. 3. Temperature Plots Output by Multiple Models.

Figure 3 displays temperature diagrams of the outputs of various models. The input of each model comprises the first eight frames, and the output contains the predicted future frames. The first row shows four images of the input data, representing the outputs at t=0, t=2, t=4, and t=6, respectively. The temperature values in the data change significantly in each three-hour interval, presenting a considerable challenge for the model to successfully capture the temperature change trend.

Table 1. Comparison of Model Performance.

Model	MSE↓	MAE↓	PSNR↑
PredRNN_V2	1.42	59.30	35.49
ConvLSTM [14]	0.85	43.22	37.91
ConvGRU [14]	0.76	40.31	38.49
E3D_LSTM [17]	0.75	42.43	38.00
MIM [16]	0.69	39.49	38.43
Phydnet [18]	0.59	35.61	39.32
PredRNN [15]	0.58	34.26	39.68
SPMD-ConvLSTMcell	0.56	33.52	39.82
SPMD-ConvGRUcell	**0.54**	**32.31**	**40.25**

The second and third rows show the output results of multiple models, with the first row being the true values, and the subsequent rows being the outputs of the models. In the following analysis, we compare the specific output results.

In Fig. 4, the red box highlights the local high-temperature area, which has a small range and a temperature gap with other regions that is not significant, making it the most challenging to capture. The experiment selects this area as a selection standard and compares the algorithms that capture this area. The results show that the algorithm can capture such details, as well as PredRNN and MIM.

We then analyze a relatively large range, as highlighted by the blue box in Fig. 4. The temperature range is concentrated in the middle, and there are several independent regions that are not connected to their adjacent areas. Observing PredRNN and MIM in the framed part of the blue box, we see that the range is more concentrated in the middle, with most of the yellow range connected together and fewer independent areas. Finally, we observe the model proposed in this article, and the overall rendering is consistent with the true values.

Additionally, since the forecast is predicting one next frame, algorithms such as PredRNN and PredRNN_V2 use mask operations for rounding, which makes long-distance forecasting more convenient by retaining a certain real value at each time step. However, such operations have no effect on the prediction of future frames. Our experiments show that these algorithms perform poorly on adjacent frames, especially PredRNN_V2, which exhibits poor performance after losing the mask operation. We also introduce the PSNR (Peak Signal to Noise Ratio) as an evaluation index, which is an objective standard for evaluating image quality. Experimental studies show that the proposed algorithm has the best image quality, which facilitates accurate judgments by meteorological observers.

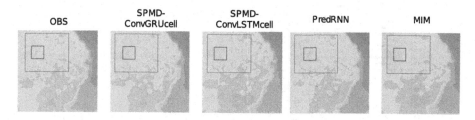

Fig. 4. Compare the forecasting effects of various models on different scales, where the red box frames the more detailed range, and the blue box frames the larger range. (Color figure online)

4.3 WeatherBench Forecasting Experiment

To predict a sufficient number of steps, we convert the number of images into the number of channels. Since temperature is a grayscale value, the number of channels after conversion equals the number of images. Using this method, we perform a temperature prediction task on the WeatherBench 5.625° dataset, forecasting the 2-meter temperature for a 5-day lead time. We compare our results with three baselines: a physical NWP model run at a coarser resolution of T42 (2.8° or 310-km resolution at the equator (NCAR, 2020)), which was initialized from ERA5, and a climatological forecast that uses either a single mean or a weekly mean computed from the training data set (1979–2016). The performance of our proposed model at a 2-meter temperature (T2m) in WeatherBench is presented in Table 2. In Fig. 5, we observe that the model's predictions are not accurate in the first few time steps. However, after 48 h, the prediction performance improves. We consider that the temperature prediction results may not only capture the change in temperature at the previous time step but also the temperature situation at the same time on the previous day. Since temperature does not change frequently, in some cases, the temperature at the same time the previous day may be a more reliable reference than the previous time step.

Table 2. WeatherBench T2m.

Model	RMSE↓ (3 d/5 d)	MAE↓ (3 d/5 d)	ACC$uparrow$ (3 d/5 d)
Climatology [29]	6.07	3.84	0
Weekly climatology [29]	3.19	2.48	0.85
IFS T42 [29]	3.21/3.69	1.99/2.53	0.87/0.83
SimVP [30]	3.04/3.12	1.94/1.98	0.0.87/0.86
Unet+resnet18	3.06/3.10	1.96/1.98	0.87/0.86
Unet+resnet32	2.97/3.10	1.95/2.00	0.87/0.85
Unet+resnet50	2.90/3.04	1.89/1.95	0.87/0.86
ours	**2.78/2.78**	**1.82/1.86**	**0.89/0.89**

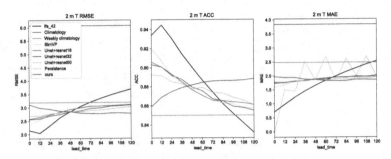

Fig. 5. Compare WeatherBench T2m in 120h(5 d).

4.4   Ablation

We propose a new mixed loss function, referred to as the equilibrium loss function, that prioritizes the generation ability of Diffusion while also ensuring the predictive ability of the RNN structure. In this subsection, we conduct ablation experiments to demonstrate the feasibility of the mixed loss function, and the experimental results are presented in Table 3. The experimental results demonstrate that the equilibrium loss function is beneficial for model learning. This function not only ensures the generation ability of Diffusion but also maintains the prediction ability of the model. Here, β is a hyperparameter, and when it is set to 1.0, SPM dominates the model training. Although the model is better at training SPM, it compromises the generation ability of Diffusion. Therefore, we set β to 0.2, favoring Diffusion, while using the SPM structure as an auxiliary to retain a certain forecasting ability of SPM and also protect the generation ability of Diffusion.

Table 3. Ablation test results.

	Model 1	Model 2	Model 3	Model 4	Model 5
$\mathbb{E}_{\mathbf{x}_0,n,\epsilon}\lVert - f_\theta(\mathbf{x}_n,n,h_t)\rVert^2$	✓	✓	✓	✓	✓
λ_t	-	✓	-	✓	✓
$\lVert g_{rnn}(\mathbf{x}_1,\mathbf{x}_2\ldots\mathbf{x}_{n-1})-\mathbf{x}_n\rVert^2\beta$	-	-	✓ $\beta=0.2$	✓ $\beta=1.0$	✓ $\beta=0.2$
MSE	0.64	0.63	0.59	0.65	0.54
MAE	37.32	35.25	34	37.3	32.31
PSNR	38.82	39.32	39.9	38.8	40.25

5   Conclusion

We propose a temperature forecasting model based on the spatiotemporal perception module (SPM) and diffusion process, which effectively learns the rules of temperature evolution and generates high-quality temperature fields. We carefully design the SPM to capture spatiotemporal dependencies in temperature fields and use it to construct an SPM-Diffusion framework. This framework uses the information captured by the SPM as the generation condition of Diffusion. We also propose two variants of SPMD, namely SPMD-ConvGRUcell and SPMD-ConvLSTMcell, which enhance the generation ability of Diffusion by leveraging SPM's grasp of long-term information dependence. Additionally, we propose a balancing loss function to balance the forecasting ability of SPM and the generative ability of Diffusion.

We conduct experiments using the SPMD dataset to verify the effectiveness of the SPMD algorithm and compare it with the latest deep learning methods. Furthermore, we design ablation experiments to prove the role of each part of the model. Finally, we compare our model with other deep learning and physical prediction models in the task of predicting the 2m temperature for the next 3/5 d on WeatherBench. Our experimental results demonstrate that our model achieves excellent forecasting performance, proving the effectiveness and generality of our model. We believe that our model provides a novel and powerful approach for the temperature forecasting field and offers valuable insights for other spatiotemporal sequence prediction problems.

References

1. Castro, R., Souto, Y.M., Ogasawara, E., et al.: STConvS2S: spatiotemporal convolutional sequence to sequence network for weather forecasting. Neurocomputing **426**, 285–298 (2021)
2. Hewage, P., Trovati, M., Pereira, E., et al.: Deep learning-based effective fine-grained weather forecasting model. Pattern Anal. Appl. **24**(1), 343–366 (2021)
3. Hewage, P., Behera, A., Trovati, M., et al.: Temporal convolutional neural (TCN) network for an effective weather forecasting using time-series data from the local weather station. Soft. Comput. **24**, 16453–16482 (2020)
4. Meti, G., GK, R.K.: Analogousness enhanced rainfall predictor using XGBoost backbone. Int. J. Intell. Syst. Appl. Eng. **11**(2), 329–335 (2023)
5. Quan Q, Hao Z, Xi feng H, et al.: Research on water temperature prediction based on improved support vector regression. Neural Comput. Appl., 1–10 (2020)
6. Ayzel, G., Heistermann, M., Sorokin, A., et al.: All convolutional neural networks for radar-based precipitation nowcasting. Procedia Comput. Sci. **150**, 186–192 (2019)
7. Sari, A.P., Suzuki, H., Kitajima, T., et al.: Short-term wind speed and direction forecasting by 3DCNN and deep convolutional LSTM. IEEJ Trans. Electrical Electron. Eng. **17**(11), 1620–1628 (2022)
8. Fernández, J.G., Mehrkanoon, S.: Broad-UNet: multi-scale feature learning for nowcasting tasks. Neural Netw. **144**, 419–427 (2021)
9. Trebing, K., Stanczyk, T., Mehrkanoon, S.: SmaAt-UNet: precipitation nowcasting using a small attention-UNet architecture. Pattern Recogn. Lett. **145**, 178–186 (2021)
10. Xie, W.H., Xu, G.J., Dong, C.M.: Research on storm surge floodplain prediction based on ConvL STM machine learning. Trans. At-mos Sci. **45**(5), 674–687 (2022)

11. Luo, C., Li, X., Ye, Y.: PFST-LSTM: a spatiotemporal LSTM model with pseudoflow prediction for precipitation nowcasting. IEEE J. Selected Top. Appl. Earth Observ. Remote Sens. **14**, 843–857 (2020)

12. Ravuri, S., Lenc, K., Willson, M., et al.: Skilful precipitation nowcasting using deep generative models of radar. Nature **597**(7878), 672–677 (2021)

13. Xu, Z., Du, J., Wang, J., et al.: Satellite image prediction relying on GAN and LSTM neural networks. In: ICC 2019–2019 IEEE International Conference on Communications (ICC), pp. 1–6. IEEE, Shanghai (2019)

14. Shi, X., Chen, Z., Wang, H., et al.: Convolutional LSTM network: a machine learning approach for precipitation nowcasting. Adv. Neural. Inf. Process. Syst. **28**, 802–810 (2015)

15. Wang, Y., Long, M., Wang, J., et al.: PredRNN: recurrent neural networks for predictive learning using spatiotemporal LSTMs. In: Proceedings of the 31st International Conference on Neural Information Processing Systems, pp. 879–888. Curran Associates, California (2017)

16. Wang, Y., Zhang, J., Zhu, H., et al.: Memory in memory: a predictive neural network for learning higher-order non-stationarity from spatiotemporal dynamics. In: Proceedings of the IEEE/CVF Conference on Computer Vision and Pattern Recognition, pp. 9154–9162. IEEE, California (2019)

17. Wang, Y., Jiang, L., Yang, M.H., et al.: Eidetic 3D LSTM: a model for video prediction and beyond. In: International Conference on Learning Representations, OpenReview.net, New Orleans (2018)

18. Guen, V.L., Thome, N.: Disentangling physical dynamics from unknown factors for unsupervised video prediction. In: Proceedings of the IEEE/CVF Conference on Computer Vision and Pattern Recognition, pp. 11474–11484. IEEE, Seattle (2020)

19. Lin, Z., Li, M., Zheng, Z., et al.: Self-attention ConvLSTM for spatiotemporal prediction. In: Proceedings of the AAAI Conference on Artificial Intelligence, pp. 11531–11538, AAAI Press, New York (2020)

20. Wang, Y., Gao, Z., Long, M., et al.: PredRNN++: towards a resolution of the deep-in-time dilemma in spatiotemporal predictive learning. In: International Conference on Machine Learning, pp. 5123–5132. PMLR, Stockholm (2018)

21. Yu, W., Lu, Y., Easterbrook, S., et al.: Efficient and information-preserving future frame prediction and beyond. In: International Conference on Learning Representations, OpenReview.net, Addis Ababa (2019)

22. Cemgil, T., Ghaisas, S., Dvijotham, K., et al.: The autoencoding variational autoencoder. Adv. Neural. Inf. Process. Syst. **33**, 15077–15087 (2020)

23. Goodfellow, I., Pouget-Abadie, J., Mirza, M., et al.: Generative adversarial networks. Commun. ACM **63**(11), 139–144 (2020)

24. Ho, J., Jain, A., Abbeel, P.: Denoising diffusion probabilistic models. Adv. Neural. Inf. Process. Syst. **33**, 6840–6851 (2020)

25. Kingma, D., Salimans, T., Poole, B., et al.: Variational diffusion models. Adv. Neural. Inf. Process. Syst. **34**, 21696–21707 (2021)

26. Nichol, A.Q., Dhariwal, P.: Improved denoising diffusion probabilistic models. In: International Conference on Machine Learning, pp. 8162–8171. PMLR, Virtually (2021)

27. Dhariwal, P., Nichol, A.: Diffusion models beat GANs on image synthesis. Adv. Neural. Inf. Process. Syst. **34**, 8780–8794 (2021)

28. Wang, Y., Wu, H., Zhang, J., et al.: PredRNN: a recurrent neural network for spatiotemporal predictive learning. IEEE Trans. Pattern Anal. Mach. Intell. (2022)

29. Rasp, S., Dueben, P.D., Scher, S., et al.: WeatherBench: a benchmark data set for data-driven weather forecasting. J. Adv. Model. Earth Syst. **12**(11), e2020MS002203 (2020)

30. Gao, Z., Tan, C., Wu, L., et al.: SimVP: simpler yet better video prediction. In: Proceedings of the IEEE/CVF Conference on Computer Vision and Pattern Recognition, pp. 3170–3180. IEEE/CVF, New York (2022)

S-SOLVER: Numerically Stable Adaptive Step Size Solver for Neural ODEs

Eliska Kloberdanz[✉][ID] and Wei Le

Department of Computer Science, Iowa State University, Ames, IA 50011, USA
{eklober,weile}@iastate.edu

Abstract. A neural ordinary differential equation (ODE) is a relation between an unknown function and its derivatives, where the ODE is parameterized by a neural network. Therefore, to obtain a solution to a neural ODE requires a solver that performs numerical integration. Dopri5 is one of the most popular neural ODE solvers and also the default solver in *torchdiffeq*, a PyTorch library of ODE solvers. It is an adaptive step size solver based on the Runge-Kutta (RK) numerical methods. These methods rely on estimation of the local truncation error to select and adjust integration step size, which determines the numerical stability of the solution. A step size that is too large leads to numerical instability, while a step size that is too small may cause the solver to take unnecessarily many steps, which is computationally expensive and may even cause rounding error build up. Therefore, accurate local truncation error estimation is paramount for choosing an appropriate step size to obtain an accurate, numerically stable, and fast solution to the ODE. In this paper we propose a novel local truncation error approximation that is the first to consider solutions of four different RK orders to obtain a more reliable error estimate. This leads to a novel solver *S-SOLVER* (Stable Solver), which is more numerically stable; and therefore accurate. We demonstrate *S-SOLVER*'s competitive performance in experiments on image recognition with ODE-Net, learning hamiltonian dynamics with Symplectic ODE-Net, and continuous normalizing flows (CNF).

Keywords: neural ordinary differential equations · numerical stability · ODE solvers

1 Introduction

Neural ODEs are continuous depth deep learning models that combine neural networks and ODEs. Since their first introduction in [5], they have been used in many applications such as: stochastic differential equations [17], physically informed modeling [25,30], free-form continuous generative models [6,8], mean-field games [24], and irregularly sampled time-series [23].

Neural ODEs parameterize the derivative of the hidden state using a neural network; and therefore, learn non-linear mappings via differential equations. A differential equation is a relation between an unknown function and its derivatives. Ordinary differential equations describe the change of only one variable

© The Author(s), under exclusive license to Springer Nature Switzerland AG 2023
L. Iliadis et al. (Eds.): ICANN 2023, LNCS 14262, pp. 388–400, 2023.
https://doi.org/10.1007/978-3-031-44201-8_32

(as opposed to multiple) with respect to time, i.e.: $dx/dt = f(t, x)$. Typically, an ODE is formulated as an initial value problem (IVP), which has the following form. Given a function derivative dx/dt, a time interval $t = (a, b)$ and an initial value (e.i.: x at time $t = a$), the solution to the IVP yields x evaluated at time $t = b$. The method for approximating $x(b)$ is numerical integration; therefore, all the various ODE solvers include different methods for performing integration.

Adaptive step size solvers are amongst the most popular solvers for neural ODEs. In fact, the default solver in *torchdiffeq* (a library of ODE solvers implemented in PyTorch) is Dopri5, the Dormand-Prince 5(4) embedded adaptive step size method of the Runge-Kutta (RK) family. Adaptive step size RK solvers perform two approximations: one of order p and another of $p-1$ and compare them to obtain the local truncation error, which is used to determine the integration step size. Specifically, the error is used to make a decision whether to accept or reject the solution step under the current step size and to decide how to modify the step size for the next step. A step size that is too large leads to numerical instability, while a step size that is too small may cause the solver to take unnecessarily many steps, which is computationally expensive and may even cause the rounding error to build up. Therefore, accurate local estimation is paramount for choosing an appropriate step size to obtain an accurate, numerically stable, and fast solution to the ODE.

The local truncation error is defined as the difference between the exact and approximate solution obtained at a given time step. All currently available adaptive step neural ODE solvers rely on estimating the local error as the difference between order p and $p - 1$ solutions, which assumes that the order p solution is exact. This is not necessarily true and if the p solution is far from the exact one, the local error estimate is inaccurate, which results in the solver making poor decisions regarding its step size.

In this paper we propose a novel local truncation error estimation that takes into account multiple orders of the RK method as opposed to just order p and $p - 1$ to obtain a more accurate estimate of the local truncation error that guides the integration step size. Specifically, we modify the local truncation error estimation of Dopri8, the Dormand-Prince 8(7) embedded adaptive step size method. Dopri8 calculates the local truncation error as the difference between its 8th and 7th order solution. Our modification computes this error as the average of the difference between both its 8th and 7th, and also 4th and 5th order solution. This leads to a new ODE solver, *S-SOLVER* (Stable Solver), a modified Dopri8 integrator with more accurate local truncation error estimation that provides more reliable information for step size calculations; and therefore, more numerically stable solution. To our best knowledge, *S-SOLVER* is the first solver that uses a multiple solution orders to estimate local truncation error for adjusting its step size.

2   Background

2.1   Neural Ordinary Differential Equations

Traditional neural networks are defined as discrete models with a discrete sequence of hidden layers, where the depth of the network corresponds to the number of layers. Neural ODEs [5] are continuous depth deep learning models, which parameterize the derivative of the hidden state using a neural network. Specifically, they are ODEs that are parameterized by a neural network, which has many benefits such as memory efficiency, adaptive computation, and parameter efficiency.

Neural ODEs are inspired by the dynamic systems interpretation of residual and other networks [9, 28]. These networks perform a sequence of transformations to a hidden state:

$$state_{t+1} = state_t + f(state_t, \theta_t), \tag{1}$$

which can be viewed as discretized forward Euler method applied to a continuous transformation. Given this interpretation, the transformation to a hidden state can be formulated as an ODE:

$$d\,state(t)/dt = f(state(t), t, \theta), \tag{2}$$

where $state(t = 0)$ is the input layer and $state(t = T)$ is the output layer. Therefore, the neural ODE is an IVP:

$$dx(t)/dt = f(t, x(t), \theta), \; for \; t_0 \le t \le t_1, \; subject \; to \; x(t_0) = x_{t_0}, \tag{3}$$

where $f(.,.,\theta)$ is the deep neural network, x_{t_0} is the input, and x_{t_1} is the output.

Neural ODEs are trainable through loss minimization, but due to their continuous nature the optimization process is slightly different from classical discrete deep learning models. The forward pass solves the ODE with an ODE solver and the backward pass computes the gradients either by backpropagating through the ODE solver or with the adjoint method [5]. In this work we focus on the forward pass, which outputs a solution to the ODE.

2.2   Neural ODE Solvers

Solving neural ODEs that we generalized in Eq. 3 requires numerical integration that can be described as follows:

$$x(t_1) = x(t_0) + \int_{t_0}^{t_1} f(t, x(t), \theta)dt \tag{4}$$

This equation can be solved with an ODE solver, which returns the value of $x(t_1)$ that represents the solution at the end of the time interval that satisfies the initial condition $x(t_0) = x_{t_0}$.

There are different types of ODE solvers that use different methods and algorithms for performing numerical integration, and the Runge-Kutta (RK) set of methods that are amongst the most popular [26]. The basic idea behind the RK integration methods is to re-write dx and dt in Eq. 3 as finite steps Δx and Δt and multiply the equations by Δt, which provides a change in x with respect to Δt. The finite time step Δt is called the step size [26] and is typically represented as h. The simplest RK method, the Euler method, illustrates this well:

$$x_{t_{n+1}} = x_{t_n} + hf(t_n, x_{t_n}) \tag{5}$$

RK methods leverage the differential equation for computing the slope k of the tangent line to the function f. The slope is then used to approximate f at the next time step $t + 1$. As shown in [2], this can be represented as:

$$x_{t_{n+1}} = x_{t_n} + h\sum_{i=1}^{S} \hat{b}_i k_i, \tag{6}$$

where

$$k_1 = f(t_n, \hat{x}_{t_n})$$

$$k_i = f(t_n + c_i h, \hat{x}_{t_n} + h\sum_{j=1}^{i-1} a_{ij}k_j) \text{ for RK stages } i = 2, ..., s \tag{7}$$

$$c_i = \sum_{j=1}^{i-1} a_{ij}$$

Since the Euler method approximates the slope only once to proceed from t to $t + 1$, it can be expressed using the general RK method shown in Eq. 6 as:

$$x_{t_{n+1}} = x_{t_n} + h(b_1 k_1) \tag{8}$$

The number of times that the slope k is approximated between t and $t + 1$ impacts the local truncation error the RK method [3,4]. The local truncation error is the difference between the exact and approximated solution and determines the order of the RK method [3]. The order of the RK method corresponds to the order of the local truncation error minus one. For example, the local truncation error for the Euler's method is $O(h^2)$, resulting in a first order numerical technique.

3 Numerical Stability of Neural ODE Solvers

When approximating the solution of an IVP, there are two primary sources of error: the roundoff error and the truncation error [1], which impact the numerical stability of the ODE solver that yields the approximate solution.

3.1 Numerical Stability

Numerical stability can be viewed property of an algorithm, which describes the sensitivity of a solution to numerical errors [10]. An unstable numerical method produces large changes in outputs in response to small changes in inputs [11], which can lead to unexpected outputs or errors. Numerical instability arises due rounding, and truncation errors [10]. Roundoff errors are caused by approximating real numbers with finite precision, while truncation errors are caused by approximating a mathematical process. Many numerical methods (e.g.: Euler's method for solving differential equations) can be derived by taking finitely many terms of a Taylor series. The terms omitted constitute the truncation error, which often depends on a parameter called the step size [10]. In this paper introduce a novel truncation error estimation used for setting an adaptive step size that achieves a numerically stable solution.

3.2 Stability of Different ODE Solvers

There are two notions of numerical stability of ODEs: zero-stability and absolute stability. Zero-stability implies that on a fixed time interval, small perturbations of data yield bounded perturbations in the solution as the step size h approaches zero [16]. Absolute stability, a stronger notion of stability, guarantees the same behavior, but for a fixed step size h as the time interval approaches infinity. Generally, a numerical method for solving initial value ODE is numerically stable if "small changes or perturbations in the initial conditions produce correspondingly small changes in the subsequent approximations" [3].

Different ODE solvers have different numerical stability. This can be demonstrated with a canonical example of an ODE that describes a swinging pendulum:

$$ml\frac{d^2\Theta(t)}{dt^2} = -mg\sin(\Theta(t)), \tag{9}$$

where $\Theta(t)$ is the angle between the pendulum and a vertical axis at a time t, l is the length of the pendulum, m is the pendulum mass, and g represents gravity. Figure 1 illustrates the varying degrees of numerical stability of three different methods that can be used to solve this pendulum IVP.

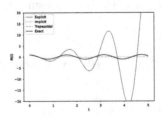

Fig. 1. Comparison of numerical stability of various ODE solvers

3.3 Analysis on Numerical Stability with Respect to Step Size

To illustrate the impact of step size on the numerical stability of ODE solvers, we provide a numerical stability analysis of the Euler method and derive its stability condition. The stability condition pertaining to explicit Euler method's step size can be derived using the *test equation*:

$$y' = ky, \quad y(0) = \alpha, \quad \alpha < 0 \tag{10}$$

Applying the forward Euler method to this ODE yields:

$$x_0 = \alpha, \quad x_{i+1} = x_i + h(kx_i) = (1 + hk)x_i \tag{11}$$

Solving for x_{i+1}:

$$x_{i+1} = (1 + hk)x_i = (1 + hk)^{i+1}x_0 = (1 + hk)^{i+1}\alpha \tag{12}$$

The exact solution is:
$$y(t) = \alpha \exp(kt) \tag{13}$$

The absolute error is the absolute difference between the exact and approximated solution:

$$|y(t_i) - x_i| = |\exp(ihk) - (1 + hk)^i| |\alpha| = |\exp(hk)^i - (1 + hk)^i| |\alpha| \tag{14}$$

If $k > 0$, the problem is unstable. If $k \leq 0$ and $|1 + hk| < 1$, the forward Euler method will be stable. This condition is called the *stability region* and pertains to the notion of absolute stability. Specifically, the analysis of the *stability region* is useful for determining a step size that can ensure absolute stability.

Illustrative Example. We demonstrate the practical application of the theoretical numerical stability analysis shown above with an illustrative example of an ODE $dy/dt = -2.3y$ with an initial value of $y(0) = 1$. Figure 2a compares the exact solution $-2.3t$ with approximate solutions obtained with the explicit Euler method with varying step sizes: $h = 1.0, 0.7, 0.1$. The solution obtained with step size $h = 1.0$ is erratic and inaccurate, while the solution with the smallest step size $h = 0.1$ yields a stable solution that is very close to the exact one. The reason for that is that kh for $h = 1.0$ and $h = 0.7$ are far away from the *stability region* represented as the blue circle in Fig. 2b. Therefore, we can observe that the step size h has a significant impact on the numerical stability and accuracy of the ODE solution.

4 Method

Prior adaptive step size solvers approximate the local truncation error as the difference between order $p - 1$ and p solution, where the p order solution is assumed to be the exact solution. This means that the error estimates are not

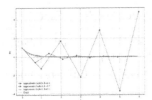
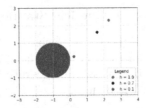

(a) The importance of step size for accu- (b) The stability region of the explicit Eu-
rate solutions   ler method

Fig. 2. The relationship between numerical stability of an ODE solution and ODE solver step size

exact, but only accurate to the leading order in h, i.e.: order p [20]. *S-SOLVER* is an adaptive step size solver with novel, more accurate local error estimation that is used for adjusting the solver step size to achieve an accurate numerically stable solution to neural ODEs.

S-SOLVER is based on Dopri8, the Dormand-Prince 8(7) embedded adaptive step size method, which is a 8th order RK method that requires 13 function evaluations per integration step [21] as shown in Eq. 15.

where
$$x_{t_{n+1}} = x_{t_n} + h \sum_{i=1}^{13} \hat{b}_i k_i, \tag{15}$$

$$k_1 = f(t_n, \hat{x}_{t_n})$$

$$k_i = f(t_n + c_i h, \hat{x}_{t_n} + h \sum_{j=1}^{i-1} a_{ij} k_j) \; for \; i = 2, ..., 12 \tag{16}$$

$$c_i = \sum_{j=1}^{i-1} a_{ij}$$

The coefficients a, b, and c in Eqs. 15 and 16 are defined using the Butcher tableau provided in [21].

In contrast to Dopri8, which calculates local error as the difference between the 7th and 8th order solution, *S-SOLVER* uses order 8, 7, 5, and 4. Specifically, given a neural ODE:

$$x(t_1) = x(t_0) + \int_{t_0}^{t_1} f(t, x(t), \theta) dt, \tag{17}$$

suppose that the solver has progressed to some time step t_n and approximated $x(t_n)$ as $\hat{x}(t_n)$. To make further progress, the solver needs to take a step forward and compute the value of x at time step $t_n + h$, where h is the step size. Suppose that this is approximated as $\hat{x}(t_n + h)$ and that the step's error is x_{error}. *S-SOLVER* computes x_{error} as an average of the difference between 8th and 7th order solution and 5th and 4th order solution to obtain a more reliable estimate:

$$x_{error} = \frac{(\hat{x}(t_n + h)_{order_8} - \hat{x}(t_n + h)_{order_7}) + (\hat{x}(t_n + h)_{order_5} - \hat{x}(t_n + h)_{order_4})}{2} \tag{18}$$

The 5th and 4th order solution is computed using a similar process, but only with 6 stages as follows:

where
$$x_{t_{n+1}} = x_{t_n} + h \sum_{i=1}^{6} \hat{b}_i k_i, \tag{19}$$

$$k_1 = f(t_n, \hat{x}_{t_n})$$

$$k_i = f(t_n + c_i h, \hat{x}_{t_n} + h \sum_{j=1}^{i-1} a_{ij} k_j) \; for \; i = 2, ..., 5 \tag{20}$$

$$c_i = \sum_{j=1}^{i-1} a_{ij},$$

where the coefficients a, b, and c are given in the Butcher tableau provided in [15]. Given a pre-defined upper bound on relative error RTOL (1e-7 default in *torchdiffeq*) and upper bound on absolute error ATOL (1e-9 default in *torchdiff*), the solver then computes an error ratio r as follows:

$$r = \left\| \frac{x_{error}}{scale} \right\|, \tag{21}$$

where *scale* is defined as:

$$scale = ATOL + RTOL \; \max(\hat{x}(t_n), \hat{x}(t_n + h)). \tag{22}$$

If $r \leq 1$ the step is accepted, otherwise it is rejected and the value of x at time step $t_n + h$ is approximated again with a smaller step size h.

5 Experiments

We implement *S-SOLVER* as a new solver that is part of the torchdiffeq library (https://anonymous.4open.science/r/S-SOLVER-EC78/ReadMe.md) and perform experiments on image recognition with ODE-Net, learning hamiltonian dynamics with Symplectic ODE-Net, and generating new distributions with continuous normalizing flows (CNF). We demonstrate the *S-SOLVER* is accurate and numerically stable thanks to better local error estimation that determines the step size, which in turn affects the numerical stability of the ODE solution as shown in Sect. 3.

5.1 Stiff Neural ODE and Error Monitoring

We first validate *S-SOLVER*'s numerical stability on solving the following stiff neural ODE obtained from page 353 of [3]:

$$dy/dt = 5 \exp(5t)(y - t)^2 + 1 \; for \; 0 \leq t \leq 1, \; subject \; to \; y(t = 0) = -1 \tag{23}$$

This ODE equation is stiff, which means that it is likely the error due to approximation is amplified and becomes dominating in the solution calculations leading to a numerically unstable solution [3,12].

As shown in Fig. 3b, the neural ODE solved with *S-SOLVER* yields a solution that is very close to the exact solution:

$$y(t) = t - exp(-5t) \tag{24}$$

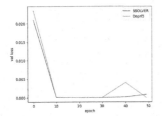
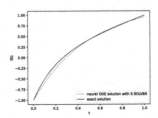

(a) Acrobot: Validation loss with *S-SOLVER* vs. Dopri5

(b) Solution to a stiff Neural ODE with *S-SOLVER*

Fig. 3. Learning Hamiltonian dynamics and solving stiff neural ODEs with *S-SOLVER*

In addition to demonstrating that *S-SOLVER* can solve stiff neural ODEs, which typically have numerical stability issues, we also examine the local error. Figure 4 shows the local error estimate produced by Dopri5 (default solver in *torchdiffeq*), *S-SOLVER*, and also a comparison of the two, which suggests that Dopri5 underestimates the local error.

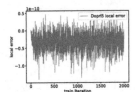
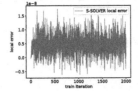
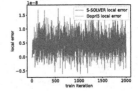

Fig. 4. A comparison of the local error produced by Dopri5 and *S-SOLVER*

5.2   Image Recognition

The next set of experiments focuses on image recognition with ODE-Nets. We train an ODE-Net with *S-SOLVER* and compare its results with an ODE-Net trained with Dopri5 (default solver in *torchdiffeq*) and also a classical ResNet on two datasets: MNIST and FASHION MNIST. Table 1 shows that the highest test accuracy on both datasets is achieved with our ODE-Net with *S-SOLVER*. The test accuracy on MNIST beats prior SOTA results in [5], who report a 0.42% test error, i.e.: 99.58% test accuracy. Using the same experiment settings as [5], thanks to *S-SOLVER* we push the test accuracy to 99.73%. Our results are also better compared to, for example, [7] who report 98.3% test accuracy that is achieved with their proposed temporal regularization.

Table 1. Results for ODE-Net with *S-SOLVER* on image recognition tasks

	MNIST			FASHION MNIST		
	train acc	test acc	loss	train acc	test acc	loss
ODE-Net with *S-SOLVER*	99.99%	**99.73%**	0.00013	97.58%	**94.00%**	0.079816
ODE-Net with dopri5	99.98%	99.69%	0.04623	97.75%	93.72%	0.055531
ResNet	99.96%	99.68%	7.2E-05	98.52%	93.94%	0.065489

5.3 Learning Hamiltonian Dynamics

We test *S-SOLVER* on Symplectic ODE-Net [30], which can learn Hamiltonian dynamics. Specifically, we choose the problem of "acrobot" [18,27], which simulates a physical system with two joints and two links, where the joint between the two links is actuated. Initially, the links are hanging downwards, and the goal is to swing the end of the lower link up to a given height. In Fig. 3a we show that the validation loss obtained with *S-SOLVER* is more stable than with Dopri5 (default solver in torchdiffeq) and therefore, preferable. We interpret this observation to be the result of *S-SOLVER*'s more reliable local estimation that controls the step size, which in turn impacts the stability of the ODE solution.

5.4 Continuous Normalizing Flows

Continuous Normalizing Flows (CNFs) are generative models introduced by [5] that leverage neural ODEs. CNFs are based on normalizing flows [22], which perform transformations of a simple probability distribution into a more complex one by a sequence of invertible and differentiable mappings [13]. We perform experiments with CNFs that use *S-SOLVER* and visualize how the model generates the Two Circles distribution from random noise in Fig. 5. Figure 5 shows the evolution of the generated distribution (samples) and probability density (log probability) with respect to the Two Circles distribution (target) over time from time-step 0.0 to 10.0. It can be observed that by the last time step, the random distribution has been transformed into the Two Circles distribution.

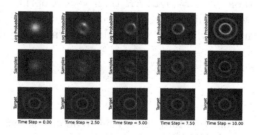

Fig. 5. CNFs for fitting the Two Circles distribution with *S-SOLVER*

6   Related Work

This paper focuses on ODE solvers for solving neural ODEs, which involves performing numerical integration. Specifically, we focus on adaptive step size ODE solvers which have become the standard for solving neural ODEs. While to our best knowledge, we are the first ones to propose a more numerically stable ODE solver that is based on more accurate local truncation error estimation, there are several prior works that also study numerical integration in neural ODEs. [31] perform numerical analysis of numerical integration in neural ODEs and propose IMDE, or inverse modified differential equations. [32] propose MALI, a new numerical integrator that is memory-efficient. [7] introduce STEER, a simple temporal regularization that randomly perturbs the numerical integration time limits. [19] propose a regularization method for adaptive ODE solvers that uses the internal cost heuristics. [29] study the robustness of the Euler method, which is the simplest, but important neural ODE solver. [14] develop a convergence test that can be used to select an ODE solver that is suitable for a particular task.

7   Conclusion

In this paper we demonstrate the importance of appropriately choosing and adapting the step size in ODE solvers for obtaining a numerically stable; and therefore, accurate solutions to a neural ODEs. To this end we propose *S-SOLVER*, a new neural ODE solver that is more numerically stable thanks to more accurate local truncation error estimation that is based on comparing multiple approximations as opposed to just two, which has been the standard approach. We provide a theoretical analysis of the impact of solver step size on numerical stability and also perform practical experiments with *S-SOLVER*. We show that *S-SOLVER* can solve a stiff neural ODE and that image recognition ODE-Nets learned with *S-SOLVER* surpass the test accuracy of prior solvers as well as classical ResNets on MNIST and FASHION MNIST. In fact, *S-SOLVER* achieves a new SOTA test accuracy on MNIST. We also show that the process of learning Hamiltonian dynamics with Symplectic ODE-Nets on the acrobot example is more stable with *S-SOLVER* than with Dopri5, the solver used in prior neural ODE works. Finally, we also show that *S-SOLVER* works well for CNFs in an experiment, where we successfully learn a new data distribution from random noise.

References

1. Abell, M.L., Braselton, J.P.: Introductory differential equations (2014)
2. Bogacki, P., Shampine, L.F.: A 3(2) pair of runge - kutta formulas. Appl. Math. Lett. **2**, 321–325 (1989)
3. Burden, R.L., Faires, J.D., Burden, A.M.: Numerical analysis. Cengage learning (2015)

4. Burrage, K., Burrage, P.M.: Order conditions of stochastic runge-kutta methods by b-series. SIAM J. Numer. Anal. **38**, 1626–1646 (2000)
5. Chen, T.Q., Rubanova, Y., Bettencourt, J., Duvenaud, D.K.: Neural ordinary differential equations. ArXiv abs/1806.07366 (2018)
6. Finlay, C., Jacobsen, J.H., Nurbekyan, L., Oberman, A.M.: How to train your neural ode: the world of Jacobian and kinetic regularization. In: ICML (2020)
7. Ghosh, A., Behl, H.S., Dupont, E., Torr, P.H.S., Namboodiri, V.: STEER: simple temporal regularization for neural odes. ArXiv abs/2006.10711 (2020)
8. Grathwohl, W., Chen, R.T.Q., Bettencourt, J., Sutskever, I., Duvenaud, D.K.: FFJORD: free-form continuous dynamics for scalable reversible generative models. ArXiv abs/1810.01367 (2019)
9. Haber, E., Ruthotto, L., Holtham, E.: Learning across scales - a multiscale method for convolution neural networks. ArXiv abs/1703.02009 (2018)
10. Higham, N.J.: Accuracy and Stability of Numerical Algorithms, second edition (2002)
11. Jong, L.D.: Towards a formal definition of numerical stability. Numer. Math. **28**, 211–219 (1977)
12. Kim, S., Ji, W., Deng, S., Ma, Y., Rackauckas, C.: Stiff neural ordinary differential equations. Chaos: Interdisc. J. Nonlinear Sci. **31**(9), 093122 (2021)
13. Kobyzev, I., Prince, S., Brubaker, M.A.: Normalizing flows: an introduction and review of current methods. IEEE Trans. Pattern Anal. Mach. Intell. **43**, 3964–3979 (2021)
14. Krishnapriyan, A.S., Queiruga, A.F., Erichson, N.B., Mahoney, M.W.: Learning continuous models for continuous physics. ArXiv abs/2202.08494 (2022)
15. Lawrence, F.S.: Some practical runge-kutta formulas. Math. Comput. **46**, 135–150 (1986)
16. LeVeque, R.J.: Finite difference methods for differential equations (2005)
17. Li, X., Wong, T.K.L., Chen, R.T.Q., Duvenaud, D.K.: Scalable gradients for stochastic differential equations. ArXiv abs/2001.01328 (2020)
18. Murray, R.M., Hauser, J.: A case study in approximate linearization: the acrobot example (2010)
19. Pal, A., Ma, Y., Shah, V.B., Rackauckas, C.: Opening the blackbox: accelerating neural differential equations by regularizing internal solver heuristics. In: ICML (2021)
20. Press, W.H., Teukolsky, S.A.: Adaptive stepsize runge-kutta integration. Comput. Phys. **6**, 188–191 (1992)
21. Prince, P.J., Dormand, J.R.: High order embedded runge-kutta formulae. J. Comput. Appl. Math. **7**, 67–75 (1981)
22. Rezende, D.J., Mohamed, S.: Variational inference with normalizing flows. In: ICML (2015)
23. Rubanova, Y., Chen, T.Q., Duvenaud, D.K.: Latent ordinary differential equations for irregularly-sampled time series. In: NeurIPS (2019)
24. Ruthotto, L., Osher, S.J., Li, W., Nurbekyan, L., Fung, S.W.: A machine learning framework for solving high-dimensional mean field game and mean field control problems. Proc. National Acad. Sci. **117**, 9183–9193 (2020)
25. Sanchez-Gonzalez, A., Bapst, V., Cranmer, K., Battaglia, P.W.: Hamiltonian graph networks with ode integrators. ArXiv abs/1909.12790 (2019)
26. Seiler, M.C., Seiler, F.A.: Numerical recipes in C: the art of scientific computing. Risk Anal. **9**, 415–416 (1989)
27. Sutton, R.S., Barto, A.G.: Reinforcement learning: an introduction. IEEE Trans. Neural Netw. **16**, 285–286 (2005)

28. Weinan, E.: A proposal on machine learning via dynamical systems (2017)
29. Yan, H., Du, J., Tan, V.Y.F., Feng, J.: On robustness of neural ordinary differential equations. ArXiv abs/1910.05513 (2020)
30. Zhong, Y.D., Dey, B., Chakraborty, A.: Symplectic ode-net: Learning hamiltonian dynamics with control. ArXiv abs/1909.12077 (2020)
31. Zhu, A., Jin, P., Zhu, B., Tang, Y.: On numerical integration in neural ordinary differential equations. In: ICML (2022)
32. Zhuang, J., Dvornek, N.C., Tatikonda, S.C., Duncan, J.S.: MALI: a memory efficient and reverse accurate integrator for neural odes. ArXiv abs/2102.04668 (2021)

TableSF: A Structural Bias Framework for Table-To-Text Generation

Di Liu[1], Weihua Wang[1,2,3(✉)], Feilong Bao[1,2,3], and Guanglai Gao[1,2,3]

[1] College of Computer Science, Inner Mongolia University, Hohhot, China
wangwh@imu.edu.cn
[2] National and Local Joint Engineering Research Center of Intelligent Information Processing Technology for Mongolian, Hohhot, China
[3] Inner Mongolia Key Laboratory of Mongolian Information Processing Technology, Hohhot, China

Abstract. Table-to-text generation is to generate a description from the tabular data. Existing methods typically encoded table content in a fixed order and relied heavily on the table row or column sequence. They generated error text descriptions when the row or column sequence changed. To solve the above problems, we proposed a novel structural bias framework that encodes tables using a modified self-attention mechanism. The framework captures the connectivity of cells in the same row or column through structural bias attention, distinguishing important cells from unimportant cells from a structural perspective. The structural bias attention will be added on top of the full self-attention, which can obtain the full structural information of the table. Experimental results show that this method generates better text descriptions on the public dataset and accomplishes a better understanding of the structured tables. This method not only obtains the relationship between cells but also improves the robustness of the pre-trained model.

Keywords: Table-to-text Generation · Self-Attention · Structural Bias Attention

1 Introduction

Tables are very common in all kinds of documents, they contain a lot of key information and convey it to the readers [1]. Table-to-text generation refers to the language model that generates text describing the table by inputting the table. Figure 1 shows an example of table-to-text generation. In this task, the model needs to understand the content and structure of the table and generate a short text that describing the table content. The generated text should be fluent in sentences, fully express the information of the table and not deviate from the facts of the table. Understanding the meaning of tables and describing their contents has potential applications such as document analysis [2], question answering [3], building dialog agents [4], and supporting search engines [5].

Most of the previous table-to-text generation tasks used the sequence-to-sequence architecture [6]. These methods represent the table as a linear structure, causing the model to rely too much on the row or column sequence of the table.

L. Iliadis et al. (Eds.): ICANN 2023, LNCS 14262, pp. 401–412, 2023.
https://doi.org/10.1007/978-3-031-44201-8_33

Name	Year	Competition	Event
Gabriele Becker	1995	World Championships	100 m
			4x100 m relay

Text: Gabriele Becker competed at the 1995 World Championships in the 100m individual and 4x100m relay.

Fig. 1. An example of table-to-text generation tasks.

These methods ignore the structural features of tables, which are key guidelines for generating accurate text. The table structure contains the relationship between each cell. However, the relationship between these cells can't be utilized by linearizing the table. Recently, pre-trained language models such as BERT [7], T5 [8], and GPT-2 [9] have shown excellent ability to encode and generate natural language text fluently and coherently, but the pre-training model can't capture the structural information of the table.

In this paper, we will improve the existing pre-trained language model method through the structural properties of tables. The structural characteristics of the table mainly refer to the relationship between the cells in the table. We propose a structural bias framework, refered as TableSF, which not only obtains the relationship between cells but also improves the robustness of the model. It encodes tables using a structure-aware self-attention mechanism and captures table structure information through self-attention and structural bias attention. This framework will add table structural bias attention on top of the full self-attention structure, which can capture the connection structure of cells belonging to the same row or column for a better understanding of the table. Our method can be applied to pre-training model, like T5, BART and etc. Experiments show that this method achieved better performance on the publicly ToTTo [10] dataset.

In particular, our contributions mainly include the following aspects:

- We illustrate the importance of table structural characteristics for generating correct text descriptions about tables and improving the robustness of the model.
- We propose a new structural bias framework to efficiently express the relationship between cells by an improved self-attention mechanism. This framework captures the table's structural information through self-attention and structural bias attention to generate accurate and fluent textual descriptions of tables.
- We evaluate our method on the ToTTo dataset and obtain better results in several domains.

2   Related Work

Table-to-text generation is to generate a description from the tabular data. Early research adapted encoder-decoder [11] frameworks for table-to-text generation tasks. To enable the model to extract the structural information from the table, Liu et al. [12] proposed a table structure-aware model. This method does not perform well in generating complex structured tables. Tables contain a significant amount of information, but the descriptions of tables typically revolve around key information. So Ma et al. [13] proposed a model centered on the key facts of the table. However, this method is not good enough for table information extraction and needs to be improved. Puduppully et al. [14] proposed a content selection and planning model to solve the problem that the table-to-text generation model performed poorly in content selection. But it can lead to incorrect facts, thus affecting the performance of the model.

The pre-training language model has an excellent performance in the field of natural language processing. Inspired by it, Harkous et al. [15] and Kale et al. [16] have achieved excellent results on different data and text benchmarks using different pre-training language models. Recently, some researchers have proposed several pre-training methods designed for table data. Deng et al. [17] propose STRUG, a weakly supervised structure-based text-to-SQL pre-training framework that can efficiently learn to capture text table alignments. But their model is only for text-to-SQL tasks, which require parallel text table data. Chen et al. [18] proposed a knowledge-based pre-training model, KGPT, which is trained based on a large knowledge-based text corpus scraped from the web. To solve the problem that the pre-trained language model is difficult to perceive the structure of the table. Zhang et al. [19] restrict attention to cells in the same row or column with attention mask, where this institutional bias is too narrow. As a result, it is impossible to directly focus on the relationship between cells in different rows or columns.

In the model mentioned above, the order of rows and columns of the table is more or less dependent, and the structural characteristics of the table are not fully utilized, which leads to the vulnerability of row or column order disturbance. But our structural bias framework, TableSF, can effectively avoid this problem.

3   Approach

3.1   Preliminaries

Table Structure Transformations. Tables are both a visual communication mode and a means of organizing data. A table consists of cells that display information in rows and columns.

We will introduce the transformation methods of the two types of tables. First, table content conversion involves modifying cell content or incorrectly exchanging any cell information in the table. This practices will change the original meaning of the table. The original table and the table with changed content are shown in Fig. 2. Secondly, transform the table layout structure without changing the table cell content, which is equivalent to the original table in a practical sense. Tables can be transposed, and entire rows or columns can be swapped. Choose one or more of the above operations to change the structure and layout of the table without changing the actual meaning of the table. The table of the transformation structure is shown in Fig. 3.

A good table-to-text generation method should generate correct descriptions for tables with the same content but different layouts.

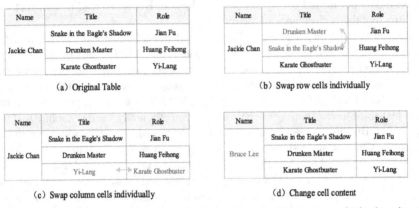

(a) Original Table

(b) Swap row cells individually

(c) Swap column cells individually

(d) Change cell content

Fig. 2. Example of table content changes. (a) is the original table structure, (b) is changing the row cells of the table alone, (c) is changing the column cells of the table alone, and (d) is changing the cell content information. Arrows indicate how the position of the table component changes. Content that does not conform to the original table is marked in red.

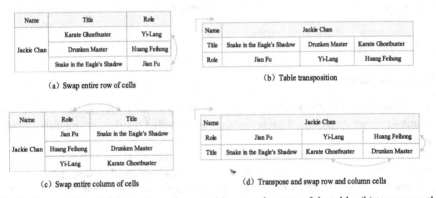

(a) Swap entire row of cells

(b) Table transposition

(c) Swap entire column of cells

(d) Transpose and swap row and column cells

Fig. 3. An example of table structure changes. (a) swaps the rows of the table, (b) transposes the table, (c) swaps the columns of the table, and (d) combines the first three ways. Arrows indicate how the position of the table component changes. Such operations are effectively equivalent to the original table contents.

Base Models. In a wide variety of generative tasks, generative models based on pre-trained Transformers perform well [20]. To make such models suitable for table-to-text generation tasks, we incorporate TableSF into them without changing the model's architecture. We use the T5 model as the base Model. The basic idea of T5 is to treat every text processing problem as a text-to-text problem, taking the text as input and generating new text as output.

3.2   TableSF: Structural Bias Framework

TableSF realizes table structural bias learning by modifying the Transformer encoder. It improves the ability of the base model to capture the structure of the table. Specifically, we introduce a self-attention mechanism with structural bias in the base model.

Structural Bias Attention. Transformer [21] employs self-attention mechanism to obtain information about all tokens in the input sequence. Each token can be connected to other tokens through attention. This attention mechanism achieves good results in sequence modeling but fails to capture table structural information.

  We integrate structural information of tables through table structural bias. According to the structural characteristics of the table, cells in the same row or column are semantically related. We consider cells that are not in the same row or column to be irrelevant to the table structure. The structural bias of the table includes the following situations: "same row", "row title to row cell", "same column", "column title to column cell", "same cell", and "title to title". In TableSF, we first get and save the attention of each token and other tokens in the table. Next, in order to extract the structural bias attention of the table, we integrate the table structure information by pruning the attention. Specifically, we remove attention from the start of the attention between cells that are not structurally related to the table, retaining attention within titles, within each cell, and between titles and cells of the same row or column. Then combine the original attention and structural bias attention to get the final attention. An example of attention used in our method is shown in Fig. 4.

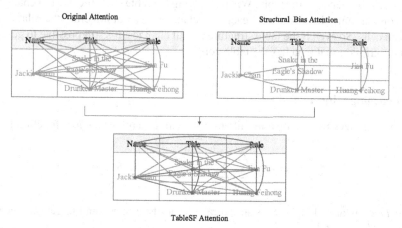

TableSF Attention

Fig. 4. Example of Original Attention, Structural Bias Attention, and TableSF Attention. In this example, we omit attention between tokens within the same cells. The red line represents the added structural bias attention.

  Each Transformer contains self-attention mechanism and each token attention to all tokens. For a single self-attention sublayer, the input X is projected by three matrices $W^Q \in \mathbb{R}^{d_{model} \times d_k}$, $W^K \in \mathbb{R}^{d_{model} \times d_k}$ and $W^V \in \mathbb{R}^{d_{model} \times d_v}$ to the corresponding representation Q, K and V vectors:

$$Q = XW^Q, K = XW^K, V = XW^V \tag{1}$$

$$\hat{A} = \frac{QK^T}{\sqrt{d_k}}, A = \hat{A} + \bar{A} \qquad (2)$$

$$Attention(X) = softmax(A)V \qquad (3)$$

where $\hat{A}$ is the original matrix capturing the similarity between queries and keys, and $\bar{A}$ is the attention bias matrix after removing structurally irrelevant cells.

In this way, we also ensure efficient extraction of the table structure, which can generate fluent sentences. It can be ensured that text descriptions generated in the case of equivalent content with varying table layouts will still accurately reflect the meaning of the table. Because the cells related to the table structure are all linked together in a specific manner.

Positional Biases. When computing attention scores between tokens, the base model usually needs their relative position in the linearization table sequence, but it can't completely obtain the positional relationship between the cells in the table, which can easily lead to positional biases between different cells. In addition, the relative position between the same token pair will change with the change in the table structure, which leads to the generation of text descriptions inconsistent with the table content. Due to the structural characteristics of the table, we should equally consider the relationship of each cell in the same row or column. Cells in the same row or column should be assigned the same relative position, no matter how far apart the cells in the same row or column are in the linear sequence of the table. When changing the table structure doesn't change the table content, only the position of each cell changes without affecting the relationship between cells. So even if the table structure layout changes, it's still possible to generate a text description that matches the table content.

3.3 Learning Objective

We use minimizes the negative log-likelihood, with N samples the loss function is

$$L = -\frac{1}{N} \sum_{i=1}^{N} \sum_{j=1}^{n_i} logP\left(y_j^i | y_{<j}^i, T_i, S_i\right) \qquad (4)$$

where T_i is linearized table, S_i is structural layout of the table, and target sentence are $Y_i = \{y_1^i, y_2^i, \ldots, y_{n_i}^i\}$.

4 Experiments and Results

In this section, we experiment with our method on the ToTTo [10] dataset. First, we introduce the dataset, baselines, evaluation metrics, and input format. Then, we compare the experimental results on TableSF and baselines. We also conduct an ablation study targeting the modified attention part. Finally, we will use a case to demonstrate the effectiveness of our method.

4.1 Dataset

ToTTo [10] is an English dataset for the table-to-text generation task. It contains 83141 Wikipedia tables, and 120761/7700/7700 sentences, for train/dev/test. Depending on whether the table exists in the train set, the development set and the test set can be further divided into two subsets, namely overlap and non-overlap. Parikh et al. [10] apply several heuristics to sample tables and candidate sentences from Wikipedia pages. They used crowd worker annotators to highlight the corresponding table cells and revise table text descriptions.

4.2 Baselines

We used the following methods as our baselines:

- **Pointer-Generator** [22]: A LSTM-based model with attention and replication mechanism. Although originally designed for summarization, it is also commonly used for data-to-text.
- **BERT-to-BERT** [23]: A Transformer-based encoder-decoder model, where the encoder and decoder are both initialized with BERT.
- **T5**: A pre-trained model based on Transformer, it was pre-processed for text-to-text tasks, and fine-tuned by linearization table to provide excellent performance.
- **TABT5** [24]: An encoder-decoder model relies on special embeddings of the input structure. The model was applied to table-to-text generation tasks and achieves state-of-the-art performance.

4.3 Evaluation Metrics

The output is evaluated using two automatic metrics:

- **BLEU** [25]: It is a commonly used evaluation metric in text generation tasks. The calculation method is designed with the core idea that the closer the generated text is to the target text, the higher the quality of the generated text.
- **PARENT** [26]: It is a metric recently proposed specifically for data-to-text evaluation that takes the table into account. Parikh et al. [10] modified it to make it suitable for the ToTTo dataset, described in the Parikh et al. [10] thesis Appendix.

4.4 Input Format

We linearize ToTTo based on Kale and Rastogi [16] linearization procedure. The input format is shown in Fig. 5. Specifically, the linearized text sequence consists of the page title, section title, table titles and many cells. Each cell in a table may have relationships with multiple rows or columns. The start and end of each field are indicated using special markers. But not quite the same as Kale and Rastogi (2020), we use the same markers to label row and column titles.

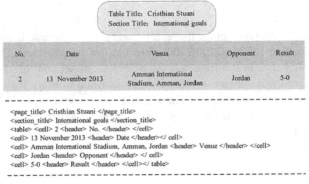

Fig. 5. An example of the input representation of the dataset, with a structured table at the top, the input format of the table in the middle, and the target text at the bottom.

4.5 Results

For the ToTTo test set, we reported the results in Table 1. We follow the official BLEU and PARENT calculation results of Parikh et al. as evaluation indicators. It can be seen from the experimental results that among all the baselines, the methods based on the pre-trained Transformer models BERT-to-BERT. T5 are better than other methods, and it performs best. Therefore we add TableSF to the T5 model. Adding our method to base models of different sizes and comparing them separately, our method consistently performs better.

Specifically, Compared with T5-small, TableSF (T5-small) improved 2.4 BLEU points and 1 PARENT points, while compared with T5-base, TableSF (T5-base) improved 1.3 BLEU points and 2.0 PARENT points. These results fully illustrate the importance of table structural information, which is nearly completely discarded by the baseline model.

On the overlap subset, TableSF (T5-small) achieves an improvement of 3.3 BLEU points and 1.6 PARENT points over the baseline model. While compared with T5-base, TableSF (T5-base) outperforms it by 0.8 BLEU points and 1.5 PARENT points improvement, showing better performance.

On the non-overlap subset, compared with T5-small, TableSF (T5-small) achieved 1.5 BLEU points and 0.4 PARENT points improvement, while compared with T5-base, TableSF (T5-base) improved 1.6 BLEU points and 2.7 PARENT points, which indicates that our method has good generalization ability.

Furthermore, comparing our method with the state-of-the-art method TABT5. TABT5 uses a large-scale dataset of 6.2M tables for pre-training, enabling TabT5 to better capture the structure of the language, thereby generating more accurate text descriptions. In this case, the PARENT of our method is higher than TABT5 by 1.1 points and 1.6 points in the overall set and non-overlap subset, but the BLUE value is not much different. TABT5 did not give results on the overlap subset.

Table 1. Results on the ToTTo test set. The best score among all methods is shown in bold. Unpublished results are represented by the '——' symbol.

Model	Overall		Overlap		Non-Overlap	
	BLUE	PARENT	BLUE	PARENT	BLUE	PARENT
Pointer-Generator	41.6	51.6	50.6	58.0	32.2	45.2
BERT-to-BERT	44.0	52.6	52.7	58.4	34.8	46.7
T5-small	45.3	57.0	52.7	61.0	37.8	53.0
TableSF(T5-small)	**47.7**	**58.0**	**56.0**	**62.6**	**39.3**	**53.4**
T5-base	47.4	56.4	55.5	61.1	39.1	51.7
TABT5-base	**49.2**	57.3	——	——	**41.0**	52.8
TableSF(T5-base)	48.7	**58.4**	**56.3**	**62.6**	40.7	**54.4**

4.6 Ablation Study

To demonstrate the role of our structural bias mechanism, we present the ablation study results in Table 2. Compared with original self-attention, only applying the structural information of the table by pruned structural bias attention can improve the overall performance by 1.8 BLEU points. After combining original attention and structural bias attention, it can bring an additional improvement of 0.2 BLEU points to the overall performance. The overlap subset and non-overlap subset results illustrate that both the tables seen and unseen during training can benefit from table structural information. The structural bias framework improves the model's ability to capture relationships between cells.

Table 2. Ablation study on ToTTo dev set. Scores are BLEU. Org + str attention is the abbreviation of the combination of original attention and structural bias attention.

Attention	Overall	Overlap	Non-Overlap
original self-attention	45.7	53.7	37.7
structural bias attention	47.5	55.5	39.5
org + str attention	47.7	55.8	39.6

4.7 Case Study

In this section, we used a case to demonstrate the effectiveness of our method. Descriptive text for tables is generated using the base model and improving the base model based on our method. We linearize table cells based on row and column sequence. It traverses row by row the table from the upper left cell to the lower right cell. For example, if the table in Fig. 6 is linearized, Huang Feihong will be located between the two movies

Drunken Master and Karate Ghostbuster. It is impossible to judge which movie Huang Feihong came from using the base model. This leads to a wrong match between the role and title relationship, thus generating wrong text descriptions. However, our method not only captures the structural information of the table, and finds the relationship between roles and titles, but also generates correct textual descriptions of the table.

Name	Year	Title	Role
		Snake in the Eagle's Shadow	Jian Fu
Jackie Chan	1978	Drunken Master	Huang Feihong
		Karate Ghostbuster	Yi-Lang

T5: In 1978, Jackie Chan played Jian Fu in Snake in the Eagle's Shadow, Huang Feihong, Karate Ghostbuster and Yi-Lang in Drunken Master.

TableSF: In 1978, Jackie Chan appeared as Jian Fu in Snake in the Eagle's Shadow, Huang Feihong in Drunken Master and Karate Ghostbuster as Yi-Lang.

Fig. 6. Use T5 and TableSF to generate the text description of the table and the roles and titles that match correctly are displayed in bold blue font.

Name	Jackie Chan		
Year	1978		
Role	Jian Fu	Yi-Lang	Huang Feihong
Title	Snake in the Eagle's Shadow	Karate Ghostbuster	Drunken Master

T5: In 1978, Jackie Chan appeared in Drunken Master, Karate Ghostbuster, Snake in the Eagle's Shadow, Huang Feihong, and as Jian Fu in Yi-Lang.

TableSF: In 1978, Jackie Chan appeared as Jian Fu in Snake in the Eagle's Shadow, Huang Feihong in Drunken Master and Karate Ghostbuster as Yi-Lang.

Fig. 7. Change the order of the cells in the table in Fig. 6 without changing the contents of the cells to form a new table. Use T5 and TableSF to generate a text description for the new table, with correctly matched roles and job titles shown in blue bold. Table structure changes significantly affected T5 results but not TableSF results.

In addition, tables with the same content can be expressed in different equivalent forms. In this case, the model is required to generate a textual description that conforms to the content of the table. Therefore, we change the layout of the table structure in Fig. 6 by transposing and exchanging the sequence of cells in the entire row and column, the modified table is shown in Fig. 7. The text description generated by the base model isn't the same as the text description generated when the cell structure is not disturbed and doesn't conform to the table facts. But this change in table structure doesn't affect our method which proves the effectiveness of our method.

5 Conclusion

We propose a structural bias framework suitable for table-to-text generation tasks. The experimental results show that our method can extract the table structure. As long as the cell content remains unchanged, no matter how the table structure layout changes, it can generate correct text descriptions about the table content. We will study how to apply our framework to the task of few-shot table-to-text generation.

Acknowledgments. This work is supported by National Natural Science Foundation of China (Nos.62066033, 61966025); Inner Mongolia Applied Technology Research and Development Fund Project (Nos.2020GG0046, 2021GG0158, 2020PT0002); Inner Mongolia Natural Science Foundation (No.2020BS06001); Inner Mongolia Autonomous Region Overseas Students Innovation and Entrepreneurship Startup Program; Inner Mongolia Discipline Inspection and Supervision Big Data Laboratory Open project (Nos.IMDBD202009).

References

1. Bao, J., Tang, D., Duan, N., et al.: Table-to-text: describing table region with natural language. In: Proceedings of the 32th AAAI Conference on Artificial Intelligence and Thirtieth Innovative Applications of Artificial Intelligence Conference, pp. 5020–5027 (2018)
2. Siddiqui, S.A., Khan, P.I., Dengel, A., et al.: Rethinking semantic segmentation for table structure recognition in documents. In: 2019 International Conference on Document Analysis and Recognition (ICDAR), pp. 1397–1402. IEEE (2019)
3. Uhar, S.K., Turney, P., Hovy, E.: Tables as semi-structured Knowledge for question answering. In: Proceedings of the 54th Annual Meeting of the Association for Computational Linguistics, pp. 474–483 (2016)
4. Yan, Z., Duan, N., Bao, J., et al.: DocChat: an information retrieval approach for chatbot engines using unstructured documents. In: Proceedings of the 54th Annual Meeting of the Association for Computational Linguistics, pp. 516–525 (2016)
5. Bao, J., Tang, D., Duan, N., et al.: Table-to-Text: Describing Table Region with Natural Language (2018)
6. Klein, G., Kim, Y., Deng, Y.T., et al.: openNMT: open-source toolkit for neural machine translation. In: Proceedings of the 55th Annual Meeting of the Association for Computational Linguistics, Vancouver, Jul 30–Aug 4, 2017, pp. 67–72. Stroudsburg, ACL
7. Kenton, J.D.M.W.C., Toutanova, L.K.: BERT: pre-training of deep bidirectional transformers for language understanding. In: Proceedings of NAACL-HLT, pp. 4171–4186 (2019)
8. Raffel, C., Shazeer, N., Roberts, A., et al.: Exploring the limits of transfer learning with a unified text-to-text transformer. J. Mach. Learn. Res **21**(140), 1–67 (2020)
9. Ethayarajh, K.: How contextual are contextualized word representations? comparing the geometry of BERT, ELMo, and GPT-2 Embeddings. In: Proceedings of the 2019 Conference on Empirical Methods in Natural Language Processing, pp. 55–65 (2019)
10. Parikh, A., Wang, X., Gehrmann, S., et al.: ToTTo: a controlled table-to-text generation dataset. In: Proceedings of the 2020 Conference on Empirical Methods in Natural Language Processing (EMNLP), pp. 1173–1186 (2020)

11. Bahdanau, D., Cho, K.H., Bengio, Y.: Neural machine translation by jointly learning to align and translate. In: 3rd International Conference on Learning Representations (2015)

12. Liu, T., Wang, K., Sha, L., et al.: Table-to-text Generation by Structure-aware Seq2seq Learning (2018)

13. Ma, S.M., Yang, P.C., Liu, T.Y., et al.: Key fact as Pivot: a two- stage model for low resource table-to-text generation. In: Proceedings of the 57th Conference of the Association for Computational Linguistics, pp. 2047–2057 (2019)

14. Puduppully, R., Dong, L., Lapata, M.: Data-to-text generation with content selection and planning. In: Proceedings of the AAAI Conference on Artificial Intelligence, vol. 33(01), pp. 6908–6915 (2019)

15. Harkous, H., Groves, I., Saffari, A.: Have your text and use it too! end-to-end neural data-to-text generation with semantic fidelity. In: Proceedings of the 28th International Conference on Computational Linguistics, pp. 2410–2424 (2020)

16. Kale, M., Rastogi, A.: Text-to-text pre-training for data-to-text tasks. In: Proceedings of the 13th International Conference on Natural Language Generation, pp. 97–102 (2020)

17. Deng, X., Hassan, A., Meek, C., et al.: Structure-grounded pretraining for text-to-SQL. In: Proceedings of the 2021 Conference of the North American Chapter of the Association for Computational Linguistics: Human Language Technologies, pp. 1337–1350 (2021)

18. Chen, W., Su, Y., Yan, X., et al.: KGPT: knowledge-grounded pre-training for data-to-text generation. In: Proceedings of the 2020 Conference on Empirical Methods in Natural Language Processing (EMNLP), pp. 8635–648 (2020)

19. Zhang, H., Wang, Y., Wang, S., et al.; Table fact verification with structure-aware transformer. In: Proceedings of the 2020 Conference on Empirical Methods in Natural Language Processing (EMNLP), pp. 1624–1629 (2020)

20. Raffel, C., Shazeer, N., Roberts, A., et al.: Exploring the limits of transfer learning with a unified text-to-text transformer. J. Mach. Learn. Res. **21**(140), 1–67 (2020)

21. Vaswani, A., Shazeer, N., Parmar, N., et al.: Attention is all you need. Adv. Neural Inform. Process. Syst. **30** (2017)

22. Gehrmann, S., Dai, F., Elder, H., et al.: End-to-end content and plan selection for data-to-text generation. In: Proceedings of the 11th International Conference on Natural Language Generation, pp. 46–56 (2018)

23. Rothe, S., Narayan, S., Severyn, A.: Leveraging pre-trained checkpoints for sequence generation tasks. Trans. Assoc. Comput. Linguist. **8**, 264–280 (2020)

24. Andrejczuk, E., Eisenschlos, J., Piccinno, F., et al.: Table-To-Text generation and pre-training with TabT5. In: Findings of the Association for Computational Linguistics: EMNLP 2022, pp. 6758–6766 (2022)

25. Papineni, K., Roukos, S., Ward, T., et al.: Bleu: a method for automatic evaluation of machine translation. In: Proceedings of the 40th annual meeting of the Association for Computational Linguistics, pp. 311–318 (2002)

26. Dhingra, B., Faruqui, M., Parikh, A., Chang, M.-W., Das, D., Cohen, W.: Handling divergent reference texts when evaluating table-to-text generation. In Proceedings of the 57th Annual Meeting of the Association for Computational Linguistics, pp. 4884–4895 (2019)

TCS-LipNet: Temporal & Channel & Spatial Attention-Based Lip Reading Network

Huanjie Chen[1], Wenjuan Li[2], Zhigang Cheng[1], Xiubo Liang[1], and Qifei Zhang[1(✉)]

[1] School of Software, Zhejiang University, Ningbo, China
{huanjiec,chengzhigang,liangxb,cstzhangqf}@zju.edu.cn
[2] School of Engineering, Hangzhou Normal University, Hangzhou, China
liwenjuan_jd@sjtu.edu.cn

Abstract. Lip-reading is the process of translating input lip-movement image sequences into text sequences, which is a task that requires both temporal and spatial information to be considered, and feature extraction is difficult. In this regard, this paper proposes a new lip reading model, TCS-LipNet, which innovatively proposes the temporal channel space attention mechanism module TCSAM, and compared with the channel space attention mechanism, TCS increases the association of channel space features in the temporal dimension and improves the performance of the model. TCS-LipNet uses the TCSAM-based ResNet18 network as the front-end module to enhance the extraction of visual features, and DC-TCN (Densely Connected Temporal Convolutional Networks) as the back-end module to address the temporal correlation of sequences. The experimental data show that TCS-LipNet achieves 92.2% accuracy on LRW, which is the highest accuracy rate currently.

Keywords: Lip reading · attention mechanism · feature extraction

1 Introduction

Lip reading is a process of understanding language through visual features and has a wide range of application scenarios. Lip reading goes through three main steps: lip visual feature extraction, sequence feature extraction, and classification.

Ideally, the visual features should contain enough valid information and show some robustness to noise in the video. Since the image features extracted by CNN have powerful representation capability, existing lip-reading models usually build front-end modules with them.

In the process of lip reading, we not only focus on the shape of the speaker's lips but also the motion of the lips and the sequential connection between visual features. Therefore, lip reading models need back-end modules to capture the lip dynamics in frames for sequence feature extraction. RNN has good modeling capability for sequence data, and RNN and its improved versions are widely used in lip reading models. However, the latest results use the time-convolutional network TCN, which performs better than RNN in all kinds of tasks. Martinez et al. [1] used MS-TCN instead of Bi-GRU to achieve SOTA results. This was followed by DC-TCN combined with the optimal training strategy to obtain a classification accuracy of 92.1% on the LRW dataset [2].

Although attention mechanisms are widely used in the back-end module of lip-reading models to improve the performance of RNNs, current research on the introduction of attention mechanisms in the front-end module has not been fully developed. Feng et al. [3] are one of the few attempts in this area, with the introduction of SE-Net [4] in the front-end module of their model. The model achieved an accuracy of 55.7% on LRW-1000, which is the most advanced on this dataset effect, but the authors do not explore the specific role of SE-Net in depth. In addition, we believe that lip reading is a task that requires simultaneous consideration of temporal and spatial information, and existing attentional mechanisms cannot fully satisfy the needs of the lip reading task.

Based on the above observations and reflections, this paper proposes the lip reading model TCS-LipNet. Front-end module of the model, we design a new attention mechanism module TCSAM, which increases the attention of channel space features in the time dimension compared with the channel space attention mechanism. The back-end module uses DC-TCN. experimental results show that our model achieves 92.2% accuracy on LRW, achieving a new highest accuracy for this dataset.

2   Related Work

2.1   Visual Feature Extraction

With the emergence of CNN architectures such as VGG [5], GoogleNet [6], AlexNet [7], ResNet [8], DenseNet [9], etc., deep convolutional neural networks have gradually become the mainstream approach in lip vision feature extraction tasks. In computer vision, 2D CNN is a better choice for processing spatial information, and it has two application methods in lip reading: one is to apply 2D convolution on each frame to extract discriminative features of the lips, and this method pays attention to the shape of the lips when speaking specific characters [10–14]; in the other method, frames are stacked and input to 2D CNN, and the model tries to capture local spatial features while capturing local temporal features [15].

Compared with 2D CNN, 3D CNN-based feature extraction methods can extract both temporal and spatial information from consecutive frames. LipNet [16] uses 3D CNN and pooling layers with different kernel sizes to extract features at different levels, combining GRU and CTC losses [17] to construct the first end-to-end lip-reading model with recognition accuracy up to 93.4% on the Grid dataset. Another popular approach is to deploy 3D counterpart blocks of 2D networks. Shillingford et al. [18] used a 3D version of VGG, which outperformed the visual modality of LipNet and WLAS [19] on the LSVSR dataset.

The combined use of 2D CNNs, which emphasize visual features, and 3D CNNs, which encode both spatiotemporal features in a sequence, can produce more powerful and discriminative features [20–22].

2.2   Attention Mechanism in Convolutional Networks

SE-Net [4] adaptively adjusts the importance of each channel by using the "squeeze-and-excitation" module. ECA-Net [23] improves on SE-Net with an efficient way to compute channel attention, significantly reducing the computational effort and number of parameters of the model. The core idea of SK-Net [24] is to introduce selective convolution between channels so that the model can better capture the relationship between different channels. CBAM [25] is built with a spatial attention module SAM and a channel attention module CAM. Aggregates the attention information of both spatial and channel. DA-Net [26] is similar to the CBAM idea, but the way to obtain the attention of both channels is different.

3   TCS-LipNet Architecture

3.1   Time and Channel and Spatial Attention Module

The lip reading task is highly dependent on both temporal and spatial information. Each image frame in the lip sequence carries part of the word information, and the focused part of the word is more capable of making a distinction between words. In the feature extraction of each lip image frame, the feature maps of different channels contain image information of different dimensions or depths, and different positions in the image space have different degrees of importance to the information provided by the task, and the lip reading should focus on the information of the lip region and reduce the attention to the chin, cheek and other regions.

For the above analysis, we propose TCSAM, which introduces attention mechanisms in three dimensions: time, channel, and space assign weights to the input data in three dimensions by convolution, filter out important information in different dimensions, and then perform information fusion. There are four forms of TCSAM, as shown in Fig. 1 and Fig. 2.

Figure 1a represents segmenting the image by sequence, each sequence unit consists of feature maps of multiple channels, performing channel and spatial attention extraction on the channel feature maps, and then extracting temporal attention after merging the images by sequence.

Figure 1b represents segmenting the image by channel, each channel unit consists of feature maps of multiple sequences, performing temporal and spatial attention extraction on the sequence feature maps, and then extracting channel attention after merging the images by channel.

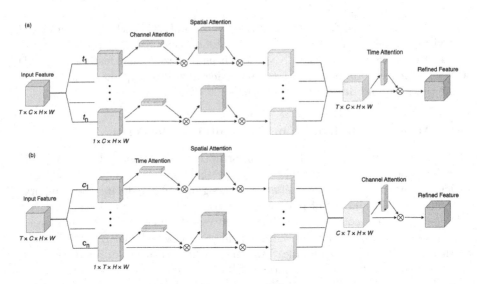

Fig. 1. The way a of TCSAM.

Figure 2a represents the segmentation of images by channel, each channel unit consists of feature maps of multiple sequences, spatial attention extraction is performed on the sequence feature maps, and then time, as well as channel attention, is extracted after merging the images by channel.

Figure 2b represents segmenting the image by channel, each channel unit consists of multiple sequences of feature maps, performing spatial attention extraction on the sequence feature maps, and then extracting the time as well as channel attention after merging the images by channel.

The channel dimension is generally understood as different depth information in the image space in the 2D image domain and different motion information in the video in the 3D video domain. The main difference between Fig. 1 and Fig. 2 is whether the channel and time are considered as two interrelated dimensions, similar to the width and height dimensions of an image, if they are not, then Fig. 1, and vice versa, then Fig. 2. The difference between a and b is which is more important for the task, the image information or the motion information. If the 2D image information is more important for the model task then it is a, and vice versa it is b. Considering that the lip reading model consists of an image feature extraction model at the front end and a temporal semantic extraction model at the back end, we choose the architecture in Fig. 1a and combine it with the ResNet18 model for feature extraction.

Given a feature map $F \in R^{T \times C \times H \times W}$ as input, TCSAM first calculates the weight feature map of channel attention for $M_c \in R^{C \times 1 \times 1}$ and the feature map of each time series unit $F_t \in R^{C \times H \times W}$, then calculates the weight feature map of spatial attention $M_s \in R^{1 \times H \times W}$, and finally combines the sequences to calculate one-dimensional temporal attention weight $M_T \in R^{T \times 1 \times 1 \times 1}$. The overall attention calculation process is shown in (1).

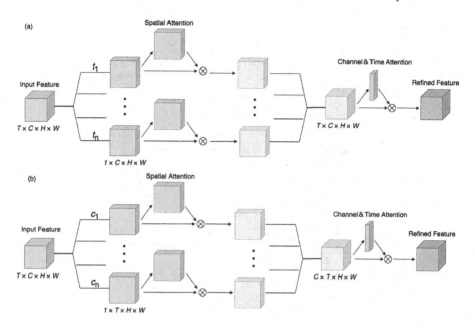

Fig. 2. The way b of TCSAM.

$$F = \{F_1, F_2, \ldots, F_T\}$$
$$F' = M_C(F_t) \otimes F_t$$
$$F_t'' = M_S(F_{t'}) \otimes F_{t'} \tag{1}$$
$$F'' = \{F_1'', F_2'', \ldots, F_T''\}$$
$$F''' = M_T(F') \otimes F''$$

where $\otimes$ denotes element-wise multiplication, during which the value of attention is multiplied by the corresponding dimension. Among them F', F_t'' is the feature map at time t, and F'' is the final output feature map. Figure 3 describes the calculation process of each attention module. Next, we mainly introduce the details of each attention module.

The calculation process of the channel attention module, as shown in Fig. 3a, performs two-dimensional average pooling and maximum pooling on a set of feature 3. A, performs two-dimensional average pooling and maximum pooling on a set of feature $F_{Avg2D}^C \in R^{C \times 1 \times 1}$ maps of each frame of the image, respectively, forming average pooling feature maps and maximum pooling features Figure $F_{Max2D}^C \in R^{C \times 1 \times 1}$, and then use the same group of 2D convolution MLPs to perform fully connected operations, add the two sets of vectors and pass through the sigmoid layer to obtain the attention weight of the same dimension as the number of channels. The formula is shown in (2), where σ represents the sigmoid function, W_0 and W_1 is MLP the shared weight in.

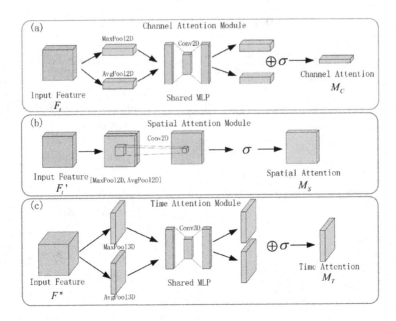

Fig. 3. Diagram of each attention sub-module

$$M_C(F_t) = \sigma(MLP(AvgPool2D(F_t)) + MLP(MaxPool2D(F_t)))$$
$$= \sigma(W_1(W_0(F^C_{Avg2D})) + W_1(W_0(F^C_{Max2D}))) \quad (2)$$

The calculation process of the spatial attention module, as shown in Fig. 3b, performs average pooling and maximum pooling in the channel dimension for a set of feature $F^S_{Avg2D} \in R^{1 \times H \times W}$ maps of each frame of the image, respectively, forming an average pooling feature map and a maximum pooling feature map $F^S_{Max2D} \in R^{1 \times H \times W}$, after the two sets of vectors are concatenated, 2D convolution is used for full connection operation, and then the attention weight of the same dimension as the image width and height is obtained through the sigmoid layer. The formula is shown in (3), whereσ represents the sigmoid function, where $f^{7 \times 7}$ represents the convolution operation with a convolution kernel size of 7×7.

$$M_S(F'_t) = \sigma(f^{7 \times 7}([AvgPool2D(F'_t); MaxPool2D(F'_t)]))$$
$$= \sigma(f^{7 \times 7}([F^S_{Avg2D}; F^S_{Max2D}])) \quad (3)$$

The calculation process of the temporal attention module, as shown in Fig. 3c, performs three-dimensional average pooling and maximum pooling on all feature maps of each frame in the image sequence to form average pooling feature maps $F^T_{Avg3D} \in R^{T \times 1 \times 1 \times 1}$ and maximum pooling feature maps $F^T_{Max3D} \in R^{T \times 1 \times 1 \times 1}$, and then use the same set of 3D convolution MLP to perform fully connected operations, add the two sets of vectors and pass through the sigmoid layer to obtain the attention weight of the same dimension as time. The formula is shown in (4), where σ represents the sigmoid function, W_0 and W_1 is MLP the shared weight in.

$$M_T(F'') = \sigma(MLP(AvgPool3D(F'')) + MLP(MaxPool3D(F'')))$$
$$= \sigma(W_1(W_0(F^T_{Avg3D})) + W_1(W_0(F^T_{Max3D}))) \tag{4}$$

3.2 Overall Model

TCS-LipNet can be divided into a front-end module and a back-end module. In the front-end module, a 3D convolutional neural network and residual network are used for lip feature extraction, and TCSAM is embedded into the residual network to obtain deeper feature extraction. In the back-end module, DC-TCN is used for temporal semantic feature extraction, and the specific architecture is shown in Fig. 4.

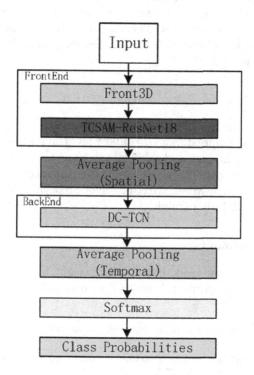

Fig. 4. TCSAM integrated with a ResBlock in ResNet

The original image sequence is changed into T * 512 * 1 * 1 high-dimensional feature data after Front3D and TCSAM-ResNet18, and the one-dimensional data of this vector are dimensionally compressed and then extracted by DC-TCN for temporal features. Input data After DC-TCN, the feature data of the same dimension as the number of classifications is output, and finally, the probability is calculated by the softmax function for the prediction and classification of results. The overall calculation formula is shown in Eq. 5.

$$y = softmax(DCTCN(x)) \tag{5}$$

4   Experiments

4.1   Datasets

The LRW dataset was proposed by the Visual Geometry team at the University of Oxford in 2016. The LRW dataset was born out of the growing need for large-scale datasets due to the rise of deep learning. The LRW dataset data is sourced from BBC radio and television programs rather than recorded by volunteers or experimenters, making the dataset a qualitative leap in data volume. The dataset selects the 500 most frequently occurring words and intercepts footage of the speaker saying these words. This dataset is widely used in the field of speech lipreading and has been evaluated and compared as a benchmark dataset in several research papers.

4.2   Pre-processing

The video images from the LRW dataset are segmented at a frame rate of 25 FPS, grayed out, and cropped to a size of 96 * 96. The images were normalized, randomly horizontally flipped, and randomly cropped to 88 * 88 size again before being input into the model. The latest lip-reading enhancement techniques such as Word Boundary, Time Mask, MixUp, Label Smooth, and cosine annealing strategy are also used during training.

4.3   Model Experiments

On the LRW dataset, we used different lightweight image feature extraction models to obtain the experimental results shown in Table 1.

Table 1. Experimental results of different lightweight models in the LRW

Front-end convolution	Feature extraction model	Acc. (%)
3D convolution	ResNet18	83.70%
	ResNet34	83.50%
	VGG-M	61.10%

The ResNet18 model with the best results among them is selected, and the comparison experiments are done for the no-attention mechanism, SE-based,

Table 2. Experimental results of different attention models

Front Model	Attention Module			Acc.(%)
	C	S	T	
ResNet18	–	–	–	89.4%
SE-ResNet18	✓	–	–	89.9%
CBAM-ResNet18	✓	✓	–	90.3%
TCSAM-ResNet18	✓	✓	✓	91.6%

CBAM, and TCSAM attention mechanism models, respectively, and the results are shown in Table 2.

It can be seen that the SE module has some improvement on ResNet, which can improve the final accuracy by 0.5% with the same back-end model, while the CBAM module improves ResNet18 better than the SE module because it has more spatial attention than the SE model, and the TCSAM with the added temporal attention mechanism obtains a higher accuracy.

In addition, we also conducted experiments on the LRW-1000 dataset. Due to the extremely uneven distribution of data in the LRW-1000 training set, we reduced the dataset and re divided the training set, verification set, and test set at a ratio of 7:2:1 for experiments.

In the experiments on the LRW-1000 dataset, the front-end module uses the Resnet18 model embedded with different attention mechanisms, and the back-end uses the unified three-layer GRU model, and the results are shown in Table 3, which shows that TCSAM has good generality.

Table 3. Comparison of different front-end modules in the LRW-1000

Front Model	Attention Module			Acc.(%)
	C	S	T	
ResNet18	–	–	–	61.7
SE-ResNet18	✓	–	–	62.04
CBAM-ResNet18	✓	✓	–	62.26
TCSAM-ResNet18	✓	✓	✓	62.47

After that, we used $5 \times 7 \times 7$ 3D convolution and TCSAM-based ResNet18 as a unified front-end model to experiment on different back-end models on the LRW dataset, and the experimental results are shown in Table 4.

Table 4. Experimental results of different back-end models

Front-end model	Back-end model	Acc. (%)
ResNet + TCSAM	DC-TCN	92.2%
	3-Bi-GRU	88.7%
	4-Bi-GRU	86.2%
	Bi-LSTM	84.3%
	MS-TCN	85.3%

5   Conclusion

In this paper, we propose the lip-reading model TCS-LipNet. In the front-end module, we design a new attention mechanism module TCSAM, which is embedded into the ResNet model to extract the lip features of the person in the image. Experiments show that our design is more effective in extracting the lip information in the image. In the back-end module, we adopt DC-TCN, which is the most effective in isolated lexical lip-reading tasks, to achieve temporal semantic extraction of character lips, and this model can reduce the interference of useless temporal sequences. TCS-LipNet achieves the current optimal accuracy of 92.2% on the LRW dataset. In the future, this model can be extended for sentence-level lip reading, applications on other linguistic datasets, and other tasks that rely on both temporal and spatial information.

References

1. Martinez, B., Ma, P., Petridis, S., Pantic, M.: Lipreading using temporal convolutional networks, pp. 6319–6323 (2020)
2. Ma, P., Wang, Y., Petridis, S., Shen, J., Pantic, M.: Training strategies for improved lip-reading. In: ICASSP 2022–2022 IEEE International Conference on Acoustics, Speech and Signal Processing (ICASSP), pp. 8472–8476. IEEE (2022)
3. Feng, D., Yang, S., Shan, S., Chen, X.: Learn an effective lip reading model without pains. arXiv preprint arXiv:2011.07557 (2020)
4. Hu, J., Shen, L., Sun, G.: Squeeze-and-excitation networks. In: Proceedings of the IEEE Conference on Computer Vision and Pattern Recognition, pp. 7132–7141 (2018)
5. Simonyan, K., Zisserman, A.: Very deep convolutional networks for large-scale image recognition. arXiv preprint arXiv:1409.1556 (2014)
6. Szegedy, C., et al.: Going deeper with convolutions. In: Proceedings of the IEEE Conference on Computer Vision and Pattern Recognition, pp. 1–9 (2015)
7. Krizhevsky, A., Sutskever, I., Hinton, G.E.: ImageNet classification with deep convolutional neural networks. Commun. ACM **60**(6), 84–90 (2017)

8. He, K., Zhang, X., Ren, S., Sun, J.: Deep residual learning for image recognition. In: Proceedings of the IEEE Conference on Computer Vision and Pattern Recognition, pp. 770–778 (2016)

9. Huang, G., Liu, Z., Van Der Maaten, L., Weinberger, K.Q.: Densely connected convolutional networks. In: Proceedings of the IEEE Conference on Computer Vision and Pattern Recognition, pp. 4700–4708 (2017)

10. Xu, K. Li, D., Cassimatis, N., Wang, X.: LCANet: end-to-end lipreading with cascaded attention-CTC (2018)

11. Yang, S., Zhang, Y., Feng, D. Yang, M., Chen, X.: LRW-1000: a naturally-distributed large-scale benchmark for lip reading in the wild. In: 2019 14th IEEE International Conference on Automatic Face Gesture Recognition (FG 2019) (2019)

12. Zhao, Y., Xu, R., Song, M.: A cascade sequence-to-sequence model for Chinese mandarin lip reading. ACM (2019)

13. Zhao, Y., Xu, R., Wang, X., Hou, P., Tang, H., Song, M.: Hearing lips: improving lip reading by distilling speech recognizers (2019)

14. Petridis, S., Stafylakis, T., Ma, P., Tzimiropoulos, G., Pantic, M.: Audio-visual speech recognition with a hybrid CTC/attention architecture. IEEE (2018)

15. Karpathy, A., Toderici, G., Shetty, S., Leung, T., Sukthankar, R., Fei-Fei, L.: Large-scale video classification with convolutional neural networks. In: Proceedings of the IEEE Conference on Computer Vision and Pattern Recognition, pp. 1725–1732 (2014)

16. Assael, Y.M., Shillingford, B., Whiteson, S., Freitas, N.D.: LipNet: end-to-end sentence-level lipreading (2016)

17. Graves, A., Fernandez, S., Gomez, F., Schmidhuber, J.: Connectionist temporal classification: labelling unsegmented sequence data with recurrent neural networks. In: Proceedings of the 23rd International Conference on Machine Learning, pp. 369–376 (2006)

18. Shillingford, B., et al.: Large-scale visual speech recognition (2018)

19. Chung, J.S., Senior, A., Vinyals, O., Zisserman, A.: Lip reading sentences in the wild. In: 2017 IEEE Conference on Computer Vision and Pattern Recognition (CVPR) (2017)

20. Stafylakis, T., Tzimiropoulos, G.: Deep word embeddings for visual speech recognition. In: 2018 IEEE International Conference on Acoustics, Speech and Signal Processing (ICASSP), pp. 4974–4978. IEEE (2018)

21. Jha, A., Namboodiri, V.P., Jawahar, C.: Word spotting in silent lip videos. In: 2018 IEEE Winter Conference on Applications of Computer Vision (WACV), pp. 150–159. IEEE (2018)

22. Zhang, X., Cheng, F., Wang, S.: Spatio-temporal fusion based convolutional sequence learning for lip reading. In: Proceedings of the IEEE/CVF International Conference on Computer Vision, pp. 713–722 (2019)

23. Wang, Q., Wu, B., Zhu, P., Li, P., Zuo, W., Hu, Q.: Supplementary material for 'ECA-net: efficient channel attention for deep convolutional neural networks. In: Proceedings of the 2020 IEEE/CVF Conference on Computer Vision and Pattern Recognition, pp. 13–19IEEE, Seattle (2020)

24. Li, X., Wang, W., Hu, X., Yang, J.: Selective kernel networks. In: Proceedings of the IEEE/CVF Conference on Computer Vision and Pattern Recognition, pp. 510–519 (2019)

25. Woo, S., Park, J., Lee, J.-Y., Kweon, I.S.: CBAM: convolutional block attention module. In: Proceedings of the European conference on computer vision (ECCV), pp. 3–19 (2018)

26. Fu, J., et al.: Dual attention network for scene segmentation. In: Proceedings of the IEEE/CVF Conference on Computer Vision and Pattern Recognition, pp. 3146–3154 (2019)
27. Lecun, Y., Bottou, L.: Gradient-based learning applied to document recognition. Proc. IEEE **86**(11), 2278–2324 (1998)
28. Chung, J., et al.: Empirical evaluation of gated recurrent neural networks on sequence modeling. Eprint Arxiv (2014)

The Dynamic Selection of Combination Methods in Classifier Ensembles by Region of Competence

Jesaías Carvalho Pereira Silva[1]([⊠]), Anne Magaly de Paula Canuto[1], and Araken de Medeiros Santos[2]

[1] Federal University of Rio Grande do Norte, Natal, RN 59.078-970, Brazil
jesayassilva@gmail.com, anne@dimap.ufrn.br
[2] Federal University of Rural do Semi-Árido, Angicos, RN 59.515-000, Brazil
araken@ufersa.edu.br

Abstract. Over the years, research has advanced in the field of classifier ensembles. Several ways to improve its efficiency have emerged, for homogeneous and heterogeneous ensembles. One challenge when using classifier ensembles is the definition of its structure. Basically, the ensemble structure selection can be done in two different ways, static and dynamic selection. Different static selection, dynamic selection defines the ensemble structure is selected for each testing instance (dynamic selection). Dynamic selection methods have been proposed in the literature, mainly for ensemble members and features, but very little effort has been done to propose dynamic selection methods for combination methods. In this paper, a dynamic combination selection is proposed in which the combination method is selected to each testing instance. The main aim of the proposed dynamic combination selection is to adapt the ensemble structure to the characteristics of each testing instance. In order to assess the feasibility of the proposed method, an empirical analysis is conducted. In this analysis, the proposed method is used along with a dynamic ensemble member selection (KNORA-Eliminate and META-DES) in order to promote more dynamicity in the ensemble structure. In this analysis, the proposed methods are compared to classifier ensemble with static combination methods and it improved the performance of all analyzed methods, for almost all analyzed scenarios.

Keywords: Classifier ensembles · Dynamic structure selection · Combination methods

1 Introduction

A classifier ensemble can be defined as a collection of individual classifiers (ensemble members), working in a parallel way, which receives the same pattern input and produces its output. A combination method receives the members outputs and provides the global output of the system [13]. In machine learning, classifier ensembles have been emerged as an efficient technique in different classification problems. In the literature, several studies have been investigated efficient ways to combine classifiers aiming at improving the classification performance in different applications. In these cases, we can find different algorithms, methods and/or practices for combining classifiers [1–5, 7, 8].

In this context, one important aspect is the definition of the ensemble structure. Several studies have proposed different ways to define the ensemble structure such as: Optimization techniques, meta-learning, among others [21, 22]. Basically, the ensemble structure definition can be done statically or dynamically. In the static selection, the ensemble structure is selected in the beginning of the training phase, and it is used throughout the whole ensemble processing. On the other hand, the dynamic selection defines the ensemble structure dynamically, in which each testing instance has its own ensemble structure. Several studies have shown that the dynamic selection tends to increase the predictive capacity of an ensemble [1, 9].

There are several studies that investigate the dynamic selection of ensemble structure, mainly for ensemble members [7, 8] and features [23] and both of them [24]. As mentioned previously, in an ensemble structure, the combination method aims at combining the outputs of all classifiers in order to provide the final output of an ensemble. Although this component plays an important role in the performance of an ensemble, very little has been done in order to define an efficient dynamic selection of this module.

Aiming at proposing an automatic decision process to select the best classification structure to a testing instance, this paper proposes a dynamic selection method for combination methods in classifier ensembles. Also known as dynamic fusion, the proposed method defines the region of competence of each candidate (combination method) for each testing instance and the most competent combination method is selected. The definition of the region of competence is made based on a pool of classifiers and it can be statically or dynamically formed. In this paper, we will apply the dynamic selection since we aim to promote dynamicity in two important parameters of an ensemble (ensemble members and combination method).

In order to assess the feasibility of the proposed method, an empirical analysis will be conducted. In this analysis, the proposed method will be used along with two well-known ensemble members dynamic selection methods, KNORA-Eliminate (KNORA-E) and META-DES. In the proposed method, a set of eight combination methods are used as candidates to be selected. Additionally, an analysis of the selection distribution of the possible candidates will be performed in order to investigate whether this selection is distributed over all possible candidates or there are one or two candidates that dominates the selection process. Finally, the proposed method will be compared to 12 ensembles in which the combination methods are selected in a static way. All the analyzed methods will be evaluated using 15 classification datasets.

2   Theoretical Concepts and Related Work

2.1   State of the Art

There are several studies that investigate the dynamic selection of ensemble structure, mainly for ensemble members [7, 8] and features [23] and both of them [10, 24].

In relation to ensemble members, in [7], for instance, a new method for dynamic ensemble member selection is presented and it uses the confidence of the base classifiers during the classification and its general credibility as selection criterion. Thus, an ensemble member is selected to compose the ensemble if its selection criterion is higher than an established threshold x. Another interesting way is to use region of competence as selection criterion, making it possible to improve the combination of classifiers, in which the most competent ones in a certain region are selected. The use of region of competence as selection criterion helps to maximize results [11, 12] by focusing only on the most competent classifiers, and examples can be found in KNORA-E [1] and META-DES [3].

In terms of dynamic feature selection, in [23], a dynamic feature select approach was proposed. The main aim of this approach is to select a different subset of features for one instance or a group of instances. The main goal of this approach is to explore the full potential of all instances in a classification problem. In [24], an initial study on how to combine these two dynamic selection techniques was performed. According to the authors, an improvement in performance was detected with the use of this integrated dynamic selection technique.

Although there are several studies to propose dynamic selection of ensemble members and feature selection, very little has been done in order to propose efficient dynamic selection of combination methods. This paper tries to bridge this gap and it proposes a dynamic selection method based on region of competence.

2.2 Classifier Ensembles

It is well-known that there is not a single classifier which can be considered optimal for all problem domains [13]. Therefore, it is difficult to select a good single classifier which provides the best performance in practical pattern classification tasks [14]. Therefore, classifier ensembles have emerged as an efficient classification structure since it combines the advantages and overcomes the limitations of the individual classifiers. Providing better generalization and performance ability, when compared to the individual classifiers [14]. In a classifier ensemble, an input pattern is presented to all individual classifiers [15, 16], and a combination method combines their outputs to produce the overall output of the system [13, 17]. The Machine Learning literature has ensured that diversity plays an important role in the design of ensembles, contributing to their accuracy and generalization [13].

One important issue regarding the design of classifier ensembles involves the appropriate selection of its structure (individual classifies and combination methods) [18]. As previously mentioned, there are basically two main selection approaches, static and dynamic. In this paper, we will focus on the dynamic approach. The next subsection will describe some existing dynamic selection methods that will be used in this paper.

2.3 Dynamic Ensemble Member Selection

The Dynamic Ensemble Selection (DES) methods perform the dynamic ensemble member selection. These methods select a subset of classifiers to classify each test instance. The selection of the classifier subset is done through the use of a selection procedure and each DES method has its own procedure. There are several DES methods proposed in the literature. In this paper, we will use two well-known DES methods, KNORA-E and META-DES.

KNORA-E: Knora [1] is a well-known DES method and it seeks to find the best subset of classifiers for a given test instance. It applies a k-Nearest Neighbors methods and the neighbors of a testing instance are selected from the validation set and the competence of each classifier is calculated. Based on a certain selection criterion, the classifier subset is selected.

KNORA-E is a knora-based method, and the selection criterion is to select a set of classifiers formed only by the classifiers that correctly classify all k neighbors of a testing instance. In the case where no classifier can correctly classify all k neighbors, the k value is decremented by one and this is done until at least one classifier can be selected [1].

META-DES: The META-DES [3] is a DES method that uses the idea of selection using meta-learning. In this method, a meta-problem is created to determine whether a classifier is competent for a given test instance. According to [10], the META-DES method uses five criteria for extracting meta-features in order to establish the new region of a meta-problem.

After that, a meta-classifier is trained, based on the defined meta-features. This meta-classifier is then used to identify whether a classifier is competent or not to classify a testing instance. Classifiers that are labeled as competent will be selected to compose the ensemble to classify the test instance.

3   The Proposed Method

The proposed method aims at selecting the combination method of a classifier ensemble dynamically. Algorithm 1 presents the main steps of the proposed method. As it can be observed, the dynamic selection of combination is performed in the testing phase. In this phase, when a testing instance is presented to the classifier ensemble, the competence of each combination method is calculated.

Algorithm 1: The proposed method.

01:	**Procedure** Dynamic Fusion
02:	**Input**: Testing instance (Ti), Validation set (V), pool of classifiers (M), combination methods (C)
03:	**Output**: The selected combination method (Cm)
04:	N = k-NN(Ti,V) % Find the neighbors of Ti
05:	**FOR** j=0 until j= size(C) **DO**
06:	Acc(Cj) = Accuracy(Cj,N)
07:	**END FOR**
08:	Cm = Max(Cj,j=1,2,...,size(C))
09:	**Return** Cm
10:	**END procedure**

This competence can be calculated in several different ways. As the use of local competence has been widely used in dynamic member selection methods, in the proposed method, the k-NN method is used to select the neighbors of the testing instance. Then, the local accuracy of each combination method is calculated in this neighborhood, and the most accurate combination method is selected.

When computing the competence region, a draw in accuracy may occur. In this case, the number of neighbours is increased by 1 ($k = k + 1$) until a winner is detected. If all instances of the Validation set is used and there is still a draw, the winner method is randomly selected.

Additionally, there are two main parameters in the proposed method, the number of neighbors of a testing instance (line 4 of Algorithm 1) and the size of the pool of classifiers. Finally, he proposed method can be applied to a pool of classifiers selected statically or dynamically. In order to provide more dynamicity for the classifier ensemble, in this paper, the proposed method will be applied to two well-known dynamic member selection methods, META-DES and KNORA-E (described in Sect. 2.3).

4 Experimental Methodology

In order to assess the feasibility of the proposed method, an empirical analysis will be conducted. The next subsections will describe the main aspects of this analysis, mainly the used datasets as well as its methods and materials.

4.1 Datasets

The datasets used in this paper are extracted from the UCI Machine Learning Repository. Table 1 describes some characteristics of the used datasets, focusing in the number of instances (Inst), number of attributes (Att) and number of classes (Class) of each dataset.

Table 1. Description of the used datasets

Dataset	Name	Inst	Att	Class
D1	Cardiac insufficiency	368	53	2
D2	Car	1728	6	4
D3	Seismic-bumps	2584	18	2
D4	Zoo	101	16	7
D5	Ionosphere	351	34	2
D6	Prognostic	198	33	2
D7	Wine	178	13	3
D8	Dermatology	366	34	6

(continued)

Table 1. (*continued*)

Dataset	Name	Inst	Att	Class
D9	Heart	303	13	2
D10	Bone marrow	187	36	2
D11	Algerian Forest Fires	244	13	2
D12	Congres Voting Records	435	16	2
D13	Maternal Health Risk	1014	6	3
D14	Risk Factors Cervical Cancer	855	28	2
D15	Phishing Website	2456	30	2

Each dataset is divided into training, Validation1, Validation2 and Testing sets, in a proportion of 50%, 16.7%, 16.7%, and 16.6%, respectively. The training set is used to generate the pool of classifiers. The testing set is used to assess the performance of the classifier ensembles. The Validation2 set is used to train the trainable combination methods (Neural Networks and Naive Bayes) while the Validation1 set is used to obtain the competence region of the proposed dynamic fusion method. This division is performed 30 times and the presented results of each ensemble configuration represent the average values over these 30 values.

4.2 Methods and Materials

In this paper, we evaluated 6 different pool sizes, 5, 10, 15, 20, 25, and 30 classifiers, in which all of them are, generated through the Bagging method. In addition, 3 different number of neighbors are assessed, 3, 7, and 11 neighbors. It is important to emphasize that the proposed method as well as both member selection techniques (KNORA-E and META-DES) use the idea of competence region. In this sense, the same number of neighbors are used for both cases, the selection of the combination method (proposed method) and the ensemble members (KNORA-E and META-DES). Finally, all ensemble configurations use Decision Trees as ensemble members.

The proposed method used a pool of 8 different combination methods, which are: Majority Vote, Sum, Geometric Mean, Naive Bayes, Edge and three Neural Networks (MLP) versions, Hard, Soft and Soft-Class. The three NN versions differ on the input information received by the ensemble members. In the Hard version, the ensemble member provides only the winner class for the testing instance. In other words, this MLP version is trained and tested using only the winner class of each ensemble member. In the other two MLP versions, the prediction probability for each class is used. In this sense, the prediction probability for each class is provided, for both MLP versions.

As the MLP input must have a fixed size and the number of selected members might vary, a strategy to define the input size must be done. In this paper, we decided to use the maximum possible size for a combination method (pool of classifier times the number of classes). In doing this, it is important to define how to handle the outputs of the unselected classifiers. The way to handle the outputs of the unselected classifiers is the main difference between Soft and Soft-Class versions. While the Soft MLP version uses -1 to all classes of an unselected classifier, the Soft-Class version uses a fixed value (1/number of total classes) as the value to all classes of the unselected classifiers.

The MLP algorithms were implemented using the Scikit-Learn [6] library with the Multi-layer Perceptron model, using 200 neurons in the hidden layer. All three neural networks followed the same configurations since this configuration provided promising results for all three NNs in a grid search method. For comparison purposes, the performance of the proposed method is compared to 12 classifier ensembles using the following combination methods: Majority Vote, Sum (Sum), Maximum (MAX), Minimum (MIN), Geometric mean, Hard MLP, Soft MLP, Soft-Class MLP, Edge, Naive Bayes, Weighted Sum and Weighted Ensemble Voting. For all analyzed ensembles, the ensemble members are dynamically selected, and the combination method is statistically selected, as originally proposed in both analyzed methods (KNORA-E and META-DES).

Additionally, the Weighted sum and weighted vote methods use weights on their functioning. The used weight is *1/(distance-of-classes)* and it is applied to the vote procedure in the Weighted Sum as well as the probability of the classifiers in the Weighted sum method.

The obtained results of all analyzed methods will be evaluated using the Friedman statistical test [20]. In cases where a statistically significant difference is detected, the Nemenyi post-hoc test is applied [20]. In order to present the obtained results by the post-hoc test, the critical difference diagram (CD) [20] is used. This diagram was selected in order to have a visual illustration of the statistical test, making it easier to interpret the obtained results. Additionally, all implemented methods are included in the DESLIB [3] library that contains both methods, KNORA-E and META-DES.

5   The Obtained Results

In this section, the obtained results are presented and analyzed. This analysis will be done in three main parts. In the first part, the accuracy of all 13 analyzed methods are assessed. The second part presents the distribution of the selected combination methods while the third part describes the results of the statistical analysis.

5.1   The Accuracy of the Analyzed Methods

Tables 2 and 3 present the accuracy results of all 13 analyzed methods for KNORA-E and META-DES, respectively. As previously mentioned, 18 different ensemble configurations (6 pool sizes and 3 different number of neighbors) and each configuration was performed 30 times. Therefore, values in Tables 2 and 3 represent the average over 540 results. Additionally, the last line in both tables represents the overall accuracy over all 15 datasets. Finally, the bold numbers represent the highest accuracy for each dataset.

For KNORA-E (Table 2), it can be observed that the proposed method (Dynamic Fusion) delivered the highest accuracy in 8 datasets, out of 15, followed by Vote and Sum (6 datasets). Furthermore, the overall accuracy achieved by the proposed method is the highest one of all analyzed methods. For META-DES (Table 3), the proposed method did not deliver the highest accuracy levels in many datasets (4 out of 15). Nevertheless, it presents the highest overall accuracy, followed by Vote and Sum. It shows that the proposed method is the best overall classifier ensemble.

The results obtained in Tables 2 and 3 show that the use of the dynamic selection of the combination methods proved to be efficient since it improves the performance of the classifier ensembles, when compared to the static selection methods. We believe that this improvement in performance is due to the fact that the dynamic fusion technique maximizes, even more, the characteristics of the ensemble members and, as a consequence, to improve the performance of the classifier ensemble. The original KNORA-E and META-DES techniques themselves already provide more efficient classifiers since the best ones are selected to classify a testing instance. Furthermore, the proposed method handles even more efficiently the classifier ensembles since it selects the combination methods that suits better to the ensemble members. Finally, we can state that the inclusion of more dynamicity in the ensemble structure can lead to an improvement in its performance.

Table 2. Results of the classifier ensembles using the KNORA-E method

Dataset	Majority Vote	SUM	MAX	MIN	Geometric average	Weighted Sum	Weighted Vote	MLP-HARD	MLP-SOFT	MLP-SOFT CLASS	Edge	Naive Bayes	Dynamic Fusion
D1	94.58	94.58	95.17	95.17	95.17	88.77	88.77	95.05	94.17	95.02	94.58	92.93	**95.66**
D2	97.30	97.30	93.35	91.81	91.81	84.90	84.90	94.29	96.12	97.15	96.39	93.85	**97.93**
D3	92.07	92.06	**93.06**	**93.06**	**93.06**	91.63	91.64	92.39	91.70	92.11	92.07	85.43	92.57
D4	93.63	93.63	93.10	89.97	89.97	76.47	76.47	90.59	88.37	92.45	90.82	76.21	**93.73**
D5	**90.97**	**90.97**	79.84	79.84	79.84	77.02	77.02	88.21	89.20	88.96	90.97	84.31	89.91
D6	69.48	69.48	44.75	44.75	44.75	62.09	62.09	69.53	68.86	69.28	69.48	71.80	**72.62**
D7	**93.68**	**93.68**	78.35	72.89	72.89	64.27	64.27	85.34	91.25	92.99	92.61	57.16	93.10
D8	**95.84**	**95.84**	90.94	84.75	84.75	78.84	78.84	90.79	93.79	95.82	94.03	78.01	95.74
D9	76.90	76.90	63.44	63.44	63.44	67.71	67.71	74.41	73.68	72.61	76.90	73.01	76.04
D10	91.70	91.70	88.39	88.39	88.39	90.97	90.97	90.13	88.48	89.78	91.70	89.18	**91.95**
D11	**97.65**	**97.65**	96.13	96.13	96.13	97.28	97.28	96.57	96.72	96.90	97.65	96.88	97.63
D12	**94.45**	**94.45**	91.70	91.70	91.70	92.46	92.46	93.11	93.51	93.36	94.45	92.80	93.94
D13	77.48	77.45	78.12	77.98	77.98	64.80	64.80	75.61	74.56	75.73	77.62	73.40	**78.69**
D14	91.47	91.47	93.21	93.21	93.21	90.97	91.00	92.57	92.17	92.36	91.47	91.05	**93.37**
D15	95.48	95.48	92.48	92.48	92.48	92.50	92.50	94.85	94.92	94.77	95.48	90.99	**95.49**
Acc Ave	90.18	90.18	84.80	83.70	83.70	81.38	81.38	88.23	88.50	89.29	89.75	83.13	**90.56**

5.2 The Selection Distribution

Once we have analyzed the accuracy of the different classifier ensembles, now we will evaluate the selection distribution made by the proposed methods. In other words, what is the proportion of selection for each combination method which was made by the proposed method in the testing phase.

Table 3. Results of the classifier ensembles using the META-DES method

Datasets	Majority Vote	SUM	MAX	MIN	Geometric average	Weighted Sum	Weighted Voting	MLP-HARD	MLP-SOFT	MLP-SOFT-CLASS	Edge	Naive Bayes	Dynamic Fusion
D1	94.23	94.23	94.52	94.52	94.52	90.43	90.43	94.07	95.09	**95.22**	9423	9130	95.01
D2	96.80	96.80	89.89	87.12	87.12	83.86	83.86	93.72	96.77	**96.99**	9568	9108	96.85
D3	92.01	92.01	93.25	**93.25**	**93.25**	92.37	92.37	92.37	92.17	92.62	9201	8259	92.66
D4	94.54	94.54	89.54	85.26	85.26	75.92	75.92	90.88	95.13	**95.26**	8980	7513	94.48
D5	90.46	90.46	80.22	80.22	80.22	76.99	76.99	88.31	89.42	88.96	9046	8357	89.67
D6	74.26	74.26	41.30	41.30	41.30	65.80	65.80	69.21	69.65	70.28	7426	5861	73.16
D7	92.84	92.84	74.37	67.87	67.87	64.39	64.39	84.39	91.97	92.45	9197	5895	92.36
D8	96.22	96.22	88.23	80.62	80.62	78.96	78.96	90.49	96.10	96.17	9385	7853	**96.32**
D9	78.54	78.54	63.02	63.02	63.02	68.59	68.59	74.18	75.70	76.46	7854	6694	**78.85**
D10	92.01	92.01	89.43	89.43	89.43	91.49	91.49	89.77	90.68	90.82	9201	8887	91.79
D11	97.75	97.75	95.86	95.86	95.86	97.42	97.42	96.58	96.82	96.78	9775	9654	97.71
D12	94.54	94.54	92.17	92.17	92.17	92.72	92.72	93.09	93.70	93.50	9454	9272	94.08
D13	77.54	77.62	77.10	76.29	76.28	64.49	64.51	75.55	76.67	77.32	7774	6805	**78.93**
D14	91.85	91.84	**93.66**	**93.66**	93.66	92.16	92.19	92.54	92.19	92.32	9185	8902	93.40
D15	95.50	95.51	92.17	92.17	92.17	92.63	92.62	94.92	95.18	95.12	9550	9036	95.40
Acc Avg	90.61	90.61	83.65	82.18	82.18	81.88	81.88	88.01	89.82	90.02	9001	8082	90.64

Tables 4 and 5 present the selection distribution for KNORA-E and META-DES methods, respectively. As it can be observed in both tables, all eight combination methods were selected by the proposed method in the testing phase. The most selected combination method is Vote, for both methods (KNORA-E and META-DES). It is an expected result since this method provided the second best accuracy level. On the other hand, the Naïve Bayes was rarely selected as the best combination method. Once again, this combination method provided one of the worst accuracy levels, for both methods (KNORA-E and META-DES). It is important to emphasize that the Sum combination method was also rarely selected since its performance is usually very similar to the Vote method and, in these datasets, the latter method was slightly better, and it was then selected. Finally, although the edge combination method obtained good accuracy levels, it is possible to observe that it was rarely selected by the proposed method.

Still in the analysis of the selection distribution, it can be seen that there is a certain equal selection distribution among five combination methods (Vote, Geometric mean, MLP-Hard, MLP-Soft and MLP-Soft-Class) which shows that there is no best combination method and that an efficient selection can improve even further the performance of the classifier ensemble. Among the NN versions, it can be observed similar selection distribution among themselves, showing a certain similarity among all three version, which together surpasses the majority vote proportion.

Based on the results of Tables 4 and 5, one can conclude that the proposed method generally biases towards the method with the highest accuracy level. This is an expected result since if a combination method is the most successful one, it is usually one of the most successful one in the dynamic fusion competence region.

5.3 Statistical Analysis

In order to evaluate the obtained results from a statistical point of view, the Friedman test [19] was applied to verify if there are statistical differences among all ensemble

Table 4. Selection distribution in the dynamic fusion when using KNORA-E

x	Sum	Majority Vote	Geometric average	MLP-HARD	MLP-SOFT	MLP – SOFT CLASS	Edge	Naive Bayes
Cardiac insufficiency	0.00	27.13	23.05	21.26	9.50	13.20	0.00	5.87
Car	0.00	30.81	1.82	12.22	11.61	26.53	7.06	9.95
Seismic-bumps	0.03	11.27	39.29	15.59	10.63	11.31	0.00	11.88
Zoo	0.69	79.94	0.80	4.57	7.43	6.20	0.19	0.19
Ionosphere	0.00	35.94	3.07	20.54	19.24	12.45	0.00	8.75
Prognostic	0.00	19.69	5.58	18.05	18.83	11.95	0.00	25.90
Wine	0.00	56.62	6.29	6.59	13.80	16.08	0.24	0.37
Dermatology	0.05	64.87	2.54	7.23	11.53	13.45	0.29	0.05
Heart	0.00	22.50	11.58	19.93	19.59	12.94	0.00	13.45
Bone marrow	0.00	46.83	18.20	15.27	6.40	6.35	0.00	6.95
Algerian Forest Fires	0.46	58.11	18.64	9.62	4.49	3.92	0.49	4.26
Congressional Voting Records	0.00	31.45	14.60	22.99	13.02	7.52	0.00	10.42
Maternal Health Risk	1.31	6.98	28.23	22.25	11.46	15.76	5.99	8.00
Risk Factors Cervical Cancer	0.00	5.50	41.65	22.76	10.29	6.90	0.00	12.89
Phishing Website	2.64	27.28	10.39	23.30	16.98	17.23	0.00	2.18
OVERALL AVERAGE	**0.35**	**34.99**	**15.05**	**16.15**	**12.32**	**12.12**	**0.95**	**8.07**

classifiers. The Friedman test is used to be able to state the hypothesis that the k-related observations derive from the same population (similar performance) or not (superiority in performance). In this test, the significance level used was set to 0.05. Hence, if the p-value is less than the established value, the null hypothesis is rejected, with a confidence level greater than 95%.

Table 6 presents the results of the Friedman test. As it can be observed in both cases (KNORA-E and META-DES) that the statistical test detected statistical differences among all analyzed methods. In this sense, the post-hoc test was applied the results are presented in the Critical Difference Diagram [20].

In the Critical Difference Diagram, the performance of a method is statistically different from another method if the difference between their average rankings is higher

Table 5. Selection distribution in the dynamic fusion when using META-DES

x	Sum	Majority Vote	Geometric average	MLP-HARD	MLP-SOFT	MLP – SOFTCLASS	Edge	Naive Bayes
Cardiac insufficiency	0.00	24.71	26.66	19.82	13.38	12.42	0.00	3.01
Car	0.00	27.53	1.87	6.19	21.72	26.59	10.34	5.74
Seismic-bumps	0.21	14.42	43.71	14.85	4.64	8.92	0.00	13.26
Zoo	0.05	86.87	0.60	3.22	8.49	0.69	0.05	0.05
Ionosphere	0.00	38.44	4.97	23.05	16.68	11.93	0.00	4.93
Prognostic	0.00	31.72	6.07	17.69	12.37	13.71	0.00	18.45
Wine	0.00	50.36	6.39	8.83	20.03	13.21	1.06	0.12
Dermatology	0.00	66.19	1.74	5.83	22.73	1.15	2.36	0.00
Heart	0.00	27.24	16.11	19.53	14.87	14.39	0.00	7.87
Bone marrow	0.00	46.72	24.43	10.99	8.14	3.52	0.00	6.20
Algerian Forest Fires	0.85	60.28	16.87	9.58	2.72	1.85	1.65	6.20
Congressional Voting Records	0.00	33.12	19.66	22.12	12.64	4.71	0.00	7.75
Maternal Health Risk	5.68	10.18	24.26	16.91	14.66	17.74	3.67	6.91
Risk Factors Cervical Cancer	0.00	12.90	50.08	14.87	8.44	2.33	0.00	11.37
Phishing Website	5.13	28.92	10.77	14.84	18.49	17.32	0.00	4.52
OVERALL AVERAGE	**0.79**	**37.31**	**16.95**	**13.89**	**13.33**	**10.03**	**1.28**	**6.42**

Table 6. Friedman test for KNORA-E and META-DES

KNORA-E				META-DES			
Chi-Squared	df	P	Kendall's W	Chi-Squared	df	P	Kendall's W
1.161.254	12	<0.05	0.358	960.454	12	<0.05	0.296

than the critical difference calculated by the Critical Difference Diagram (CD). In this case, when two methods are similar, there is a horizontal line linking these two methods.

Figure 1(a) shows the CD diagram for KNORA-E. As it can be observed in this figure, the superiority of the proposed method was detected by the statistical test. It shows that the improvement in performance was strong enough to be detected by the statistical test, when compared to all other analyzed methods.

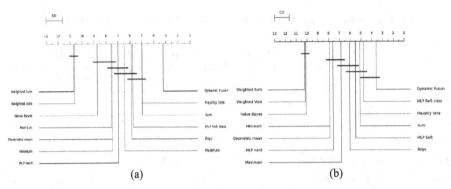

(a)   (b)

Fig. 1. Critical Difference Diagram for KNORA-E (a) and META-DES (b)

Figure 1(b) presents the CD diagram for META-DES. In this method, unlike KNORA-E, the superiority in performance delivered by the proposed method was not detected by the statistical test. As it can be observed, the CD diagram detected that the accuracy of dynamic fusion, sum, majority vote, and soft class MLP provide similar performance. For the remaining methods, the proposed method provided higher accuracy levels, detected by the statistical test.

6   Final Remarks

This paper proposed a method to dynamically select combination methods for a classifier ensemble. The combination methods are selected for each testing instance based on the competence region of the analyzed combination methods. The dynamic combination method selection was used along the dynamic ensemble member methods in order to include more dynamicity in the ensemble structure selection and, as a consequence, leading to more efficient ensembles.

In order to assess the feasibility of the proposed method, an empirical analysis was conducted. In this analysis, the dynamic combination method selection was made among eight combination methods: Majority Vote, Sum, Geometric Average, Edge, Naive Bayes, and three types of MLP. Additionally, the proposed method was used in two different dynamic ensemble member methods, KNORA-E and META-DES.

Through this analysis, it can be observed that the proposed method provided the highest overall accuracy levels among all analyzed methods, for both methods (KNORA-E and in META-DES). Additionally, we could observe that the proposed method selected almost equally five combination methods (out of 8), showing that it is indeed important to apply different combination methods in the classifier ensemble structures. Finally, the statistical test proved that the superiority in performance of the proposed method was detected by the statistical test, for KNORA-E.

In general, the proposed technique showed promising results and, indeed, improvements in performance, when compared to the static selection of combination methods. We believe that this improvement in performance is due to the fact that the dynamic fusion technique maximizes, even more, the characteristics of the ensemble members and, as a consequence, to improve the performance of the classifier ensemble.

This empirical was limited to 15 classification databases. As future analysis, it is necessary to expand this analysis using another selection approaches and to perform a more detailed analysis with more datasets and different ensemble configurations. It will also be investigated the best number of neighbors to define the dynamic fusion competence region and to expand the tests for KNORA-Union [1] and Overall Local Accuracy (OLA) [9], among others. Finally, different approaches to define the competence of a method will be analyzed.

References

1. Ko, A.H.R., Sabourin, R., Britto, A.S., Jr.: From dynamic classifier selection to dynamic ensemble selection. Pattern Recogn. **41**(5), 1718–1731 (2008)
2. Cavalin, P.R., Sabourin, R., Suen, C.Y.: Dynamic selection approaches for multiple classifier systems. Neural Comput. Appl. **22**, 673–688 (2013)
3. Cruz, R.M.O., et al.: META-DES: a dynamic ensemble selection framework using meta-learning. Pattern Recogn. **48**(5), 1925–1935 (2015)
4. Oliveira, D.V.R., Cavalcanti, G.D.C., Sabourin, R.: Online pruning of base classifiers for dynamic ensemble selection. Pattern Recogn. **72**, 44–58 (2017)
5. Cruz, R.M.O., Sabourin, R., Cavalcanti, G.D.C.: METADES. Oracle: meta-learning and feature selection for dynamic ensemble selection. Inform. Fusion **38**, 84–103 (2017)
6. Pedregosa, F., et al.: Scikit-learn: machine learning in python. J. Mach. Learn. Res. **12**, 2825–2830 (2011)
7. Nguyen, T.T., et al.: Ensemble selection based on classifier prediction confidence. Pattern Recogn. **100**, 107104 (2020)
8. Cruz, R.M.O., et al.: Deslib: a dynamic ensemble selection library in python. J. Mach. Learn. Res. **21**(1), 283–287 (2020)
9. Woods, K., Kegelmeyer, W.P., Bowyer, K.: Combination of multiple classifiers using local accuracy estimates. IEEE. 405–410 p (1997)
10. Dantas, C.A.: An integration analysis of dynamic selection techniques for a classification system building. (PhD thesis) Federal University of Rio Grande do Norte (2021)
11. Cruz, R.M.O., et al.: Dynamic ensemble selection vs k-nn: why and when dynamic selection obtains higher classification performance? In: IEEE 2017 Seventh International Conference on Image Processing Theory, Tools and Applications (IPTA), pp. 1–6 (2017)
12. Cruz, R.M.O., Sabourin, R., Cavalcanti, G.D.C.: Dynamic classifier selection: Recent advances and perspectives. Inform. Fusion **41**, 195–216 (2018)
13. Kuncheva, L.I.: Combining pattern classifiers: methods and algorithms. Wiley (2004)
14. Dietterich, T.G.: Ensemble methods in machine learning. Multiple Classifier Systems: First International Workshop, MCS 2000 Cagliari, Italy, June 21–23, 2000 Proceedings 1. Springer, Berlin, Heidelberg (2000)
15. Kuncheva, L.I.: A theoretical study on six classifier fusion strategies. IEEE Trans. Pattern Anal. Mach. Intell **24**(2), 281–286 (2002)
16. Brown, G., et al.: Diversity creation methods: a survey and categorisation. Inform. fusion **6**(1), 5–20 (2005)
17. Braga, L.P.V.: Introdução à Mineração de Dados-2a edição: Edição ampliada e revisada. Editora E-papers (2005)
18. Canuto, A.M.P.: Investigating the influence of the choice of the ensemble members in accuracy and diversity of selection-based and fusion-based methods for ensembles. Pattern Recogn. Lett. **28**(4), 472–486 (2007)

19. Friedman, M.: A comparison of alternative tests of significance for the problem of m rankings. Ann. Math. Stat. **11**(1), 86–92 (1940)
20. Demšar, J.: Statistical comparisons of classifiers over multiple data sets. J. Mach. Learn. Res. **7**, 1–30 (2006)
21. Feitosa, A.A., Canuto, A.M.P.: An exploratory study of mono and multi-objective metaheuristics to ensemble of classifiers. Appl. Intell. **48**(2), 416–431 (2018)
22. Kordík, P., Cerný, J., Frýda, T.: Discovering predictive ensembles for transfer learning and meta-learning. Mach. Learn. **107**(1), 177–207 (2018)
23. Nunes, R.O., et al.: An unsupervised-based dynamic feature selection for classification tasks. In: 2016 International Joint Conference on Neural Networks (IJCNN). IEEE (2016)
24. Dantas, C., et al.: Instance hardness as a decision criterion on dynamic ensemble structure. In: 2019 8th Brazilian Conference on Intelligent Systems (BRACIS). IEEE (2019)

The Progressive Detectors and Discriminative Feature Descriptors Combining Global and Local Information

Siyuan Liang, Baolu Gao$^{(\boxtimes)}$, Bingjie Zhang, Xiaoyang Li, and Hao Wang

Taiyuan University of Technology, Taiyuan, China
85389301@qq.com

Abstract. Point cloud registration plays a critical role in many computer vision applications. Nevertheless, despite numerous feature-based registration methods that have been presented recently, the majority concerns learning local features, which unavoidably suffers from an insufficient discriminative ability of the point cloud feature descriptors. Thus, this paper proposes a more discriminative feature descriptor by combining global and local information and adding an intermediate supervision mechanism. Unlike previous methods, we introduce a Local-Nonlocal Module that focuses on the local information of the point cloud and captures the global information, thus improving the discriminative ability of the feature descriptors for repetitive structures. To obtain more robust keypoints, we utilize the progressive scoring mechanism to detect keypoints that are the most significant in the neighborhood and channels and range from a coarse to a detailed scope to provide progressive detectors (PD). Additionally, we utilize the multi-level supervision mechanism to provide stronger supervision signals. Finally, we train and evaluate the proposed model on the indoor dataset 3DMatch, with the experimental results indicating that our method outperforms related techniques.

Keywords: Local-Nonlocal features · Multi-level supervision mechanism · Progressive scoring mechanism · Point cloud registration

1 Introduction

The point cloud registration methods can be classified into optimization-based and feature-based. **Optimization-based registration methods** are represented by ICP-based methods, which mainly estimate the transformation matrix through two-step optimization strategies. First, they search for the nearest neighbor points to obtain correspondences and then estimate the transformation matrix between the two point clouds based on the obtained correspondences. The above two steps are performed iteratively to calculate the best transformation matrix. However, this method is susceptible to poor initial relative pose. **The feature-based registration methods**, which have received much attention in recent years, can be divided into two categories according to the data type: learning on volumetric data and point cloud. Such methods typically involve three

L. Iliadis et al. (Eds.): ICANN 2023, LNCS 14262, pp. 439–455, 2023.
https://doi.org/10.1007/978-3-031-44201-8_36

steps. First, the point cloud feature descriptors are obtained through the network. Then keypoint descriptors of higher significance are extracted based on the feature detectors. Finally, the correspondences and the transformation matrices between the point clouds are calculated through the keypoint descriptors.

However, the existing feature-based methods mainly extract local feature descriptors and calculate the feature of each point utilizing the neighboring points, and thus are constrained to the local point cloud information. For example, FCGF [8] extracts local features of sparse point clouds using the Minkowski engine, and 3DMatch [36] extracts local features using the 3D voxel data after point cloud conversion. However, there may be some repetitive structures in a point cloud, forcing the feature descriptors obtained from the local area to be insufficiently discriminative, affecting the feature similarity of 3D data. To improve the discriminative nature of similar structures and products and enhance the features' descriptiveness, we introduce a Local-Nonlocal Module that combines local and global information of the point cloud. This enables the network to learn the point cloud distribution as a whole. Additionally, the traditional single-level supervision methods cannot provide adequate supervision signals for the point cloud registration, and the keypoint detectors disregard minute detail information. Given this problem, the multi-level supervision mechanism is introduced to provide stronger supervision signals. Moreover, to obtain more robust keypoints, we utilize the progressive scoring mechanism that gradually shifts from a coarse scope to a detailed scope to combine the regional significance and the channel significance of keypoints into keypoint scores. The progressive scoring mechanism combines the detection results at different density scopes to make the keypoint scoring information more accurate.

In summary, this paper's contributions are threefold:

1. We propose a Local-Nonlocal Module to combine local and global information and improve the discriminative ability of feature descriptors for repetitive structures.
2. We propose a multi-level supervision mechanism to provide stronger supervision signals and a progressive scoring mechanism to provide more accurate keypoint scores.
3. Our method achieves better results on the indoor dataset 3DMatch than related techniques.

2   Related Work

2.1   Point Cloud Registration Methods

Current point cloud registration methods can be divided into optimization-based and feature-based methods. Next, we will introduce the milestone methods of each of these two categories, and then introduce multi-level supervision, which is a method that effectively improves the model effect.

Optimization-Based Registration Methods. The key idea of the optimization-based methods is to develop a complex optimization strategy to obtain an optimal solution to the point cloud registration problem. The classic implementation strategies for this approach are ICP-based methods. The ICP-based registration methods can be classified as point-to-point ICP [3], point-to-plane ICP [5], and plane-to-plane ICP [4] according to the different distance metric employed. Calculating the transformation matrix based on the correspondences can be divided into four methods: SVD-based [3], Lucas-Kanade (LK) [2], LM-ICP method [12], and Procrustes analysis [11]. This type of methods is sensitive to the initial relative poses, i.e., poor initial relative poses can lead the algorithm to a local optimum, forcing the model not to converge to the best registration result through iterations.

The Feature-Based Registration Methods. Feature-based registration methods are a mainstream registration category that is divided into two categories according to the data type: learning on volumetric data and point cloud. Several works have tackled this problem by learning volumetric data jointly. For instance, 3DMatch [36] converts RGB-D images into 3D voxel data and inputs it into a neural network to obtain local feature descriptors. 3DSmoothNet [13] firstly adjusts the pose of point clouds by an estimated local reference frame (LRF), then computes the 3D volumetric data based on the point clouds, and finally feeds the volumetric data into the convolutional neural network to extract the feature descriptors. FCGF [8] utilizes UNet-like network [21] and Minkowski Engine [7] to extract feature descriptors based on volumetric data, providing a larger receptive field while being computationally efficient. CGF [16] proposes a unique method for learning feature descriptors that represent the local geometric information of each point in an unstructured point cloud and then feeding the hand-crafted descriptors into the neural network to obtain the learning-based 3D local feature descriptors. O-CNN [28] first transforms the point clouds into a voxelized octree model and then constructs the neural network with modified convolution to extract feature descriptors. OctNet [20] utilizes an unbalanced octree to partition the space according to a hierarchy, stores the pooled feature representation with the octree leaves, and then extracts the feature descriptors by a modified neural network. These methods for learning volumetric data mainly start from the perspective of local point cloud information and ignore the repetitiveness of structures in the global perspective.

Besides, several works have learnt features on point clouds jointly [9,10,30, 34,38]. PPF-FoldNet [9] utilizes an unsupervised method to address the limitation of requiring labeled data. The basic idea is to utilize PointNet [19] to encode features and then utilize a decoder to obtain local feature descriptors that are consistent with the input dimension. SiamesePointNet [38] extracts feature descriptors utilizing a hierarchical coder-decoder network containing a global shape constraint module and a feature transformation operator integrating global and local contextual information. DGCNN [31] dynamically updates the graph structure between different levels to learn the semantic information of point sets at different levels and then extracts the local shape features of point clouds that satisfy the registration invariance. Yang [33] proposes a hybrid feature representation involving color moments for each point to save point cloud information. Then it extracts feature descriptors from point clouds utilizing a supervoxel segmentation algorithm.

Methods such as FCGF [8], PPFNet [10], PPF-FoldNet [9], and D3feat [1], extract local information as feature descriptors. Thus, these methods consider only the point cloud's local information and ignore each point's information from a global perspective. Opposing current methods, we present a Local-Nonlocal Module that extracts local and global features simultaneously.

2.2   Multi-level Supervision

Multi-level supervision is a novel approach in deep learning that directly adds supervision signals to the network's intermediate layers instead of supervising at the output layer of the network. This concept is widely utilized in artificial intelligence tasks. For example, Wang [26] is the first to apply a multi-level supervised method to deep convolutional neural networks to solve image classification tasks. The author successfully demonstrates that adding auxiliary supervision branches to several intermediate layers enhances the model's generalization ability. He [14] proposes a fictional teacher-student method and utilizes intermediate supervision signals in the teacher network to improve the inferential ability of the student network. Wang [27] utilizes intermediate supervision for adversarial learning, which improves the network's recognition ability in the intermediate layer, and explores the structural consistency between semantics and depth. Li [17] and Shi [24] suggest that inferential tasks usually have fixed intermediate representations that can improve the model's generalization ability. Therefore, they utilize dense intermediate supervision to improve the sensitivity of the backbone convolutional neural network to treat all regions. Note that all studies above demonstrate the extraordinary effectiveness of multi-level supervision in deep networks.

Given the successful practice of multi-level supervision in recent years, we utilize a multi-level supervision mechanism to provide a stronger supervision signal. In addition, more accurate keypoints are obtained through a progressive scoring mechanism that combines keypoint scores in different receptive fields.

3   Method

Most feature-based methods [8–10] calculate the transformation matrices using local information from the point clouds, which inevitably ignores global information. However, there may be several repetitive structures in a point cloud, and feature descriptors solely extracted using local point cloud information can degrade the feature descriptors' discriminative ability. Therefore, this paper combines the global and local information of the point cloud, enabling the network to learn the point cloud structural distribution in the global space and enhance differentiating similar structures by generating more discriminative feature descriptors(DFD). Additionally, a multi-level supervision mechanism and progressive scoring mechanism are utilized to obtain more accurate correspondences and more robust transformation matrices.

3.1 Problem Definition

Point cloud registration has non-convex characteristics [18], and thus the best transformation matrix and the most appropriate correspondences cannot be computed simultaneously through a simple method. However, if we first derive the correspondences by the Euclidean distance between two point cloud feature descriptors, the point cloud registration problem can be converted to an L2-distance minimization problem.

$$\arg\min_{R\in\mathcal{SO}(3),t\in\mathbb{R}^3} f(x) = [\frac{1}{N} \cdot \|P - (RQI + t)\|], \tag{1}$$

where $R \in \mathcal{SO}(3)$ denotes the rotation matrix and $t \in \mathbb{R}^3$ is the translation vector. $I \in \mathbb{R}^{N \times N}$ is an indicator function matrix with a value of 1 when the v-th point in Q is the corresponding point of the u-th point in P, and a value of 0 otherwise.

3.2 Network Structure

We construct a UNet-like [21] network structure that comprises a five-layer encoder structure and a four-layer decoder structure, utilizing skip links to fuse the corresponding feature descriptors in encoding and decoding. The local and the computed nonlocal feature descriptors are fused in the last three layers of the encoder network. Additionally, supervision signals are added in the last two layers of the decoder network, and the keypoint scores obtained by the detectors in the last two layers are fused, providing the final keypoint scores. Figure 1 illustrates the proposed network architecture.

3.3 Feature Descriptor

Recently, global information has been widely utilized [6,37]. Inspired by [29,32], which introduces global information for registration tasks, we combine the local and global information of the point cloud to obtain feature descriptors with higher discrimination. Next, will present the details of the point clouds' local and nonlocal feature descriptors.

Local Feature Descriptor. A local feature descriptor is extracted by a new convolution type named KPConv [25], which will be introduced in the following paragraphs.

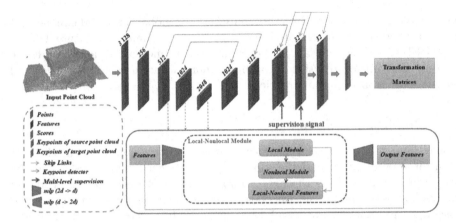

Fig. 1. The network architecture comprises a UNet-like network with five encoding layers and four decoding layers. The features are extracted in the last three layers of the encodings part utilizing the Local-Nonlocal Module. A multi-level supervision mechanism is utilized in the last two layers of the decoding part, and a progressive scoring mechanism is employed to fuse scores in different scopes and obtain more robust keypoint scores.

First, we calculate the weight coefficient $h(y_i, \tilde{x}_i)$ based on the relative distance from the kernel points corresponding to the weight matrix to each neighbor point. The smaller the relative distance, the greater the weight of the neighboring point feature, with the maximum value being 1. Then, we represent the weight parameter $g(y_i)$ of each neighboring point feature by a kernel function.

$$h(y_i, \tilde{x}_i) = max(0, 1 - \frac{\|y_i - \tilde{x}_k\|}{\sigma}), \tag{2}$$

$$g(y_i) = \sum_{k<K} h(y_i, \tilde{x}_i) \cdot W_k, \tag{3}$$

where $y_i = x_i - x$ denotes the decentralized neighbor point, $\tilde{x}_k$ is the kernel point represented by a special position computed according to the specific rules, and W_k is the kernel point weight matrix representing the weights of the kernel points.

Finally, we calculate the local feature descriptor of each point utilizing the weight parameter $g(y_i)$ and the features f_i of each neighboring point, which are calculated as follows:

$$(F \cdot g)(x) = \sum_{x_i \in N_X} g(x_i - x) \cdot f_i, \tag{4}$$

where F denotes the feature of each point corresponding to the neighboring points, with each point having N_x neighboring points, and the weight coefficients are calculated by the kernel function g.

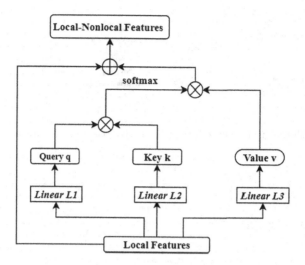

Fig. 2. Extraction method of the local and nonlocal feature descriptors. The notation $\otimes$ and $\oplus$ represent matrix multiplication and concatenation. Both source and target point clouds extract features using this method.

Nonlocal Feature Descriptor. As depicted in Fig. 2, we utilize the attention mechanism to compute the nonlocal feature descriptors for each point concerning the whole point cloud. For each point feature $f_1, ..., f_k \in N_k$, its corresponding nonlocal feature is $F_1, ..., F_k \in M_k$, where N_k and M_k are the local and nonlocal features of the current point cloud, respectively. The nonlocal features can be written as:

$$F_i = \mathcal{A}(R(f_i, f_j)\gamma(f_k), \forall f_j, f_k \in N_k), \tag{5}$$

We utilize the paired function R to compute a high-dimensional relationship matrix between the features of different points, representing the similarity between the feature descriptors of different points. The dimension of the initial feature changes with a unary function γ, changing from D_{in} to D_{out}. Besides, $\mathcal{A}$ denotes a connectivity function. In the experiment, we define the linear fully connected function as $\gamma(f) = W_\gamma \cdot f$ and utilize the matrix dot product to calculate the function $R(f_i, f_j)$ that represents the feature similarity of two points. The following equation expresses this similarity, and softmax [15] is utilized to normalize the result.

$$R(f_i, f_j) = Softmax(\Phi_1(f_i)^T \cdot \Phi_2(f_j)/D_{out}), \tag{6}$$

where Φ_1 and Φ_2 are two independent linear fully connected functions utilized to compute the output features of a specific dimension D_{out} from the original feature dimension D_{in}. Here D_{in} and D_{out} denote the original feature dimension and the computed feature dimension, respectively.

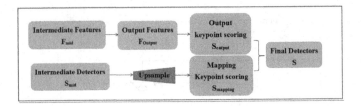

Fig. 3. Detectors via the progressive scoring mechanism.

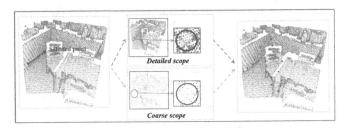

Fig. 4. Schematic diagram of keypoint detection.

In summary, we propose a Local-Nonlocal Module to extract local and global features of the point cloud respectively, and then fuse the obtained features by matrix addition to obtain more discriminative feature descriptors (DFD).

3.4   Feature Detector

Progressive Scoring Mechanism in Training. To obtain more accurate keypoints, we present the progressive scoring mechanism that gradually shifts from a coarse to a detailed scope to combine the regional and channel significance of the keypoints into the keypoint scores. The keypoint scores S_{mid} and S_{output} of the intermediate layer features F_{mid} and output layer features F_{output} are calculated separately by the following method. Then the intermediate layer scores S_{mid} are mapped to the dense keypoint score $S_{mapping}$. Finally, the keypoint scores ($S_{mapping}$ and S_{output}) of the coarse and detailed scopes are superimposed to obtain the final point cloud keypoint score S. The details are illustrated in Fig. 3 and Fig. 4.

$$s_i = \max_k(\alpha_i^k \cdot \beta_i^k), \tag{7}$$

$$s_j = \max_k(\alpha_j^k \cdot \beta_j^k), \tag{8}$$

where i and j denote the subscript of a point in the point cloud of the intermediate and the output layer, and k denotes the channel subscript of a specific point.

Then, we utilize the keypoint scores s_{mid} in the intermediate layer combined by s_i and downsample the indexes to obtain the mapping keypoint scores s'_{final}. After that, we fuse the above mapping scores s'_{final} and network output keypoint scores s_{final} combined by s_j to calculate the final keypoint scores. The details are given below.

The regional saliency score α_i^k is utilized to evaluate the significance of each point relative to the points in its neighborhood. The relative significance of each point within a certain local area is evaluated by calculating the difference between each point feature D_i^k and the average feature of the points in its neighborhood. To prevent the scores from being affected by local sparsity, the calculated regional saliency scores are processed utilizing the softplus function in PyTorch. In particular, the number of nonzero features is utilized to normalize the features, preventing gradient explosion caused by significantly large values. The specific calculation equation is as follows:

$$\alpha_i^k = ln(1 + exp(D_i^k - \frac{1}{\|N_{x_i}\|} \cdot \sum_{x_j \in Nx_i} D_j^k)). \tag{9}$$

The channel saliency score β_i^k is calculated by the magnitude of each point relative to the maximum channel eigenvalue, assessing the saliency of different channels for each point, as follows:

$$\beta_i^k = \frac{D_i^k}{max_t(D_i^t)}. \tag{10}$$

Keypoint Scoring Method in Testing. The keypoints in the testing point cloud must be the most significant in their neighborhood and in the channels, based on the following calculations. Besides, we also utilize the progressive scoring mechanism to combine the scores under different scopes during testing.

$$i = \arg\max_{j \in N_{x_i}}[\max_t(D_j^t)], \tag{11}$$

where N_{x_i} denotes the set of points of the i-th point in the specified radius. Specifically, we first select the most significant channel k (with the largest eigenvalue) for each point and then utilize whether the eigenvalue of this point in channel k is the maximum eigenvalue of the points in the neighborhood on channel k as the judgment criterion for the keypoints. Finally, the keypoints with the highest scores can be selected as the final keypoints.

3.5   Multi-level Supervision Mechanism

First, the source and target point clouds in the intermediate layer are extracted from the considered point set (the source and target point clouds are downsampled to obtain the point set of the intermediate layer according to the given radius). The source point cloud is translated and rotated utilizing the ground truth transformation. Finally, the KD-tree built with the target point clouds is utilized to perform a radial search and obtain the correspondences between the source and target point clouds. Following that, the corresponding source and target point cloud features utilized in the intermediate layer are extracted from the complete features for a multi-level supervision mechanism.

The supervision signal is divided into two parts. The first part involves the feature descriptors' supervision in the intermediate and final layers, represented as L_{mid} and L_{final}. The second part is the supervision of the detectors for the keypoint score combinations in different network layers, represented as L_{det}. The final loss function is the sum of the two types of losses in the case of different weights.

$$Loss = W_{desc} \cdot (L_{mid} + L_{final}) + W_{det} \cdot L_{det}. \tag{12}$$

Feature Descriptor Loss. The supervision of feature descriptors is divided into two parts, i.e., in the intermediate layer and the final layer. The supervision of a certain feature descriptor is obtained by superimposing the supervision on positive and negative sample points, respectively.

$$L_{desc} = \frac{1}{n} \sum_{i=1}^{n} (L_{pos} + L_{neg}), \tag{13}$$

$$L_{pos} = max(0, d_{pos}(i) - M_{pos}), \tag{14}$$

$$L_{neg} = max(0, M_{neg} - d_{neg}(i)), \tag{15}$$

where M_{pos} and M_{neg} are the boundary values of positive and negative point cloud pairs, $d_{pos}(i)$ denotes the Euclidean distance between corresponding point features, and $d_{neg}(i)$ is the Euclidean distance between non-corresponding point features, which is calculated as follows:

$$d_{pos}(i) = \|d_{A_i} - d_{B_i}\|_2, \tag{16}$$

$$d_{neg}(i) = min\|d_{A_i} - d_{B_j}\|_2 \text{ s.t. } \|B_i - B_j\|_2 > R, \tag{17}$$

where R denotes the safe distance and B_j is the negative sample outside the full distance of the true correspondences.

Feature Detector Loss. The feature detector loss can be calculated from the keypoint scores after fusing the scores in the intermediate and the final layers. The specific calculation method can be represented as follows,

$$L_{det} = \frac{1}{n} \sum_{i=1}^{n} [(d_{pos}(i) - d_{neg}(i)) \cdot (s_{A_i} + s_{B_i})]. \tag{18}$$

In the above formulation, if two points are corresponding, i.e., $d_{pos}(i) - d_{neg}(i) < 0$, the smaller the feature detector loss, the higher the score of the point pair. Similarly, if two points are not corresponding, i.e., $d_{pos}(i) - d_{neg}(i) > 0$, the smaller the feature detector loss, the lower the score of the point pair. Through the deep learning back-propagation mechanism, the detector loss will become smaller, which means the scores of positive sample pairs will increase, the scores of the negative sample pairs will reduce, and finally, the most appropriate point cloud score will be obtained.

4 Experiment

4.1 Dataset

The 3DMatch dataset [2] is a common indoor registration dataset, commonly utilized to extract keypoints and feature descriptors of 3D point clouds, and conduct point cloud registration, classification, and segmentation tasks. This dataset collects data from 62 scenarios, of which 54 were utilized to train the model and 8 to evaluate the model. The dataset consists of three main components: 3D coordinate data of the point clouds, overlap rate between the point cloud pairs, and correspondence pairs between the two point clouds. We down-sample 3DMatch point clouds using a voxel grid filter of size 0.03 m in our experiment. Several point clouds of the dataset has been shown in the first column of Fig. 6.

4.2 Evaluation Metrics

We utilize three metrics, i.e., feature matching recall, inlier ratio, and registration recall, to evaluate the performance of the feature descriptors the network provides. Similar to the related literature, we briefly discuss these evaluation metrics as follows. Refer to [1] for more details of the evaluation metrics.

Feature matching recall measures the accuracy of the correspondences obtained by the feature descriptors of the point cloud pairs after being registered by the ground truth transformations.

Inlier ratio is the metric that judges the requested correspondences by the proportion of the Euclidean distance between the corresponding point cloud pairs within a distance threshold after registration utilizing the ground truth transformations.

Registration recall defines the proportion of overlapping regions that can be correctly registered by the transformation matrix derived from RANSAC[39] for the standard transformation matrix fragment pairs.

4.3 Experimental Details

All experiments are conducted on a PC with an Intel Core i7 @ 3.6 GHz, 20 GB RAM, and an NVIDIA RTX 3090 GPU. We utilize point cloud pairs with an overlap of over 30% for training, construct the network structure according to the PyTorch framework, and set the initial voxel radius for downsampling to 3 cm. During training, we optimize the model parameters utilizing gradient descent loss with an initial learning rate of 0.01 and update the learning rate dynamically utilizing an exponential decay strategy. The maximum training epoch is set to

150, and the model converges at the 47-th epoch. To solve the emergent gradient explosion problem, we utilize a gradient cropping method to control the gradient values in the range of $[-10, 10]$ before back-propagation.

4.4   Comparison with Related Methods

We compare our method's evaluation results with the representative techniques on the 3DMatch dataset, by selecting 5000 sampling points to compare the registration effect. The developed method uses 5000 keypoints obtained from the detector scores for testing. As reported in Table 1, the proposed method attains the best results.

Table 1. Results of FMR and STD in different methods.

	FMR (%)	STD
FPFH [22]	35.9	13.4
SHOT [23]	23.8	10.9
3DMatch [36]	59.6	8.8
CGF [16]	58.2	14.2
PPFNet [10]	62.3	10.8
PPF-FoldNet [9]	71.8	10.5
PerfectMatch [13]	94.7	2.7
FCGF [8]	95.2	2.9
D3feat [1]	95.8	2.9
Ours	**96.3**	**2.61**

4.5   Model Performance Under Different Numbers of Points

To obtain more comprehensive evaluation results, we further evaluate the results of the three evaluation metrics under a different number of sampling points and extend during testing the number of points from 5000 to 2500, 1000, 500, and 250. As reported in Table 2, our method achieves better results in most cases.

4.6   Ablation Experiments

To evaluate the validity of our proposed methods, we conduct ablation experiments on the 3DMatch dataset. As highlighted in Table 3, we compare 1) the registration results utilizing the method proposed in D3feat [1], 2) Model-V1: the registration results utilizing our method without intermediate supervision, 3) Model-V2: the registration results utilizing intermediate supervision mechanism with local features and 4) the registration results integrating global and local features and utilizing intermediate supervision mechanism. We conclude from the experimental results that the new proposed feature descriptors and the intermediate supervised mechanism lead to more robust registration results.

Table 2. Evaluation results of the 3DMatch under a different number of points.

# Keypoints	250	500	1000	2500	5000
Feature Matching Recall (%)					
PerfectMatch [13]	82.9	90.1	92.6	94.2	94.7
FCGF [8]	89.9	93.0	94.6	95.5	95.2
D3feat [1]	90.6	92.8	94.4	94.8	95.8
UKPGAN [35]	92.6	93.5	94.2	94.7	95.5
Ours	**94.6**	**95.3**	**96.0**	**96.2**	**96.3**
Registration Recall (%)					
PerfectMatch [13]	50.9	64.8	73.4	77.5	80.3
FCGF [8]	73.0	81.0	85.8	85.8	87.3
D3feat [1]	75.4	83.0	86.6	88.2	89.4
UKPGAN [35]	69.7	77.1	81.4	82.8	83.8
Ours	**85.8**	**89.7**	**91.7**	**92.0**	**92.6**
Inlier Ratio (%)					
PerfectMatch [13]	19.1	23.0	28.3	34.5	37.7
FCGF [8]	34.7	43.3	**49.1**	**54.5**	**56.9**
D3feat [1]	30.8	35.3	38.6	41.1	42.1
UKPGAN [35]	33.1	34.0	35.5	38.8	39.3
Ours	**41.7**	**43.5**	44.3	43.0	43.7

Table 3. Ablation experiments.

# Keypoints	250	500	1000	2500	5000
Feature Matching Recall (%)					
D3feat [1]	90.6	92.8	94.4	94.8	95.8
Model-V1	92.8	93.8	94.7	95.6	92.8
Model-V2	93.5	94.2	95.4	95.5	95.5
Ours	**94.6**	**95.3**	**96.0**	**96.2**	**96.3**
Registration Recall (%)					
D3feat [1]	75.4	83.0	86.6	88.2	89.4
Model-V1	81.3	86.2	88.4	89.4	89.6
Model-V2	84.4	89.1	90.9	91.5	92.1
Ours	**85.8**	**89.7**	**91.7**	**92.0**	**92.6**
Inlier Ratio (%)					
D3feat [1]	30.8	35.3	38.6	41.1	42.1
Model-V1	36.2	38.8	40.7	41.8	42.4
Model-V2	40.9	43.2	43.5	41.9	42.3
Ours	**41.7**	**43.5**	**44.3**	**43.0**	**43.7**

4.7 Visualization

As can be observed from Fig. 5, the keypoints are mainly distributed in the regions of the edges and vertices of the point cloud. By utilizing the keypoints selected by the progressive detectors to calculate the transformation matrix, we can obtain the transformation matrix with smaller registration errors for point clouds in different poses.

Fig. 5. Results on the 3DMatch dataset, visualizing the complete point cloud and the selected keypoints (500 are in red and the rest in blue). (Color figure online)

We select some fragment pairs and register them with our proposed method, D3feat [1] and FCGF [8]. The results before and after registration are shown in Fig. 6. From the results, we can conclude that: 1) Point cloud registration task can be accomplished by the proposed method, 2) The point cloud reregistrated by the proposed method can achieve better results compared to D3feat [1] and FCGF [8].

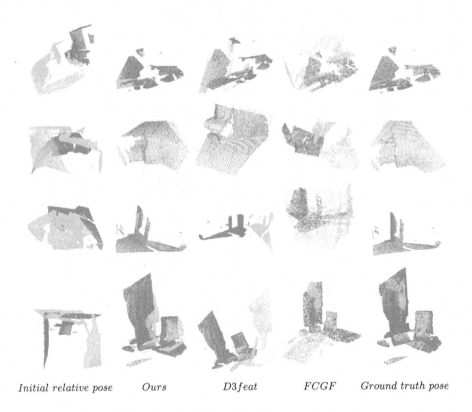

Initial relative pose   *Ours*   *D3feat*   *FCGF*   *Ground truth pose*

Fig. 6. Quantitative test results in the 3DMatch dataset.

5   Conclusion

This paper proposes an efficient feature descriptor by combining global and local information. A stronger supervision signal can also be provided to the feature descriptors by applying a multi-level supervision mechanism and a progressive scoring mechanism. The developed method selects more accurate keypoints, leading to more robust point cloud registration. Extensive experiments on the 3DMatch dataset demonstrate that our model outperforms some existing methods, especially when selecting fewer keypoints.

References

1. Bai, X., Luo, Z., Zhou, L., Fu, H., Quan, L., Tai, C.L.: D3Feat: joint learning of dense detection and description of 3D local features. In: Proceedings of the IEEE/CVF Conference on Computer Vision and Pattern Recognition, pp. 6359–6367 (2020)
2. Baker, S., Matthews, I.: Lucas-Kanade 20 years on: a unifying framework. Int. J. Comput. Vision **56**(3), 221–255 (2004)
3. Besl, P.J., McKay, N.D.: Method for registration of 3-D shapes. In: Sensor Fusion IV: Control Paradigms and Data Structures, vol. 1611, pp. 586–606. SPIE (1992)
4. Brenner, C., Dold, C., Ripperda, N.: Coarse orientation of terrestrial laser scans in urban environments. ISPRS J. Photogramm. Remote. Sens. **63**(1), 4–18 (2008)
5. Chen, Y., Medioni, G.: Object modelling by registration of multiple range images. Image Vis. Comput. **10**(3), 145–155 (1992)
6. Cheng, S., Chen, X., He, X., Liu, Z., Bai, X.: PRA-Net: point relation-aware network for 3d point cloud analysis. IEEE Trans. Image Process. **30**, 4436–4448 (2021)
7. Choy, C., Gwak, J., Savarese, S.: 4D spatio-temporal convnets: Minkowski convolutional neural networks. In: Proceedings of the IEEE/CVF Conference on Computer Vision and Pattern Recognition, pp. 3075–3084 (2019)
8. Choy, C., Park, J., Koltun, V.: Fully convolutional geometric features. In: Proceedings of the IEEE/CVF International Conference on Computer Vision, pp. 8958–8966 (2019)
9. Deng, H., Birdal, T., Ilic, S.: PPF-FoldNet: unsupervised learning of rotation invariant 3D local descriptors. In: Proceedings of the European Conference on Computer Vision (ECCV), pp. 602–618 (2018)
10. Deng, H., Birdal, T., Ilic, S.: PPFNet: global context aware local features for robust 3D point matching. In: Proceedings of the IEEE Conference on Computer Vision and Pattern Recognition, pp. 195–205 (2018)
11. Dryden, I.L., Mardia, K.V.: Statistical Shape Analysis: With Applications in R, vol. 995. Wiley, Hoboken (2016)
12. Fitzgibbon, A.W.: Robust registration of 2D and 3D point sets. Image Vis. Comput. **21**(13–14), 1145–1153 (2003)
13. Gojcic, Z., Zhou, C., Wegner, J.D., Wieser, A.: The perfect match: 3D point cloud matching with smoothed densities. In: Proceedings of the IEEE/CVF Conference on Computer Vision and Pattern Recognition, pp. 5545–5554 (2019)
14. He, G., Lan, Y., Jiang, J., Zhao, W.X., Wen, J.R.: Improving multi-hop knowledge base question answering by learning intermediate supervision signals. In: Proceedings of the 14th ACM International Conference on Web Search and Data Mining, pp. 553–561 (2021)

15. Joulin, A., Cissé, M., Grangier, D., Jégou, H., et al.: Efficient softmax approximation for GPUs. In: International Conference on Machine Learning, pp. 1302–1310. PMLR (2017)
16. Khoury, M., Zhou, Q.Y., Koltun, V.: Learning compact geometric features. In: Proceedings of the IEEE International Conference on Computer Vision, pp. 153–161 (2017)
17. Li, C., Zia, M.Z., Tran, Q.H., Yu, X., Hager, G.D., Chandraker, M.: Deep supervision with intermediate concepts. IEEE Trans. Pattern Anal. Mach. Intell. **41**(8), 1828–1843 (2018)
18. Li, H., Hartley, R.: The 3D-3D registration problem revisited. In: 2007 IEEE 11th International Conference on Computer Vision, pp. 1–8. IEEE (2007)
19. Qi, C.R., Su, H., Mo, K., Guibas, L.J.: PointNet: deep learning on point sets for 3D classification and segmentation. In: Proceedings of the IEEE Conference on Computer Vision and Pattern Recognition, pp. 652–660 (2017)
20. Riegler, G., Osman Ulusoy, A., Geiger, A.: OctNet: learning deep 3D representations at high resolutions. In: Proceedings of the IEEE Conference on Computer Vision and Pattern Recognition, pp. 3577–3586 (2017)
21. Ronneberger, O., Fischer, P., Brox, T.: U-net: convolutional networks for biomedical image segmentation. In: Navab, N., Hornegger, J., Wells, W.M., Frangi, A.F. (eds.) MICCAI 2015. LNCS, vol. 9351, pp. 234–241. Springer, Cham (2015). https://doi.org/10.1007/978-3-319-24574-4_28
22. Rusu, R.B., Blodow, N., Beetz, M.: Fast point feature histograms (FPFH) for 3D registration. In: 2009 IEEE International Conference on Robotics and Automation, pp. 3212–3217. IEEE (2009)
23. Salti, S., Tombari, F., Di Stefano, L.: SHOT: unique signatures of histograms for surface and texture description. Comput. Vis. Image Underst. **125**, 251–264 (2014)
24. Shi, L., Zhang, Y., Cheng, J., Lu, H.: Action recognition via pose-based graph convolutional networks with intermediate dense supervision. Pattern Recogn. **121**, 108170 (2022)
25. Thomas, H., Qi, C.R., Deschaud, J.E., Marcotegui, B., Goulette, F., Guibas, L.J.: KPConv: flexible and deformable convolution for point clouds. In: Proceedings of the IEEE/CVF International Conference on Computer Vision, pp. 6411–6420 (2019)
26. Wang, L., Lee, C.Y., Tu, Z., Lazebnik, S.: Training deeper convolutional networks with deep supervision. arXiv preprint arXiv:1505.02496 (2015)
27. Wang, P., et al.: A tooth surface design method combining semantic guidance, confidence, and structural coherence. IET Comput. Vision **16**, 727–735 (2022)
28. Wang, P.S., Liu, Y., Guo, Y.X., Sun, C.Y., Tong, X.: O-CNN: octree-based convolutional neural networks for 3D shape analysis. ACM Trans. Graph. (TOG) **36**(4), 1–11 (2017)
29. Wang, X., Girshick, R., Gupta, A., He, K.: Non-local neural networks. In: Proceedings of the IEEE Conference on Computer Vision and Pattern Recognition, pp. 7794–7803 (2018)
30. Wang, Y., Solomon, J.M.: Deep closest point: learning representations for point cloud registration. In: Proceedings of the IEEE/CVF International Conference on Computer Vision, pp. 3523–3532 (2019)
31. Wang, Y., Sun, Y., Liu, Z., Sarma, S.E., Bronstein, M.M., Solomon, J.M.: Dynamic graph CNN for learning on point clouds. ACM Trans. Graph. (tog) **38**(5), 1–12 (2019)

32. Yan, X., Zheng, C., Li, Z., Wang, S., Cui, S.: PointASNL: robust point clouds processing using nonlocal neural networks with adaptive sampling. In: Proceedings of the IEEE/CVF Conference on Computer Vision and Pattern Recognition, pp. 5589–5598 (2020)
33. Yang, Y., Chen, W., Wang, M., Zhong, D., Du, S.: Color point cloud registration based on supervoxel correspondence. IEEE Access **8**, 7362–7372 (2020)
34. Yew, Z.J., Lee, G.H.: RPM-net: robust point matching using learned features. In: Proceedings of the IEEE/CVF Conference on Computer Vision and Pattern Recognition, pp. 11824–11833 (2020)
35. You, Y., Liu, W., Ze, Y., Li, Y.L., Wang, W., Lu, C.: UKPGAN: a general self-supervised keypoint detector. In: Proceedings of the IEEE/CVF Conference on Computer Vision and Pattern Recognition, pp. 17042–17051 (2022)
36. Zeng, A., Song, S., Nießner, M., Fisher, M., Xiao, J., Funkhouser, T.: 3DMatch: learning local geometric descriptors from RGB-D reconstructions. In: Proceedings of the IEEE Conference on Computer Vision and Pattern Recognition, pp. 1802–1811 (2017)
37. Zhou, H., Feng, Y., Fang, M., Wei, M., Qin, J., Lu, T.: Adaptive graph convolution for point cloud analysis. In: Proceedings of the IEEE/CVF International Conference on Computer Vision, pp. 4965–4974 (2021)
38. Zhou, J., Wang, M., Mao, W., Gong, M., Liu, X.: SiamesePointNet: a Siamese point network architecture for learning 3D shape descriptor. In: Computer Graphics Forum, vol. 39, pp. 309–321. Wiley Online Library (2020)

Towards Better Dialogue Utterance Rewriting via a Gated Span-Copy Mechanism

Qingqing Li[1,2] and Fang Kong[1,2(✉)]

[1] Laboratory for Natural Language Processing, Soochow University, Suzhou, China
20214227029@stu.suda.edu.cn, kongfang@suda.edu.cn
[2] School of Computer Science and Technology, Soochow University, Suzhou, China

Abstract. Dialogue rewriting aims to reconstruct the incomplete utterance from dialogue history. It is a challenge task due to the frequent phenomena of coreference and ellipses in dialogue. Although the conventional encoder-decoder architecture has shown the effectiveness for dialogue rewriting, there are still two issues should be addressed. Firstly, the objects referred to or omitted are usually mentions, represented as spans. So the traditional word-by-word copy mechanism, which is widely used in current models, can lead to incompletion, repetition and disorder problems. Secondly, words in dialogue history and common vocabulary list have different effects on rewriting the current utterance. Intuitively, semantically and cohesively matched spans are more important. In this paper, we propose a novel Gated Span-level Copy Mechanism (GSCM) that aims to retrieve the omitted or co-referred spans contained in history dialogue and recover them for the incomplete utterance. The experimental results on the Cam-Rest676 and RiSAWOZ corpora show that our GSCM can significantly improve the performance of dialogue rewriting.

Keywords: Copy Mechanism · Dialogue Rewriting · Ellipsis Recovery · Coreference Resolution

1 Introduction

In daily conversations, objects that are repeatedly referred to or are well known, tend to pronoun or be omitted. It is normal for humans, but hard for machines to understand. The task of dialogue utterance rewriting (Su et al. [13]; Pan et al. [7]) aims to reconstruct the latest utterance using dialogue history. The obtained utterance is semantically equivalent to the original one and can be understood without historical information.

Table 1 illustrates a typical example. For the incomplete utterance $x_3(usr)$, the expression '*Suzhou*' is omitted to avoid repetition (Ellipsis), and the pronoun '*this*' in $x_3(usr)$ refers to '*always cloudy raining*' in $x_2(sys)$ (Coreference).

Currently, A series of models of generative-based have been studied for multi-turn systems. The conventional encoder-decoder architecture has been widely used in dialogue rewriting task with great success (Su et al. [13]; Pan et al. [7]; Quan et al. [10];

L. Iliadis et al. (Eds.): ICANN 2023, LNCS 14262, pp. 456–468, 2023.
https://doi.org/10.1007/978-3-031-44201-8_37

Table 1. An example of multi-turn human-to-machine dialogue, including the dialogue history utterances (x_1, x_2), the incomplete utterance (x_3) and the complete utterance(x_3^*). Purple means ellipsis and orange means co-reference.

Turn	Utterance (*Translation*)
$x_1(usr)$	苏州最近天气怎么样 *How is the recent weather in Suzhou*
$x_2(sys)$	苏州最近经常阴天下雨 *Suzhou is always cloudy raining recently*
$x_3(usr)$	冬天就是这样 *Winter is like this*
x_3^*	苏州冬天就是经常阴天下雨 *It is always cloudy raining in winter Suzhou*

Zhang et al. [15]; Ni et al. [6]). Some studies focus on how to better model the conversation history to improve the rewriting performance, while others focus on better generation (i.e.,decoding) with techniques such as pointer networks, copy mechanisms, and so on. Although recent work on dialogue rewriting has been achieving impressive progress, there are still two issues should be addressed. Firstly, just as noted in Table 1, we can find that the omitted or co-referred objects are mentions (i.e., spans), which can be found in dialogue history in most cases. However, most generation models are currently based on the word level, which inevitably leads to in-completion, repetition and disorder problems. Secondly, intuitively, what is referred or omitted is usually the current focus of the dialogue. During decoding stage, all words without prior focus are considered equivalently may result in performance degradation.

In this paper, we propose a novel Gated Span-level Copy Mechanism (GSCM) to retrieve the omitted or co-referred spans contained in history dialogue and recover them for the incomplete utterance. It tracks the copying history and copies the next word from the input based on its relevance with previously generated tokens. In particular, during encoding stage, we use the encoder to predict the span-copy labels. Then filtered history dialogue spans will be integrated into the original history dialogue. So that we can effectively extract and aggregate the omitted or co-referred expressions into history dialogue as extra guidance. During decoding stage, we use the decoder to predict the span-copy labels to get the span-copy distribution. Then the span-copy distribution is used to generate the Gated Span-Copy distribution to work for generation. Our model achieves the state-of-the-art results on CamRest676 and RISAWOZ datasets.

2 Related Work

Recently, building a chatbot with data-driven approaches in open-domain has drown significant attention [4,12]. However, it is hard for machines to understand the real intention from the original incomplete utterance. Then sentence rewriting task is proposed to generate complete utterances. Xing et al. [14] proposed a hierarchical recurrect network using sentence-level attention and word-level attention mechanisms to get the history dialogue being copied distribution. Kumar et al. [5] and Su et al. [13] used the framework of sequence-to-sequence learning to generate complete questions from a non-sentential question, given previous question and answer. Quan et al. [10] first attempted to provide both solution and dataset for ellipsis and coreference resolution in multi-turn dialogue. Pan et al. [7] propose a cascade frame of "pick-and-combine" to restore the incomplete utterance from history, then use extra guidance from context to help the generation during decoding time. We also use this method to do experiment. Ni et al. [6] proposed the ELD which solves such restoration task in an end-to-end way. It employs a speaker highlight dialogue history encoder and uses the same architecture in [14] to use both the sentence-level and word-level attentions. To mask full use of the characteristic of coreference and ellipsis, since the object omitted or co-referred objects are mentions (i.e., spans), we propose the GSCM to make model learn to copy consecutive spans.

3 Constructing Span-Copy Labels

The gold span-copy labels for utterance rewriting is not naturally available. To address this problem, We construct the span-copy tags based on the alignment between the input u_i and reference utterances u'_i. We firstly match the u_i and u'_i using longest common

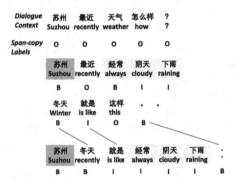

Fig. 1. An example of constructing span-copy tags.

sub-sequence(LCS) algorithm to get the span alignments(the black lines in Fig. 1). Then we get span-copy labels following rules:(i) For the aligned spans in both u_i and u'_i, the first word (e.g. "。 (.)") in each span is assigned the label B, which means the beginning of the aligned span. If one span (e.g. "冬天就是 (winter is like)") contains more than one word, the following words (e.g. " 就是 (is like)") after first word are assigned the label I, which means the word is the intermediary in the aligned span. (ii) For each unaligned span (e.g. the spans in blue and yellow in Fig. 1) in u'_i, if there are multiple candidate spans can be matched from dialogue context, we choose the closest span (e.g. "苏州 (Suzhou)") to avoid long-range dependency. The matched span (e.g. " 经常阴天下雨 (always cloudy raining)") in both u_i and u'_i are assigned labels following (i) Synchronously. (iii) If no candidate can be found, the token are assigned label O.

4 Approach

We formulate utterance rewriting task as a sequence-to-sequence generative problem. Given n-th user utterance $U_n = (u_1, u_2, ..., u_s)$ and its dialogue history $H =$

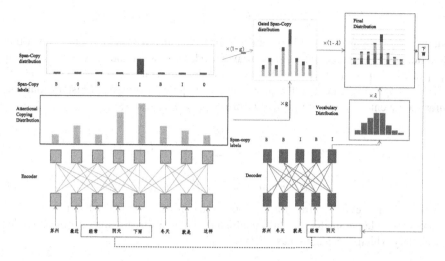

Fig. 2. The framework of GSCM model that copies what is relevant to the previous copied words. The red boxes indicates the being copied 3-gram. (Color figure online)

$\{(U_1, R_1), (U_2, R_2), ..., (U_{n-1}, R_{n-1})\}$ corresponding to all previous dialogue turns, where R_i represents the system response of the i-th turn, the goal is to recover the ellipsis or coreference for the original user utterance U_n. The dialogue ellipsis and coreference resolution task can be formulated as $((H, U_n) \rightarrow U_c)$ where each token of U_c is generated from current user utterance or its dialogue history. Our model architecture is shown in Fig. 2 which mainly consists of three components: (i) utterance encoder; (ii) Gated Span-Copy Mechanism; (iii) decoder with gated copy mechanism.

4.1 Seq2Seq Baseline Architecture

We adopt GECOR [10] Seq2seq architecture as our baseline. We get the hidden states H_c and H_u from GRU encoder. $H_c = \{h_{c1}, h_{c2}, ..., h_{cm}\}$, $H_u = \{h_{u1}, h_{u2}, ..., h_{un}\}$, in the decoder, the attention distribution is calculated as in [1], the previous hidden state s_{t-1} and the hidden states H_{u_i} of token u_i are used to produce attention distribution a^t. Then the attention distribution a^t is used to calculate a weighted sum of the representation H_{u_i}, which is known as context vector h_t^*.

$$attn_i^t = v^T \tanh(w_1 H_{u_i} + w_2 s_{t-1} + b_1) \tag{1}$$

$$a^t = \text{Softmax}(attn^t) \tag{2}$$

$$h_t^* = \sum_i a^t H_{u_i} \tag{3}$$

where w_1, w_2, b_1, v are learn-able parameters. Then the auto-regressive generation is described as follows:

$$o_t, s_t = \text{GRU}([e_{t-1}; h_t^*], s_{t-1}) \tag{4}$$

$$P_{vocab}(y_t|y_{1:t-1}) = w_3 h_t^* + w_4 o_t + b_3 \tag{5}$$

where w_3, w_4, b_3 are learn-able parameters and h_t^* is then fed into the single-layer uni-directional GRU together with the previous decoder state s_{t-1} and the word embedding e_{t-1} of previous generated word to obtain the decoder state s_t, o_t. Word-copy mechanism is applied to calculate the probability of copying words from history dialogue information enhanced by the explicit information as follows:

$$P_{copy}(y_t|y_{1:t-1}) = \sum_{i:c_i=y_t}^{|C|} \frac{1}{Z} e^{\psi c^{(c_i)}}, y_t \in C \tag{6}$$

$$\psi_c(y_t = c_i) = \sigma(w_5 H_c + b_5)s_t \tag{7}$$

where ψ_c is the score function for the copy mode and Z is the normalization term. w_5, b_5 are learn-able parameters. At last, the final probability distribution over the extended vocabulary which is calculated as follows:

$$P(y_t|y_{1:t-1}) = P_{vocab}(y_t) + P_{copy}(y_t), y_t \in V \cup C \tag{8}$$

The gated word-copy mechanism is introduced to regulate the contribution of the generation and copy mode to the final prediction to generate the generation probability distribution $P(y_t|y_{1:t-1})$.

$$\lambda = \sigma(w_6[h_t^*; e_{t-1}; s_t] + b_6) \tag{9}$$

$$P(y_t|y_{1:t-1}) = \lambda P_{vocab} + (1 - \lambda)P_{copy} \tag{10}$$

where λ is a gate to regulate the contribution of the generation and copy mode to the final prediction. σ is the sigmoid function. w_6, b_6 are learn-able parameters. Both the generation probability over the entire vocabulary and the copy probability over all words are taken into account for predicting the complete user utterance.

4.2 Gated Span-Copy Mechanism

We propose the Gated Span-Copy Mechanism(GSCM) that takes advantages of span-copy labels and at each time step, explicitly encourages the model to copy the context word that is relevant to the previously copied tokens. For an example in Fig. 2, in order to predict the current token "下雨 (raining)", the model first predicts its span-copy label equals I, which indicates the current token constitute a 3-gram with the predicted tokens "经常", "阴天". Then we search the potential 3-grams from the context, and '下雨' is the only valid candidate. Finally, the span-copy distribution except "下雨 (raining)" are all masked as zero, gate g is adapted to regulate the contribution of attention copying distribution and span-copy distribution to generate the Gated Span-copy distribution P^{span} as Eq. (11):

We employ a 3-class classification network on s_t to generate the span-copy labels in inference time.

$$P_j^{span}(y_t|z_t) = \begin{cases} 0 & c_j \notin cans \\ \sum_{i:c_i=y_t}^{|C|} \frac{1}{Z} e^{\psi c^{(c_i)}} & c_j \in cans \end{cases} \tag{11}$$

- If the span-copy label is B(eg. "苏州 (Suzhou)" in both Fig. 1 and Fig. 2) or O, the gated span-copy distribution is followed by attentional copying distribution. The *cans* equals to all the context word list.
- If the span-copy label is I(eg. "下雨 (raining)" in Fig. 1), which indicates the current generating token constitute a n-gram(n is calculated according to the number of generated tokens labeled I)with the predicted tokens as we calculate the copied token number. The BI-labeled generated words before time t("经常阴天" (always cloudy) in Fig. 1) are worked as a prefix. We use the prefix to find the matching next word in dialogue history and mask the word which cannot constitute the any n-gram of history dialogue using the prefix, which can ensure the words of BI labeled is a span copied from dialogue history. The next word lists constitute the set *cans* (eg. "下雨 (raining)" in Fig. 1).

The Eq. (6) is replaced by Eq. (13):

$$g = \sigma(w_7[h_t^*; e_{t-1}; s_t] + b_7) \tag{12}$$

$$P_{copy}(y_t|y_{1:t-1}) = g \sum_{i:c_i=y_t}^{|C|} \frac{1}{Z} e^{\psi c^{(c_i)}} + (1-g) P^{span}(y_t) \tag{13}$$

5   Experimentation

In this section, we systematically evaluate our proposed gated span-copy mechanism approach to dialogue ellipsis and coreference restoration.

5.1   Experimental Settings

Same as previous work [10], all experiments are conducted in the data from the English corpus CamRest676 [10] and the Chinese corpus RiSAWOZ [11]. CamRest676 include three types of data: the ellipsis CamRest676 dataset where only ellipsis version utterances from the annotated dataset was used, the co-reference CamRest676 where only co-reference version utterances from the annotated dataset were used and the mixed CamRest676 dataset where we randomly selected a version for each user utterance from ellipsis, co-reference, complete. We employed the 50-dimension word embeddings provided by Glove [9] for CamRest676 and 300 dimensional fastText [2] word vectors to initialize word embeddings for RiSAWOZ. We set the vocabulary size V to 800 and 12000 respectively. The size of hidden states was set to 128 and 256 respectively. The learning rate was set to be 3e-3. The batch size and dropout was set to 16 and 0.5 respectively. The standard cross-entropy loss is adopted as the loss function. We use exact match rate(EM) which measures whether the generated utterances exactly match the gold utterances, F1 score which is a balance between word-level precision(Prec) and recall(Rec), and Bilingual Evaluation Understudy(BLEU) [8] is used for evaluating the quality of generated utterances at n-grams and word level.

Table 2. The main results on mixed CamRest676 dataset of our generative method and other methods. † denotes the duplicated systems.

Model	EM	BLEU	F1	Prec	Rec
GECOR1†	66.48	82.39	95.75	98.12	93.49
GECOR2†	66.73	83.79	96.53	**98.40**	94.73
ELD†	68.05	85.04	96.43	98.24	94.70
GSC1	68.97	85.22	96.82	98.06	95.04
GSC2	69.65	**99.29**	**96.86**	98.34	**95.42**
ELDGSC	**70.68**	85.07	96.07	97.61	94.57

Table 3. The main results on ellipsis and coreference CamRest676 dataset of our generative method and other methods. † denotes the duplicated systems.

Model	Ellipsis					Coreference				
	EM	BLEU	Prec	Rec	F1	EM	BLEU	Prec	Rec	F1
GECOR1†	67.78	83.32	96.40	**98.39**	94.49	71.35	85.89	96.49	98.19	94.86
GECOR2†	66.36	83.39	96.46	98.25	94.74	71.18	85.93	97.09	**98.46**	95.76
ELD†	68.16	84.17	96.42	98.35	94.58	72.47	88.01	96.99	98.38	95.63
GSC1	**72.01**	**84.87**	96.34	98.23	94.53	72.68	88.11	**97.30**	97.45	**97.16**
GSC2	72.00	84.82	**96.54**	98.17	**94.96**	73.18	87.59	97.24	97.45	97.04
ELDGSC	70.09	84.44	96.22	97.95	94.55	**74.14**	**88.14**	96.61	97.53	95.70

5.2 Compared Methods

In this paper, we compare our proposed system with the following competitive models on the CamRest676 and RiSAWOZ corpus:

- **GECOR1**: an end-to-end generative model proposed by Quan et al. [10] that uses the plus copy mechanism proposed by Gu et al. [3] to recover omission and coreference. Using our GSCM after GECOR1 called GSC1.
- **GECOR2**: whose architecture is as the same as GECOR1, but uses the gated copy mechanism. Using our GSCM after GECOR2 called GSC2.
- **ELD** [6]: It employs a speaker highlight dialogue history encoder, a top-down hierarchical copy mechanism and a gated copy mechanism as the same as GECOR2. Which works on probability of coping words from history dialoguee, our GSCM works after the gated copy mechanism is called ELDGSC.

5.3 Main Results

The main results on CamRest676 are as shown in Table 2, 3 respectively. The performance of our proposed models on mixed data has been improved on CamRest676 corpora. All the model with GSCM get better performance original model where gaps are 2.49, 2.92 and 2.63 EM points. The results prove the necessity of GSCM.

The performance on coreference data has been improved on CamRest676 corpora. The GSC1 and GSC2 models can improve performance by 1.33 and 2 EM points, compared with GECOR1, GECOR2 respectively. And the BLEU score is improved by 2.22

Table 4. The main results on RiSAWOZ test set of our generative method and other methods. †
denotes the duplicated systems.

Model	EM	BLEU	F1	Prec	Rec
GECOR1†	59.26	87.88	97.52	98.05	97.01
GECOR2†	58.33	87.67	97.02	97.05	96.01
ELD†	64.89	88.68	98.02	98.09	97.01
GSC1	63.01	88.67	97.32	97.75	96.88
GSC2	62.14	88.24	97.39	97.64	97.15
ELDGSC	**65.24**	**88.95**	**98.37**	**98.60**	**98.14**

Table 5. The main results on mixed CamRest676 dataset of our method with extra guidance. †
denotes the duplicated systems.

Model	EM	BLEU	F1	Prec	Rec
GSC1	68.97	85.22	96.82	98.06	95.04
GSC1+ex	71.18	85.64	96.97	98.51	95.51
GSC2	69.65	85.31	96.86	98.34	95.42
GSC2+ex	**71.43**	**87.08**	**97.33**	**98.57**	**96.13**
ELDGSC	70.68	85.07	96.07	97.61	94.57
ELDGSC+ex	70.81	86.87	96.71	98.04	95.42

points and 1.66 points respectively. And surprisingly the ELD model with GSCM can
achieve the better score in EM and BLEU. As we suppose, the speaker highlight mechanism can make the model pay more attention to user-aware or system-aware sentence
flow in history dialogue, because of which the model can find the best coreference link
in the history dialogue. The comparative experimental results on the two corpora provide strong support and verify the effectiveness of the improved method.

The results on RiSAWOZ are in Table 4. Our GSCM can make the model achieve
better EM, BLEU and F1. The GSC1 and GSC2 models can improve performance by
0.79 and 0.57 BLEU points, compared with GECOR1 and GECOR2 respectively. And
surprisingly the ELD model with GSCM can achieve the SOTA result on all metrics, in
which the word-level and utterance-level attention are helpful to especially Chinese corpus because of the complex structure in Chinese. Moreover, we can find that our GSCM
is more helpful in terms of the fragment or sequence-based metrics (i.e., BLEU and
EM) than in terms of the word-level metrics (i.e., F1, Prec, and Rec). Which matches
our span-level rather than word-level hypothesis.

5.4 Effect of Extra Guidance

Following [7], all the B-labeled and I-labeled words encoder hidden states H_{BI} c(eg.
"苏州 (Suzhou)", "经常阴天下雨 (always cloudy raining), "冬天就是(Winter is)"
and "。(.)") in dialogue context in Fig. 1) are filtered out as extra guidance, which

corresponds to the missing semantic information. There are three different guidance ways: The first two are to concatenate H_{BI} into the original history dialogue hidden states and the user utterance hidden states respectively. The last one is to do the above two ways together. Table 5 shows the experimental results of our method with extra guidance. The GSC1+ex means the GSC1 with the best one of the three guidance ways. When confronted with the model, extra guidance can greatly enhance performance on all five metrics. We intuitively believe that adding extra guidance can give the model the ability to pay more attention to the missing semantic information and restore the semantic expression related to the omitted and correlative information.

5.5 Case Studies

A given utterance is semantically complete when it requires no additional information to understand and contains no references or omissions that may cause ambiguity. In mixed dataset, about 53.36% utterances are semantically complete, while incomplete utterances occupy about 46.64%. We analyze our models for complete and incomplete utterances.

For each complete utterance, our model needs to confirm that the utterance is semantically complete, just leave it in its original state. Our GSC1 can generate 98.94% utterances that exactly match the input utterances, only 1.06% utterances do not match the input utterances perfectly. Most unmatched cases can be grouped into three types, i.e., missing words, repetition and missed tone auxiliary. Following illustrates the corresponding examples for each type.

- Missing words
      User: Can I get a Korean restaurant in the town centre?
      GEOCOR: Can I get a Korean restaurant in the town?
      GSCI: Can I get a Korean restaurant in the town centre?
- Repetition
      User: OK, thank you. That is all for today then.
      GEOCOR: OK, thank you. That is all for today for today then.
      GSCI: OK, thank you. That 's all for today then.
- Missed tone auxiliary
      User: 再帮我找家川菜吧，中等的就行，告诉我评分和人均消费。

      GSC1: 再帮我找家川菜吧，中等的就行，告诉我的评分和人均消费。

From these examples, we can conclude that our GSC1 model can retrieve the missing word and the repetition problems due to the employment of GSCM. Copying spans from history dialogue, our model can keep a high consistency with the history dialogue. However, our model is unable to deal with the problem of missed tone auxiliary. In Chinese, the tone auxiliaries are always missed or generated in wrong places.

When the input user utterances are incomplete, our model needs to find the elements that may be ambiguous and replace them from the conversation history. At the same time, our model should also keep the unambiguous parts as they are. Result analysis of our model shows that, the GSC1 model can generate 43% utterances that exactly match the reference utterances, about 57% do not match perfectly. An in-depth analysis on the unmatched cases shows that, excluding the same three kinds of problems for complete utterances, there are additional three kinds of problems closely related to ellipsis and coreference for incomplete utterances, i.e., paraphrase, partial resolution, and lack of resolution. Table 6 lists some examples.

Among them, we find that paraphrases occupy the majority of the unmatched cases. Example (1)–(3) are associated with this category. Sometimes the generated utterances cover even more detail information than the reference, just as Example (1) and (2) indicate. Additionally, there are some spans generated in different positions. In fact, these positions are legal, just as Example (3) notes. In general, we think, the paraphrased complete utterances generated by GSC1 are acceptable for understanding. Partial res-

Table 6. Examples for incomplete utterances.

Example (1)
User: Any will be fifine.
GSC1: any cheap restaurant in the north part of town will be fine.
Reference: Any type of restaurant will be fifine.
Example (2)
user:这家店的营业时间是几点到几点？
GSC1:那 川菜馆 名叫 江边 城外 烤 全鱼 的 营业时间 是 几点 到 几点？
Reference: 那 江边 城外 烤 全鱼 的 营业时间 是 几点 到 几点？
Example (3)
user: 听 起来 不错 呢， 电话 是 多少 啊
GSC1: 东吴 面馆 听 起来 不错 呢， 电话 是 多少 啊
Reference: 听 起来 不错 呢， 东吴 面馆 电话 是 多少 啊
Example (4)
User: I do not care about them.
GSC1: I do not care about the price range.
Reference: I do not care about the price range or location.
History:
usr: I would like a barbeque restaurant.
sys:Where would you like to search for a restaurant, and what price range would you prefer?
Example (5)
User: 噢 噢， 了解 了， 你 再 帮 我 看看 第二天 有没有 厦门 回 北京 的 飞机 。
GSC1: 噢 噢， 了解 了， 你 再 帮 我 看看 第二天 有没有 厦门 回 北京 的 飞机 。
Reference: 噢 噢， 了解 了， 你 再 帮 我 看看 下周一 有没有 厦门 回 北京 的 飞机 。

olution means our model only conducts a partial resolution for the pronoun referring to more than one items. Just as Example (4) shows, referring to the dialogue history, we can find the pronoun "them" means both "location" and "price range" of a restaurant. However, our model only recovers one item "price range". Lack of resolution means some anaphors are ignored. In Example (5), the anaphora between the mention

" 第二天/the second day" and "下周一/next monday" is missing. In fact, this may require additional knowledge beyond the content of the conversation (i.e., today is Sunday).

6   Effect on Different Window Size of Gram for BLEU Score

As we have found the BLEU score has getting better with our GSCM. Which shows our model effectiveness on word-level(1-gram). We want to further investigate that has our model learned to copy more accurately (especially for the consecutive copying). We employ GSC2 and GECOR2 for a fair comparison in which the difference is only GSCM. Figure 3 shows that GSC2 model contain a higher rate of 'correct' n-grams(those appear both in the generated sentence and reference) than the GECOR2, especially, with the rise of the gram window size, our GSC2 work better than indicating that learning to copy spans from the copying history is beneficial to generate consecutive spans.

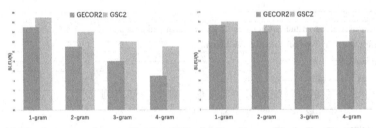

(a) Results on coreference CamRest676.   (b) Results on ellipsis CamRest676.

Fig. 3. The BLEU scores of different n-grams.

7   Conclusion

In this paper, we propose a novel Gated Span-level Copy Mechanism that aims to retrieve omitted or co-referred spans contained in history and recover them for the incomplete utterance. Experimental results demonstrated the effectiveness of our proposed model.

Acknowledgments. This work was supported by the Projects 62276178 under the National Natural Science Foundation of China, the National Key RD Program of China under Grant No.2020AAA0108600 and the Priority Academic Program Development of Jiangsu Higher Education Institutions.

References

1. Bahdanau, D., Cho, K., Bengio, Y.: Neural machine translation by jointly learning to align and translate. In: Bengio, Y., LeCun, Y. (eds.) 3rd International Conference on Learning Representations, ICLR 2015, San Diego, CA, USA, 7–9 May 2015, Conference Track Proceedings, pp. 1–15 (2015)

2. Grave, E., Bojanowski, P., Gupta, P., Joulin, A., Mikolov, T.: Learning word vectors for 157 languages. In: Calzolari, N., et al. (eds.) Proceedings of the Eleventh International Conference on Language Resources and Evaluation, LREC 2018, Miyazaki, Japan, 7–12 May 2018, pp. 1–5. European Language Resources Association (ELRA) (2018)

3. Gu, J., Lu, Z., Li, H., Li, V.O.K.: Incorporating copying mechanism in sequence-to-sequence learning. In: Proceedings of the 54th Annual Meeting of the Association for Computational Linguistics, ACL 2016, 7–12 August 2016, Berlin, Germany, Volume 1: Long Papers, pp. 1631–1640. The Association for Computer Linguistics (2016)

4. Ji, Z., Lu, Z., Li, H.: An information retrieval approach to short text conversation. arXiv:abs/1408.6988 (2014)

5. Kumar, V., Joshi, S.: Non-sentential question resolution using sequence to sequence learning. In: Proceedings of COLING 2016, the 26th International Conference on Computational Linguistics: Technical Papers, Osaka, Japan, pp. 2022–2031. The COLING 2016 Organizing Committee (2016). http://aclanthology.org/C16-1190

6. Ni, Z., Kong, F.: Enhancing long-distance dialogue history modeling for better dialogue ellipsis and coreference resolution. In: Wang, L., Feng, Y., Hong, Yu., He, R. (eds.) NLPCC 2021. LNCS (LNAI), vol. 13028, pp. 480–492. Springer, Cham (2021). https://doi.org/10.1007/978-3-030-88480-2_38

7. Pan, Z.F., Bai, K., Wang, Y., Zhou, L., Liu, X.: Improving open-domain dialogue systems via multi-turn incomplete utterance restoration. In: Inui, K., Jiang, J., Ng, V., Wan, X. (eds.) Proceedings of the 2019 Conference on Empirical Methods in Natural Language Processing and the 9th International Joint Conference on Natural Language Processing, EMNLP-IJCNLP 2019, Hong Kong, China, 3–7 November 2019, pp. 1824–1833. Association for Computational Linguistics (2019)

8. Papineni, K., Roukos, S., Ward, T., Zhu, W.: Bleu: a method for automatic evaluation of machine translation. In: Proceedings of the 40th Annual Meeting of the Association for Computational Linguistics, 6–12 July 2002, Philadelphia, PA, USA, pp. 311–318. ACL (2002)

9. Pennington, J., Socher, R., Manning, C.D.: Glove: global vectors for word representation. In: Moschitti, A., Pang, B., Daelemans, W. (eds.) Proceedings of the 2014 Conference on Empirical Methods in Natural Language Processing, EMNLP 2014, 25–29 October 2014, Doha, Qatar, A meeting of SIGDAT, a Special Interest Group of the ACL, pp. 1532–1543. ACL (2014)

10. Quan, J., Xiong, D., Webber, B., Hu, C.: GECOR: an end-to-end generative ellipsis and coreference resolution model for task-oriented dialogue. In: Inui, K., Jiang, J., Ng, V., Wan, X. (eds.) Proceedings of the 2019 Conference on Empirical Methods in Natural Language Processing and the 9th International Joint Conference on Natural Language Processing, EMNLP-IJCNLP 2019, Hong Kong, China, November 3–7, 2019, pp. 4546–4556. Association for Computational Linguistics (2019)

11. Quan, J., Zhang, S., Cao, Q., Li, Z., Xiong, D.: Risawoz: a large-scale multi-domain wizard-of-oz dataset with rich semantic annotations for task-oriented dialogue modeling. In: Webber, B., Cohn, T., He, Y., Liu, Y. (eds.) Proceedings of the 2020 Conference on Empirical Methods in Natural Language Processing, EMNLP 2020, Online, 16–20 November 2020, pp. 930–940. Association for Computational Linguistics (2020)

12. Ritter, A., Cherry, C., Dolan, W.B.: Data-driven response generation in social media. In: Proceedings of the 2011 Conference on Empirical Methods in Natural Language Processing, Edinburgh, Scotland, UK, July 2011, pp. 583–593. Association for Computational Linguistics (2011). http://aclanthology.org/D11-1054

13. Su, H., Shen, X., Zhang, R., Sun, F., Hu, P., Niu, C., Zhou, J.: Improving multi-turn dialogue modelling with utterance rewriter. In: Korhonen, A., Traum, D.R., Màrquez, L. (eds.) Proceedings of the 57th Conference of the Association for Computational Linguistics, ACL

2019, Florence, Italy, July 28- August 2, 2019, Volume 1: Long Papers. pp. 22–31. Association for Computational Linguistics (2019)

14. Xing, C., Wu, W.Y., Wu, Y., Zhou, M., Huang, Y., Ma, W.Y.: Hierarchical recurrent attention network for response generation. In: AAAI Conference on Artificial Intelligence (2017)

15. Zhang, X., Li, C., Yu, D., Davidson, S., Yu, Z.: Filling conversation ellipsis for better social dialog understanding. In: The Thirty-Fourth AAAI Conference on Artificial Intelligence, AAAI 2020, The Thirty-Second Innovative Applications of Artificial Intelligence Conference, IAAI 2020, The Tenth AAAI Symposium on Educational Advances in Artificial Intelligence, EAAI 2020, New York, NY, USA, 7–12 February 2020, pp. 9587–9595. AAAI Press (2020)

TSP Combination Optimization with Semi-local Attention Mechanism

Hua Yang[✉]

School of Software, Tsinghua University, Beijing 100084, China
yang-h17@mails.tsinghua.edu.cn

Abstract. The Traveling Salesman Problem (TSP) is a canonical NP-hard combinatorial optimization problem. The attention mechanism has shown promising performances in natural language processing (NLP) and computer vision (CV). But on the TSP combinatorial optimization problems, the attention mechanism has not achieved satisfactory performance. Therefore, this paper proposes a new attention mechanism, termed a semi-local attention mechanism, to solve combinatorial optimization problems such as the TSP road network graph problem. This paper trains a Long Short-Term Memory (LSTM) network to predict a distribution over different city permutations with the input of a set of city node coordinates, uses negative tour length as the reward, and optimizes the parameters of the LSTM network with Adam optimizer and utilizes a stochastic gradient descent and a policy gradient method to train the model. The extensive experiments demonstrate that the semi-local attention mechanism achieves more close to optimum solutions than the local attention and globe attentional mechanism on 2D TSP combinatorial optimization problem graphs with 200 nodes.

Keywords: combinatorial optimization · attention mechanism · TSP · reinforcement learning · deep learning

1 Introduction

Combinatorial Optimization Problems (COP) [6,11,18,23] are well studied discrete optimization problems. The Traveling salesman problem (TSP) [4,9,15] is a canonical Combinatorial Optimization Problem. Given a graph of city nodes, one needs to search the city node permutations to find the optimal solution of nodes with minimal total tour length [32].

The traditional methods of solving combinatorial optimization problems have the following categories:

- **Exact approaches** [31] To ensure that the best solution is discovered, the exact algorithm examines the whole solution space. Because the search space is too vast, pruning techniques can be used to minimize it. Modeling integer programming (IP) or mixed-integer programming (MIP) is a frequent method. The problem can be solved using branch-and-bound, branch-and-cut, and constraint programming techniques. By continually picking and dividing

L. Iliadis et al. (Eds.): ICANN 2023, LNCS 14262, pp. 469–481, 2023.
https://doi.org/10.1007/978-3-031-44201-8_38

nodes and working with pruning, branch and bound effectively construct the search space into the shape of a tree and successfully locate the ideal answer. Many heuristics have been developed to determine how to specify nodes and assign values to them, which has a substantial impact on the speed with which the solution is found.

- **Approximate methods** [1] The goal of an approximation algorithm is to discover a sub-optimal or near-optimal solution with a particular degree of optimality guarantee. For example, it can ensure that the worst-case answer is many times the optimal solution. There are several polynomial complexity algorithms for the Near-optimal solution, despite the fact that there is no polynomial complexity method for the ideal answer. The greedy algorithm, dynamic programming, primal-dual method, randomized technique, and other ways are examples of such approaches. Christofides algorithm [5] is a prominent example of this solution for the TSP, which is addressed by computing the minimal spanning tree and minimum weight perfect match. The time complexity is polynomial $O(n^3)$.

- **Heuristic algorithms** [19] The purpose of a heuristic algorithm is to discover an approximate solution; however, unlike an approximation algorithm, it has no theoretical guarantee of optimality, which means it cannot guarantee the quality of the solution. However, it can discover a better solution than the approximation approach in most cases. It also features a diverse range of options. The first is to build the solution using a problem-related heuristic, such as Nearest Neighbor or Minimum Spanning Tree; the second is local search, which modifies the intermediate solution locally using the heuristic and searches the solution space in an iterative manner; the third is to use meta-heuristic, such as simulated annealing, tabu search, particle swarm optimization, and so on. The state-of-the-art algorithm for the TSP in this type of method is Lin-Kernighan-Helsgaun (LKH) [10], and the scale of the TSP that it can solve can reach tens of thousands.

However, the drawback of the traditional approaches is that it is intractable when the scale of problems becomes large due to insufficient memory of Graphic Processing Unit (GPU) or Central Processing Unit (CPU). Therefore, recently one tries to find the solutions to the TSP using machine learning. Moreover, many researchers have achieved rather satisfactory results [13,24]. And the attention mechanism has shown promising performances in natural language processing (NLP) and computer vision (CV). But it does not do better on Combinatorial Optimization Problem. This paper tries to make up for it, proposing a new attention method, named the semi-local attention mechanism.

The main contributions of our work are the following:

(1). **Present a new attention mechanism:** We propose a new attention mechanism, a semi-local attention mechanism, to tackle combinatorial optimization problem. This attention mechanism is closer to the optimal solution than the vanilla attention mechanism in combinatorial optimization problems and shows better performance.

(2). **Attention mechanisms play a better role in the field of combinatorial optimization:** The attention mechanism [2,20,26] not only shows good results in computer vision and natural language processing, but also shows better and better performance in the field of combinatorial optimization, we make the attention mechanism [2,20,26] play a better role in the field of combinatorial optimization, digging into the application field of attention mechanism.

2   Related Works

In this section, we review the application of attention mechanism in combinatorial optimization, especially in the TSP. The work [26] proposed a global attention and a local attention mechanism. The global attention always pays to all source input sequences, and the local attention only looks at a selection of source input sequences at a time [20]. One usually classifies Attention-based models into two categories, a local attention based model and a global attention based model. These classes differ in terms of whether the "attention" is placed on all source inputs or on only a few source inputs.

Solving combinatorial optimization problems [6,11] using neural networks dates back to Hopfield [12], who first applied a Hopfield-network for solving the traveling salesman problem instances (TSP) [32]. Deep learning [3] has recently been employed in an offline setting to learn about a whole category of problem instances. Deep reinforcement learning [27] has demonstrated promising results [13,21,24,29,32] when used to solve combinatorial challenges.

In 2015, Google's paper "Order Matters: Sequence to sequence for sets" [30] focused on those scenarios where the order of input and output data is important for learning models, and experimented with sorting and estimating the joint probability distribution in the unknown graph model problem.

In 2017, Vaswani'paper "Attention Is All You Need" [29] caused a huge response from the industry. The modeling of serialized data at that time was mostly based on Recurrent Neural Network (RNN), Long Short-Term Memory (LSTM) or Convolutional Neural Networks (CNN). The Transformer model is proposed in [29], which only uses the attention mechanism, and the model is more accurate, easier to parallelize, and faster to train. The Transformer [29] continues the encoder-decoder architecture, and its encoder and decoder networks are composed of stacked self-attention and point-wise fully connected layers.

In 2018, Nazari et al. [22] extended the method of Bello et al. [3] to vehicle routing problem (VRP), adds a dynamic change part of processing requirements. The basic idea is similar to Bello et al. [3]. It is also based on reinforcement learning. The model is also based on Pointer Network. For VRP, its difficulty is that its problem input is dynamically changing.

In 2018, the paper of Deudon et al. [7] was based on the main idea of Bello et al. [3], which is to solve the TSP based on reinforcement learning. It is still based on Pointer Network's structure output, but its network structure has absorbed the essence of Transformer. The Encoder encodes all city coordinates into a

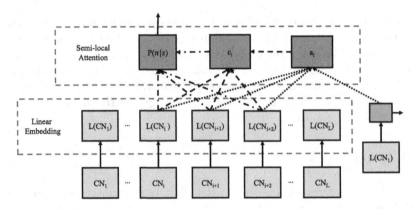

Fig. 1. The proposed semi-local attention architecture. Assuming that the node i is the center, we only take the 3 nodes to the right of the i-th node for linear embedding transformation, then calculate the attention a_i and the score function c_i, and finally calculate the probability of each node.

corresponding number of action vectors based on the structure in the Transformer. The decoder obtains the query vector based on the last three actions, and the result is obtained through the Pointing mechanism together with the action vector output by the encoder. In the experimental, it is compared with Christofides algorithm [5], OR_tools [8] and other industry solutions, and the solution quality and running time are comparable. It also performed well when the model trained on TSP50 was directly used on TSP100, indicating its generalization ability. When combined with local search 2-opt heuristic, it can also quickly improve the effect, showing the benefits of combining machine learning with traditional operations research.

In 2019, the paper of Kool et al. [17] was also based on the Transformer model. Compared with the original Transformer model, positional encoding is not used in the encoder, which makes node embedding independent of the input order. The other parts basically use the stacked multi-head attention (MHA) and feed-forward structures in the Transformer architecture to get the node embedding corresponding to each city node graph. The average of node embedding is regarded as graph embedding. This embedding will be output to the decoder. Decoder uses the classic autoregressive mode. In each step, the output of the current step is based on the embedding of the encoder and the output of the previous step. The Decoder network is also based on the attention mechanism. A big difference from the previous work is that it introduces a context node to represent the context vector during decoding. Finally, the decoder structure has a single attention head (MHA with m = 1), and the output through softmax is the output of the current step. The difference here is that the baseline function is obtained through the rollout method [32].

The graph attention network [7,16,17] is used to extract the features of each node in graph structure. An explicitly forgetting mechanism is introduced to construct a solution which only requires the last three selected nodes per step. Then the constructed solution is improved by 2OPT local search. A context vector is introduced to represent the decoding context and the model is trained by the REINFORCE algorithm [27] with a deterministic greedy rollout baseline [27].

3 Model Architecture

Our proposed semi-local attention mechanism architecture illustrated in Fig. 1, including input layer, which is L ($L \in R^2$, node number, sequence length) city nodes CN_L, linear embedding layer, which transformates the input layer into hidden layers h_t, and semi-local attention layer, which comprises a variable-length vector a_i, a context vector c_i, and a probability distribution $p(\pi|s)$. The semi-local attention mechanism we proposed means that at time step $t = i$, we only consider half of the length of a quarter of the input after i, rather than the entire interval centered on a city point of the local attention mechanism, this is because the city node before the i-th time step of the TSP has been visited and does not need to participate in the calculation. As shown in Fig. 1, we assume that the input length is 12, $t = i$, and we only take the 3 input nodes after i to participate in the operation, rather than the 6 nodes centered on i to participate in the operation.

At each time step t, the model will first enter the hidden state h_t at the top level of the LSTM. Then, our goal is to derive a context vector c_t, which captures the coordinate information of the city node of the relevant data source to help predict the city node information h_t output by the current target. Although these models differ in the way they derive the context vector c_t, they share the same subsequent steps. Note that considering the target hidden state h_t and the source context vector c_t, we use a simple connection layer to combine the information from the two vectors to produce an attention hidden state Eq. 1. The attention vector $Hidden_t$ is then fed through the softmax layer to produce the predictive distribution Eq. 2. i.e.

$$Hidden_t = \tanh(W_c[c_t; h_t]), \tag{1}$$

$$q_\theta(\pi|s) = \text{softmax}(W_s Hidden_t). \tag{2}$$

When calculating the context vector c_t, a standard global attentional model takes into account all of the encoder's hidden states. By comparing the current target decode hidden state h_t with each source input encode hidden state h_s, a variable-length vector a_t Eq. 3 is created, whose size equals the number of time steps on the source side. Here, the scoring function is referred to as a content-based function for which Eq. 4 are considered.

Global attention has a disadvantage that it must process all source coded input city nodes for each target city node. In order to solve this defect, the local attention mechanism only focuses on a small part of the source input node of each target decoding output.

$$a_t(s) = \frac{\exp(\text{score}(h_t, h_s))}{\sum_{s'} \exp(\text{score}(h_t, h_s))}, \tag{3}$$

$$\text{score}(h_t, h_s) = V \text{softmax}(\frac{QK^T}{\sqrt{d_k}}). \tag{4}$$

The vanilla local attention mechanism selectively focuses on a small context window. This method avoids the expensive calculations caused by soft attention [20] and is easier to train than hard attention methods [32]. In concrete details, the model first generates an aligned position p_t for each target input at time t. The context vector c_t is then derived as a weighted average over the set of source hidden states within the window$[p_t - w, p_t + w]$; w is empirically selected Unlike the global approach, the local alignment vector a_t is now fixed-dimensional.

4   Model Training

In terms of the TSP, we define a TSP instance s as a network with n nodes, with node $i \in \{1, 2, 3, ..., n\}$ represented by features x_i , which is the coordinate of node i. Input graphs are represented as a series of n cities in a two-dimensional space $s = \{x_i\}$. We are interested in discovering a tour technique, which is a permutation of the nodes π. The length of a tour defined by a permutation π as

$$L(\pi|s) = \sum_{i=1}^{n-1} \|x_{\pi_i} - x_{\pi_{i+1}}\|_2 + \|x_{\pi_1} - x_{\pi_n}\|_2. \tag{5}$$

A tour $\pi = (\pi_1, \pi_2, \pi_3, ..., \pi_n)$ is defined as a solution with a permutation of the nodes, thus $\pi_i \in \{1, 2, 3, ..., n\}$. Our attention-based encoder-decoder model [2] defines $p(\pi|s)$ as a stochastic policy for finding a solution given a problem instance s. It is factorized and parameterized by θ as

$$p_\theta(\pi|s) = \prod_{i=1}^{n} p_\theta(\pi_i|\pi_{1...i-1}, s). \tag{6}$$

Because the input length of the pointer network is changeable, we utilized it as an input to the model. Our training goal function is the average tour length (ATL) given an input graph s, which is defined as Eq. 7.

$$C(\theta|s) = \mathbb{E}_{p_\theta(\pi|s)} L(\pi|s). \tag{7}$$

We use stochastic gradient descents (SGD) and policy gradient methods to optimize the parameters [32]. The gradient of Eq. 8 is formulated using the well-known REINFORCE algorithm [27],

$$\nabla_\theta C(\theta|s) = \mathbb{E}_{p_\theta(\pi|s)}[(L(\pi|s) - b(s))\nabla_\theta \log p_\theta(\pi|s)], \tag{8}$$

Table 1. The average tour length of the TSP with a semi-local attention mechanics. "Att" is the abbreviation of "Attention". Difference Length, left column is global attention subtract optimal length, middle column is local attention subtract optimal length, right column is semi-local attention of $k = L/4(L = 20, 50, 100, 200)$ equal 25 subtract optimal length. Optimal Gap Ratio, the left column is the first column of Difference Length divided by optimal length, the middle column is the second column of Difference Length divided by optimal length, the right column is the third column of Difference Length divided by optimal length.

Task	Example Numbers	Global Att	Local Att	Optimal Length	semi-local Attention k = 5, 12, 25, 50	Difference Length	Optimal Gap Ratio(%)
TSP20	1280	4.03	3.89	3.84	3.91, 3.95, 3.89, 3.92	0.19, 0.05, 0.05	4.95, 1.30, 1.30
	12800	3.94	3.95	3.84	3.94, 3.95, 3.94, 3.96	0.10, 0.11, 0.10	2.60, 2.86, 2.60
	128000	4.03	3.86	3.84	3.94, 3.91, 3.87, 3.93	0.19, 0.02, 0.03	4.95, 0.52, 0.78
	1280000	4.25	4.07	3.83	3.98, 3.99, 3.95, 3.97	0.42, 0.24, 0.12	10.97, 6.27, 3.13
TSP50	1280	5.82	5.92	5.73	5.94, 5.91, 5.83, 5.92	0.09, 0.19, 0.10	1.57, 3.32, 1.73
	12800	5.89	5.94	5.73	5.93, 5.91, 5.87, 5.86	0.16, 0.21, 0.13	2.79, 3.66, 2.27
	128000	5.83	5.84	5.74	5.88, 5.94, 5.85, 5.90	0.09, 0.10, 0.11	1.57, 1.74, 1.91
	1280000	5.93	5.83	5.72	5.88, 5.91, 5.77, 5.78	0.21, 0.11, 0.05	3.67, 1.92, 0.87
TSP100	1280	8.91	8.98	7.82	8.69, 8.71, 8.57, 8.72	1.09, 1.16, 0.75	13.93, 14.83, 9.59
	12800	8.41	8.63	7.83	8.01, 8.11, 8.04, 8.19	0.58, 0.80, 0.21	7.41, 10.21, 2.68
	128000	7.95	8.21	7.77	7.98, 8.02, 7.83, 7.99	0.18, 0.44, 0.06	2.32, 5.66, 0.77
	1280000	7.84	7.91	7.75	7.94, 8.05, 7.87, 7.93	0.09, 0.16, 0.12	1.16, 2.06, 1.55

where $b(s)$ denotes a baseline, being independent on π and estimates the average tour length (ATL) to reduce the variance of the gradients [32]. Our selection is the critic network which learns a value function with the Asynchronous Advantage Actor-Critic (A3C) algorithm [27]. We take a look at the graphs $s_1, s_2, ..., s_B \sim S$, the gradient in Eq. 8 is estimated with Monte Carlo sampling:

$$\nabla_\theta C(\theta) = \frac{1}{B} \sum_{i=1}^{B} (L(\pi_i|s_i) - b(s_i)) \nabla_\theta \log p_\theta(\pi_i|s_i). \tag{9}$$

5 Experiments

We conducted experiments to verify our proposed model architecture, semi-local attention mechanism, also considered 100 2D Euclidean TSP tasks, where the number of nodes is 20, 30, 50, 80, 100, and 200. City node coordinates are randomly generated from a uniform distribution in units of unit square [0,1]*[0,1].

All of our models are trained on a single Geforce RTX 2080Ti GPU with 11GB of GPU memory, 32GB of CPU memory, and a single layer LSTM with 256 hidden units, mini-batches of 128 sequences, LSTM cells with 256 hidden units, and embedding the two coordinates of each point in a 256-dimensional space. We utilize the Adam optimizer to train our models and use an initial learning rate of 10^{-3} for TSP20, TSP50, and TSP100, which we decay by a factor of 0.96 every 5000 steps. Our parameters are evenly initialized at random within the range $[-0.08, 0.08]$, and our gradients' L2 norms are clipped to 2.0. We can employ up to two attention glimmers at a time.

We report the two kinds of metrics, average tour length (ATL) and optimality gap ratio (OGR) which is the average percentage ratio of the predicted tour length relative to optimal solutions, to evaluate performance of our model and other baselines.

Table 2. The Comparison of the semi-local attention mechanism with various solvers, several heuristic algorithms and the work of other similar authors. The number of city nodes in the TSP graph are 20, 30, 50, 100 and 200. The abbreviation "ATL" stands for "Average Travel Length". The abbreviation "OGR" stands for "Optimal Gap Ratio".

Method	TSP20		TSP30		TSP50		TSP100		TSP200	
	ATL	OGR	ATL	OGR	ATL	OGR	ATL	OGR	ATL	OGR
Concorde	3.83	0.00%	4.56	0.00%	5.71	0.00%	7.77	0.00%	10.53	0.00%
Gurobi	3.83	0.00%	4.56	0.00%	5.71	0.00%	7.77	0.00%	10.53	0.00%
LKH3	3.83	0.00%	4.56	0.00%	5.71	0.00%	7.77	0.00%	10.53	0.00%
OR-Tools	3.84	0.26%	4.60	0.88%	5.80	1.57%	7.95	2.32%	11.74	11.49%
Random Insertion	4.06	6.01%	4.89	7.24%	6.25	9.46%	8.53	9.78%	14.28	35.61%
Nearest Insertion	4.38	11.75%	5.27	15.57%	6.75	18.21%	9.46	21.75%	16.82	58.40%
Farthest Insertion	3.89	1.31%	4.79	5.04%	6.03	5.60%	8.37	7.72%	13.99	32.86%
Nearest Neighbor	4.43	13.05%	5.73	25.66%	6.88	20.49%	9.67	24.45%	14.83	41.12%
Cheapest insertion	4.21	9.92%	5.04	10.53%	6.39	11.91%	9.37	20.59%	15.16	43.97%
Christofides	4.11	7.31%	5.21	14.25%	6.21	8.76%	9.51	22.39%	14.92	41.69%
Bello et al. [3]	3.85	0.52%	4.78	4.83%	5.89	3.15%	8.31	6.95%	13.42	27.45%
Dai et al. [16]	3.89	1.31%	4.72	3.51%	5.96	4.38%	8.28	6.56%	15.87	50.71%
Kool et al. [17]	3.86	0.78%	4.68	2.63%	5.76	0.86%	7.98	2.70%	13.25	25.83%
Nazari et al. [22]	3.97	3.66%	4.87	6.80%	6.08	6.48%	8.44	8.62%	14.62	38.84%
Deudon et al. [7]	3.84	0.26%	4.80	5.26%	5.81	1.75%	8.85	13.90%	14.99	42.36%
Qiang Ma et al. [21]	3.84	0.26%	4.69	2.85%	5.78	1.23%	8.05	3.60%	13.89	31.91%
Joshi et al. [14]	3.84	0.26%	4.73	3.73%	6.14	7.53%	8.05	3.60%	12.94	22.89%
Sultana et al. [25]	3.87	1.04%	4.72	3.51%	5.85	2.45%	8.31	6.95%	13.93	32.29%
semi-local(ours)	**3.84**	**0.26%**	**4.68**	**2.63%**	**5.77**	**1.05%**	**7.93**	**2.06%**	**12.84**	**21.94%**

5.1   Results and Analysis

For each problem, we report performance on 100 test instances. At inference time we use greedy decoding where we select the best action at each step, or sampling decoding where we sample 100 solutions and report the best. More sampling improves solution quality at the cost of increased computational complexity. In Table 2 we use the solutions of various solvers as the baselines for comparison of other methods, and compare greedy decoding against baselines which also construct a single solution, and compare sampling against baselines that also consider multiple solutions with sampling, beam search or local search. For each problem, we also report the "best possible solution": either optimal via Concorde, Gurobi, LKH3, OR-tools or a problem specific state-of-the-art algorithm.

The comparison of the vanilla global attention mechanism, the vanilla local attention mechanism [20] and the semi-local attention mechanism we proposed is shown in Table 1, which demonstrates the performance differences of various attention mechanisms on the TSP, and we use the average travel length of 100 random test cases [32]. As shown in Table 1, when the task is TSP20, in Optimal Gap Ratio, except when the training sample is 128000 our semi-local attention mechanis is not the best, the test results of the other three training samples, the Optimal Gap Ratios of our semi-local attention mechanis solution are 1.30%, 2.60%, and 3.13%, respectively, which are lower than the corresponding global attention and local attention 4.95%, 2.60%, 10.97%, 1.30%, 2.86%, and 6.27%. Our semi-local attention mechanis solution is closer to the optimal solution than others. In TSP100, when the training examples are 128000, the Optimal Gap Ratio of our semi-local attention mechanis solution is 0.77%, but global attention is 2.32% and local attention is 5.66%.

In Table 2, the performance of our semi-local attention mechanism compared with a variety of baselines: a variety of solvers; open source software for combinatorial optimisation, Google OR-Tools [8] which is a mature and widely used solver for combinatorial optimisation problems based on meta-heuristics; learning models using supervised techniques; and learning methods using reinforcement learning. We compare against Christofied local search, Cheapest, Nearest, Random and Farthest Insertion, as well as Nearest Neighbor in Table 2. We also focus our comparison to the recently proposed deep learning methods [3,7,13,16,17,21,22] using their publicly released implementations. The description of baseline experimental procedures is as follows:

- Concorde: Concorde [28] is a computer code for the symmetric TSP and some related network optimisation problems. Concorde's TSP solver has been used to obtain the optimal solutions for all random instances.
- LKH3: LKH [10] is an effective implementation of the Lin-Kernighan heuristic for solving the traveling salesman problem. LKH3 is an extension of LKH for solving constrained traveling salesman problems and vehicle routing problems.
- OR-Tools: Google Optimisation Tools OR-Tools [8] is an open-source solver for combinatorial optimisation problems. OR-Tools contains one of the best available vehicle routing problem solver, which is a generalisation of the TSP and implemented many heuristics for finding an initial solution and meta-heuristics, we use it as our baseline.
- Nearest Insertion: The nearest insertion will insert the node into the nearest set of nodes, because this insertion operation has the lowest cost in the total stroke length.
- Farthest Insertion: The farthest insertion needs to select two cities and connect them to get the lowest cost tour, and then find the farthest city in this tour. Repeat this step until each city has to complete the tour.

In Table 2, we compare the semi-local attention mechanism with various solvers, several heuristic algorithms, and the similar work of other authors. The number of city nodes in the TSP graph are 20, 30, 50, 100 and 200. The abbreviation "ATL" stands for "Average Travel Length". The abbreviation "OGR" stands for "Optimal Gap Ratio". We chose the most commonly used solvers in the field of combinatorial optimization: Concode, Gurobi, LKH3, Google OR-Tools. We report optimal results by Gurobi, and by Concorde which is faster than Gurobi as it is specialized for the TSP, as well as LKH3 which is a state-of-the-art heuristic solver that empirically also finds optimal solutions in time comparable to Gurobi. Compared with other performances, various heuristic algorithms including Random Insertion, Nearest Insertion, Farthest Insertion, Nearest Neighbor, Cheapest insertion and Christofides have the longest average travel length and the worst performance. We compare against Nearest, Cheapest, Random and Farthest Insertion as well as Nearest Neighbor which is the only non-learned baseline algorithm that also constructs a tour directly in order.

We report on 20, 30, 50, 100 and 200 node graphs, respectively. In the TSP30 instance, compared with similar work of other authors, the performance of the semi-local attention mechanism is notably improved for both Bello et al. (2.20%), Dai et al. (0.88%), Kool et al. (0.0%), Nazari et al. (4.17%), Deudon et al. (2.63%), Qiang Ma et al. (0.22%), Joshi et al. (1.10%) and Sultanan et al. (0.88%). In other TSP instance, compared with similar work of other authors, the performance of semi-local attention mechanism significantly outperforms other baseline models as well.

Selecting TSP20 and TSP100 tasks, we compare the solution of the semi-local attention mechanism with the solution of the optimal solver Concorde. In TSP20 task, we test the model with random sampling search, which is the training model for 1280000 examples and 10 epoches. The average tour length of a semi-local attention mechanism is 3.84, which is about equal to optimal tour length 3.83. When the number of the city node is 100, we test the model with beam search with size 10, which is the training model for 128000 examples and 5 epoches. The average tour length of a semi-local attention mechanism is 7.93, but its optimal tour length 7.77.

5.2   Greedy Search and Beam Search

In this experiment, we used three different decoders:

- Greedy decoder: In each decoding step, the node with the highest probability is selected as the next destination node.
- Sampling randomly decoder: We sample 100 solutions and report the best. More sampling improves solution quality at increased computation time. We use polynomial distribution to select a city node and compare greedy decoding against baselines that also construct a single solution.
- Beam search decoder: Beam search (BS) decoder, tracks the most probable path, and then chooses the one with the minimum tour length. Our results show that by applying the beam search algorithm, the quality of the solution can be improved with only a slight increase in calculation time.

For faster training and generating feasible solutions, we have used a masking scheme which sets the log-probabilities of infeasible solutions to -10^8 if a particular condition is satisfied. In decoder, the predicted probabilities are used to select the next node at the current step via sampling or greedily selecting the most probable node. Since decoders directly output probabilities over all nodes independent of one-another, we can obtain valid TSP tours to traverse the graph starting from a random node and masking previously visited nodes which is a semi-local attention.

During inference test, we can increase the capacity of greedy search via limited width breadth-first beam search. Meanwhile, we can sample b solutions from the learnt policy and select the shortest tour among them. Naturally, searching longer or sampling more solutions allows trading off run time for solution quality. However, it has been noted that using large b for search or sampling or local search during inference test may overshadow an architecture's inability to a semi-local attention. To better understand a semi-local attention, we focus on using greedy search and beam search or sampling with small $b \in [5, 100]$.

6   Conclusion

Solving Combinatorial Optimization is difficult in general. Thanks to decades of research, solvers for the TSP are highly efficient, able to solve large instances. With little engineering and no labels, Neural Networks trained with Reinforcement Learning are able to learn clever heuristics for the TSP. This paper proposes that the semi-local attention mechanism is applied to solve the traveling salesman problem in typical combinatorial optimization problems, and deep reinforcement learning is used to construct the network structure. Through comparison with various solvers, heuristic algorithms, and similar work by other authors, it is found that the semi-local attention mechanism can achieve the state-of-the-art results and the optimal gap ratio is the closest to the optimal solution.

References

1. Arora, S.: The approximability of NP-hard problems. In: Proceedings of the Thirtieth Annual ACM Symposium on Theory of Computing, pp. 337–348 (1998)
2. Bahdanau, D., Cho, K., Bengio, Y.: Neural machine translation by jointly learning to align and translate. arXiv preprint arXiv:1409.0473 (2014)
3. Bello, I., Pham, H., Le, Q.V., Norouzi, M., Bengio, S.: Neural combinatorial optimization with reinforcement learning. arXiv preprint arXiv:1611.09940 (2016)
4. Boese, K.D.: Cost versus distance in the traveling salesman problem. Citeseer (1995)
5. Christofides, N.: Worst-case analysis of a new heuristic for the travelling salesman problem. Carnegie-Mellon Univ Pittsburgh Pa Management Sciences Research Group, Technical report (1976)
6. Cook, W., Lovász, L., Seymour, P.D. (eds.): Combinatorial Optimization: Papers from the DIMACS Special Year, vol. 20. American Mathematical Soc., Providence (1995)

7. Deudon, M., Cournut, P., Lacoste, A., Adulyasak, Y., Rousseau, L.-M.: Learning heuristics for the TSP by policy gradient. In: van Hoeve, W.-J. (ed.) CPAIOR 2018. LNCS, vol. 10848, pp. 170–181. Springer, Cham (2018). https://doi.org/10.1007/978-3-319-93031-2_12

8. Google, I.: Google optimization tools(or-tools) (2018). https://github.com/google/or-tools

9. Gutin, G., Punnen, A.P.: The Traveling Salesman Problem and Its Variations, vol. 12. Springer, New York (2006). https://doi.org/10.1007/b101971

10. Helsgaun, K.: An extension of the Lin-Kernighan-Helsgaun TSP solver for constrained traveling salesman and vehicle routing problems: Technical report (2017)

11. Hochba, D.S.: Approximation algorithms for NP-hard problems. ACM SIGACT News **28**(2), 40–52 (1997)

12. Hopfield, J.J., Tank, D.W.: Neural computation of decisions in optimization problems. Biol. Cybern. **52**(3), 141–152 (1985)

13. Joshi, C.K., Cappart, Q., Rousseau, L.M., Laurent, T., Bresson, X.: Learning tsp requires rethinking generalization. arXiv preprint arXiv:2006.07054 (2020)

14. Joshi, C.K., Laurent, T., Bresson, X.: An efficient graph convolutional network technique for the travelling salesman problem. arXiv preprint arXiv:1906.01227 (2019)

15. Jünger, M., Reinelt, G., Rinaldi, G.: The traveling salesman problem. Handbooks Oper. Res. Manage. Sci. **7**, 225–330 (1995)

16. Khalil, E., Dai, H., Zhang, Y., Dilkina, B., Song, L.: Learning combinatorial optimization algorithms over graphs. In: Advances in Neural Information Processing Systems, pp. 6348–6358 (2017)

17. Kool, W., Van Hoof, H., Welling, M.: Attention, learn to solve routing problems! arXiv preprint arXiv:1803.08475 (2018)

18. Li, W., Ding, Y., Yang, Y., Sherratt, R.S., Park, J.H., Wang, J.: Parameterized algorithms of fundamental np-hard problems: a survey. HCIS **10**(1), 1–24 (2020)

19. Lin, S., Kernighan, B.W.: An effective heuristic algorithm for the traveling-salesman problem. Oper. Res. **21**(2), 498–516 (1973)

20. Luong, M.T., Pham, H., Manning, C.D.: Effective approaches to attention-based neural machine translation. arXiv preprint arXiv:1508.04025 (2015)

21. Ma, Q., Ge, S., He, D., Thaker, D., Drori, I.: Combinatorial optimization by graph pointer networks and hierarchical reinforcement learning. arXiv preprint arXiv:1911.04936 (2019)

22. Nazari, M., Oroojlooy, A., Snyder, L., Takác, M.: Reinforcement learning for solving the vehicle routing problem. In: Advances in Neural Information Processing Systems, pp. 9839–9849 (2018)

23. Papadimitriou, C.H., Steiglitz, K.: Combinatorial Optimization: Algorithms and Complexity. Courier Corporation, North Chelmsford (1998)

24. Peng, B., Wang, J., Zhang, Z.: A deep reinforcement learning algorithm using dynamic attention model for vehicle routing problems. In: Li, K., Li, W., Wang, H., Liu, Y. (eds.) ISICA 2019. CCIS, vol. 1205, pp. 636–650. Springer, Singapore (2020). https://doi.org/10.1007/978-981-15-5577-0_51

25. Sultana, N., Chan, J., Sarwar, T., Qin, A.: Learning to optimise general TSP instances. Int. J. Mach. Learn. Cybern. **13**, 2213–2228 (2022)

26. Sutskever, I., Vinyals, O., Le, Q.V.: Sequence to sequence learning with neural networks. In: Advances in Neural Information Processing Systems, vol. 27, pp. 3104–3112 (2014)

27. Sutton, R.S., Barto, A.G.: Reinforcement Learning: An Introduction. MIT Press, Cambridge (2018)

28. Chvatal, V., Applegate, D.L., Bixby, R.E., Cook, W.J.: Concorde TSP solver (2006). https://www.math.uwaterloo.ca/tsp/concorde/
29. Vaswani, A., et al.: Attention is all you need. In: Advances in Neural Information Processing Systems, pp. 5998–6008 (2017)
30. Vinyals, O., Bengio, S., Kudlur, M.: Order matters: sequence to sequence for sets. arXiv preprint arXiv:1511.06391 (2015)
31. Woeginger, G.J.: Exact algorithms for NP-hard problems: a survey. In: Jünger, M., Reinelt, G., Rinaldi, G. (eds.) Combinatorial Optimization — Eureka, You Shrink! LNCS, vol. 2570, pp. 185–207. Springer, Heidelberg (2003). https://doi.org/10.1007/3-540-36478-1_17
32. Yang, H.: Extended attention mechanism for TSP problem. In: 2021 International Joint Conference on Neural Networks (IJCNN), pp. 1–8. IEEE (2021)

UDCGN: Uncertainty-Driven Cross-Guided Network for Depth Completion of Transparent Objects

Yutao Hu[1], Zheng Wang[2]([⊠]), Jiacheng Chen[1], Yutong Qian[1],
and Wanliang Wang[1]

[1] College of Computer Science and Technology, Zhejiang University of Technology,
Hangzhou 310023, Zhejiang, China
[2] School of Computer and Computational Sciences, Zhejiang University City College,
Hangzhou 310015, Zhejiang, China
wang-cc23@caai.cn

Abstract. In the field of robotics, most perception methods rely on depth information captured by RGB-D cameras. However, the ability of depth sensors to capture depth information is hindered by the reflection and refraction of light on transparent objects. Existing methods of completing transparent objects' depth information are usually impractical due to the need for fixtures or unacceptably slow inference speeds. To address this challenge, we propose an efficient multi-stage architecture called UDCGN. This method progressively learns completion functions from sparse inputs by dividing the overall recovery process into more manageable steps. To enhance the interaction between different branches, Cross-Guided Fusion Block (CGFB) is introduced into each stage. The CGFB dynamically generates convolution kernel parameters from guided features and convolutes them with input features. Furthermore, the Adaptive Uncertainty-Driven Loss Function (AUDL) is developed to handle the uncertainty issue of sparse depth. It optimizes pixels with high uncertainty by adapting different distributions. Comprehensive experiments on representative datasets demonstrate that UDCGN significantly outperforms state-of-the-art methods in terms of both performance and efficiency.

Keywords: Transparent object · Depth completion · Neural network

1 Introduction

Depth completion is a vital task in computer vision, involving the conversion of sparse depth images to dense depth images. This task is critical for numerous downstream applications, including autonomous driving [1], robot navigation [2], and robot manipulation [3]. However, transparent objects pose a significant challenge for RGB-D sensors due to their reflective and refractive qualities, as demonstrated in Fig. 1. Despite recent advances in depth completion techniques,

© The Author(s), under exclusive license to Springer Nature Switzerland AG 2023
L. Iliadis et al. (Eds.): ICANN 2023, LNCS 14262, pp. 482–495, 2023.
https://doi.org/10.1007/978-3-031-44201-8_39

Fig. 1. UDCGN is proposed to complete the depth information of transparent objects from an RGB-D image.

accurately reconstructing the geometry of transparent objects remains an ongoing research problem.

Some of previous works on estimating the geometry of transparent objects have been studied under restricted conditions [4,5], which makes it difficult to apply to other scenarios. Based on the assumption that the item is rotational and symmetric, Phillips et al. [4] estimate the geometry of transparent objects from two calibrated views of a scene. To determine the geometry of reflective objects, Qian et al. [5] solve an optimizer function that imposes a position-normal consistency constraint. Nevertheless, it requires a fixed background under the assumption that the rays refract only twice.

Convolutional Neural Networks (CNNs) have gained popularity because of their success in learning generalized priors for massive amounts of data. In this situation, ClearGrasp [3] is the first CNN-based method for the deep completion of transparent objects and it achieves excellent results. However, it may be difficult to use in real-time applications due to the expensive nature of its global optimization. Furthermore, Zhu et al. [6] propose Local Implicit Depth Function (LIDF), a two-stage framework that makes use of local implicit functions. A local implicit neural representation based on ray-voxel pairs and a self-correcting refinement model to progressively enhance depth completeness are the essential components of LIDF. It further improves the precision and speed of deep completion.

Our study builds a multi-stage architecture to speed up the depth completion algorithm's inference process even further. More specifically, the multi-stage aims to complete depth progressively. There are two branches, the RGB branch and the depth branch, in our proposed architecture. Using an RGB image as its input, the RGB branch creates dense depth maps that are somewhat accurate near object boundaries, but they might be overly sensitive to changes in texture or color. The depth branch takes sparse depth images as inputs that, while generally reliable, were hampered by the dense noise present around object boundaries in the sparse input.

In addition, the Cross-Guided Fusion Block (CGFB) is inserted as a flexible plugin to help the kernel capture more representative patterns and fuse features. The guided features, which are the output of another branch, are used to generate modulated kernel parameters. After that, modulated kernel convolute with the input features. To further improve the effectiveness and efficiency of the optimization, the Adaptive Uncertainty-Driven Loss (AUDL) is suggested to model the uncertainty of data by taking into the inherent noise in the data. Our method produces superior results while using fewer model parameters, and the inference speed satisfies the real-time needs of the robot.

The main contributions of this work are summarized below:

1. We propose UDCGN, a multi-stage architecture for depth completion of transparent objects.
2. A Cross-Guided Fusion Block (CGFB) is effective at aggregating RGB features and depth features by dynamic convolution.
3. An Adaptive Uncertainty-Driven Loss (AUDL) that models the inherent noise in the data, i.e., back-propagation is performed by adaptively assigning different weights to each pixel by considering the uncertainty of the data.
4. We compared our UDCGN to current state-of-the-art methods. The results are encouraging in accuracy and speed. We further provide detailed ablation studies to demonstrate the effectiveness of the proposed module.

2   Related Work

2.1   Depth Completion

Depth completion is a task that involves taking a sparse depth image obtained by depth sensors and completing a dense depth image. Depending on whether or not there is a guide image, it can be separated into RGB guided depth completion and unguided depth completion. The RGB-guided depth completion takes a sparse depth image and its corresponding RGB image as input [7–10], whereas the unguided methods use only a sparse depth image to predict the dense images [11–13]. RGB-guided approaches usually outperform unguided depth completion methods due to the abundance of semantic cues offered by RGB images. Whereas, for transparent objects that are common in daily life, it's more challenging to complete the depth image due to their distinctive optical features. To solve the issue, Sajjan et al. [3] use surface normal and occlusion boundaries as intermediate stereoscopic information. Zhu et al. [6] introduce a local implicit function built on ray-voxel pairs to help complete the depth information. As with the above method, our method belongs to late fusion with RGB images guided. We designed a multi-stage architecture to complete the depth image progressively. The dual-branch is designed for handling RGB and depth information separately.

2.2   Feature Fusion

Depending on the fusion methods used, RGB-guided depth completion can be characterized as early fusion [14–17] or late fusion [18–20]. Early fusion models directly concatenate the sparse depth image and RGB image before passing through the model [14,15], or aggregate features after the first convolutional layer [16,17]. Late fusion techniques, by contrast, usually employ two sub-networks to handle different modalities [20] or the RGB and depth features are extracted by using two encoders independently, and then fused and fed to the decoder [18,

19]. However, some methods fuse features directly by addition or concatenation, which is far from effective. To this end, dynamic convolution [21] is employed in UDCGN to fuse features more closely and effectively.

2.3 Uncertainty Estimation

Since the uncertainty-driven method was initially introduced [22], numerous research have attempted to model uncertainty in order to improve the performance and robustness of neural networks in many tasks [23–25]. The uncertainty can be divided into epistemic uncertainty and aleatoric uncertainty [22]. The epistemic uncertainty, which expresses how uncertain the model is regarding its predictions, is related to the model and is caused by incomplete training. This uncertainty can theoretically be eliminated if it is given more training data to compensate for the lack of knowledge in the existing model. The observed data's inherent noise causes another sort of uncertainty, known as aleatoric uncertainty. This uncertainty cannot be eliminated. The uncertainty-driven loss is designed to model the aleatoric uncertainty. Earlier approaches for uncertainty-driven loss, however, only used one probability distribution. We propose AUDL that can choose various distributions based on the threshold value.

3 Method

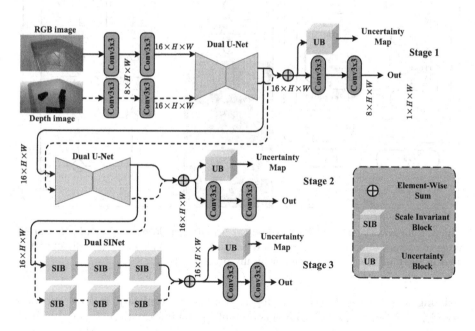

Fig. 2. Architecture of UDCGN for depth completion of transparent objects. Our UDCGN consists of a multi-stage design incorporating efficient fusion modules.

The proposed UDCGN, as shown in Fig. 2, comprises two branches and three stages which is designed to progressively complete depth images and efficiently integrate RGB and depth information. To prevent interfering with the completion, we first utilize a single U-Net to predict the mask of transparent objects from the color image. The mask is used for remove incorrect depth information.

UDCGN takes a sparse depth image $D \in \mathbb{R}^{H \times W \times 1}$ and its corresponding RGB image $I \in \mathbb{R}^{H \times W \times 3}$ as input. The uncertainty map $S \in \mathbb{R}^{H \times W \times 1}$ and dense depth image $\hat{D} \in \mathbb{R}^{H \times W \times 1}$ is output in each stage, and then passed to Formula.9 to calculate loss. During test, the sparse depth image, which is generated in stage3, is used to calculate metrics. Then, we go into depth about our methodology, which has three main parts: (a) the architecture of UDCGN (Sect. 3.1); (b) a Cross-Guided Fusion Block (CGFB) (Sect. 3.2); and (c) an Adaptive Uncertainty-Driven Loss Function (AUDL) (Sect. 3.3).

3.1   Overview

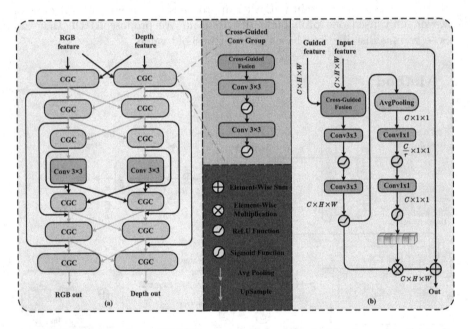

Fig. 3. Subnetworks of our UDCGN are: (a) An encoder-decoder is used in the earlier stage to extract multi-scale contextual data, and (b) the scale-invariant subnetwork is used in the final stage to provide a spatially precise output.

Existing single-stage CNNs for depth completion typically use an encoder-decoder architecture, which can encode multi-scale information efficiently. However, due to downsampling operations, it generally sacrifices spatial detail information. On the other hand, the single-scale feature network produces images with preserved spatial detail, and yet it cannot gather global information. Therefore, the proposed UDCGN incorporates two various network designs in accordance with a multi-stage architecture.

In addition, As there are two types of input images: RGB and depth images, the dual-branch is designed to process different modalities. Since all of the branches have the same network architecture, for the sake of simplicity, we only illustrate a separate branch. Given an input image, Each branch first applies two 3×3 convolutional layers to extract low-level features and then passes the features into subnetworks. The first two stages are based on encoder-decoder subnetworks that learn the global contextual information. By contrast, the fine texture is preserved in the final stage, which uses a scale-invariant subnetwork that runs at the same resolution.

Dual-UNet. To acquire information globally, UNet [26] is utilized as the encoder-decoder subnetworks. Input features are turned into output features via a four-level symmetric encoder-decoder, as shown in Fig. 3(a). The CGFB is inserted at each encoder-decoder level to fuse features. The encoder expands channel capacity while hierarchically reducing spatial size starting with the high-resolution input. The decoder gradually recovers the high-resolution representations from the input of low-resolution latent features. We use avgpooling and bilinear interpolation procedures for feature upsampling and downsampling. By skipping connections, the encoder features are combined with the decoder features to benefit the recovery process.

Dual-SINet. In order to preserve spatial detail, the scale-invariant network (SINet) is introduced in the last stage. SINet produces spatially-enriched high-resolution features without using any downsampling operations. In other words, it performs the convolution operation without modifying the resolution. SINet is made up of multiple scale-invariant blocks (SIBs), each of which comprises a CGFB, two 3×3 convolution layers and SE block [27], as illustrated in Fig. 3(b). The SE block prioritizes more crucial channel-level information by giving channel weights.

3.2   Cross-Guided Fusion Block

Since RGB and depth images need to be processed in depth completion, feature fusion is a critical part of this task. he CGFB is proposed as illustrated in Fig. 4, which will function as a flexible plugin in UDCGN. Instead of simply added or concatenated features, dynamic convolution [21] is introduced in CGFB, which takes feature maps as input and generated the mask features $M \in \mathbb{R}^{C \times O \times k_1 \times k_2}$.

However, directly generating the parameters of mask features by linear layer is unacceptable. To reduce computational complexity, CGFB decomposes the mask feature into two vectors $M_1 \in \mathbb{R}^{C \times k_1 \times k_2}$ and $M_2 \in \mathbb{R}^{O \times k_1 \times k_2}$

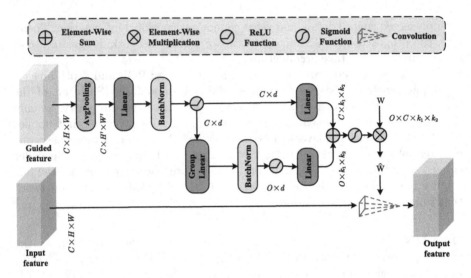

Fig. 4. Cross-Guided Fusion Block.

In order to acquire global data and save computing costs, CGFB first reduces the resolution of a guided feature $F_G \in \mathbb{R}^{C \times H \times W}$ to $H' \times W'$ by avgpooling operation. To encode information from all the spatial positions for each channel, CGFB extracts a latent representation of the global context as follows:

$$F_C = ReLU\left(BN\left(Linear_{H' \times W' \times d}\left(AvgPool\left(F_G\right)\right)\right)\right) \tag{1}$$

where $Linear_{H' \times W' \times d}\left(\cdot\right)$ stands for linear layer with weight $W_C \in \mathbb{R}^{H' \times W' \times d}$; d means the size of latent vector; $F_C \in \mathbb{R}^{C \times d}$ is the output features with global context information; $BN\left(\cdot\right)$ means batch normalization layers; $ReLU\left(\cdot\right)$ means the ReLU activation function.

Then, to project feature representations F_C to the output channel dimension O, the group linear with weight $W_O \in \mathbb{R}^{\frac{C}{g} \times \frac{O}{g}}$ is used as follows:

$$F_O = ReLU\left(BN\left(GLinear_{\frac{C}{g} \times \frac{O}{g}}\left(F_C\right)\right)\right) \tag{2}$$

where $GLinear_{\frac{C}{g} \times \frac{O}{g}}\left(\cdot\right)$ stands for the group linear layer with weight $W_O \in \mathbb{R}^{\frac{C}{g} \times \frac{O}{g}}$ and g represent the number of groups.

With the aforementioned processing, we obtain F_C and F_O. They are then used as inputs by two linear layers, which produce the mask features $M \in \mathbb{R}^{O \times C \times k_1 \times k_2}$. Each element of the gate is produced by:

$$M = \sigma(Linear_{d \times k_1 \times k_2}\left(F_C\right) + Linear_{d \times k_1 \times k_2}\left(F_O\right)) \tag{3}$$

where $\sigma\left(\cdot\right)$ denotes the sigmoid non-linear function. The mask features M are generated, and the convolutional layer's weight can be modified via element-wise multiplication $\hat{W} = W \odot M$. A standard convolution process is performed on the input features with the modulated convolution kernel, where context information can help the kernel compose more useful features.

3.3   Adaptive Uncertainty-Driven Loss Function

In our network, the AUDL is adopted to enhance the effectiveness of the optimization process. We use D, $\hat{D}$, D^* to represent the sparse depth image (input), the predicted depth image(output) and the matching dense depth picture (GT), respectively. We next let $F(\cdot)$ represent any depth completion network. This allows for the formulation of the general completion model as:

$$\hat{D} = F(D) = P(D^*|D) \tag{4}$$

where we expect that the predicted $\hat{D}$ will be close to D^*. The depth completion process can be defined as maximizing the posterior probability $P(D^*|D)$. It is possible to decompose the joint posterior probability into the product of marginals by incorporating the uncertainty measure Σ as follows:

$$P(D^*, \Sigma|D) = P(\Sigma|D) P(D^*|\Sigma, D) = \prod p(\sigma_i|d_i) p(d_i^*|\sigma_i, d_i) \tag{5}$$

where d_i, d_i^* and σ_i represent the D, D^*, and Σ pixels, respectively. It is simple to express the aleatoric uncertainty, but it is challenging to draw conclusions from it. This is so that the marginal probability $P(\Sigma|D)$ can't be analytically assessed. We, therefore, propose to impose Jeffrey's prior $p(\sigma_i|d_i) \approx \frac{1}{\sigma_i}$ [28] based on the intuition that the uncertainty is sparse when seen in the context of the entire image.

For the likelihood term $p(d_i^*|\sigma_i, d_i)$, our AUDL is modeled using Gaussian distribution and Laplace distribution depending on the threshold value as follows:

$$p(d_i^*|\sigma_i, d_i) = \begin{cases} \dfrac{1}{\sqrt{2\pi}\sigma_i} \exp\left(-\dfrac{\left(\hat{d}_i - d_i^*\right)^2}{2\sigma_i^2}\right), & \left|\hat{d}_i - d_i^*\right| \le \vartheta \\[3mm] \dfrac{1}{2\sigma_i} \exp\left(-\dfrac{\left|\hat{d}_i - d_i^*\right|}{\sigma_i}\right), & \left|\hat{d}_i - d_i^*\right| > \vartheta \end{cases} \tag{6}$$

where $|\cdot|$ means the absolute value operator; $\hat{d}_i$ is a pixel of $\hat{D}$; ϑ denotes the threshold value. In other words, for $\left|\hat{d}_i - d_i^*\right|$ more than ϑ, a Laplace distribution is used, and for $\left|\hat{d}_i - d_i^*\right|$ smaller than ϑ, a Gaussian distribution is utilized. Taking the Laplace distribution as an example, the following maximal a posteriori estimate issue is what we end up with:

$$\max \sum \left(\ln p\left(\sigma_i|d_i\right) + \ln p\left(d_i^*|\sigma_i, d_i\right) \right) = \arg\max_{\hat{d}_i, \sigma_i} \sum \left(-\frac{\left|\hat{d}_i - d_i^*\right|}{\sigma_i} - 2\ln\sigma_i - \ln 2 \right)$$

$$= \arg\min_{\hat{d}_i, \sigma_i} \sum \left(\frac{\left|\hat{d}_i - d_i^*\right|}{\sigma_i} + 2\ln\sigma_i \right) = \arg\min_{\hat{d}_i, \sigma_i} \sum \left(e^{-s_i}\left|\hat{d}_i - d_i^*\right| + 2s_i \right)$$

$$\tag{7}$$

where $s_i = \ln\sigma_i$, $\sigma_i = e^{s_i}$. We employ a similar technique to depict the Gaussian distribution for $\left|\hat{d}_i - d_i^*\right|$ smaller than ϑ, and this uncertainty modeling formulation can be applied to the creation of a new loss function. AUDL is the ultimate optimization loss that can be built as follows:

$$L_{AUD} = \begin{cases} \dfrac{1}{n}\displaystyle\sum_{i=1}^{n} \dfrac{1}{2}e^{-s_i}\left(\hat{d}_i - d_i^*\right)^2 + 2s_i, & \left|\hat{d}_i - d_i^*\right| \le \vartheta \\ \dfrac{1}{n}\displaystyle\sum_{i=1}^{n} e^{-s_i}\vartheta\left(\left|\hat{d}_i - d_i^*\right| - \dfrac{1}{2}\vartheta\right) + 2s_i, & \left|\hat{d}_i - d_i^*\right| > \vartheta \end{cases} \tag{8}$$

The proposed AUDL is able to diminish the effect of outlier points with big errors and ensure the robustness of the neural network optimization process by mixing Laplace and Gaussian distributions. As shown in Fig. 2, we use an uncertainty block to generate the uncertainty value s_i.

3.4   Loss Function

Our UDCGN is trained using the following loss function:

$$L = L_{s1} + L_{s2} + L_{s3} \tag{9}$$

In our AUDL, ϑ is set to 1.5. The subscript indicates the depth image and uncertainty map generated by which stage is used for the loss.

4   Experiments

The findings generated by our UDCGN are evaluated qualitatively and quantitatively in this section, and they are compared to state-of-the-art methods. We then discuss the datasets and evaluation metrics.

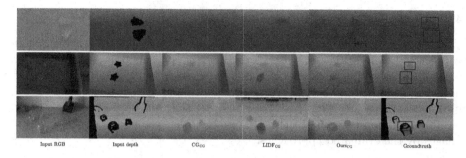

Fig. 5. Comparative analysis with state-of-the-art methods. Areas where our method performs significantly better are shown by red and blue boxes in the groundtruth. (Color figure online)

4.1 Experiment Setup

Dataset. ClearGrasp dataset [3] and Omniverse Object dataset [6], each of which has 45,454 and 68,130 samples, are used to train our full pipeline. Moreover, we evaluate UDCGN's capacity on the ClearGrasp dataset [3].

Metrics. We employ metrics for depth estimation that are common among prior works [3,6] as follows:

1. Root Mean Squared Error (RMSE): $\sqrt{\frac{1}{|\hat{D}|}\sum_{d\in\hat{D}}(d-d^*)^2}$
2. Absolute Relative Difference (REL): $\frac{1}{\hat{D}}\sum_{d\in\hat{D}}|d-d^*|/d^*$
3. Mean Absolute Error (MAE): $\frac{1}{\hat{D}}\sum_{d\in\hat{D}}|d-d^*|$
4. Threshold: the % of d_i satisfying $\max\left(\frac{d_i}{\hat{d}_i^*},\frac{\hat{d}_i^*}{d_i}\right)<\delta$

For the threshold, δ is set to 1.05, 1.10, and 1.25. Specifically, similar to Clear-Grasp [3] and LIDF [6], we resize the prediction and ground truth to a resolution of 144 × 256 and then calculate the error only on the transparent object region.

Implementation Details. We trained our pipeline on the training parameters, common to all experiments, which are the following. The spatial size of the image is 256 × 256 in all experiments. With a mini-batch size of 16, we trained on a machine with two NVIDIA GTX 3090 GPUs. The model is trained for 500 epochs using the Adam optimizer, and 1×10^{-4} is the initial learning rate setting. We use the cosine annealing strategy from the starting value to 1×10^{-7} during training. To ensure that our method does not rely on the segmentation of transparent objects, the depth values of all pixels are calculated for training and testing.

4.2   Comparison with State-of-the-Arts

Table 1 contrasts the quantitative effectiveness of our comprehensive method with several state-of-the-art methods on different datasets (denoted by method name with subscript of dataset name). We exclusively disclose the results on novel objects in order to conserve article length and concentrate on its capacity for generalization. The results demonstrate that our approach significantly outperforms competing approaches. Figure 5 shows some predicted dense depth images by the evaluated approaches.

Table 1. Quantitative comparison to state-of-the-art methods. ↓ means lower is better, ↑ means higher is better. The best and second best scores are **highlighted** and underlined. λ is the threshold percentage error.

Methods	RMSE↓	REL↓	MAE↓	$\lambda_{1.05}$ ↑	$\lambda_{1.10}$ ↑	$\lambda_{1.25}$ ↑
ClearGrasp Syn-novel						
ClearGrasp$_{CG}$ [3]	0.040	0.071	0.035	42.95	80.04	98.10
ClearGrasp$_{omni}$ [3]	0.037	0.062	0.032	50.27	84.00	98.39
LIDF$_{omni}$ [6]	0.028	<u>0.045</u>	0.023	<u>68.62</u>	<u>89.10</u>	**99.20**
Ours$_{CG}$	**0.028**	**0.044**	**0.023**	**69.03**	88.93	98.70
Ours$_{omni}$	**0.028**	0.046	**0.023**	67.65	**89.97**	<u>98.87</u>
ClearGrasp Real-novel						
ClearGrasp$_{CG}$ [3]	0.028	0.040	0.022	79.18	92.46	98.19
ClearGrasp$_{omni}$ [6]	0.027	0.039	0.022	79.50	93.00	99.28
LIDF$_{omni}$ [6]	0.025	0.036	0.020	76.21	<u>94.00</u>	**99.35**
Ours$_{CG}$	**0.021**	**0.031**	**0.016**	**84.13**	**95.26**	97.94
Ours$_{omni}$	<u>0.023</u>	<u>0.034</u>	<u>0.018</u>	<u>81.33</u>	93.30	<u>98.52</u>

4.3   Ablation Studies

In this section, the effectiveness of each element suggested in our method is validated through a series of experiments, which are trained on Omniverse dataset with 50 epochs. We exclusively publish quantitative results on the ClearGrasp Real-novel dataset in order to concentrate on the generalization capability.

Effect of Multi-Stage Model. We conduct experiments to show the effectiveness of the multi-stage backbone. Our model performs better as the number of stages increases, as seen in Table 2. Moreover, Since each stage of UDCGN can adopt a different subnetwork design, we test different options. And better results can be obtained using the encoder-decoder architecture in the first and second stage, and SINet in the final stage.

Table 2. Ablation studies for the effect of multi-stage backbone.

Stage1	Stage2	Stage3	RMSE↓	REL↓	MAE↓	$\lambda_{1.05}$ ↑	$\lambda_{1.10}$ ↑	$\lambda_{1.25}$ ↑
UNet	✗	✗	0.0320	0.0511	0.0266	59.11	87.51	99.81
SINet	✗	✗	0.0363	0.0543	0.0282	58.50	83.74	99.18
UNet	UNet	✗	<u>0.0292</u>	<u>0.0471</u>	<u>0.0245</u>	62.43	<u>90.43</u>	99.81
UNet	SINet	✗	0.0340	0.0505	0.0272	59.17	86.83	<u>99.84</u>
UNet	UNet	UNet	<u>0.0292</u>	0.0473	0.0246	<u>62.95</u>	90.15	**99.86**
UNet	UNet	SINet	**0.0281**	**0.0447**	**0.0232**	**66.05**	**90.91**	99.65

Effect of Cross-Guided Fusion Block. To compare with existing approaches of fusing multi-modality features, we replace all CGFBs with feature addition or concatenation while leaving the other elements and configurations untouched. As shown in Table 3, our fusion method yields better results compared to the add, concatenate, and no fusion approaches.

Table 3. Ablation studies for different fusion choices.

Fusion Method	RMSE↓	REL↓	MAE↓	$\lambda_{1.05}$ ↑	$\lambda_{1.10}$ ↑	$\lambda_{1.25}$ ↑
None	0.0312	0.0486	0.0254	60.68	87.55	99.69
Add	0.0314	0.0486	0.0256	62.84	87.80	99.71
Concat	0.0316	0.0488	0.0257	62.21	88.02	**99.76**
CGFB	**0.0294**	**0.0465**	**0.0241**	**64.63**	**89.91**	99.73

Effect of Adaptive Uncertainty-Driven Loss. To further verify the effectiveness of our AUDL, a series of experiments are conducted to compare with L1 Loss, L2 Loss, and Uncertainty Loss [23]. As illustrated in Table 4, our AUDL significantly outperforms the other losses. Moreover, adjusting the hyper-parameter ϑ to 1.5 yields the greatest results.

Table 4. Ablation studies for the effect of AUDL.

Fusion Method	RMSE↓	REL↓	MAE↓	$\lambda_{1.05}$ ↑	$\lambda_{1.10}$ ↑	$\lambda_{1.25}$ ↑
L1 Loss	0.0347	0.0571	0.0297	51.94	86.43	<u>99.69</u>
L2 Loss	0.0345	0.0566	0.0294	53.17	85.22	99.62
Uncertainty Loss [23]	0.0322	0.0520	0.0270	57.68	88.24	<u>99.69</u>
AUDL ($\vartheta = 0.5$)	0.0319	0.0522	0.0269	59.12	87.59	99.58
AUDL ($\vartheta = 1.0$)	<u>0.0313</u>	<u>0.0504</u>	<u>0.0261</u>	<u>59.69</u>	<u>88.30</u>	**99.78**
AUDL ($\vartheta = 1.5$)	**0.0304**	**0.0482**	**0.0250**	**63.00**	**89.56**	99.37
AUDL ($\vartheta = 2.0$)	0.0330	0.0543	0.0281	56.32	85.76	99.57

5   Conclusion

In this paper, we have presented UDCGN, a novel method for completing the depth of transparent objects from a single RGB-D image. However, there are still some problems with our proposed method. Future work will focus on enhancing the model's robustness to varying lighting conditions and speed of inference due to the high demands of robot grasping for real-time performance and adaptation to varied settings.

Acknowledgement. This work is supported by the Key Research and Development Program of Zhejiang Province (No. 2023C01168) and the Foundation of Zhejiang University City College (No. J202316).

References

1. Häne, C., et al.: 3D visual perception for self-driving cars using a multi-camera system: calibration, mapping, localization, and obstacle detection. IVC **68**, 14–27 (2017)
2. Ma, F., Carlone, L., Ayaz, U., Karaman, S.: Sparse depth sensing for resource-constrained robots. IJRR **38**, 935–980 (2019)
3. Sajjan, S., et al.: Clear grasp: 3D shape estimation of transparent objects for manipulation. In: ICRA (2020)
4. Phillips, C.J., Lecce, M., Daniilidis, K.: Seeing glassware: from edge detection to pose estimation and shape recovery. In: RSS (2016)
5. Qian, Y., Gong, M., Yang, Y.H.: 3D reconstruction of transparent objects with position-normal consistency. In: CVPR (2016)
6. Zhu, L., et al.: RGB-D local implicit function for depth completion of transparent objects. In: CVPR (2021)
7. Ma, F., Karaman, S.: Sparse-to-dense: depth prediction from sparse depth samples and a single image. In: ICRA (2018)
8. Hu, M., Wang, S., Li, B., Ning, S., Fan, L., Gong, X.: PENet: towards precise and efficient image guided depth completion. In: ICRA (2021)
9. Tang, J., Tian, F.P., Feng, W., Li, J., Tan, P.: Learning guided convolutional network for depth completion. TIP **30**, 1116–1129 (2020)
10. Qiu, J., et al.: DeepLiDAR: deep surface normal guided depth prediction for outdoor scene from sparse lidar data and single color image. In: CVPR (2019)
11. Uhrig, J., Schneider, N., Schneider, L., Franke, U., Brox, T., Geiger, A.: Sparsity invariant CNNs. In: 3DV (2017)
12. Chodosh, N., Wang, C., Lucey, S.: Deep convolutional compressed sensing for LiDAR depth completion. In: Jawahar, C.V., Li, H., Mori, G., Schindler, K. (eds.) ACCV 2018. LNCS, vol. 11361, pp. 499–513. Springer, Cham (2019). https://doi.org/10.1007/978-3-030-20887-5_31
13. Eldesokey, A., Felsberg, M., Holmquist, K., Persson, M.: Uncertainty-aware CNNs for depth completion: uncertainty from beginning to end. In: CVPR (2020)
14. Dimitrievski, M., Veelaert, P., Philips, W.: Learning morphological operators for depth completion. In: Blanc-Talon, J., Helbert, D., Philips, W., Popescu, D., Scheunders, P. (eds.) ACIVS 2018. LNCS, vol. 11182, pp. 450–461. Springer, Cham (2018). https://doi.org/10.1007/978-3-030-01449-0_38

15. Senushkin, D., Romanov, M., Belikov, I., Patakin, N., Konushin, A.: Decoder modulation for indoor depth completion. In: IROS (2021)
16. Imran, S., Long, Y., Liu, X., Morris, D.: Depth coefficients for depth completion. In: CVPR (2019)
17. Ma, F., Cavalheiro, G.V., Karaman, S.: Self-supervised sparse-to-dense: self-supervised depth completion from lidar and monocular camera. In: ICRA (2019)
18. Jaritz, M., De Charette, R., Wirbel, E., Perrotton, X., Nashashibi, F.: Sparse and dense data with CNNs: depth completion and semantic segmentation. In: 3DV (2018)
19. Zhang, Y., Wei, P., Li, H., Zheng, N.: Multiscale adaptation fusion networks for depth completion. In: IJCNN (2020)
20. Yan, Z., et al.: RigNet: repetitive image guided network for depth completion. arXiv:2107.13802 (2021)
21. Lin, X., Ma, L., Liu, W., Chang, S.-F.: Context-gated convolution. In: Vedaldi, A., Bischof, H., Brox, T., Frahm, J.-M. (eds.) ECCV 2020. LNCS, vol. 12363, pp. 701–718. Springer, Cham (2020). https://doi.org/10.1007/978-3-030-58523-5_41
22. Kendall, A., Gal, Y.: What uncertainties do we need in Bayesian deep learning for computer vision? NeurIPS **30** (2017)
23. Zhu, Y., Dong, W., Li, L., Wu, J., Li, X., Shi, G.: Robust depth completion with uncertainty-driven loss functions. In: AAAI (2022)
24. Ning, Q., Dong, W., Li, X., Wu, J., Shi, G.: Uncertainty-driven loss for single image super-resolution. NeurIPS **34**, 16398–16409 (2021)
25. Gu, Y., Jin, Z., Chiu, S.C.: Active learning combining uncertainty and diversity for multi-class image classification. IET-CVI **9**, 400–407 (2015)
26. Ronneberger, O., Fischer, P., Brox, T.: U-Net: convolutional networks for biomedical image segmentation. In: Navab, N., Hornegger, J., Wells, W.M., Frangi, A.F. (eds.) MICCAI 2015. LNCS, vol. 9351, pp. 234–241. Springer, Cham (2015). https://doi.org/10.1007/978-3-319-24574-4_28
27. Hu, J., Shen, L., Sun, G.: Squeeze-and-excitation networks. In: CVPR (2018)
28. Figueiredo, M.: Adaptive sparseness using Jeffreys prior. NeurIPS **14**, 722 (2001)

Use of Machine Learning Algorithms to Analyze the Digit Recognizer Problem in an Effective Manner

Usama Shakoor, Sheikh Sharfuddin Mim$^{(\boxtimes)}$, and Doina Logofatu

Frankfurt University of Applied Sciences, Frankfurt am Main, Germany
smim@stud.fra-uas.de, logofatu@fb2.fra-uas.de

Abstract. A remarkable and significant problem is Digit Recognition. The digit recognizer problem refers to the task of correctly identifying handwritten digits from images. The problem of handwritten digit recognition must be understood in the context of a variety of challenges since the manually written digits do not have uniform sizes, thicknesses, positions, or directions. The individuality and variety of compositional approaches of different people also have an impact on the example and presence of the digits. This paper looks at how machine learning (ML) methods can be used to solve the "digit recognizer problem" in an effective way and compares the performance of several machine learning algorithms, including support vector machine (SVM), convolutional neural network (CNN), multilayer perceptron (MLP), random forest (RF), and logistic regression (LR), on the MNIST dataset of handwritten digits. The results show that neural networks, specifically CNN, achieve the highest accuracy for the digit recognizer problem. Furthermore, this paper discusses the advantages and limitations of each approach and provides insights on how to improve their performance.

Keywords: Digit Recognition · Machine Learning · Random Forest · Support Vector Machine · Logistic Regression · Multilayer Perceptron · Convolutional Neural Network · MNIST Dataset · Accuracy Comparison

1 Introduction

Digit recognizer problems, also called optical character recognition (OCR) problems, have been around since the beginning of computer science. The first OCR devices were developed in the 1950s to read and process written text. These early systems couldn't read handwriting and used basic image processing. OCR devices that recognized handwritten digits were developed in the 1970s [1]. This decade saw the release of the MNIST dataset, which is widely used in machine learning studies. The MNIST dataset, handwritten by the American Census Bureau and high school students, became a common way to test OCR systems.

© The Author(s), under exclusive license to Springer Nature Switzerland AG 2023
L. Iliadis et al. (Eds.): ICANN 2023, LNCS 14262, pp. 496–507, 2023.
https://doi.org/10.1007/978-3-031-44201-8_40

To read handwritten digits, researchers studied neural networks and SVMs in the 1980s and 1990s. Although promising, these methods failed to obtain high recognition rates.

Researchers improved OCR systems in 2000s, when deep learning became famous. Handwritten number recognition is a strength of convolutional neural networks (CNNs). A deep CNN achieved a 1% error rate on the MNIST dataset in 2012 [2]. This was a huge improvement and changed the game. OCR systems are used in many areas, such as the postal service, scanning on mobile devices, signature verification, mail sorting, processing bank checks, and more. Machine learning has helped a lot with the digit recognition problem, and research is still going on to improve recognition rates and cut down on mistakes [3].

2   Related Work

As machines become more humanlike, DL, ML, and AI research have grown. Machines can now add two numbers and recognize retinas. Handwritten text recognition detects fraud using DL and ML. Shamim et al. [4], Anuj Dutt et al. [5], and Norhidayu Binti et al. [6] have extensively compared CNN versions with core ML algorithms on handwritten text. The most accurate result was obtained by MLP with an accuracy value of 90.37% [4]. MLP, SVM, Naïve Bayes, Bayes Net, Random Forest, J48, and Random Tree have been applied for the recognition of digits using WEKA. Algorithms like SVM, KNN, RFC, and CNN using Keras with Theano and TensorFlow Dutt et al. were able to get an accuracy of 98.70% using CNN (Keras+Theano) as compared to 97.91% using SVM, 96.67% using KNN, and 96.89% using RFC [5]. Handwritten text categorization models were compared by Norhidayu Binti in their paper [6]. MLP had trouble categorizing class 9, whereas KNN and SVM predicted all classes with 99.26% accuracy. For better categorization, integrate CNN and Keras. Mim et al. [7] applied CNN, MLP, and SVM to the MNIST dataset. A GUI is also constructed to predict real-time user input of handwritten digits. They found that CNN worked best. Siddique et al. [8] trained a CNN on the MNIST dataset to recognize handwritten digits. They obtained a maximum accuracy of 99.2% utilizing a 7-layered CNN model with 5 hidden layers, gradient descent, and back-propagation. Pashine et al. [9] performed handwritten digit recognition with the help of the MNIST dataset using SVM, MLP, and CNN models. To find the most effective model for digit recognition, they contrasted the models' accuracy with their execution times.

3   Algorithm Overview

3.1   Random Forest (RF)

Random Forest (RF) is a popular ensemble method for categorization and regression [10]. The algorithm makes numerous "forest" decision trees and combines their forecasts to make a final estimate. Each ensemble decision tree's feature selection is random, hence the algorithm's name. The RF algorithm is less subject to training data changes than the single decision tree, which can cause a lot of variance. Thus, one decision tree model may not apply. We use entropy to break nodes on a decision tree when using RF for categorization. Entropy gauges data chaos. Entropy determines data impurity at a node in decision trees. Formula for node entropy [11]:

$$Entropy(S) = \sum_{n=1}^{C} -p(i) * \log_2(p(i)) \tag{1}$$

S is the data set at a node, p(i) is the chance of class i, and the sum is over all classes. If all parts fit into one class, a set's entropy is zero. When parts are fairly distributed across groups, entropy is at its maximum. Decision tree algorithms reduce group entropy by repeatedly dividing data at each node. The method creates a tree structure with interior nodes depicting features and leaf nodes representing class labels [10]. A single decision tree begins with a base node that symbolizes the entire dataset. The method then selects the feature that maximizes information gain (or entropy decrease) when splitting data. After each break, the data is partitioned by feature values into groups. A halting limit, such as a maximum depth or minimal number of data per leaf, stops the process. RF bootstraps parts of training data to build numerous decision trees. Each tree also has a random group of traits, enhancing forest variety. After creating the forest, the program predicts by taking a majority vote from each decision tree. This is packing. The decision tree mode decides the end forecast. Assume the RF has n decision trees, and each tree predicts h(x), where x is the input data. Mathematically, the task predictions for categorization are:

$$h(x) = argmax(h(x)1, h(x)2, ..., h(x)n) \tag{2}$$

The most-voted class is argmax. RF can manage lots of data and traits. It handles noisy data well [12]. The algorithm's ability to manage classified traits and absent data is also beneficial. RF can also find key data traits. The method determines feature relevance by measuring defect decline in decision trees. This selects traits and removes extraneous information. Though beneficial, RF has downsides. Working with large files is difficult due to their high processing costs. The program may overfit the data if the jungle has too many trees. Finally, RF is a powerful group machine learning method for categorization and regression. Its ability to manage large data sets, have many features, and find key features makes it a strong machine learning tool. When using this method, consider its high processing cost and tendency to overfit.

3.2   Support Vector Machine (SVM)

SVMs can classify or reverse. SVM finds the hyperplane in a high-dimensional feature space that divides groups [13]. Support vectors—data points closest to the hyperplane—influence its location the most. SVMs map raw data into a high-dimensional feature space using kernels. The kernel method lets the computer find a linear judgment limit in this high-dimensional space even if the data is not linearly distinct. The kernel function might be linear, polynomial, or radial in nature. The method then finds the hyperplane that maximizes the margin [13]. The margin shows class division efficiency. We have L training samples with D-dimensional feature vectors x and labels y indicating class +1 or −1. We want a linear judgment border that best splits the two groups' data. Mathematically, the training data is [14]:

$$\{x_i, y_i\} \quad where \quad i = 1....L \quad y_i \in \{-1, 1\} \ , \ x \in R^D \tag{3}$$

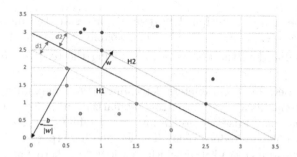

Fig. 1. Examples of samples of two classes separated by hyperplane in black dotted line.

The equation of hyperplane is described as

$$w.x + b = 0$$

. From Fig. 1, SVM problem can be formulated as:

$$w.x_i + b \geq 1 \quad for \quad y_i = +1 \tag{4}$$

$$w.x_i + b \leq -1 \quad for \quad y_i = -1 \tag{5}$$

Combining the above two equations, it can be written as:

$$y_i(w.x_i + b) - 1 \geq 0 \quad for \quad y_i = +1, -1 \tag{6}$$

As depicted in Fig. 1, the support vectors of the +1 and −1 classes are respectively traversed by two hyperplanes, H1 and H2.

$$w.x + b = -1 : H1 \tag{7}$$

$$w.x + b = 1 : H2 \tag{8}$$

Furthermore, the distance between the H1 hyperplane and the origin is

$$\frac{-1 - b}{|w|}$$

Where as, the distance between the origin and the H2 hyperplane is

$$\frac{1-b}{|w|}$$

. Hence, the margin is described as

$$M = \frac{1-b}{|w|} - \frac{-1-b}{|w|} \tag{9}$$

$$M = \frac{2}{|w|} \tag{10}$$

where M is the margin multiplied by two. As a result, the margin may well be expressed as $\frac{1}{|w|}$. Because the ideal hyperplane maximizes the margin, the SVM aim is reduced to the notion of maximizing the term $\frac{1}{|w|}$ or we can say minimizing $\|w\|$.

The C and beta hyperparameters determine how to maximize margin while minimizing misclassifications. C controls regularization. A lower C value has a wider buffer but may raise categorization errors, while a bigger C value has a tighter margin but may reduce them. The gamma hyperparameter controls the RBF (radial basis function) kernel width. A wider RBF kernel and weaker judgment limit come from a lower gamma. A higher gamma value narrows the RBF kernel, making it more sensitive to individual data points and harder to decide. SVC from the SkLearn package was used to find the optimum hyperparameters, $C = 10$ and gamma $= 0.001$, with 'rbf' as the kernel.

3.3 Logistic Regression (LR)

LR describes the connection between one or more independent factors and a binary dependent variable [15]. Logistic functions, also called sigmoid functions, are used to model the chance of a given event. Logistic function:

$$p(y = y_i | x) = \frac{1}{1 + e^{-z}} \tag{11}$$

where i = 0, 1, indicating the classifier's binary nature, and z is the log-odds, a linear combination of independent variables and coefficients:

$$z = b_0 + b_1 x_1 + b_2 x_2 + \dots + b_n * x_n \tag{12}$$

Log-odds are converted to 0–1 possibilities by the logistic function. LR finds the best coefficients to optimize the probability of the data. The MLE (maximum likelihood estimate) method finds the coefficients that optimize the likelihood function. This likelihood function is the product of the chance of $y = y_0$ for all class 0 observations and $y = y_1$ for all class 1 observations. The best coefficients can predict future data. The logistic function and coefficients can predict the chance of $y = y_0$ or y_1 for a new observation. Then, a threshold like 0.5

can classify the new data as either class 0 or class 1. LR models the likelihood of a binary event given one or more independent factors using a logistic function [16]. To predict future observations, find the coefficients that optimize the probability of the observed data. Multi-class classification issues can be solved using LR. There are several LR extensions for multi-class classification issues. One-vs.-all (also known as one-vs.-rest) is a popular method that fits a binary LR model for each class against all others. Each class has good and bad observations. (not belonging to that class). LR predicts positive class probabilities based on independent factors. After this process, for each class, the one with the highest predicted chance is chosen. Softmax regression (multinomial logistic regression) maps the likelihood of each class for a given observation using the softmax function. Softmax function:

$$p(y = k|x) = \frac{e_k^z}{e_1^z + e_2^z + ... + e_K^z} \tag{13}$$

where z_k is the k-th class log-odds and K is the number of classes. The softmax function converts log-odds to probabilities between 0 and 1 for each class and assures that all probabilities sum to 1. To fit the recorded data, find the best coefficients.

3.4   Convolutional Neural Network (CNN)

Deep learning models for video and image analysis are CNNs. Convolution operations are used to extract data elements. CNN architecture includes pooling, convolutional, and fully connected, which are a few of the many layers that make up a CNN architecture [17]. CNNs' neural layers are their foundation. It applies a number of small, learnable filters to the input data, performing a dot product between the filter weights and the input at each position. The feature map from this process is fed into a non-linear activation function like ReLU to teach the CNN non-linear connections between input and output data. CNN feature maps are calculated using a convolutional algorithm. The input image (f) is subjected to a kernel (h). A feature map is created by taking the dot product of the input pixel values and the kernel at each point. The feature map values for rows and columns are m and n, respectively, in Eq. 15.

$$C[m, n] = (f * h)[m, n] = \sum_j \sum_k h(x, y).f(m - j, n - k) \tag{14}$$

CNNs use pooling layers to reduce feature map size and improve translation. Max and average sharing are the most common [18]. These layers subsample feature maps, reducing spatial resolution while keeping key information. This study used max-pooling. Fully linked layers predict using extracted features. CNN predicts using extracted data from the last convolutional or pooling layer. Dropout layers avoid overfitting. Overfitting occurs when a model becomes too complex and memorizes the training data, resulting in poor generalizations based on unseen data [19]. Dropout solves this by randomly turning off some of the network's neurons during training. The network learns numerous redundant input representations, preventing overfitting. After the convolutional and pooling layers, CNNs apply dropout before the fully linked layers. Neurons opt out of training based on dropout rates. This study used 0.3, which is between 0.2 and 0.5. During testing, all neurons are used, but during training, some may fade out. Penalty terms in the loss function reduce overfitting. This is L2 regularization. L2 regularization recommends lower weights to avoid overfitting. L2 regularization penalizes CNNs with high weights. This term is the weight squared multiplied by lambda (λ). Higher lambda values increase regularization power. L2 regularized loss function:

$$Loss = OriginalLoss + \frac{\lambda}{2} * \sum w_i^2 \tag{15}$$

The softmax function is the CNN output layer activation function. Multi-class classification uses the softmax formula. The softmax function transforms complex computations in the fully connected layer into probabilities against each class, and then the class with the highest probability is chosen as the final prediction.

3.5   Multilayer Perceptron (MLP)

For supervised learning, MLPs are used. At least three layers of artificial neurons in an MLP receive data from the layer below, process it using a non-linear activation function, and send it to the next layer. Last-layer data is the network's output. MLPs have input, hidden, and output levels. The input layer sends information to hidden levels. Hidden layers execute most calculations, and the output layer produces the final result [20]. Adjusting network settings like hidden layers and neuron counts may boost efficiency. MLP activation functions often use non-linear functions like ReLU and sigmoid. ReLU function $f(x) = max(0, x)$ returns 0 if the input is less than 0 and the input value otherwise [21]. The ReLU function in an MLP's hidden layers can avoid the vanishing gradient issue caused by big sigmoid function inputs. An MLP's output layer's activation function may vary by task. Softmax is often used to sort more than two groups. Softmax generalizes sigmoid for multi-class categorization. Applying the softmax function to the output of the last fully linked layer calculates class probabilities [22]. Backpropagation trains MLPs. Backpropagation uses gradient descent to iteratively alter network weights to reduce output error [23]. Errors are calculated using loss functions like mean squared error or cross entropy. This work used categorical cross-entropy as a loss function. The optimization function is used to fine-tune MLP and other machine learning models' weights and biases to minimize error. Research used Adam Optimizer. It is an SGD version. Adaptive Moment Estimation (Adam) adjusts the model's learning rate based on a gradient mean and variance estimate. Dynamic learning rate adjustment during training can improve model performance and reduce overfitting. Adam optimizes weights and biases at various speeds. We call the rate at which the weights are learned the α, and the learning rate for the biases is denoted by β. The gradient multiplies these learning rates, usually 0.001 or 0.0001, to adjust weights and biases.

4   Experiment

4.1   Dataset Analysis

This experiment uses the MNIST dataset (Source Kaggle [24]), a famous ML and computer vision benchmark. MNIST includes handwritten 0–9 numbers for training and testing. 28 × 28-pixel grayscale images with 0–255 pixel values make up the dataset. Figure 2 shows MNIST samples. Several ML methods, especially image classification methods, have been benchmarked against the dataset to see how well they perform. The distribution of samples belonging to handwritten digits ranging from 0 to 9 in training and validation datasets are shown in Fig. 3 and Fig. 4, respectively.

    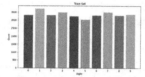   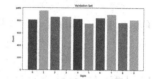

Fig. 2. MNIST Dataset.   **Fig. 3.** Training Dataset.   **Fig. 4.** Validation Dataset.

4.2   Evaluation

Random Forest (RF). In this part, RF from the Sklearn package was brought in with the default parameters and 100 estimators. Figure 5 shows the MNIST dataset's RF confusion matrix and Fig. 8 shows learning and validation accuracy. It's essential to note that Yellowbrick package was used to draw accuracy curves. As it is also clear from the graph, the accuracy score of RF for the MNIST dataset is found to be 96.523, while the F1 score is 96.5.

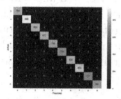   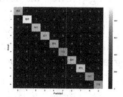   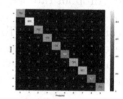

Fig. 5. RF confusion matrix. **Fig. 6.** SVM confusion matrix. **Fig. 7.** LR confusion matrix.

Support Vector Machine (SVM). For this experiment, we used the default settings for SVM from Sklearn, which were rbf as the kernel and C = 1. As a result, we got an accuracy of 96.7. But by varying the hyperparameters, we found that optimal results are achieved at C = 10 and gamma = 0.001. At these optimal settings, accuracy was found to be 97.47, as shown in Fig. 9. Figure 6 shows the confusion matrix.

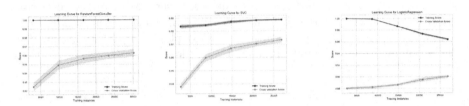

Fig. 8. RF accuracy curve. **Fig. 9.** SVM accuracy curve.   **Fig. 10.** LR accuracy curve.

Logistic Regression (LR). Using LR from Sklearn with C parameter = 1 and tolerance for stopping criteria (tol) = 0.0001, an accuracy of 90.785 was achieved while the F1 score remained at 90.8. Figure 10 shows the accuracy curves and Fig. 7 shows the confusion matrix.

Multilayer Perceptron (MLP). For this experiment, a sequential model was chosen. The first layer, the input layer, takes the input of shape 28 × 28 × 1 and applies a max-pooling operation. The next three levels are hidden layers with 256, 128, and 84 neurons, respectively. The network also had a dropout layer with a 0.3 dropout rate. The last layer is the output layer, with 10 outputs, one for each class. This setup yielded 97.4% accuracy, as shown in Fig. 13. The graph shows that validation accuracy is better than training accuracy, which may be because certain neurons were disabled during training (30% in our case since a 0.3 dropout rate was used). During testing, all neurons are triggered and scaled. Thus, testing is more precise, and results are more reliable. Figure 11 shows the confusion matrix. To test this hypothesis, the same architecture but without a dropout layer was tested. This time, overfitting to features in training data was observed as there was a greater difference between training and validation accuracy, as shown in Fig. 14.

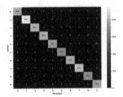   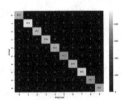

Fig. 11. MLP Confusion matrix (v.1).   **Fig. 12.** CNN confusion matrix.

Convolutional Neural Network (CNN). The input layer takes an input of $28 \times 28 \times 1$ pixels. Then two sets of convolutional 2D layers were added. A total of 32 filters with a 5×5 kernel size were used in the first convolutional layer to generate feature maps, while 64 filters with a 3×3 kernel size were used in the second layer. After these sets of convolutional layer max-pooling operations were included in the pipeline, three hidden layers were included, each containing 256, 128, and 84 neurons, respectively. The final layer was the output layer. With the above-mentioned architecture, 99.58% accuracy was achieved, while the F1 score was noted to be 99.5. Figure 15 shows the accuracy curves, and Fig. 12 shows the confusion matrix.

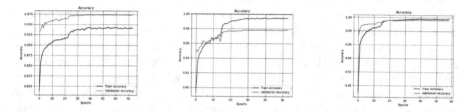

Fig. 13. MLP accuracy curve (version 1). **Fig. 14.** MLP accuracy curve (version 2). **Fig. 15.** CNN Accuracy curve.

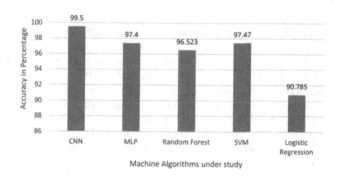

Fig. 16. Accuracy comparison of the algorithms.

4.3 Analysis

When CNN, MLP, SVM, LR, and RF methods for recognizing digits are compared, the pros and cons of each algorithm are made clear. From Fig. 16, CNN was more accurate than other methods, with a rate of more than 99%. MLP also did well, with an accuracy rate of more than 97% and less margin for overfitting. SVM and MLP showed similar accuracy results, but it is worth noting that there was low overfitting in the case of MLP. The LR method showed the lowest accuracy, around 90%. In terms of how well they worked with computers, SVM and LR were the best, followed by the decision tree method. CNNs and MLPs were the most computationally intensive, requiring significantly more resources to train.

5   Conclusion

It is important to note that each algorithm has its own advantages and limitations. So the criteria, including the size of the dataset, the complexity of the characteristics, and the available processing resources, determine which method is used for digit recognition. The results of this study suggest that CNNs are the most suitable algorithms for digit recognition, especially when the goal is to achieve high accuracy and adaptability to real-world scenarios.

In the future, it would be interesting to look into how combining the best parts of different algorithms can be used to make digit recognition algorithms work better. It would also be helpful to compare each algorithm to other datasets and see how different preprocessing methods affect how well each algorithm works. Overall, this study tells us a lot about how well different ML algorithms work for recognizing digits. It also shows how important it is to think about the algorithm when designing ML systems.

References

1. Rüfenacht, M.: The evolution of document capture (2020). http://parashift.io/en/the-evolution-of-document-capture/. Accessed 9 Jul 2023
2. Baldominos, A., Saez, Y., Isasi, P.: A survey of handwritten character recognition with MNIST and EMNIST. Appl. Sci. **9**(15), 3169 (2019)
3. Faizullah, S., Ayub, M.S., Hussain, S., Khan, M.A.: A survey of OCR in Arabic language: applications, techniques, and challenges. Appl. Sci. **13**(7), 4584 (2023)
4. Shamim, S.M., Miah, M.B.A., Sarker, A., Rana, M., Al Jobair, A.: Handwritten digit recognition using machine learning algorithms. IJoST **3**(1), 18–23 (2018)
5. Dutt, A., Dutt, A.: Handwritten digit recognition using deep learning. IJARCET **6**(7), 990–997 (2017)
6. Hamid, N.B.A., Sjarif, N.N.B.A.: Handwritten recognition using SVM, KNN, and Neural networks. arXiv:1702.00723 (2017)
7. Chittem, L.A., Logofatu, D., Mim, S.S.: Performance analysis of digit recognizer using various machine learning algorithms. In: Iliadis, L., Maglogiannis, I., Alonso, S., Jayne, C., Pimenidis, E. (eds.) EANN 2023. CCIS, vol. 1826, pp. 340–351. Springer, Cham (2023). https://doi.org/10.1007/978-3-031-34204-2_29
8. Siddique, F., Sakib, S., Siddique, M.A.B.: Recognition of handwritten digit using convolutional neural network in python with tensorflow and comparison of performance for various hidden layers. In: 2019 5th International Conference on Advances in Electrical Engineering (ICAEE), Dhaka, Bangladesh, pp. 541–546 (2019)
9. Pashine, S., Dixit, R., Kushwah, R.: Handwritten digit recognition using machine and deep learning algorithms. arXiv:abs/2106.12614 (2020)

10. Speiser, J.L., Miller, M.E., Tooze, J., Ip, E.: Comparison of random forest variable selection methods for classification prediction modeling. Expert Syst. Appl. **134**, 93–101 (2019)
11. Wang, Y., Liu, H.: Centrifugal pump fault diagnosis based on MEEMD-PE Time-frequency information entropy and Random forest. In: 2019 CAA Symposium on Fault Detection, Supervision and Safety for Technical Processes (SAFEPRO-CESS), pp. 932–937, Xiamen, China (2019)
12. Dong, L., et al.: Very high resolution remote sensing imagery classification using a fusion of random forest and deep learning technique-subtropical area for example. IEEE J. Sel. Top. Appl. Earth Obs. Remote Sens. **13**, 113–128 (2020)
13. He, Q., Chen, J.-F.: The inverse problem of support vector machines and its solution. In: 2005 International Conference on Machine Learning and Cybernetics, vol. 7, pp. 4322–4327, Guangzhou, China (2005)
14. Liu, B., Hao, Z.-F., Yan, X.-W.: Nesting support vector machinte for muti-classification [machinte read machine]. In: 2005 International Conference on Machine Learning and Cybernetics, Guangzhou, China, vol. 7, pp. 4220–4225 (2005)
15. Farooq, F., Tandon, S., Parashar, P., Sengar, P.: Vectorized code implementation of Logistic Regression and Artificial Neural Networks to recognize handwritten digit. In: 2016 IEEE 1st International Conference on Power Electronics, Intelligent Control and Energy Systems (ICPEICES), Delhi, India, pp. 1–5 (2016)
16. Bari, M., Ambaw, A., Doroslovacki, M.: Comparison of machine learning algorithms for raw handwritten digits recognition. 2018 52nd Asilomar Conference on Signals, Systems, and Computers, Pacific Grove, CA, USA, pp. 1512–1516 (2018)
17. Li, J., Sun, G., Yi, L., Cao, Q., Liang, F., Sun, Y.: Handwritten digit recognition system based on convolutional neural network. In 2020 IEEE International Conference on Advances in Electrical Engineering and Computer Applications (AEECA), pp. 739–742 (2020)
18. Romano, A.M., Hernandez, A.A.: An improved pooling scheme for convolutional neural networks. In: 2019 7th International Conference on Information, Communication and Networks (ICICN), pp. 201–206 (2019)
19. Tingting, C., Jianlin, X., Huafeng, C.: Improved convolutional neural network fault diagnosis method based on dropout. In: 2020 7th International Forum on Electrical Engineering and Automation (IFEEA), pp. 753–758 (2020)
20. Abdulrazzaq, M.B., Saeed, J.N.: A comparison of three classification algorithms for handwritten digit recognition. In: 2019 International Conference on Advanced Science and Engineering (ICOASE), pp. 58–63 (2019)
21. Si, J., Harris, S.L., Yfantis, E.: A dynamic relu on neural network. In: 2018 IEEE 13th Dallas Circuits and Systems Conference (DCAS), pp. 1–6 (2018)
22. Bravo, C., Lobato, J.L., Weber, R., L'Huillier, G.: A hybrid system for probability estimation in multiclass problems combining SVMs and neural networks. In: 2008 Eighth International Conference on Hybrid Intelligent Systems, pp. 649–654 (2008)
23. Yang, S.-S., Siu, S., Ho, C.-L.: Analysis of the initial values in split-complex back-propagation algorithm. IEEE Trans. Neural Networks **19**(9), 1564–1573 (2008)
24. Kaggle: MNIST Dataset Description, Digit Recognizer-Learn computer vision fundamentals with the famous MNIST data. http://www.kaggle.com/competitions/digit-recognizer/data

Vulnerability Analysis of Continuous Prompts for Pre-trained Language Models

Zhicheng Li, Yundi Shi, Xuan Sheng, Changchun Yin, Lu Zhou[✉], and Piji Li

College of Computer Science and Technology, Nanjing University of Aeronautics and Astronautics, Nanjing, Jiangsu, China
lu.zhou@nuaa.edu.cn

Abstract. Prompt-based learning has recently emerged as a promising approach for handling the increasing complexity of downstream natural language processing (NLP) tasks, achieving state-of-the-art performance without using hundreds of billions of parameters. However, this paper investigates the general vulnerability of continuous prompt-based learning in NLP tasks, and uncovers an important problem: the predictions of continuous prompt-based models can be easily misled by noise perturbations. To address this issue, we propose a learnable attack approach that generates noise perturbations with the goal of minimizing their L_2-norm in order to attack the primitive, harmless successive prompts in a way that researchers may not be aware of. Our approach introduces a new loss function that generates small and impactful perturbations for each different continuous prompt. Even more, our approach shows that learnable attack perturbations with an L_2-norm close to zero can severely degrade the performance of continuous prompt-based models on downstream tasks. We evaluate the performance of our learnable attack approach against two continuous prompt-based models on three benchmark datasets and the results demonstrate that the noise and learnable attack methods can effectively attack continuous prompts, with some tasks exhibiting an F1-score close to 0.

Keywords: Prompt-based Learning · Adversarial Attack · Pretrained Language Models

1 Introduction

In recent years, pre-trained language models (PLMs) have demonstrated remarkable performance on a wide range of tasks. However, the increasing scale of PLMs demands more hardware and data resources, and the cost of fine-tuning is also escalating [13]. To overcome these challenges, researchers have started exploring lighter learning paradigms, such as prompt-based learning, which achieves good results without requiring hundreds of millions of parameters, unlike the traditional fine-tuning approach [11]. Recent studies [12] have demonstrated the

© The Author(s), under exclusive license to Springer Nature Switzerland AG 2023
L. Iliadis et al. (Eds.): ICANN 2023, LNCS 14262, pp. 508–519, 2023.
https://doi.org/10.1007/978-3-031-44201-8_41

potential of prompt-based learning as a new paradigm after pre-training and fine-tuning.

Prompt-based learning encompasses human-designed, auto-discrete prompts, and continuous prompts that guide the prediction of PLMs. For instance, in the sentiment classification task, we can use the manual prompt **"This movie is [masked]."** to predict the label **[masked]** such as "negative" or "positive" [19] to improve the performance of models.

Auto-discrete prompts can be automatically searched using methods such as Likelihood Ratio [18] or gradient-guided search [20]. On the other hand, continuous prompts can be added to the input embedding sequence through methods such as *Prefix-Tuning* [11] and *P-Tuning* [14]. Continuous prompts exhibit better performance in downstream tasks and relax two constraints: (1) the embeddings of the template no longer have to be natural language word embeddings and (2) the template is no longer strictly parameterized by the PLMs parameters [12].

The impressive results achieved by prompt-based learning in NLP and the widespread use of prompts in security-sensitive applications. Numerous studies [7,11,12,14,19,20] have shown that the choice of prompts can have a significant impact on the models' performance. **Small differences in the prompts can lead to large differences in the model performance.** This poses significant security risks, making the vulnerability of models based on continuous prompts become a new research focus on model attack and defense research. Therefore, it is necessary for in-depth research to investigate the security risks of models based on continuous prompts.

As still in the prompts security early stage, many problems remain unexplored regarding the attack of continuous prompts. Among these, this paper aims to explore the vulnerability of models with continuous prompts. We initially explored the sensitivity of models to various types and magnitudes of noise attacks to continuous prompts. Subsequently, we have devised a learnable attack method to generate perturbations that minimize L_2 - **norm** of the noise and achieve the desired attack performance.

Our contributions can be summarized as follows:

- We validate that continuous prompts are susceptible to attacks by various types and magnitudes of noise and propose a learnable attack method.
- Our learnable attack method minimizes the L_2-norm perturbations to the continuous prompts, significantly reducing the model's effectiveness.
- We conduct numerous experiments on different datasets and models to verify the effectiveness of existing noises and find that learnable perturbations with minimal L_2-norm are also effective.

2   Related Work

2.1   Prompt-Based Learning

Manual prompts in prompt-based learning are typically built based on human natural language knowledge and are easy to understand [5]. However, several methods have been proposed to automate the template design process. Many studies propose methods for automatically generating prompts [6, 8, 20] and continuous prompts [10, 11, 23]. Here, we focus on methods based on continuous prompts due to their fewer limitations and better performance.

Li et al. [11] proposed *Prefix-Tuning*, a continuous prompts creation method for table-to-text and summary tasks. *P-Tuning* [15] and *P-Tuning v2* [13] are also typical methods for constructing continuous prompts, transforming template construction problems into optimization problems with continuous vectors. The *OptiPrompt* [23] method uses *AutoPrompt* [20] to automatically search for discrete prompts as the initialization of continuous prompts and verifies that the effect of this method is better than that of random initialization. Qin et al. [17] optimize the ensemble of prompts, learning more effective prompts and their combinations. Brian Lester et al. [10] proposed prompt tuning and showed its competitiveness with the fine-tuning method in the field of large-scale language models.

2.2 Attack Prompt Methods

Several attack methods can be used on prompt language models. Lei et al. [22] discover that prompt-based learning inherits the vulnerability of the pre-train stage, and explores the general vulnerability of prompt-based methods. The work considers two types of attacks: *AToP* (adversarial triggers on prompt-based learning) and *BToP* (backdoor triggers on prompt-based learning). *BadPrompt* [3] investigates the vulnerability of continuous prompt learning models to backdoor attacks. It generates candidate triggers that predict the target label and are distinct from the non-target label samples. And then *BadPrompt* uses an adaptive trigger optimization algorithm to select the most efficient trigger. However, the vulnerability of continuous prompts learning models to perturbation has not been studied.

3   Methodology

During the development process of continuous prompts, researchers did not consider the potential security risks of the model. As a result, the continuous prompts are vulnerable to attacks that cause failure to complete tasks effectively. Intuitively, constructing a malicious continuous prompt can be viewed as the adversarial sample for images. Therefore, we select the existing noise as the perturbation to influence continuous prompts to interfere with the model. Additionally, we propose a learnable attack method for continuous prompt language models and investigate the vulnerability of these models to such attacks.

3.1   Existing Noise Attack

In this section, we introduce a method for verifying whether adding noise directly to the continuous prompts can effectively reduce prediction accuracy. We also describe two types of noise used in our experiments: Gaussian noise and Poisson noise. Deliberately introducing noise to the prompt can cause the model

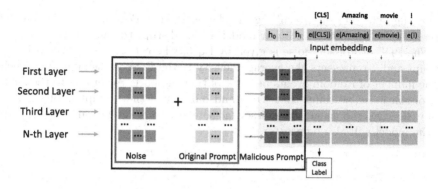

Fig. 1. Overview of the method of existing noise attack.

to output incorrect answers with high confidence levels. Applying noises from different distributions to the prompt to generate **malicious prompt** $\hat{P}$ through Eq. 1 can cause a decrease in the model's accuracy. Here, P represents the **original prompt**, ϵ is the noise parameter, $N(\cdot)$ is the added noise, and d is the probability distribution of the used noise. The overall framework of the process of existing noise attack is shown in Fig. 1. The orange blocks refer to the noise, the light green blocks are the original continuous prompts, and the brown blocks represent malicious prompts caused by noise attacks.

$$\hat{P} = P + \epsilon * N(d) \tag{1}$$

Gaussian Noise. Gaussian noise is commonly present in images from natural sources [2]. It is difficult for the trainer to visually detect its presence when Gaussian noise is used as an adversarial noise in image classification tasks. Thus Gaussian noise is a popular choice for testing the sensitivity of the model to perturbations. In view of this, we opted to use Gaussian noise to investigate the vulnerability of continuous prompts, hoping that it would also disrupt the fitting process of text-based models.

Gaussian noise is a type of noise whose probability density function (PDF) follows a Gaussian distribution. The PDF of Gaussian noise is defined by Eq. 2, where σ represents the standard deviation and μ represents the mean value. The mean value in Gaussian noise determines the degree of brightness and is equivalent to an offset of the mean value of the prompt. The larger the variance, the more dispersed the data and the more influential the noise.

$$P_{Gaussian}(x) = \frac{e^{-\frac{1}{2}(\frac{x-\mu}{\sigma})^2}}{\sigma\sqrt{2\pi}} \tag{2}$$

Poisson Noise. Poisson noise arises due to fluctuations in light intensity. Discretization causes greater fluctuations in the number of photons received with increasing light intensity, resulting in a larger level of Poisson noise. When the discrete noise is added to a linear model, it can disrupt the model [1].

The PDF of Poisson noise is given by Eq. 3, where P represents the original prompt and k represents the average density in the Poisson distribution, which is the number of random events per unit of time or space. According to the PDF of Poisson noise, we infer that when and only when the prompt is bigger and more effective, the generated Poisson noise will also be larger, and the impact on the model will also be greater.

$$P_{Poisson}(x = k) = \frac{P^k * e^{-P}}{k!} \tag{3}$$

3.2 Learnable Perturbation Attack

This part presents a learnable perturbation attack method that aims to generate specific and effective disturbances for a given task. And we ensure that the perturbation has a significant attack effect even when minimizing L_2-norm. To achieve this, the method introduces a new loss function L in Eq. 4 that combines the Cross-Entropy loss function and the Euclidean Distance between the malicious prompt and the original prompt.

$$L((x, \hat{P}), Label) = L_f(P, \hat{P}) - L_C((x, \hat{P}), Label) \tag{4}$$

$$= \|\hat{P} - P\|_k + \sum_{i=0}^{n} log(C_i((x, \hat{P}), Label))$$

where L_f represents the Euclidean Distance between the perturbed prompt $\hat{P}$ and the great prompt P and L_C is a kind of class Cross-Entropy loss. If the classifier correctly predicts the class $Label$, it will punish the generation network. L_f is the norm of the difference between P and $\hat{P}$, which ensures that the similarity between the original prompt and the attack prompt is very high, that is, the added disturbance is very small. The selection of k should ensure that it does not promote sparsity, otherwise, residual sediments will accumulate in small areas and will be obvious. We select to use $k = 2$ because adversarial attacks with L_2-norm are a popular choice. L_2-norm attacks can be more stealthy, making them harder to detect by humans. According to Eq. 4, when the L_f is less and the L_C is larger, the loss function L is minimal. When the Euclidean Distance between the original prompt and the attack prompt is smaller, the L_f is smaller which is L_2-norm. When the difference between the output result of the model and the real $Label$ is larger, the misclassification loss L_C is larger. Therefore, when the loss function continues to decrease, the L_2-norm will gradually decrease and the misclassification loss will gradually increase, which is consistent with the original intention of designing the loss function.

The overall framework for generating learning noise is illustrated in Fig. 2. In the figure, V is the initialized noise vector, NET represents the neural network, V' denotes the final perturbation that learns from the neural network, P shows the original continuous prompt, and $\hat{P}$ refers to the **malicious prompt** obtained

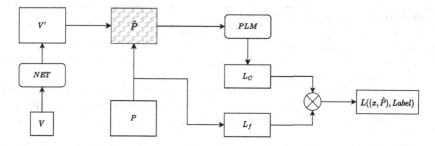

Fig. 2. Overview of the method of adding learnable perturbation.

by adding perturbation V' to the continuous prompt P. PLM represents the pre-training language model, *Label* is the real label, L_f denotes the L_2-norm between P and $\hat{P}$, which mainly indicates the degree of similarity. L_C represents the Cross-Entropy loss function between the model prediction label and the real label, and L denotes the loss function determined by both the L_2-norm and the Cross-Entropy loss function. By optimizing the L loss function, we can guide the generation of small and offensive perturbations. The whole process is shown in the Algorithm 1.

In summary, the learnable perturbation attack method can produce specific and effective perturbation for giving tasks. The attack is efficient even under small values of L_2-norm by minimizing the loss function, the perturbation can be updated in each iteration and adapted to the specific task.

4   Experiments

To evaluate the effectiveness of the proposed method for adding noise to the continuous prompt, we conduct experiments on various pre-training models and natural language understanding tasks.

4.1   Experimental Settings

Tasks and Datasets. We mainly focus on two natural language understanding tasks: natural language inference (NLI) and named entity recognition (NER). We conduct experiments on three datasets based on these tasks. The datasets used in the experiments are **Recognizing Textual Entailment** (RTE), **CONLL04** [4], and **OntoNotes 5.0** [21], which have been widely used in continuous prompts. The RTE dataset is used for NLI tasks to judge if two sentences have an implicative relationship. The CONLL04 dataset is used for NER tasks and contains four entity types and five relationship categories. The main entities in the CONLL04 dataset are Person, Organization, and Location, as well as relationships between entities such as Work For and ORGBased. OntoNotes 5.0 is a corpus that includes various text types in three languages: English, Chinese, and Arabic. It is also used as a dataset for NER tasks.

Algorithm 1. Learnable perturbation attack

Input: Original prompt: P; Datasets: D; Iterations: K
Output: Malicious prompt: $best\_\hat{P}$

1: $best\_metric = 0$ ▷ Initialize $best\_metric$
2: **for** $i = 0; i < K; i + +$ **do**
3:     $x = random(\text{D})$ ▷ Randomly select a sentence x from dataset D
4:     $V_0 = embedding(x)$ ▷ Initialize each block of perturbation
5:     $V_1 = V_0.repeat()$ ▷ Copy perturbation blocks and generate perturbation for
    each layer
6:     $V = V_1.repeat()$ ▷ Copy each layer of perturbation and generate the overall
    perturbation
7:     $V' = Net(V)$ ▷ Generate final perturbation after learning
8:     $\hat{P} = P + V'$ ▷ Get malicious prompt
9:     $metric = train\_metric(D, \hat{P})$ ▷ Evaluate metric
10:     $cross\_loss = L_C(\hat{P}, Label)$
                        ▷ Compute loss between model result and real label $Label$
11:     $trigger\_loss = L_2(\hat{P}, P)$
                    ▷ Compute Euclidean Distance between $\hat{P}$ and P
12:     $loss = trigger\_loss - cross\_loss$ ▷ Get current loss
                                    ▷ Through Back-propagation
13:     **if** $metric < best\_metric$ **then**
14:         $best\_metric = metric$
15:         $best\_\hat{P} = \hat{P}$
16:     **end if**
17: **end for**
18: **return** $best\_\hat{P}$

Victim Models. The victim models comprise both PLMs and a prompt model. We use BERT-large [9] and RoBERTa-large [16] as the main victim model of P-Tuning v2 the continuous prompt method.

Baseline. We have selected the P-Tuning v2 method by Xiao et al. [13] as the baseline, as our proposed method in this chapter is built upon this approach. We evaluate the impact of adding noise to the continuous prompt on the models' accuracy under the same conditions and compare it with the baseline to ascertain the vulnerability of the continuous prompt.

Metric. For the RLI task, we use accuracy as the evaluation metric. For NER tasks, we use Micro-F1 as the metric. The Micro-F1 score is calculated based on precision and recall, which evaluate the accuracy of the model in identifying these entities.

4.2   Results and Analysis

In this section, experiments are conducted in a fully supervised environment for NLU tasks. The impact of noise on the performance of the continuous prompt model is investigated by introducing existing and learnable perturbations to the prompts.

Experiment Results of the Existing Noise Attack. This section presents experimental results on various models and datasets using the method of adding existing noise, which verifies the vulnerabilities of prompt-based language models.

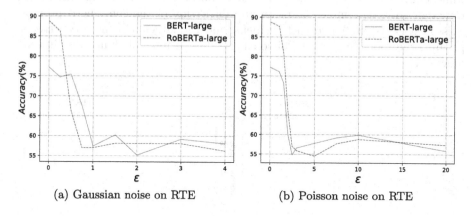

(a) Gaussian noise on RTE   (b) Poisson noise on RTE

Fig. 3. Influence of Gaussian noise and Poisson noise on P-Tuning v2 on RTE dataset.

The experimental results presented in Figs. 3, 4, and 5 demonstrate that *P-Tuning v2* with continuous prompts exhibits a certain level of robustness, but its sensitivity to different types of noise varies. Specifically, introducing noise to the continuous prompt can have a significant impact on the model's performance when ϵ is larger.

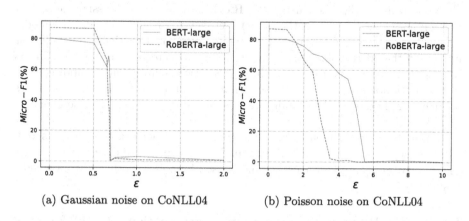

(a) Gaussian noise on CoNLL04   (b) Poisson noise on CoNLL04

Fig. 4. Influence of Gaussian noise and Poisson noise on P-Tuning v2 on CoNLL04 dataset.

These results illustrate that the model based on the prompt is more sensitive to **Gaussian noise** than Poisson noise. For Gaussian noise, the influence of the model accuracy tends to remain stable when the ϵ is less than **1**. On the contrary, Poisson noise does not significantly affect the continuous prompts and the accuracy of the model is close to that of the original model when the ϵ is **1**. This can be attributed to the fact that Gaussian noise is a continuous distribution, while Poisson noise follows a discrete distribution. The mean and variance of Gaussian noise determine the mean and dispersion of the continuous prompt. Poisson noise is related to each element, and the larger and more effective of prompt, the more impact of Poisson noise due to its probability distribution function.

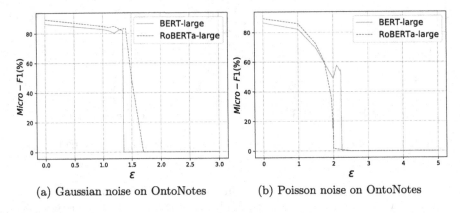

(a) Gaussian noise on OntoNotes   (b) Poisson noise on OntoNotes

Fig. 5. Influence of Gaussian noise and Poisson noise on P-Tuning v2 on OntoNotes 5.0 dataset.

As seen in Fig. 3, when using the **RTE** dataset, both Gaussian noise and Poisson noise can only affect the model accuracy to around 55% and the model cannot be reduced to a lower level. Notably, noise has a particularly significant impact on the NER task, causing the F1-score to decrease to below 5%. This is because *P-Tuning v2* is trained in a fully supervised environment, so adding noise to the continuous prompt can cause significant variations in the characteristics of each sample during the training process, leading to a considerable effect on the F1-score.

Through the experiments, we found that only ϵ reaches a certain threshold, and the accuracy of the model drops rapidly. It is difficult to determine whether the fluctuating changes in accuracy are caused by noise or other factors when ϵ is small.

Experiment Results of the Learnable Perturbation Attack. From the experimental results in the previous section, it can be concluded that adding noise to P-Tuning v2 can reduce the model's accuracy and successfully attack the model. This section carries out experiments to verify the experimental results of adding learnable perturbation. It mainly needs to be proved through experiments that: (1) The learnable perturbation method can successfully attack the model and reduce the model evaluation metrics, and the effect is better than or equivalent to adding noise directly; (2) A smaller amount of perturbation of learnable perturbation attack method can achieve better performance.

First, the experiment of adding learnable perturbation on three datasets and two pre-training language models is carried out in this section. The experiment results are shown in Table 1. The $Difference$ in the table is the attack success rate where a larger value indicates a stronger attack.

Table 1. Experiment results of adding the learnable perturbation.

Dataset	Task	PLM	P-Tuning v2	Learnable	$Difference$
RTE	**NLI**	BERT-large	77.2%	46.6%	**30.6%**
		RoBERTa-large	88.8%	48.7%	**40.1%**
CoNLL04	**NER**	BERT-large	80.2%	2.3%	**77.9%**
		RoBERTa-large	87%	3.3%	**83.7%**
OntoNotes 5.0	**NER**	BERT-large	86.5%	0.8%	**85.7%**
		RoBERTa-large	89.4%	1.0%	**88.4%**

From the data in Table 1, it can be seen that the accuracy of the **RTE** dataset can be reduced to 48%. And the F1-score of the **CoNLL04** dataset and **OntoNotes** dataset can be reduced to a single digit, or even close to 0. These results demonstrate the effectiveness of the learnable perturbation proposed in this paper, which can successfully reduce the indicators of the model, and achieve certain effects on the attack on the model.

Compared with the data of the existing noise attack method that only reduces the accuracy of the model to about 55% on the **RTE** dataset, while learnable perturbation can reduce the accuracy to about 48%. This proves that the learnable perturbation attack on the RTE dataset can achieve better results than the existing noise attack. On the **CoNLL04** dataset and **OntoNotes** dataset, both learnable perturbation and directly added noise can reduce the F1-score to a value close to 0, which proves that both attacks can achieve the same good effect.

To verify that the L_2-norm of the learnable perturbation attack is smaller than that existing noise attack method under the same attack effect. Table 2 shows the difference of the L_2-norm between the original prompt and the malicious prompt. When the L_2-norm value is smaller, the perturbation is smaller, indicating that the malicious prompt is more similar to the original prompt.

Table 2. Comparison of disturbance size between existing noise and learnable perturbation

Dataset	Task	PLM	Gaussian	Poisson	Learnable
RTE	**NLI**	BERT-large	0.7639	0.8807	**0.0152**
		RoBERTa-large	2.4730	3.8907	**0.0201**
CoNLL04	**NER**	BERT-large	1.3784	1.5029	**0.0159**
		RoBERTa-large	3.5471	4.3746	**0.0187**
OntoNotes 5.0	**NER**	BERT-large	0.6540	0.7047	**0.0218**
		RoBERTa-large	1.9369	2.5749	**0.0174**

According to Table 2, it can be observed that regardless of the task or PTM used, the learnable perturbation results in the smallest perturbation size. The Euclidean Distance between the original and malicious prompts can be as small as about 0.02, while the Gaussian noise and Poisson noise are greater than 1. Therefore, it can be verified that the learnable perturbation attack proposed in this section can successfully reduce the model performance when the perturbation is small.

To sum up, the learnable perturbation attack can reduce the accuracy of the model with little interference, and achieve the same or even better effect as the existing noise attack. Thus, we have achieved the objective of designing learnable perturbation and verifying the effectiveness and feasibility of the method in this chapter.

5   Conclusion

In this paper, we investigate the vulnerability of continuous prompts to noise perturbations from the perspective of attackers. To reveal the general vulnerability of the continuous prompt-based learning paradigm in noise, we verify the effectiveness of existing noise and propose a smaller magnitude and task-adaptive learnable attack method. The massive experiments demonstrate the excellence of the learnable attack method. In future work, we will investigate how to defend against attacks targeted at continuous prompts. We believe that our work will pave the way for the future development of prompt-based learning.

Acknowledgement. This research is supported by the National Key R&D Program of China (Grant No.2021YFB3100700), the National Natural Science Foundation of China (Grant No.62272228, No.BK20200418, No.62106105), Shenzhen Science and Technology Program (Grant No.JCYJ20210324134408023), the CCF-Tencent Open Research Fund (No.RAGR20220122), the CCF-Zhipu AI Large Model Fund (No.CC F-Zhipu202315), the Scientific Research Starting Foundation of Nanjing University of Aeronautics and Astronautics (No.YQR21022), and the High Performance Computing Platform of Nanjing University of Aeronautics and Astronautics.

References

1. Boyat, A.K., Joshi, B.K.: A review paper: noise models in digital image processing. arXiv preprint arXiv:1505.03489 (2015)
2. Buades, A., Coll, B., Morel, J.M.: A review of image denoising algorithms, with a new one. Multiscale Model. Simul. **4**(2), 490–530 (2005)
3. Cai, X., Xu, H., Xu, S., Zhang, Y., et al.: Badprompt: backdoor attacks on continuous prompts. Adv. Neural. Inf. Process. Syst. **35**, 37068–37080 (2022)
4. Carreras, X., Marques, L.: Introduction to the CONLL-2004 shared task: semantic role labeling, CONLL-2004. MI USA, Ann Arbor (2005)
5. Cui, L., Wu, Y., Liu, J., Yang, S., Zhang, Y.: Template-based named entity recognition using bart. arXiv preprint arXiv:2106.01760 (2021)
6. Gao, T., Fisch, A., Chen, D.: Making pre-trained language models better few-shot learners. arXiv preprint arXiv:2012.15723 (2020)

7. Gu, Y., Han, X., Liu, Z., Huang, M.: PPT: pre-trained prompt tuning for few-shot learning. arXiv preprint arXiv:2109.04332 (2021)
8. Jiang, Z., Xu, F.F., Araki, J., Neubig, G.: How can we know what language models know? Trans. Assoc. Comput. Linguist. **8**, 423–438 (2020)
9. Kenton, J.D.M.W.C., Toutanova, L.K.: Bert: Pre-training of deep bidirectional transformers for language understanding. In: Proceedings of NAACL-HLT, vol. 1, p. 2 (2019)
10. Lester, B., Al-Rfou, R., Constant, N.: The power of scale for parameter-efficient prompt tuning. In: Proceedings of the 2021 Conference on Empirical Methods in Natural Language Processing, pp. 3045–3059 (2021)
11. Li, X.L., Liang, P.: Prefix-tuning: optimizing continuous prompts for generation. arXiv preprint arXiv:2101.00190 (2021)
12. Liu, P., Yuan, W., Fu, J., Jiang, Z., Hayashi, H., Neubig, G.: Pre-train, prompt, and predict: a systematic survey of prompting methods in natural language processing. ACM Comput. Surv. **55**(9), 1–35 (2023)
13. Liu, X., Ji, K., Fu, Y., Du, Z., Yang, Z., Tang, J.: P-tuning v2: prompt tuning can be comparable to fine-tuning universally across scales and tasks. arXiv preprint arXiv:2110.07602 (2021)
14. Liu, X., et al.: P-tuning: prompt tuning can be comparable to fine-tuning across scales and tasks. In: Proceedings of the 60th Annual Meeting of the Association for Computational Linguistics (Volume 2: Short Papers), pp. 61–68 (2022)
15. Liu, X., et al.: GPT understands, too. arXiv:abs/2103.10385 (2021)
16. Liu, Y., et al.: Roberta: a robustly optimized Bert pretraining approach. arXiv preprint arXiv:1907.11692 (2019)
17. Qin, G., Eisner, J.: Learning how to ask: querying LMs with mixtures of soft prompts. In: Proceedings of the 2021 Conference of the North American Chapter of the Association for Computational Linguistics: Human Language Technologies, pp. 5203–5212, (2021)
18. Schick, T., Schmid, H., Schütze, H.: Automatically identifying words that can serve as labels for few-shot text classification. arXiv preprint arXiv:2010.13641 (2020)
19. Schick, T., Schütze, H.: Exploiting cloze questions for few shot text classification and natural language inference. arXiv preprint arXiv:2001.07676 (2020)
20. Shin, T., Razeghi, Y., Logan IV, R.L., Wallace, E., Singh, S.: Autoprompt: eliciting knowledge from language models with automatically generated prompts. arXiv preprint arXiv:2010.15980 (2020)
21. Weischedel, R., et al.: Ontonotes release 5.0 ldc2013t19. linguistic data consortium, philadelphia, pa (2013)
22. Xu, L., Chen, Y., Cui, G., Gao, H., Liu, Z.: Exploring the universal vulnerability of prompt-based learning paradigm. In: Findings of the Association for Computational Linguistics: NAACL 2022, pp. 1799–1810 (2022)
23. Zhong, Z., Friedman, D., Chen, D.: Factual probing is [MASK]: learning vs. learning to recall. In: Proceedings of the 2021 Conference of the North American Chapter of the Association for Computational Linguistics: Human Language Technologies, pp. 5017–5033 (2021)

Author Index

© The Editor(s) (if applicable) and The Author(s), under exclusive license
to Springer Nature Switzerland AG 2023
L. Iliadis et al. (Eds.): ICANN 2023, LNCS 14262, pp. 521–523, 2023.
https://doi.org/10.1007/978-3-031-44201-8

Printed in the United States
by Baker & Taylor Publisher Services